A GUIDE TO
Microsoft® Windows NT®
Server 4.0

Michael J. Palmer, Ph.D.

COURSE
TECHNOLOGY

ONE MAIN STREET, CAMBRIDGE, MA 02142

an International Thomson Publishing company I(T)P®

Cambridge • Albany • Bonn • Boston • Cincinnati • London • Madrid • Melbourne • Mexico City
New York • Paris • San Francisco • Singapore • Tokyo • Toronto • Washington

A Guide to Microsoft Windows NT Server 4.0 is published by Course Technology.

Managing Editor:	Kristen Duerr
Senior Product Manager:	Jennifer Normandin
Production Editor:	Nancy Shea
Development Editor:	Deb Kaufmann
Technical Editors:	Clint Saxton, Robert Bruce Sinclair
Composition House:	GEX, Inc.
Text Designer:	GEX, Inc.
Cover Designer:	Wendy J. Reifeiss
Marketing Manager:	Tracy Foley

© 1998 by Course Technology—I**T**P®

For more information contact:

Course Technology
One Main Street
Cambridge, MA 02142

ITP Europe
Berkshire House 168-173
High Holborn
London WCIV 7AA
England

Nelson ITP Australia
102 Dodds Street
South Melbourne, 3205
Victoria, Australia

ITP Nelson Canada
1120 Birchmount Road
Scarborough, Ontario
Canada M1K 5G4

International Thomson Editores
Seneca, 53
Colonia Polanco
11560 Mexico D.F. Mexico

ITP GmbH
Königswinterer Strasse 418
53227 Bonn
Germany

ITP Asia
60 Albert Street, #15-01
Albert Complex
Singapore 189969

ITP Japan
Hirakawacho Kyowa Building, 3F
2-2-1 Hirakawacho
Chiyoda-ku, Tokyo 102
Japan

Trademarks

Course Technology and the Open Book logo are registered trademarks and CourseKits is a trademark of Course Technology. Custom Edition is a registered trademark of International Thomson Publishing.

I**T**P® The ITP logo is a registered trademark of International Thomson Publishing.

Some of the product names and company names used in this book have been used for identification purposes only and may be trademarks or registered trademarks of their respective manufacturers and sellers.

Disclaimer

Course Technology reserves the right to revise this publication and make changes from time to time in its content without notice.

ISBN 0-7600-5875-X

Printed in the United States of America

1 2 3 4 5 6 7 8 9 BH 02 01 00 99 98

BRIEF TABLE OF CONTENTS

TABLE OF CONTENTS

CHAPTER ELEVEN

Remote Access

PREFACE

Career opportunities abound for well-prepared server administrators. This book is designed as your doorway to server administration through Microsoft Windows NT Server 4.0. If you are new to Windows NT Server or server administration, you hold in your hand a ticket to an exciting future. Others who have prior experience with Windows NT Server will find that the book adds depth and breadth to that experience. The book also provides the knowledge you need to prepare for Microsoft's certification exam #70-067, Implementing and Supporting Microsoft Windows NT Server 4.0. Passing this exam grants you certification as a Windows NT Server Product Specialist and is a crucial step toward becoming a Microsoft Certified Systems Engineer (MCSE).

Although Windows NT Server is young as a network operating system, it is mature in what it can accomplish for large and small organizations. It provides the cornerstone on which to build a business, an Internet Web site, or access to information-rich data sources. The success of Windows NT Server is reflected in the huge number of software vendors and developers in this environment or who have switched from other environments to Windows NT Server.

When you complete this book, you will be at the threshold of a server administration career that can be very fulfilling and challenging. This is a rapidly advancing field that offers ample opportunity for personal growth and to make a contribution to your business or organization. The book is intended to provide you with knowledge that you can apply right away as well as a sound basis for understanding the changes that you will encounter in the future. It also is intended to give you the hands-on skills you need to be a valued professional in your organization.

This book is filled with hands-on projects that cover every aspect of installing and managing Windows NT Server. The projects are designed to make what you learn come alive through actually performing the tasks. Besides the hands-on projects, each chapter gives you realistic experience through case projects that put you in the shoes of a Windows NT server consultant working in all kinds of situations to fulfill clients' needs. Also, every chapter includes a range of practice questions to help prepare you for the Microsoft certification exam. All of these features are offered to reinforce your learning so you can feel confident in the knowledge you have gained from each chapter. For those who do not have access to the Windows NT Server operating system, simulations are available with the book, enabling you to practice important activities, such as installing Windows NT Server or setting up an account.

Chapter 1, "Networking with Microsoft Windows NT Server," explains the history and current capabilities of Windows NT Server. It also shows how Windows NT Server can be home to Internet and intranet applications. In **Chapter 2**, "Basic Network Design and Protocols," you learn the fundamentals of how networks work and how you can plan and design your own network with NT Server. **Chapter 3**, "Server Hardware," gives you detailed information about how to select a computer on which to install Windows NT Server. In Chapter 3, you learn about computer architecture, how to select a network interface card, and how to choose disk storage.

After learning about hardware, you are ready to install the Windows NT Server operating system in **Chapter 4**, "Server Installation." This chapter shows you how to plan in advance for a successful installation and then how to execute it. In **Chapter 5**, "Server Configuration," you learn how to configure the server for specialized monitors, keyboards, network communications, and many other needs. **Chapter 6**, "Configuring Server Storage, Backup, and Performance Options," continues with configuration issues for server disk storage, backups, and performance enhancement. It also shows you how to protect against lost data and equipment power failures.

In **Chapter 7**, "Server Clients," you learn how to set up network computers to communicate with a network and with Windows NT Server. Also, different client operating systems are compared to help you decide which best suit your work situation. **Chapter 8**, "Managing the Server Through Accounts and Groups," marks your introduction into server management by establishing how users access the server. In **Chapter 9**, "Managing Server Folders, Permissions, and Software Installation," you continue learning server management by setting up folders and software for users to access.

Chapter 10, "Printer Management," shows how Windows NT Server takes much of the headache out of managing network printing. It shows you how to set up and manage all types of printers. In **Chapter 11**, "Remote Access," you learn how to turn a Windows NT Server into a tool that can be accessed from home by telecommuters or by users who travel from city to city. This chapter also shows you how to set up server administration tools so you can access them remotely.

Chapter 12, "Interoperating with Novell NetWare," explains how to set up Windows NT Server to communicate with NetWare servers and how user can access a NetWare server through an NT Server. Internet and intranet services are the focus of **Chapter 13**, "Internet and Intranet Services." In this chapter you learn how to make a Windows NT Server function as a full-featured Internet Web site.

The last three chapters of the book show you how to enhance the performance of Windows NT server and how to troubleshoot problems. In **Chapter 14**, "Server and Network Monitoring," you learn how to use Windows NT Server tools to track server performance. **Chapter 15**, "Performance Tuning," includes information about how to tune vital server elements such as memory, file system cache, disk storage, and network communications. In **Chapter 16**, "Troubleshooting," you learn how to troubleshoot a full range of problems that can emerge, including hardware and network problems. Finally, **Appendix A** provides supplementary information about Windows NT Server utilities that can be purchased from Microsoft and third-party sources. **Appendix B** provides a full summary of Windows NT Server commands.

FEATURES

To aid you in fully understanding Windows NT concepts, there are many features in this book designed to improve its pedagogical value.

- **Chapter Objectives** Each chapter in this book begins with a detailed list of the concepts to be mastered within that chapter. This list provides you with a quick reference to the contents of that chapter, and is a useful study aid.

- **Illustrations and Tables** Numerous illustrations of server screens and components aid you in the visualization of common setup steps, theories, and concepts. In addition, many tables provide details and comparisons of both practical and theoretical information.

- **Hands-on Projects** Although it is important to understand the theory behind server and networking technology, nothing can improve upon real-world experience. To this end, each chapter provides, along with theoretical explanations, numerous hands-on projects aimed at providing you with real-world implementation experience.

- **Chapter Summaries** Each chapter's text is followed by a summary of the concepts it has introduced. These summaries provide a helpful way to recap and revisit the ideas covered in each chapter.

- **Review Questions** End-of-chapter assessment begins with a set of review questions that reinforce the ideas introduced in each chapter. These questions not only ensure that you have mastered the concepts, but are written to help prepare you for the Microsoft certification examination.

- **Case Project** Located at the end of each chapter is a continuous running case. In this extensive case example, as a consultant at the fictitious Aspen Consulting, you implement the skills and knowledge gained in the chapter through real-world server setup and administration scenarios.

TEXT AND GRAPHIC CONVENTIONS

Wherever appropriate, additional information and exercises have been added to this book to help you better understand what is being discussed in the chapter. Icons throughout the text alert you to additional materials. The icons used in this textbook are described below.

The **Note icon** is used to present additional helpful material related to the subject being described.

Each hands-on activity in this book is preceded by the Hands-On icon and a description of the exercise that follows.

Tip icons present advice from the author's experience. Tips provide extra information about how to attack a problem, how to set up Windows NT Server for a particular need, or what to do to in certain real-world situations.

Caution icons help you anticipate potential mistakes or problems so you can prevent them from happening.

Case Project icons mark the running case project. These are more involved, scenario-based assignments. In this extensive case example, you are asked to implement independently what you have learned.

INSTRUCTOR'S MATERIALS

The following supplemental materials are available when this book is used in a classroom setting. All of the supplements available with this book are provided to the instructor on a single CD-ROM.

Electronic Instructor's Manual The Instructor's Manual that accompanies this textbook includes:

- Additional instructional material to assist in class preparation, including suggestions for lecture topics, suggested lab activities, tips on setting up a lab for the hands-on assignments, and alternative lab setup ideas in situations where lab resources are limited.

- Solutions to all end-of-chapter materials, including the Project and Case assignments.

Course Test Manager 1.1 Accompanying this book is a powerful assessment tool known as the Course Test Manager. Designed by Course Technology, this cutting-edge Windows-based testing software helps instructors design and administer tests and pre-tests. In addition to being able to generate tests that can be printed and administered, this full-featured program also has an online testing component that allows students to take tests at the computer and have their exams automatically graded.

PowerPoint presentations This book comes with Microsoft PowerPoint slides for each chapter. These are included as a teaching aid for classroom presentation, to make available to students on the network for chapter review, or to be printed for classroom distribution. Instructors, please feel at liberty to add your own slides for any additional topics you introduce to the class.

Simulations The Instructor's Resource Kit CD-ROM features several simulations, written in Visual Basic, which animate key concepts including starting a server service; sharing a folder as a network resource; setting up a network (shared) printer; setting up TCP/IP network protocol properties; creating and modifying user accounts for network management; setting up network account policies (password and account lockout management policies); setting up account auditing; setting up rights policies; and installing the Network Monitor Agent. Also, the Windows NT Server Installation Simulator, which simulates an actual installation, is provided. These simulations work in conjunction with many of the hands-on exercises in the book, and can be run in a 16-bit or 32-bit environment. The host workstation operating system and setup are unaffected by running the simulation software.

TRANSCENDER CERTIFICATION TEST PREP SOFTWARE

Bound into the back of this book is a disk containing Transcender Corporation's Implementing and Supporting Microsoft Windows NT Server 4.0 certification exam preparation software with one full exam that simulates the Microsoft exam (Exam 70-067).

Acknowledgments

A book is a rewarding effort that involves many key people. I am very grateful to Kristen Duerr, managing editor at Course Technology, for her support and for providing the opportunity to work on this book. Deb Kaufmann is a great colleague as development editor, providing insight, advice, and wisdom each step of the way. Jennifer Normandin, Nancy Shea, and Lisa Ayers of Course Technology have played a vital role in the production of the book and in the production of supplementary materials.

Also, I want to thank the technical reviewers, Clint Saxton of Hewlett-Packard and Robert Bruce Sinclair of the University of Wyoming, for very careful reading and advice. Finally, I am grateful to my family for their constant support and patience.

Dedication

In memory of Arthur Weisbach, a great teacher.

PREPARING FOR MICROSOFT CERTIFICATION

Microsoft offers a program called the Microsoft Certified Professional (MCP) program. Becoming a Microsoft Certified Professional can open many doors for you. Whether you want to be a network engineer, product specialist, or software developer, obtaining the appropriate Microsoft Certified Professional credentials can provide a formal record of your skills to potential employers. Certification can be equally effective in helping you secure a raise or promotion.

The Microsoft Certified Professional program is made up of many courses in several different tracks. Combinations of individual courses can lead to certification in a specific track. Most tracks require a combination of required and elective courses. One of the most common tracks for beginners is the Microsoft Certified Product Specialist (MCPS). By obtaining this status, your credentials tell a potential employer that you are an expert in a specialized computing area such as Personal Computer Operating Systems on a specific product, like Microsoft Windows 95.

HOW CAN TRANSCENDER'S TEST PREP SOFTWARE HELP?

To become a Microsoft Certified Professional, you must pass rigorous certification exams that provide a valid and reliable measure of technical proficiency and expertise. The disk contained in this book, Transcender Corporation's Limited Version certification exam preparation software, can be used in conjunction with the book to help you assess your progress in the event you choose to pursue Microsoft Professional Certification. The Transcender disk presents a series of questions that were expertly prepared to test your readiness for the official Microsoft Certification examination on Implementing and Supporting Windows NT Server 4.0 (Exam 70-067). These questions were taken from a larger series of practice tests produced by the Transcender Corporation—practice tests that simulate the interface and format of the actual certification exams. Transcender's complete product also offers explanations for all questions. The rationale for each correct answer is carefully explained, and specific page references are given for Microsoft Product Documentation and Microsoft Press reference books. These page references enable you to study from additional sources.

Practice test questions from Transcender Corporation are acknowledged as the best available. In fact, with their full product, Transcender offers a money-back guarantee if you do not pass the exam. If you have trouble passing the practice examination included on the enclosed disk, you should consider purchasing the full product with additional practice tests and personalized feedback. Details and pricing information are available at the end of this section. A sample of the full Transcender product is on the disk on the inside back cover, including remedial explanations.

The Transcender product is a great tool to help you prepare to become certified. If you experience technical problems with this product, please e-mail Transcender at *course@transcender.com* or call (615) 726-8779.

WANT TO KNOW MORE ABOUT MICROSOFT CERTIFICATION?

There are many additional benefits to achieving Microsoft Certified status. These benefits apply to you as well as to your potential employer. As a Microsoft Certified Professional (MCP), you will be recognized as an expert on Microsoft products, have access to ongoing technical information from Microsoft, and receive special invitations to Microsoft conferences and events. You can obtain a comprehensive, interactive tool that provides full details about the Microsoft Certified Professional program online at *www.microsoft.com/train_cert/cert/certif.htm*. For more information on texts at Course Technology that will help prepare you for certification exams, visit our site at *www.course.com*.

When you become a Certified Product Specialist, Microsoft sends you a Welcome Kit that contains:

- An 8½×11" Microsoft Certified Product Specialist wall certificate. Also, within a few weeks after you have passed any exam, Microsoft sends you a Microsoft Certified Professional Transcript that shows which exams you have passed.

- A Microsoft Certified Professional Program membership card.

- A Microsoft Certified Professional lapel pin.

- A license to use the Microsoft Certified Professional logo. You are licensed to use the logo in your advertisements, promotions, proposals, and other materials, including business cards, letterheads, advertising circulars, brochures, yellow page advertisements, mailings, banners, resumes, and invitations.

- A Microsoft Certified Professional logo sheet. Before using the camera-ready logo, you must agree to the terms of the licensing agreement.

- A Microsoft TechNet CD-ROM.

- A 50% discount toward a one-year membership in the Microsoft TechNet Technical Information Network, which provides valuable information via monthly CD-ROMs.

- Dedicated forums on CompuServe (GO MECFORUM) and The Microsoft Network, which enable Microsoft Certified Professionals to communicate directly with Microsoft and one another.

- A one-year subscription to Microsoft Certified Professional Magazine, a career and professional development magazine created especially for Microsoft Certified Professionals.

- A Certification Update subscription. Certification Update is a bimonthly newsletter from the Microsoft Certified Professional program that keeps you informed of changes and advances in the program and exams.

- Invitations to Microsoft conferences, technical training sessions, and special events.

- Eligibility to join the Network Professional Association, a worldwide association of computer professionals. Microsoft Certified Product Specialists are invited to join as associate members.

A Certified Systems Engineer receives all the benefits mentioned above as well as the following additional benefits:

- Microsoft Certified Systems Engineer logos and other materials to help you identify yourself as a Microsoft Certified Systems Engineer to colleagues or clients.

- Ten free incidents with the Microsoft Support Network and a 25% discount on purchases of additional 10-packs of Priority Development and Desktop Support incidents.

- A one-year subscription to the Microsoft TechNet Technical Information Network.

- A one-year subscription to the Microsoft Beta Evaluation program. This benefit provides you with up to 12 free monthly beta software CDs for many of Microsoft's newest software products. This enables you to become familiar with new versions of Microsoft products before they are generally available. This benefit also includes access to a private CompuServe forum where you can exchange information with other program members and find information from Microsoft on current beta issues and product information.

CERTIFY ME!

So you are ready to become a Microsoft Certified Professional. The examinations are administered through Sylvan Prometric (formerly Drake Prometric) and are offered at more than 700 authorized testing centers around the world. Microsoft evaluates certification status based on current exam records. Your current exam record is the set of exams you have passed. To maintain Microsoft Certified Professional status, you must remain current on all the requirements for your certification.

Registering for an exam is easy. To register, contact Sylvan Prometric, 2601 West 88th Street, Bloomington, MN, 55431, at (800) 755-EXAM (3926). Dial (612) 896-7000 or (612) 820-5707 if you cannot place a call to an 800 number from your location. You must call to schedule the exam at least one day before the day you want to take the exam. Taking the exam automatically enrolls you in the Microsoft Certified Professional program; you do not need to submit an application to Microsoft Corporation.

When you call Sylvan Prometric, have the following information ready:

- Your name, organization (if any), mailing address, and phone number.

- A unique ID number (e.g., your Social Security number).

- The number of the exam you wish to take (#70-67 for the Implementing and Supporting Microsoft Windows NT Server4.0 exam).

- A payment method (e.g., credit card number). If you pay by check, payment is due before the examination can be scheduled. The fee to take each exam is currently $100.

READ THIS BEFORE YOU BEGIN

To the Student

This book comes with an NT Server installation simulator, available from your instructor, that enables you to practice the installation steps from any computer with Windows 3.1 or higher. Your instructor also can provide electronic simulations to help you practice important server setup activities. Each chapter of the book ends with review questions, hands-on projects, and case assignments. Your instructor can provide you with answers to the review questions and additional information about the hands-on projects. When you complete the case assignments you can submit them electronically or in written form. The Student Work Disk contains a Microsoft Word file for each end of chapter project. You can enter your answers in the space provided within the file and submit them to your instructor by disk, by printing out your answers, through the network, or through e-mail.

To the Instructor (Please refer to the Instructor's Resource Kit that accompanies this text for more details.)

Setting up the classroom or lab file server To complete the projects and assignments in the book, the students will need access to a file server. To maximize the learning experience, it is recommended that you have one or more file servers which can be dedicated for classroom use. Each server need not be an expensive model, but should be on Microsoft's Hardware Compatibility List. There is an advantage in having several servers for student projects so that the students have more flexibility in their practice. Every server should be equipped with Microsoft Windows

NT Server 4.0 and have enough licenses for all students who need to access them. The Instructor's Resource Kit contains many suggestions about how to set up a lab, including how to equip and manage a lab in which there are limited resources. It also contains alternative projects and assignments for students.

Internet Assignments A few projects require Internet access for information searches. These projects are not mandatory, however, the projects will help train the student in using this resource as a prospective server administrator.

Accepting assignments electronically The project files on the Student Work Disk are in Microsoft Word format. This enables you to accept assignments electronically, if appropriate to your classroom setting. For more details, please refer to the Instructor's Manual.

System Requirements The recommended software and hardware configurations are as follows:

Workstation Clients

- Windows 3.11 or higher (Windows 95 or Windows NT Workstation are preferred)
- 386 or higher processor with 4 MB of RAM (486 or higher preferred with 8+ MB of RAM)
- VGA monitor
- Mouse or pointing device
- Network interface card cabled to the classroom file server
- Hard disk with at least 10 MB free
- At least one high density 3.5-inch floppy disk drive
- Internet access and a browser (recommended but not required for selected research assignments)

File Server

- Listed in Microsoft's Hardware Compatibility List
- 32-bit bus computer with an 80486 25 MHz or faster processor
- VGA or better resolution monitor
- Mouse or pointing device
- High density 3.5-inch floppy disk drive
- CD-ROM drive
- 16 MB or more memory
- One or more hard disks with at least 500 MB of disk storage
- Network interface card for network communications
- Tape system (recommended but not required)
- Modem (recommended but not required)
- Printer (to practice setting up a network printer)

System Requirements for Transcender Corporation's Test Prep Software

- 8 MB RAM (16 MB recommended)
- VGA/256 Color display or better
- 3.5" Disk Drive
- Microsoft Windows 3.1, Windows for Workgroups 3.11, Windows NT 3.51, Windows NT 4.0, or Windows 95

Upgrade to the full version of ServerCert 4.0

What you get with the full version:

- Three full-length exams
- Detailed answer explanations for every question
  - *each explanation gives specific citations to common study references for easier study*
- Documentation that includes a study outline
- Money Back if You Don't Pass Guarantee
  - *see our website for guarantee details*

ServerCert 4.0 is one of an entire line of Microsoft exam simulations designed to help you attain Microsoft certification. Transcender offers simulations of exams for every certification – MCSE (Microsoft Certified Systems Engineer), MCSD (Solution Developer), MCPS (Product Specialist) and MCT (Trainer). See our website at **http://www.transcender.com** for detailed product information and to download product demos.

To order your upgrade, mail us:

The coupon below, filled out with your information (no reproductions or photocopies please)

A check or money order, made out to Transcender Corporation, for $129, plus $6 shipping ($25 outside U.S.)

Terms and Conditions:

Maximum one upgrade per person. Prepayment by check, money order, or credit card, payable to Transcender Corporation. For your own protection, do not send currency through the mail. Allow 4–6 weeks for delivery.

Send to: Upgrade Program
Transcender Corporation
242 Louise Avenue
Nashville, TN 37203

Please send me the ServerCert 4.0 Upgrade. Enclosed is my check or credit card number, payable to Transcender Corporation for $129 plus $6 ($25 outside U.S.). TN residents add $10.64 for sales tax.

Name _____   School_____

Address_____   Credit Card: VISA   MC   AMEX   DISC

City_____State _____   CC# _____

Zip _____Country _____   Expiration _____

Phone _____   Name on Card _____

E-Mail _____   Signature_____

_____ CRS598

CHAPTER ONE

NETWORKING WITH MICROSOFT WINDOWS NT SERVER

Each day millions of people turn on their computers and log into the Internet for information about stocks or to see the latest selections at their favorite online clothing store. At work, people use their computers to add a new employee to the payroll, to check the company's budget, to check on inventory, or to design a bridge. Chances are that those people link into a computer running Microsoft Windows NT Server. When you use the Internet for home banking services to make a cash transfer from one account to another, you may be on a Windows NT Server. When you make a telephone call to order flowers for someone two states away, the customer service representative assisting with your order may be logged on to an NT Server database.

AFTER READING THIS CHAPTER AND COMPLETING THE EXERCISES YOU WILL BE ABLE TO:

- EXPLAIN WORKGROUP NETWORKING

- EXPLAIN DOMAIN NETWORKING AND THE ADVANTAGES OF FILE SERVER OPERATING SYSTEMS

- PRESENT A HISTORY OF HOW WINDOWS NT SERVER EVOLVED

- DESCRIBE THE CAPABILITIES OF MICROSOFT NT SERVER

- COMPARE DIFFERENT FILE SYSTEMS USED BY MICROSOFT NT SERVER

- DISCUSS HOW MICROSOFT NT SERVER IS INTEGRATED WITH INTERNET AND INTRANET APPLICATIONS

Microsoft Windows NT Server is used throughout the world by small and large businesses, government groups, and schools. It is used by researchers to access information about developing countries, find medical diagnostics databases, review food safety data, and research plant growth statistics. Housed in a computer that may look like the one you have at home, Windows NT Server has taken over many functions that once were performed only on mainframe computers in units that filled huge rooms with machinery and support equipment. Today's Windows NT Server computer may look unassuming, but it is at the heart of vital information processing throughout the world. This book is your opportunity to join the computer professionals who manage Windows NT Server installations that compose a huge web of exciting information management applications.

WORKGROUP NETWORKING

Microsoft Windows NT Server is a **network operating system**. It is used to coordinate the way people access a network and the resources available to them on the network. Networks can link users who are in the same office or on different continents.

There are different kinds of networks. A **peer-to-peer** network is one of the simplest ways to network. On a peer-to-peer network, PCs called **workstations** communicate with one another through their own operating systems. Microsoft calls this type of networking the **workgroup model**. A **workgroup** is a grouping of computer users who share one or more resources, such as files or printers, in a decentralized way. Windows 95 is an example of an operating system that can be used for peer-to-peer network communications. Files, folders, printers, and the contents of entire disk drives can be made available on one computer for others to access. No special computer, such as a mainframe computer or server, is needed to enable workgroup members to communicate and share resources (see Figure 1-1). Windows NT Server can also be used for peer-to-peer networking, but it is designed to operate in a domain, a more centralized networking model discussed in the next section.

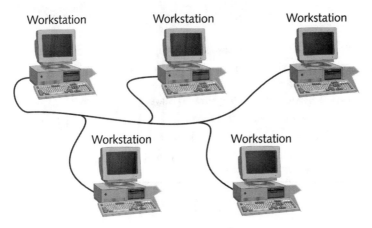

Figure 1-1   A simple peer-to-peer workgroup

1

Strict peer-to-peer or workgroup networking can be effective for very small networks, but there are problems when resource management is totally decentralized. For example, if workgroup members turn off their computers, no one can access them. Another problem is that a workstation operating system is not designed to handle a growing load of clients in the same way as a server operating system.

One situation where peer-to-peer networking can be effective is in a small office. For example, in a group with five tax accountants and one office assistant, each accountant can share a drive on his or her computer containing client tax files. Every accountant can access the client files of any other accountant. The office assistant also can access files to prepare mailings to all clients.

When the workgroup grows to over about 10 members, however, peer-to-peer networking is much less effective for several reasons:

- It offers only moderate network security. Access to information can be limited to a certain drive or directory, but not to individual files.

- There is no centralized storage or account management. As the number of network users grows, so does the need to have a central place to store and manage information. It is much easier to manage files by locating them on a central file server for all to access.

- Network management becomes more difficult because there is no point of centralized administrative control from which to manage users and critical files, including backing up important files.

- Peer-to-peer networks can soon experience slow response because this model is not optimized for heavy multiple access to one computer. If many workgroup members decide to access one shared drive or other shared resources at the same time, all are likely to experience slow computer response from the load.

NETWORKING IN A DOMAIN

Microsoft Windows NT Server is a more robust network operating system than Windows 95. As with Windows 95, you can run programs on Windows NT Server and use desktop features such as My Computer to view files, and Network Neighborhood to see computers on the network (try Hands-on Project 1-1 at the end of this chapter). But Windows NT Server offers much more because it enables computers to operate as part of a domain. An NT **domain** is a collection of resources and of users who have access to the resources. In a domain, all computers access a central database of information about user accounts and security; in a workgroup, each computer has more haphazard access granted through an array of decentralized resources. A single domain can have one or more servers as members. Also, users can be set up into groups to control who has access to what resources. The domain offers a way to manage resources, workstations, software, and the network from one central location. For the network administrator, this offers a way to manage the network resources with minimum confusion and time expenditure.

Domains can include file servers. A **file server** is a single computer that provides multiuser access. The file server is designed to handle several hundred or more users at once, resulting in faster response when delivering the shared resource, and less network congestion as multiple workstations wait to access that resource. Figure 1-2 illustrates a domain with a file server.

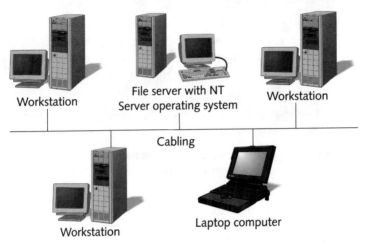

Figure 1-2   A file server on a network

The domain model offers many options for multiple network applications. For instance, a Windows NT file server can offer the following advantages:

- All members can share computer files.

- Printers and other resources can be shared; they can also be located in a central place for convenience.

- Access to resources can be centrally controlled and administered.

- All members can have electronic mail (e-mail) and send messages to other office members through the network and file server.

- Members can share software applications, such as an accounting package or word-processing software. This provides an opportunity to have everyone using the same software (and the benefits of common support for one software package).

- All computers can be backed up more easily. With a network and file server, the backups can be done from one location and regularly scheduled to run from the server. The server can be backed up, too.

- The sharing of computer resources can be arranged to reflect the work groupings within the domain. For example, managing partners can be one group for the purpose of sharing management and financial information on the server.

- The network administrator can save time when installing future software upgrades. For example, to implement the latest version of Microsoft Word, the administrator upgrades only the software at the server. The Microsoft Word users can upgrade their versions from the server.

- More detailed network monitoring and performance analysis can be done from a central location.

A HISTORY OF MICROSOFT WINDOWS NT

Work on Windows NT began in 1988, when Microsoft already had two operating systems on the market, MS-DOS/Windows version 2 and OS/2, which IBM and Microsoft developed jointly. The design for Windows NT focused on providing broader capabilities in areas key to business and network users. Table 1-1 summarizes the goals originally set for Windows NT and where progress toward those goals stands today.

Table 1-1   Original Windows NT Development Goals and their Implementation

Goal	Today's Implementation
Reliability, to support demanding business applications, such as database operations	Programs cannot interfere with the operating system or with other programs, making the system more crashproof
Security, to meet government specifications and to satisfy business auditing requirements	Meets the requirements for government C2 security, which includes security levels up to top secret
Scalability, the option to scale the system to larger computers, including those with multiprocessing architectures	Runs on 80486, Pentium, Pentium Pro, and RISC systems
Extensibility, with protected links into the operating system to accommodate a wide range of hardware **drivers** for extended networking, electronic mail, or other purposes	Uses drivers, application programming interfaces, and other methods to extend capabilities for hardware and software development
Portability, through a system **kernel** that can be ported to computers other than those based on the 8086 processor family, such as million instructions per second (MIPS) computers like the DEC Alpha or IBM RISC computers	Program kernel is written for portability to a growing number of hardware platforms
Compatibility with the many MS-DOS and Windows programs already implemented	Not as compatible as Windows 95 with older MS-DOS programs because of the 32-bit architecture and security requirements, but compatible with Windows-based programs
Distributability, for applications used on a network	Extensively network-compatible with network communication protocols, remote access services, and Internet/intranet services
Government certification, to meet demanding federal government standards	Conforms to open systems and security requirements of the federal government

The first release of Windows NT, in 1991, was for a small group of about 200 developers (Table 1-2). Because this operating system was created from scratch, many programming issues had to be addressed, and the software was not released to the general public until 1993. The public release came in two versions, Windows NT 3.1 and Windows NT 3.1 Advanced Server. Windows NT had a graphical user interface (GUI) similar to that of Windows 3.1 and was issued with the same release number. Later, in 1994, Microsoft added many networking and remote-access improvements to version 3.5, along with the new names Windows NT Workstation and Windows NT Server, which were used to help end confusion over the purpose of each version. Both NT Server and NT Workstation are built with a strong networking foundation, and both can be used for servers or workstations. The primary difference is in the number of supported users connected while the operating system is in the server mode. Windows NT Workstation is designed for about 10 simultaneous users, while Windows NT Server supports several thousand. NT Workstation has become an advanced workstation operating system preferred by corporate, research, and educational users who run demanding or **mission-critical** applications. NT Server is a network operating system that is challenging the dominance once held by Novell NetWare and other network operating systems.

Table 1-2   Windows NT Milestones

Date	Windows NT Release
Late 1991	First release to a small group of developers
Mid-1992	Release to a large group of developers
Fall 1992	First beta version release
Early 1993	Second beta version release
Mid-1993	Released to the public as version 3.1
Mid-1994	Networking and remote-access improvements
Mid-1996	Implementation of new desktop interface, enhanced networking, Internet, directory services, and installation features

MICROSOFT WINDOWS NT SERVER CAPABILITIES

Microsoft Windows NT Server is equipped with a range of capabilities that makes it a versatile network operating system. Because of these capabilities, it is at home acting as a file server, a Web server, or a center for client/server applications. NT Server capabilities include the following:

- Sharing resources
- Managing resources
- Security

- Scalability and compatibility
- Reliability
- Distributability
- Client/server applications
- Electronic mail
- Fault tolerance

SHARING RESOURCES

Data files, software, and print services are examples of resources that a file server can make available on a network. Before file servers, PC users carried files on disk from office to office (a method sometimes called the "SneakerNet"). At one university, a budget officer created disks of budget information that were then distributed to each department. Every department would review the disk files, make changes, and send its disk back to the budget officer to be incorporated in the calculations for the next budget. Creating a university-wide budget involved lots of work as over a hundred disks were carried back and forth to distribute original data and make corrections or additions.

The implementation of a network and Windows NT Server changed the effort to create a new budget each year. With a network, the budget officer could put data files on the file server. Each department could access its own budget information, share it with others in the department, adjust the data, and return it, all without asking anyone to leave his or her office.

A Windows NT file server enables files that need to be used by several people to be stored at one location for all to access. Those who have accounts or authorized access to the file server can quickly obtain shared files. Storing information in one place means that controls can be set up to ensure that everyone obtains consistent data. It is easier to back up data, too, because of its central location.

Microsoft NT servers provide options to share files by creating a shared folder. When a shared folder is available through the network, users with the right authorization can **map** that folder as though it were a drive on his or her computer (Figure 1-3). The Hands-on Projects 1-2 and 1-3 demonstrate folder shaving and how to map a folder.

Windows NT Server print services enable many kinds of printers to be shared on a network. For example, a printer connected to the server can be shared with all network users or only with a designated group of users. Print services to other shared network printers also can be managed from the server.

Many offices find that network print services save on making a substantial investment in printing equipment. For example, in an office with six people working in close proximity, all can share a single network printer, as shown in Figure 1-4, instead of using six individual printers. In another example, an architecture firm can save by sharing one expensive plotter for printing building drawings, instead of purchasing a lower-quality plotter for each architect.

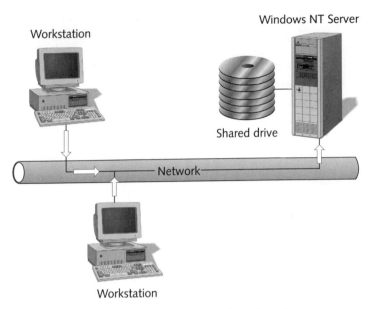

Figure 1-3   Workstations accessing a shared NT Server
hard drive

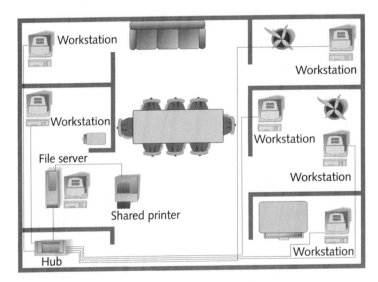

Figure 1-4   Workstations sharing one printer

Another advantage of Windows NT Server is the ability to load or run software applications
on workstations across the network. A site license can be purchased to have one shared copy
of a word processor or one shared copy of an entire suite of programs, such as Microsoft
Office, installed on the server. For example, if the site license is for 400 users, then that many

users have the option to install it from the file server to their workstation over the network. Another option is to run a network version of the software, which means that only a few utility files are permanently loaded at the workstation, while the main program files are always loaded from the server each time the program is started. The advantage of this method is that it saves workstation disk space. A disadvantage is that it may create an excessive load on the server and the network, if there are several hundred users who have network installations.

Using application services on a network can save the network administrator or client support people hours of work. When a software upgrade is released, the network administrator loads one copy on the server that can be shared by all users. This represents hours of savings when compared to purchasing individual licenses and loading the software at each workstation—in our example of 400 users, for instance. Also, using the file server as the central application program source makes it easier to ensure that all users have the same software and version level. This saves many hours for client support people by reducing the need to support an extensive range of software and different software versions.

Microsoft offers a Windows NT Server BackOffice product called Systems Management Server (SMS) that can automatically upgrade software on client workstations, such as late at night when workstations are not in use (providing that the workstations are left logged on to the server).

 When software applications are selected, their compatibility for networking should be determined before the purchase is final. Some software applications can slow file server or network response for all users.

MANAGING RESOURCES

A Microsoft-based network consists of **resources** that can be managed through Windows NT Server. NT Server offers a way to centralize management of network resources, allowing a network administrator to simplify network management tasks. The network resources are file servers, workstations, shared printers, and shared folders. With an NT server, the network administrator can manage access to software, the Internet, print services, data files, and other network services.

SECURITY

At one time computer security was given little attention. Today, security is an important issue. File servers house sensitive data that must be protected from intruders who gain access through a local network or via the Internet. Windows NT 4.0 Server has a C2 top secret security rating from the United States government. The C2 rating means that the NT Server network operating system provides security at many levels, as follows:

- File and folder protection
- Account passwords
- File, folder, and account auditing
- File server access protection on a network
- File server management controls

SCALABILITY AND COMPATIBILITY

Most users want a system that can grow as their organization's needs grow. **Scalability** is the ability of a computer operating system to function on a range of computers from small to large. For example, you might start out with a single-processor Pentium server and 100 users. In a year, you might grow to 400 users and find that you need a more powerful server, such as a dual-processor RISC computer. When you move from the Pentium to the RISC computer you'll want to move the operating system also, in order to keep your investment in software.

NT Server can be scaled to handle substantial growth. The operating system can support from 1 to 15,000 user connections. It works on both single-processor and multiprocessor computers, including 80486s, Pentiums, **symmetric multiprocessor (SMP)** computers, and **reduced instruction set computers (RISCs)**. NT Server 4.0 can run on servers that have up to 32 processors, depending on the capability of the hardware, and it runs on more than 5,000 different brands of computers.

NT Server also can handle small and large databases. Microsoft Access is an example of a small database system that works with NT Server. Larger database capabilities are fulfilled by relational database systems such as Microsoft SQL Server. A single database on an NT Server can hold more than 200 GB of information and have more than 5,000 users accessing it at the same time.

Another result of growth is the need to communicate with a wider range of computers and networks. Microsoft NT communicates with IBM, Novell, UNIX, Banyan, DEC, and other server and host systems. Also, it can be accessed by any of the following types of workstations:

- MS-DOS clients
- Windows 3.x clients
- Windows 95 clients
- Windows NT clients
- Macintosh clients
- UNIX clients
- NetWare clients

RELIABILITY

1

Several features of Windows NT Server make it reliable and powerful. One feature is that the Windows NT Server operating system kernel runs in **privileged mode**, which protects it from problems created by a malfunctioning program or process. Privileged mode gives the operating system an extra level of security from intruders and prevents system crashes because of out-of-control applications.

When a user runs an MS-DOS program on Windows NT Server, the operating system uses the **NT Virtual DOS Machine (NTVDM)** component. The virtual DOS machine tricks the MS-DOS application into responding as though it were the only application running. Each virtual DOS machine session runs in a separate memory space, and several MS-DOS programs can be running at once, each within a different virtual DOS machine session. If a program attempts to make a direct call to memory or to a hardware component, and the operating system detects an error condition or an exception to security, the program may be stopped by Windows NT.

Windows NT Server also runs 16-bit Windows applications by using the virtual DOS machine. When the 16-bit program is started, Windows NT starts a virtual machine session and then starts a 16-bit version of Windows within that session. If more than one 16-bit Windows program is started, all will run in the same virtual DOS machine session, sharing the same memory space allocated for that session. If there is an error in one of the programs, the 16-bit Windows session may be shut down, causing all of the programs in that session to stop. When a 16-bit Windows program is started using the Windows NT RUN utility from the command prompt, an option can be checked to have the program Run in its own virtual DOS machine session. MS-DOS programs also run in the virtual DOS machine, but the difference is that each MS-DOS program always runs in its own virtual DOS machine session and memory space.

Another powerful feature of NT Server is that it takes full advantage of the multitasking and multithreading capabilities of modern Pentium computers. **Multitasking** is the ability to run two or more programs at the same time. For example, Microsoft Word prints a document at the same time that a Microsoft Excel spreadsheet is calculating the sum of a column of numbers. **Multithreading** is the capability of programs written in 32-bit code to run several program code blocks, or threads, at the same time. For instance, a Microsoft Access database query runs a thread to pull data out of the database while another thread generates a subtotal of data already obtained.

The multitasking in Windows NT is preemptive. That means that each program runs in an area of memory separate from areas used by other programs. Early versions of Windows used cooperative multitasking, in which programs shared the same memory area. The advantage of preemptive multitasking is that it reduces the risk of one program interfering with the smooth running of another program.

DISTRIBUTABILITY

There are many software applications written to distribute functions among computers. For example, a sales analysis program might use programs at one computer, databases from two other computers, and special information display screens at a user's computer. The process of dividing computer functions across many computers is called **distributability**.

Windows NT Server handles distributability through the **Distributed Component Object Model (DCOM)**, a capability designed for client/server networks to allow software applications to be integrated across several computers. For example, DCOM makes it possible to integrate a payroll system for a company with multiple locations, housing Windows NT file servers and workstations at each location. The payroll applications and database information can be maintained at and coordinated among all locations.

CLIENT/SERVER APPLICATIONS

The DCOM capability of Windows NT Server makes this operating system a major player in client/server applications. Client/server applications began appearing in the late 1980s as a means to provide more information to users than could previously be provided by traditional mainframe or file-server-based application systems. Mainframe solutions have not been successful in fully meeting the reporting and data query needs of users. File server systems alone have not been efficient in handling large databases of information. Client/server applications are designed to fill the gaps left by mainframe and file server approaches.

Client/server applications have focused on quickly bringing data to customers. Users are able to build queries and reports to meet their information needs without writing complex computer code. These applications are made possible by a combination of technological tools that includes the following:

- Relational databases
- Graphical user interfaces (GUIs)
- Rapid application development (RAD) tools
- Powerful reporting tools
- More powerful PC workstations
- Networks

Relational databases have made it possible to store large amounts of data on a server. These databases can be designed for fast access to data for updating, querying, or reporting. Modern relational databases can store voice and video information as well as data. They also provide open access paths (standard guidelines for reaching data) so that a variety of reporting and development tools can access the data. This connectivity has created an active market for companies that offer RAD development tools and GUI reporting tools.

Today, 90% of client/server applications are developed in the Microsoft Windows GUI environment with RAD development tools such as Microsoft Visual Basic. The GUI environment is easy for the customer to use, and the RAD tools are easier for programmers to work with than older development methods. More powerful PC workstations have made it possible to use GUI and to access large amounts of data held in relational databases.

Networks provide the link to the applications and to the data. Many client/server systems are designed to be three-tiered, meaning that there are three critical pieces (Figure 1-5). One piece is the PC client workstation, which contains the GUI presentation logic seen by the user. Another piece is the application server, which stores client/server applications and reports (business process logic) used by the client. The third piece is the database server, which provides data-related services, including security.

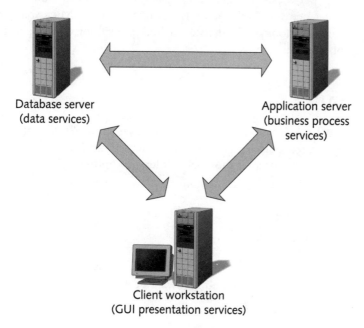

Database server
(data services)

Application server
(business process
services)

Client workstation
(GUI presentation services)

Figure 1-5   Client/server application system

The demands for client/server applications will continue to grow. GUI reporting tools make it possible for more clients to write their own database queries quickly. As more clients transport more ad hoc report data, network and server demands increase. This is particularly true when that data is video or voice information. The GUI format also is very data-intensive and puts demand on the network and on servers.

RAD tools are reducing application development cycles, so developers can place more applications with more functionality on the network. Since the applications are developed in GUI format, they attract new customers who did not use computers in the past. This introduces more people to network computing, resulting in more network and server demand, such as for powerful servers.

ELECTRONIC MAIL

Microsoft NT Server can be configured to provide e-mail services similar to those of a post office. **Electronic mail (e-mail)** has become a critical application on networks. Many organizations rely on their e-mail services to communicate about projects, to discuss sales strategies, and to prepare for meetings. College professors are contacted by their students through e-mail for information about tests and assignments, and some prefer to have assignments submitted by e-mail. Many software vendors provide assistance to their customers by e-mail. Television viewers can even contact their favorite news organizations through e-mail.

A major advantage of e-mail is that it is fast and convenient. Another advantage is that mail distribution lists can be built, allowing many people at different locations to receive the same message. Also, many networked organizations offer calendar and appointment software to complement e-mail. Microsoft NT Server is compatible with Microsoft Exchange, Microsoft Mail, Microsoft Outlook, and Microsoft Schedule+, all software applications that provide e-mail and appointment services.

FAULT TOLERANCE

Computer software and hardware sometimes fail, for many reasons. Protection from these failures is called fault tolerance. NT Server comes with many fault-tolerance capabilities, as you will learn later in this text. Some of those fault-tolerance options are as follows:

- Recovery from hard disk failures
- Recovery from lost data in a file
- Recovery from system configuration errors
- Protection from power outages
- Advanced warning about system and hardware problems
- Recovery from network connectivity failures

SERVER FILE SYSTEMS

Windows NT 4.0 Server primarily supports two file systems: the file allocation table (FAT) file system and NT file system (NTFS). It also supports conversion of the High Performance File System (HPFS) to NTFS.

FAT

The **file allocation table (FAT) file system** is an older file system that is suited for computers with small disk systems, such as early computers with 20, 40, 100, 250, or 500 MB of disk storage. Most computers sold today come with much larger disk storage, such as 2, 3, or 4 GB, or more. Because today's applications and data files quickly consume disk space, many computer owners are purchasing additional disk drives.

FAT was developed to use with MS-DOS and is compatible with Windows NT, Windows 95, OS/2, and various UNIX computer operating systems. FAT disk drives are set up in a series of allocation units (previously called clusters) to form a partition. An allocation unit may consist of two, four, or eight sectors on a disk. Files are created from one or more allocation units. The operating system keeps track of used and unused allocation units in a disk area called the file allocation table, which is kept in the beginning allocation units of the partition. (See Chapter 6 for an explanation of partitions.) The file allocation table has one of four types of entries for each allocation unit, as follows:

- A mark indicating that the unit is available to be used
- A number showing the next allocation unit occupied by a file
- An end-of-file mark showing the last allocation unit for a file using several allocation units
- A mark indicating that the allocation unit is damaged or cannot be read

A FAT system also contains lists of associated files that form a directory. A directory tracks the following information about its files:

- Name
- Time and date of creation or last update
- Attributes, such as read-only
- Size
- Number of the first allocation unit it occupies

FAT has several advantages:

- It is a simple file system that is supported by many small computer operating systems.
- It has a low operating system overhead.
- It can support partitions up to 4 GB.

Some important disadvantages of FAT are:

- It becomes corrupted over time as files are spread among disjointed allocation units, and pointers to each unit are lost.
- FAT does not offer many file or directory security or auditing options.
- It does not support long filenames; filenames are limited to 11 characters, 8 for the main name and 3 for an extension.

The FAT system has been upgraded in newer versions of MS-DOS and in Windows 95 to support long filenames. The upgrade is called VFAT.

NTFS

The **NT file system (NTFS)** is the native Windows NT file system, a modern system designed for the needs of a network server environment. As a full-featured network file system, NTFS is equipped with security features that meet the US government's C2 security specifications. C2 security refers to high-level "top secret" standards for data protection, system auditing, and system access that are required by some government agencies. NTFS also incorporates such features as:

- Long filenames
- File compression
- Large file capacity
- File activity tracking
- POSIX support

NTFS enables the use of filenames of up to 256 characters. This is an advantage over the older FAT system, because files can more easily be named to reflect their contents.

NTFS security accomplishes several purposes. One is to create security measures to determine what type of access is allowed for users of folders and of files within folders. The file and folder access can be tailored to the particular requirements of an organization. For example, the system files on a server can be protected so that only the server administrator has access. A folder of databases can be protected with read access, but no authority to change data; a public folder can give users in a designated group authority to read and update files, but not to delete files.

File compression is a process that significantly reduces the size of a file by a method similar to the MS-DOS DoubleSpace technique, but Windows NT compression is used on folders rather than on entire volumes. Some files can be compressed by more than 40%, saving important disk space for other storage needs. This is particularly useful for files that are accessed infrequently. NTFS provides the ability to compress files as needed (Figure 1-6).

File compression can be used on specified files after an NT server is set up. A disadvantage is that compressed files take longer to access because they must be decompressed when retrieved.

NTFS can be scaled to accommodate very large files, particularly for database applications. A Microsoft SQL Server database file might be 20 GB or larger. This means that an organization can store pictures, scanned images, and sound clips in a single database. The NTFS system can support files up to 64 GB.

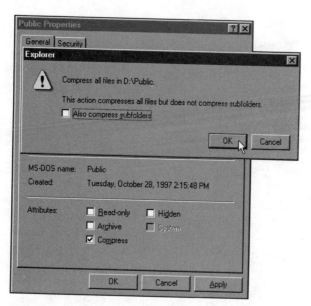

Figure 1-6   NTFS file compression

Another NTFS feature is that it keeps a log or journal of file system activity. This is a critical process should there be a power outage or hard disk failure. Important information can be retrieved and restored in these situations. FAT does not have this capability.

A last NTFS feature is support of the **Portable Operating System Interface (POSIX)**. POSIX is a set of standards to enable portability of applications from one computer system to another, and has been used particularly for UNIX systems. Windows NT follows the POSIX1 standard, which includes case-sensitive filenames and use of multiple filenames (called hard links). For example, the files Myfile.doc and MYFile.doc are considered different files (except when using NT Explorer or the MS-DOS command prompt window).

A limitation of NTFS is that it is designed for Windows NT systems. For example, if you set up a computer to run Windows NT and Windows 95 (called a dual-boot system), Windows 95 will not recognize the NTFS files when it is running.

HPFS

The **High Performance File System (HPFS)** is a file system used by the OS/2 operating system. HPFS was developed as an alternative to FAT to provide larger file-storage capability and faster access to data through a B-tree directory system similar to fast data-search routines used by programmers to find data in a database. HPFS also has better security than FAT and better recovery from disk errors. When a disk error occurs, HPFS uses a "hot fix" technique that quickly grabs the data on the damaged portion and writes it to an undamaged part of the disk. HPFS was supported by Windows NT Server through version 3.51, but is not supported by version 4.0. HPFS is a step up from FAT, but it does not match NTFS in large-file support, security through permissions, and transaction logging for data recovery. Also, NTFS has hot fix capabilities that match HPFS. There is little value in continued support of HPFS, other than to convert it to NTFS. The conversion program for that purpose is CONVERT.EXE and is available from Microsoft.

CHOOSING A FILE SYSTEM

If Windows NT Server is intended for a computer with only one disk drive that has 500 MB or less of disk storage, then the FAT file system may be sufficient. But that is rarely the case for the type of users who purchase NT Server, because they need a system that can handle demanding applications with high memory and disk requirements. For systems with over 500 MB of disk storage or more than one hard drive, NTFS is the best choice. NTFS is better at handling file operations on large disks and can combine multiple drives so that they are recognized under one drive letter, such as one logical drive C. Also, for users who anticipate extremely large disk requirements, NTFS supports a much larger total volume size of 2 terabytes (TB) compared to a 4 GB maximum for FAT.

Security is another important consideration in the selection of a file system on a server. FAT has limited security capabilities, such as setting an attribute to make a file read-only or hidden. NTFS has extensive security based on permissions. Permissions are a security property that can be placed on a drive, folder, or file. For example, access to a folder can be restricted to a certain group of users so that any group member has authority to read a file and add new files to the folder. Non-group members can be prevented from accessing the folder entirely. Also, the NTFS system enables a folder or file to be audited, so that there is a record of the number of times a file has been successfully opened.

If Windows NT Server is implemented on a RISC computer, the FAT file system and NTFS must be combined, because the RISC-based system files must reside in a FAT partition. The remainder of the disk storage can be formatted for NTFS, including the boot partition of the computer.

Another advantage of NTFS that many administrators prefer is transaction logging. If a disk error occurs while a file is being updated, the data is recovered in an instant. FAT uses file caching, which also enables it to recover data after a disk problem. But the FAT recovery may not be as quick or as accurate if there have been many updates recorded in cache.

A disadvantage of using NTFS is that the server contents cannot be converted back to FAT, should there be a need. However, a FAT partition can be converted to NTFS on a one-time basis. Table 1-3 compares the FAT and NTFS file systems.

Table 1-3   FAT and NTFS Compared

Feature	FAT	NTFS
Total volume size	4 GB	2 TB
Maximum file size	4 GB	64 GB
Filename length	11 characters (except for VFAT, which supports 256)	256 characters
Security	Limited security based on attributes	C2-rated extensive security options
File compression	Supported with extra utilities	Supported as part of NTFS
File activity tracking	None	Tracking via a log
POSIX support	None	POSIX1 support
Hot fix	Limited	Supports hot fix
Large database support	Limited	Yes
Multiple disk drives in one volume	No	Yes

INTERNET INTEGRATION AND ELECTRONIC COMMERCE

Many organizations are interested in offering information or services on the World Wide Web (WWW) through the Internet. NT Server is designed as a home for Microsoft's Web server software called Internet Information Server (IIS). IIS gives organizations the ability to take advantage of intranet software as well as Internet software. The **Internet** is a collection of thousands of smaller networks tied together around the globe by a vast array of network equipment and communications links. An **intranet** is a private network within an organization; it uses the same Web-based software as the Internet but is highly restricted from public access. Intranets are currently used to enable managers to run high-level reports, to enable staff members to update human resources information, and to provide access to other forms of private data.

IIS for NT Server has a built-in service called Index Server. This software automatically indexes the information created for intranet access within a company. Index information is created for **Hypertext Markup Language (HTML)** pages, text files, or Microsoft Office documents, such as Microsoft Word. The Index Server enables quick searches for the indexed topics while using low network overhead.

Microsoft is making a strong commitment to Web development. It offers IIS for Windows NT Server, Peer Web Services for Windows NT Workstation and Windows 95, FrontPage for Web development, and HTML formatting options built into Microsoft Office 97.

The Internet has become a major source of commerce, allowing people to order just about anything online. With an account number or credit card handy, you can order practically any type of product, including flowers, a boat, books, art, computer equipment, shoes, or a mountain bike. Thousands of companies have scrambled to establish Web sites from which to advertise and sell products. Many publications are now electronic only, available through subscription on the Internet.

CHAPTER SUMMARY

- Windows NT 4.0 Server is an operating system meant for networking. Peer-to-peer networking is an important advancement for network operations, but the full-featured NT 4.0 Server operating system offers many advantages. Peer-to-peer networking can be slow, as more demands are placed on the individual workstations. By using Windows NT 4.0 Server you have many more options for network productivity and growth. NT Server offers many resource options for shared folders, printers, and other network resources. It also provides network management facilities through domains and groups. NT Server is a reliable operating system with built-in protection from unexpected crashes.

- Once you invest in NT Server, you have options to scale up to larger and more powerful hardware as demands grow through the addition of users and more information stored at the server. With DCOM compatibility, NT Server offers a solid foundation for distributed application servers such as client/server applications. Windows NT Server also makes a reliable e-mail server for a network.

- NT Server supports both the FAT and NTFS file systems. The system that is best for a particular installation depends on several factors, such as file sizes, volume size, security needs, and the purpose of the server and number of users.

- NT Server offers access to and integration of Internet and intranet services through Microsoft's Web server software, Internet Information Server (IIS), and built-in Index Server service.

KEY TERMS

- **Component Object Model (COM)** — Standards that enable a software object, such as a graphic, to be linked from one software component into another one. COM is the foundation that makes object linking and embedding (OLE) possible.

- **Distributed Component Object Model (DCOM)** — A standard built upon COM to enable object linking to take place over a network.

- **distributability** — Dividing complex application program tasks among two or more computers.

- **domain** — A grouping of network users and file servers to make common administrative and security management tasks more efficient.

■ **driver** — Software that enables a computer to communicate with devices such as network interface cards, printers, monitors, and hard disk drives. Each driver has a specific purpose, such as to handle network communications.

■ **electronic mail (e-mail)** — Using mail software on a client to compose a message and send it to mail or post office software on one or more servers that forward the message to the intended destination. E-mail is possible because of networks and can span the globe thanks to the Internet.

■ **file allocation table (FAT) file system** — A file system based on the use of a file allocation table, a flat table that records the allocation units (clusters) used to store the data contained in each file stored on disk. FAT is used by several operating systems, including MS-DOS, Windows 95, and Windows NT. Advanced security and auditing are not supported on FAT partitions.

■ **High Performance File System (HPFS)** — A file system used by the OS/2 operating system. Although previous versions of Windows NT supported HPFS, Windows NT 4.0 does not.

■ **Hypertext Markup Language (HTML)** — A formatting process that is used to enable documents and graphics images to be read on the World Wide Web. HTML also provides for fast links to other documents, to graphics, and to Web sites. The World Wide Web is a series of file servers with software, such as Microsoft's Internet Information Server (IIS), that make HTML and other Web documents available for workstations to access.

■ **Internet** — A global network of diverse WWW and information servers offering voice, video, and text data to millions of users.

■ **intranet** — A private network within an organization. It uses the same Web-based software as the Internet but is highly restricted from public access. Intranets are currently used to enable managers to run high-level reports, to enable staff members to update human resources information, and to provide access to other forms of private data.

■ **kernel** — An essential set of programs and computer code that allows a computer operating system to control processor, disk, memory, and other functions central to the basic operation of a computer.

■ **mapped drive** — A disk volume or folder that is shared on the network by a file server or workstation. It gives designated network workstations access to the files and data in its shared volume or folder. The workstation, via software, determines a drive letter for the shared volume, which is the workstation's map to the data.

■ **mission-critical** — A computer software application or a hardware service that has the highest priority in an organization.

■ **multitasking** — The capability of a computer to run two or more programs at the same time.

■ **multithreading** — Running several program processes or parts (threads) at the same time.

■ **network operating system** — Software that enables computers on a network to communicate and to share resources and files.

- **NT file system (NTFS)** — The native Windows NT file system, which has a more detailed directory structure than FAT and supports security measures not found in FAT. It also supports large disks, long filenames, and file compression.

- **NT Virtual DOS Machine (NTVDM)** — In Windows NT, a process that emulates an MS-DOS window in which to run MS-DOS or 16-bit Windows programs in a designated area of memory.

- **peer-to-peer network** — A network where any computer can communicate with other networked computers on an equal or peer-like basis without going through an intermediary, such as a server or host.

- **Portable Operating System Interface (POSIX)** — Standards set by the Institute of Electrical and Electronics Engineers (IEEE) for portability of applications.

- **reduced instruction set computer (RISC)** — Computers that have CPUs that require fewer instructions for common operations. The processor works faster because the commands to the CPU are reduced.

- **resource** — On an NT server network, a file server, shared printer, or shared directory that can be accessed by users. On a workstation, a resource is an IRQ, I/O address, or memory that is allocated to a computer component, such as a disk drive or communications port.

- **scalable** — A computer operating system that can be used on small to large computers, such as those with a single Intel-based processor, and on larger computers, such as those with multiple Intel or RISC processors.

- **symmetric multiprocessor (SMP)** — A type of computer with two or more CPUs that share the processing load.

- **workgroup** — As used in Microsoft networks, a number of users who share drive and printer resources in an independent peer-to-peer relationship.

- **workstation** — A computer that has its own CPU and may be used as a standalone computer for word processing, spreadsheet creation, or other software applications. It also may be used to access another computer such as a mainframe computer or file server, as long as the necessary network hardware and software are installed.

- **World Wide Web (WWW)** — A vast network of servers throughout the world that provide access to voice, text, video, and data files.

REVIEW QUESTIONS

1. The ability of Windows NT 4.0 Server to run on Intel- and RISC-based computers is called

   a. distributability

   b. scalability

   c. retrofitting

   d. partitioning

2. You are installing NT Server on a computer that has two 4.5 GB hard disks, and you want to configure them into one volume with the drive letter C:. Which file system would you select?

   a. FAT

   b. HPFS

   c. NTFS

   d. all of the above

   e. only b and c

3. Which of the following is a network drive on a computer?

   a. drive C:

   b. a CD–ROM drive

   c. a mapped drive

   d. a local drive

4. File servers are an example of a _____ system.

   a. multimedia

   b. multiuser

   c. single user

   d. restricted user

5. Which of the following plays a role in the distributability features of Windows NT 4.0?

   a. DCOM

   b. COM

   c. fault tolerance

   d. POSIX

6. Which types of application is (are) an example of distributability?

   a. Microsoft Word

   b. Microsoft PowerPoint

   c. client/server

   d. all of the above

   e. only a and b

7. Which of the following does using a server on a network enable you to do?

   a. share files

   b. create electronic workgroups

   c. save time installing software

   d. all of the above

   e. only b and c

8. Protection from unexpected system crashes in Windows NT Server is provided by

   a. the privileged mode.

   b. fault examination.

   c. the real mode.

   d. using dual processors.

9. Printing and looking up Help information at the same time in Microsoft Word is accomplished in Windows NT Server by

   a. creating folder properties.

   b. multitasking.

   c. multithreading.

   d. mapping.

10. Windows NT Server recognizes which of the following file systems?

    a. NTFS

    b. FAT

    c. UNIX

    d. all of the above

    e. only a and b

11. Which of the following is a set of core programs and program code in an operating system?

    a. command window

    b. external subroutine sets

    c. kernel

    d. Component Object Model

12. Which of the following was not an initial development goal of Windows NT?

    a. reciprocation

    b. security

    c. scalability

    d. reliability

13. You are installing an NT server for a government agency that requires the highest level of security. Which file system would you use?

    a. FAT

    b. NTFS

    c. HPFS

    d. UNIX

1

14. Which of the following computers might have two or more CPUs?

    a. symmetric multiprocessor (SMP)

    b. reduced instruction set computer (RISC)

    c. Intel-based 80486 with an exchangeable socket

    d. all of the above

    e. only a and b

15. A workstation running which of the following operating systems can connect to Windows NT Server?

    a. Macintosh

    b. MS-DOS

    c. Windows 95

    d. all of the above

    e. only b and c

16. Which of the following is an example of fault tolerance?

    a. recovery of data on a hard disk

    b. setting access protections on a folder

    c. using auditing on a folder

    d. all of the above

    e. only b and c

17. A _____ is software that enables a computer to communicate with an attached monitor or printer.

    a. text file

    b. driver

    c. performance enhancer

    d. display subroutine

18. A long filename can be up to _____ characters.

    a. 244

    b. 256

    c. 11

    d. 100

19. In Windows NT 4.0 Server, a 16-bit Windows program runs

    a. like any 32-bit program

    b. with a maximum of 640 KB memory allocated to it

    c. in the virtual DOS machine

    d. about 32% slower than 32-bit Windows programs

20. A Web site can be established in Windows NT 4.0 Server using

    a. Web client/server

    b. COM

    c. HTML server

    d. Internet Information Server

21. As the server administrator, you can locally run an MS-DOS program in Windows NT Server 4.0 through _____.

    a. the virtual DOS machine in its own memory space

    b. by sharing a memory space with 16-bit Windows programs that are running

    c. by sharing a memory space with 32-bit Windows programs that are running

    d. only by first starting native MS-DOS when the server is booted

22. One user logged onto Windows NT Server is accessing the Internet Information Server while at the same time the server administrator is logged on locally to use the Notepad editor. This is an example of _____.

    a. dual processing

    b. process starting

    c. multitasking

    d. mapping

HANDS-ON PROJECTS

 PROJECT 1-1

This activity gives you an opportunity to view the drives on a Windows NT 4.0 Server through My Computer, a utility used to view the contents of drives and folders. You need access to a computer running Windows NT 4.0 Server (using NTFS) and the password to the Administrator's account or to an account with the same privileges as the Administrator's account. Remain logged on after completing this activity, so that you can easily complete the other hands-on activities in this section.

To use My Computer:

1. Log on to Windows NT Server by pressing **[Ctrl]-[Alt]-[Del]**.

2. Enter the username and password and click **OK**.

3. Double-click **My Computer** on the desktop (Figure 1-7).

4. Double-click drive **C:** to view its folders and files (Figure 1-8).

5. Close My Computer.

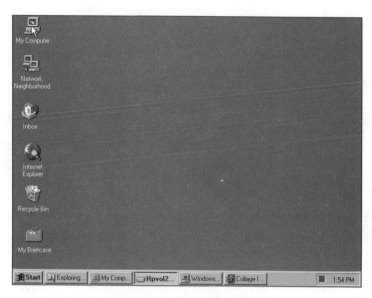

Figure 1-7 Opening My Computer

Figure 1-8 Viewing drive C: contents

PROJECT 1-2

In this activity, you use Windows NT Explorer to view files on NT Server and then to view the properties of a folder created in NTFS.

To use NT Explorer:

1. Click the **Start** button, **Programs**, and **Windows NT Explorer** (Figure 1-9).

2. Notice there are two scroll boxes of information, All Folders and Contents of (C:) (Figure 1-10).

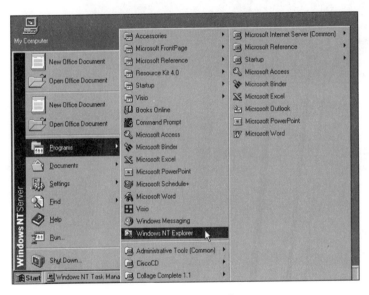

Figure 1-9   Opening Windows NT Explorer

3. Scroll down to view files in the Contents of (C:) scroll box.

4. Scroll to the Winnt folder. Every folder created in NTFS contains properties, such as information about the folder size, sharing, and security options. Right-click the **Winnt** folder and click the **Properties** option on the shortcut menu (Figure 1-11).

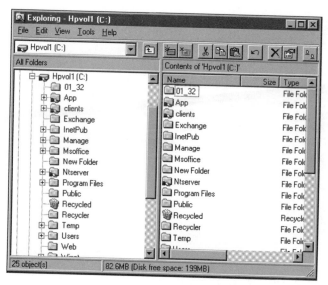

Figure 1-10   Viewing drive C: contents

5. Notice the information in the General tab, such as folder statistics and attributes (Figure 1–12).

6. Click to view the **Sharing** tab and then the **Security** tab. Notice the options on each tab.

7. Click **Cancel** to close the Properties dialog box.

8. Close NT Explorer.

Figure 1-11   Viewing a folder's properties

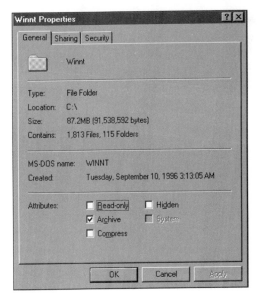

Figure 1-12   General tab information

 **PROJECT 1-3**

In this activity, you use Network Neighborhood to view workstations and servers connected to a Microsoft-based network.

To use Network Neighborhood:

1. Double-click **Network Neighborhood** on the desktop.

2. Double-click one of the computer icons in Network Neighborhood (the icons in your display will differ from Figure 1-13). This step enables you to view folders, printers, and other resources that the computer is sharing on the network (Figure 1-14).

Figure 1-13   Viewing the shared resources
             on a networked computer

1

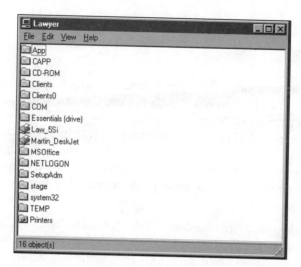

Figure 1-14 Listing of shared resources
on a networked computer

3. Notice that shared folders are indicated by a folder icon, and that shared printers have a printer icon.

4. To view how to map a shared folder, right-click a folder in the dialog box, and then click **Map Network Drive**.

5. Notice that you can assign a drive letter to the mapped folder in the Drive: list box, and that you can click the box Reconnect at Logon to automatically map this drive each time you log on (Figure 1-15).

Figure 1-15 Mapping a drive

6. Click **Cancel** in the Map Network Drive dialog box.

7. Close the listing of shared resources.

8. Close Network Neighborhood.

ASPEN CONSULTING: EXPLORING NT 4.0 SERVER

You are a Windows NT Server consultant for Aspen Consulting, which operates from the West Coast in the United States and has an office in Vancouver, Canada. Your boss is Mark Arnez, one of the managing partners of Aspen Consulting. Aspen Consulting has over 50 consultants, who specialize in networking, server operating systems implementation, and support of Microsoft computer operating systems. Your company has clients throughout the United States and Canada. The work is challenging because your clients are very diverse, such as accounting firms, manufacturing companies, colleges, universities, law firms, mail-order houses, and publishing companies.

Today Mark asks you to work with a large bookstore, OPUS Books, that has 82 employees and that wants to begin sales over the Internet. OPUS Books occupies an eight-story building in Seattle and already has installed network cable. There are 62 Windows 95 workstations that will connect to the network. They want your help in selecting a network operating system.

1. OPUS Books knows that they can connect the Windows 95 computers using peer-to-peer networking. Do you recommend this type of setup, or should they consider installing a server? Explain your recommendations.

2. The bookstore manager, Vicki Sanchez, wants to know the advantages of using Windows NT Server. Describe five features of this operating system that would benefit OPUS Books.

3. OPUS Books wants to establish a huge database of their inventory, possibly as large as 8 GB. If they purchase Windows NT 4.0 Server, what file system would you recommend? What are the advantages of this file system?

4. Vicki Sanchez has some questions about mapping a shared drive. Explain how she can view shared network resources and map a shared drive to her computer.

5. Vicki has mapped the drive, but it is not displayed each time she connects. What do you advise?

6. Explain what Internet software can be used with Microsoft NT Server and how this might help OPUS Books expand their sales.

BASIC NETWORK DESIGN
AND PROTOCOLS

A Windows NT server needs a network to communicate with workstations and other computers. Fortunately there is very little mystery to a basic network; mainly, it is computers connected to communications cable. Network devices such as routers, switches, and hubs simply join different networks, strengthen the communications signal sent between computers, direct the signal to the right place, and provide techniques to send the signal as quickly as possible.

The most important element in designing a network is meeting the needs of the organization it serves. A Windows NT server on a well-designed network can be a powerful source of information, while helping people be more productive in their work. Networking is your opportunity to be a success in your organization by applying basic design skills that yield effective results. This chapter teaches you fundamental skills for planning a network, such as choosing the right cable, selecting a modern network layout, and incorporating effective communications between a Windows NT server and the workstations it reaches.

AFTER READING THIS CHAPTER AND COMPLETING THE EXERCISES YOU WILL BE ABLE TO:

- PLAN A NETWORK
- EXPLAIN NETWORK TOPOLOGIES
- DESCRIBE NETWORK COMMUNICATIONS MEDIA
- EXPLAIN HOW NETWORK CABLE CONNECTS TO A COMPUTER
- DESCRIBE THE ETHERNET AND TOKEN RING TRANSPORT METHODS
- DESCRIBE MICROSOFT NETWORKING SERVICES AND PROTOCOLS
- DETERMINE HOW TO SELECT THE TOPOLOGY AND COMMUNICATIONS CABLE FOR A GIVEN INSTALLATION
- DETERMINE HOW TO SELECT THE RIGHT PROTOCOL FOR A GIVEN INSTALLATION

AN OVERVIEW OF NETWORKS

Early networks connected users in close proximity, such as in the same office area or floor of a building. These were truly **local area networks (LANs)** with a limited area of service. A LAN is a series of interconnected computers, printers, and other computer equipment that shares hardware and software resources. The service area is usually limited to a given floor, office area, or building. Figure 2-1 is an example of a simple LAN linking workstations and a server in two school computer labs.

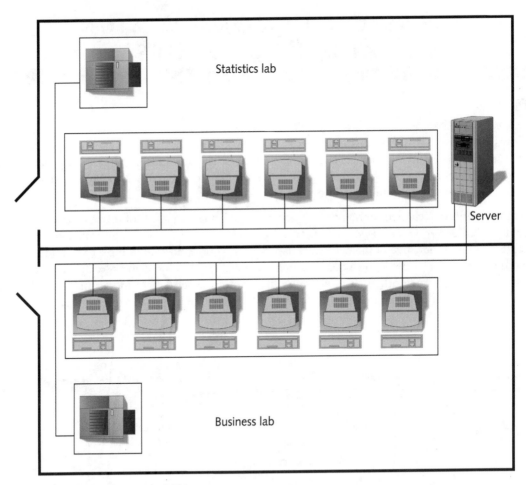

Figure 2-1   A sample LAN

Once LANs became a reality, the push was on to find ways to connect one LAN to another, for instance to connect a LAN in one building to a LAN in an adjacent building or in a building across town. Connecting multiple LANs within a city or metropolitan region creates a **metropolitan area network (MAN)**. A state university in one city is a MAN when it links several research centers and other facilities throughout the same city. A large business campus might have LANs used for administrative processing connected to LANs used for scientific research. Both of these also are examples of **enterprise networks** because they link separate LANs with different computer resources into one large connected unit. An enterprise network reaches throughout a large area, such as a college campus, a city, or across several states, connecting many kinds of local area networks and network resources, including mainframes, minicomputers, servers, printers, plotters, and fax equipment.

The reach of networks has grown to extend across continents and oceans. These **wide area networks (WANs)** give college students at the University of Washington the ability to use supercomputers housed at the University of Illinois. A commercial vendor in Rochester, New York, can send software application updates to clients in Colorado and in London, England, via network connections. Figure 2-2 illustrates enterprise networks in Toronto, Chicago, and Detroit linked into a WAN.

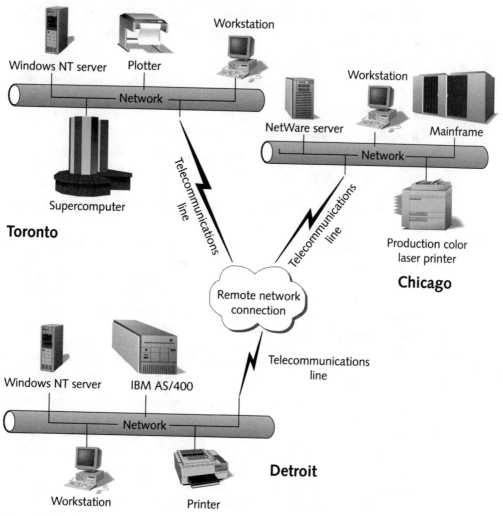

Figure 2-2   Enterprise networks connected into a WAN

Network technology is pervasive and has blurred the distinctions between LANs and WANs. It is now difficult to define where a LAN ends and a WAN begins. The distinctions are growing more vague as television cable companies partner with telephone companies to bring networking into every home.

PLANNING A NETWORK

Before you begin running cable and connecting workstations, develop a network plan. The first step in network planning is to assess the business or organizational needs for which the network is to be used. These include the following:

- Size and purpose of the organization
- Potential growth of the organization in terms of people and services
- Number of mission-critical applications on the network
- Important cycles for the business or organization
- Relationship of the network resources to the mission of the business or organization
- Security needs
- Amount budgeted for network and computer resources

There are many other considerations, but these provide a good start. For example, if you are working with a large organization that is likely to grow, there will be a particular emphasis on planning for extra cabling and high-capacity network options. For a small network, such as a 15-person dental office, the network design needs to be reliable and easy to manage on a small budget.

Some organizations, such as accounting and payroll departments or banks, work with very sensitive financial information, requiring a high degree of reliability, security, and fault tolerance. Also, those organizations have especially urgent business cycles, including daily electronic transmission of money transactions, daily account balancing, month-end and year-end accounting cycles, income tax reporting, and regular audits from independent financial auditors. Your network planning and management must always take into account those important cycles. For example, you do not want to upgrade the accounting server to the next version of the operating system in the middle of year-end processing, or replace the telecommunications equipment just before an electronic transmission to the Federal Reserve.

In many cases, the network and computing resources are a cornerstone in the business strategy of an organization. A president of a subscription company that markets collectible items regards the computer capabilities of his company as the key reason the company stays ahead of the competition. Computing resources enable that company to provide the fastest customer service and delivery of products. When a customer places an order, a series of inventory, billing, customer profiling, promotional, manufacturing, and product shipping events occur automatically through the computer systems. For colleges, computer systems play an important role in attracting and retaining students, in recruiting, admitting, and registering students, and providing grade and degree progress information.

At one time, security was not a priority on many computers and networks, because few people knew how to intrude into systems. Times have changed, and responsible network planning always includes a blueprint for security. Besides guarding against intrusions, security also includes backing up data, planning for computer failures, and having a plan for disaster recovery.

Organizations rarely have all of the budget they want for computer and network resources. As a responsible network administrator, you can help by planning a network that allows the investment to be retained for many years. For example, you might spend a few dollars more to install top-grade high-speed cable even though your current needs do not require a high-speed network.

From the start, learn how the network is related to the needs of its users, determine what resources already exist, and plan a secure network positioned for growth. A given in networking is that once a network is successfully implemented and managed, the requests to expand its capabilities start immediately.

DEVELOPING A PLAN

Most organizations have a business plan, a long-range plan, or a mission statement. Incorporate this information into your planning process. Develop your own network plan to describe the current resources and what is needed for the future. As you develop your plan, take the following into account:

- Number and kinds of workstations and their operating systems
- Number and kinds of server and host computers and their operating systems
- All software applications that will be networked
- Characteristics of offices and the building layout
- Network management needs
- Cabling types and topologies

Many organizations that are planning a new network or a major expansion write planning documents to send to vendors. These documents are a **request for information (RFI)** and a **request for proposal (RFP)**. An RFI is written as an initial attempt to define in general terms what is needed. It usually describes the organization, existing resources, and the type of services wanted from the vendor. Part of the description of services may be as general as: "The vendor will install network cable and equipment in every room of the building." The RFI is sent to vendors, who respond with information about their products and how they meet the organization's needs as set forth in the RFI. The organization may choose to select a vendor based on that vendor's response to the RFI, or it may choose to send out a follow-up RFP. An RFP uses cumulative information from the returned RFIs to establish exact specifications that may later be binding in a contract. Such a specification might be: "The vendor will install category 5 cable for a 10BASE-T network to every room with two connections per room. The vendor will test every connection after the installation is complete and sign a verification that each connection is working."

NETWORK TOPOLOGIES

There are several ways to plan and design a network to accommodate the needs of those who will be using it. Once a network is in place and fulfilling user needs, a significant investment has been made. This investment includes cabling, network equipment, file servers, workstations, software, and training. Network design and protecting the user's investment in a network are two interrelated concerns. The network design impacts the life of the investment in the network. Some designs are low in cost, but expensive to maintain or upgrade. Other designs are more expensive in the beginning, but are easy to maintain and offer simple upgrade paths.

The best starting point for understanding a network is its topology. The **topology** is the physical layout of a network, combined with its logical characteristics. The physical layout is like an overhead picture or map of how the cabling is laid in the office, building, or campus. This is often called the **cable plant**. The logical side of the network is the way the signal is transferred from point to point along the cable.

The network layout may be decentralized, with cable running between each station on the network, or the layout may be centralized, with each station physically connected to a central device that dispatches data from workstation to workstation. Centralized layouts are like a star with individual rays reaching out to each network station. Decentralized layouts resemble a team of mountain climbers, each at a different location on the mountain, but all joined by a long rope. The logical side of a topology consists of the path taken by the data as it moves around the network.

There are three main topologies: bus, ring, and star. The important task of selecting the best topology depends on the questions addressed by your planning document, such as what software will be used, what computers will be connected, what networks will connect to yours, and what security is needed.

For example, the applications intended to be used on a network influence the number and frequency of data to be transmitted, which is known as **network traffic**. If the network users are primarily accessing word-processing software, the network traffic will be relatively low, and most of the work will be performed at workstations, rather than on the network. Client/server applications generate a medium to high level of network traffic, depending on the client/server software design. Networks on which there is frequent exchange of database information, such as Microsoft Access or SQL Server files, have medium to high network traffic. Scientific software and publications software generate high levels of traffic because they involve extremely large data files.

The influence of hosts and servers on a network is closely linked to the type of software applications that are used. For example, a database server that is constantly accessed to generate reports of financial and sales figures is likely to cause more network traffic than a file server that is occasionally used to access business letters or templates for letters.

Whether other networks will be connected to the network also affects the topology used. The network topology for a small business that will never use more than four computers will be different from the topology required by an industrial campus. The small business is unlikely to connect to additional networks, except for perhaps an outside connection to the Internet. The industrial campus may consist of several interconnected networks, such as a network to control machines in the plant, a network for the business systems, and a network for the research scientists. Some topologies permit better network interconnectivity than other topologies.

Another question that the network administrator should ask is whether or not the applications on the network are mission-critical. If the network is used for a company's payroll, then it is mission-critical. This type of network topology will need to include system redundancy. For example, the network must include alternate routes for data transmission, so that failure of one part of the network will not prevent the payroll from running.

Some networks, such as those on which large files are transmitted, need high-speed data transmission capabilities. The network speed is important to the productivity of the users. High-speed capability is particularly needed when images, graphics, and other large files need to be transported over long distances.

Security is another issue that influences network design. Security is protection of data so that only authorized individuals have access to confidential information. Security involves network implementations that permit restrictions on who can access folders, files, printers, file servers, and applications software. It also may include data encryption, which encodes packets and allows only authorized nodes to decode packets. On high-security networks, fiber-optic cable is used to minimize the risk that unauthorized persons will be able to tap into the cable and capture packets.

Network topology directly influences the network's potential for growth. Once a network is installed, it is very common for an organization to need to add more users in the same office or from additional offices or floors. As a network administrator, you will find that your successful network implementation attracts more and more people who want to be networked.

BUS TOPOLOGY

The **bus topology** consists of running cable from one PC or file server to the next, in a pattern similar to a city bus route. A city bus has a starting point and an ending point on its route, and along the way it visits each possible pick-up station.

In a bus topology, a terminator is connected to each end of a bus cable segment. Like the city bus, a data packet stops at each station on the line. Also like the city bus, a packet has a given amount of time to reach its destination, or it is considered late. A bus network segment must be within the **Institute of Electrical and Electronics Engineers (IEEE)** length specifications to ensure that packets arrive in the expected time. The IEEE is an organization of scientists, engineers, technicians, and educators that has played a leading role in developing standards for network cabling and data transmissions. Figure 2-3 shows a simple bus network.

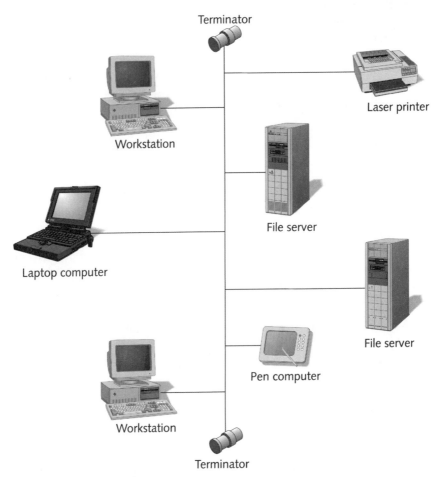

Figure 2-3   Bus topology

The terminator is critical on bus networks because it signals the physical end to the segment. A terminator is really an electrical resistance or block to the signal when it reaches the end of the network, and may be a separate cable component or contained in the network equipment. Without a terminator, a segment violates IEEE specifications, and signals are unreliable because the signal can be mirrored back, reflected on the same path it just covered.

The traditional bus design shown in Figure 2-3 works well for small networks and is relatively inexpensive to implement. At the start, costs can be minimized because it requires less cable than other topologies. It is also easy to add another workstation to extend the bus for a short distance within a room or office. The disadvantage is that management costs can be high. For example, it is difficult to isolate a single malfunctioning node or cable segment and associated connectors—and one defective node or cable segment and connectors can take down the entire network (although modern networking equipment discussed later in this chapter makes this less likely). Another disadvantage is that the bus can become very congested with network traffic, requiring the addition of bridges and other equipment to control the traffic flow.

RING TOPOLOGY

The **ring topology** is a continuous path for data with no logical beginning or ending point, and thus no terminators. Workstations and file servers are attached to the cable at points around the ring (Figure 2-4). When data is transmitted onto the ring, it goes from node to node until the destination node is reached. Because the destination node may be reached before the data has gone full circle, the data often does not pass through all stations.

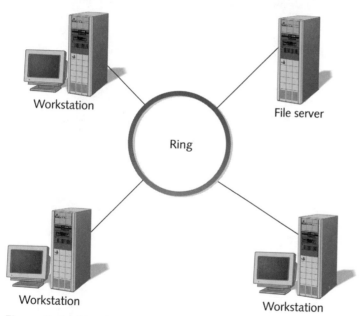

Figure 2-4   Ring topology

When it was first developed, the ring topology permitted data to go in one direction only, stopping at the node that originated the transmission. New high-speed ring technologies consist of two loops for redundant data transmission in opposite directions.

An advantage of the ring topology is that it is easier to manage than the bus. The network equipment used to build the ring makes it easier to locate a defective node or cable problem. This topology is well suited for transmitting signals over long distances on a LAN, and it handles high-volume network traffic better than the bus topology. Overall, the ring topology enables more reliable communications than the bus.

A disadvantage is that the ring topology is more expensive to implement than the bus. Typically, it requires more cable and network equipment at the start. Another disadvantage is that the ring is not used as widely as the bus topology, so there are fewer equipment options and fewer options for expansion to high-speed communications.

STAR TOPOLOGY

The **star topology** is in the shape of a physical star. This is the oldest communications design method, with its roots in telephone switching systems. Although it is the oldest design method, advances in network technology have made the star topology a good option for modern networks. The physical layout of the star topology consists of multiple nodes attached to a central hub (Figure 2-5). A **hub** is a central device used in the star topology that joins single cable segments or individual LANs into one network. Some hubs are also called concentrators or access units. Single communications cable segments radiate from the hub like a star.

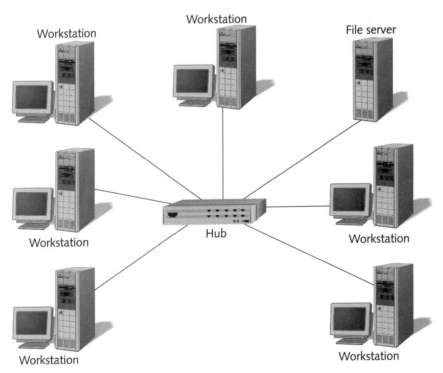

Figure 2-5   Star topology

The startup costs of the star topology are now lower than those of a bus network and comparable to those of the ring network. This is because costs for network equipment are greatly reduced from what they were a few years ago, and vendors have increased costs for bus network components. Like the ring topology, however, the star is easier to manage than the traditional bus network, because malfunctioning nodes can be identified quickly. If a node or a cable run is damaged, it is easily isolated from the network by the network equipment, and service to the other nodes is not affected. The star is easier to expand for connecting additional nodes or networks. It also offers the best avenues to expand into high-speed networking. For these reasons, the star is the most popular topology today, which means that there is a wider variety of equipment made for this topology.

A disadvantage is that the hub is a single point of failure; if it fails, all connected nodes are unable to communicate (unless there is redundancy built into the hub to include backup measures). Another disadvantage is that the star requires more cable to be run than do bus designs.

BUS NETWORKS IN A PHYSICAL STAR LAYOUT

Modern networks combine the logical communications of a bus with the physical layout of a star. In this topology, each ray radiating from the star is like a separate logical bus segment, but with only one or two computers attached. The segment is still terminated at both ends, but the advantage is that there are no exposed terminators. On each segment, one end is terminated inside the hub, and the other is terminated at the device on the network.

Another advantage of the bus-star network topology is that multiple hubs can be connected to expand the network in many directions (Figure 2-6). The connection between hubs is a backbone, often using high-speed communications between hubs. A **backbone** is a high-capacity communications medium that joins networks and central network devices on the same floor in a building, on different floors, and across long distances.

Hubs are available with built-in intelligence to help detect problems. Also, there are expansion opportunities for implementing high-speed networking. Because this is a popular alternative, there is a wide range of equipment available for bus networks in the shape of a star.

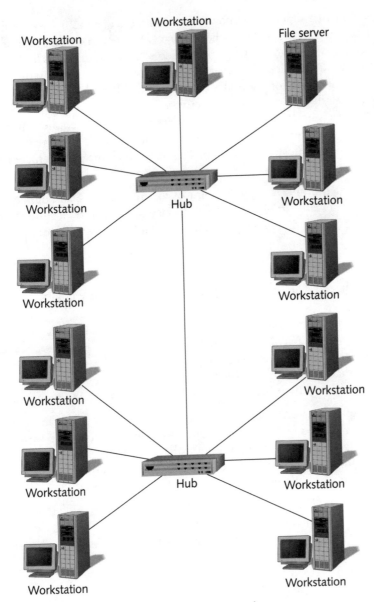

Figure 2-6 Expanding a bus-star network

NETWORK COMMUNICATIONS MEDIA

The communications media on a network are literally the tie that binds everything together. The media used in network communications include the following:

- Thick coaxial cable
- Thin coaxial cable
- Shielded twisted-pair cable
- Unshielded twisted-pair cable
- Fiber-optic cable

The characteristics of each media type make them suitable for different types of networks. The most commonly used cabling is twisted-pair. Coaxial cable, though still common, is used mainly in older LANs. Fiber-optic cabling is used primarily to connect computers that demand high-speed access and to connect networks between different floors and buildings.

When choosing the best medium for a network, you need to consider the characteristics of the different media, such as the following:

- Data transfer speed
- Use in specific network topologies
- Distance requirements
- Cable and cable component costs
- Additional network equipment that is required
- Ease of installation
- Immunity to interference from outside sources
- Upgrade options

COAXIAL CABLE

Coaxial cable (usually called coax) comes in two varieties, thick and thin. Thick coaxial cable was used on early networks, particularly as a backbone to join different networks. It is used infrequently today because there are better alternatives, such as fiber-optic cable. Thin coaxial cable has a much smaller diameter than thick coaxial cable and is used on networks to connect to desktop workstations.

Thick Coaxial Cable

Thick coaxial cable (Figure 2-7) has a copper or copper-clad aluminum conductor as the core. The conductor has a relatively large diameter, as compared with thin coaxial cable.

The conductor is surrounded by insulation, and an aluminum sleeve is wrapped around the outside of the insulation. A polyvinyl chloride (PVC) or Teflon jacket covers the aluminum sleeve.

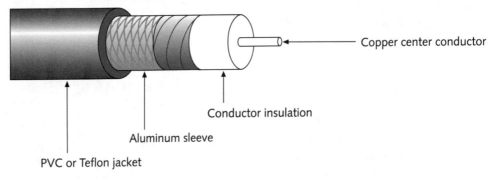

Copper center conductor

Conductor insulation

Aluminum sleeve

PVC or Teflon jacket

Figure 2-7   Thick coaxial cable

The cable jacket is marked every 2.5 meters to show where a network connecting device can be attached. If devices are attached more closely than this, network errors will result. This type of cable is also called RG-8 cable (RG means radio grade).

Thick coaxial cable is difficult to bend, and a minimum bend radius must be followed, because of the large diameter of the copper conductor. However, this cabling has better electrical interference immunity than thin coaxial because of the large-diameter conductor and the aluminum shielding.

Thick coaxial cable works on bus networks normally using transmission speeds of 10 megabits per second (Mbps). According to IEEE standards, the maximum cable length, or run, is 500 meters. The shorthand for these specifications is 10BASE5. The 10 indicates that the cable transmission rate is 10 Mbps. BASE means that baseband transmission is used. A baseband transmission is one in which the entire channel capacity of the medium is used by one data signal. Thus, only one node transmits at a time. The 5 indicates 5 × 100 meters for the longest cable run.

Thick coaxial is not as popular as other cabling because of its diameter and the difficulty in manipulating and terminating it. It is also expensive to purchase and install. On the plus side, thick coax is very durable and reliable, with great resistance to signal interference.

Thin Coaxial Cable

Thin coaxial cable resembles television cable. However, unlike those of television cable, the electrical characteristics of network cable must be very precise and meet the specifications established by the IEEE. This coaxial cabling is labeled with the notation "RG–58A/U" (Radio Grade 58). Thin coax is called 10BASE2 (or thinnet or cheapernet), which means that it has a maximum theoretical network speed of 10 Mbps, can have wire runs up to 200 meters, and uses baseband-type data transmission. Although 10BASE2 cable runs can be up

2

to 200 meters, a maximum of 185 meters is preferred to allow for extra cabling needs required by network equipment. It is important to follow cable specifications carefully, to ensure reliable data communications.

Thin coax cabling has a copper or copper–clad aluminum conductor at the core and an insulating foam material that surrounds the core. High-quality cable has an aluminum foil between the mesh and the foam around the core. A woven copper mesh and aluminum foil sleeve wraps around the insulating foam material and is covered with an outside PVC or Teflon jacket for insulation. It looks similar to the thick coaxial, but is much smaller in diameter.

Coaxial cable is attached to a **bayonet navy connector (BNC)**, which is then connected to a T-connector. The middle of the T is connected to the computer or network device. If that computer or device is the last node at the end of the cable, a terminator is connected to one end of the T-connector, as shown in Figure 2-8.

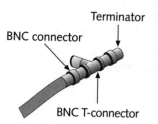

Figure 2-8   A T-connector with a terminator at one end

Thin coaxial cable is easier and cheaper to install than thick coaxial, but twisted-pair cable is much easier still to install and use, because it has better flexibility. This is one reason that coaxial is now used on a limited basis.

Twisted-Pair Cable

Resembling telephone wire, **twisted-pair** cable is the most popular communications medium. Twisted-pair is more flexible than coaxial cable for running through walls and around corners. If it is attached to the right network equipment and the right category of cable is used, this cable can be adapted for high-speed communications of 100 Mbps. For most applications, the maximum length to extend twisted-pair cable is 100 meters.

Twisted-pair cabling is connected to network devices with RJ-45 plug-in connectors, which resemble the RJ-11 connectors used on telephones. These connectors are less expensive than T-connectors and less susceptible to damage when moved. They also are easy to connect and allow more flexible cable configurations than coaxial cable.

The two kinds of twisted-pair cable are shielded and unshielded. Unshielded cable is preferred because of its lower cost and high reliability.

Shielded Twisted-Pair Cable

Shielded twisted-pair (STP) cable consists of pairs of insulated solid wires surrounded by a braided or corrugated shielding. Braided shielding is used for indoor wire, and corrugated shielding is used for outside or underground wiring. Shielding reduces interruptions of the communication signal caused by electrical interference. Twisting the wire pairs also helps reduce interference, but not to the same extent as the shield. This type of cabling is used in situations where heavy electrical equipment or other strong sources of interference are nearby. Figure 2-9 shows an example of shielded and unshielded twisted-pair cable.

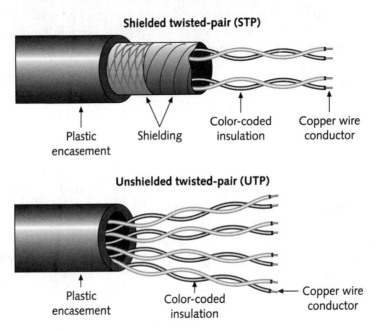

Figure 2-9   Twisted-pair cable

Unshielded Twisted-Pair Cable

Unshielded twisted-pair (UTP) cable is the most frequently used network cabling because of its low cost and relatively easy installation. UTP consists of wire pairs within an insulated outside covering. As with STP, each inside strand is twisted with another strand to help reduce interference to the data-carrying signal. An electrical device called a media filter is built into the network equipment, workstation, and file server connections to reduce electrical interference.

UTP is popularly called 10BASE-T cable, which means that it has a maximum transmission rate of 10 Mbps (although actual cable specifications can be up to 16 Mbps for some data transmissions), uses baseband communications, and is twisted-pair. A newer version of UTP cable, called category 5 UTP, can transmit data at up to 100 Mbps and is used in 100BASE-X communications.

 Category 5 twisted-pair cable is the best choice for new cable installations because it has high-speed networking capabilities and is only slightly higher in cost than other categories of cable.

FIBER-OPTIC CABLE

Fiber-optic cable consists of a central glass cylinder encased in a glass tube, called cladding. The central core and cladding are surrounded by a PVC cover (Figure 2-10). The cable core carries optical light pulses as transmitted by laser or light-emitting diode (LED) devices. The glass cladding is designed to reflect light back into the core. Fiber-optic cable is well suited for high-speed network transmissions of 100 Mbps to over 1 Gbps. It is used in cable plant backbones, such as between floors in a building, between buildings, and beyond. The most common use for fiber-optic cable in a campus environment is to interconnect different buildings.

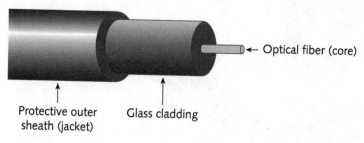

Protective outer sheath (jacket)   Glass cladding   ← Optical fiber (core)

Figure 2-10   Fiber-optic cable

An advantage of fiber-optic cable is its high bandwidth and low signal loss, which allow it to carry a large amount of data over long distances. Because the data travels by means of optical light pulses (on or off), there is no problem with electrical interference. Another advantage is that it is very difficult for someone to place unauthorized taps into the cable, since cable installation requires a high level of expertise. Disadvantages of this cable are that it is very fragile and relatively expensive, and that it requires specialized training to install.

Fiber-optic cable comes in two modes: single-mode and multimode. Single-mode cable is used mainly for long-distance communications. Multimode cable can support simultaneous transmission of multiple light waves, and the transmission distance is not as great as for single-mode cable.

NETWORK INTERFACE CARD

The device used to connect a workstation, file server, or other network equipment to the communications cable is called a **network interface card (NIC)**. The NIC contains a transmitter/receiver, or transceiver, for sending and receiving data signals on the cable. Each NIC comes with a set of software drivers to encode and decode the data so that it is readable by the workstation or server. NICs also have built-in memory chips to provide temporary storage while the data is waiting to be transmitted or to be sent to the station's CPU for processing.

NICs are designed for coaxial, twisted-pair, or fiber-optic cable. Some NICs come with adapters for both coaxial and twisted-pair cable. Figure 2-11 shows a NIC with the capability to connect to twisted-pair or coax cable (although you must not connect both at the same time). Many vendors sell computers with the NIC already installed, for college and business customers.

Figure 2-11   Connecting cable to a NIC

TRANSPORTING DATA ON THE COMMUNICATIONS CABLE

When a computer needs to send data, it separates the data into individual units, and packages the data into packets or frames. A **packet** is the complete unit of formatted data ready to be placed on the communications cable. The packet normally consists of a header containing information about its source and destination, the data to be transmitted, and a footer containing error-checking information. One word-processing file may be transmitted as hundreds of packets.

2

Two common ways to format and move a packet along a network are the Ethernet and token ring data transport methods. Ethernet is used in more installations than token ring because it offers more network design options and more options for high-speed networking implementations, and because it is more widely supported by an array of network devices. Token ring is used by many because it offers highly reliable network communications, particularly on busy networks.

ETHERNET

Ethernet transport takes advantage of the bus and star topologies. Standard Ethernet transmits data at a rate of 10 Mbps, and the newer Fast Ethernet transmits at 100 Mbps. This transport system uses a control method known as **Carrier Sense Multiple Access with Collision Detection (CSMA/CD)**. CSMA/CD is an algorithm (computer logic) that transmits and decodes formatted data frames. Using CSMA/CD, the Ethernet sending node encapsulates the frame to prepare it for transmission. All nodes that wish to transmit a frame on the cable are in contention with one another. No single node has priority over another node. The nodes listen for any packet traffic on the cable. If a packet is detected, the non-sending nodes go into a "defer" mode. The Ethernet protocol permits only one node to transmit at a time. Signal transmission is accomplished by carrier sense. **Carrier sense** is the process of checking communications cable for a specific voltage level indicating the presence of a data-carrying signal. When no signal traffic is detected on the communications medium for a given amount of time, any node is eligible to transmit.

Occasionally, more than one node will transmit at the same time. This is called a **collision**. The transmitting node detects a collision by measuring the signal strength. A collision has occurred if the signal is at least twice the normal strength. A transmitting node uses the collision detection software algorithm to recover from packet collisions. This algorithm causes the stations that have transmitted to continue their transmission for a designated time. The continued transmission is a jam signal of all binary ones that enables all listening nodes to determine that a collision has occurred. The software at each node generates a random number that is used as the interval to wait until transmitting. This ensures that no two nodes will attempt to transmit again at the same time.

Packets find their way to a particular destination through addressing. Each workstation and server has a unique address associated with its NIC. That address is burned into a programmable read-only memory chip (PROM) in the NIC. To prevent confusion on the network, it is important that no two network cards have the same address. If this should happen, and both NICs are active, network communications become unreliable. It is difficult for the network to determine if packets are being sent or received by a single, distinguishable node.

The computer logic that performs these functions is compiled into programs and related files that are called network drivers. Every NIC requires specific network drivers suited for the network access method, data encapsulation format, cabling type, and addressing method. The driver is installed on the computer.

Ethernet networks are widely supported by computer vendors that offer a vast array of equipment options. One reason for the popularity of Ethernet is that it offers many expansion paths to high-speed networking. For example, a 10 Mbps Ethernet network can be upgraded to 100 Mbps Fast Ethernet, often by using the NICs and cable plant already in place. Also, there are many network testing and management tools available for Ethernet.

TOKEN RING

The **token ring** access method was developed by IBM in the 1970s and remains a primary LAN technology. Data transmission in token ring is 4 Mbps for older versions and 16 Mbps for newer versions. IBM also is releasing a new 100 Mbps token ring technology. The token ring transport method uses a physical star topology, but with the logic of the ring topology. Although each node is connected to a central hub, the packet travels from node to node as though there is no starting or ending point. Nodes are joined by use of a **multistation access unit (MAU)** (Figure 2-12). The MAU is a specialized hub that ensures that the packet is transmitted around the ring of computers. Because the packets travel as though in a ring, there are no terminators at the workstations or in the MAU.

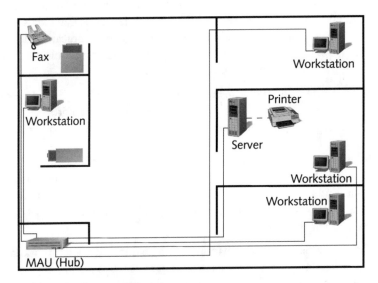

Figure 2-12   Token ring network

A specialized token is continuously transmitted on the ring, to coordinate when a computer can send a packet. In most implementations, there is only one token available on the ring, although the IEEE specifications permit two tokens for networks operating at 16 Mbps or faster. When a node wishes to transmit, it must capture the token. No other node can capture the token and transmit until the active node is finished. The station that captures the token builds a frame of data to send as a packet. The resulting packet is sent around the ring until it is read by the target node. It continues around the ring until the original transmitting station picks it up and checks the token to determine if it was received. The transmitting station then encapsulates the next frame of data with the token, or it builds a token without data to return to the ring so that a different station will grab it.

Token ring networks are extremely reliable, and are used in some mission-critical situations for this reason. One advantage of token ring networks over Ethernet networks is that broadcast storms and workstation interference are rare. **Broadcast storms** sometimes occur on Ethernet networks when a large number of computers or devices attempt to transmit at once, or when computers or devices persist in transmitting repeatedly. Network interference also occurs on Ethernet networks when a damaged NIC continues to broadcast transmissions regardless of whether or not the network is busy. These problems are rare on token ring networks, since only one node is able to transmit at a time.

PROTOCOLS

Data transported via Ethernet or token ring is sent in the form of a language called a protocol. A **protocol** is a set of rules that might be compared to grammar in a spoken language. In conjunction with the transport method, a protocol determines how the data is packaged to be read by the receiving computer. For example, it determines how to include information about the computer that sent the packet, which computer is to receive the packet, the type of data in the packet, the packet size, the amount of data it contains, and the means to detect a packet or transmission error. Just as there are many spoken languages, such as English, Spanish, Swedish, and Chinese, there are also several network protocols. The protocols used most are TCP/IP, NetBEUI, and IPX/SPX. Microsoft equips servers and workstations with these protocols.

Microsoft operating systems use several protocols to provide network services over Ethernet and token ring networks: NetBIOS/NetBEUI, NDIS, NWLink, ODI, TCP/IP, DLC, and AppleTalk. The services provided by these tools are summarized in Table 2-1 and described in detail in the following sections.

NETBIOS AND NETBEUI

NetBIOS Extended User Interface (NetBEUI) is a communications protocol that is native to Microsoft network communications. First developed by IBM in 1985, it is an enhancement of **Network Basic Input/Output System (NetBIOS)**. NetBIOS, which is not a protocol, is a method for interfacing software with network services. It also provides a naming convention.

Table 2-1   Microsoft Tools for Ethernet and Token Ring Communications

Service	Function
NetBIOS (Network Basic Input/Output System)	A link to programs that use the NetBIOS interface
NetBEUI (NetBIOS Extended User Interface)	Software drivers for a data transport protocol used on small Microsoft-based networks
NDIS (Network Driver Interface Specification)	A specification for, and software drivers to enable, Microsoft-based network protocols to communicate with a NIC
ODI (Open Datalink Interface)	Novell-developed software drivers for communications with Novell NetWare networks
NWLink (NetWare Link)	Microsoft-developed drivers for communications with Novell NetWare networks
TCP/IP (Transmission Control Protocol/Internet Protocol)	Software drivers for TCP/IP communications with mainframes, UNIX computers, and Internet servers
DLC (Data Link Control Protocol)	Software drivers for communications with IBM mainframes and minicomputers
AppleTalk	Software drivers for communications with Apple Macintosh computers

NetBIOS

When a software application is written for compatibility with the NetBIOS interface, it calls the NETBIOS.DLL file, which links the software to a transport driver. The transport driver communicates with NetBEUI for network transmissions. Microsoft Windows 3.1, 3.11, and 95 are most compatible with older programs requiring the NetBIOS interface. Microsoft NT uses a NetBIOS emulator (a program that simulates NetBIOS) for communications between NetBIOS and NetBEUI. Figure 2-13 illustrates the communication flow from NetBIOS applications to NetBEUI in order to transport data over a network.

NetBIOS names are used to name objects on a network, such as a workstation, server, or printer. For example, your workstation might use your last name for identification to other network users, the network printer you access might be named HPLaser, and the server you access might be named Netserver. These names make it easy for human beings to identify a particular network resource. They are translated into an address for network communications by the NetBIOS Name Query services.

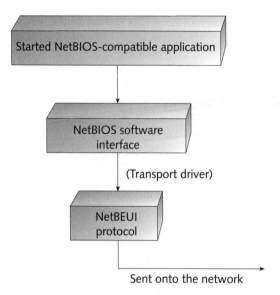

Figure 2-13 NetBIOS/NetBEUI communications

There are two important elements to remember about NetBIOS names. First, each name must be unique. No network object can have the same name as another object. If it could, there would be great confusion about how to communicate with objects having the same name. Second, names are no more than 16 characters. The first 15 characters are for a user to assign a name, and the last character is used to identify the type of network resource, such as a server or printer. The operating system handles this, using a hexadecimal number.

Name workstations, servers, and printers so that others can quickly recognize them. For example, if a workstation has your last name, it is easier to associate it with you than if you name it Hoss or BigCool.

NetBEUI

NetBEUI was developed when computer networking primarily meant local area networking for a relatively small number of computers, from a couple of computers to about 200. It was not developed to take into account enterprise networks where frames are directed from one network to another through routing and routers. For this reason, NetBEUI is well suited for small LANs using Microsoft or IBM operating systems such as the following:

- Microsoft Windows 3.1 or 3.11
- Microsoft Windows 95
- Microsoft LAN Manager
- Microsoft LAN Manager for UNIX

- Microsoft Windows NT
- IBM PCLAN
- IBM LAN Server

NetBEUI on a computer running Windows NT is also called NBF, which is an acronym for NetBEUI Frame.

NetBEUI is a good choice on small Microsoft networks for several reasons. First, it is simple to install and it is very compatible with Microsoft workstation and server operating systems. Second, it can handle nearly limitless communication sessions on one network, because the 254-session limitation of earlier versions is removed. Microsoft specifications, for example, show that a Windows NT server can support 1,000 sessions on one NIC. Third, NetBEUI has low memory requirements and can be quickly transported over small networks. Fourth, it has solid error detection and recovery.

The inability to route NetBEUI is a major disadvantage for medium and large networks, including enterprise networks. This means that a NetBEUI frame cannot be forwarded by a router (a network device) from one network to another, because there is not enough information in the NetBEUI frame to identify specific networks. Another disadvantage is that there are fewer network analysis tools for it than for other protocols. NetBEUI also is not widely supported by computers running non-Microsoft operating systems.

Consider two different networking situations. In the first situation, you are responsible for setting up a network for a credit union that has 52 workstations, four network printers, and one Microsoft NT server. The network is a bus-star topology containing no routers. This is a good context for using NetBEUI as the sole protocol. In a second situation, you are setting up communications on a busy college network with 520 nodes, including an IBM mainframe, 10 Microsoft NT servers, and Internet access. That network also is a bus-star topology, but has four routers linking different LANs across campus. NetBEUI is not a good choice in this situation; another protocol, such as TCP/IP (discussed later in this chapter), would be the best choice.

NDIS

The **Network Driver Interface Specification (NDIS)** is a software driver specification that enables Microsoft network protocols to communicate with a NIC. When you bind a protocol to a NIC, the binding is accomplished through the NDIS driver. A **network binding** is a process that identifies a computer's NIC with one or more network protocols, to achieve optimum communications with network services. For Microsoft operating systems, you should always bind a protocol to each NIC that is installed (Figure 2-14).

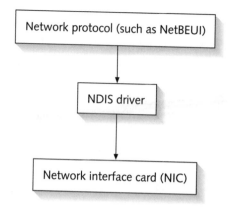

Figure 2-14   Binding a protocol to a NIC

NDIS can bind one or more protocols to a single NIC, allowing each protocol to be sending information at the same time. For example, you may have one process sending information using the NetBEUI protocol, while another process is sending information using the IPX/SPX protocol to communicate with a Novell NetWare server. Try Hands-on Project 2-1 to view the protocol and NIC setup in Windows NT.

ODI

Another driver that can be used to transport multiple protocols is the **Open Datalink Interface (ODI)** driver. This driver is used on Novell NetWare networks to support communications with NetWare file servers, mainframes and minicomputers, and the Internet. ODI communications can be used on a Microsoft network, but this is not advised. The Microsoft implementation of the ODI driver is an older 16-bit application, compared to NDIS, which can support the 16-bit and the more advanced 32-bit drivers.

NWLINK AND IPX/SPX

Novell adapted one of the early LAN protocols, the **Xerox Network System (XNS)** protocol, for use with its NetWare file server operating system. XNS was introduced by the Xerox Corporation as a means to communicate over Ethernet. In the early 1980s, several vendors implemented their own versions of XNS. Novell's adaptation is called the **Internet Packet Exchange (IPX)** protocol for use with NetWare.

One advantage that IPX has over NetBEUI is that it has routing capabilities, so data is transported over multiple networks in an enterprise. Also, along with IPX, Novell implemented a companion protocol called **Sequence Packet Exchange (SPX)**. SPX enables the exchange of application-specific data with greater reliability than IPX. One use of SPX is for exchange of database data on the network. Novell's remote console utility and print services also take advantage of SPX. The remote console utility enables a workstation to display the same information that appears on a NetWare file server monitor. With the remote console software, the workstation user can execute file server console commands without having to be at the file server keyboard.

IPX/SPX can be deployed on a Microsoft network in one of two ways. One way is to install the ODI driver instead of NDIS at workstations and servers. Because this offers limited 16-bit support, the better way is to use NetWare Link (NWLink). **NWLink** is a network protocol used on Microsoft networks to emulate IPX/SPX.

 To use NWLink you must first install the NDIS driver.

The best way to install NWLink is to install it as part of Client Service for NetWare, which installs three elements as follows:

- Client Service for NetWare
- NWLink IPX/SPX Compatible Transport
- NWLink NetBIOS

NWLink offers several advantages, such as routing over enterprise networks. It is easy to install and provides more effective communications with NetWare file servers than the ODI driver. Its disadvantages are that it is not transported as fast as NetBEUI. Also, IPX/SPX and the NWLink emulation are really designed as proprietary protocols used mainly on NetWare networks. Another disadvantage is that IPX/SPX is a "chatty" protocol, in that each packet transmitted must be acknowledged by the receiving node. Hands-on Project 2-2 enables you to view statistics on network protocol traffic.

The most common situations for using Microsoft's NWLink to emulate IPX/SPX are (1) to enable a workstation running Microsoft Windows 95 or NT Workstation to communicate with one or more NetWare servers, and (2) to set up a Microsoft Windows NT server as a gateway to one or more NetWare servers. For example, assume that you are configuring workstations running Windows 95 for a network with five Novell NetWare servers and no other host computers. In this situation, you would configure all workstations to use NWLink. However, consider another situation in which you have one NetWare server and four Windows NT servers on a network where some print services are to be handled through the Windows NT servers. One solution would be to configure all Windows-based workstations for NWLink and NetBEUI. Depending on the need for access to the NetWare server, a better solution would be to configure one of the Windows NT servers for NWLink and set it up to act as a gateway to NetWare by installing Microsoft's Gateway Service for NetWare. Now the workstations would only need to use NetBEUI, because they would access the NetWare server through the Windows NT server gateway. In this instance, the gateway functions to make the NetWare directories appear as a shared folder on the Windows NT server.

Installing Client Service for NetWare and Gateway Service for NetWare are covered in Chapter 12, "Interoperating with Novell NetWare."

2

TCP/IP

Many network users need to connect to a host computer, such as a mainframe running IBM's MVS operating system or a minicomputer with UNIX. Another common need is to connect to a host computer providing access to the Internet or to a Web server. The protocol for these jobs is **Transmission Control Protocol/Internet Protocol (TCP/IP)**. TCP/IP is used around the globe for reliable network communications. TCP/IP is many protocols wrapped into one, all working together to establish the most error-free communications possible. The TCP portion was originally developed to ensure reliable connections on government, military, and educational networks. It performs extensive error checking to ensure that data is delivered successfully. The IP portion of the protocol provides network addressing to ensure that data packets quickly reach the correct destination. It uses the dotted decimal notation system of addressing that consists of four numbers separated by a period, such as 129.77.15.182. In this scheme, the first two numbers identify the network, and the last two compose the host number, such as a server or workstation. TCP/IP is a protocol particularly well suited for medium and large networks.

For example, if you need to access an IBM mainframe connected to your network, you would configure your workstation to use TCP/IP. As a start, the workstation needs a unique IP address, either specified at the workstation or obtained from a server that assigns temporary addresses for a communication session. Depending on the mainframe and application software in use, you might also need special software to emulate an IBM terminal, such as an IBM 3270 terminal emulator. A **terminal** is a device consisting of a monitor and keyboard, used to communicate with a host computer that runs the programs. The terminal does not have a processor to use for running programs locally. The emulation software runs on the workstation, so it responds in a way similar to a terminal.

Before setting up TCP/IP, you need to make some decisions about how to set up IP addressing on the network. The options are to use what Microsoft calls static addressing or dynamic addressing. **Static addressing** involves assigning a dotted decimal address that is each workstation's permanent, unique IP address. This method is used on many networks, large and small, where the network administrator wants direct control over the assigned addresses. Direct control may be necessary where network management software is used to track all network nodes, and the software depends on each node having a permanent, known IP address. Permanent addresses give consistency to monitoring network statistics and to keeping historical network performance information. The disadvantage is that IP address administration can be a laborious task on a large network. Most network administrators have an IP database to keep track of currently assigned addresses and of unused addresses to assign as new people are connected to the network.

Dynamic addressing automatically assigns an IP address to a computer each time it is logged on. An IP address is leased to a particular computer for a defined period of time. This addressing method uses the **Dynamic Host Configuration Protocol (DHCP)**, which is a convention supported by Microsoft for dynamic addressing. The protocol is used to enable a Windows NT server with DHCP services to detect the presence of a new workstation and assign an IP address to that workstation. On your network, this would require you to load DHCP services onto a Microsoft NT server and configure it to be a DHCP server. It would still act as a file server, but with the added ability to automatically assign IP addresses to work-stations. A Windows NT DHCP server leases IP addresses for a specified period of time, which might be one week, one month, one year, or a permanent lease. When the lease is up, the IP address is returned to a pool of available IP addresses maintained by the server. On NT servers that provide Internet communications, when an NT DHCP server is configured, **Windows Internet Naming Service (WINS)** can also be installed (but is not required) so that the NT server is both a DHCP and a WINS server. A WINS server is able to trans-late a workstation name to an IP address for Internet communications, such as translating the workstation name Palmer to its IP address, 129.77.15.182.

 One advantage to using a WINS on a TCP/IP-based network is that it cuts down on network traffic. On a network without WINS, each computer must send a broadcast message to the entire network to locate another computer. WINS reduces this traffic by providing quick IP-to-computer name translations.

TCP/IP Advantages and Disadvantages

There are several advantages that TCP/IP offers:

- It is very well suited for medium to large networks and enterprise networks.
- It is designed for routing and has a high degree of reliability.
- It is used worldwide for directly connecting to the Internet and by Web servers.
- It is compatible with standard tools for analyzing network performance.
- The parallel ability to use DHCP and WINS through a Microsoft NT server is another strong reason for using TCP/IP.

TCP/IP does have some disadvantages as well:

- It is more difficult to set up and maintain than NetBEUI or IPX/SPX.
- It is somewhat slower than IPX/SPX and NetBEUI on networks with light to medium traffic. (However, it may be faster on heavy-volume networks where there is a high frequency of routing frames.)

One situation where you would use TCP/IP is on a large enterprise network, such as on a college or business campus where there is extensive use of routers and connectivity to main-frame or UNIX computers. You also would use it on a smaller network where 100–200 Windows-based workstations access intranet or Internet services through an NT server offering Web services from Microsoft's Internet Information Server.

Protocols Associated with TCP/IP

Complementing the main protocols are four application services provided through TCP/IP:

- Telnet
- File Transfer Protocol (FTP)
- Simple Mail Transfer Protocol (SMTP)
- Domain Name Service (DNS)

Telnet is an application protocol within TCP/IP, providing support for terminal emulation, such as for an IBM 3270 terminal or a DEC VT220 terminal. Telnet enables a user to connect to a host computer so that the host responds as though it were connected to a terminal. For example, Telnet with a 3270 emulator can connect to an IBM ES9000 mainframe like a terminal. The ES9000 requires a logon ID and password, just as though it were directly connected to a terminal.

Another TCP/IP application protocol, the **File Transfer Protocol (FTP),** is an algorithm that enables the transfer of data from one remote device to another, using TCP and Telnet protocols. Through FTP, a user in England can use the Internet to log on to a host computer in California and download one or more data files from the host. (The user first must have an authorized user ID and password on the host.)

FTP is designed to transfer entire files only, in bulk. It does not provide the capability to transfer a portion of a file or records within a file. The FTP transmission is composed of a single stream of data concluded by an end-of-file delimiter. FTP can transfer binary files and ASCII text files.

A popular alternative to FTP is the **Network File System (NFS)** software offered by Sun Microsystems. NFS sends data in record streams instead of in bulk file streams. NFS is used by UNIX computers for file transfers, sharing disk storage, and enabling a UNIX workstation to act as a file server.

The **Simple Mail Transfer Protocol (SMTP)** is designed for the exchange of electronic mail between networked systems. UNIX, MVS, and other computer operating systems can exchange messages if they have TCP/IP accompanied by SMTP.

SMTP provides an alternative to FTP for sending a file from one computer system to another. This is handy since SMTP does not require use of a logon ID and password for the remote system. All that is needed is an e-mail address for the receiving end. SMTP is limited to sending ASCII text files, so files in other formats must be converted to text before they are placed in an SMTP message.

Messages sent through SMTP have two parts: an address header and the message text. The address header can be very long, because it contains the address of every SMTP node through which it has traveled and a date stamp for every transfer point. If the receiving node is unavailable, SMTP can "bounce" the mail back to the sender.

SMTP establishes rules for how the sending and receiving computers need to format and exchange mail. One method employed by SMTP is to create a queue in a file directory. The queue serves as a "post office" for local users on the machine where it resides. If the queue contains messages for another computer system, it notifies the SMTP application on that system and forwards the message.

Another application protocol is **Domain Name Service (DNS)**, which is used to translate domain computer names, such as *microsoft.com*, to an IP address. The DNS software runs on one or more computers that act as a network server for the address translations. The process of translating names to addresses is called **resolution**, a process you have already used if you access the Internet.

CONNECTING TO IBM MAINFRAMES WITH DLC

Another way to connect to an IBM mainframe is to use the **Data Link Control Protocol (DLC)**. Microsoft Windows NT 4.0 Workstation and Server and Windows 95 offer a DLC driver that can be installed. DLC is needed to connect to IBM computers when TCP/IP is not available. It does this by providing connectivity to IBM's communication system, called Systems Network Architecture (SNA). Another use for DLC is to communicate with printers directly connected to the network, such as a Hewlett-Packard laser printer equipped with print services and network connectivity.

The main advantage to using DLC is that it is an alternative to TCP/IP. A disadvantage is that the protocol is not routable. Also, DLC is not truly designed for peer-to-peer communications between workstations, but only for connectivity to a computer such as an IBM ES9000 mainframe or AS/400 minicomputer.

CONNECTING TO MACINTOSH COMPUTERS WITH APPLETALK

Macintosh computer networks use a peer-to-peer network protocol called **AppleTalk**. AppleTalk is only supported in very limited ways on non-Macintosh networks. On a Microsoft network, Macintosh computers are linked in by setting up the Windows NT Server Services for Macintosh. The NT server becomes a file server for Macintosh computers as well as for computers running Microsoft operating systems. It also is able to communicate with the Macintosh computers through the AppleTalk protocol and to operate as a print server.

A separate disk volume can be created on the Windows NT server for Macintosh files, resembling a shared volume. Access permissions can be set up and logon authentication can be performed to ensure that only authorized users have access.

SELECTING THE RIGHT TOPOLOGY AND COMMUNICATIONS CABLE

The network topology you select depends on the size and needs of your network, whereas the cable selection depends on the topology. For example, suppose that you are planning a network for a mortgage company that occupies the first floor in a four-story building and has 22 employees. For this type of installation you could use any of the following:

1. A simple Ethernet bus network design and thin coax cable

2. A token ring network, MAU, and twisted-pair cable

3. An Ethernet bus-star network, hub, and twisted-pair cable

Option 1, the simple Ethernet bus network, is the weakest choice because new thin coax installations are least preferred. Coax cable and its connectors are now more expensive than twisted-pair, and the cable is harder to install because it is less flexible than twisted-pair. Also, troubleshooting problems on this type of network is more difficult because problems at one connection may affect the entire network. The second option is feasible if there is a strong need for network reliability. However, there are fewer equipment options for token ring, higher equipment costs, and fewer high-speed expansion options than for Ethernet. High-speed networking might be needed at this installation if they work with large image or picture files, storing images of contracts or pictures of homes in a database, for instance. Option 3 is the best selection because it combines the flexibility of twisted-pair with the vast range of equipment available for Ethernet. Network troubleshooting is easier on a bus-star network than on a simple bus. Also, converting an initial 10 Mbps network to a 100 Mbps network is likely to be easier than converting the token ring network to high-speed networking. One advantage of the wider range of equipment for the star-based network is that there are more options for Internet connectivity, should the company decide to have a Web site. Another advantage is that the bus-star network can use centralized network management and can be more readily expanded to other floors in a building or to other buildings. (Use Hands-on Project 2-3 to learn more about how a hub or MAU is employed).

Next, suppose that you are networking a company that makes scientific instruments. They have a five-story building that houses the research and business functions. Their plant is next door in a sprawling one-story building. The Ethernet bus-star design also matches the needs of this situation. Each floor in the five-story building would be wired with category 5 UTP cable. Fiber-optic cable would be used between floors and between the buildings, providing the fastest possible data transmissions along a backbone. The plant would be wired with twisted-pair cabling, using STP in areas with high electrical interference from machinery. The bus-star design has a particular advantage in this situation because it uses a series of centralized hubs that make network management, expansion, and troubleshooting easier than with other designs. The fiber-optic cable offers high-speed communications along the paths most likely to have intense network traffic, and the category 5 twisted-pair cable makes it possible to establish one workstation link or an entire floor with 10 Mbps or 100 Mbps communications.

SELECTING THE RIGHT PROTOCOL

The protocols you employ on a network depend on several factors:

- Do frames need to be routed?
- Is the network small (under 100 connections), medium (100 to 500 connections), or large (over 500 connections)?
- Are there Microsoft NT servers?
- Are there mainframe host computers?
- Are there NetWare servers?
- Is there direct access to the Internet or to Web-based intranet applications?
- Are there mission-critical applications?

If there is a need to route packets, such as on an enterprise network, your best choice is likely to be TCP/IP because it is designed for routing and is used on many types of networks. For a small nonrouted network with only Microsoft NT servers, NetBEUI is a good choice because it is native to Microsoft networking and it provides fast, reliable communications. A NetWare-only network would use IPX/SPX, while a network with a combination of NetWare and NT servers would need to employ NetBEUI and IPX/SPX. (You could also use only IPX/SPX for a routed or nonrouted network of 200 to 500 users.) NWLink is a good choice for NetWare client communications from workstations running a Microsoft operating system.

Connectivity to Internet or Web-based services requires that TCP/IP be implemented, and TCP/IP is also necessary to allow FTP services to be used to transfer files. TCP/IP also is the first choice for connectivity to mainframe and UNIX computers. The Telnet terminal emulation available through TCP/IP may be needed to connect to the mainframe. DLC is another option for IBM mainframe and minicomputer communications, if TCP/IP cannot be used.

TCP/IP is the protocol of preference for medium to large networks. It can be routed, is reliable for mission-critical applications, and has solid error checking. Network monitoring and analysis become very important on these networks, and TCP/IP has associated protocols to accomplish these activities, too.

In many cases it is necessary to use a combination of protocols for different types of network applications. Modern networks often combine use of the major protocols, TCP/IP, NetBEUI, and IPX/SPX.

In multiprotocol networks, the order in which protocols are used is critical. Protocol order is set at the workstations and on servers, such as through Windows 95 or Windows NT operating systems. For example, if most workstations use NetBEUI more than TCP/IP, NetBEUI should be set at a higher order for better network performance.

Chapter Summary

- A Windows NT server operates in the context of a network. A LAN is the most basic kind of network. Other more complex networks, such as enterprises and WANs, are built by joining different types of LANs. The main ingredient in preparing a network is solid planning, taking into account factors such as the needs of the organization that will use the network, software that will be used, existing computer equipment, and security requirements.

- Network design employs the bus, ring, and star topologies. The most versatile topology is a combination bus and star implementation. The communications cable used on networks includes coax, twisted-pair, and fiber-optic cable. Twisted-pair is used most frequently because it is flexible, and because the category 5 version of the cable supports transmission rates up to 100 Mbps. Fiber-optic cable is used to connect networks between floors in a building and between buildings.

- Communications on networks are enabled through network transport methods such as Ethernet and token ring. Ethernet is used in many types of situations because it offers a variety of expansion and high-speed networking options. Token ring is used because it offers reliable communications and is a time-proven technology.

- Protocols such as NetBEUI and TCP/IP establish a communications format that is understood by the computers on a network. Microsoft networks support many different protocols for different network sizes and requirements.

Key Terms

- **AppleTalk** — A peer-to-peer protocol used on networks for communications between Macintosh computers.

- **backbone** — A high-capacity communications medium that joins networks on the same floor in a building, on different floors, and across long distances.

- **bayonet navy connector (BNC)** — A connector used for coax cable that has a bayonet-like shell. The male BNC connector has two small knobs that attach to circular slots in the female connector. Both connectors are twisted on for a connection.

- **broadcast storm** — Saturation of network bandwidth by excessive broadcasts from devices attached to that network.

- **bus topology** — A network configured so that nodes are connected to a segment of cable in the logical shape of a line, with a terminator at each end.

- **cable plant** — The total cabling that composes a network.

- **carrier sense** — The process of checking a communications medium, such as cable, for a specific voltage level indicating the presence of a data-carrying signal.

- **Carrier Sense Multiple Access with Collision Detection (CSMA/CD)** — A network transport control mechanism used in Ethernet networks, regulating transmission by sensing the presence of packet collisions.

- **coaxial cable** — Also called coax, a cable with a copper core, surrounded by insulation. The insulation is surrounded by another conducting material, such as braided wire, which is covered by an outer insulating material.

- **collision** — A situation that occurs when two or more packets are present at the same time on an Ethernet network.

- **Data Link Control Protocol (DLC)** — Available through Microsoft NT 4.0 and Windows 95, this protocol enables communications with an IBM mainframe or mini-computer.

- **Domain Name Service (DNS)** — A TCP/IP application protocol that resolves domain computer names to IP addresses, or IP addresses to domain names.

- **dynamic addressing** — An addressing method in which an IP (Internet Protocol) address is assigned to a workstation without the need for the network administrator to "hard code" it in the workstation's network setup.

- **Dynamic Host Configuration Protocol (DHCP)** — A network protocol that provides a way for a server to automatically assign an IP address to a workstation on its network.

- **enterprise network** — A network that reaches throughout a large area, such as a college campus, a city, or across several states, connecting many kinds of local area networks and network resources.

- **Ethernet** — A transport system that uses the CSMA/CD access method for data transmission on a network. Ethernet is typically implemented in a bus or star topology.

- **fiber-optic cable** — A cabling technology that uses pulses of light sent along a light-conducting fiber to transfer information from sender to receiver. Fiber-optic cable can send data in only one direction, so two cables are required to permit any two network devices to exchange data in both directions.

- **File Transfer Protocol (FTP)** — Available through the TCP/IP protocol, FTP enables files to be transferred across a network or the Internet between computers or servers.

- **hub** — A network device that acts as a central unit to link workstations, servers, networks, and network equipment.

- **Institute of Electrical and Electronics Engineers (IEEE)** — An organization of scientists, engineers, technicians, and educators that issues standards for electrical and electronic devices, including network interfaces, cabling, and connectors.

- **Internet Packet Exchange (IPX)** — A protocol developed by Novell for use with its NetWare file server operating system.

- **local area network (LAN)** — A series of interconnected computers, printers, and other computer equipment that share hardware and software resources. The service area is usually limited to a given floor, office area, or building.

- **metropolitan area network (MAN)** — A network that links multiple LANs within a large city or metropolitan region.

- **multistation access unit (MAU)** — A central hub that links token ring nodes into a topology that physically resembles a star but where packets are transferred in a logical ring pattern.

- **NetBIOS Extended User Interface (NetBEUI)** — A communications protocol native to Microsoft network communications. It is an enhancement of NetBIOS, which was developed for network peer-to-peer communications among workstations with Microsoft operating systems installed on a local area network.

- **Network Basic Input/Output System (NetBIOS)** — A combination software interface and network naming convention. It is available in Microsoft operation systems through the file NETBIOS.DLL.

- **network binding** — A process that identifies a computer's network interface card or a dial-up connection with one or more network protocols to achieve optimum communications with network services. For Microsoft operating systems, you should always bind a protocol to each NIC that is installed.

- **Network Device Interface Specification (NDIS)** — A set of standards developed by Microsoft for network drivers. It enables communication between a NIC and a protocol, and enables the use of multiple protocols on the same network.

- **Network File System (NFS)** — A UNIX-based network file transfer protocol that ships files as streams of records.

- **network interface card (NIC)** — A PC adapter board designed to connect a workstation, file server, or other network equipment to some sort of network medium.

- **network traffic** — The number, size, and frequency of packets transmitted on the network in a given amount of time.

- **NWLink** — A network protocol that simulates the IPX/SPX protocol for Microsoft Windows 95 and NT communications with Novell NetWare file servers and compatible devices.

- **Open Datalink Interface (ODI)** — A driver that is used by Novell NetWare networks to transport multiple protocols on the same network.

- **packet** — A unit of data formatted for transmission over a network. A packet normally consists of a header containing information about its source and destination, the data to be transmitted, and a footer containing error-checking information.

- **protocol** — A strictly defined set of rules for communication across a network.

- **request for information (RFI)** — A general planning document that is sent to vendors to obtain information about what services and products they can offer. It may be used to develop an RFP (request for proposal).

- **request for proposal (RFP)** — A detailed planning document, often developed from responses to an RFI (request for proposal), that is sent to vendors to inform them of the exact specifications for services and products that an organization intends to purchase.

- **resolution** — A process used to translate a computer's domain name to an IP address, and vice versa.

- **ring topology** — A network in the form of a continuous ring, or circle, with nodes connected around the ring.

- **Sequence Packet Exchange (SPX)** — A Novell connection-oriented protocol used for network transport where there is a particular need for data reliability.

- **shielded twisted-pair (STP)** — Cable that contains pairs of insulated wires that are twisted together and surrounded by a shielding material for added EMI and RFI protection, all inside a protective jacket.

- **Simple Mail Transfer Protocol (SMTP)** — An e-mail protocol used by systems having TCP/IP network communications.

- **star topology** — A network configured with a central hub and individual cable segments connected to the hub in the shape of a star.

- **static addressing** — An IP (Internet Protocol) addressing method that requires the network administrator to manually assign and set up a unique network address on each workstation connected to a network.

- **Telnet** — A TCP/IP application protocol that provides terminal emulation services.

- **terminal** — A device that consists of a monitor and keyboard, used to communicate with a host computer that runs the programs. The terminal does not have a processor to use for running programs locally.

- **token ring** — Using a ring topology, a network transport method that passes a token from node to node. The token is used to coordinate transmission of data, because only the node possessing the token can send data.

- **topology** — The physical layout of the cable and the logical path followed by network packets sent on the cable.

- **Transmission Control Protocol/Internet Protocol (TCP/IP)** — A protocol that is particularly well suited for medium and large networks. The TCP portion was originally developed to ensure reliable connections on government, military, and educational networks. It performs extensive error checking to ensure that data is delivered successfully. The IP portion consists of rules for packaging data and ensuring that it reaches the correct destination address.

- **twisted-pair** — Flexible communications cable that contains pairs of insulated copper wires that are twisted together for reduction of EMI and RFI and covered with an outer insulating jacket.

- **unshielded twisted-pair (UTP)** — Communications cable that has no shielding material between the pairs of insulated wires twisted together and the cable's outer jacket.

- **wide area network (WAN)** — A far-reaching system of networks that can extend across state lines and across continents.

- **Windows Internet Naming Service (WINS)** — A Windows NT Server service that enables the server to convert workstation names to IP addresses for Internet communications.

- **Xerox Network System (XNS)** — A protocol developed by Xerox in the early networking days for Ethernet communications.

REVIEW QUESTIONS

1. Ethernet communications use what transport method?
   a. CSMA/CD
   b. token sharing
   c. token passing
   d. flow processing

2. A(n) _____ is used to connect a computer running Windows NT Server to communications cable.
   a. attachment interface
   b. L-connector
   c. network interface card (NIC)
   d. file transfer card (FIC)

3. Microsoft's NWLink emulates which protocol?
   a. TCP/IP
   b. DLC
   c. IPX/SPX
   d. NetBEUI

4. You are setting up Windows NT 4.0 Server as the only server on a network that services 75 Windows 95 users on a nonrouted network. Which of the following protocols would you use on the network?

   a. TCP/IP

   b. DLC

   c. IPX/SPX

   d. NetBEUI

5. Which type of cable uses a BNC connector?

   a. thin coax

   b. unshielded twisted-pair

   c. fiber-optic

   d. shielded twisted-pair

6. Which of the following would you consider when planning a network?

   a. software to be used

   b. types of computers to connect

   c. business needs and cycles

   d. all of the above

   e. only a and b

7. You need to connect to the Internet. Which protocol would you use?

   a. TCP/IP

   b. DLC

   c. IPX/SPX

   d. NetBEUI

8. Which of the following protocols cannot be routed?

   a. TCP/IP

   b. IPX/SPX

   c. NetBEUI

   d. none of the above can be routed

   e. only a and c cannot be routed

9. You are planning a network in a building in which there are many places where cable must go in tight spots and around sharp corners. Which of the following types of cable has the most flexibility for this situation?

   a. thick coax

   b. thin coax

   c. twisted-pair

   d. fiber-optic

10. Your company wants to connect the networks in two buildings that are in the same block. Which communications cable would be the best choice?

    a. thick coax

    b. thin coax

    c. twisted-pair

    d. fiber-optic

11. Which type of communications cable is least susceptible to electrical interference?

    a. thin coax

    b. shielded twisted-pair

    c. unshielded twisted-pair

    d. fiber-optic

12. Which type of cable would be used with a 10BASE2 network?

    a. thick coax

    b. thin coax

    c. twisted-pair

    d. fiber-optic

13. Ethernet transmits at which of the following rates?

    a. 10 Mbps

    b. 100 Mbps

    c. 1 Gbps

    d. all of the above

    e. only a and b

14. Twisted-pair cable uses which type of connector?

    a. RJ-11

    b. BNC

    c. RG-58

    d. RJ-45

15. You plan to use both TCP/IP and NetBEUI for communications on your network. Which of the following drivers would you implement on your NT server to communicate using both protocols?

    a. NDIS

    b. ODI

    c. Multilink

    d. all of the above

    e. only b and c

16. Which of the following would use a MAU?

    a. Ethernet

    b. token ring

    c. DLC

    d. AppleLink

17. Fast Ethernet communications are at:

    a. 1 Gbps

    b. 100 Mbps

    c. 10 Mbps

    d. 4 Mbps

18. You are setting up Windows NT Server on a network that has workstations using Windows NT, Windows 95, and an IBM LAN server. Which protocol would you set up to use?

    a. TCP/IP

    b. DLC

    c. IPX/SPX

    d. NetBEUI

19. One application of DLC is to communicate with

    a. an IBM mainframe

    b. Novell NetWare

    c. MS-DOS computers using NetBIOS

    d. Ethernet networks

20. Which part of TCP/IP is responsible for addressing?

    a. TCP

    b. IP

    c. SMTP

    d. FTP

HANDS-ON PROJECTS

 PROJECT 2-1

In this project you view information about the protocol and NIC setup on a networked computer running Windows NT 4.0 Server or NT 4.0 Workstation.

To view protocol and NIC setup information:

1. Click **Start**, **Settings**, and **Control Panel** (Figure 2-15).

Figure 2-15 Opening Control Panel

2. Double-click the **Network** icon (Figure 2-16).

Figure 2-16 Selecting the Network icon

3. Click the **Protocols** tab to view the protocols already installed (Figure 2-17).

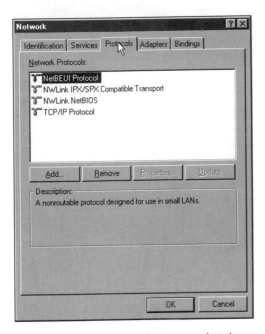

Figure 2-17   Viewing the Protocols tab

4. Click the **Adapters** tab to see what NIC is installed on the computer (Figure 2-18).

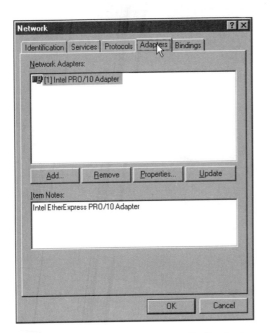

Figure 2-18   Viewing the installed adapter

5. Click the adapter and then the **Properties** button.
6. Notice the properties associated with your NIC, including configuration information.
7. Click **Cancel** on the NIC Setup dialog box.
8. Click **Cancel** on the Network dialog box to exit.

PROJECT 2-2

In this Hands-on project you view network activity statistics that are continuously gathered by a NIC and reported to the Windows NT operating system.

To view the statistics:

1. Click the **Start** button, **Programs**, **Administrative Tools**, and **Windows NT Diagnostics** (Figure 2-19).

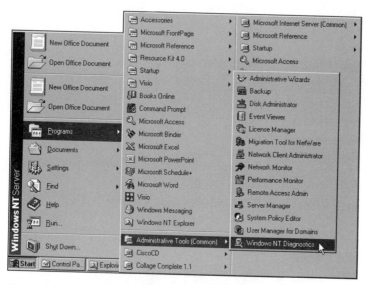

Figure 2-19 Opening Windows NT Diagnostics

2. Click the **Network** tab and click the **Transports** button to view information about protocols and their bindings to the NIC.

3. Click the **Statistics** button to view transmission statistics collected by the NIC, such as Bytes Received and Bytes Transmitted (Figure 2-20).

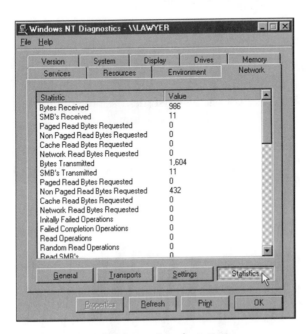

Figure 2-20   Viewing network statistics

4. These statistics will not mean much to you now, but they give you an idea of how much network activity goes through the NIC.

5. Click **OK** on the Windows NT Diagnostics dialog box to exit.

PROJECT 2-3

In this project you view how a hub or MAU links workstations on a network.

To view the hub or MAU:

1. Visit a lab or the computer center at your school, or contact a network administrator at a local business. Ask to see a working hub or MAU.
2. Observe the cable and connectors into the hub.
3. Observe how the cabling connects to a workstation on the network.
4. Determine what type of cable is used.
5. If the network administrator is available, ask what network topology is used.
6. Ask if you can view a diagram of the network or of a portion of the network.

ASPEN CONSULTING: NETWORK DESIGN AND PROTOCOLS

In the following assignments you are working with two clients, Andrews Chemicals and Flight Dynamics. Andrews Chemicals is a large chemical company that has just purchased new NT servers and needs configuration advice. Flight Dynamics is a small company that grew large overnight and needs recommendations about network setup and design.

1. One of your clients, Andrews Chemicals, has just purchased four new NT servers to place on an enterprise network. The network has 522 users, who have Windows 3.11, Windows 95, and Windows NT. Besides the NT servers, the network contains an IBM mainframe, a UNIX server, and two NetWare servers. What drivers and protocols would you configure on the NT servers? What drivers and protocols would you configure on the workstations? Explain your answers.
2. Mark Arnez has asked you to work with Flight Dynamics. This small company consists of eight engineers who perform consulting work for aircraft builders. They have configured their Windows NT server so that each engineer can connect via NetBEUI. They also have a telecommunications link to the Internet and have set up a Web site using the Internet Information Server (IIS). The problem is that no one on the Internet can contact the Web site. What might be the problem? Why?
3. Two weeks after you solve the Web site problem for Flight Dynamics, Mark informs you that they have been purchased by a venture capital company that wants them to move into a new three-story building in Los Angeles. The venture capital company plans to expand the original eight engineers to 95. They also want to add a business

department and a human resources department for another 10 employees. All employees will use Windows NT Workstation and connect to two Windows NT 4.0 servers, one for business information and one for research use. In a few months, they will add another NT server as a dedicated Web server. Mark wants you to make some general recommendations about:

- Network topology
- Transport method
- Communications cable
- Protocol and driver selection

4. Flight Dynamics has asked one of the original engineers to take over as network administrator until one is hired. That engineer, Jason Brown, is asking that you prepare a table showing protocols available through Microsoft networking services and the situations in which they are implemented. Prepare a table using two columns, the left column to record the protocol, and the right column to record information about how it is used. When you finish, explain to Jason how two or more protocols might be supported.

5. Jason has called back and wants to know more about Ethernet and token ring communications. Provide him with a basic explanation of how each works. Also, summarize the advantages and disadvantages of each.

SERVER HARDWARE

A well-designed server computer is as important as a strong network foundation when you install Windows NT Server. This chapter shows you how to select a server computer and computer components. You'll learn about CPU sizing, computer buses, peripheral adapters, disk storage, and tape storage. These lessons are important in two ways: First, the installation of Windows NT 4.0 Server is smoothest on a well-planned computer system. Second, the performance of your server is closely tied to how well you have selected the hardware.

AFTER READING THIS CHAPTER AND COMPLETING THE EXERCISES YOU WILL BE ABLE TO:

- DESCRIBE THE BASE SYSTEM REQUIREMENTS FOR WINDOWS NT 4.0 SERVER

- EXPLAIN HOW TO SELECT HARDWARE THAT IS COMPATIBLE WITH WINDOWS NT 4.0 SERVER

- DETERMINE THE APPROPRIATE CPU SIZE, BUS ARCHITECTURE, AND AMOUNT OF MEMORY REQUIRED FOR AN NT SERVER

- SELECT A NIC FOR THE SERVER

- SELECT THE APPROPRIATE DISK STORAGE, DISK STORAGE FAULT TOLERANCE, AND TAPE SYSTEM FOR NT SERVER

- SELECT A CD-ROM DRIVE OR CD-ROM ARRAY

- SET UP AND TEST A SERVER

The adage "you get what you pay for" applies to many aspects of computing, but especially to computer hardware. Consider two examples of server purchases. In the first case, a department head purchased a new computer as a server for a library checkout system. She carefully researched the requirements for NT Server, the workstation load, and the anticipated software needs. On the basis of her research preparations, she purchased a name-brand computer sized to meet the expected server load. Her server was installed and is working flawlessly. In another case, a systems analyst provided a server for a vacation and sick-leave tracking system to be used by hundreds on a college campus. He selected an on-hand, two-year-old 80486 computer with 500 MB of disk space. The server he selected was undersized for the job, causing long waits to enter and retrieve data.

SYSTEM REQUIREMENTS

The most basic step in selecting a server is to review the minimum system requirements for Microsoft Windows NT 4.0 Server. The requirements tell you the base on which you will need to build; they are shown in Table 3-1 for Intel and RISC-based computers.

 Keep in mind that these are *minimum* requirements for installation. Additional hard disk space is required for applications and data files, and additional memory may be required for some applications and for increasing performance.

Table 3-1   Minimum Hardware Requirements to Install Windows NT

Component	Intel	RISC
Processor	32-bit bus 80486/25 or higher	MIPS R4x00 or higher, Digital Alpha AXP, PowerPC
Display	VGA or better	VGA or better
Memory	16 MB (the system can run on 12 MB, but 16 MB is recommended)	16 MB (24 MB recommended)
Hard disk space	124 MB	158 MB
Floppy disk drive	High-density 3.5-inch	High-density 3.5-inch
CD-ROM drive	Required for installations not performed over the network	Required for installations not performed over the network
Network interface card (NIC)	Required to connect to the network	Required to connect to the network
Mouse or pointing device	Optional	Optional

With these requirements in mind, you need to plan hardware that exceeds the minimums to accommodate the workstations that will use the server, extra software besides the operating system, and data stored on the server. You will need to plan a server with enough CPU horsepower, disk storage, RAM, and backup resources for a system fully loaded to match the intended use.

WINDOWS NT 4.0 SERVER COMPATIBILITY

Your first stop in selecting hardware should be to check Microsoft's **Hardware Compatibility List (HCL),** a document that comes with the Windows NT Server software. The most up-to-date version is available on the Microsoft Web site, *http://www.microsoft.com.*

3

Microsoft reviews all types of hardware to determine whether they will work with Windows NT Server and Windows NT Workstation. The HCL includes information on the following hardware:

- Single-processor computers

- Multiprocessor computers

- RISC computers

- Processor upgrades

- PCMCIA hardware

- SCSI adapters and drives

- Video adapters

- Network adapters

- Audio adapters

- Modems

- Printers

- Tape devices

- Uninterruptible power supplies (UPSs)

The best step you can take in avoiding NT Server installation difficulties is to select well-known brand names from the HCL and to avoid hardware from small companies that build individual computers from generic parts. Most established computer manufacturers have products compatible with Windows NT Server, though their prices are somewhat higher than those of the smaller companies. Cutting expenses when buying server hardware could prove to be costly later on, if it results in unreliable equipment and difficult software installations.

CPU SIZING

Most Intel-based servers sold at this writing are Pentium Pro and Pentium II computers with a CPU clock speed of 200 megahertz (MHz) or faster. The **clock speed** is the rate at which the CPU sends data through the **buses,** or data pathways, inside the computer. A high clock speed helps ensure that the CPU does not become bottlenecked with more processing requests than it can handle. Buses come in different capacities, measured in terms of bits. For example, Pentium computers can send data in 32-bit streams. A typical character, such as the letter *r* or the number *5*, is packaged as 8 bits (1 byte). Thus, a 32-bit bus can carry 4 characters in each clock cycle.

80486 AND PENTIUM COMPUTERS

NT Server will work using an Intel-based 80486 CPU with a 25 MHz or higher clock speed. Many organizations have implemented 80486 servers with positive results. But the limitations of an 80486 become apparent as the server demand grows. The slower clock speed puts these servers at a disadvantage compared to a Pentium-based computer.

Windows NT Server takes advantage of the Pentium's fast clock speeds and 32-bit bus to provide better server response. Windows NT also uses Pentium-enabled features such as multithreading and multitasking. A high clock speed is recommended because this increases the speed at which the computer can internally transfer data, between the CPU and a disk or tape drive, for instance.

MULTIPROCESSOR COMPUTERS

Windows NT Server is designed to fully exploit the capabilities of multiprocessor computers. Many computer vendors make Pentium-based multiprocessor computers to be used specifically as servers. These symmetric multiprocessor (SMP) computers have two, three, four, or more processors to share the processing load.

 If you purchase an SMP computer, make sure that you understand the requirements for adding CPUs. Some use an architecture that requires CPUs to be added in multiple numbers, such as in pairs, making CPU upgrades expensive. Also, make sure that the SMP computer you purchase is compatible with Windows NT Server. If it has over four processors, you will need to obtain a custom version of NT Server.

RISC COMPUTERS

RISC computers are more powerful than Intel-based systems, although this distinction is becoming less true because of the expanding use of Intel-based SMP computers. A RISC computer uses fewer instructions per CPU operation than other large systems. With fewer instructions, there is less traffic along the CPU's bus, which speeds processing. Also, RISC CPUs come with clock speeds faster than those of most Intel-based servers, at 300 MHz and higher (another distinction that is becoming less and less true).

Two other advantages of RISC servers are that they can issue four CPU instructions for each clock cycle and that they support larger buses (more traffic lanes for data) than Intel servers. Manufacturers of RISC computers that are compatible with NT Server include Acer, DEC, IBM, and NEC. Two examples of RISC-based computers are DEC's Digital

Alpha System and IBM's RISC System/6000. RISC computers come with single and multiple CPU configurations.

A common business application for RISC computers is client/server computing. Large multigigabyte client/server databases require CPU power for data queries, updates, and high-volume user access. In these situations the RISC server is needed to prevent CPU bottlenecks.

3

BUS ARCHITECTURES

Computers have two buses. The internal bus carries instructions about computer operations to the CPU. The external bus carries data to be processed, such as data for mathematical operations. The server's speed is influenced by the size of the bus. Pentium servers have a 32-bit bus, and RISC servers have a 64-bit bus.

NT Server is a 32-bit operating system, which means that it can take advantage of a 32-bit or larger bus design. With this in mind, there are several bus types from which to choose: **Industry Standard Architecture (ISA)**, **Extended Industry Standard Architecture (EISA)**, **Microchannel Architecture (MCA)**, or **Peripheral Computer Interface (PCI)**.

ISA is an older expansion bus design dating back to the 1980s, supporting 8-bit and 16-bit cards and having a data transfer rate of 8 MB per second. Many computers have ISA or EISA expansion slots for older adapter cards. An EISA bus is an enhancement to ISA, supporting faster information throughput by means of the ability to have more than one process occurring at the same time. EISA internal and external buses support 8-, 16-, and 32-bit data transfer. The EISA bus permits several interface cards, such as two NICs, to transfer data without contention. This is possible through **bus mastering**, which enables some processing activities to take place on interface card processors instead of on the CPU.

The MCA bus is used in some Intel-based IBM computers. This bus has the same advantages as EISA, but it is capable of slightly faster data transfer rates. One advantage is that EISA is supported by many computer manufacturers that have defined this as a bus standard. A large variety of computer interface cards and add-ons is available for EISA because it is widely manufactured. A disadvantage of EISA and MCA is that they are not as fast as PCI.

The newer PCI bus supports 32-bit and 64-bit data transfer. This architecture enables a much faster data transfer speed than EISA or MCA, and nearly matches the speed of the CPU. Also, PCI has a local bus design that provides separate buses for disk storage and network interfaces. The local bus capability is designed to significantly speed the server by reducing contention on the bus. A disadvantage is that PCI adapters tend to be more expensive than EISA or MCA cards. Table 3-2 provides a summary of the bus standards.

 PCI bus servers are a good choice to protect your server hardware investment as new resource-intensive software applications continue to emerge, creating more demand for speed.

Table 3-2   Bus Architectures

Bus	Description
ISA	8-bit and 16-bit bus architecture dating to the early 1980s
EISA	32-bit bus built on the ISA architecture with faster throughput by means of bus mastering
MCA	32-bit bus proprietary to IBM computers and having a slightly faster transmission rate than EISA
PCI	32-bit and 64-bit bus with the fastest data transfer rate and local bus capability

SELECTING A NETWORK INTERFACE CARD (NIC)

The NIC is a server's window to the network, because all incoming and outgoing data passes through this card. Originally NICs were 8-bit cards designed for ISA buses. Today you can purchase 16-bit and 32-bit NICs.

When you develop specifications for a server, plan to purchase one with PCI expansion slots and a 32-bit PCI NIC. A NIC with fast throughput is critical to your server. One way to think about the importance of a fast NIC is to compare it to having 16 small doorways into a large stadium. With 16 doors, thousands of people would have to line up waiting to enter the stadium. However, with 32 doors, twice as many can go through in the same amount of time, providing faster entry with fewer bottlenecks.

 In addition to being slow, 16-bit NICs are likely to be unreliable on Pentium computers.

Purchase a NIC from a brand-name vendor in the Microsoft HCL. If the NIC is prein-stalled in the computer, make sure in advance that it is compatible with Windows NT and the type of network in which the server will be used, such as Ethernet or token ring.

Ethernet NICs come in 10 Mbps and 100 Mbps versions, or may support both speeds. The same applies to token ring NICs for 4 Mbps or 16 Mbps networks. Also, NICs are manu-factured for coax, twisted-pair, or a combination of these. To retain your investment in a NIC, consider one that offers a combination of options, such as a 10/100 Mbps Ethernet card with both coax and twisted-pair connectivity (try Hands-on Project 3-3).

Although Microsoft Windows NT Server includes drivers for many brands of NICs, make sure you obtain the most recent driver from the NIC manufacturer. Enhancements are made to NICs for which the latest driver is necessary. Also, an old NIC driver may contain software "bugs" that are corrected by a newer version. Some NIC vendors provide regular updates to their drivers to ensure against transmission problems, and many distribute these updates through the Internet. The ability to receive frequent updates from a quick, online source is very important, because network drivers are historically problematic.

Windows NT Server does not fully support **Plug and Play (PnP)** technology that enables you to install a card and have the operating system automatically recognize it when the computer is turned on. You may need to consult the NIC documentation about how to configure the card for your computer. In some cases you may need to set jumpers or DIP switches on the card. In other cases, the driver installation automatically configures the card. Figure 3-1 illustrates how a card is installed in a computer. Also, Hands-on Project 3-2 shows where a NIC is set up in Windows NT Server.

3

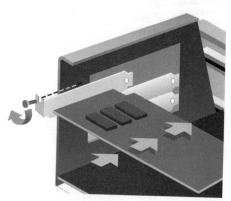

Figure 3-1   Example installation of a server NIC

MEMORY REQUIREMENTS

Another factor that influences how well a server performs is the amount of memory available to the server. The minimum RAM recommended for Windows NT Server is 16 MB, even though it is possible to boot the system with only 12 MB. Memory is one of the most critical components of a server. Each time a workstation connects to the server, a portion of memory is allocated to that connection. At the same time, memory is allocated to the following:

- Operation system kernel

- Services such as the Server service

- Processes

- Programs

- CPU functions

An inexpensive way to boost server performance is to install extra RAM. Estimating the amount of RAM needed is not an exact science, but some basic rules apply. First, determine the minimum amount of memory needed for the server operating system (16 MB). Next, determine the number of people who will be accessing the system at the same time. Finally, determine the average software requests per user and the amount of memory required for the requests. For example, consider a system with 100 maximum users who need an average of 2 MB per connection to access word-processing, spreadsheet, and program files. The calculation of memory is as follows:

16 MB for the operating system + (100 users × 2 MB average memory use) = 216 MB of memory.

In this case it is prudent to increase the memory to 256 MB as a growth factor for the future. Also, when purchasing memory, it is safest to purchase **error checking and correcting (ECC)** memory chips. That type of chip keeps some memory in reserve for when problems occur. It also makes an automatic correction if a parity error is detected, preventing the file server from crashing in the event of a memory parity error.

Server memory often is installed in modules called single inline memory modules (SIMMs). Most Pentium computers use 72-pin SIMMs in which the modules come in megabyte sizes of 1 MB, 4 MB, 8 MB, 16 MB, 32 MB, and so on. Figure 3-2 shows an example of a SIMM.

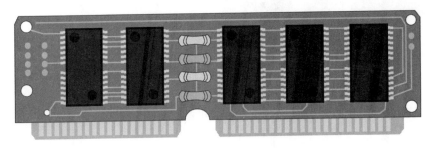

Figure 3-2   A 72-pin SIMM

On many systems, SIMMs are installed in banks located on the main circuit board. SIMMs generally must be installed in combinations recommended by the computer manufacturer that are based on a computer's design. Also, all SIMMs in the computer must be rated at the same speed. For example, if the initial SIMMs operate at 70 nanoseconds (ns), memory upgrades must operate at that speed. Figure 3-3 illustrates how a SIMM is installed. Also, try Hands-on Project 3-4 to practice installing a SIMM.

If you install SIMMs to upgrade a computer, make sure that you wear a wrist grounding strap to prevent electrostatic discharge. One end of the strap attaches to an unpainted metal area on the computer chassis, and the other is a strap that goes around your wrist. An alternative is to touch an unpainted chassis area before beginning the installation.

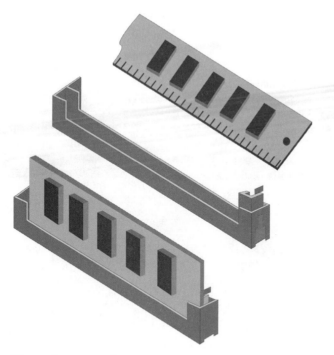

Figure 3-3   Installing a SIMM

DISK STORAGE

Choosing the right hard disk drive is just as important as selecting the right bus. Hard disk access on a file server is far more frequent than on a typical workstation. This constant activity leads to congested data paths and the malfunctioning of overused disk drive parts. In choosing a server hard drive, you will need to make decisions about capacity, contention, and fault tolerance.

DISK CAPACITY

Estimating hard disk capacity is based on calculating space for the following:

- Operating system files
- Software files
- Data and database files
- User files
- General public files
- Utility files
- Server management files

Most network administrators calculate a general figure based on the total number of bytes needed. Table 3-3 illustrates how the number of bytes might be calculated for a law office consisting of 12 users.

Table 3-3   Calculating Disk Capacity

Operating System Files	Estimated Size
Microsoft NT Server (depending on the accessories and services installed)	150 MB
Subtotal	150 MB
Application Software	**Estimated Size**
Microsoft Office	100 MB
Microsoft Exchange	100 MB
WordPerfect	10 MB
Lotus 1-2-3	12 MB
Accounting software	250 MB
Legal time accounting software	200 MB
Client databases	75 MB
Court forms	52 MB
Contracts forms	42 MB
Tax law forms	41 MB
Wills legal forms	45 MB
Bankruptcy legal forms	35 MB
Database query software	24 MB
Subtotal	986 MB
User Directories	**Estimated Size**
Each user 100 MB × 12	1200 MB
Subtotal	1200 MB
Public Directories	**Estimated Size**
Shared directories containing word-processing files, spreadsheets, and data	290 MB
Utility directories	50 MB
Subtotal	340 MB
Server Management Software	**Estimated Size**
Extra utilities for server and network management	150 MB
Subtotal	150 MB
Total	2,826 MB

Table 3–3 shows a total of 2.826 GB required in estimated disk space. An additional amount should be added to accommodate anticipated growth, such as extra space needed by users and for new software that will be installed. Also, in this situation, the law firm should take into account expected growth in the databases, accounting data, and legal time software. Each time the firm bills a client or records information about a new client, data in these areas will grow. Also, some users may need larger allocations for user directories. A margin of growth in this situation might be calculated at 50% for the next two years. Adjusting the capacity requirements for growth yields the following estimate:

$$2.826 \text{ GB} + (2.826 \text{ GB} \times 0.5) = 4.239 \text{ GB}$$

DISK CONTENTION

Disk contention is the number of simultaneous requests to read or write data onto a disk. The number of requests processed by a file server can be quite large when there are many users, such as 100 or 200. Disk contention can be reduced through the design of the server disk storage. The primary design issues are:

- Speed of the individual disks

- Speed of the disk controllers

- Speed of the data pathway to the disks

- Number of disk pathways

- Disk caching

The speed of the disk is called **disk access time**, measured in milliseconds (ms). This is the time it takes for the read/write heads on the disk to reach the data for reads or updates. A fast disk access time can reduce disk contention. Disk drives manufactured today have fast access times of 15 ms or less. Access time is important, but because most disks are built to be fast, it is not as important as how quickly the data reaches the disk.

The speed of the data pathway or channel is called the **data transfer rate**, measured in megabytes per second (Mbps). The data transfer rate is determined by the type of disk controller used in the server. The disk controller is the board that acts as the interface between the disk drives and the computer. Figure 3–4 shows a disk controller. Many computer systems come with **Integrated Device Electronics (IDE)** or **Enhanced Small Device Interface (ESDI)** disk controllers. These controllers provide average data transfer rates and traditionally have been a viable choice for older servers.

Server   Disk controller   Disk drive

Figure 3-4 Disk controller connecting a disk drive

The best choice for a modern server is to implement a **small computer system interface (SCSI)** adapter, which takes advantage of the 32-bit bus architecture of Pentium computers. SCSI interfaces rely less on the main system CPU than IDE and ESDI controllers, freeing the CPU for other work. Data transfer rate enhancements continue to be implemented for SCSI devices. The standard SCSI-1 interface has a data transfer rate of 5 Mbps, which is many times that of IDE or ESDI. The second-generation SCSI-2 interfaces come with narrow and wide bus options. The wide interfaces have about twice the data transfer speed, 20 Mbps, as the narrow ones, at 10 Mbps. Today, Ultra SCSI and wide Ultra SCSI adapters are used on Pentium-based servers because they transfer data at 20 Mbps and 40 Mbps, respectively. Servers soon will be equipped with Ultra2 SCSI adapters that have just emerged on the market, offering 80 Mbps data transfer. SCSI-3 adapters are made for RISC computers and have speeds up to 100 Mbps. Table 3-4 summarizes the SCSI interface speeds.

Table 3-4 SCSI Interface Data Transfer Rates

Interface	Data Transfer Rate
SCSI-1	Up to 5 Mbps
Narrow SCSI-2	Up to 10 Mbps
Wide SCSI-2	Up to 20 Mbps
Ultra SCSI	Up to 20 Mbps
Wide Ultra SCSI	Up to 40 Mbps
Ultra2 SCSI	Up to 80 Mbps
SCSI-3 (RISC)	Up to 100 Mbps

Several disk drives or other devices, such as a tape drive or CD-ROM drive, can be daisy-chained on the cable of a SCSI adapter. Wide Ultra SCSI or Ultra2 SCSI provides the best performance when devices are daisy-chained. Also, it is important to make sure that each device connected to the interface has a unique address, with the first device addressed as 0. Problems occur if two devices have the same address. The SCSI cable must be terminated with a SCSI terminator after the last device that is connected.

Omitting the cable terminator is a common problem when connecting several devices to one SCSI adapter. If you experience difficulty recognizing hard disk storage during the Windows NT Server installation, check to make sure that the terminator is connected to the last device on the SCSI cable.

Computers designed as servers generally come equipped with SCSI-2 adapters or higher. Watch for new developments with SCSI adapters, particularly in extending data transfer rates over 100 Mbps for Pentium-based computers.

The controller of a SCSI device is directly attached to the device. This design makes it possible to mix different devices on the same interface. The SCSI interface plugs into one of the computer's open expansion slots on the main board. A cable is run in daisy-chain fashion from the adapter to the controller card for each device, with a terminator at the last device. Several disk drives, a tape drive, and other SCSI devices can be attached to one adapter, as shown in Figure 3-5.

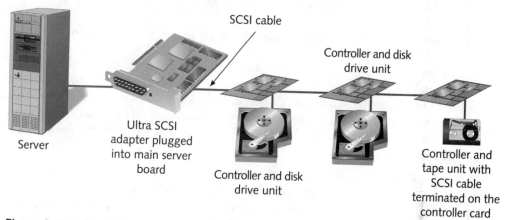

Figure 3-5   Ultra SCSI adapter connected to two disk drives and a tape drive

When you configure a server, be cautious about placing too much demand on access to hard disk storage. If you purchase only one drive, all the users will contend for data on that drive. If you purchase two drives to place on one SCSI adapter, the data contention on the single pathway may be excessive. One solution is to purchase a server with an Ultra SCSI or Ultra2 SCSI interface and put both drives on the same pathway. A better solution is to create two separate pathways with two adapters, as shown in Figure 3-6.

 One method to significantly increase performance on a server is to purchase two or more hard disk drives and divide the flow of data between two or more data pathways by placing the drives on different adapters.

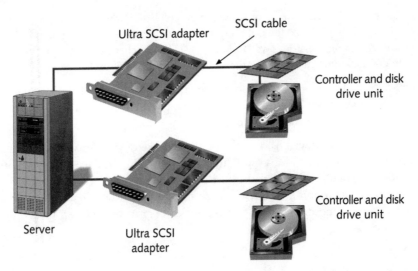

Figure 3-6 Using two SCSI adapters to create separate data paths for hard disk drives

In the Table 3-3 example presented earlier, one way to implement the 4.239 GB of total storage is to purchase two drives, each with 2.2 GB or more capacity, and place each on its own SCSI adapter. Even though two disks and two adapters will increase the cost of the server, the benefits from increased performance will override the cost factor. Another advantage is that if one SCSI interface malfunctions, you can move its disk drive to the remaining interface for a fast recovery.

Disk caching is another way to improve disk response time. Cache is memory allocated to a device so that the device can store frequently used information or the last information used. Because data access to memory is faster than access to disk, caching saves time. The purchase of a controller with a large disk-caching capability will permit faster data access.

DISK STORAGE FAULT TOLERANCE

Because hard disk drives are prone to failure, one of the best data security measures is to plan for disk redundancy in servers and host computers. This is accomplished in two ways: by installing backup disks and by installing RAID drives.

One fault-tolerance option common to many server and host computer operating systems is **disk mirroring** to store redundant data. With disk mirroring, there are two separate drives for each disk volume of data. One is the main drive used to handle all of the user's requests to access or write data. The second drive contains a mirror image of the data on the first. Each time there is an update or deletion, it is made on the main drive and replicated on the second. If the main drive fails, the mirrored drive takes over with no data loss. In disk mirroring, both drives are attached to the same disk controller or SCSI adapter (Figure 3-7). For example, one SCSI adapter plugged into a slot on the computer's main board might have two disk drives, the main drive and a mirrored drive.

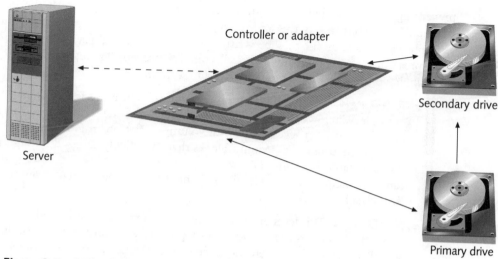

Figure 3-7 Disk mirroring

Disk mirroring has a weakness, because it leaves the data inaccessible if it is the controller or adapter that fails. To compensate for that weakness, **disk duplexing** is another fault-tolerance method, combining disk mirroring with redundant adapters or controllers. Each disk is still mirrored by using a second backup disk, but the backup disk is placed on a controller or adapter that is separate from the one used by the main disk (Figure 3-8). If the main disk, controller, or adapter fails, users may continue their work on the redundant one. Some operating systems can switch from the main to the backup disk without interruption in service to the users, while others require that the server or host computer be rebooted to use the mirror drive instead of the failed main drive.

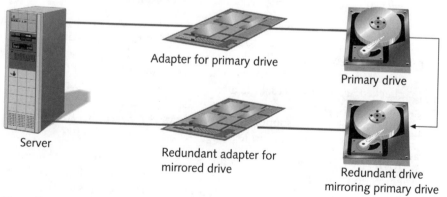

Figure 3-8 Disk duplexing

Another approach to disk redundancy is through the use of a **redundant array of inexpensive disks (RAID)**. RAID is a set of standards for lengthening disk life and preventing data loss. There are eight levels of RAID, beginning with the use of disk striping. **Disk striping** is the ability to spread data over multiple disk volumes. For example, part of a large file may be written to one volume and part to another. The goal is to spread disk activity equally across all volumes, preventing wear from being focused on a single volume in a set. The eight RAID levels are as follows:

- *RAID level 0:* Striping with no other redundancy features is RAID level 0. For example, Windows NT Server supports level 0 to extend disk life and to improve performance. Data access on striped volumes is fast on an NT server because of the way the data is divided into blocks that are quickly accessed through multiple disk reads and data paths. NT Server can stripe data across 2 to 32 disks. A significant disadvantage to using level 0 striping is that if one disk fails, you can expect a large data loss on all volumes.

- *RAID level 1:* This level employs simple disk mirroring and is used on smaller networks. Windows NT Server also supports level 1, but includes disk duplexing as well as mirroring. If there are three or more volumes to be mirrored or duplexed, this solution is more expensive than the other RAID levels. However, this option is sometimes preferred by network administrators because disk mirroring has better read and write performance than RAID methods other than level 0. Also, disk mirroring and disk duplexing offer the best guarantee of data recovery when there is a disk failure.

- *RAID level 2:* This level uses an array of disks with the data striped across all disks in the array. Also, in this method all disks store error-correction information that enables the array to reconstruct data from a failed disk. The advantages of level 2 are that disk wear is reduced and data is reconstructed if a disk fails.

- *RAID level 3:* Like level 2, RAID level 3 uses disk striping and stores error-correcting information, but the information is only written to one disk in the array. If that disk fails, the array cannot rebuild its contents.

- *RAID level 4:* This level stripes data and stores error-correcting information on all drives, in a manner similar to level 2. An added feature is its ability to perform checksum verification. The checksum is a sum of bits in a file. When a file is recreated after a disk failure, the checksum previously stored for that file is checked against the actual file after it is reconstructed. If the two do not match, the network administrator will know that the file may be corrupted. RAID levels 2 through 4 are not supported by Windows NT Server because they do not offer the full protection found in level 5.

- *RAID level 5:* Level 5 combines the best features of RAID, including striping, error correction, and checksum verification. NT Server supports level 5, calling it "stripe sets with parity." Whereas level 4 stores checksum data on only one disk, level 5 spreads both error correction and checksum data over all of the disks, so there is no single point of failure. An added feature of level 5 is that a network administrator can replace a failed disk without shutting down the other drives. This level uses more memory than other RAID levels, with 16 MB recommended as additional memory for system functions. In addition, level 5 requires at least three disks in the

RAID array. Recovery from a failed disk provides roughly the same guarantee as with disk mirroring, but takes longer with level 5.

 RAID level 5 is slower than the other two levels supported by NT Server, levels 0 and 1.

- *RAID level 6:* This level is similar to level 5, but creates two sets of error-correction and checksum data on all of the disks in the array. In level 6, two disks in the array can fail simultaneously without loss of data.

- *RAID level 10:* Level 10 is disk mirroring, as in level 1, but also stripes the disks when there are multiple sets of main and mirrored disks (similar to level 0).

On a Windows NT server, mirrored disks or RAID drives are set up using the Disk Administrator, a central tool for managing the server disk and CD-ROM drives (Try Hands-on Project 3-1). The Disk Administrator offers several disk management options, as follows:

- Viewing status information about drives, including file system information
- Creating an NTFS partition on a new disk drive
- Combining two physical drives into one logical drive
- Changing drive letter assignments
- Formatting drives
- Extending a partitioned drive to include any free space not already partitioned
- Creating a mirrored drive set
- Creating a striped drive set

SELECTING DISK STORAGE FAULT TOLERANCE

The disk storage fault-tolerance method you use depends on factors such as:

- The importance of the data stored on the server
- How soon a server must be working after a disk problem
- The amount of data stored on the server
- Budget constraints

Consider three different situations for planning fault tolerance. In the first, you are a planning a server to be used by a team of 10 software developers for a full-featured human resources hiring system used by large department stores. None of the software on this server is used in a live environment, because the server is strictly for testing and development. Also, the developers work only with limited test data, not with a large human resources database.

However, the application developers are under rigid deadlines for completing each phase of the software. In this situation, the disk storage requirements are not large, and a disk crash is unlikely to cause them to lose data that cannot be replaced. The main concern is to have the server quickly working again after a disk failure, so that the developers can keep up with their deadlines. In this situation, disk mirroring or RAID level 1 is likely to meet their needs. If the main disk drive is lost, the mirrored disk can quickly take over, and they will not lose precious time. Disk duplexing is another alternative, if there is a concern that they may lose an adapter or disk controller and sacrifice time as a result of this type of failure.

In another example, an NT Server is used by tellers and loan officers in a small bank with 15 employees. The bank cannot afford to risk loss of data or downtime because of a failed disk drive or controller. Also, during certain peak periods, they experience heavy disk read and write activity. The bank is likely to benefit from dividing data between two disk drives on different SCSI adapters, with a mirrored drive for each main drive. The disk load is spread between two drives for faster access during peak times at the bank. If one disk drive fails, the mirrored drive can take over. If an adapter fails, both of the drives on that adapter can be switched to the remaining adapter until the failed adapter is replaced. Another option, if access speed is not a concern, is to connect two small RAID level 5 arrays to two different adapters. This provides two paths for better disk response and the advantage of disk redundancy should one of the RAID drives fail. Also, if an adapter fails, its RAID drive can be switched temporarily to the working adapter.

A third scenario is a mail-order company that sells clothes. This company has 55 customer service representatives who take telephone orders and enter the data into an interactive order entry database on a Windows NT server. Customer service representatives work around the clock, and any server downtime costs hundreds of dollars a minute. Also, the company cannot afford any data loss due to a failed drive, because it could cost them thousands of dollars. This is a good application for multiple data paths and large RAID level 5 or 6 arrays. The multiple data paths will help the server respond to aggressive disk demands, and the RAID level 5 or 6 arrays will prevent data loss if a drive in an array fails. Also, this setup prevents downtime, because the disk array continues working even though a drive has crashed.

SELECTING A TAPE SYSTEM

Another form of redundancy to protect data is to equip a server with a tape backup system. For example, a tape drive used to back up NT servers on a network can be mounted inside a server, or it can be an external unit. For best server response, consider purchasing a SCSI-based tape drive, making it the only device connected to the SCSI adapter (Figure 3-9).

 If hard disks also are on the SCSI interface, server access to the disks may be slowed by the high traffic through that SCSI adapter during backups.

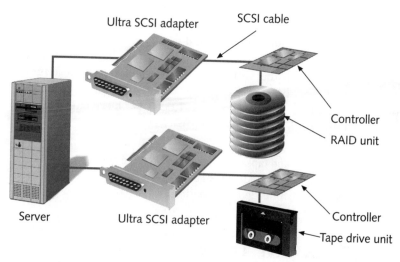

Figure 3-9   Connecting a tape drive to a separate SCSI adapter

Windows NT servers typically use quarter-inch cartridge (QIC), digital audio tape (DAT), or digital linear tape (DLT) backup. Cartridge backup systems have the smallest storage capability, in the gigabyte range of 2 to 4 GB. Use of QIC tapes for backups has decreased over the past several years because the storage capacity is limited.

Much more popular among server administrators is DAT technology, which stores data in the medium gigabyte range. Most administrators have moved from the initial 4 mm tape, which holds 2 to 9 GB per tape, to the newer 8 mm format, which holds 4 to 25 GB.

Server administrators with high-capacity backup needs are also moving to the DLT systems, which store data in the 10 to 40 GB range. DLT tapes are more resistant to damage than DAT or QIC tapes and have a longer shelf life of up to 30 years. DLT systems write information to tape about three times faster than DAT.

To help you plan for tape systems on different types of networks, consider two different situations. In one example, an independent insurance agency uses three Windows NT servers, each with 8 to 12 GB of disk storage. The agency is very active during the day, but there is little network activity in the evening. In this situation, you can use one tape drive for all of the NT servers. The network traffic will be greater than if you install one tape drive per server, but since the network is hardly used at night, you can run tape backups in the evening. The traffic is greater with one tape drive because backups on the servers to which the drive is not attached must go over the network to the server that has the drive. A high-capacity 8 mm DAT or a DLT tape system is a reliable choice in this situation. For example, using a 40 GB DAT system would enable you to back up all servers to one tape. You would be able to insert the backup tape and have the built-in NT scheduler start the backup any time during the night, freeing you from staying late to start the backups manually.

In another situation, assume that you are planning a network that will have 10 NT servers for a liberal arts college. Each server has 20 to 25 GB of disk storage. Three of the servers are used by college administrators and faculty, with the remaining servers used for student labs. On some evenings, particularly before midterm and final exams, the servers are busy until 1:00 A.M., which is when the labs are closed for the evening. In this situation, you might equip each of the three administrative and faculty servers with its own tape drive to reduce the network load during their backups. Backups on these servers might be started after 9:00 P.M., depending on the work patterns of the faculty and administration. You might also purchase two or three tape drives to be used for the student lab computers. Backups for these computers would start after 1:00 A.M. DLT tape systems are a good choice in this situation for reliability and tape capacity.

Reliable tape systems and tapes are one of the best investments you can make. The expense of tape backup equipment and tapes is small compared to the cost of the human resources needed to reconstruct lost data.

CHOOSING A CD-ROM DRIVE

The CD-ROM drive is necessary to load the NT Server operating system, unless you choose to load the system over the network. Another good reason for having the drive is to run software that is only available on CD-ROM. In the law office example used earlier, the CD-ROM drive might by used to make legal forms software available to all attorneys and paralegals connected to the server.

Another way to implement CD-ROM access is to purchase a CD-ROM "jukebox" or server that can be connected to the Windows NT server by using a SCSI adapter (Figure 3-10). CD-Technology, DEC, NEC, Plextor, Sony, and Toshiba are examples of CD-ROM vendors on Microsoft's HCL. CD-ROMs come in various speeds ranging up to 24X and faster. Most server-grade computers have at least a 6X or 8X CD-ROM drive. If you plan to use multiple CD-ROMs for sharing through a server, investigate the many options for CD-ROM arrays. The arrays offer throughput that can match Ultra SCSI speeds. CD-ROM arrays come in various configurations, such as 7, 10, 14, and 32 CD-ROM drives in a single tower array. One user can be connected to one or more CD-ROMs in the array.

Figure 3-10   A CD-ROM server array

SETTING UP AND TESTING THE SERVER

There are several steps you can take once your new server arrives, which will help you prepare for Windows NT 4.0 installation. A first step is to boot the computer to make sure it works. As the server boots, it is likely to go through a test of the banks of RAM.

If you need to install the NIC, turn off the computer, unplug it from the wall outlet, and remove the monitor, mouse, and keyboard. Next, remove the cover according to the manufacturer's instructions. Locate an empty slot for the NIC. The circuit board slots are usually located at the rear of the main circuit board or on a separate board that connects to the main board. At the end of each slot, there is a slot cover on the frame of the server. Remove the slot cover before installing the NIC. Consult the manual to be certain which are 32-bit EISA and PCI slots. Make sure to plug the NIC into the appropriate type of slot, which will depend on the type of NIC (EISA or PCI).

After removing the slot cover, check to make sure that your wrist grounding strap is on securely. Remove the NIC from its antistatic protective bag and firmly install it into a slot. You may hear a slight click as the card goes into place against the bottom of the slot.

Plan to execute a fast test of the NIC to be certain that the NIC is installed properly. Reattach the monitor, mouse, keyboard, and power cord. Once the computer is on, run the test software included with the NIC. The test program should indicate that the NIC is installed correctly and is ready to be used.

Repeat the same type of procedures if you also need to install one or more SCSI adapters. Install SCSI adapters in the appropriate EISA or PCI expansion slots. If possible, leave space between boards inside the server (empty slots between occupied slots). This allows better air circulation and reduces the impact of heat generated by the computer. It also helps to prolong the life of the boards.

After the SCSI adapters are installed, boot the computer again to make sure that it boots properly. If the adapter manufacturer has included test software, make sure to use it to test the installation. Once you are certain that the newly installed components are working, let the computer run for several days as a "burn in" period. Any defective components are likely to fail after you run the computer for several days. If there is a defective component, such as a monitor or floppy disk drive, you will have the opportunity to get it replaced before starting the Windows NT Server installation. This is much easier than puzzling over NT Server installation problems due to defective hardware.

CHAPTER SUMMARY

- The best way to start a server installation is to begin with hardware selected to match the role the server will play on the network. It is better to start with too much server than with too little. A server that begins its job undersized will quickly become a source of problems. At first, an undersized server may appear to be a network problem because of slow response and delays at the server. You may spend hours locating the problem, and your users will quickly lose confidence in the installation. A well-sized computer enables you to get a fast start so you can proceed with the next steps in managing the server. Also, the server will quickly generate confidence, enabling users to enjoy productivity gains right away.

- The first step in selecting hardware is to check the Microsoft Hardware Compatibility List (HCL) to make sure that all components will work with Windows NT 4.0 Server. One reason for taking this step is to ensure that drivers are available for each hardware component and that they are compatible with the operating system installation. Your choice of CPU from the list depends on the anticipated server load. In many cases a Pentium-based CPU is a good selection for small and medium-sized installations (a few users to several hundred). If the installation is for a demanding client/server system or for a large number of users (300 and over), a large SMP computer or RISC-based computer is likely to be needed.

- Computers use different types of bus architectures, such as ISA, EISA, MCA, and PCI. For most installations a combination of EISA and PCI expansion buses works best. The EISA slots are compatible with many types of adapters, while the PCI slots provide high throughput for critical components, such as the NIC. The selection of the NIC depends on network and computer requirements. If the network is 100 Mbps Ethernet using twisted-pair cable, the NIC will need to match those requirements. Also, the NIC needs to match the type of expansion slots in the computer, such as EISA and PCI.

- The selection of disk storage depends on factors such as capacity, speed, and data transfer rate. SCSI adapters are generally used to connect hard disks to the computer because of their fast throughput at up to 80 Mbps. Fault-tolerance options also need to be considered when disk storage is selected. Disk mirroring, duplexing, and RAID are fault-tolerance methods supported by Windows NT 4.0 Server. Installing a tape system is another way to implement fault tolerance so that data on hard disks can be backed up regularly.

- Most servers have at least one CD-ROM drive. Options are available to connect an array of CD-ROM drives for situations in which the server makes multiple CD-ROMs available to users. CD-ROM drives vary in speed from 2X to 24X. A low-speed drive can be used if its purpose is mainly to load software and drivers on the server. High-speed access in the 24X range is desirable for drives that are shared among network users.

- The last stage in preparing the server hardware is to install components such as NICs, SCSI adapters, RAM, and tape drives (if they are not preinstalled by the manufacturer). Each device should be tested after it is installed. The server and components should have a burn-in period of several days to make sure that all parts are functional before the Windows NT 4.0 Server operating system is loaded.

KEY TERMS

- **bus** — A pathway in a computer used to transmit information. This pathway is used to send CPU instructions and other information for data transfer within the computer.

- **bus mastering** — A process that reduces the reliance on the CPU for input/output activities on a computer's bus. Interface cards that have bus mastering can take control of the bus for faster data flow.

- **clock speed** — Rate at which the CPU sends bursts of data through a computer's buses.

- **data transfer rate** — Speed at which data moves through the disk controller along the data channel to a disk drive.

- **disk access time** — Amount of time it takes for a disk drive to read or write data by moving a read/write head to the location of the data.

- **disk duplexing** — A fault-tolerance method similar to disk mirroring in that it prevents data loss by duplicating data from a main disk to a backup disk, but disk duplexing places the backup disk on a different controller or adapter than is used by the main disk.

- **disk mirroring** — A fault-tolerance method that prevents data loss by duplicating data from a main disk to a backup disk. Some operating systems also refer to this as disk shadowing.

- **disk striping** — A data storage method that breaks up data files across all volumes of a disk set to minimize wear on a single volume.

- **Enhanced Small Device Interface (ESDI)** — An early device interface for computer peripherals and hard disk drives.

- **error checking and correcting memory (ECC)** — Memory that can correct some types of memory problems without causing computer operations to halt.

- **Extended Industry Standard Architecture (EISA)** — A computer bus design that incorporates 32-bit communications within a computer. It is an industry standard used by several computer manufacturers.

- **Hardware Compatibility List (HCL)** — List of computer hardware tested by Microsoft and determined to be compatible with Windows NT 4.0.

- **Integrated Device Electronics (IDE)** — An inexpensive hard disk interface that is used on Intel-based computers from the 80286 to Pentium computers.

- **Industry Standard Architecture (ISA)** — An older expansion bus design dating back to the 1980s, supporting 8-bit and 16-bit cards and with a data transfer rate of 8 MB per second.

- **Microchannel Architecture (MCA)** — A bus architecture that is used in older IBM Intel-based computers. It provides 32-bit communications within the computer.

- **Peripheral Computer Interface (PCI)** — A computer bus design that supports 32-bit and 64-bit bus communications for high-speed operations.

- **Plug and Play (PnP)** — Ability of added computer hardware, such as an adapter or modem, to identify itself to the computer operating system for installation.

- **redundant array of inexpensive disks (RAID)** — A set of standards to extend the life of hard disk drives and to prevent data loss from a hard disk failure.

- **small computer system interface (SCSI)** — A 32- or 64-bit computer adapter that transports data between one or more attached devices, such as hard disks, and the computer. There are several types of SCSI adapters, including SCSI, SCSI-2, SCSI-3, SCSI wide, SCSI narrow, and Ultra SCSI. All are used to provide high-speed data transfer to reduce bottlenecks within the computer.

REVIEW QUESTIONS

1. A basic system requirement in order to load Windows NT 4.0 Server is _____ .

   a. 80486 computer or faster

   b. VGA monitor

   c. 16 MB RAM

   d. all of the above

   e. only a and b

2. Which RAID level is the same as disk mirroring?

   a. RAID level 0

   b. RAID level 1

   c. RAID level 2

   d. RAID level 5

3. What hard disk fault-tolerance method provides insurance against an adapter failure?

   a. duplexing

   b. mirroring

   c. defragmenting

   d. sectoring

4. You are planning a server that will experience heavy disk access by 90 telephone marketers. Which of the following actions would help manage the load?

   a. purchase ISA adapters

   b. disable disk caching

   c. create two or more data paths

   d. all of the above

   e. only a and c

5. Which type of memory can correct errors?

    a. ESDI

    b. ECC

    c. equal access RAM

    d. module RAM

6. Wide Ultra SCSI transfers data at _____.

    a. 5 Mbps

    b. 10 Mbps

    c. 20 Mbps

    d. 40 Mbps

7. Which of the following RAID levels consists only of disk striping?

    a. RAID level 0

    b. RAID level 1

    c. RAID level 2

    d. RAID level 5

8. Which of the following bus types has a fast data transfer rate plus local bus capability?

    a. ISA

    b. PCI

    c. MCA

    d. EISA

9. An adapter with _____ reduces the reliance on the CPU for I/O operations.

    a. bus mastering

    b. local caching

    c. data pairing

    d. imaging

10. The speed of data along a disk pathway or channel is called _____.

    a. bus rate

    b. line rate

    c. data transfer rate

    d. data interval

11. Which of the following is compatible with 32-bit bus architecture?

    a. MCA

    b. PCI

    c. EISA

    d. all of the above

    e. only b and c

12. Which tape technology has the largest tape capacity?

    a. DAT

    b. QIC

    c. DLT

    d. 3480

13. Which SCSI technology is best suited for RISC computers?

    a. SCSI-1

    b. SCSI-2

    c. SCSI-3

    d. Universal SCSI

    e. only a and b

14. 4 mm or 8 mm tape would best describe which of the following?

    a. DAT

    b. QIC

    c. DLT

    d. 3480

15. Which of the following affects disk contention?

    a. disk access time

    b. RAM

    c. CPU size

    d. all of the above

    e. only b and c

16. A SIMM is _____.

    a. a RAID array

    b. RAM

    c. a bus

    d. an interactive CPU component

17. You need to back up 10 GB of information on a server each night. Which of the following tape systems would most likely meet your needs?

   a. QIC

   b. DLT

   c. DAT

   d. all of the above

   e. only b and c

18. RAM is measured in _____.

   a. bits per second

   b. megabits per second

   c. nanoseconds

   d. megahertz

19. The speed at which data travels to and from the CPU on a computer's buses is _____.

   a. clock speed

   b. access rate

   c. CPU timing ratio

   d. bus ratio

20. Pentium computers support which of the following?

   a. 32-bit bus

   b. multitasking

   c. multithreading

   d. all of the above

   e. only b and c

21. Which RAID level(s) is (are) supported by Windows NT Server?

   a. RAID level 0

   b. RAID level 3

   c. RAID level 5

   d. all of the above

   e. only a and c

22. You have set up a server connecting two disk drives to one SCSI adapter. Each drive has its own controller. Which of the following fault-tolerance methods would you set up?

   a. disk marking

   b. disk copying

   c. disk duplexing

   d. disk striping with parity

HANDS-ON PROJECTS

PROJECT 3-1

In this activity you view where to set hard disk fault tolerance on a computer running Windows NT 4.0 Server. You need access to the Administrator account or an account with the same privileges. (Another option is to use Remote Administration Tools from a computer running Windows 95 or NT.)

To view where to set hard disk fault tolerance:

1. Click **Start**, **Programs**, **Administrative Tools (Common)** and **Disk Administrator** (Figure 3-11).

2. Click the **Fault Tolerance** menu and notice the options Establish Mirror and Create Stripe Set with Parity. (Figure 3-12).

3. Close the Disk Administrator.

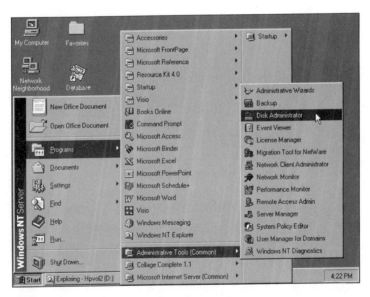

Figure 3-11   Starting the Disk Administrator

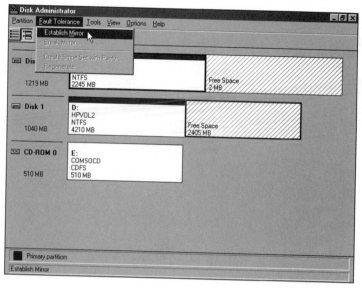

Figure 3-12   Viewing fault-tolerance options

PROJECT 3-2

In this activity you view where to set up a NIC in Windows NT Server, once the NIC and operating system are installed.

To view where to install a NIC:

1. Click the **Start** button, **Settings,** and **Control Panel**.
2. Double-click the **Network** icon.
3. Click the **Adapters** tab.
4. Click the **Add** button (Figure 3–13).
5. Notice the list of adapters that can be installed on Windows NT Server (Figure 3–14).
6. Use the scroll bar to view a sampling of adapters.
7. Click **Cancel** when you are finished viewing the list.
8. Click **Cancel** on the Network dialog box to exit.
9. Close the Control Panel.

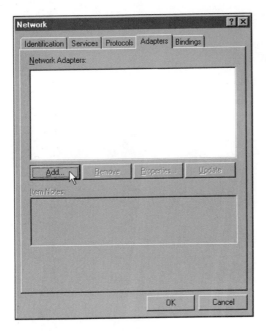

Figure 3-13   Adding a NIC

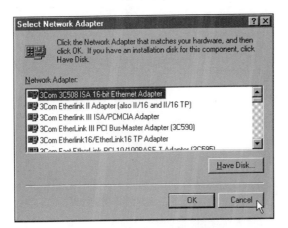

Figure 3-14   NICs that can be installed

3

PROJECT 3-3

In this activity you visit the Web site of a NIC manufacturer to determine NIC options. Two example Web sites are *www.3com.com* and *www.intel.com*. You need access to Microsoft Internet Explorer in Windows 95 or Windows NT. (If you use another Web browser, open that instead of Internet Explorer in Step 1.)

To find the NIC information on the Web:

1. Double-click **Internet Explorer** on the desktop or click **Start**, **Programs**, and **Internet Explorer**.

2. Enter any dial-up networking information that may be required to use the Internet, such as a telephone number, your username, and password.

3. Enter **http://www.3com.com** as the address.

4. Click **Products** (Figure 3-15).

5. Click to view **Network Interface Cards**.

6. Find an option to view information about 10/100 Mbps Ethernet cards.

7. Create a document to record information about the cards, such as what bus types are used and what communications cable is used to connect the cards to a network.

8. Determine if any of these cards will work using category 5 twisted-pair cable.

9. Close the Internet Explorer when you are finished.

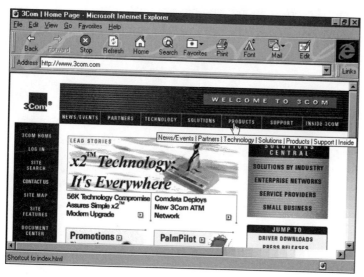

Figure 3-15   Accessing a NIC vendor's Web site

Project 3-4

In this activity you practice installing extra memory in a computer. You need a computer with empty RAM expansion slots and a SIMM.

To install a SIMM:

1. Make sure the computer is turned off. Remove the power cord, keyboard cable, mouse, and monitor cable. Remove any other cables that might be connected to the computer.

2. Remove the cover on the computer, following the manufacturer's instructions.

3. Find the memory banks on the main board in the computer.

4. Obtain a compatible SIMM to install in the computer.

5. Remove the SIMM from its protective antistatic container.

6. Attach a wrist grounding strap around your wrist or touch an unpainted portion of the computer.

7. Hold the SIMM at a 45-degree angle over the first available slot (see Figure 3-3).

8. Guide the chip into the notches on either side of the slot.

9. Once the module is aligned with the notches, gently snap the module into the slot, so that it is perpendicular with the main board. Install a second module, if required for your computer.

10. Put the computer cover back on.

11. Attach the monitor, keyboard, mouse, and power cord.

12. Turn on the computer and watch the memory diagnostics as the computer comes on.

13. Make sure that the computer recognizes the new memory in the diagnostics.

ASPEN CONSULTING: SERVER HARDWARE SPECIFICATIONS

This week you are working again with Flight Dynamics, helping them with several issues regarding server hardware selection. Also, you will help the alumni and college development association for Fall River College, which needs you to provide specifications for servers used in a client/server system.

1. Flight Dynamics is planning to install two new servers after the new expansion of the company is complete. Create specifications for their business and human resources computer, so that it will accommodate at least 10 users. Include in your specifications:

   - CPU type and size

   - RAM

   - Disk storage (capacity, type, and other factors relating to hard disk performance)

   - NIC

   Take into account your recommendations from Case Project question 3 in Chapter 2, "Basic Network Design and Protocols," when you determine what type of NIC to recommend. Use the following information from Table 3-5 on the next page for disk capacity calculations.

2. Jason Brown at Flight Dynamics has some questions about bus designs and SCSI adapters. Explain the different types of bus designs. Explain the options available for different kinds of SCSI adapters.

3. What type of fault tolerance do you recommend for Flight Dynamics' business and human resources server? As you plan redundancy, take into account that the business accounting group performs a daily reconciliation of accounting information each night at 5:00 P.M. They also perform a weekly closing each Friday night, and a month-end closing on the last working day of each month. Each closing must be accurate to the penny and completed before the accounting system can be started the next working day. The human resources group runs a payroll on the second to last working day of each month. They are legally obligated to have the payroll out on time.

4. The Flight Dynamics computers have arrived for both the business (accounting, marketing, and human resources) and the research servers. The NICs, hard disk, and tape adapters will have to be installed separately. Explain the steps Jason will need to take in order to prepare the server computers for the Windows NT Server installation.

Table 3-5   Information for Disk Calculations in Case Project 1

Operating System Files	Estimated Size
Microsoft NT Server (depending on the accessories and services installed)	150 MB
Application Software	**Estimated Size**
Microsoft Office	120 MB
Microsoft Exchange	80 MB
Accounting software	275 MB
Accounting databases	172 MB
Human resources software	322 MB
Human resources databases	242 MB
Marketing and sales software	195 MB
Marketing databases	455 MB
Word-processing files and letters	75 MB
Spreadsheet files	192 MB
User Directories	**Estimated Size**
Each user 200 MB × 10	2000 MB
Public Directories	**Estimated Size**
Shared directories containing word-processing files, spreadsheets, and data	52 MB
Utility directories	74 MB
Server Management Software	**Estimated Size**
Extra utilities for server and network management	90 MB

5. The alumni and college development association for Fall River College has 170,000 paying members. The association has fund drives and other money-raising activities taking place every three months. They use a sophisticated client/server system to track detailed information on every member and to account for every dollar donated to the college. The system consists of three four-processor SMP Pentium servers. One server is used strictly to run software applications that interface with the alumni and development databases. A second is used to store the main databases for update and accounting activity. The third server contains copies of the main databases that are used strictly to generate reports and queries by the 20-member staff of development officers and office associates. The databases on the third server are automatically updated from the second server at noon and each evening, to ensure that data is as up to date as possible for accurate reporting. What hard disk fault-tolerance methods would you recommend for each of the three servers?

SERVER INSTALLATION

Installing Windows NT 4.0 Server is a smooth process as long as you fully prepare in advance, by carefully selecting and preparing the server hardware, for instance. Wise hardware selection is the single most effective way to launch a problem-free operating system installation. The Windows NT 4.0 Server installation is very straightforward, compared to earlier network operating system installations. At one time, network operating system installations were confusing, often leading the installer through a maze of frustrating dead ends. Microsoft has removed much of the installation frustration by using character-based and graphical screens that logically proceed step by step.

This chapter describes the decisions and preparations you should make before starting the installation, as well as different installation options, such as installing from a CD-ROM and installing over a network. You will also learn to troubleshoot installation problems, although you already have performed important troubleshooting if you have followed the recommendations in Chapter 3, "Server Hardware," for at least the minimum hardware requirements and for ensuring that all hardware is listed on the HCL.

AFTER READING THIS CHAPTER AND COMPLETING THE EXERCISES YOU WILL BE ABLE TO:

- MAKE ADVANCE PREPARATIONS TO INSTALL WINDOWS NT 4.0 SERVER, INCLUDING LISTING HARDWARE INFORMATION AND MAKING DECISIONS REGARDING INSTALLATION SETUP PARAMETERS
- CREATE AN EMERGENCY REPAIR DISK
- PERFORM NT SERVER INSTALLATION USING DIFFERENT METHODS
- TROUBLESHOOT INSTALLATION PROBLEMS
- REMOVE WINDOWS NT SERVER

ADVANCE PREPARATIONS

As is true for any important undertaking, the Windows NT Server installation will be most successful if you have made a few preparations. For example, the installation requires the following:

- Information about what hardware components are installed
- Information about where the operating system files will be installed
- The name of the server
- An installed NIC

Before you begin the installation, review the preparations in the following sections that apply to your circumstances and consider recording preparation information to have at your side for the installation.

SERVER HARDWARE COMPONENTS

Begin by compiling a list of hardware component information such as computer type, monitor and adapter, SCSI adapters, keyboard type, hard disk drive capacity, CD-ROM drive and adapter, tape drive and adapter, and NIC information. Table 4-1 is an example of how you might prepare this information to have it available during the installation.

Table 4-1   Server Hardware Component Information Form

Hardware Component	Description
CPU type (Pentium, Pentium II, Pentium Pro, SMP, RISC)	
Type of buses in the computer	
Amount of RAM	
Hard disk and adapter type (manufacturer and model information)	
Mouse or pointing device	
Monitor and monitor adapter (manufacturer and model information)	
Keyboard type	
Floppy drive type	
Tape drive and adapter (manufacturer and model information)	
NIC (manufacturer, model, specifications)	

In addition to making a hardware list, record the **basic input/output system (BIOS)** configuration settings on the computer. The BIOS is a program on a read-only memory chip that establishes basic communications with components such as the monitor and disk drives. The BIOS setup is accessed differently on each computer, such as by pressing F1 or some combination of keys when the computer is booted. Most BIOS setup menus are character-based screens holding information about the BIOS version and manufacturer, hardware components, the drive the computer boots from first, drive statistics such as the size and number of cylinders per disk, floppy drive type, and so on. It is possible for a computer to lose its setup as a result of a defective battery or some other system problem. You can quickly restore the setup if you have a record of the settings. Figure 4-1 is an example BIOS setup screen.

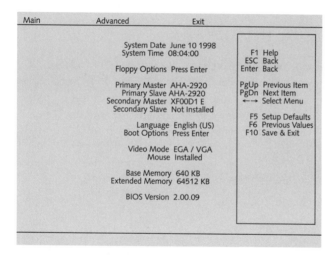

Figure 4-1 BIOS setup screen

 The BIOS setup program usually has an option to specify the boot drive order. This is the order in which the computer checks drives for an operating system boot sector. Most server administrators have the BIOS check drives in the order of the drive letters: A, B, C, D, and so on. This provides the option to boot first from a floppy drive, in case there is a need to use a floppy setup or diagnostic disk. If the floppy drives are empty, the computer boots from drive C.

Another hardware preparation task is to make sure that you have the most up-to-date drivers for hardware such as SCSI adapters, RAID drives, the NIC, and CD-ROM drives. The drivers usually are included on a floppy disk or CD-ROM that accompanies the hardware. If the drivers are not with the hardware, contact the manufacturer or obtain the drivers from a Web page. Place driver files on a floppy disk for easiest use during installation.

If you are installing on an SMP computer, obtain the most recent copy of the **Hardware Abstraction Layer (HAL)** from the manufacturer. The HAL is a set of program routines used to control specific hardware components from within the operating system kernel. Special HAL drivers may be needed to install Windows NT Server on a multiprocessor SMP computer.

 If you have a problem installing Windows NT Server after carefully selecting and preparing the server computer, it most likely will be related to a missing or out-of-date driver. Obtaining current drivers before you start the installation enables you to address this problem on the spot.

MAKING DECISIONS IN ADVANCE

There are several decisions you need to make before starting the installation. If you wait to make the decisions during the installation, you may have to undo your choices later. The decisions you make in advance will save you time, and make the installation go faster. Also, some decisions may require input from a supervisor or management committee, such as the name of the server and the server domain. The decisions you need to consider are the following:

- How to partition the disk(s)
- What file system(s) to use
- Where system files will be located
- What the server name will be
- What the password for the Administrator account will be
- What protocol(s) will be selected
- What the domain name will be
- How the server will function

Disk Partition Selection

You have the option to partition the server hard disks for Windows NT only, or for a combination of operating systems, such as MS-DOS and Windows NT. **Partitioning** is a process in which a hard disk section or a complete hard disk is set up for use by an operating system. A disk can be formatted after it is partitioned. **Formatting** is an operation that marks small disk sections, called tracks and sectors, for use by a specific file system.

Some server administrators like to create a **dual-boot system**, partitioning a few megabytes of disk space for MS-DOS. The reason for having an MS-DOS partition is to provide a way to boot the server and run diagnostic and repair utilities, in case one or more NT boot files are damaged as the result of some other difficulty. Also, some hardware can only be set up through MS-DOS programs or utilities.

A Windows NT Server installation allows you to leave another operating system on the server to create a dual-boot system. Compatible operating systems are MS-DOS, Windows 3.x, Windows 95, and others that are FAT compatible. You can run only one operating system at a time. Also, FAT-based operating systems such as MS-DOS and Windows 95 cannot view NTFS files used by Windows NT Server, unless a third-party driver is loaded, such as NTFSDOS. FAT volumes are limited to 2 GB in Windows NT Server (although you likely will only want to allocate a few megabytes for FAT). FAT volumes over 2 GB (the theoretical maximum is 4 GB) may display a message that 0 bytes are available.

If you select to partition for FAT and NTFS, plan to partition the FAT portion before starting the NT Server installation. Use the MS-DOS FDISK utility to partition a FAT area, and then use the MS-DOS FORMAT command to format the partition. Size the partition so that it will be large enough to hold the utility programs you need plus the MS-DOS operating system files.

On single- and dual-boot systems, the Windows NT boot loader is placed by the NT setup program on the partition from which the computer boots, such as drive C. The boot loader recognizes that there are two or more operating systems on that computer. When you boot, it displays a character-based screen that enables you to select which operating system you want to start (Figure 4-2). There are always two entries for Windows NT. These exist in case you reconfigure Windows NT after the installation and cannot get the system to boot afterward. For example, you might reconfigure to use the wrong video display. The [VGA mode] option uses a basic set of configuration parameters to make sure that you can reboot NT Server in this type of situation.

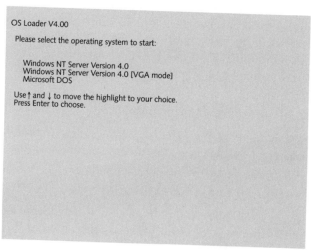

Figure 4-2   Startup screen for a dual-boot server

The contents of the Windows NT boot loader menu are specified in the BOOT.INI text file, which is marked as read-only. You can edit the file (remove its read-only designation using the *attrib −r* command) to remove an operating system reference or to change the menu display. The file contains two sections: [boot loader] and [operating systems]. The [boot loader] section specifies a timeout value in seconds for selecting an operating system, and a default operating system that is booted if a selection is not made before the timeout value is reached. The [operating systems] section lists the operating systems that can be started. For example, if Windows NT Server and Windows 95 are both loaded, the BOOT.INI file might look as follows:

```
[boot loader]

timeout=30

default=multi(0)disk(0)rdisk(1)partition(1)\WINNT

[operating systems]

multi(0)disk(0)rdisk(1)partition(1)\WINNT="Windows NT
Server Version 4.00"

multi(0)disk(0)rdisk(1)partition(1)\WINNT="Windows NT
Server Version 4.00 [VGA mode]" /basevideo /sos

C:\="Microsoft Windows"
```

The operating system location for Windows NT Server is specified in terms of the Advanced RISC Computing (ARC) pathname. In this example, the multi() shows a non-SCSI drive is installed, which always has the value 0. The disk() value also is always 0 for non-SCSI drives. The rdisk() value is always 0 or 1 (counting from 0) for single channel controllers that can have up to two disks. Rdisk() can be 0 to 3 for dual-channel controllers that can have up to four disks attached. Partition() is the number of the partition, which is 1 to 4 (counting from 1). If SCSI drives are used scsi() replaces multi() and the value inside the brackets is determined by the SCSI driver. Also on a SCSI disk the disk() value is the ID of the disk in the chain of devices connected to the SCSI adapter. The rdisk() value is usually 0 for SCSI disks. For example, the line

```
multi(0)disk(0)rdisk(1)partition(1)\WINNT
```

means the operating system is in folder \WINNT on a non-SCSI disk (multi(0)disk(0)), on the second disk in the channel path (rdisk(1)) and on the first partition of that disk (partition(1)). The line

```
scsi(1)disk(2)rdisk(0)partition(1)\WINNT
```

means that the operating system is in folder \WINNT on a SCSI disk designated as 1 by its driver (scsi(1)), on the third disk in the SCSI chain (disk(2); counting from 0), and on the first partition (partition(1); counting from 1).

NT Server File Systems

In Chapter 1, "Networking with Microsoft Windows NT Server," you learned the differences between the FAT and NTFS file systems. In nearly all installations, it is recommended that you install the more robust NTFS because it is meant for networking. NTFS offers the best security, performance, and file handling for network users. This is particularly true if you anticipate that the server will need to handle large files, such as databases. NTFS also has features such as logging and file compression, which are not included with FAT.

File Location and NT Directory Name

Another decision you will make is where to place the NT Server operating system files. This is particularly important if you plan to have a dual-boot system. NT Server can easily coexist with other operating systems, but you do not want to put the NT Server system files in the same directory with files for other operating systems, such as MS-DOS. If you do, it is difficult to determine which files belong with which operating system. This can be a problem later if you need to remove one of the operating systems.

When you run the Windows NT installation, the setup program recommends that you place the system files in the root directory of the boot disk in a folder called Winnt. It is recommended that you take this default option instead of placing the files on a secondary disk or specifying a different folder name. This is particularly important because you may not be the only one who supports the server. Also, it is easier because many NT software utilities anticipate finding the operating system files in this folder.

Server Name

Because the server name affects everyone who uses the server, you may want to solicit input from a supervisor or management team. This helps ensure their support of the project, and it ensures that an appropriate name is selected. The server name is seen in Network Neighborhood and in other network utilities. There are some general guidelines to consider when selecting a name:

- Use a name that is relatively short, so that it is easy to type.
- Make the name describe the server's function or reflect the organization that uses it.
- Select a name that is easy for everyone to remember and use.
- Make sure that the name is not used already by another network computer.

If there are several servers on a network, develop a naming scheme such as one that identifies servers by department, function, or location. For example, if one server is used by the accounting department, one by marketing, and another for research, you might name them ACCOUNT, MARKET, and RESEARCH. This is easier for users than if you name them SERVER1, SERVER2, and SERVER3. In a school with lab servers in the library, student union, and fine arts building, you might name them LIBRARY, UNION, and

ARTS. These types of naming schemes are important to network administrators as well as to users. They make it easier to identify and manage servers on a network that may have 10, 20, or more servers.

Administrator Account Password

At the time of installation, NT Server creates a master account called the Administrator account. This account has access to all areas of the server, including security administration, file administration, and control of user accounts. Entry into the Administrator account is controlled by a password that is established at the time the NT Server is installed. The password can be changed later, but it saves time to have a password ready before starting the installation. Select a password that is difficult to guess, and avoid using information that can be identified with you, such as your nickname, favorite car, favorite food, or the name of a family member. A long password, such as 10 characters or more, is appropriate for this sensitive account. Windows NT Server accepts passwords up to 14 characters. Make sure you remember the password, because you will need it to log on to the Administrator account as soon as the operating system is installed.

Protocol Selection

As you learned in Chapter 2, "Basic Network Design and Protocols," you need to select a protocol to use for communicating with the server. NetBEUI is appropriate for small nonrouted networks of under 200. For a larger network or a routed network, consider using TCP/IP. Also, the server will need TCP/IP if you intend to use Internet connectivity, such as through the Internet Information Server (IIS). If the server will be used as a gateway to NetWare, you need to install Client Service for NetWare (CSNW) and NWLink.

Fortunately you do not need to make all of these decisions from the start. You can configure additional protocols after the server is set up. However, you do need at least one protocol to start. NetBEUI is the easiest to set up initially. If you need to set up TCP/IP, you will need an IP dotted decimal address for the server and a subnet mask (see Chapter 5, "Server Configuration"). Obtain this from a network administrator. If you are the network administrator, you may keep a database to show the next available address. If you are just starting out, contact a network professional or an Internet service provider for more information.

Server Domains

Microsoft employs the concept of the domain to identify the members of a group. As you learned in Chapter 1, domains are used to identify users, check their authorizations, and give access to resources.

Domains also simplify server management. They make it possible for accounts, privilege levels, and user information to be managed from one place. A network can have more than one domain, as a means to divide users into different network groups, particularly on a WAN.

For example, a statewide bank with 20 branches might identify the computer resources at each branch by using different domains. One or more servers can belong to a single domain to simplify their management.

When you install Windows NT Server you can specify a domain name or a workgroup name. As you learned in Chapter 1, domains offer more powerful management options than peer-to-peer workgroups. It is recommended that you use the domain structure when you install Windows NT Server.

4

Microsoft domains consist of clients and resources used by the clients. User accounts and user groups compose the client side. File servers, print servers, and other network services are the resources. One or more groups can be defined to the domain, with a user having membership in any or all groups. The concept of the domain preserves the idea of work groupings, without the headaches of managing them individually from multiple workstations and file servers. For example, if a business is interested in creating an executive management group with access to the accounting, sales, and inventory software, a group can be created to include each manager on that team. If a supervisor is promoted to a manager's position on the team, she or he is easily added.

The domain concept saves time as the network administrator sets up users, privileges, and groups. One or more domains can be created to suit the management needs and styles of an organization. A domain is a powerful management tool because one domain can support as many as 40,000 objects, 26,000 users, and 250 groups. Multiple domains can bring many more thousands of users and resources together for centralized management, and work well for businesses or colleges with branch sites in different cities or states. Multiple domains also work well for organizations with foreign and domestic locations. With network administration centralized at the domain level, only one user security database is needed to store information about all users and their security privileges.

Choose a domain name with the same care as the server name. Many organizations incorporate their domain name into e-mail addressing over the Internet. Because it is a public representation of your organization, you may want to select a name that reflects the nature of the organization. If your organization is a college, the domain name might be the college initials, such as NU for Northern University, or it might be Northern. If your company manufactures radios, your domain name might be LISTENUP or MUSIC. The domain name must be different from any other computer or server names used on the network, including the server name you use when you install Windows NT Server.

 If NT Server is installed on a computer that is not connected to the network during installation, it cannot check for duplicate domain or server names.

Server Functions

Before centralized management through domains, users logged on to each network server individually. One user might have to log on to three servers: one for word-processing and spreadsheet applications, one for CAD applications, and one for accounting data. That user would have an account on each server. Access rights and other services would have to be set on each server, with every server having its own record of the user's privileges. When networks were small, having a few servers was manageable, but time-consuming. As networks have grown, individual server management is not productive for administrators or users, hence the importance of having one domain and one security-checking mechanism.

Microsoft NT Servers centrally store information about the domain, accounts, groups, and access privileges in one database called the **security accounts manager (SAM) database**. Every domain must have at least one server that houses the SAM. That server is called the **primary domain controller (PDC)**, which contains the master copy of the SAM. Each time users log on, their account and access privileges are verified through the SAM. If there is more than one server in a domain, selected servers can be designated to keep a backup copy of the SAM. These are called **backup domain controllers (BDCs)**. The PDC and BDCs can check the authorization of any user attempting to log on to a server in the domain.

When the administrator creates a new account or modifies an existing account, that account information is immediately updated in the SAM on the PDC for that domain. At regular intervals, the Windows NT Server operating system automatically replicates the updated SAM to all of the BDCs in the domain, so that their information is current. BDCs offer fault-tolerance, because there always is a backup copy of the SAM on the domain BDCs. Also, if the PDC server is disabled, any one of the BDCs can be promoted to act as the PDC. Figure 4-3 illustrates how the PDC backs up the SAM to the BDCs.

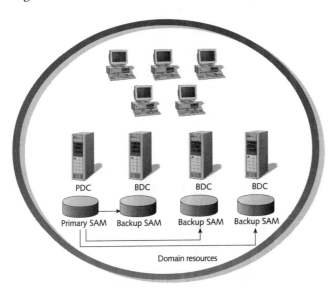

Figure 4-3   Backing up the PDC with BDCs

 The first server you set up must always be designated as the PDC, because there must be a primary server with a SAM to authenticate users when they log on. A BDC server can only be designated when there already is a PDC on the network.

A third server type is called a **member server**. This type of server does not handle logon or security validations. The most typical case is a client/server operation in which one server is used strictly to store the databases. The database server does not need to handle logon checking because the information it houses is accessed indirectly through software applications on a PDC or BDC server that checks the logon permissions. Another role of a member server is to handle print, CD-ROM, or fax services.

The fourth type of server is a **standalone server**, one that is not part of a domain. This type of server might be dedicated to supporting a particular workgroup, such as a group of software developers who use the computer for testing purposes and do not want others in the domain to have access.

4

CREATING AN EMERGENCY REPAIR DISK

At the end of the installation, NT Server provides the opportunity to create an **Emergency Repair Disk (ERD)**. Plan to have a high-density 1.44 MB 3.5-inch floppy disk ready for this step. Microsoft highly recommends creating the disk, because it can be used to repair and troubleshoot problems if they occur. The ERD is used to fix problems with drivers, the NTFS file system, and the NT Server operating system. Plan to update the ERD each time you install software, make a server configuration change, install a new adapter, add a NIC, restructure a partition, or upgrade the operating system.

You can create or update the ERD at any time after Windows NT Server is installed. Windows NT includes a utility in the \System32\Config folder called RDISK for this purpose. Always run RDISK using the /s option to update the SAM and Registry information. (Enter <u>RDISK /s</u> from the Start menu Run option.) Hands-on Project 4-5 enables you to practice creating an ERD.

Table 4-2 lists the information contained on the ERD.

Table 4-2   Contents of the Emergency Repair Disk

Disk File	Purpose
Autoexec.nt	Initializes MS-DOS
Config.nt	Initializes MS-DOS
Default._	Holds compressed setup and system profile information
Ntuser.DA_	Used by the NT repair process
Sam._	Compressed copy of the SAM
Setup.log	Keeps a log of installed files and holds repair information
Software._	Compressed information about installed software configurations
System._	Compressed information about the system configuration

INSTALLATION OPTIONS

There are several ways to install Windows NT Server. The method you choose depends on the resources of your computer. For example, if the computer is not equipped with a CD-ROM drive, you can perform an installation over a network. No matter what method you select, you must have software licenses for the server and the number of users who will access the server. The primary installation methods are as follows:

- Floppy disk and CD-ROM

- Network installation

- Network Client Administrator installation

- Unattended installation

The installation methods are described in the sections that follow. The Hands-on Projects at the end of the chapter enable you to practice the different installation methods. Each of the installation methods consists of techniques to boot the computer and enable you to load the installation files. Even though the startup techniques vary, such as performing the installation from CD-ROM or over a network, in every case you start the setup by running either WINNT.EXE or WINNT32.EXE. Winnt and Winnt32 perform the same function, but Winnt32 runs in the 32-bit Windows NT environment.

 WINNT.EXE is used if your computer is started from a disk made through the Client Administrator or if the computer already has an operating system loaded, such as MS-DOS, Windows 3.1, Windows 3.11, or Windows 95. Use WINNT32.EXE if the computer is already loaded with a version of Windows NT Server or Windows NT Workstation.

There are several switches that can be used with either Winnt or Winnt32, shown in Table 4–3. For example, if you want to start the installation and create copies of the floppy disks used for the combined floppy disk and CD-ROM installation method, enter *Winnt /OX*. If you want to specify a location for the installation files that is different than the directory from which you start WINNT.EXE or WINNT32.EXE, use the switch */S* and specify the drive and directory after the switch, such as *Winnt /S:D:\I386*.

Table 4-3   Command-line Switches for WINNT.EXE and WINNT32.EXE

Switch	Purpose
/?	Lists the switches for Winnt
/B	Used to install NT Server without floppy disks, such as on a workstation without a floppy drive (the switch /S: must also be used to indicate where to locate the installation files)
/C	Omits the check for free space on the boot floppy disks (only used with WINNT.EXE)
/E:command	Executes a command after the Windows portion of the setup, such as to start a program or open the Control Panel
/F	Causes Setup to copy files to the floppy disks without verifying the copy (used to save time during the installation and only available in WINNT.EXE)
/I:initialization filename	Specifies that you are using an initialization file other than the default, DOSNET.INF (this initialization file shows where installation files are located)
/O	Creates a set of three floppy disks from which to boot for the installation (requires the Windows NT Server CD-ROM and does not start the installation)
/OX	Creates a set of three floppy disks from which to boot for the installation and starts the installation (requires the Windows NT Server CD-ROM)
/R:folder	Creates an optional folder of files copied from the Windows NT Server CD-ROM, such as a directory of installation files for another type of computer
/RX:folder	Creates an optional folder of files copied from the Windows NT Server CD-ROM, such as a directory of add-on files (Microsoft Internet Information Server or Microsoft FrontPage)
/S:drive:\folder /S:\\ server\share\folder	Specifies the use of a path for the installation files other than the current path
/T:drive\folder	Copies the temporary files used by the installation to a specified location (otherwise they are copied to the target drive of the installation)
/U:script file	Used in an unattended installation to specify the name of the script file containing installation commands
/X	Begins a regular installation from floppy disks (does not reproduce the disks)

The Windows NT Server CD-ROM contains different installation folders for each type of computer: Alpha, I386, Mips, and Ppc. The I386 folder contains installation files for 80486, Pentium, Pentium II, and Pentium Pro computers using Intel, Cyrix, or AMD processors. The Alpha directory is for Digital Equipment Corporation (DEC) computers that use the Alpha processor. The Mips folder has installation files for RISC computers that use MIPS processors and the Ppc folder is for IBM's PowerPC RISC computers.

FLOPPY DISK AND CD-ROM INSTALLATION

One of the most common ways to start the Windows NT Server setup is by using the three floppy disks and Windows NT Server CD-ROM that accompany your purchase of Windows NT Server 4.0. The steps for using this method are outlined in this section.

 Be certain to have all the Windows NT Server floppy disks and the CD-ROM handy for the installation, as well as the information you recorded about the computer's components. Also, keep the CD-ROM case available because it has the identification key printed on a sticker, and you will need this information for the installation.

1. Make sure that the computer's BIOS is set to attempt to boot first from floppy drive A:.

2. Power off the computer.

3. Insert Setup Disk #1 into drive A:.

4. Turn on the computer, allowing it to boot from Setup Disk #1, then insert the CD-ROM into the CD-ROM drive.

5. This method automatically starts WINNT.EXE, and then follow the instructions on the screen.

NETWORK INSTALLATION

Network installation enables you to perform the Windows NT Server installation from a shared network directory on another computer. This method is useful if you have a computer that does not have a CD-ROM drive. Also, the method is useful if you operate a large network and plan to implement many NT Servers. The network installation can be fast, and you can set up to install all of the servers in the same way.

 Before you start, make sure that you have an appropriate number of software licenses for the servers you create.

The network method requires a prospective server computer that is connected to the network and can access a shared drive, such as one running Windows 3.11, Windows 95, or Windows NT. Another alternative is to use the Network Client Administrator on a Windows NT Server to create a floppy from which to boot the computer and connect to the network.

Follow these general steps to start a network installation:

1. Copy the installation files to the host computer that will offer the shared folder, such as an existing NT server. To copy the files, first create the folder on the host computer, calling it, for example, \I386. Insert the Windows NT Server CD-ROM in the host computer and copy the files from the appropriate directory (see Hands-on Project 4-1).

2. Share the host's folder, giving it Read or Change share permissions (you will learn about share permissions in Chapter 9 "Managing Server Folders, Permissions, and Software Installation").

3. To start the installation, map the prospective server computer to the shared folder. Run the WINNT.EXE program, using the switches that match your needs, such as /OX (see Hands-on Project 4-3).

4

NETWORK CLIENT ADMINISTRATOR INSTALLATION

You can install Windows NT Server over the network, even if your prospective server computer has no operating system. To do this, run Network Client Administrator on an existing Windows NT server to create a network startup floppy disk. You then use the network boot disk to connect the prospective server to the network share and begin the installation. Hands-on Project 4-2 takes you through the steps of a Network Client Administrator installation.

UNATTENDED INSTALLATION

An unattended installation is usually performed over the network and enables you to specify a set of parameters before the Windows NT Server installation begins. The parameters enable you to provide a script or **answer file** that provides responses to questions that come up in the installation. The unattended installation is started from a batch file, such as UNATTEND.BAT, that you create. The batch file runs Winnt or Winnt32 with the /U and /S switches, as follows:

```
winnt /S:<path to installation files>/U<answer file>
```

The /S: switch indicates where to find the installation files, such as on a network computer (/S:\\ *server\share\folder*) or in a local folder (/S:*drive:\folder*). The /U: switch provides the name of the answer file, such as UNATTEND.TXT, for the unattended installation. You can use the Setup Manager tool that comes with Windows NT Server to create the unattended answer file, or you can use a text editor such as Notepad. This file contains predetermined answers to questions asked by Windows NT Server Setup, such as information about the computer hardware, what software components to install, which drivers to use, and what protocol to use. An example answer file is included by Microsoft on the Windows NT CD-ROM, such as the UNATTEND.TXT file in the \I386 folder. The following is an example of several answers than can be provided in the answer file:

```
[Unattended]
NtUpgrade = no
ConfirmHardware = yes
TargetPath = Winnt


[UserData]
Fullname = "Anne Nishida"
OrgName = "Nishida and McGuire"
ComputerName = NISHIDA
```

To further customize an unattended installation, you can create a **uniqueness database file (UDF)**. The UDF works in conjunction with the answer file, allowing you to create a unique answer set for each server setup. For example, the UDF might contain the server name. Each server would have a uniqueness ID in the database associated with its information. The uniqueness ID is specified by the /UDF<uniqueness id> command used with the Winnt command.

Because you want to make sure that each step of an installation is performed as you intend, the unattended installation techniques are not recommended for creating servers; however, they can save time when setting up multiple Windows NT workstations.

STEPPING THROUGH AN INSTALLATION

Once you have gathered all your information and determined which options you will use to install Windows NT, you can proceed with the installation. The next sections outline an installation using the floppy disk and Windows NT Server CD-ROM method. The installation is divided into two parts. In the first part, character-based Setup screens are presented. This part primarily focuses on detecting the hardware and loading installation files onto the computer. The second part is a graphical display that uses Windows-based dialog boxes that enable you to configure information specific to the server, such as the registration information, server name, server type, and NIC setup (try Hands-on Project 4-4).

INSTALLATION PART 1 (TEXT-BASED)

After you start Winnt or Winnt32 as detailed earlier in the section "Floppy Disk and CD-ROM Installation," the text-based Setup goes through the following stages:

1. Setup checks the system configuration and requests you to insert Setup Disk #2 and press Enter (the mouse doesn't work on the initial setup screens).

2. The four NT Server Setup options appear: learn more about NT Setup, continue with setup, repair a previously installed version, or quit. Press Enter to continue the installation.

3. Setup attempts to automatically detect mass storage device controllers, such as ESDI, IDE, and SCSI. The mass storage detection process requires Setup to load a large number of device drivers from many hardware vendors. Setup Disk #3 contains the device drivers. As requested, insert Disk #3 and press Enter.

4. If Setup has problems detecting SCSI adapters for hard drives and CD-ROM drives, you might need a supplementary driver disk from the manufacturer to install drivers for certain SCSI adapters. Press S if you need to manually select a driver from those suggested by Setup, or to install a driver from a manufacturer's disk.

If Setup does not detect a SCSI adapter that is non-critical for the installation, such as a tape drive, you can install it later using the Windows NT Server Control Panel.

5. Press Enter to continue the installation. The next prompt is to insert the CD-ROM labeled Windows NT Server CD-ROM, and then press Enter.

6. Setup loads the Microsoft license agreement. The agreement is in English and French. When finished reading you can agree to the terms of the license by pressing F8.

7. If there is already a version of Windows NT loaded, Setup displays an upgrade choice. If there is an earlier version of NT Server installed, such as 3.51, press Enter to upgrade.

If Setup detects that Windows NT Workstation is already loaded on the computer, press N to cancel the upgrade and install a fresh copy of Windows NT. If you use the Windows NT Server installation files to upgrade Windows NT Workstation, the resulting server is limited to being a member or standalone server, not a full-fledged PDC or BDC.

8. Setup verifies information about the core computer parts, such as the type of PC, the display type, the keyboard, the keyboard type (English or a foreign language), and the pointing device. If a change needs to be made, use the arrow keys to highlight the selection, and press Enter to view the list of alternatives. If the information is correct, highlight "No Changes: The above list matches my computer," and press Enter to move to the next screen.

9. The detected disk drives and partitions are displayed, and Setup asks where you'd like to install Windows NT. Select the partition on which you'd like to install it, and press Enter. Figure 4-4 shows two partitioned disks, drives C and D, detected. The partitioned portion of drive C (the volume already partitioned by the vendor, using the FAT file structure) is highlighted as the default by the Setup program. In this case you would leave that drive highlighted, so that it will be home to the NT Server system files, and press Enter to accept the choice and advance to the next screen.

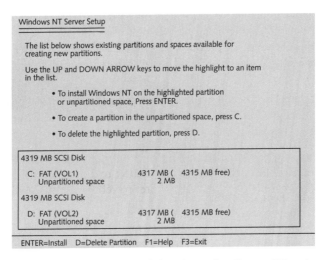

Figure 4-4   Selecting a disk volume for the partition to house NT Server files

You could also choose to press D to delete the FAT partition, and later repartition the drive for NTFS. This would be an extra step, because Setup provides an opportunity to convert the partition to NTFS on the next screen. Also note that deleting a partition will permanently erase all data on the partition.

10. Setup confirms the drive location for the NT Server partition and lists the following choices:

   ■ Format the partition using the FAT file system.

   ■ Format the partition using the NTFS file system.

   ■ Convert the partition to NTFS.

   ■ Leave the current file system intact (no changes).

If you have decided to use NTFS instead of FAT, you can choose either to format the partition for NTFS or to convert the partition. Either choice is appropriate. However, if you want to leave a portion of the disk for MS-DOS or Windows 95, you will not want to format or convert the partition.

11. Highlight a selection (such as C to convert the partition to NTFS). Press Enter to continue. If you select to format the drive, a confirmation screen appears so that you can be certain the correct drive is selected. Press F to continue.

12. Setup shows the default directory path and name for the NT Server files. It is recommended that you accept the default by pressing Enter; however, you can enter another directory path and name if you need to change it.

13. There is an option to press Enter to perform a thorough test of the hard disk storage. This selection is advisable to make sure that the disk is fully functional. The test takes several minutes, and upon completion a message appears that shows the files are being copied to the hard disk.

14. When the copying is finished, there is an instruction to remove all media from the floppy and CD-ROM drives and press Enter to reboot the machine. This is the end of the text-based portion of the installation.

INSTALLATION PART 2 (GRAPHICAL)

Once the computer reboots, there is a prompt to load the NT Server CD-ROM and click OK. This initiates the GUI part of the installation; from this point forward, you can use the mouse. When the CD-ROM is loaded, the computer loads files, and then the NT Server Setup Wizard starts.

Figure 4-5 shows the Setup Wizard dialog box with instructions for the next three parts of Setup: (1) gathering information about the computer, (2) installation of NT networking, and (3) the wrap-up steps to complete the installation. From this dialog box, you can click Back to retrace previous installation steps or Next to continue with the installation.

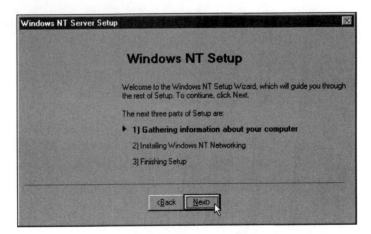

Figure 4-5 Gathering information about the computer

The steps of the graphical-mode setup are as follows:

1. Enter your name and the your organization's name. This information is used to identify the owner of the software licenses and to customize selected screens. Click Next to continue.

2. Enter the CD key code from the sticker on the back of the NT Server CD-ROM case. Like many software programs, NT Server is protected from unauthorized use by a key code unique to the license holder. Click Next.

3. Provide licensing information. There are two ways to license NT Server: purchase a specific number of licenses per server, or purchase separate "seat" licenses for each workstation. Select the appropriate option and click Next.

 In larger settings, such as a company or university, where there are many servers, it may be more cost-effective to purchase a license for each workstation. This way, the licensed workstation is billed only for access to those servers for which it has security authorization. However, in most smaller office settings where there is only one server, a server license with a set number of workstations makes more sense.

4. Enter the name of the server and click Next to proceed.

5. Specify the server type, such as primary domain controller (PDC). If this is the first server installed, there is no option for a member server. Click Next.

6. Enter the Administrator account password. Enter the password again in the confirmation box, to make certain that the password is entered correctly, and then click Next.

7. Select the option to create an Emergency Repair Disk (ERD), if desired. If you click this option, the ERD will be created toward the end of the installation.

8. Specify software components to add at the time of installation. The Setup Wizard automatically marks the most commonly used components for installation during setup, as shown in Figure 4-6. To accept the components listed, click Next.

Start with the software components already selected by Setup. This keeps your initial installation simple and reduces problems. Other components can be added later as you need them.

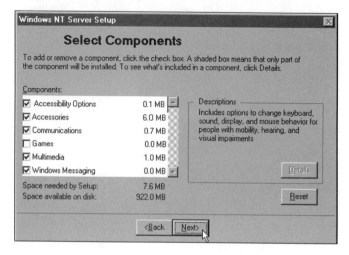

Figure 4-6 Selecting the components to install

9. Specify network connection options. Indicate whether the server is directly connected to a network, used for dial-up access, or both. In most cases you will click Wired to the network. If a modem is installed, you might also click the Remote access to the network option, which enables you to later set up remote access service. Click Next after making the selection.

10. Select the option to install Microsoft's Internet Information Server (IIS) software, if desired, and click Next.

11. Click Start Search to have Setup automatically search and detect the server NICs. Once the NICs are identified, click Next.

12. Select the protocol or protocols to be installed, and click Next. You may select all protocols or only one, such as NetBEUI. If you select TCP/IP you will need to enter the IP address information on another dialog box.

13. Specify the services to install, as shown in Figure 4-7. Select main services such as NetBIOS Interface, Workstation, and Server. The NetBIOS interface is for older MS-DOS programs that use NetBIOS. The Workstation service is critical in that it enables you to perform work on the server. The Server service enables others to connect to the server as users. Microsoft IIS can be installed at this point, too. The RPC (remote procedure call) configuration is used to remotely run jobs on UNIX or other large systems.

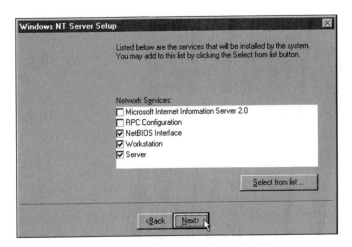

Figure 4-7   Selecting network services

14. Click Next to confirm that the selections made so far are correct, or click Back to go back and change selections made earlier.

15. Setup starts the installation of network components by automatically detecting the system settings for the NIC. Confirm the settings or change any as needed.

16. Confirm or change network bindings as desired. You can disable the preselected network bindings or set them manually. It is best to go with the defaults and make any necessary changes later. Click Next to accept the automatic selections made by Setup.

Network bindings are part of the NT Server system used to coordinate the software communications among the NIC, the network protocols, and network services. Bindings ensure that communications are established to optimize the performance of the hardware and software. Setup automatically configures the bindings for highest performance.

17. Setup is ready to start network communications and to complete the installation. At this point make sure that the server is connected to the network. A dialog box is displayed in which you can click Next to start the network, or click Back to review the setup to this point. Click Next to start the network.

18. Enter the domain name and click Next. Because the network is started, Setup now checks for any identical domain or computer names. Click Finish. A short message informs you that the software is configuring the server.

19. Adjust the date, time, and time zone in the Date/Time Properties dialog box. The system date and time are important on a server because this information is used to put a creation time on files and data. Click the Close button.

 The time, date, and video settings can be reset from the Control Panel once NT Server is running.

20. Click OK to verify the display settings for the video monitor attached to the server. Click the Test button to check that the color and resolution are accurate. Once the test is complete, click Yes if you saw the test screen properly.

21. Click OK in the Display Settings dialog box, and then click OK in the Display Properties dialog box.

22. Setup informs you that it is installing program shortcuts, security, and messaging services. When these tasks are finished, a message appears asking that the blank disk for the Emergency Repair Disk be inserted into drive A:. Insert the disk and click OK.

23. The last screen in Setup is a button announcing that the process is complete. Remove any floppy disks, and click the Restart Computer button. The server is rebooted so that all of the installed software can be put to use.

TESTING THE NEW SERVER

When the new server restarts, a logon screen appears with a message to press the Ctrl-Alt-Del keys at the same time. When NT Server boots, the Ctrl-Alt-Del combination is used to start the logon screen and does not reboot the server. Press the keys, enter Administrator as the account, and enter the password you supplied during the installation. The NT Server desktop appears, as shown in Figure 4-8.

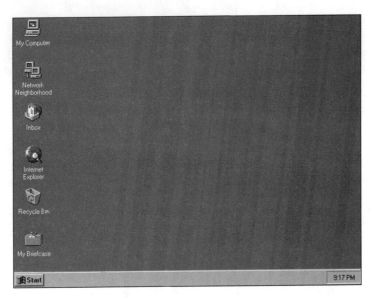

Figure 4-8   NT Server desktop

TROUBLESHOOTING INSTALLATION PROBLEMS

In most cases the installation goes smoothly, but installers sometimes experience problems. Often, difficulties are prevented by making the advance preparations explained earlier in this chapter. Some examples of preventive steps are as follows:

- Ensure that you purchase a processor and hardware components that are on Microsoft's HCL.

- Test all hardware before installing Windows NT.

- Compile and record information about the hardware components and BIOS setup before starting.

- Run a comprehensive test of the hard disk to ensure that it is functioning properly.

Sometimes prevention is not enough, and installation problems do occur. Most problems are related to hardware drivers or to the actual hardware. For example, the PC may contain a CD-ROM drive or display adapter that is newly marketed and not contained in the installation selection list. If the Windows NT Setup does not contain the driver, or it is not included on a disk with the hardware, it is necessary to contact the PC vendor for a new driver. Sometimes an adapter card (such as a NIC or hard disk adapter) is loosened when the PC is moved, and the card simply needs to be reseated.

If SCSI adapters are used, the SCSI cable may be loose, or it may not be properly terminated. A network interface card or sound card driver may be needed, since new models are often introduced to the market. Table 4-4 provides a list of problem descriptions and steps to take to solve the problems.

Table 4-4 Troubleshooting a Windows NT Server Setup

Problem Description	Solution Steps
Setup did not find any mass storage devices on the computer. OR There is an Inaccessible Boot	Check to make sure that all adapters and controllers are working properly. Check power to all devices. Reseat adapters and controllers.
	For SCSI devices ensure that : (1) the SCSI cabling is properly installed, (2) SCSI devices are terminated, (3) SCSI devices are Device message. correctly addressed, and (4) the BIOS correctly recognizes all SCSI adapters. Also, be sure that the SCSI boot drive is addressed as 0. Check the manufacturer's recommendations for configuring SCSI adapters and hard disk drives. Try replacing the adapter before replacing the drive(s).
	For EIDE drives: (1) check the controller, (2) ensure that file I/O and disk access are set to standard, and (3) ensure that the boot drive is the first device on the controller.
	For IDE and ESDI drives: (1) check the cabling and controller, (2) check the drive setup in the BIOS for master/slave relationships, and (3) ensure that the drive is properly recognized in the BIOS.
There is a disk error on one of the three floppy setup disks.	Start the installation over, making new setup disks.
A problem is reported with HAL.DLL.	Start the installation from the Windows NT boot disk. When Setup examines the hardware configuration, press F5 to view computer types. Select the appropriate computer type from the list, or use a version of HAL supplied on a floppy disk by the manufacturer.
The installation fails when installing the network components.	Check the network interface card to ensure that it is working. Reseat or replace the card and start Setup again. Use the diagnostic software provided with the card to test for problems. If this does not work, try a card from a different manufacturer, in case there is a hardware incompatibility.
A problem is reported with NTOSKRNL.EXE.	The BOOT.INI file needs to be changed to indicate where to find Windows NT (if other than on the primary boot drive).
A device driver is not available in Setup for a given component, such as a NIC, sound card, video card, or other adapter.	Obtain the most recent driver from the manufacturer.
A STOP message appears during the installation.	Start the installation again. If the STOP message appears a second time, check the IRQ and I/O settings for conflicts on hardware components and cards. If the STOP message appears a third time, record the message and consult a Microsoft technician.
Computer locks up.	Check the IRQ and I/O settings for conflicts among hardware components and cards.

UNINSTALLING WINDOWS NT SERVER

Sometimes it is necessary to uninstall Windows NT Server, such as when new server hardware is purchased and you want to pass along the old hardware to someone else. For example, to remove NT Server and install Windows 95, you might use the following steps:

1. Purchase a new copy of Windows 95, or use the disks from a licensed copy not presently used by someone else.

2. Perform a complete backup of all files on the server computer.

3. Start the BIOS setup program and set it to boot from drive A: before trying to boot from drive C: (consult the computer documentation on how to use its BIOS setup program).

4. Power off the server and insert the Windows 95 boot disk into drive A:.

5. Boot the computer from the Windows 95 boot disk.

6. Use the FDISK and FORMAT utilities on the boot disk to delete the NTFS partition, to partition the workstation drive(s) for FAT, and to format the drive(s).

7. Use the Windows 95 installation disk set or CD-ROM to install Windows 95.

8. Install the appropriate applications software and data files onto the computer.

If your version of FDISK cannot delete the NTFS partition, an alternative is to insert the Windows NT Server CD-ROM or Setup Disk #1 and start an installation. When Setup identifies the existing NTFS partition, highlight the partition and type D to delete it.

CHAPTER SUMMARY

- With a little advance preparation, the installation of Windows NT 4.0 Server is likely to be trouble-free. One way to prepare is to record information about the server hardware components. Keep this information on hand as a reference when you start the installation. Another way to prepare is to have current drivers for hardware in the server, particularly for the NIC and SCSI adapters.

- As you plan the installation, make important decisions before you start. Determine how you want to partition the server boot drive and what file system to use. Also, decide on names for the server and its domain. Have IP address information ready, if you are planning to configure the server for TCP/IP. As a last step, prepare an Emergency Repair Disk (ERD).

- There are several installation methods you can use, depending on the server hardware. A common method is to use the floppy disks and CD-ROM included with Windows NT Server. Another way is to install the software over the network from a shared directory. If your computer does not have an operating system from which to start the installation, you can use the Network Client Administrator to make a boot disk.

If your preparations are thorough, problems are unlikely to develop. Most problems are due to out-of-date drivers, and can be solved by having current drivers available for the installation. If other problems occur, consult the troubleshooting table in this chapter for solutions.

KEY TERMS

4

- **answer file** — A text file that contains a complete set of instructions for installing Windows NT.

- **backup domain controller (BDC)** — An NT server that acts as a backup to the primary domain controller and has a copy of the security accounts manager database containing user account and access privilege information.

- **basic input/output system (BIOS)** — A program on a read-only memory chip that establishes basic communications with components such as the monitor and disk drives.

- **dual-boot system** — A computer set up to boot from two or more different operating systems, such as Windows NT Server and MS-DOS.

- **Emergency Repair Disk (ERD)** — A disk created when you install Windows NT and updated after the installation, containing repair, diagnostic, and backup information in case there is a problem with Windows NT.

- **format** — An operation that marks disk sections, called tracks and sectors, for storage of files by a specific file system, such as NTFS.

- **Hardware Abstraction Layer (HAL)** — A set of program routines that enables an operating system to control a hardware component, such as the processor, from within the operating system kernel.

- **member server** — An NT server that does no account logon verification and that is used as a special-purpose server, such as a database server.

- **network binding** — Part of the NT Server system used to coordinate the software communications among the NIC, the network protocols, and network services. Bindings ensure that communications are established to optimize the performance of the hardware and software.

- **partition** — A process in which a hard disk section or a complete hard disk is set up for use by an operating system. A disk can be formatted after it is partitioned.

- **primary domain controller (PDC)** — An NT server that acts as the master server when there are two or more NT servers on a network. It holds the master database (called the SAM) of user accounts and access privileges.

- **security accounts manager (SAM) database** — Also called the directory services database, stores information about user accounts, groups, and access privileges on a Microsoft Windows NT server. The master database is kept on the PDC (primary domain controller) and regularly backed up to the BDCs (backup domain controllers).

- **standalone server** — A server that is not part of an existing domain.

- **uniqueness database file (UDF)** — A text file that contains an answer set of unique instructions for installing Windows NT.

REVIEW QUESTIONS

1. A domain server that does no account logon authentication is called a

   _____.

   a. primary domain controller

   b. standalone server

   c. backup domain controller

   d. member server

2. Which of the following operating systems can coexist on the same computer with Windows NT Server?

   a. MS-DOS

   b. Windows 95

   c. Windows 3.11

   d. all of the above

   e. only b and c

3. During an installation you can set up networking for _____.

   a. cable connection

   b. a remote connection through a modem

   c. clients of the NT Server

   d. all of the above

   e. only a and b

4. What NIC information can you set up during an installation?

   a. type or model of NIC

   b. IRQ use

   c. amount of memory

   d. all of the above

   e. only a and b

5. Which of the following is (are) true about the server name?

   a. It should have the same name as the network administrator's account name.

   b. It should reflect the purpose of the server or organization.

   c. It must be over 20 characters in length.

   d. all of the above

   e. only b and c

6. Which of the following protocols can be set up during an installation?

a. NetBEUI

b. NWLink IPX/SPX Compatible

c. TCP/IP

d. all of the above

e. only a and c

7. Which type of account has access to all areas of an NT server?

a. Administrator

b. Guest

c. Anonymous

d. Supervisor

8. Windows NT Server Setup can automatically detect which type(s) of controller or adapter?

a. IDE

b. SCSI

c. ESDI

d. all of the above

e. only a and b

9. Which of the following hard disk operations can be performed through Window NT Server Setup?

a. formatting

b. mirroring

c. striping

d. all of the above

e. only a and b

10. Which installation program is used when there already is a version of Windows NT on the target computer?

a. Win

b. Winnt

c. Winnt32

d. Setup /nt

11. Which method(s) can be used to install Windows NT 4.0 Server?

    a. floppy disk and CD-ROM

    b. over the network

    c. complete floppy disk set made from the Network Client Administrator

    d. all of the above

    e. only a and b

12. Which of the following licensing methods is (are) used by NT Server?

    a. licenses per server

    b. licenses per seat

    c. licenses per shared volume

    d. all of the above

    e. only a and b

13. Which of the following is not a software component installed through Windows NT Server Setup?

    a. multimedia software

    b. accessory software

    c. accessibility software

    d. office software

14. Which of the following switches for the Winnt command enables you to make a set of three floppy boot disks during an installation?

    a. /O

    b. /RX

    c. /C

    d. /?

15. Windows NT Server Setup is having difficulty recognizing a SCSI drive. How might you try to fix the problem?

    a. change all device addresses to 0

    b. replace the SCSI cable with an RS–232S cable

    c. check to make sure that the cable is terminated

    d. all of the above

    e. only b and c

16. Which of the following should be enabled during the network portion of the NT Server installation?

    a. network bindings

    b. network Wizards

    c. I/O memory error correction

    d. IRQ time slices

17. An unattended installation uses which of the following switches?

   a. /R

   b. /U

   c. /X

   d. /A

18. What would you use to create an answer file for an unattended installation?

   a. Notepad

   b. Setup Manager

   c. Client Manager

   d. all of the above

   e. only a and b

19. What tool would you use to create a boot disk for a computer without an operating system?

   a. User Manager

   b. Setup Manager

   c. Network Client Administrator

   d. Boot Maker

20. The statement *TargetPath = Winnt* might be found in

   a. an unattended installation answer file

   b. an unattended installation switch

   c. an executable file on a boot disk

   d. a NET.CFG file for an over-the-network installation

21. You have installed Windows NT Server and have just added a new SCSI adapter and hard disk drive. What program and switch would you use to update the Emergency Repair Disk?

   a. VDISK /a

   b. VDISK /r

   c. REPAIR /r

   d. RDISK /s

22. In the ARC path, *scsi(1)disk(0)rdisk(0)partion(1)\WINNT*, which disk in the chain of SCSI devices contains the operating system?

   a. the first disk

   b. the second disk

   c. the third disk

   d. the last disk

HANDS-ON PROJECTS

PROJECT 4-1

In this activity you create a shared folder from which to load Windows NT Server over the network. You need a computer running Windows NT Server or NT Workstation and the Windows NT 4.0 Server CD-ROM.

To create a shared folder from which to install Windows NT Server:

1. Log on to the Administrator account or an account with the same privileges.
2. Insert the Windows NT 4.0 Server CD-ROM in the computer.
3. Click **Start**, **Programs**, and **Windows NT Explorer**.
4. Double-click the CD-ROM drive in Windows NT Explorer.
5. Right-click the **I386** folder and click **Copy** on the shortcut menu (Figure 4-9).

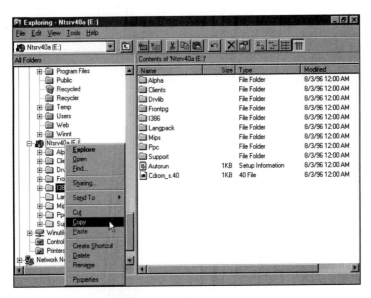

Figure 4-9   Copying the I386 folder

6. Right-click drive **C:** or another available drive in Windows NT Explorer.
7. Click **Paste** on the shortcut menu.

8. Right-click the new **I386** folder under drive C: and click **Sharing**.

9. Click the **Shared As:** radio button.

10. Leave the share name as I386.

11. Click the **Allow** _____ **Users** radio button and enter **1** in the scroll box.

12. Click the **Permissions** button.

13. Set Type of Access: to **Change** on the Access Through Share Permissions dialog box (Figure 4-10).

14. Click **OK**.

15. Click **OK** on the I386 Properties dialog box.

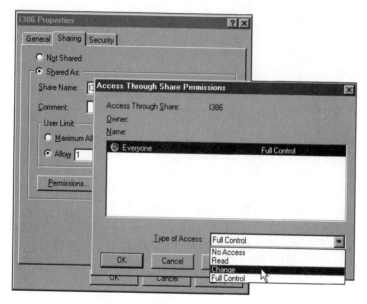

Figure 4-10   Setting up a shared drive

PROJECT 4-2

In this activity you make a network boot disk using Network Client Administrator. You need a computer running Windows NT Server (or access to Windows NT Server Remote Administration Tools from a shared directory on an NT server). You also need a formatted floppy disk with the system files (format the disk using the *Format a: /s* command from the MS-DOS window).

To make a network boot disk using Network Client Administrator:

1. Log on to Windows NT Server using the Administrator account or one with the same privileges.

2. Click **Start**, **Programs**, and **Administrative Tools (Common)**, **Network Client Administrator**.

3. Click the radio button for **Make Network Installation Startup Disk** (Figure 4-11), and then click **Continue**.

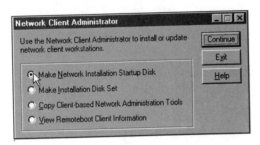

Figure 4-11   Network Client Administrator

4. Click the **Share Files** radio button, and accept the default share name and path. Click **OK**. The Network Client Administrator will tell you that it is making the client configuration files available on the network share.

5. Click the floppy disk type you have in your server, such as **3.5"**, and then select **Network Client v3.0 for MS-DOS and Windows**.

6. In the Network Adapter Card list in the Target Workstation Configuration dialog box, select the type of NIC that is in the target workstation and click **OK**.

7. In the Network Startup Disk Configuration dialog box, enter a name for the computer on which you will install NT Server. The default account and domain information will be filled in.

8. Select a network protocol that the computer will use to connect to the server. NetBEUI is the simplest network protocol. If you choose TCP/IP, you may have to enter additional information (TCP/IP address, subnet mask, etc.). You must select a protocol supported by your server. Click **OK**.

9. Insert the floppy disk formatted with DOS system files in drive A:, set the destination path as **\A:**, and click **OK** to confirm your selections.

10. Click **OK** after Network Client Administrator tells you that the files have been successfully copied.

11. Click the **Exit** button on the Network Client Administrator dialog box, and then click **OK** again. Leave the floppy disk in the drive.

12. Open the floppy drive icon from the desktop (double-click **My Computer**, then double-click the floppy drive icon).

13. Right-click the **AUTOEXEC.BAT** file and select **Edit**. This opens the file in Notepad for editing.

14. Edit the **Net Use** line. The Net Use command should refer to the name of the share where the installation files are located. If you are installing to an Intel-based computer, the share name will be I386.

The Net Use command accepts the Universal Naming Convention (UNC) format for specifying the share name as *server**sharename*, such as Net Use \\\\ourserver\\ i386. You also can enter a password at the end of the Net Use command for the account you specified when you made the client boot disk.

15. Select **File, Save** from the Notepad menu, and then exit Notepad (**File, Exit**).

16. After the disk is made, set the BIOS on the client computer to boot first from drive A:.

17. Turn off the client computer, insert the client disk in drive A:, and boot the computer.

18. Run **WINNT.EXE** from the shared network drive to install Windows NT on the client.

PROJECT 4-3

In this activity you practice the steps to run an installation over the network from the I386 shared folder you created in Hands-on Project 4-2. These steps also are intended to create installation floppy disks. Begin by logging on to a networked computer running Windows 95 or Windows NT.

To start the network installation:

1. Double-click **Network Neighborhood**.

2. Locate the computer with the shared folder and double-click it.

3. Right-click the **I386** folder and click **Map Network Drive** (Figure 4–12).

Figure 4-12 Mapping a drive

4. In the Map Network Drive dialog box, enter the letter of a drive that is not already mapped, and click **OK**.

5. Click **Start**, **Run**, and the **Browse** button.

6. Find the I386 shared folder.

7. Click **Winnt** so that it appears in the File name: box, or type in the file name.

8. Click **Open** in the Browse dialog box.

9. Enter the **/OX** switch after Winnt in the Open box.

10. Click **Cancel** so that you do not actually start the installation.

 PROJECT 4-4

In this activity you practice an installation using the Windows NT Server Installation Simulator that accompanies this book.

To start the Installation Simulator:

1. Load the files **WINNTSIM.EXE** and **VBRUN300.DLL**, from the disk accompanying this book or from your instructor, into a directory on your computer.

2. Click **Start**, **Run**, and the **Browse** button.

3. Locate the **Winntsim** file and click it.

4. Click **Open** in the Browse dialog box.

5. Click **OK**.

6. Click **Continue** in the Simulator.

7. Follow the instructions in the dialog boxes to run the Simulator.

PROJECT 4-5

In this activity you create an Emergency Repair Disk (ERD). You need access to a computer running Windows NT Server or NT Workstation. Also, obtain a formatted floppy disk and insert it into drive A:.

To create the ERD:

1. Click **Start**, **Programs**, and **Windows NT Explorer**.
2. Double-click the **Winnt** folder.
3. Double-click the **System32** folder.
4. Double-click **RDISK.EXE**.
5. Click the **Create Repair Disk** button in the Repair Disk Utility dialog box.
6. Click **OK**.
7. Click the **Exit** button.

 # ASPEN CONSULTING: INSTALLING WINDOWS NT 4.0 SERVER

Press Plastics is a company that molds sheet plastic into different shapes for containers, food packaging, computer memory chip packaging, and audio equipment packaging. Their molded plastic forms protect against damage when products are transported. Mark Arnez asks you to work with the network administrator to install 15 Windows NT file servers.

1. Prepare a list of decisions that should be made before Windows NT Server is installed on the 15 file servers. Explain each item on the list. Experiment with the Windows NT Server Installation Simulator included with this book to determine if you have missed any topics that ought to be on the list. Also, develop a list of data that should be obtained about the server hardware components.

2. Press Plastics' network administrator is not sure what installation methods can be used with Windows NT Server. Explain the installation methods. Which method do you recommend for Press Plastics?

3. The network administrator is practicing an installation on one of the servers. During the installation, Setup does not properly recognize the NIC. What troubleshooting steps do you recommend for this situation?

4. On another server computer, Setup does not detect a new SCSI adapter. What troubleshooting steps should be taken for this situation?

5. After installing Windows NT Server on a computer, the network administrator's boss has decided that the computer should be temporarily lent to the company president, who is waiting for a newly ordered state-of-the-art computer. The computer on which you installed Windows NT Server also has Windows 95 installed. Explain how you would remove Windows NT Server from that computer and prepare it for the president.

6. One of the computers that Press Plastics is using for a server was purchased at a discount. It is made of generic parts and was put together by a local computer store. The computer has previously been in service running Windows 95 on someone's desktop, but has not been networked. When the network administrator attempts to install Windows NT Server on that computer, Setup is unable to recognize one of the hard drives. The administrator replaces the hard drive adapter with another one, which seems to solve the problem. However, now Setup recognizes that there is a NIC in the computer, but it is having trouble determining the model of the NIC. Explain possible sources of these problems. What are your recommendations about what to do next?

SERVER CONFIGURATION

Now that Windows NT Server is successfully installed, it is time to make it network- and user-ready. One of the reasons for purchasing Windows NT Server is to take advantage of the many ways it can be configured and used on a network. As a start, the mouse, video, and keyboard can be customized to match the models of those devices used on the server. Additional protocols can be added and configured. More NICs can be installed to provide extra access to the server. Also, additional networking services can be implemented. Microsoft provides a large array of server software that can be installed, such as network communication alternatives, remote access capabilities, Internet software, and gateway software to other computer systems.

AFTER READING THIS CHAPTER AND COMPLETING THE EXERCISES YOU WILL BE ABLE TO:

- Explain how to configure the server environment through the Control Panel
- Configure network connectivity such as NWLink IPX/SPX and TCP/IP
- Add a network service
- Resolve a NIC conflict
- Set up multiple NICs
- Install a tape drive and SCSI adapter

When you configure a server, make a mental note of the work you need to perform before you make the server available to users. Another option is a make a list of items you can check off one by one. The projects ahead include the following:

- Configure the server and server components
- Set up performance-enhancement options
- Set up the clients to access the server
- Set up accounts and groups
- Create folders, load the software, and set security
- Set up network printing
- Set up utilities such as remote access, Novell NetWare access, and performance monitoring

In this chapter you start with the basic configuration tasks, such as configuring the mouse, video, and keyboard. You will also configure protocols, NICs, SCSI adapters, tape drives, and Windows NT services. All of the work you embark on from this point teaches you how Windows NT Server works and how to set up your server for the maximum benefit in its assigned role on the network.

SETTING UP THE SERVER ENVIRONMENT

Many of the Windows NT configuration options are contained in the Control Panel. The Control Panel is similar to a control center where you can customize NT Server for devices, network connectivity, dial-up capabilities, and many other functions. Plan to thoroughly learn the Control Panel options because they are vital to the role of a server administrator.

CONTROL PANEL

The Control Panel is accessed by clicking the Start button, highlighting the Settings option, and then clicking Control Panel. Two other ways to access the Control Panel are from the Windows NT Explorer window that displays drives and folders, and from My Computer on the Windows NT desktop. Each tool in the Control Panel is represented by an icon. To customize the display, click the View menu, which has options similar to the ones in Windows NT Explorer. From the View menu, you can customize the size of the icons, the display of details, and the arrangement of icons. You also can select to activate a toolbar at the top of the Control Panel. Figure 5-1 illustrates the Control Panel with the view set to list icons and a description of each one.

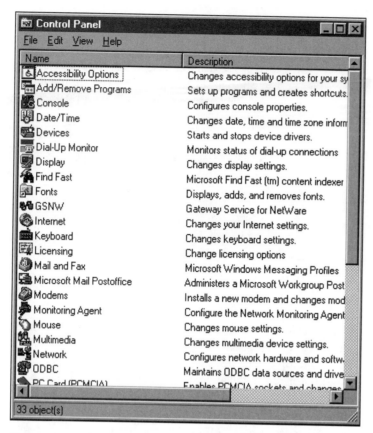

Figure 5-1   The Windows NT Control Panel

The content of the Control Panel is influenced by which software applications were installed during the original Windows NT Server setup and by applications that have been added or removed since the setup. For example, if e-mail and fax services are installed, there is a Control Panel icon to manage them. When dial-up communications are installed, a Dial-Up Monitor icon is included in the Control Panel. If a database that employs open database standards has been installed, there will be an icon to create and manage connections to databases on database servers.

Modern relational databases use a common set of open standards, so the techniques used to access one vendor's database can be applied to a different vendor's database. For example, the Structured Query Language (SQL) that accesses data in Microsoft's SQL Server database works in the same way to access data in a Sybase database or an Oracle database.

More than 30 Control Panel tools can be installed in Windows NT Server. The sections that follow provide summaries of some of the Control Panel tools, along with representations of their icons. Using the Control Panel is often the best and most immediate way for a server administrator to set a parameter or to adapt a server to a unique need.

Accessibility Options

The Accessibility Options tool enables a computer to accommodate the particular visual, audio, and sensory needs of the user. Keyboard and mouse button options can be used to set up the workstation for easier access. Special SerialKey devices can be installed to provide alternatives to keyboard and mouse use. Table 5-1 lists the options and their purposes.

Table 5-1 Accessibility Options

Accessibility Option	Purpose
General	Sets alternative keyboard and mouse access features and provides notification when an accessibility feature is turned off
Keyboard	Provides alternative touch and sound options for keyboard functions
Sound	Displays visual warnings and captions for sounds
Mouse	Enables the keyboard keypad to act as a pointing device

Add/Remove Programs

Software applications are installed and uninstalled with the Add/Remove Programs tool. For example, using the Windows NT Setup tab, an application that was not installed at the time of the Windows NT Server setup can be installed, such as Microsoft Exchange or the Phone Dialer. The server administrator can install any new software, such as Microsoft Office, using the Install/Uninstall tab.

Pre-Windows software or "legacy" MS-DOS software cannot be loaded with the Add/Remove Programs tool. To load legacy software, use the Run option from the Start menu.

Console

The Console tool controls the display of the emulated MS-DOS Command Prompt window. When an MS-DOS program is run on Windows NT Server, it runs within the NT virtual DOS machine component (the virtual DOS machine was introduced in Chapter 1, "Networking with Microsoft Windows NT Server"). Because Windows NT Server does not have MS-DOS, it uses the virtual machine to simulate an MS-DOS window in which to run an MS-DOS program. The Console tool customizes the window display. Font size can be changed, color contrasts customized, and the window size enhanced. Those options make the window more accessible and easier to use.

When a user runs an MS-DOS program on Windows NT Server, the operating system uses the NT virtual DOS machine component. Each virtual machine session runs in a separate memory space, and several MS-DOS programs can be running at once, each in its own virtual machine session.

Date/Time

With the Date/Time tool, you can set the calendar date, time, and time zone. This is an important tool for date-stamping files in order to track software versions, updates to financial information, and logon and access history data on a server or a workstation. Date information can be valuable in determining when a problem first occurred, and for reconstructing corrupted data. Documents, files, and other important information are permanently imprinted by a **date stamp** to record their creation date and time and to record modification dates and times.

 ## Devices

The types of devices on a Windows NT Server include disk drives, CD-ROM drive, processor, modem, keyboard, video, sound, and others. The Devices tool shows the status of those devices and enables their device drivers to be started or stopped. For example, it might be necessary to stop a device driver and start it again if that device (such as a SCSI adapter or NIC) is not responding, or appears to be hung. Also, if there are problems with the response of a protocol, you can stop and start its driver in an effort to correct the problem without rebooting the server.

You can set a device driver to start automatically when the server is booted, or you can start a device driver manually (Figure 5-2). You also can use this icon to disable devices—for example, when PCMCIA slots are not in use. (PCMCIA is defined later in this chapter.)

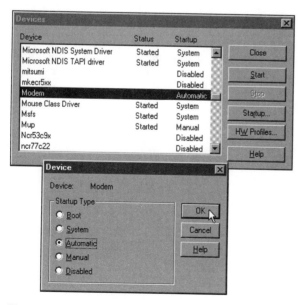

Figure 5-2   Control Panel Devices tool

Dial-Up Monitor

Windows NT Server can host users who dial into it from a modem or an ISDN telecommunications line. The Dial-Up Monitor is used to view information about dial-up sessions.

Display

The Display tool is used to set video characteristics, including the desktop background, display colors and resolution, the appearance of the title bar, screen-saver parameters, and other options. There also are settings to help accommodate a user's visual impairments. Table 5-2 lists the Display options.

Table 5-2   Display Properties

Display Option	Purpose
Appearance	Sets appearance of desktop entities such as title bars, application background, window borders, and icons
Background	Sets the display pattern and wallpaper
Plus!	Sets visual parameters for icons and indicates which icons to associate with the desktop functions
Screen Saver	Sets up a screen saver and controls screen saver parameters
Settings	Sets up the color palette and pixel desktop area

Find Fast

The Find Fast tool is used to build indexes for finding topics or documents and is set up when Microsoft Office products are installed. It is compatible with all Microsoft Office products such as Word, Excel, Access, and Outlook. Another useful feature is that it can be used for a rapid Web search through Microsoft Office. Find Fast is an example of a tool that comes with an add-on application for Windows NT Server.

Fonts

Windows NT Server supports a huge number of fonts and point sizes, and software vendors offer additional fonts for Windows. Fonts are installed or removed with the Fonts tool. Installed fonts are contained in the \Winnt\Fonts folder.

GSNW

The GSNW (Gateway Service for NetWare) icon is added when you set up NT Server to act as a gateway for one or more NetWare file servers. Users running Windows 3.11, Windows 95, and Windows NT can access NetWare folders and files as an NT Server shared folder, instead of logging on to a NetWare server. This tool provides a way to manage the gateway services.

Internet

Dial-up Internet access may require that a proxy server be established through which Internet access is managed. The Internet tool provides a way to specify the name and location of the proxy server. A **proxy server** assists a name server in handling the **resolution** of network names, such as the workstation name Wilkins, to a network Internet Protocol (IP) address. For example, when you use dial-up networking to connect to CompuServe, you specify the name of CompuServe's proxy server, which assists in correlating your CompuServe ID to IP communications on the Internet. You will learn more about IP addressing later in this chapter.

Keyboard

With the Keyboard tool, you can customize the keyboard setup for key repeat rate, cursor blink rate, language, and keyboard type. Also, you can install a new keyboard driver using the tool.

Licensing

After you install Windows NT Server, you may decide to purchase additional licenses to match the growth in network use. The Licensing tool enables you to add new licenses and to remove licenses. It also lets you specify the licensing mode, either per server or per seat (Figure 5-3). (Chapter 9 gives more information on licensing.)

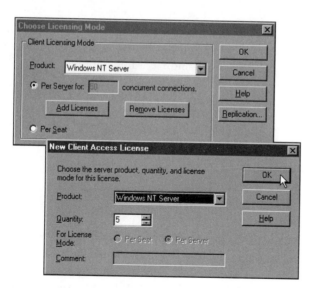

Figure 5-3 The Licensing tool

Mail and Fax

A Mail and Fax tool is included if a network mail system, such as Microsoft Mail or Exchange, is in use. It is used to configure the mail setup, mail services, and address book location, along with fax information.

Microsoft Mail Postoffice

The Postoffice tool is installed on the NT server through Microsoft messaging services. Microsoft post offices, users, mail security information, and other functions are managed here.

Modems

Modem configuration, such as modem type, speed, and other modem characteristics, is set up with this tool. If a new modem is added, the tool starts the New Modem Wizard to install it. You use the Modems tool to check that installed modems are set to their maximum speed, and that communications parameters such as data bits, parity, and stop bits are set correctly. Usually data bits are set to 8, parity is none, and stop bits equal 1. Data bits are the number of bits used to represent one character, such as the letter a. Parity is a method to check for errors, and the stop bit is a character used to indicate that the transmission of a byte of data is complete.

Mouse

With the Mouse tool, left-handed users, those who want a different scheme of mouse pointer symbols, and those who want to slow down mouse response can customize the mouse. This utility and the Display tool are two of the most frequently used Control Panel icons.

Multimedia

Windows NT Server supports audio, music, video, digital camera, multimedia compression, MIDI, and other devices. These devices, including drivers, are added and removed through the Multimedia tool. The tool also has playback and recording controls.

Network

Administrators become very familiar with the Network access features of Windows NT Server. This tool sets protocols, configures network adapters, and installs network drivers and new networking services. You will become much better acquainted with this tool later in the chapter.

ODBC

Open Database Connectivity (ODBC) is a widely used standard to provide open access to Microsoft Access, Microsoft SQL Server, Oracle, Sybase, and other databases. There are two versions of ODBC, one for 16-bit and one for 32-bit database applications. The ODBC Control Panel icon is a powerful tool that is used to install drivers, make database connections, and perform data queries. ODBC is a set of rules used to create an interface with a database to enable data to be read or updated. It ensures not only access but also conformance to SQL.

PC Card (PCMCIA)

The PC Card tool shows information about whether a **Personal Computer Memory Card International Association (PCMCIA)** is correctly installed, including resource and resource conflict information. A workstation's resources include the **interrupt request (IRQ) line**, which is a channel for communications with the CPU, and other elements such as the **I/O address** and reserved memory range. For example, a computer contains a limited number of IRQ lines, such as 01–15. The video display, each disk drive, each serial and parallel port, and the sound card use a dedicated IRQ to communicate with the processor. Each also needs reserved memory addresses for I/O operations. A PCMCIA card, which is about the size of a credit card, enables a modem, a NIC, a CD-ROM, or other peripheral device to connect to a computer. Originally intended for portables, these cards also are used in desktop computers.

5

> The term **resource** has two meanings in a Microsoft network. In this context, the term refers to elements linked to the physical components on a workstation: the IRQs, the I/O addresses, and the memory that can be allocated to a computer component such as a disk drive or a communications port. When the term is applied to a network, it refers to a file server, a shared printer, or a shared folder that can be accessed by users.

Ports

Serial ports are configured by using the Ports tool to establish settings such as the port speed, the I/O address, and the IRQ (Figure 5-4).

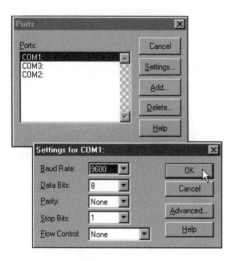

Figure 5-4 The Ports tool

Printers Folder

This is the same Printers folder that can be accessed from the Start button Settings option. It contains the Add Printer Wizard for installing a new printer, plus controls for managing one already set up. (Printer management is covered in Chapter 10, "Printer Management.")

Regional Settings

Users who prefer to view time in 24-hour notation use this tool to customize the display. The Regional Settings tool also enables international customization of numbers, the date and time formats, currency, and language.

SCSI Adapters

The SCSI Adapters tool provides a view of installed SCSI adapters and the devices connected to them. Also, SCSI device drivers are installed here. For example, if you install a SCSI adapter for a disk drive, a tape drive, or a scanner, you use this tool to load the driver. IDE CD-ROM drivers are loaded using this icon, as well. Windows NT Server has many drivers included on the Windows NT Server CD-ROM, or a driver from the manufacturer may be on a disk included with the hardware.

Server

Windows NT Server has many server capabilities, which are enabled through the Server service. Using the Server tool, the administrator can view the user connections and shared resources in use, set parameters for automatic copying of folders, set up problem alerts to server administrators, and disconnect users from the network, if necessary.

Services

Many services run in the background of Windows NT Server to enable particular functions, such as the Server service and the Print Spooler service. The Services tool provides a place to start, stop, and manage the startup method of services, and it should be used with caution. The Server service, for example, enables NT Server to function as a server to computers connected to the network. The Print Spooler service is used to process print jobs in the background, so that a server administrator can run a program or perform another task at the same time that a file is printing. Also, if a network printer is shared from the server, the spooler handles print requests from workstations that use the network printer.

Sounds

Special sound effects are provided with Windows NT Server, such as musical chords, dinging bells, "tada!," and others. New sounds can be purchased and added. The Sounds tool enables the server administrator to associate a sound with a specific event, such as when a new mail message is received or when the computer is shut down. Of course, to use sounds, the computer needs a sound card and speakers.

System

The server environment and performance are managed from the System tool (Figure 5-5). Windows NT 4.0 Server has advanced capabilities to set up hardware and user profiles, which is useful when the server functions as a means to provide a common desktop to some or all server users. Desktop settings can be customized so that users see the same desktop no matter which computer they use to log on to the server. Also, different hardware profiles can be set up to match changing situations, such as when the server sometimes uses a remote monitor and keyboard, and sometimes uses its own monitor and keyboard. Remote setups are used in machine rooms in which there are 10, 20, or more servers, all connected through a switchbox to be accessed from a single monitor and keyboard.

5

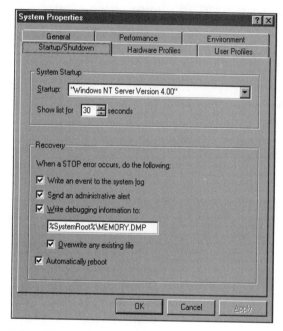

Figure 5-5 The System tool

Tape Devices

When a tape drive is attached to the workstation, an accompanying driver needs to be installed. The Tape Devices tool is the place to install the driver and to have the server detect the tape drive.

Telephony

The Telephony tool stores information about telephone services used through the computer, such as the local area code and the country. This tool is mainly intended for a portable computer that uses Windows NT Workstation, in which a telephony profile can be established for each location from which it is used. Drivers can be installed for special telephone services, such as cell phones.

UPS

Many server administrators attach their server to an uninterruptible power supply because the server is used for critical services and cannot be out of service because of power problems. An **uninterruptible power supply (UPS)** is one or more batteries that provide backup power to electrical devices for several minutes when the main power goes out. Many UPSs are housed in separate device units that have a number of sockets to provide power for equipment such as computers, disk arrays, and tape-backup systems.

The UPS tool offers a way to set up communications between the UPS and the server in order to sound alarms, provide warnings, initiate an orderly shutdown of the server, and specify interface voltage levels.

Additional Control Panel Tools

Besides the primary Control Panel tools, others can be installed for special management purposes. For example, some print server devices use software that allows the devices to be controlled through an icon on the Control Panel. Specialized video capabilities can be managed with a Control Panel icon from a vendor.

CONFIGURING THE DISPLAY

One of the first server components to configure is the display. For example, you might decide to use a specialized monitor, such as a 15-inch or 17-inch monitor that requires the installation of a new video adapter and driver. Also, you likely will install a screen saver for the display. A new display driver is installed from the Settings tab after opening the Display tool (Figure 5-6). Click the Display Type button and then the Change button to install the driver. Select the display manufacturer and model, and have the driver disk or CD-ROM ready to insert. (You practice installing a display driver in Hands-on Project 5-1).

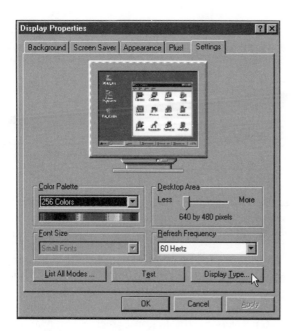

Figure 5-6   Installing a display driver

Installing a screen saver has two important advantages: it extends the life of the display monitor, and it provides security when you step away from the server after logging on. Screen savers are especially important for extending the life of a typical monitor, which functions much like a television screen. The monitor contains a cathode-ray tube with a gun that shoots electrons at a phosphorus-coated screen inside the tube. The electrons are fired in patterns to form images on the screen. When the same screen image is displayed continuously for hours, on a word-processing screen, for example, the repeated shooting of the electrons to the same areas can "burn" that image into the screen. A screen saver produces constant change on the screen, causing the electron gun to fire at more random screen locations, instead of at the same spot.

A screen saver also can provide security when you are away from the server, but have not logged off from an account, such as Administrator, which has extensive access to the entire network and its resources. With security enabled, you must enter a password to close the screen saver and return to the work screen. That prevents anyone without the password from accessing the server.

Microsoft Windows NT Server supports **OpenGL**, which is a standard for multidimensional graphics. Several interesting OpenGL-based screen savers are available for Windows NT, including a few already bundled with the operating system (Table 5-3). These graphics add a pleasing touch to screen savers.

Table 5-3   Three-Dimensional OpenGL Screen Savers Included with Windows NT Server

OpenGL Screen Saver	Screen Pattern
Flower Box	A cube that transforms into a ball and then into a flower
Flying Objects	An animated Microsoft flag
Maze	Similar to moving through a maze in a computer game
Pipes	Builds connected pipes on the screen
Text	Moving text (you specify the text that is displayed)

Choose a screen saver carefully. Some screen savers are CPU-intensive, which means that they can slow down user and background processes on a server. Microsoft warns that this is a problem with the 3D Pipes screen saver included in Windows NT.

To set up a screen saver with a password, double-click the Display icon in the Control Panel and click the Screen Saver tab, as shown in Figure 5-7, then select Beziers as the screen saver. Beziers places a relatively low demand on the processor and provides a random display across the screen. Other low-demand screen savers are the Logon Screen Saver, Marquee Display, Mystify, and Starfield Simulation.

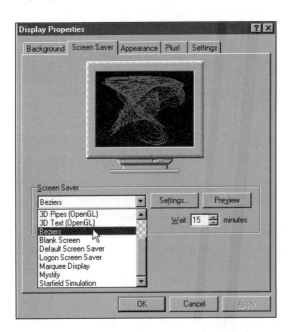

Figure 5-7   Screen Saver tab on the Display Properties
dialog box

Next, click the Settings button, from which you can regulate the size of the graphic on the screen and the speed of the changing display; for instance, you can leave the default settings for length and width but modify the speed so that the change rate is a little slower (Figure 5-8). Click OK to return to the Display Properties screen. From there, change the screen saver to start within the time you specify, such as after less than 15 minutes of inactivity. This is done by using the Wait ____ minutes option. Although not visible on the Screen Saver tab shown in Figure 5-7, there is a box to set password protection below the Screen Saver list box. Because you are now back on the tab without the list box open, click the "Password protected" box to implement security. The password is the same as the logon password for the currently logged-on server account. Click Apply to implement the changes, and then click OK.

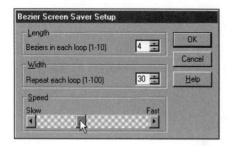

Figure 5-8 Screen Saver Setup dialog box

CONFIGURING THE MOUSE AND POINTING DEVICES

The Mouse icon in the Control Panel provides a way to customize mouse features and to install a driver for a particular type of pointing device, such as a trackball. The customization options are shown in Table 5-4.

Table 5-4 Mouse Setup Options

Option	Purpose
Buttons	Sets right-handed and left-handed options plus the double-click speed
General	Sets up a new mouse and driver
Motion	Controls the mouse speed and sets the mouse to snap to the default confirmation or notification buttons in dialog boxes.
Pointers	Customizes the pointer icons displayed with specific functions such as Busy or Text Select.

To change the mouse speed, click the Motion tab and adjust the pointer speed bar between slow and fast (Figure 5-9). If you are installing a new mouse driver, click the General tab and then the Change button. Click the radio button to Show all devices, and select the device you want to install. Insert the pointing device manufacturer's disk containing the drivers and click OK or Have Disk to install the drivers. Provide the path to the drivers disk and click OK or Continue (depending on the options in the dialog box). (Hands-on Project 5-2 is an exercise to practice installing a mouse driver.)

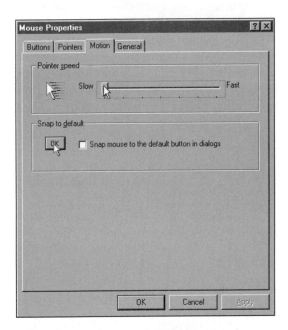

Figure 5-9 Adjusting the pointer speed

CONFIGURING THE KEYBOARD

The Keyboard icon in the Control Panel provides a way to change keyboard characteristics or to install a driver for a specialized keyboard. For example, if you find the key repeat rate is too fast, click the Speed tab and move the Repeat rate bar to a slower setting (Figure 5-10). If you are using a specialized keyboard that comes with its own drivers, click the General tab and the Change button. If your keyboard is not displayed, click the Show all devices radio button. Highlight the keyboard, insert the drivers disk and press Have Disk. Click OK to complete the installation. Table 5-5 summarizes the keyboard Setup options. In Hands-on Project 5-3, you will configure keyboard options.

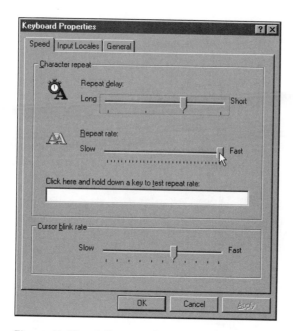

Figure 5-10   Adjusting the keyboard repeat rate

Table 5-5   Keyboard Setup Options

Option	Purpose
General	Installs a new keyboard driver
Input Locales	Sets up language and other keyboard properties for locales that use different languages, such as English and Swedish
Speed	Sets up keyboard characteristics such as repeat delay, repeat rate, and cursor blink rate

USING THE CONTROL PANEL TO CONFIGURE NETWORK CONNECTIVITY

The Windows NT 4.0 Server installation steps in Chapter 4, "Server Installation," have already illustrated how to set up NetBEUI. However, you may need to use the Network icon to set up the server to communicate using other protocols, such as IPX/SPX and TCP/IP. You might use IPX/SPX to communicate with a particular network printer, such as an older Hewlett-Packard laser printer, or you might need to set up NT Server to communicate as a client or gateway with a Novell NetWare server. TCP/IP is needed for access to mainframes, UNIX computers, and the Internet.

INSTALLING NWLINK IPX/SPX COMPATIBLE TRANSPORT

NWLink IPX/SPX Compatible Transport is installed from the Control Panel Network icon by selecting the Protocols tab (Figure 5-11). Click the Add button to display a list of protocols, highlight NWLink IPX/SPX Compatible Transport, and click OK. As with other installations, you need to insert the Windows NT Server CD-ROM, provide its path, and click to continue. (Try Hands-on Project 5-4 for practice.) Make sure that you bind the protocol to the NIC by clicking the Bindings tab before you leave the Network dialog box.

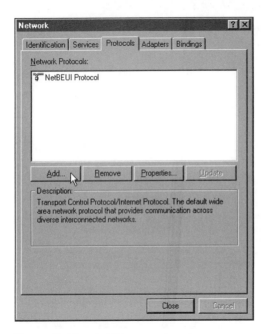

Figure 5-11   Adding a protocol

After configuring the protocol, make sure that the right network number and frame type are implemented to work with Novell NetWare. Depending on the version, NetWare may be using Ethernet frame type 802.2, 802.3, Ethernet II, or Ethernet SNAP. The NT Server should be using the same frame type as the NetWare servers on the network. To check this information, click the Protocols tab and highlight the newly installed NWLink IPX/SPX Compatible Transport. Click the Properties button to view the dialog box in Figure 5-12. Enter the same network number as is used by the NetWare servers (consult the NetWare administrator for the network number). Also, click the Auto Frame Type Detection radio button so that the server can automatically detect and use a compatible frame type. If you are more comfortable manually selecting the frame type, click the Manual Frame Type Detection radio button and then click Add. Select the frame type in the Manual Frame

Detection dialog box, click Add, and click Apply in the NWLink IPX/SPX Properties dialog box. Close the Network dialog box and reboot the server for the new settings to be implemented. (For more information on NetWare connectivity, see Chapter 12, "Interoperating with Novell NetWare.")

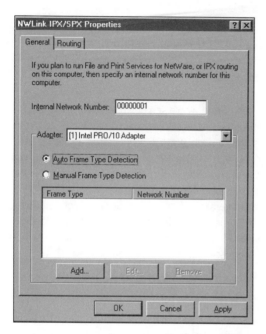

Figure 5-12   Setting the NWLink IPX/SPX Compatible Transport

CONFIGURING TCP/IP

Configuring TCP/IP also is performed from the Control Panel Network icon. However, installing TCP/IP can be more complex than installing NetBEUI or NWLink IPX/SPX, depending on whether dynamic or static addressing is used on the network. As you learned in Chapter 2, "Basic Network Design and Protocols," static addressing is used on many networks, large and small, where the network administrator wants direct control over the assigned addresses. Direct control might be necessary where network management software is used to track all network nodes, and the software depends on each node having a permanent, known IP address. As you learned, an IP address uses the dotted decimal notation system of addressing, which consists of four numbers separated by periods, such as 129.77.15.182. Permanent addresses give consistency to monitoring network statistics and to keeping historical network performance information. The disadvantage is that IP address administration can be a laborious task on a large network. Most network administrators have an IP database to keep track of currently assigned addresses and of unused addresses to assign as new people are connected to the network.

With dynamic addressing, an IP address is leased to a particular computer for a defined period of time. This addressing method uses the Dynamic Host Configuration Protocol (DHCP), which is a convention supported by Microsoft for dynamic addressing. The protocol is used to enable a server with DHCP services to detect the presence of a new workstation and to assign addressing data to that workstation.

If you have a DHCP server on the network, then you specify this during the TCP/IP setup, and your work is greatly reduced because DHCP can configure other parameters for you, depending on how it is set up. If static addressing is used on your network, you need to determine the following information before installing TCP/IP:

Plan to keep the IP information associated with a server limited to one address per NIC. The Control Panel Network icon enables you to enter up to five IP addresses for one NIC (by using the Advanced button in the TCP/IP Properties dialog box). It also is possible to edit the Windows NT Registry and enter more. A computer having multiple addresses is called a multihomed computer. Multihoming is not recommended because of the increased network traffic problems and added problems in the performance and management of network routing equipment. Most importantly, NetBIOS over TCP/IP limits to one the number of addresses that can be bound to a NIC. Also, the NetBIOS-based computer name information used on a Microsoft network uses only the first IP address associated with a NIC.

- *IP address:* The server needs a unique IP address that is compatible with your network and not assigned to any other network computer.

- *Subnet mask:* A **subnet mask** is a method to show which part of the IP address is a unique identifier for the network and which part uniquely identifies the computer. On a simple network that does not connect with other networks, the subnet mask is likely to be 255.255.0.0. This means that the first two sets of digits (the 255s) are the network identification for the computers on that network, and the third and fourth sets of digits (the 0s) are used as the workstation or server identification. For example, your network might have a network identification of 122.44. All workstations and servers on your network will have IP addresses that start with 122.44 (and will usually have a 0 in the third place), such as 122.44.0.1, 122.44.0.2, and so on. If your network is composed of several networks combined into one, such as occurs on a large college campus, the subnet mask might be 255.255.255.0. In this case, the 255 in the third position is used to identify each smaller network or subnetwork. In a college campus, this might mean that there is a subnetwork for the administration buildings (122.44.1), one for the classroom buildings (122.44.2), and another for the dorms (122.44.3). In the dorms, your IP address might be 122.44.3.20, and your neighbor across the hall might have 122.44.3.21. Your professor in a classroom building might have the address 122.44.2.54, and the academic dean in the administration building might have 122.44.1.5.

- *Domain name service (DNS) server:* As you learned in Chapter 2, this is a network server that converts names to IP addresses. For example, if your network has a mainframe called ADMIN, that mainframe also has an IP address, such as 122.44.1.5. When you send e-mail or some other communication to mainframe ADMIN, a DNS network server converts that name to 122.44.1.5, enabling the communication to be transferred along the network in a format that computers and network devices understand. A DNS server also can convert the IP address back to the name, for the sake of human users.

- *Windows Internet Naming Service (WINS) server:* In Chapter 2, you learned that a Microsoft NT server can double as a WINS server. A WINS server converts names to IP addresses, and vice versa, on the local network. When you configure TCP/IP, you can specify the IP address of a domain name server, a Microsoft WINS server, or both. Many NT server administrators prefer to use the WINS server because of its Microsoft compatibility and convenience, and the fact that it can help reduce traffic on a busy network.

- *Default gateway:* A **default gateway** is a computer or router that forwards a network communication from one network to another. By specifying the IP address of the default gateway, you enable the server to communicate with workstations on another network. Transmitted data goes from your server to the gateway. The gateway then routes the data to the network it is intended to reach, where it is forwarded to the destination computer.

Begin installing TCP/IP by opening the Network icon and clicking the Protocols tab and the Add button. Highlight TCP/IP Protocol and click OK (Figure 5-13). Insert the Windows NT Server CD-ROM and click OK or Continue. If there is a DHCP server, click Yes to have the server determine the IP address and associated information. If you click No, you will need to enter the IP address and subnet mask. If there are DNS, WINS, or both kinds of servers, enter their IP addresses.

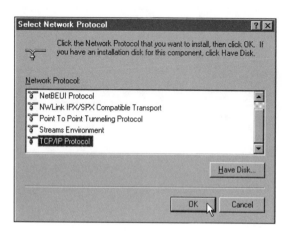

Figure 5-13 Selecting the TCP/IP protocol

Load the TCP/IP drivers from the Windows NT Server CD-ROM. Use the Bindings tab to bind the new drivers to the NIC (this is done automatically if you do not click the tab, but the step is a good precaution). Once the binding process is complete, the Network dialog box is again available. On the Protocols tab, highlight the TCP/IP protocol and click the Properties button. Use the IP Address, WINS Address, and DNS tabs to enter IP, subnet, WINS, and DNS information.

Make sure you enter both the IP address and subnet mask in the IP Address tab (if there is no DHCP server). There may be more than one WINS server on the network, in which case you can enter two IP addresses, one for a primary WINS server and one for a secondary WINS server. Apply the changes and reboot the computer when you are finished. You will practice installing TCP/IP in Hands-on Project 5-5.

USING THE NETWORK ICON TO ADD A SERVICE

Additional network services can be loaded from the Network icon Services tab. This is the place to load Microsoft DHCP, DNS, and WINS server services. To load a service, click the Add button, highlight the service, and click OK. You will need the Windows NT Server CD-ROM in order to load the service. Follow the on-screen directions for loading a particular service from the dialog box. (There will be opportunities to load network services in several chapters later in the book.) Figure 5-14 shows the dialog box from which to select a service to load.

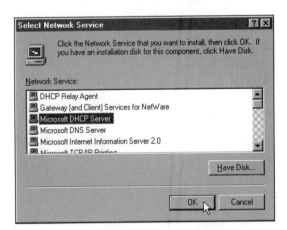

Figure 5-14   Adding a network service

RESOLVING A NIC RESOURCE CONFLICT

Sometimes there are resource conflicts when a network adapter is configured during the initial Windows NT Server installation. There is a way to check for a resource conflict, something you should do because a conflict can be manifested in several ways. For example, an IRQ conflict prevents the NIC from working properly. A subtle address conflict may simply result in puzzling intermittent connection problems.

To check the NIC, open the Network icon and click the Adapters tab. On the Adapters tab, four action buttons in the middle perform the following functions:

- Add is used to install an adapter.

- Remove uninstalls an adapter.

- Properties shows the resource settings of the currently highlighted adapter.

- Update is used to reconfigure a card for a new driver.

Highlight the adapter and click Properties. The Setup dialog box for the adapter appears, showing the resource configuration, as in Figure 5-15. A resource conflict would be indicated on the screen with a message. For example, both an adapter and a serial port may be assigned to use IRQ 3. To correct the conflict, you would click the Change button and assign a different interrupt, such as IRQ 5, to the adapter. The Test button on the dialog box sends packets onto the network and checks packets that are received back. The Test button is a good place to start when checking for card or cable problems. If the test fails, a message is displayed showing the packet transmission statistics and possible causes of the failure. (Test and setting options can vary, depending on the drivers that come with a NIC.)

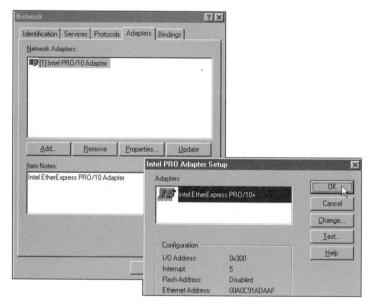

Figure 5-15   Resource configuration

Often a resource conflict is more subtle than two devices using the same IRQ. A common example occurs when the I/O address range of one device overlaps slightly the range of another device, such as a serial port using the range 02F8-0300 and a network interface card using 0300-030F. In that case, both devices are using location 0300, and the Network icon or the Ports icon on the Control Panel should be used to reset the range for either the adapter or the serial port.

Intel computers have 15 IRQs that can be used by devices. One way to determine which IRQs are already in use is to view the assigned resources in Windows NT Diagnostics. Windows NT Diagnostics is started by clicking the Start button, Programs, and Administrative Tools (Common). Open Windows NT Diagnostics and click the Resources tab, as shown in Figure 5-16.

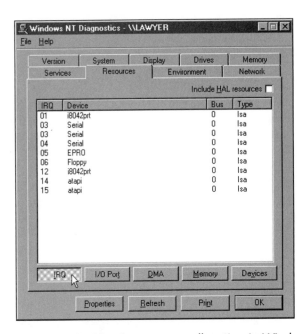

Figure 5-16 Viewing resource allocation in Windows NT Diagnostics

Computer manufacturers vary in how they assign IRQ and I/O port address ranges on computers, but generally they work to follow a common scheme. Table 5-6 shows typical IRQ assignments, and Table 5-7 (on the page following) shows common I/O port assignments, for an Intel-based computer.

Table 5-6 Common Intel IRQ Assignments

IRQ	Typical Device Assignment	Comment
0	Timer	Hardwired on the motherboard; cannot be changed
1	Keyboard	Hardwired on the motherboard; cannot be changed
2	Cascade from IRQ9	Might or might not be available, depending on how the motherboard is designed. Avoid using this IRQ because some old VGAs might use it for autoswitching.
3	COM2 or COM4	Available, unless used for a second serial port such as COM2, COM4, or a bus mouse (a mouse that runs directly to the bus, not via a serial port)
4	COM1 or COM3	
5	LPT2	Available (unless used for a second parallel port such as LPT2 or a sound card)
6	Floppy-disk controller	
7	LPT1	
8	Real-time clock	Hardwired to the motherboard; cannot be changed
9	Cascaded to IRQ2	Wired directly to IRQ2, so does not exist as separate interrupt. Sometimes when you set a board to IRQ2, you have to tell the software that you set it to IRQ9 to make it work.
10		Available
11		Available
12	Mouse	Used for in-port mice, a built-in port made for a mouse
13	Math coprocessor	Used to signal detected errors in the coprocessor
14	Hard-disk controller	
15		Available (on non-IDE systems)

5

Table 5-7   Common Intel I/O Port Assignments

Port	Device	Port	Device
200-20F	Game port	300-30F	NIC (network interface card)
210-21F		310-31F	NIC
220-22F		320-32F	
230-23F	Bus mouse	330-33F	
240-24F		340-34F	
250-25F		350-35F	
260-26F		360-36F	
270-27F	LPT3	370-37F	LPT2
280-28F		380-38F	
290-29F		390-39F	
2A0-2AF		3A0-3AF	
2B0-2BF		3B0-3BF	LPT1
2C0-2CF		3C0-3CF	EGA/VGA
2D0-2DF		3D0-3DF	CGA/MCGA and EGA/VGA color video modes
2E0-2EF		3E0-3EF	
2F0-2FF	COM2	3F0-3FF	Floppy-disk controller, COM1

When working to resolve a NIC conflict, you may overlook a setting or make another change to the Windows NT setup that causes the server to lock up when you reboot it. To return to the Last Known Good Configuration (the previous configuration that enabled you to successfully boot the computer), press Ctrl-Alt-Del, then press the spacebar when you see the following message: "Press spacebar NOW to invoke Last Known Good Menu." The resulting menu provides different options for booting the server. Press L to boot using the Last Known Good Configuration.

ADDING A NIC

An NT server can use more than one NIC, which accomplishes two purposes. The first is to provide two routes into the server, which can provide better access on a busy server. The second advantage is that the second NIC is a form of fault tolerance, so if one NIC is malfunctioning there is still a way to access the server. A busy company that relies heavily on its server can benefit from having multiple NICs.

To install another NIC, shut down the server and insert the NIC in an appropriate expansion slot. Reboot the server and use the Network icon Adapters tab to install the NIC driver. Click the Add button and select the NIC from the list in the Network Adapter: box. Insert the manufacturer's drivers disk or the Windows NT Server CD-ROM and click OK. Specify the path to the disk in the Windows NT Setup dialog box and click Continue. Once the drivers are loaded, check to make sure that there is no resource conflict by examining the NIC's properties (see Figure 5-15). Next, click the Bindings tab to bind previously installed protocols to the new NIC. Click Close in the Network dialog box and reboot the computer.

INSTALLING A TAPE DRIVE WITH A SCSI ADAPTER

At this point you have a significant amount of time and effort invested in preparing a server. This is a good time to install and set up a tape drive so that there is a way to back up your work. The two immediate steps to take in preparing to use the tape drive are to install the SCSI adapter and to install the drivers for the tape drive.

First, install the SCSI adapter for the tape drive in an open expansion slot in the computer. Next, reassemble the computer, reboot, and install the driver for the adapter by double-clicking the SCSI Adapters icon in the Control Panel. Click the Drivers tab and click Add to create a list of available drivers in the Install Driver dialog box. Highlight the appropriate vendor in the Manufacturers box, as shown in Figure 5-17, and select the adapter model from the list in the SCSI Adapter box. Insert the drivers disk provided by the manufacturer and click Have Disk. In the Install from Disk dialog box, enter A:\ (or another drive path to the drivers) to show where to obtain the driver, and click OK. When it finishes loading, click OK to leave the SCSI Adapters dialog box. (Try Hands-on Project 5-6 for practice.)

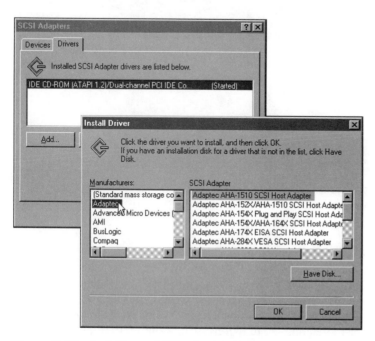

Figure 5-17   Installing a SCSI adapter driver

After the SCSI driver is installed, shut down the server and use a SCSI cable to connect the tape drive to the adapter. Reboot and make sure that the adapter and driver are detected correctly. If they are not, Windows NT Server displays a warning, shortly after rebooting, that they were not detected. The warning appears prominently in the foreground on the desktop.

Next, install the driver for the tape drive by double-clicking the Tape Devices icon in the Control Panel. Click the Drivers tab, then the Add button. A list of manufacturers is created, from which to select a tape device, as shown in Figure 5-18. Insert the manufacturer's driver disk in drive A: and click Have Disk. In the Install from Disk dialog box, use the default path (or provide a path to the driver disk) and click OK. The driver is loaded. Back in the Tape Devices dialog box, click the Devices tab. Click the Detect button, and the new tape drive is detected by NT Server. Click OK to leave the Tape Devices dialog box. You now have a new tape drive ready to use for backups.

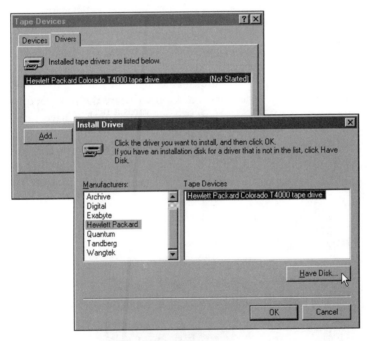

Figure 5-18   Installing a tape device driver

CHAPTER SUMMARY

- Once NT Server is installed, there is still work to be done configuring the server. One of the most powerful configuration resources is the Control Panel. It contains a large variety of tools for server configuration. You can configure basic functions, such as the date and time, or more complex functions such as the TCP/IP protocol and installing a SCSI adapter.

- In this chapter, you have learned how to set up the display, keyboard, and pointing devices. For example, you can use a screen saver to extend the life of a monitor and to secure the server. Key repeat rate and other keyboard features can be customized through the Control Panel. Another feature that can be customized is the speed of the mouse as you move its pointer across the screen. Drivers for new display, keyboard, and pointing devices also are installed through the Control Panel.

- Another important function of the Control Panel is its central role in setting up network connectivity. Through the Control Panel, new protocols are installed and configured. A range of network services can be installed, such as Microsoft DHCP and WINS. The Control Panel also is the place to install an additional NIC or to resolve a resource conflict at a NIC.

5

KEY TERMS

- **date stamp** — Documents, files, and other important information are permanently imprinted by a date stamp to record their creation date and time and to record modification dates and times.

- **default gateway** — A computer or router that forwards a network communication from one network to another, acting as a gateway between networks.

- **interrupt request (IRQ) line** — A hardware line that a computer component, such as a disk drive or serial port, uses to communicate to the processor that it is ready to send or receive information. Intel-based computers have 16 IRQ lines, with 15 of those available for computer components to use.

- **I/O address** — The address in memory through which data is transferred between a computer component and the processor.

- **Open Database Connectivity (ODBC)** — A set of rules developed by Microsoft for accessing databases and providing a standard doorway to database data.

- **OpenGL** — A standard for multidimensional graphics used in Microsoft's 3D screen savers.

- **Personal Computer Memory Card International Association (PCMCIA) card** — A credit-card-sized adapter used in portable computers and in desktops to connect disk drives, CD-ROM drives, network interfaces, and other computer peripherals.

- **proxy server** — A server used to help convert a workstation or logon ID to an IP address.

- **resolution** — A process used to translate a computer's domain name to an IP address, and vice versa.

- **resource** — (1) On a workstation or server, an IRQ, an I/O address, or memory that is allocated to a computer component, such as a disk drive or communications port. (2) On an NT server network, a resource is a file server, shared printer, or shared directory that can be accessed by users.

- **subnet mask** — A method to show which part of the IP address is a unique identifier for the network and which part uniquely identifies the workstation.
- **uninterruptible power supply (UPS)** — A device built into electrical equipment or a separate device that provides immediate battery power to equipment during a power failure or brownout.

REVIEW QUESTIONS

1. From where would you stop a driver for a SCSI adapter?

   a. Devices tool

   b. Adapter tool

   c. System tool

   d. Tape Drive tool

2. To change the speed of the mouse, use the _____.

   a. Mouse icon General tab

   b. Display icon General tab

   c. Mouse icon Motion tab

   d. Services icon Speed tab

3. You have configured NWLink IPX/SPX, but there are problems connecting to NetWare. What might you check to resolve the problems?

   a. that TCP/IP is not configured on the same server

   b. the frame type in use by the NetWare server

   c. the NetWare icon Setting tab Test button

   d. all of the above

   e. only a and b

4. What is IRQ3 most likely to be used for?

   a. NIC communications

   b. COM2 or COM4

   c. display adapter

   d. floppy-drive controller

5. Which of the following can resolve the name *course.com* to an IP address?

   a. DNS server

   b. WINS server

   c. DHCP server

   d. all of the above

   e. only a and b

6. You have installed a SCSI adapter using the driver included on the Windows NT Server CD-ROM, but the server is having trouble recognizing the SCSI adapter. What might you try to resolve the problem?

a. try a driver for a different card

b. set a SCSI protocol through the Network icon

c. use the driver that came with the SCSI drive

d. all of the above

e. only a and c

7. You have installed a new modem and need to set it up in Windows NT Server. What tool would you use?

a. Modems tool

b. Telephony tool

c. Device tool

d. Adapter tool

8. Which of the following would help you to determine the IRQs that are already in use?

a. Windows NT Explorer

b. Network icon

c. Windows NT Diagnostics

d. Services icon

9. Which of the following is (are) an example of a resource on a server?

a. IRQ

b. port memory

c. memory speed in nanoseconds

d. all of the above

e. only a and b

10. How might you provide security on a Windows NT Server console?

a. use the keyboard security feature

b. use monitor blanking

c. disable the mouse

d. set up a screen saver password

11. If your network has DHCP, then _____.

a. it is not necessary to set up the IP address for TCP/IP

b. it is not necessary to specify the subnet mask for TCP/IP

c. TCP/IP is automatically installed without administrator intervention

d. all of the above

e. only a and b

12. You have changed the resource settings on the server's NIC, but when you reboot, the server locks up. What should you do?

    a. reinstall Windows NT Server

    b. use the Emergency Repair Disk

    c. reseat the NIC and boot again

    d. reboot using the Last Known Good option

13. From where in the Control Panel would you set up a connection to a Microsoft SQL Server database?

    a. Network icon

    b. ODBC icon

    c. System icon

    d. Server icon

14. Which of the following routes communications from one network to another?

    a. WINS Server

    b. default gateway

    c. net linker

    d. DHCP resolving

15. For which protocol(s) might you configure information about WINS?

    a. NWLink IPX/SPX

    b. NetBEUI

    c. TCP/IP

    d. all of the above

    e. only b and c

16. When the subnet mask is 255.255.255.0, which part of the IP address identifies a workstation or server on the network?

    a. 0

    b. 255.255

    c. 255.255.255

    d. none of the above

17. Which type of software cannot be loaded through the Add/Remove Programs icon?

    a. old MS-DOS programs

    b. Windows 2.x programs

    c. Windows 3.x programs

    d. all non-32-bit programs

18. What I/O port assignment might be used for a NIC?

    a. 210–21F

    b. 350–35F

    c. 2AF–2FF

    d. 300–30F

19. One caution about using a screen saver is:

    a. Some screen savers can crash Windows NT Server.

    b. Some screen savers are resource intensive and can slow down a server.

    c. Some screen savers actually burn out the monitor.

    d. Some screen savers can hang Windows NT Server.

20. Which tool is an example of an icon that is added into the Control Panel by a software application that you install?

    a. Display icon

    b. Keyboard icon

    c. Find Fast icon

    d. UPS icon

21. How many IP addresses can be bound to a single NIC in Windows NT Server?

    a. five

    b. four

    c. three

    d. two

    e. one

HANDS-ON PROJECTS

PROJECT 5-1

In this activity you practice installing a display driver. You need a computer running Windows NT Server or Windows NT Workstation and access to an account with Administrator privileges. You also need the Windows NT Server CD-ROM (or you can click Cancel at this step).

To install the display driver:

1. Install the new driver before installing the new display adapter (if a new adapter is needed) and monitor by clicking the **Start** button, **Settings**, and **Control Panel**.

2. Double-click the **Display** icon and the **Settings** tab.

3. Click the **Display Type** button, then the **Change** button (Figure 5-19).

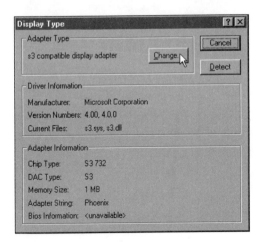

Figure 5-19   Installing a display driver

4. In the Change Display dialog box, highlight the display manufacturer and the display model in the Manufacturers: and Display: boxes. Next, click the **Have Disk** button (Figure 5-20).

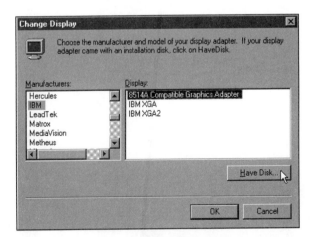

Figure 5-20   Selecting the type of display

5. Insert the Windows NT Server CD-ROM or the manufacturer's driver disk included with the monitor and adapter. Enter the path to the driver disk (e.g., **A:**) and click **OK** (or click **Cancel** if you are just practicing).

6. Click the **Settings** tab and move the Desktop Area bar to the lowest setting. Next, change the Color Palette to 256 colors. (Both these low settings help ensure that you can view the screen after the new adapter and monitor are installed.)

7. Shut down the computer and turn off the power.

8. Install the new adapter card (wear a wrist grounding strap) and the new monitor, according to the manufacturer's instructions.

9. Reboot the computer. If the Windows portion of the boot process cannot be viewed, reboot again using the VGA option.

10. Open the Control Panel **Display** icon and click the **Settings** tab. Set up the display according to the manufacturer's specifications. Use the **Test** button to check the settings.

11. Shut down and reboot again to make sure that the new settings work properly (if they do not, use the VGA option to boot and check the Display settings).

PROJECT 5-2

In this activity you install a mouse or pointing device driver.

To install the mouse or pointing device driver:

1. Click **Start**, **Settings**, and **Control Panel**. Next, double-click the **Mouse** icon.

2. Click the **General** tab and the **Change** button.

3. Highlight the new pointing device in the Select Device dialog box and click **Have Disk** (Figure 5-21). (If your device is not displayed, click the Show all devices radio button and look for the device in the dialog box.)

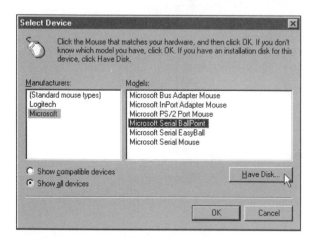

Figure 5-21   Installing a mouse driver

4. Insert the Windows NT Server CD-ROM or the manufacturer's driver disk included with the pointing device. Enter the path to the driver disk (e.g., **A:**) and click **OK** (or click **Cancel** if you are only practicing and do not want to install the driver).

5. Use the **Buttons**, **Pointers**, and **Motions** tabs to configure the new device according to the manufacturer's instructions.

6. Click **Close** in the Mouse Properties dialog box.

7. Shut down the computer and turn off the power.

8. Attach the new pointing device and reboot the computer.

 PROJECT 5-3

In this activity you install a keyboard driver for a new keyboard to attach to a server.

To install the keyboard driver:

1. Click **Start**, **Settings**, and **Control Panel**. Next, double-click the **Keyboard** icon.

2. Click the **General** tab, then click **Change**.

3. In the Select Device dialog box, highlight the new keyboard and click **Have Disk** (Figure 5-22). (If your keyboard is not displayed, click the Show all devices radio button and then look for the device in the dialog box.)

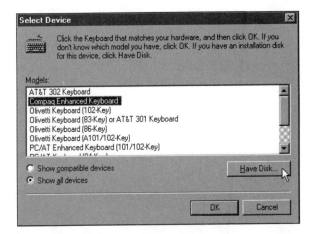

Figure 5-22   Installing a keyboard driver

4. Insert the Windows NT Server CD-ROM or the manufacturer's driver disk included with the keyboard. Enter the path to the driver disk (e.g., **A:**) and click **OK**.

5. Click **Close** in the Keyboard Properties dialog box.

6. Shut down and turn off the computer.

7. With the computer turned off, attach the new keyboard, turn on the computer and reboot.

PROJECT 5-4

In this activity you install NWLink IPX/SPX Compatible Transport.

To install the NWLink IPX/SPX Compatible Transport protocol:

1. Click **Start**, **Settings**, **Control Panel**, and double-click the **Network** icon.
2. Click the **Protocols** tab and click **Add**.
3. Double-click **NWLink IPX/SPX Compatible Transport** (Figure 5-23).

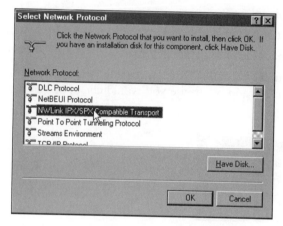

Figure 5-23 Adding the NWLink IPX/SPX Compatible
Transport protocol

4. Insert the Windows NT Server CD-ROM and provide a path to it in the Path box. Click **OK** or **Continue** (depending on your dialog box display).
5. If Remote Access Service is installed, specify if you want to bind NWLink to it for dial-up networking.
6. Click the **Bindings** tab to automatically bind the protocol to the NIC.
7. Close the Network dialog box.
8. Click **Yes** to reboot the computer so that the new settings can be implemented.

PROJECT 5-5

In this activity you install TCP/IP on a Windows NT server. You will need advance information about whether or not there is a DHCP server and the IP addresses of any DNS and WINS servers. (You can still practice even if you do not know this information, but make sure you cancel your changes.)

To install TCP/IP:

1. Click **Start**, **Settings**, and **Control Panel**.
2. Double-click the **Network** icon.
3. Click the **Protocols** tab in the Network dialog box, then click **Add**.
4. Highlight the **TCP/IP Protocol** option and click **OK**.
5. Determine if there is a Windows NT DHCP server on the network (Figure 5-24). If there is one, you would click Yes, and otherwise you would click No. For this practice session, click **No**.

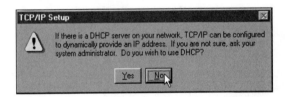

Figure 5-24   Query about DHCP services when installing TCP/IP

6. Insert the Windows NT Server CD-ROM as requested, enter the path to the CD-ROM drive and **\I386**, and click **Continue**. (If Remote Access Service is installed, there is a dialog box that enables you to click Yes to configure for this service.)
7. The installation program returns to the Protocols tab after the files are loaded. Click the **Bindings** tab to automatically configure the NIC for TCP/IP.
8. Click the **Protocols** tab, highlight **TCP/IP Protocol**, and click the **Properties** button, as shown in Figure 5-25.

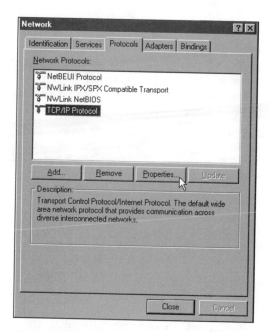

Figure 5-25 Configuring the TCP/IP properties

9. Click the **IP Address** tab and enter the IP address and the network subnet mask (Figure 5-26).

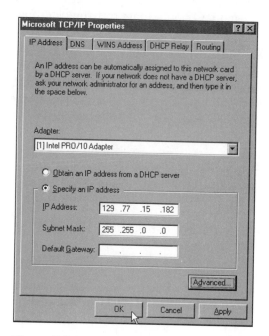

Figure 5-26 Entering the IP address and subnet mask

10. If there is a DNS server, click the **DNS** tab and complete the Host Name and Domain boxes.

11. If there is a WINS server, click the **WINS Address** tab and enter the addresses of the primary and secondary WINS servers. Also, if you specified a DNS server, click the box **Enable DNS for Windows Resolution** (this enables DNS servers also to be used to convert names and IP addresses). Click **Apply** and then **OK**.

12. Click **Close** in the Network dialog box.

13. Windows NT will perform a binding review.

14. Click **Yes** to restart the computer to have the new protocol take effect.

 PROJECT 5-6

In this activity you install a SCSI adapter.

To install a SCSI adapter and driver:

1. Open Windows NT Diagnostics (click **Start, Programs, Administrative Tools (Common), Windows NT Diagnostics**).

2. Click the **Resources** tab to determine which IRQ and I/O port addresses are in use. Write down available IRQ and I/O port addresses.

3. Check the documentation included with the SCSI adapter, and set DIP switches and jumpers (if required) with the IRQ and I/O port settings that you determined are not in use, in Step 2.

4. Turn off the server and install the adapter per the manufacturer's instructions, using a SCSI cable to connect any devices, such as a hard disk, tape drive, or CD-ROM drive. (Wear a wrist grounding strap to reduce static electricity while you are working inside the computer.) Make sure that the SCSI cable is terminated at the last attached device. Also, make sure that each attached device has a different device address, starting with 0 for the first device.

5. Boot the server and check the BIOS setup to make sure that the SCSI adapter is recognized. If it is not, reseat the adapter, reattach the SCSI cable, and try again. Otherwise, consult with the server or SCSI device manufacturer.

6. Continue booting to start Windows NT Server.

7. Click the **Start** button, **Settings**, and **Control Panel**. Next, click the **SCSI Adapters** icon.

8. Click the **Drivers** tab and **Add**.

9. Highlight the manufacturer and model of the adapter, such as Manufacturers: **Adaptec** and SCSI Adapter: **Adaptec AHA-2920 SCSI Host Adapter**. Click **Have Disk**.

10. Insert the drivers disk from the manufacturer or the Windows NT Server CD-ROM, enter the path to the driver (e.g., **A:**), and click **OK**. (If there is a CD-ROM, CD-ROM array, or disk array attached to the adapter, it might be necessary to use a special driver set for the adapter and attached device. Consult the manufacturer's documentation on what driver disk to insert.)

11. Click **Yes** to restart the computer. (If there is a resource conflict when you start the computer, open the Control Panel **SCSI Adapters** icon, click the **Devices** tab, highlight the adapter, and click the **Properties** button to adjust those settings. Also change the jumpers and switches on the adapter, if necessary.)

5

ASPEN CONSULTING: CONFIGURING WINDOWS NT 4.0 SERVER

You are still helping the Press Plastics network administrator to set up the 15 Windows NT file servers they have installed. These assignments focus on configuring the servers.

1. The server administrator of Press Plastics has purchased a specialized control system that enables all of the servers to be connected to one centralized control box having one 17-inch VGA monitor and an ergonomic keyboard with a built-in touch pad and trackball. The administrator has correctly hooked all of the servers to the centralized device, but there are video display problems, such as the wrong colors and size of display on the screen. Also, there are unexpected responses when typing some keyboard characters, and the touch pad does not work at all. What action or actions do you recommend that the administrator take? Create a step-by-step document explaining what the administrator should do.

2. The document that you created to solve the problem in Case Project 1 worked; however, the administrator has another question. The Windows NT servers are located in a computer room in which there are other central computers, and printers attached to those computers. Employees often come into the machine room to talk with the computer operator who manages the computers and distributes printouts. The administrator has found an occasional employee trying out the servers, as though they were on display in a department store. Explain how the administrator might set up security in this situation. Also provide some step-by-step instructions.

3. Press Plastics has a laser printer that uses IPX/SPX to communicate with workstations. Also, they have several UNIX computers that use TCP/IP. What information do you need to help the administrator set up these protocols on the servers? Explain how to set up the protocols.

4. One of the servers seems to have a resource conflict with its NIC. The NIC will not communicate, and the mouse port does not work. How would you find this conflict and solve it?

5. The administrator has installed a new SCSI adapter in one of the servers and attached a tape drive. Unfortunately, the LPT1 printer port now does not work, and the computer does not recognize the new adapter or its tape drive. Explain how you would troubleshoot this situation and properly set up each component. Include information about IRQs and I/O port addresses.

6. Your day is almost over, but the Press Plastics server administrator is on the telephone with another question. The question is about using multiple NICs in some of the servers. They have several extra NICs and are wondering if there is any reason to use them in the servers. Also, they are curious about how to install a second adapter, if they decide to use the extra NICs. What are your recommendations about using and possibly installing those NICs?

CONFIGURING SERVER STORAGE, BACKUP, AND PERFORMANCE OPTIONS

Not long ago 1 GB of disk storage meant filling a specialized computer room with refrigerator-sized cabinets that contained huge sealed disk modules protecting disk platters. One hard disk platter was larger than a Frisbee, and a mainframe disk controller was the same size as a hard disk cabinet. Today hard disks come in 2 GB, 4 GB, and larger sizes, but are housed in a compact unit that can slide into a PC, leaving plenty of room for other components. RAID disk arrays that contain several gigabytes of data are housed in compact, tower-like cabinets that are the same size as a tower PC. A disk controller is the same size or smaller than other PC boards and usually is attached directly to the hard drive. The small size and versatility of hard disks means that it is easy to swap, add, and extend disk storage on a server. Some disk arrays enable you to replace a defective drive without shutting down the computer or the disk array.

AFTER READING THIS CHAPTER AND COMPLETING THE EXERCISES YOU WILL BE ABLE TO:

- PARTITION AND FORMAT HARD DISKS
- EXPLAIN PRIMARY AND EXTENDED DISK PARTITIONS
- CREATE VOLUME SETS
- EXTEND A DISK VOLUME
- DESCRIBE THE FILES NEEDED TO START WINDOWS NT SERVER
- IMPLEMENT DISK REDUNDANCY THROUGH STRIPED SETS, STRIPED SETS WITH PARITY, AND MIRRORED SETS
- PERFORM DISK BACKUPS
- DEVELOP A TAPE ROTATION SCHEME
- CONFIGURE SERVER MEMORY TO IMPROVE PERFORMANCE
- CONFIGURE WINDOWS NT SERVER FOR A UPS

Versatile hard disk storage requires a computer operating system that can take advantage of modern disk features. NT Server has many disk management options. It supports disk fault-tolerance methods such as disk mirroring, duplexing, and striping. NT Server also offers ways to combine disks with different file systems in one server. When disk space starts running out, new disks can be installed and added to an existing disk set. Multiple disks can be combined under one drive letter or divided among several drive letters. Complementing disk storage are two methods to protect data. The first, server backup, is critical for making a copy of data in case one or more disks fail and data cannot be recovered. A UPS is the second method; it prevents disk data loss by providing temporary power when the local power goes out. A UPS also reduces the damage to disk drives and other components due to power failures. In this chapter you learn about configuring and maintaining disk drives, maintaining security through various backup techniques, and configuring server memory to improve performance.

HARD DISK BASICS

When a hard disk is delivered from the manufacturer, it is low-level formatted. A **low-level format** is a software process that marks the location of disk tracks and sectors. Every disk is divided into **tracks**, which are like a number of circles around a disk. To visualize tracks, it helps to think of an old phonograph record filled with grooves. The number of tracks on a hard disk depends on the disk size and manufacturer, just as an old 45 rpm record (one song per side) is smaller and has fewer grooves that a 33.3 rpm record (six or seven songs per side). Each track is divided into sections of equal size called **sectors**. Figure 6-1 illustrates a hard disk divided into tracks and sectors.

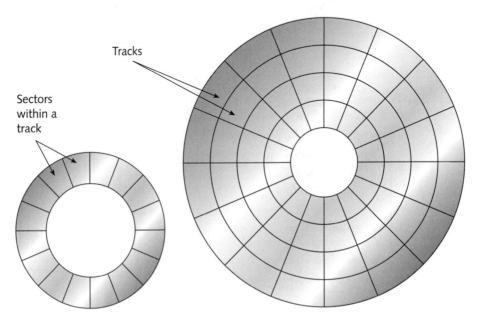

Tracks

Sectors
within a
track

Figure 6-1   A disk divided into tracks and sectors

DISK PARTITIONS

A hard disk that is low-level formatted can be set up for one or more file systems, such as FAT or NTFS. The process of marking or "blocking" a group of tracks and sectors in preparation for a file system is called **partitioning**. Each partition appears as a logical drive—for example, a single disk can be partitioned into drive C for FAT and drive D for NTFS. A partition is made out of **free space** on the disk, that is, space not yet partitioned for use by any file or operating system.

When a drive is partitioned, a **master boot record (MBR)** and a **partition table** are created in the beginning track and sectors on the disk. The MBR is located in the first sector and track of the hard disk and has startup information about partitions and how to access the disk. The partition table contains information about each partition created, such as the type of partition, size, and location. Also, the partition table provides information to the computer about which partition to access first.

A partition is created by using the Windows NT Disk Administrator, which is started from the Administrative Tools (Common) menu (Figure 6-2). Hands-on Project 6-1 at the end of the chapter takes you step by step through creating a partition.

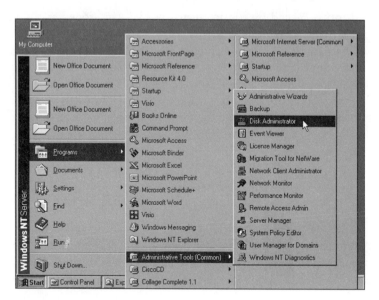

Figure 6-2 Opening the Disk Administrator

There are two views available in the Disk Administrator, Volumes and Disk Configuration. In most cases, you want to use the Disk Configuration view, which is selected from the View menu or by pressing Ctrl-D.

There are two ways to save your changes made through the Disk Administrator. One is to use the Commit Changes Now option to have the change take effect immediately. The other is to close the Disk Administrator instead of using the Commit Changes Now option.

You can delete a partition using the Disk Administrator as well. To delete a partition, click the partition you want to delete. The partition will have a black border to indicate that you have selected it. Open the Partition menu and click Delete. The Disk Administrator gives you a warning that data will be lost. Click Yes to continue the delete process. Click Commit Changes Now on the Partition menu and Yes to confirm the deletion (or exit the Disk Administrator).

PRIMARY AND EXTENDED PARTITIONS

A partition may be set up as primary or extended. A **primary partition** is one from which you can boot an operating system, such as MS–DOS or Windows NT Server. Or it may simply hold files in a different file system format. When you boot from a primary partition, it contains the operating system startup files in a location at the beginning of the partition. For example, the startup files for Windows 95 include IO.SYS and MSDOS.SYS. For Windows NT, those files include BOOT.INI, NTLDR, and NTDETECT.COM (these files are discussed later in this chapter). A partition containing the startup files is called a **system partition**. A single disk must have one primary partition and can have up to four.

An **extended partition** is created from space that is not yet partitioned and is added onto a primary partition. The purpose of an extended partition is to enable you to exceed the four-partition limit of a hard disk. On some computers, an extended partition is not bootable (cannot be a system partition). However, either a primary or an extended partition can hold the Windows NT operating system files, which are the files you loaded into the \Winnt\System32 folder during the installation as described in Chapter 4, "Server Installation." The partition containing the operating system files is called the **boot partition** by Microsoft (even though you might not actually boot the computer from that partition).

 There can be only one extended partition on a single disk.

You create an extended partition in a way that is similar to creating a primary partition. Open the Disk Administrator and click the Partition menu. Click Create Extended and enter the size of the partition (Figure 6-3). Click OK. Open the Partition menu and click Commit Changes Now, then click Yes to confirm that you want to create the partition.

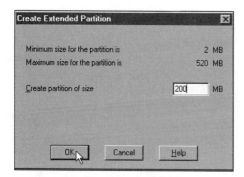

Figure 6-3 Entering the partition size

6

A computer with multiple partitions boots from the partition that is designated as the **active partition**, which must also be a system partition containing the startup files. To determine which partition is designated as active, click each partition and check the status bar at the bottom of the Disk Administrator, as shown in Figure 6-4.

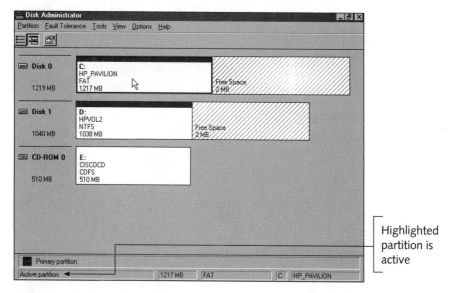

Highlighted partition is active

Figure 6-4 Checking the active partition

Hands-on Project 6-2 shows how to use the Disk Administrator to mark a partition as the active partition.

FORMATTING

After a partition is created, it needs to be formatted for a particular file system. As you learned in Chapter 1, "Networking with Microsoft Windows NT Server," Windows NT supports the FAT and NTFS file-system formats. **Formatting** is a process that creates a table containing file and folder information for a specific file system in a partition. The process also creates a root directory (folder) and a volume label. Once a partition is formatted, it is called a **volume** and can be assigned a drive letter. Assigning a drive letter, such as C, makes it easier to refer to the volume.

 By Microsoft's definition, a volume is any of the following: primary partition, drive in an extended partition, volume set, stripe set, stripe set with parity, and mirrored set. You will learn about all of these types of hard disk setup options in the sections that follow.

To format a partition, open the Disk Administrator and click the partition to be formatted. Click the Tools menu and then click Format (Figure 6-5). The complete steps for formatting a drive are given in Hands-on Project 6-3.

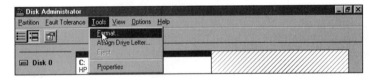

Figure 6-5   Formatting a hard drive partition

 When you format a partition, avoid using the Quick Format option because it does not check for bad sectors during the format.

You can assign a different drive letter to a partition by using the Disk Administrator Tools menu shown in Figure 6-5. To assign a new drive letter to a partition or volume, first select it in the Disk Administrator. Next, click the Tools menu and Assign Drive Letter (Figure 6-6). Select the desired drive letter and click OK.

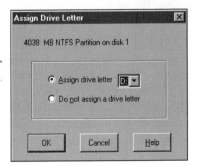

Figure 6-6   Assigning a drive letter

Use caution when reassigning drive letters on an established volume, since there may be programs that rely on a particular drive letter assignment.

Whenever you make a change in the Disk Administrator, for example to partition a drive, format a partition, or assign a new drive letter, update the Emergency Repair Disk (ERD) to reflect the change. Insert the ERD and enter *rdisk /s* from the command line (Start menu, Run option) to update the Emergency Repair Disk. (The RDISK.EXE utility is found in \Winnt\System32.)

6

CREATING VOLUME SETS

A **volume set** consists of two or more partitions that are combined to look like one volume with a single drive letter. For example, you might create a volume set if you have three small hard disks, 1 GB, 1.5 GB, and 2 GB. All three can be partitioned and combined as a set under the single drive letter C. Another reason to use a volume set is if you have several small free partitions scattered throughout the server's disk drives. You might have a 600 MB free partition on one drive, a 150 MB partition on another, and a 70 MB partition on a third. All of these partitions can be formatted and combined into a single 820 MB volume set with its own drive letter.

The advantage of creating volume sets is the ability to manage several small disk drives more easily or to maximize the use of scattered pockets of disk space across several disks. The disadvantage is that if one disk in the volume set fails, the entire volume is inaccessible. For this reason, avoid placing mission-critical data and applications on a volume set. The volume set might be used to store data that is already backed up on another medium, such as tape. For instance, a previous year's accounting data might be stored on a volume set. The data is already saved on tape, but a copy is left on disk for fast lookup and reporting.

Creating a volume set requires only a few steps. In the Disk Administrator, hold down Ctrl and click each partition that will be included in the volume set. Formatted partitions must have the same file system to be placed in the same volume set. Open the Partition menu and click Volume Set. Enter the size of the volume set and click OK.

EXTENDING A VOLUME

Sometimes the capacity of a particular NTFS disk drive is at a premium because it contains a frequently used application with growing data files or because the number of users who access that disk increases. One way to expand the capacity is to add another disk, creating an extended volume set consisting of the original disk and the new disk. When you consider this option, remember that it comes with the same risks as a volume set. If one disk fails, the set cannot be accessed. However, in some situations it is one solution for quickly extending a full disk until larger disk drives are purchased.

Extending a volume is set similarly to creating a volume set. In the Disk Administrator, press and hold down Ctrl, clicking the volume you want to extend. While still holding down Ctrl, click each partition that will be in the extended volume set. From the Partition menu, select Extend Volume Set. Click OK. Use the Partition menu option Commit Changes Now, or exit Disk Administrator, to implement the new extended volume set.

FILES NEEDED AT STARTUP

The system partition must have several files in the root directory for the computer's startup procedures. The NT Loader (NTLDR) is one of those files. NTLDR is run before the Windows NT kernel is started. It initiates the operating system selection on a dual-boot system, for example, and it performs hardware detection. The file BOOTSECT.DOS is needed if there are other operating systems besides NT on the computer. The operating system selection options presented by NTLDR are determined by the contents of the BOOT.INI file. If no operating system is selected after a specified time, NTLDR boots the operating system specified as the default by BOOT.INI.

 RISC computers use the file OSLOADER, located in the \OS\Nt40 folder, instead of NTLDR. OSLOADER does not use BOOTSECT.DOS, BOOT.INI, or NTD.ETECT.COM because these functions are built into OSLOADER.

After an operating system is selected, NTDETECT.COM checks the computer's hardware, such as bus and adapter types, video, ports, keyboard, floppy disk, and pointing device. If you are using SCSI adapters, it may be necessary for NTBOOTDD.SYS, which is used as the driver for the SCSI adapters, to be in the root directory.

 NTBOOTDD.SYS is normally created from the manufacturer's driver disk. Copy the manufacturer's driver to the root directory and rename that file NTBOOTDD.SYS.

After the hardware is detected, the Windows NT kernel, NTOSKRNL.EXE, is loaded from the boot partition by NTLDR. At the same time, the HAL.DLL (Hardware Abstraction Layer) is loaded from the boot partition. NTLDR also loads the device drivers for the computer hardware. Each time the operating system loads, it also checks the system key to validate your authorization (license) to use Windows NT Server. Table 6-1 summarizes the components needed to boot Windows NT Server from one or more hard disks.

Table 6-1   Windows NT Server Startup Files

System Component	Purpose	Location
NTLDR	Initiates the startup process, operating system selection, and hardware detection	Root directory of the system partition
BOOTSECT.DOS	Used for dual-boot systems	Root directory of the system partition
BOOT.INI	Used by NTLDR to obtain startup information, such as which operating systems are available	Root directory of the system partition
NTDETECT.COM	Detects the computer's hardware	Root directory of the system partition
NTBOOTDD.SYS	Driver for SCSI adapters, if present	Root directory of the system partition
NTOSKRNL.EXE	Windows NT kernel	Winnt\System32 folder in the boot partition
HAL.DLL	Hardware Abstraction Layer	Winnt\System32 folder in the boot partition
Hardware device drivers	Drivers for communication between hardware and the Windows NT kernel	Winnt\System32 folder in the boot partition

6

IMPLEMENTING DISK REDUNDANCY

Windows NT has several options to protect data on a server's hard disks. The hot fix is one of the most basic protective features. Other features include techniques for striping and mirroring disks. Each of these is described in the sections that follow.

OPERATING SYSTEM DISK PROTECTION

One of the most important hard disk protection features in Windows NT Server is the ability to perform a hot fix for data when a bad spot is located on a disk. In a **hot fix**, the operating system temporarily stores data that cannot be written immediately because of a disk problem at that location, such as damage to the disk surface. The operating system next locates another disk area that is free from damage, and writes the stored data there. Many server operating systems perform hot fix operations instantaneously and without intervention from the server administrator. The instantaneous action prevents users from experiencing an interruption in service, guarantees that the data is not lost, and prevents error messages such as "I/O Error" and "Abort, Retry, Fail?"

The Windows NT file system on an NT server performs hot fixes in one of two ways: sector sparing and cluster remapping. **Sector sparing** is available only on disk drives connected to a SCSI adapter. It also requires that mirrored disks or a striped RAID array be set up through the Disk Administrator. In sector sparing, the operating system designates certain sectors as reserved, or as spares, to be used when a disk write problem occurs. Information about which sectors are spares is kept by the hard disk's device driver. When a bad disk sector is discovered, the operating system obtains a copy of the data to be written by accessing the mirrored or RAID backup drives, and writes it to a spare sector on the drive to which the operating system originally tried to write it. It also keeps a record of the bad sector so that there are no further attempts to write to it. Sector sparing is supported for FAT and NTFS.

On non-SCSI drives, Windows NT uses a technique called **cluster remapping**. When a damaged disk area is discovered, the operating system designates the disk cluster with the bad sector as damaged. It finds an undamaged cluster and writes the information there. The locations of bad clusters are recorded into the operating system file $BadClus. Cluster remapping is only available on volumes that use NTFS.

A cluster may contain one or more sectors, depending on how disk resources are allocated by the operating system. Windows NT keeps information about how the sectors are allocated into clusters in the file $Bitmap.

DISK STRIPING

As you learned in Chapter 3, "Server Hardware," RAID level 0 is disk striping. The main purpose for striping disks is to extend the life of hard disk drives by spreading data equally over two or more drives. Spreading the data divides the drive load so that one drive is not working more than any other. Another advantage of striping is that it increases disk performance. Contention among disks is equalized, and data is accessed faster for both reads and writes than when it is on a single drive. Striping has been used successfully on mainframes and minicomputers for years, as a way to enhance disk performance. Both FAT and NTFS support striping.

In Windows NT, striping requires at least two disks and can be performed over as many as 32. The total number of striped disks is called a striped set. Equal portions of data are written in 64 KB blocks in rows or stripes on each disk. For example, suppose that you have set up striping across five hard disks and are working with a 720 KB data file. The first 64 KB portion of the file is written to disk 1, the next 64 KB portion is written to disk 2, the third portion is written to disk 3, and so on. After 320 KB are spread in the first data row across disks 1 through 5, the next 320 KB are written in 64 KB blocks in the second row across the disks. Finally, there will be 64 KB in the third row on disk 1, and 16 KB in the third row on disk 2 (Figure 6-7).

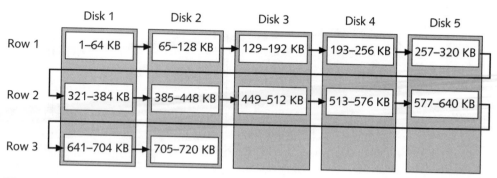

Figure 6-7 Disk striping

Because of its high performance, striping is useful for volumes that store large databases or for data replication from one volume to another. Striping is not a benefit when most of the data files on a server are very small, such as under 64 KB. Also, data can be lost when one or more disks in the stripe set fail, because the system has no automated way to rebuild data. If you use striping to increase disk performance for a critical database, consider frequently backing up that database on tape or through Microsoft's directory replication service, which is described in Chapter 9, "Managing Server Folders, Permissions, and Software Installation."

A **stripe set** is created through the Disk Administrator. To create a stripe set, first ensure that the disks are partitioned. Press Ctrl and click each partition to be in the stripe set. Next, open the Partition menu, click Create Stripe Set, and enter the size of the set. Click OK and either exit the Disk Administrator or use the Commit Changes Now option in the Partition menu to implement the changes.

STRIPING WITH PARITY

Fault tolerance is better for a **stripe set with parity** than for a simple stripe set. Striping with parity requires a minimum of three disk drives. Parity information is distributed on each disk so that if one disk fails, the information on that disk can be reconstructed. The parity used by Microsoft is Boolean logic containing information about the data contained in each row of 64 KB data blocks on the striped disks. Using the example of storing a 720 KB file across five disks, one 64 KB parity block is written on each disk. The first parity block is always written in row 1 of disk1, the second is in row 2 of disk 2, and so on, as illustrated in Figure 6-8.

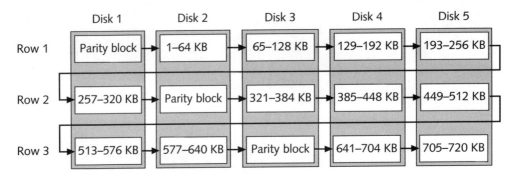

Figure 6-8   Striping with parity

When you set up striping with parity, the performance is not as fast as with striping without parity, because it takes longer to write the data and calculate the parity block for each row. However, accessing data through disk reads is as fast as for striping without parity. Striping with parity is a viable fault-tolerance choice for mission-critical data and for applications, when full mirroring is too expensive. It works well with disk arrays that are compatible with RAID level 5. Striping with parity is particularly useful in a client/server system that uses a separate database for queries and creating reports, because it provides fast disk read performance for obtaining data. In applications such as a customer service database that is constantly updated with new orders, disk read performance will be slower than with striping without parity.

If you use striping with parity, consider adding 12 MB or more of RAM, because striping with parity uses more memory than mirroring. Stripe sets with parity take up disk space for the parity information. The amount of storage space used is based on the formula $1/n$ where n is the number of physical disks in the set. For example, if there are four disks, the amount of space taken for parity information is 1/4 of the total space allocated in the disk partitions. This means you get more usable disk storage if there are more disks in the set. A set of eight 2 MB disks yields more usable storage than a set of four 4 MB disks in a stripe set with parity.

Use the Disk Administrator to create a stripe set with parity. Press Ctrl and click each partition for the set, then click the Fault Tolerance menu, and choose Create Stripe Set with Parity. Enter the size of the set and click OK. Close the Disk Administrator to initiate the change.

Make sure you use partitions of equal size to create stripe sets with parity. If the partitions are different sizes, the Disk Administrator creates stripes using the size of the smallest partition. However, the physical disks containing the partitions do not need to be of equal size.

DISK MIRRORING

As you learned in Chapter 3, disk mirroring involves creating a shadow copy of data on a backup disk, and it is RAID level 1. It is the most guaranteed form of disk fault tolerance because the data on a failed drive is instantly recovered from the mirrored drive. Also, disk read performance is the same as for reading data from any single disk drive. The disadvantage of mirroring is that the time needed to create or update information is doubled because the data is written twice, once on the main disk and once on the shadow disk. However, disk writing in mirroring is normally faster than writing to disk when you use stripe sets with parity.

Disk mirroring is particularly well suited for situations in which data is mission-critical and cannot be lost under any circumstances, such as customer files at a bank. It also is valuable in situations in which computer systems cannot be down for long, such as in medical applications or in 24-hour manufacturing. The somewhat slower update time is offset by the assurance that data will not be lost and that the system will be quickly back on line after a disk failure. However, if fast disk updating is the most important criterion for disk storage, as is the case for copying files or in taking orders over a telephone, then disk striping may be a better choice than mirroring.

The NT Server system and boot partitions can be in a mirrored set, but they cannot be in a volume set, stripe set, or a stripe set with parity. If the system partition is on a mirrored set, create a floppy disk containing the Windows NT startup files, because you cannot boot from the mirrored disk until it has the startup files and has been made the active partition. Also, for best performance use identical disks for mirroring and identical disk controllers for duplexed disk mirroring.

Hands-on Project 6-4 shows you how to use the Disk Administrator to create a mirrored set.

INCREASING DISK PERFORMANCE AND LONGEVITY

Disk drives that are over 80% full also are subject to increased mechanical wear. When a disk drive failure occurs, it is most likely to be due to a read head that has physically touched the disk platter. In all cases this causes damage to the platter, sometimes resulting in the release of metal fragments within the sealed module of the disk unit. One way to increase disk performance and extend the life of hard disks is to make sure that one disk is not accessed and working harder than other disks in a multiple-disk server. Striping and striping with parity are two ways to equalize the disk load. If neither of these methods is employed, then you should consider monitoring disk usage and manually relocating files on a periodic schedule. By relocating files you can distribute disk access more evenly.

Extensive fragmentation of files on a disk is another cause of extra wear. **Disk fragmentation** exists when the files on a disk gradually become spread over the hard drive, with empty pockets of space scattered throughout. Fragmentation occurs normally over time, the result of creating new files and deleting files. Full and fragmented drives cause the read head to move across the disk more extensively than in situations where disks are maintained regularly. **Defragmenting** a disk is a process used to reorganize files to reduce the number of empty spaces between files. Windows NT does not come with defragmenting software, but you can purchase it from other software companies. Disk defragmenting software is a sound investment as a way to extend the life of disk drives.

On a busy server, drives should be defragmented every week to two weeks. On less busy servers, defragment the drives at least once a month. Also, encourage users to defragment their workstation drives once a month.

DISK SECURITY THROUGH BACKUP TECHNIQUES

One of the best ways to make sure that you do not lose valuable information on a hard disk is to back up information to tape. In Chapter 3, you learned how to select and install a tape drive and SCSI adapter. Tape backups can be performed from the server or from a workstation connected to the server. There are several advantages to performing backups from a tape drive installed in the server:

- There is no extra load on the network due to traffic caused by transferring files from the server to a tape drive on a workstation.

- By equipping each server with its own tape drive, you have a way to perform backups on a multiple server network even if one of the tape drives fails on a server. Backups can be performed from the tape drive on one of the other servers.

- Backing up from a tape drive on a server provides more assurance that the Registry is backed up, since access to the Registry is limited, except for backups performed at the server.

The **Registry** contains vital information about a server's setup. The advantage of performing backups on a workstation connected to the server is that you can perform all backups from one place, instead of walking to each server to start backups. Besides the extra network load, a disadvantage is that there is a possibility that an intruder can tap into the network and obtain backup data going from the server to the workstation.

In general it is easiest to perform backups on a tape drive connected to the server, especially on large networks where traffic and risks from intruders are a concern.

Once the tape hardware is installed and you have installed Windows NT Server, the next step is to establish tape backup procedures. There are several types of backups from which to choose. Most popular is a **full backup**, in which all volumes, directories, and files are backed up. One form of the full backup is to create an exact image of the disk files on tape. Image backups are performed in binary format, storing the information bit by bit. Image backups are fast, but have the disadvantage that if only a few files on the hard disk are accidentally deleted or corrupted, all files must be restored from tape. There is no option to restore only selected files or selected directories. A more widely used full backup procedure is called file-by-file, whereby data is stored as files on tape. In this format, the network administrator and backup operators can restore single files or selected directories as needed. The backup software that accompanies NT Server has file-by-file backup options, but no image backup capabilities. Backup software from tape system vendors may come with image backup options.

Another method is the **incremental backup,** which backs up only those files that have changed since the previous backup, as indicated by the archive attribute on the file. Many organizations combine full and incremental backups because there is not enough time to back up all files after each workday. One method is to perform full file-by-file backups on a Friday night or a weekend day, when there is less activity on servers. During the week, incremental backups are performed at the end of each workday. If a disk fails on Wednesday, the restore procedure is to first restore the volume from the previous weekend's full backup. Then restore from Monday's incremental backup, followed by Tuesday's incremental backup.

The NT Server backup software recognizes five backup options, which are variations of full or incremental backups. The first is called the normal backup, which is the same as a full file-by-file backup. The advantage of performing full backups each night is that all files are on one tape or tape set. Another NT option is the copy backup, which backs up only the files or directories selected. The archive attribute, showing that a file is new or updated, is left unchanged. For example, if the archive attribute is present on a file, the copy backup does not remove it. Copy backups are used in exceptional cases where a backup is performed on certain files, but the regular backup routines are unaffected because the copy backup does not alter the archive bit.

Windows NT has an incremental option that backs up only files that have the archive attribute. When it backs up a file, the incremental backup removes the archive attribute. A differential backup is the same as an incremental, but it does not remove the archive attribute. Incremental or differential backups are often mixed with full backups. The advantage of the differential backup is that only the most recent full backup and the most recent differential are required to restore data. That saves time over incremental restores, which require the full backup and all incrementals dating back to the last full backup.

The daily backup option backs up only files that have been changed or updated on the day the backup is taken. It leaves the archive attribute unchanged, so that regular backups are not affected. A daily backup is valuable when there is a failing hard disk and little time to save the day's work up to that point. It enables the administrator to save only that day's work, instead of all changed files, which may span more than a day.

To perform a tape backup of all files on drive C, for example, you need to have the tape system installed, and you need enough formatted blank tapes to hold the information you plan to back up from the server. Before starting a backup it may be necessary to format a new tape or retension new and used tapes. Both tasks can be performed from the Operations menu in the NT Backup utility. Backup is started from the Administrative Tools (Common) menu (see Figure 6-2). Formatting deletes existing information and automatically retensions a tape. Retensioning makes sure that the tape starts from the beginning of the reel.

Once the tape is inserted and ready, highlight drive C and click the Select menu and then click Check (Figure 6-9). Click the Backup button and complete the information in the Backup Information dialog box. Make sure that you select the option to back up the Registry, which contains vital information about the server setup and user accounts. The complete process for backing up a disk to tape is covered in Hands-on Project 6-5 at the end of the chapter.

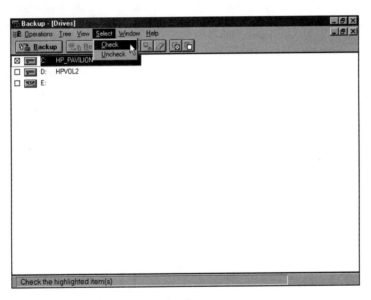

Figure 6-9   Starting a tape backup

TAPE ROTATION

Many server administrators develop a tape rotation method to ensure alternatives in case there is a bad or worn tape. One common tape rotation method is called the Tower of Hanoi procedure. This method rotates tapes so that some are used more frequently than others. If one of the frequently used tapes is bad, a less frequently used tape is likely to be intact (although some recent data cannot be restored). In a given week the tapes are rotated Monday through Saturday, as shown in Figure 6-10, which is an example rotation scheme for one server that requires one tape for the backup and requires that a full backup be performed each day.

Sunday	Monday	Tuesday	Wednesday	Thursday	Friday	Saturday
1	2 Tape 1, Set 1 (Set 2 in Bank)	3 Tape 2, Set 1	4 Tape 1, Set 1	5 Tape 3, Set 1	6 Tape 2, Set 1	7 Tape 4, Set 1
8	9 Tape 1, Set 2 (Set 1 in Bank)	10 Tape 2, Set 2	11 Tape 1, Set 2	12 Tape 3, Set 2	13 Tape 2, Set 2	14 Tape 4, Set 2
15	16 Tape 1, Set 1 (Set 2 in Bank)	17 Tape 2, Set 1	18 Tape 1, Set 1	19 Tape 3, Set 1	20 Tape 2, Set 1	21 Tape 4, Set 1
22	23 Tape 1, Set 2 (Set 1 in Bank)	24 Tape 2, Set 2	25 Tape 1, Set 2	26 Tape 3, Set 2	27 Tape 2, Set 2	28 Tape 4, Set 2
29	30 Tape 1, Set 1 (Set 2 in Bank)					

Figure 6-10   An example tape rotation schedule

In this example, there are two sets of tapes with four tapes in each set. Each complete set is rotated every week, and the four tapes within a set are rotated each day of the week. For instance, during the first week of the month, set 1 is in use while set 2 is stored away from harm in a bank vault or safe deposit box. In the second week, set 1 is stored and set 2 is put to use. On Monday of the first week, the first tape in set 1 is used. On Tuesday, the second tape in set 1 is used, and so on. Tapes 1 through 4 are rotated throughout the week, but some tapes are used more than others. This method has several advantages. First, tapes 3 and 4 in each set are used half as much as tapes 1 and 2. If there is a problem with tape 1 or 2, tapes 3 and 4 are likely to be usable. If any one of the tapes in the set is bad, it is unlikely that you will lose more than a single day's work. By having one complete set in a bank vault, you are protected if there is a fire, flood, or theft at the office. The most you would lose is a week of work. Storing tapes in a vault is one example of planning for disaster recovery.

 Store tapes carefully to avoid damage from excessive heat or from sitting in the sun. Also, tapes can be damaged by placing them next to the power supply of a PC or on top of a video monitor.

CONFIGURING A SERVER TO IMPROVE PERFORMANCE

Besides properly setting up disk resources for fault tolerance and performance, you can tune memory to improve the server's performance. Two ways to tune memory are to configure virtual memory and to set memory to match the number of users on the server.

CONFIGURING VIRTUAL MEMORY

Virtual memory is disk storage that Windows NT Server uses to expand the capacity of the physical RAM installed in the PC. When the currently running programs and processes exceed the RAM, they treat disk space allocated for virtual memory just as if it really is memory. The disadvantage is that memory activities performed through virtual memory are not as fast as those performed in RAM (although disk access and data transfer speeds can be quite fast). Virtual memory works through a technique called **paging**, whereby blocks of information, called pages, are moved from RAM into virtual memory on disk. On a Pentium computer, data is paged in blocks of 4 KB. For example, if the system has a 7 KB block of code that it is not presently using, it will divide the code block into two pages, each 4 KB in size (part of one page will not be completely full). Next, both pages will be moved to virtual memory on disk until needed. When the processor calls for that code block, the pages are moved back into RAM.

Before virtual memory can be used, it must first be allocated for this purpose by tuning the operating system. The area of disk that is allocated for this purpose is called the **page file**. A default amount of virtual memory is always established when Windows NT Server is installed, but the amount should be checked by the administrator to ensure that it is not too large or too small.

Besides size, the location of the page file is important. For example, server performance is better if the page file is not placed on the boot partition (containing the system files). However, if there are multiple disk drives, performance is improved by placing a page file on each drive, but not on the drive containing the boot partition. Also, Microsoft does not recommend putting a page file on volumes set up as a stripe set with parity or on the mirrored (backup) disk in a mirrored set.

 The page file is called PAGEFILE.SYS and can be viewed at the root level by using NT Explorer or My Computer.

A general rule for sizing a page file is to start with the amount of installed RAM plus 12 MB. For a server with 120 MB of RAM the page file should be at least 132 MB (120 MB RAM and 12 MB extra). To set virtual memory, open the Control Panel and click the System icon and then the Performance tab. Click the Change button to adjust the allocation. Highlight the drive that will contain the page file. Set the initial page file size to match your calculation for the size that is needed. Set the maximum size so that it affords plenty of room for growth, such as 50 MB or more over the initial size you calculated.

Windows NT always starts at the initial size and only uses additional space as needed. Click the Set button to implement the change (Figure 6-11).

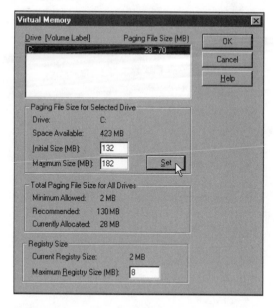

Figure 6-11   Configuring virtual memory

Also, there is a box to set the maximum size for the Registry file. As a general rule, the maximum Registry size is 25% of the initial page file size, which is 33 MB for a page file size of 132 MB (132 * 0.25). Click OK to save the changes, and click OK again to leave the System Properties dialog box.

CONFIGURING MEMORY TO MATCH THE USER LOAD

Memory is divided between server functions and network connectivity functions. The server functions include software applications, printing, and currently running services. Network connectivity is related to the number of user connections at a given time. Server functions use RAM and paging. The network connectivity functions only use RAM. If the server performance is slow because memory is busy, the network memory parameters should be checked and tuned.

If the initial size of server memory is set too small, server performance can be affected. The constant expansion of the page file to a larger size causes disk fragmentation, and applications take longer to start.

Network memory is adjusted from the Network icon on the Control Panel. Double-click the Network icon and then click the Services tab. Highlight the Server service and click the Properties button, as shown in Figure 6-12.

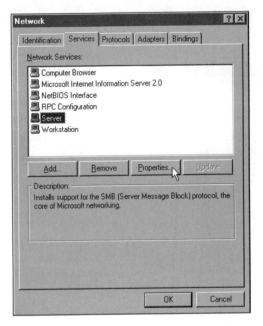

Figure 6-12   The Network Services tab

The memory optimization settings on the Server dialog box are described in Table 6-2. For example, if a server has 120 users who regularly access files, the Maximize Throughput for File Sharing option should be checked; if there are only 32 users on a small network, check the Balance radio button. (You can practice tuning memory in Hands-on Project 6-6.)

Table 6-2   Configuring Server RAM

Optimizing Memory Settings	Purpose
Minimize Memory Used	Optimizes the memory used on servers with 10 or fewer simultaneous network users
Balance	Optimizes memory use for a small LAN with 64 or fewer users.
Maximize Throughput for File Sharing	Used for a large network with 64 users or more where file serving resources need more memory allocation to make the server efficient
Maximize Throughput for Network Applications	Used on dedicated database servers in a client/server application environment, such as one using Microsoft's SQL Server database
Make Browser Broadcasts to LAN Manager 2.x Clients	Used for networks that have both NT Server and Microsoft's early server operating system, LAN Manager

The memory settings shown in Table 6-2 are based primarily on how caching is handled compared to working sets. Caching involves storing often-used information, such as the contents of a file, in memory. A working set involves assigning physical memory to a process, such as to software application code. The Minimize Memory Used setting simply uses the minimum amount of memory for logged on users. Balance equally divides memory use between caching and working sets. Maximize Throughput for File Sharing gives caching most priority for use of available memory. Maximize Throughput for Network Applications gives working sets most memory and caching least memory.

UPS FAULT TOLERANCE

6

Disk drives, memory, and other key server components can sustain damage from power outages and fluctuations, such as brownouts. Also, the server may lose valuable data when a sudden power problem causes it to shut down without the opportunity to save data. A **UPS (uninterruptible power supply)** is the best fault-tolerance method to prevent power problems from causing data loss and component damage.

There are two kinds of UPS systems commonly marketed: online and offline. **Online UPS** systems provide electrical power to equipment directly from their batteries. Their batteries are always charging from city power, until a power failure strikes. An **offline UPS** connects city power directly to the electrical equipment until it senses a sudden reduction in power, at which time it switches over to batteries. The advantage of an offline UPS is that it is less expensive than the online variety, and batteries often last longer. The disadvantage is that it may not switch to battery power in time to fully protect equipment during a sudden power failure. For this reason, many people prefer online systems for more guaranteed protection.

All UPS systems are designed to provide power for a limited time period, such as 10 to 20 minutes, so a decision can be made about how long the power failure is likely to last and about whether or not to shut down computers immediately. Of course, the amount of time the batteries can provide power depends on how much and what kind of equipment is attached to the UPS. This is why most people attach only critical equipment to a UPS, such as computers and monitors, external disk arrays, and tape drives.

 Some manufacturers recommend against plugging laser printers into a UPS, because those printers draw excessive power when turned on, risking damage to the UPS.

For an extra cost, a UPS system may include circuitry to guard against power surges in which so much power is sent through electrical lines that it may damage motors, power supplies, or electronic components in equipment. Additional circuits may be present in offline UPSs to protect against power brownouts or sags, during which not enough power is available. An online UPS normally regulates power to provide insurance against brownouts as well as outages. Also, many systems have protection for modem lines in case lightning strikes telephone lines. Another feature of modern UPS systems is the ability to communicate information to the computers they support, such as a warning that the power is out or that the UPS batteries are low.

Before connecting a server to a UPS, unpack the equipment and inspect it. Check to be sure that a serial cable is included for communication with the server. After the inspection, shut down the server, attach the UPS serial cable to a serial communications port on the server, such as port 2 (COM2). Plug the UPS into the wall outlet, and plug the server, monitor, and tape drive power cords into the UPS. Turn on the UPS and then power up the server.

After the server boots, log on and open the Control Panel. In the Control Panel, double-click the UPS icon, which is at the bottom of the list. In the UPS dialog box, shown in Figure 6-13, complete the information that applies to the UPS. For example, click the check box, "Uninterruptible Power Supply is installed on:," click the down arrow, and select the communications port, such as COM2. If the UPS can send a message that the batteries are low, check the "Power failure signal" box. Also, check the appropriate interface voltage, positive or negative. Next, indicate the expected battery life and recharge time before selecting the next UPS options, entering that information in the boxes provided on the left side of the dialog box.

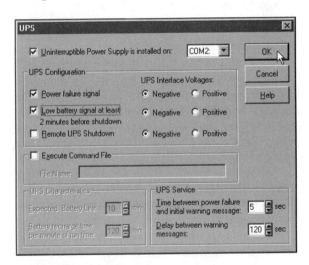

Figure 6-13   The UPS dialog box

If the UPS can send a low battery signal, check the box, "Low battery signal at least 2 minutes before shutdown" and click the appropriate interface voltage. The remote UPS shutdown means that the UPS battery or batteries can accept a signal from the computer to the UPS to instruct them to shut down. Click that option if it is appropriate to the UPS, and indicate the interface voltage. You also can check Execute Command File to set up a command file that automatically runs on notification of a power failure. The command file can be used to run a predefined set of actions before shutting down the computer, such as closing active windows and then starting the shutdown.

In the UPS Service area, you can enter the number of seconds to wait before issuing a notification through the computer that the power is out. Also, when the power goes out, the system will send repeated notifications to logged-on users at a specified interval, such as every 120 seconds.

The UPS capabilities are dependent upon the UPS service, which must be running. In the Control Panel, double-click the Services icon. In the Services dialog box, use the down arrow to scroll to the UPS service. If the UPS service is set to start manually, adjust it to start automatically. Highlight the UPS service and click the Startup button. In the Service dialog box (Figure 6-14), click Automatic as the Startup Type. Click OK to save this information. From now on, the UPS service will start automatically when the server boots. If you want to start the service now, highlight the UPS service and click the Start button. Click OK to leave the Services dialog box.

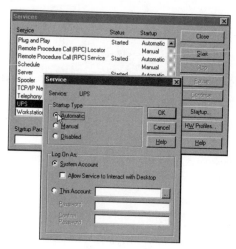

Figure 6-14   Configuring the UPS service

CHAPTER SUMMARY

- The disk storage on a server is the bread and butter of the system because it makes available to network users a wealth of applications, data, and utilities. Properly setting up disk storage is as important as selecting it. The starting point is to partition disk drives through the Disk Administrator. One disk drive can have a combination of primary and extended partitions. Partitions can be used alone or combined, such as in a volume set or in a volume extension.

- A partition is formatted through the Disk Administrator for the file system that is to be used on the server. After partitions are set up and formatted, the next step is to implement a fault-tolerance method. Windows NT supports disk striping, striping with parity, and disk mirroring. Each fault-tolerance method has performance advantages and disadvantages, depending on how the server is used. Disk performance also is affected by fragmentation and by the way in which files are distributed across multiple disks. Configuring RAM and virtual memory are two other methods used to increase server performance.

- After disk drives are set up and ready to accept data, plan to establish a tape backup method to guard against data loss. Windows NT offers a variety of backup options to match an organization's particular needs, including full and partial backup techniques. As you develop a backup scheme, include tape rotation to build in alternatives in case a backup tape cannot be used. Another method for protecting the server's data is to attach the server to a UPS so that data is not lost when there is a local power problem. The UPS also helps guard hardware components from power-related damage.

KEY TERMS

- **active partition** — Partition from which a computer boots, or starts.
- **boot partition** — Partition that holds the Windows NT \Winnt folder containing the system files.
- **cluster remapping** — A fault-tolerance technique used by Windows NT that flags a damaged cluster and finds an undamaged cluster on which to write data.
- **defragmentation** — A software process that rearranges data to fill in the empty spaces that develop on disks and makes data easier to obtain.
- **disk fragmentation** — A normal and gradual process in which files become spread throughout a disk, and empty pockets of space develop between files.
- **extended partition** — Partition that is created from unpartitioned disk space and is linked to a primary partition in order to increase the available disk space.
- **format** — A process that prepares a hard disk partition for a specific file system.
- **free space** — Disk space not yet partitioned for use by a file or operating system.
- **full backup** — A backup of an entire system, including all system files, programs, and data files.
- **hot fix** — A data recovery method that automatically stores data when a damaged area of disk prevents that data from being written. The computer operating system finds another, undamaged area on which to write the stored data.
- **incremental backup** — A backup of new or changed files.
- **low-level format** — A software process that marks tracks and sectors on a disk. A low-level format is necessary before a disk can be partitioned and formatted.
- **master boot record (MBR)** — Data created in the first sector of a disk, including startup information and information about disk partitions.
- **offline UPS** — Battery backup device that waits until there is a power decrease or sag before switching to battery power.
- **online UPS** — Battery backup device that provides power to equipment directly from its batteries at all times.

- **page file** — Disk space reserved for use when memory requirements exceed the available RAM.

- **paging** — Moving blocks of information from RAM to virtual memory on disk.

- **partition** — Blocking a group of tracks and sectors to be used by a particular file system, such as FAT or NTFS.

- **partition table** — Table containing information about each partition on a disk, such as the type of partition, size, and location. Also, the partition table provides information to the computer about how to access the disk.

- **primary partition** — Partition or portion of a hard disk that is bootable.

- **Registry** — A database used to store information about program setup, configurations, devices, and drivers, and information used by NT Server.

- **sector** — A portion of a disk track. Disk tracks are divided into equal segments, or sectors.

- **sector sparing** — Available in Windows NT Server and Workstation for SCSI drives, a fault-tolerance method that reserves certain hard disk sectors so that they can be used when a bad sector is discovered.

- **stripe set** — Two or more disks set up so that files are spread in blocks across the disks.

- **stripe set with parity** — Three or more disks in which files are spread across the disks in blocks, and a parity block is written on each disk to enable data recovery should one disk in the set fail.

- **system partition** — Partition that contains boot files, such as BOOT.INI and NTLDR in Windows NT Server.

- **tracks** — Concentric rings that cover an entire disk like grooves on a phonograph record. Each ring is divided into sectors in which data is stored.

- **uninterruptible power supply (UPS)** — A device built into electrical equipment or a separate device that provides immediate battery power to equipment during a power failure or brownout.

- **virtual memory** — Disk space allocated to link with memory to temporarily hold data when there is not enough free RAM.

- **volume** — A partition that has been formatted for a particular file system, a primary partition, a volume set, an extended volume, a stripe set, a stripe set with parity, or a mirrored set.

- **volume set** — Two or more formatted partitions (volumes) that are combined to look like one volume with a single drive letter.

6

REVIEW QUESTIONS

1. A low-level disk format marks which of the following?

   a. sectors

   b. tracks

   c. partitions

   d. all of the above

   e. only a and b

2. One disk can have how many partitions?

   a. 1

   b. 2

   c. 3

   d. 4

3. Which tool(s) do you use to format a partition?

   a. Network icon in the Control Panel

   b. System icon in the Control Panel

   c. Disk Administrator

   d. Drive Formatter

   e. only a and b

4. When a disk is partitioned, a _____ is automatically created.

   a. file allocation table

   b. master boot record

   c. startup floppy disk

   d. drive table

5. The NTLDR file is located on the _____.

   a. system partition

   b. boot partition

   c. extended partition

   d. start partition

6. Sector sparing is an example of _____.

   a. formatting

   b. partitioning

   c. hot fixing

   d. spindle mapping

7. You have 240 MB of RAM in a server. How large should you make the page file?

   a. 120 MB

   b. 240 MB

   c. 252 MB

   d. There is no formula for sizing the page file.

8. From where do you configure the page file?

   a. Control Panel System icon

   b. Control Panel Server icon

   c. Windows NT Diagnostics

   d. Windows Backup utility

9. How many extended partitions can be on a single disk?

   a. 1

   b. 2

   c. 3

   d. 4

10. You are working on a server that has three 2 GB disks, and you want to combine them under the drive letter C. What technique would you use to combine the disks?

    a. create three partitions, assigning each the same drive letter

    b. create a volume set

    c. create a drive C linked set

    d. create three partitions and use the Combine Format option

11. Which of the following backup options will not remove the archive attribute?

    a. copy

    b. differential

    c. incremental

    d. all of the above

    e. only a and b

12. Which disk setup offers the fastest overall performance?

    a. mirroring

    b. duplexing

    c. striping with parity

    d. striping

6

13. You are configuring a server that is accessed by a maximum of eight users. Which of the following RAM configurations would you use?

    a. Balance

    b. Minimize Memory Used

    c. Maximize Throughput for Network Applications

    d. Maximize Throughput for File Sharing

14. What is the name of the page file?

    a. NTPAGE.SYS

    b. NETCOM.DAT

    c. PAGEFILE.SYS

    d. PAGEFILE.COM

15. Using disk space to help extend RAM is called _____.

    a. linked RAM

    b. virtual memory

    c. extended memory

    d. Disk space cannot be used to extend RAM.

16. _____ is the name of the Windows NT startup file used by RISC computers.

    a. NTDETECT

    b. NTLDR

    c. OSLOADER

    d. NTBOOTDD

17. A _____ Windows NT backup saves all of the selected files to tape.

    a. complete

    b. differential

    c. incremental

    d. normal

18. The Windows NT kernel file is _____.

    a. NTOSKRNL.EXE

    b. BOOT.EXE

    c. KERNEL.EXE

    d. KERNEL.COM

19. Which technique gives you alternatives for restoring data even when a backup tape is damaged and cannot be used?

    a. tape retensioning

    b. tape rotation

    c. tape formatting

    d. tape regeneration

20. Which utility enables you to start the UPS service?

    a. UPS icon on the Control Panel

    b. System icon on the Control Panel

    c. Services icon on the Control Panel

    d. Media icon on the Control Panel

21. Which of the following RAM configurations involves most use of caching?

    a. Balance

    b. Minimize Memory Used

    c. Maximize Throughput for Network Applications

    d. Maximize Throughput for File Sharing

22. You have created a stripe set with parity containing five physical disks each having a 500 MB partition in the stripe set. How much disk space is usable to store files and other information?

    a. 2.5 GB

    b. 2 GB

    c. 1.5 GB

    d. 1 GB

23. A server administrator that you know has neglected to expand the page file to meet demand on a server. What problems might result from this?

    a. the server will boot using a smaller set of processes in the kernel

    b. applications will take longer to start

    c. the disk containing the page file will become fragmented

    d. all of the above

    e. only b and c

24. You have three disks on a server as drives C, D, and E. Drive C contains the Windows NT system files. On which of these disks should you place the paging file?

    a. drive C only

    b. the first two drives, C and D

    c. drives D and E only

    d. any of the drives

HANDS-ON PROJECTS

 PROJECT 6-1

In this activity you create a disk partition. You need access to a computer running Windows NT Server or Windows NT Workstation as well as an account with Administrator privileges.

To partition a disk:

1. Click **Start**, **Programs**, and **Administrative Tools (Common)**.
2. Click **Disk Administrator**.
3. Click the **View** menu and click **Disk Configuration** (or press **[Ctrl]-[D]**).
4. Click the free space on the disk that you want to partition.
5. Click the **Partition** menu and click **Create** (Figure 6-15).

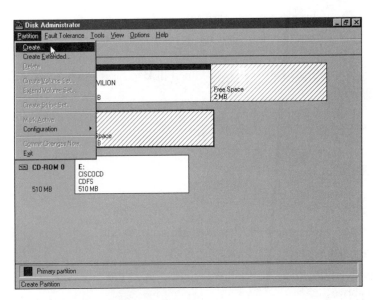

Figure 6-15   Creating a partition

6. Since this is not likely to be the first primary partition, click **Yes** to confirm that you want to create the partition.
7. Enter the size of the partition you want to create, and click **OK** (or click Cancel and stop at this point if you do not want to actually create a partition) (refer to Figure 6-3).
8. Click the **Partition** menu and click **Commit Changes Now**. Click **Yes** to confirm. (Or close the Disk Administrator for the partition to be created.)
9. Note that the partition you have created is a primary partition.

PROJECT 6-2

In this activity you make a partition active.

To designate a partition as the active partition:

1. Click **Start**, **Programs**, and **Administrative Tools (Common)**.

2. Click **Disk Administrator**.

3. Click the **View** menu and click **Disk Configuration** (or press **[Ctrl]-[D]**).

4. If there are two or more partitions, determine which partition is active. Click the first partition and check the status bar at the bottom of the screen. Notice whether or not that partition is designated as active.

5. Repeat Step 3 for each partition on the computer.

6. Click one of the partitions on the computer that is not marked as active. (If there is only one partition, click it).

7. Click the **Partition** menu and click **Mark Active** (Figure 6-16; notice that if the partition is active already, you will have to stop here because Windows NT has disabled the Mark Active option).

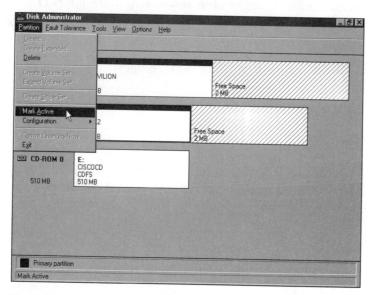

Figure 6-16   Marking a partition active

8. A message warns that the partition has been marked active, and that the computer will in the future boot from the operating system on that partition.

9. Click **OK**.

10. Close the Disk Administrator for the change to take place.

12. Click **Yes** in the Confirm dialog box to save the change or click **No** if you are just practicing and do not want to make the partition active.

PROJECT 6-3

In this activity you format a partition.

To format a partition:

1. Click **Start**, **Programs**, and **Administrative Tools (Common)**.
2. Click **Disk Administrator**.
3. Click the **View** menu and click **Disk Configuration** (or press **[Ctrl]-[D]**).
4. Click the newly created partition you want to format.
5. Click the **Tools** menu and **Format**.
6. Specify the file system for the format.
7. Enter a volume label.
8. Click the option to **Enable Compression**, if you want to use this NTFS feature.
9. Click **Start** to begin the format (or click Cancel to discontinue at this point).
10. Click **OK** and **OK** again.
11. Close the Disk Administrator when the format is complete.

PROJECT 6-4

In this activity you have an opportunity to set up disk mirroring. You need a computer running Windows NT Server. The computer should have two installed disk drives, with the second drive having an amount of unpartitioned free space equal to or greater than the amount of space on the main drive.

To mirror a drive:

1. Click **Start**, **Programs**, and **Administrative Tools (Common)**.
2. Click **Disk Administrator**.
3. Click the **View** menu and click **Disk Configuration** (or press **[Ctrl]-[D]**).
4. Click the main drive partition, such as drive **C**. A black border appears around the box containing the drive information.

5. Press **[Ctrl]** and simultaneously click a free area on another disk, such as on Disk 1. The free area must be at least as large as the volume to be mirrored. This is disk space that is not partitioned, until it is designated as a mirror volume and partitioned for that purpose.

6. Click the **Fault Tolerance** menu and **Establish Mirror** (Figure 6-17).

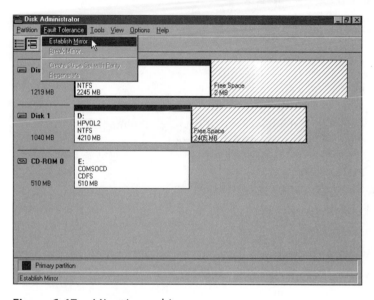

Figure 6-17   Mirroring a drive

7. Click **OK** to confirm that you want to establish the mirror.

8. Close the Disk Administrator.

9. Click **Yes** to restart the computer for the new mirroring to go into effect.

PROJECT 6-5

This activity gives you practice backing up a hard drive on a Windows NT server from the Administrator's account or equivalent. You need a server with the tape drive already set up.

To back up a drive to tape using the NT Backup utility:

1. Make sure that there is a formatted tape in the tape drive and that the drive is turned on.

2. Click **Start**, **Programs**, **Administrative Tools (Common)**, **Backup**. The Backup option automatically detects a previously installed tape drive each time it starts.

3. Highlight one of the drives on the screen, such as drive **C**, click the **Select** option on the menu bar, and click **Check** to check the box in front of the drive (refer to Figure 6-9).

4. Choose **Operations, Backup** from the menu, or click the **Backup** button under the menu bar.

5. On the Backup Information dialog box, check the **Backup Registry** box.

6. Enter a description of the backup, such as **Drive C backup**.

7. Enter **Normal** as the Backup Type:.

8. Click **OK** to start the backup.

 PROJECT 6-6

In this activity you configure the server RAM to match the number of users on a network. Assume that there are 45 users who access the server.

To configure RAM:

1. Click **Start**, **Settings**, and **Control Panel**.

2. Double-click the **Network** icon.

3. Click the **Services** tab.

4. Highlight the **Server** service and click the **Properties** button (refer to Figure 6-12).

5. Click the **Balance** radio button (Figure 6-18).

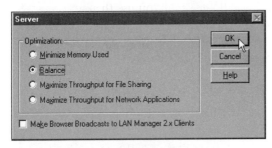

Figure 6-18   Configuring server RAM

6. Click **OK** on the Server dialog box and then **OK** on the Network dialog box.

ASPEN CONSULTING: CONFIGURING DISK STORAGE AND SERVER PERFORMANCE

This week you have two new clients, Micro Electronics and Beckwith College. Both need your help in setting up disk storage and in working with server performance.

1. Micro Electronics is a 24-hours-a-day manufacturing company in Vancouver that is configuring three Windows NT servers on a network. The servers are used for a client/server manufacturing system. One server, equipped with two 8 GB disk drives will hold the client/server application programs, e-mail mailboxes for each user, and user files. A second server will be used for constant updates to a large database and has four 8 GB disk drives. The third server will contain a duplicate of the database on the second server, which will be updated twice a day. The third server also has four 8 GB disk drives and will be used only for reporting and specialized queries of information in the database. Their server administrator is asking for your advice about setting up disk storage on all three servers. Provide your recommendations along with an explanation of what you recommend.

2. Explain what tools you would use to implement the recommendations you made in Case Project 1, including step-by-step instructions for how to set up the disk storage.

3. The server administrator from Beckwith College is experiencing slow performance on the administrative computing server. The problems seem to be related to memory rather than to disk access. What would you advise the administrator to check? What NT Server tools would you use, and how would you use them?

4. Micro Electronics is calling back to report that they have set up the server disk storage according to your recommendations. Now they want to develop a tape backup plan. Devise a plan for them.

5. Beckwith College has a new problem. The Division of Natural Sciences wants to put four large databases on one of the college's academic servers, in order to start a research project for which they have just received funding. The academic server has one 5 GB hard drive, but the server administrator also has a spare 5 GB drive that is not installed in a server. The main purpose of the databases is to provide research information for statistics queries. Explain how the administrator can quickly set up the spare drive so that only one drive letter is used to refer to the old and new drives. Describe step-by-step how you would implement the addition of another drive.

6. Explain the fault-tolerance method you would use on the academic server in Case Project 5.

6

CHAPTER SEVEN

SERVER CLIENTS

Windows NT Server is made to host clients. It is never too early to begin setting up clients to connect to the server, particularly your own workstation and any others that will be used to help test your server installation before it is released to the public. Many different kinds of clients are able to log on to a Windows NT server; however some client operating systems are more suited to a particular organization or purpose than others. For instance, users of older 16-bit Windows software may find the software works better in Windows 95 than in Windows NT.

In this chapter, you examine client operating system options, comparing their advantages and disadvantages. Also, you learn how to set up client operating systems using tools that accompany Windows NT Server. You learn how to set up client protocols, computer names, and other configuration options for a client. On the server side, you learn how profiles are established for organizations in which users want to have identical desktop setups when they access the server.

AFTER READING THIS CHAPTER AND COMPLETING THE EXERCISES YOU WILL BE ABLE TO:

- Describe and compare the client operating systems that work with Windows NT Server
- Discuss client requirements and options for processors, memory, disk storage, and NICs
- Use Network Client Administrator to create a boot disk and enable workstations to install operating systems over the network
- Set up a Windows 95 client, including resolving resource conflicts and configuring the client protocol
- Set up Windows NT Server for Macintosh clients
- Create user and roaming profiles

CLIENT OPERATING SYSTEMS COMPATIBLE WITH NT SERVER

Many types of client workstation operating systems can connect to Windows NT Server, including MS-DOS, Windows 3.1, Windows 3.11 (Windows for Workgroups), Windows 95, and Windows NT Workstation. Some of those operating systems are more compatible with NT Server than others, however. The operating systems and compatibility issues are discussed in the following sections.

 Other operating systems work with NT Server, too, such as OS/2, UNIX, and Macintosh.

MS-DOS

In some cases, it is necessary to have an MS-DOS client to run older, specialized software. One example is a popular address-correction program that is used for mass postal mailings. The program is unreliable when run from an MS-DOS window and so must be run using native MS-DOS. Unfortunately, MS-DOS has many disadvantages for networking, and it is not designed to fully take advantage of a network operating system like NT Server. For example, an MS-DOS client cannot fully accommodate networking features such as establishing a workgroup and offering a shared network drive to other network users. Also, MS-DOS has limited network protocol support.

WINDOWS 3.1 AND 3.11

With its GUI interface, Windows 3.1 is a significant step up from MS-DOS, but its networking abilities are almost as limited. With Windows for Workgroups (WFW or Windows 3.11), Microsoft added significant network capabilities to Windows, such as options to have workgroups and to set up a shared drive (Figure 7-1). WFW represents Windows' true initiation into networking. It is a true peer-to-peer network operating system, which means that each computer on a network can communicate with other computers on the same network. As you learned in Chapter 1, "Networking with Microsoft Windows NT Server," peer-to-peer communications open the way for sharing resources such as files and folders. For example, the File Manager application in Windows was upgraded in WFW to include icons for sharing directories with others.

Although WFW is a network operating system, it still has several disadvantages compared to a full-fledged network-capable operating system like Windows 95 or Windows NT. As is true for Windows 3.1, WFW is designed to run 16-bit applications and has the same 640 KB **conventional memory** limitation. Applications from many software vendors are now written for 32-bit operating systems without the 640 KB memory limit. For instance, WFW is not compatible with the full range of Web tools from either Microsoft or Netscape Communications.

Also, Microsoft's support for WFW is not as comprehensive as it is for Microsoft's later operating systems. This is particularly important for obtaining specialized software drivers, such as NIC drivers.

 Early small computers and operating systems, such as MS-DOS and Windows 3.1, reserved memory above 640 KB and below 1 MB for system use.

Figure 7-1   Drive sharing on a network

WINDOWS 95

Windows 95 is a solid client for NT Server because it has full peer-to-peer and network communications features. It has a greater capacity for disk sharing, printer sharing, network communications, workgroup activities, and other network operations than earlier versions of Windows. Windows 95 introduces an improved GUI interface, with new utilities such as Windows Explorer.

Because it is a 32-bit operating system, Windows 95 can run both 16-bit and 32-bit software applications. This makes it compatible with newer 32-bit software, such as the 32-bit version of Internet Explorer. It also is compatible with new versions of Microsoft Office, new mail systems, and other new 32-bit software, and it offers improved components to handle e-mail communications for MS Mail and MS Exchange.

Another advantage of Windows 95 is compatibility with Plug and Play (PnP), so that when you add hardware to a computer, the hardware is instantly recognized. This is handy when you install a NIC or an additional disk drive. Once the new component is installed, a computer running Windows 95 detects the presence of the component, as long as that component is designed for Plug and Play.

Microsoft also provides stronger technical support for Windows 95 than it does for earlier versions of Windows. Many printer, NIC, and other hardware drivers are available for Windows 95, and if you need a new driver or an enhancement, such as the Dial-Up Scripting Tool for building Netscape or Internet Explorer scripts for dial-up connections, you can download it from Microsoft's Web site, *www.microsoft.com*.

NT WORKSTATION

NT Workstation has all the peer-to-peer and network communications advantages of Windows 95, and with version 4.0, Microsoft equipped NT Workstation with nearly the same updated GUI interface used in Windows 95. As is true for Windows NT Server, the NT Workstation operating system runs in a privileged mode to insulate it from "crashes" caused by software applications. This characteristic has given it a reputation as a reliable workstation operating system for business applications. A disadvantage is that some 16-bit programs will not run in NT Workstation because they attempt to access hardware components directly, an activity not permitted in the privileged mode.

A unique advantage of NT Workstation is that it can act as a small server on a network. Up to 10 computers can access NT Workstation for network file services, such as running software or storing data files.

 Windows NT Workstation can host more than 10 clients, but it is only optimized for 10, which is one of the key differences between NT Workstation and NT Server. Windows 95 can also act as a server through sharing resources such as folders and printers, but does not have the same server capabilities or operating system architecture as Windows NT.

NT WORKSTATION VS. WINDOWS 95

Windows NT Workstation is well suited to situations in which the client runs demanding 32-bit software, such as client/server and complex reporting applications. Also, it is a solid choice as a research workstation for engineering, design, and statistics uses. Because it can be implemented to use the NTFS file system, it also has better security than Windows 95. Many server administrators use Windows NT Workstation because it is resistant to crashes and is compatible with most network management software.

Windows 95, however, is a better choice for situations in which MS-DOS and 16-bit Windows applications are used. Also, Windows 95 requires slightly less memory and fewer disk resources and is less expensive to implement. There are more hardware drivers for Windows 95, particularly for older computer components and devices. Table 7-1 compares Windows 95 and Windows NT Workstation 4.0.

Table 7-1 Windows 95 and Windows NT Workstation 4.0 Compared

Windows 95	NT Workstation 4.0
Extensive 16-bit application support	Some 16-bit applications will not work
Limited security	Advanced security
Susceptible to crashes	Virtually crashproof
Supports one CPU	Supports dual CPU processors
No robust built-in server capability (no accounts, server services, or NTFS security)	Can be a server to about 10 accounts simultaneously
Has the new Windows interface	Has the new Windows interface
Extensive network compatibility	Extensive network compatibility
32-bit operating system	32-bit operating system
Requires less memory and disk storage	Requires more memory and disk storage

7

CLIENT REQUIREMENTS

The following sections detail the requirements and options for clients of a Windows NT Server in terms of CPU, memory, disk storage, and NICs.

PROCESSOR

Windows NT Server can have many kinds of computers as clients, ranging from 8086 computers running MS-DOS to Pentium II computers running Windows NT Workstation. The most important consideration in selecting the client CPU is the work that the client's user needs to perform. Networks and network operating systems are designed to help make users productive. However, users running Windows 3.11 on an 80386 computer cannot benefit from a Windows NT Server network as much as those using a Pentium-based computer and Windows 95 or Windows NT. The Windows 3.11 environment on the 80386 computer is dramatically slower and does not support modern 32-bit software. Contrast that environment to a fast Pentium computer that can run Office 97 software and the latest version of Microsoft Internet Explorer or Netscape Communicator.

When you size a client workstation, consider the software that the user needs to access, both currently and in the near future. For example, a mail presorting application may work adequately in MS-DOS on an 80386 computer, but upgrades to that software are likely to be 32-bit and designed for networking and modern versions of Windows. Also, the 80386 cannot take full advantage of workgroup and domain resource sharing when running MS-DOS. New computers designed for Windows and GUI applications are simply faster, and they offer dynamic opportunities to customize the desktop to make their users' lives easier and more productive. Saving money by keeping an old computer is likely to be far more expensive in lost productivity than purchasing up-to-date equipment. Most users simply do not have the patience or the time to wait several minutes for a job on an older computer and operating system when the same job can be done in seconds on modern equipment.

WORKSTATION MEMORY

The best way to ensure workstation performance on a network is to have adequate RAM. For example, Windows 95 requires a minimum of 8 MB and Windows NT Workstation needs at least 12 MB. The performance of both operating systems is much better if the workstation has at least 16 MB of memory, and preferably 24 to 32 MB. Installing extra RAM is an inexpensive way to achieve very significant performance increases. Resource-intensive applications such as Microsoft Access and PowerPoint respond much more rapidly when extra memory is used. Large print files and scanned images also are handled better through added RAM.

Both Windows 95 and Windows NT Workstation use page files for virtual memory, as is true for Windows NT Server. The page file size for Windows NT Workstation is configured in the same way as for Windows NT Server (refer to Chapter 6, "Configuring Server Storage, Backup, and Performance Options"). In Windows 95, the system can be set to automatically determine the size of the page file, or you can set the size. In general, the page file size for Windows 95 should equal the amount of RAM in the computer plus 8 MB.

If you choose to set the page file size in Windows 95, open the System icon in the Control Panel. Click the Performance tab in the System Properties dialog box and click the Virtual Memory button (Figure 7-2). (Turn to Hands-on Project 7-1 for the complete instructions for configuring the page file size in Windows 95.)

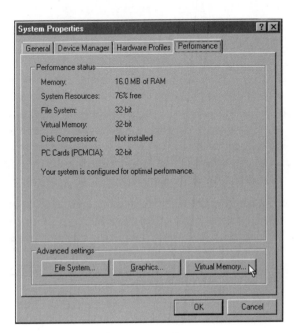

Figure 7-2   Configuring virtual memory in Windows 95

DISK STORAGE

Windows 95 needs about 100 MB or more to store system files on the workstation's hard disk. Windows NT Workstation needs at least 117 MB of disk space. Many early 80486 computers have 250 to 500 MB of disk storage. Early Pentium computers may have 500 MB to 1 GB of disk storage, and more recent Pentium II and Pentium Pro computers come with well over 2 GB. While a client with 250 MB of disk storage can successfully connect to Windows NT Server, this amount does not provide much room after Windows 95 or Windows NT is loaded. If the network employs Microsoft Office or other 32-bit applications, plan on equipping workstations with at least 500 MB to 1 GB of storage, or more if feasible. Disk storage is used up fast on workstations.

SELECTING A WORKSTATION NIC

7

The performance of a network workstation is influenced by its NIC. Older workstations may have 8-bit NICs, while more recent workstations have 16-bit or 32-bit NICs. As is true for the server, the NIC is the workstation's doorway to the network. Consider purchasing 32-bit ISA or PCI NICs for network workstations. A NIC with high throughput increases productivity because a user does not have to wait for the NIC to transfer and receive files.

If your budget allows for the extra expense, purchase a PCI NIC for clients that participate in high-traffic network applications, such as transporting databases over the network. The PCI NIC is faster than an ISA NIC. Also, avoid using old 8-bit NICs with Pentium computers because there may be compatibility problems.

If the workstation is to be connected to an Ethernet network, purchase combination 10/100 Mbps NICs for new workstations, making sure that the NIC matches the network cable media (coaxial or twisted-pair). When purchasing a NIC for token ring, match the NIC speed to that of the network (4 Mbps or 16 Mbps).

Many new workstations come with the NIC built-in. Consider the NIC capacity and options before you purchase a workstation, so you can be certain that the NIC matches the communication needs of the user and the network. Also, always run the test software that comes from the manufacturer to make sure that the NIC is working after it is installed. Run the test software even on systems in which the NIC is preinstalled.

USING NETWORK CLIENT ADMINISTRATOR

Setting up a workstation to communicate on the network is a multiple-step process. First the workstation must have a NIC and an operating system that is capable of network communications. Next it is necessary to install network communications devices, such as the NIC drivers, and to establish network protocols and setup information.

One way to establish connectivity for network workstations is with the assistance of Network Client Administrator in Windows NT Server. As you learned in Chapter 4, "Server Installation," Network Client Administrator creates client boot disks and can be used to install or update client workstation operating systems. It contains operating system installation files for the following clients:

- Windows 95
- MS-DOS version 3.0
- Microsoft LAN Manager for MS-DOS version 2.2c
- Microsoft LAN Manager for OS/2 version 2.2c
- Microsoft TCP/IP-32 for Windows for Workgroups
- Remote Access Server (RAS)

Network Client Administrator is particularly useful when there are tens or hundreds of computers to set up in a short time, such as in a computer lab or when a business has moved to a new building and users need to be online immediately. Before the client operating system is installed or updated, make sure that a license is purchased for the operating system on the workstation.

Network Client Administrator contains options to install operating systems in a shared folder and to create a disk from which to boot a client for a particular operating system. For example, one way to quickly set up clients is to create a boot disk for each client and then log on to Windows NT Server from the client to load the client operating system. The procedures for installing a client in this way are similar to those used in Chapter 4 for performing a Windows NT Server installation over the network. The general steps are as follows:

1. Install the operating system files on a Windows NT server and create a shared directory.

2. Create a floppy boot disk for a particular operating system, such as for Windows 3.11 or Windows 95. (Specific steps for Windows 95 are given in Hands-on Project 7-7 at the end of the chapter.)

3. Use the boot disk to boot the client workstation, and then access the network to load the operating system files from the shared NT server directory. (See Hands-on Project 7-8.)

To complete the first step, start Network Client Administrator from the Administrative Tools (Common) menu. Select the option to install the operating system files. Click the radio button to Copy Files to a New Directory in the Share Network Client Installation Files dialog box. Indicate a folder path for the shared files, such as \Client and enter a directory share name, such as Client. Insert the Microsoft Windows NT Server CD-ROM, specify the path to the CD-ROM, and click OK to load the operating system files. After the files are copied, Windows NT Server automatically sets up the shared folder containing the operating system files. Table 7-2 lists the subfolders created in the shared folder.

Table 7-2   Windows NT Server Network Client Administrator Shared Folders

Subfolder	Contents
Lanman	Microsoft LAN Manager for MS-DOS 2.2c
Lanman.OS2	Microsoft LAN Manager for OS/2 version 2.2c
Msclient	Microsoft MS-DOS 3.0 for network clients
RAS	Remote access files for MS-DOS
\Srvtools\win95	Network administration tools for Windows 95 clients
\Srvtools\winnt	Network administration tools for Window NT Workstation clients
\Tcp32wfw	TCP/IP software for Microsoft Windows 3.11
\Win95	Microsoft Windows 95

To create the boot disk, start Network Client Administrator from the Administrative Tools (Common) menu. In the Network Client Administrator dialog box, click the option to Make Network Installation Startup Disk (Figure 7-3). Follow the steps as indicated in Hands-on Project 7-7 to finish creating the boot disk.

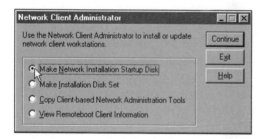

Figure 7-3   Making a boot disk for a client

The third step is to install the operating system files on the client (an existing operating system can also be updated using these steps). First back up the workstation, if it already contains an operating system and work files. Check the BIOS of the workstation and make sure that it is set to boot from drive A: first (refer to Chapter 4). Turn off the workstation, insert the boot disk you made into drive A:, and power on the workstation, which will boot from the disk in drive A:. Access the shared folder on the server that contains the operating system files. Run Setup.exe (for Windows 95 or lower) or Winnt.exe (for Windows NT Workstation) to install the operating system files on the client. (See Hands-on Project 7-8.)

SETTING UP AN EXAMPLE CLIENT

As a rule, the client operating system needs to be configured for network connectivity. Windows 95 offers a good example because it has many network connectivity options. When you set up Windows 95, begin by installing the NIC driver from the Network icon in the Windows 95 Control Panel.

The Windows 95 Network dialog box is somewhat different from the Network dialog box in Windows NT, in that there are three tabs for Windows 95: Configuration, Identification, and Access Control. The Configuration tab is used to set up particular network components, such as a NIC or a protocol. The Identification tab is used for setting up the workstation's network name. The Access Control tab is where workstation owners can specify how others are allowed to access information at their workstation, such as how folders are shared. Select the Configuration tab and click the Add button to install the NIC driver (Figure 7-4).

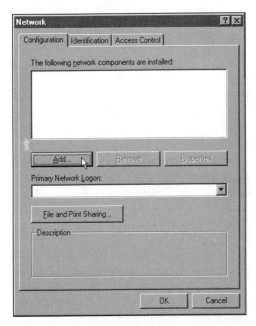

Figure 7-4   The Configuration tab in the Network dialog box

The next dialog box shows suggested network components, including Client, Adapter, Protocol, and Service. Double-click Adapter to install the NIC. The next dialog box shows a wide range of network adapter manufacturers on the left, such as 3COM, AST, Cabletron, Compaq, Hewlett-Packard, IBM, and Intel, with their corresponding cards shown in a box on the right. Highlight the NIC manufacturer and then the model (Figure 7-5). Click the Have Disk button to load the drivers from the floppy disk that came with the NIC.

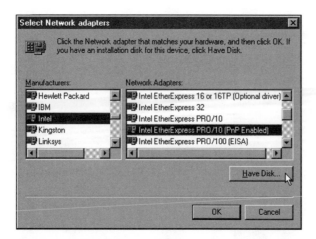

Figure 7-5   Selecting the NIC

In the Install From Disk dialog box, specify the path from which to load the driver, such as A:\. Insert the driver disk and then click OK to load the driver. After the driver is loaded, the Network dialog box Configuration tab is displayed again, but with the NIC now shown in the box entitled "The following network components are installed" (see Figure 7-4). Highlight the NIC and click the Properties button to configure the NIC. The Properties dialog box has four tabs: Driver Type, Bindings, Advanced, and Resources. Click the Driver Type tab and click the radio button Enhanced mode (32-bit and 16-bit) NDIS driver. As discussed in Chapter 2, "Basic Network Design and Protocols," the best selection for a Windows NT Server network is the 32-bit and 16-bit NDIS drivers, because they take most advantage of Windows networking. This selection positions the client to use communications for Windows NT Server, Novell NetWare, TCP/IP, and other network protocols. The option for Real mode (16-bit only) does not take advantage of Windows 95 32-bit capability, and the Real mode (16-bit) ODI driver option is for connecting to older Novell NetWare servers using IPX/SPX. (Try configuring a NIC yourself in Hands-on Project 7-3.)

The Advanced tab shows information about the duplex setting, power management, and transceiver type for the NIC. The duplex setting determines whether or not the NIC can send and receive signals at the same time. This should be set to **half duplex** (which means that the NIC will not send and receive simultaneously) unless there are network hubs that support **full duplex** for sending and receiving at the same time. Power Management is the ability to have the NIC automatically shut off when the computer does, if the computer has power management to save electricity. As a rule, consider leaving NIC power management turned off, which means that the NIC will continue to receive network signals even when the computer is using power management. If users step away from their desks and power management shuts down the monitor and disk drive, it is still desirable for the computer to communicate with the network uninterruptedly. As Figure 7-6 shows, the transceiver type is set for Auto-Connector, which means that it will automatically detect the cable type. Another option would be to specify the transceiver type, such as twisted-pair or coaxial.

7

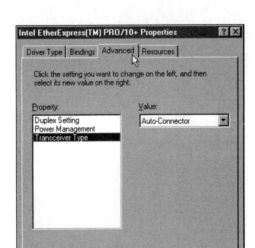

Figure 7-6   Advanced settings for the NIC

Click the Resources tab to be sure that no conflicts are detected with the automatic hardware configuration through the PnP detection of the NIC. A hardware conflict is indicated by an asterisk (*) next to one of the settings. A conflict occurs when the NIC uses a resource already allocated to a disk controller, communications port, or other hardware component (refer to Chapter 5, "Server Configuration"). As the dialog box in Figure 7-7 shows, there are no conflicts for the IRQ and I/O address range.

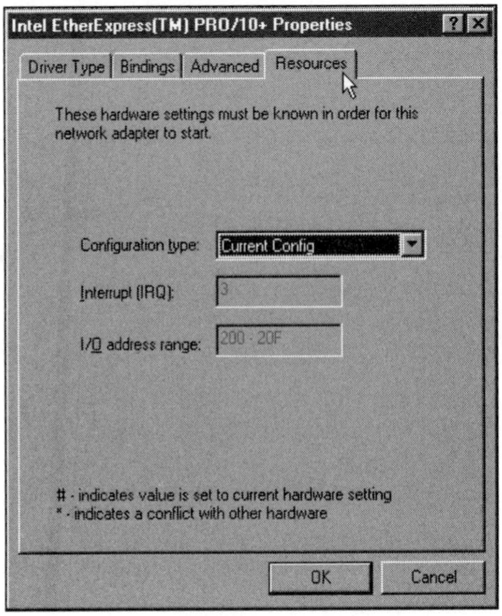

Figure 7-7   Resources used by the NIC

RESOLVING A WINDOWS 95 RESOURCE CONFLICT

If the dialog box in Figure 7-7 had shown a conflict, there is an option to fix the conflict on that screen. A box with a resource in conflict not only shows an asterisk, but it also becomes active, with up and down arrows that allow you to scroll through other resource options. An option without a conflict is indicated by the absence of an asterisk.

Another way to resolve a resource conflict in Windows 95 is to start the Control Panel and double-click the System icon. From there, select the Device Manager tab to view devices (Figure 7-8). Details about device components appear when you double-click a particular component. For example, double-clicking Ports (COM & LPT) displays all of the communications and printer ports. If the NIC, for example, is using IRQ 3 and has a conflict with communications port 4 (COM4), you can assign another IRQ to that port by highlighting the port and clicking the Properties button to change the resources on the Resources tab. Another option is to disable that communications port if it is not in use.

Figure 7-8   Windows 95 System Device Manager

To disable the port, double-click the Ports (COM & LPT) icon, highlight the COM4 icon on the Device Manager tab, and click the Properties button. Click the General tab (the default), and remove the check in the Original Configuration (Current) box under Device usage. Click OK to save the change. You can verify that the device is disabled by returning to the Device Manager screen, which shows an X through the COM4 icon.

CONFIGURING THE WORKSTATION AS A MICROSOFT CLIENT

With the NIC installed, next configure the workstation as a network client. This installs drivers for accessing network resources and for sharing resources from the client, such as folders and printers. From the Control Panel, click the Network icon. On the Network Configuration tab, click the Add button to display the Select Network Component Type dialog box. On that dialog box, highlight the Client option, and click the Add button to add parameters for accessing the NT Server network. In the Manufacturers: list box, select Microsoft, and in the Network Clients list box, choose Client for Microsoft Networks, and click OK.

The network client now requires a computer name to identify that computer to others on the network. The computer name is actually a NetBIOS name for an object on the network (refer to Chapter 2). The name can be up to 15 characters long (the 16th character is reserved) and should make the workstation easily identifiable to others. Some organizations use the last name of the workstation user. Others use a name that identifies the user's function in an organization. Many organizations develop naming guidelines for users to follow. Also, some server administrators keep track of network computer names in a spreadsheet or database.

To set up a computer name, open the Network icon in the Windows 95 Control Panel. Click the Identification tab in the Network dialog box. Enter the name you have chosen in the Computer Name: box. The Domain name you selected when installing Windows NT Server is entered in the Workgroup: box. A description of the computer is optionally entered in the Computer Description: box. (See Hands-on Project 7-4 at the end of the chapter.)

Entering the domain name simply causes Windows 95 to use that domain as the default to browse when accessing an account on one or more servers in the domain.

CONFIGURING A PROTOCOL

The next step in configuring the workstation is to set up a protocol, such as NetBEUI. The protocol is installed via the Control Panel Network icon. In the Network Properties dialog box, click the Configuration tab and the Add button. Double-click Protocol in the Select Network Component Type dialog box (Figure 7-9). Click Microsoft as the manufacturer and NetBEUI for the protocol. Click OK and insert the Windows 95 CD-ROM or setup disk in the computer, as requested, and click Continue or OK.

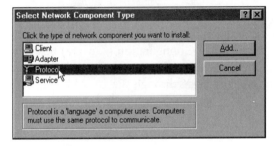

Figure 7-9   Installing a protocol

After the protocol is loaded, bind it to the NIC. From the Configuration tab, highlight the NIC and click the Properties button. Click the Bindings tab and put a check in the box for NetBEUI. Click OK on the NIC Properties dialog box, and click OK to exit the Network Properties dialog box. (Try Hands-on Projects 7-2 and 7-3 at the end of the chapter.)

SETTING UP WINDOWS NT SERVER FOR MACINTOSH CLIENTS

Macintosh computer networks use a peer-to-peer network protocol called **AppleTalk**. AppleTalk is supported only in very limited ways on non-Macintosh networks. On a Microsoft network, Macintosh computers are linked in by setting up the Windows NT Server Services for Macintosh. The NT server becomes a file server for Macintosh computers as well as for computers running Microsoft operating systems. It also is able to communicate with the Macintosh computers through the AppleTalk protocol.

A separate disk volume, resembling a shared volume, can be created on the Windows NT server for Macintosh files. Access permissions can be set up and logon authentication can be performed to ensure that only authorized users have access. Windows NT Server Services for Macintosh is installed from the Windows NT Server Control Panel. Open the Network icon and click the Services tab and then the Add button. In the Network Service: scroll box, click Services for Macintosh, and then click Have Disk. Insert the Windows NT Server CD-ROM, provide the path, and click Continue or OK to load the services.

CUSTOMIZING CLIENT ACCESS WITH PROFILES

Client access to Windows NT Server can be customized through user and roaming profiles. A **user profile** consists of desktop settings that are customized for one or more clients who log on locally to the server. For example, if there are two server administrators and two backup operators, who primarily run backups, you might want to create one profile for the administrators and a different one for the backup operators. That can be useful if each type of account needs to have certain program icons, startup programs, or some other prearranged desktop settings. Also, a user profile can be set up so that it is downloaded to the client workstation each time a specific account is logged on. This is a **roaming profile**, which enables a user to start off with the same desktop setup, no matter what computer on the network she or he uses.

Profiles are used in Microsoft operating systems to provide a consistent working environment for one or more users. A user profile is a particular desktop setup that always starts in the same way and is stored on the local computer. A roaming profile is a desktop setup that starts in the same way from any computer used to access an account, including remote connections from home or on the road. A **hardware profile** provides a consistent hardware setup for a user at the server console, including such features as keyboard, display type, and other hardware components. Hardware profiles are not used much in Windows NT Server, but are used more commonly in NT Workstation to facilitate portable computing.

When a user profile is associated with a server account, it becomes a roaming profile for that account. The profile is stored on the server in the \Winnt\Profiles*accountname* folder and a local copy is loaded to the user's workstation the first time the account is accessed. Then each time the user logs on, the server compares its copy of the roaming profile to the one stored locally on the workstation. If the server copy is more recent, the server updates the local copy on the workstation. Also, if the user makes a change to the desktop, the user has the option when logging off to reflect that change in the roaming profile stored on the server.

However, in some circumstances the server administrator needs to set up profiles so that certain users cannot change their profiles. This is done by creating a **mandatory user profile** in which the user does not have permission to update the folder containing his or her profile. A mandatory user profile overrides the user's locally stored profile if it has been changed from the version stored on the server. To make a user profile (either local or roaming) mandatory, rename the user's NTUSER.DAT file in the user's Profile folder as NTUSER.MAN.

If the server administrator does not assign a profile to a user's account, a default user profile is loaded by the server when a user logs on. Located in the \Winnt\Profiles\Default User folder, the default user profile is also loaded automatically when an account's assigned profile cannot be accessed. However, if a mandatory profile cannot be accessed for some reason, the user will *not* be able to log on because the default profile is not loaded in this situation.

An easy way to set up a profile is to first set up a generic account on the server as a model with the desired desktop configuration, including desktop icons, shortcut folders, and programs in the Startup folder to start when the client workstation starts (you will learn about creating accounts in Chapter 8, "Managing the Server Through Accounts and Groups"). Then copy the model to the \Winnt\Profiles folder, giving it a permanent name, such as Administrators or Usersall. The profile can be used for each account or only for selected accounts created on the server.

For example, you can use the Guest account that is automatically created when Windows NT Server is installed. You log on to the Guest account and set up desktop icons, shortcuts, color preferences, a background, and other desktop settings, then use the System Control Panel applet, User Profiles tab to set up the profile. Complete steps are given in Hands-on Project 7-5 at the end of the chapter.

Normally, profiles are stored in the \Winnt\Profiles folder or in a subfolder under that path.

You can also use the System icon to create a roaming profile by clicking the User Profiles tab and the profile that is to be used as a roaming profile. Hands-on Project 7-6 details the steps.

CHAPTER SUMMARY

- Windows NT Server network users are particularly affected by the way their client workstations are set up to take advantage of network resources. There are many elements to consider when you select and set up a client computer. Although many kinds of clients can access a Windows NT server over the network, not all clients take equal advantage of network resources. An 80386 computer running MS-DOS or Windows 3.11 does not deliver as much power or as many options as a Pentium computer running Windows 95 or Windows NT. Few users have the time to wait for an older computer to process information.

- As you set up client computers, equip them generously with memory and disk storage. The client computer's performance is improved not only by having a powerful CPU, but also by having enough memory for the software it must run. Memory is an easy way to enhance performance. Disk storage capacity on a client also is a consideration because modern operating systems and software quickly consume storage. Storage is particularly important if the client uses databases or large graphics files. The network performance is affected by the capability of the NIC inside the client. For instance, 32-bit NICs provide faster response than 16-bit NICs.

- Microsoft Windows NT Server offers Network Client Administrator as a tool for installing client operating systems on a large scale. Network Client Administrator has the ability to create client boot disks and to enable clients to load or update operating systems such as Windows 95. Of course, you need to obtain client licenses before loading operating systems from Network Client Administrator.

- This chapter provided an example of a client installation of Windows 95. In Windows 95 you can configure paging and other resources for optimum client performance. Windows 95 includes the ability to specify a network name for the client and to configure different protocols.

- On the Windows NT Server side, you can configure the server for Macintosh clients in situations in which Apple computers are used. Also, user and mandatory roaming profiles can be set up for Windows-based users who need to use the same desktop characteristics for continuity from computer to computer.

KEY TERMS

- **AppleTalk** — A peer-to-peer protocol used on networks for communication between Macintosh computers.

- **conventional memory** — The lower 640 KB of memory on a PC, designated for software applications. Early small computers and operating systems reserved memory above 640 KB and below 1 MB for system use.

- **full duplex** — Sending and receiving signals at the same time.

- **half duplex** — Having the ability to send or receive signals, but not simultaneously.

- **hardware profile** — A consistent setup of hardware components associated with one or more user accounts.

- **mandatory user profile** — A user profile, assigned by an administrator, that cannot be modified by the user. A user with a mandatory profile can make changes to user environment settings during a single logon session, but these changes are not saved when the user logs off. Each time the user logs on, the settings revert to those from the mandatory profile. Mandatory user profiles are created by renaming the user's NTUSER.DAT file to NTUSER.MAN.

- **roaming profile** — Desktop settings that are associated with an account, so that the same settings are employed no matter what computer is used to access the account (the profile is downloaded to the client).

- **user profile** — A desktop setup that is associated with one or more accounts and determines what startup programs, additional desktop icons, and other customizations are used. A user profile is local to the computer in which it is stored.

REVIEW QUESTIONS

1. Which of the following does not use a GUI interface?
   a. MS-DOS
   b. Windows 3.1
   c. NT Workstation
   d. Windows 95

2. A client boot disk can be created from _____.
   a. User Manager for Domains
   b. Windows NT Diagnostics
   c. Disk Administrator
   d. Network Client Administrator

3. Which of the following is (are) designed for peer-to-peer communications?
   a. MS-DOS
   b. Windows 3.1
   c. Windows 95
   d. all of the above
   e. both b and c

4. Which of the following can run 32-bit software applications?
   a. Windows 3.11
   b. Windows NT Workstation
   c. Windows 95
   d. all of the above
   e. only b and c

5. Which client operating system(s) is (are) most crashproof?

   a. Windows 3.11

   b. Windows NT Workstation

   c. Windows 95

   d. all of the above

   e. only a and b

6. Which of the following means that signals cannot be sent and received at the same time?

   a. half duplex

   b. full duplex

   c. single plexing

   d. auto-connecting

7. From where might you resolve an IRQ conflict involving a NIC in Windows 95?

   a. Control Panel Network icon

   b. Control Panel System icon

   c. Control Panel Devices icon

   d. all of the above

   e. only a and b

8. From where do you set up a user profile in Windows NT Server?

   a. Control Panel System icon

   b. Control Panel Server icon

   c. Control Panel Profile icon

   d. all of the above

   e. only a and c

9. In Windows 95, an X through a device's icon in the Device Manager means
   _____.

   a. the device driver needs to be upgraded

   b. the device is disabled

   c. there is another device just like it installed

   d. the device is not PnP-compatible

10. As server administrator, you work on client workstations throughout a large organization and decide that you want to use the same desktop setup wherever you log on to Windows NT Server from a client. How might you accomplish that?

    a. set up a revolving account

    b. set up a roaming profile

    c. set up a hardware profile

    d. run the desktop initiator when you log on

11. From where would you configure a client's computer name in Windows 95?

    a. Configuration tab in the Network icon

    b. Identification tab in the Network icon

    c. Computer Name tab in the System icon

    d. a client computer name is set through Windows NT Server and not through Windows 95

12. Which type of NIC provides the best performance?

    a. 24-bit PnP NIC

    b. 16-bit EISA NIC

    c. 32-bit ISA NIC

    d. 32-bit PCI NIC

13. Which of the following clients can connect to NT Server?

    a. MS-DOS

    b. Windows 3.1

    c. OS/2

    d. all of the above

    e. only a and b

14. You need to enable computers using AppleTalk to access an NT Server. How would you provide this capability?

    a. create an Apple page file of 64 MB in Windows NT Server

    b. use the ODI drivers in Windows NT Server

    c. install Services for Macintosh in Windows NT Server

    d. configure the Macintosh computer to use the Data Link Control (DLC) protocol

15. Which operating system is best suited to run 16-bit Windows applications?

    a. Windows 95

    b. MS-DOS 4.0

    c. Windows NT Workstation

    d. Windows NT Server

16. A computer name can have up to _____ characters.

    a. 8

    b. 15

    c. 24

    d. 256

17. Which operating system(s) can be installed on a client from Windows NT Server?

    a. Windows 95

    b. MS-DOS

    c. UNIX

    d. all of the above

    e. only a and b

18. From where is a protocol set up in Windows 95?

    a. Control Panel Network icon

    b. Control Panel NIC icon

    c. Control Panel System icon

    d. Control Panel Connection icon

19. Windows NT Workstation is optimized as a server for up to _____ users.

    a. 5

    b. 10

    c. 25

    d. 40

20. You want to improve the performance of a network workstation. Which of the following is likely to have the most immediate impact?

    a. set the serial port speed to 56 Kbps

    b. set up two page files on each hard disk

    c. increase the RAM

    d. add more communication buffers for the NIC

HANDS-ON PROJECTS

PROJECT 7-1

In this activity you practice configuring the page file size in Windows 95.

To configure the page file size:

1. Click **Start**, **Settings**, and **Control Panel**.

2. Double-click the **System** icon.

3. Click the **Performance** tab in the System Properties dialog box and then the **Virtual Memory** button.

4. Click the radio button **Let me specify my own virtual memory settings**.

5. Enter your virtual memory calculation in the Minimum: box (the amount of RAM plus 8 MB).

6. Enter a Maximum: value, such as 20 MB over your Minimum: entry (the maximum cannot exceed the amount of disk space left on the computer) (Figure 7-10).

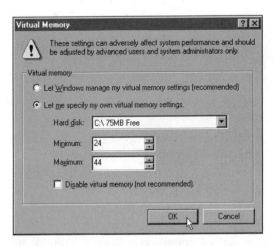

Figure 7-10   Configuring virtual memory for Windows 95

7. Click **OK** in the Virtual Memory dialog box, and click **Close** in the System Properties dialog box.

8. Make sure your work is saved, then click **Yes** to restart the computer.

PROJECT 7-2

This activity shows you how to install the NetBEUI protocol in Windows 95, and Project 7-3 shows how to set up a NIC to work with it. You need a computer with Windows 95 and with a NIC already installed. This activity uses the Intel EtherExpress Pro 100 NIC as an example. Before starting, obtain the NIC driver software disk or plan to use a driver from the Windows 95 installation disk or CD-ROM.

To set up the NetBEUI protocol for Windows 95:

1. Click the **Start** button, **Settings**, and **Control Panel**.

2. Double-click the **Network** icon.

3. Click the **Configuration** tab, and then the **Add** button.

4. Double-click the **Client** selection on the Select Network Component Type dialog box.

5. Highlight **Microsoft** in the Manufacturers: text box and double-click **Client for Microsoft Networks** in the Network Clients: box.

6. If a dialog box is displayed asking for a Windows 95 disk or CD-ROM, insert the disk or CD-ROM, provide the path, if asked, and click **OK** or **Continue** (depending on the dialog box that is displayed).

7. After the drivers are loaded and you return to the Configuration tab, click **Add**.

8. Double-click the **Protocol** selection in the Select Network Component Type dialog box (Figure 7-11).

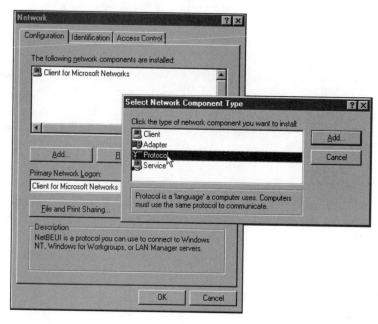

Figure 7-11   Setting up a protocol

9. Click **Microsoft** in the Manufacturers: text box, and double-click **NetBEUI** in the Network Protocols: text box in the Select Network Protocol dialog box.

10. If a dialog box is displayed asking for a Windows 95 disk or CD-ROM, insert the disk or CD-ROM, provide the path, if asked, and click **OK** or **Continue**.

PROJECT 7-3

After setting up NetBEUI in Windows 95 (complete Project 7-2), you can configure the NIC for your computer.

To configure a NIC in Windows 95:

1. Double-click the **Network** icon in the Control Panel if it is not already open.

2. Click the **Configuration** tab in the Network dialog box.

3. Click the **Add** button.

4. Double-click **Adapter** in the Select Network Component Type dialog box.

5. Select the vendor of your NIC adapter in the Manufacturers: text box, and double-click the type of NIC in the Network Adapters: text box.

6. Insert the NIC driver disk and enter the path to the disk, such as **A:**, in the Copy manufacturers files from: text box (or use the Windows 95 installation disk or CD-ROM). Click **OK**.

7. Back on the Configuration tab, highlight the NIC, which now appears on the tab, and click the **Properties** button.

8. Click the **Driver Type** tab and click the radio button for **Enhanced mode (32 bit and 16 bit) NDIS driver** (Figure 7-12). Click the **Bindings** tab and check the box for **NetBEUI** (Figure 7-13).

9. Click **OK** on the NIC Properties dialog box, and click **OK** on the Network dialog box.

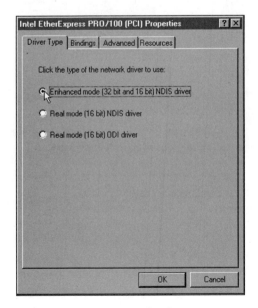

Figure 7-12   Entering the driver type

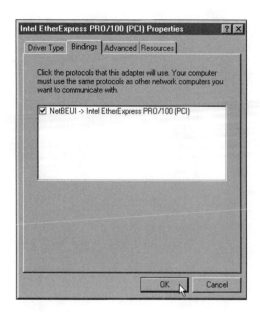

Figure 7-13   Binding NetBEUI

 PROJECT 7-4

In this activity you provide a computer and domain name to a Windows 95 client.

To configure a computer and domain name for a Windows 95 client:

1. Click the **Start** button, **Settings**, and **Control Panel**.
2. Double-click the **Network** icon on the Control Panel.
3. Click the **Identification** tab (Figure 7-14).
4. Enter your workstation's name in the Computer name: text box.
5. Enter a domain name (although you may not have one yet), such as **MyGroup** in the Workgroup: text box.
6. Enter a description of the computer, such as **Desktop workstation** in the Computer Description: text box.
7. Click **OK** in the Network dialog box.

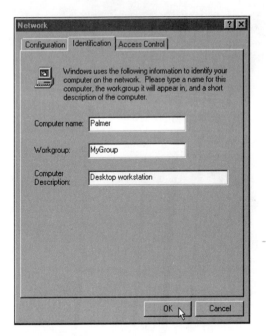

Figure 7-14   Configuring the computer name and domain name

 PROJECT 7-5

In this activity you practice creating a user profile. By granting access to Everyone, you can later assign this profile as a roaming profile when new accounts are created. You need access to a computer running Windows NT Server and to the Guest account.

To create a user profile in Windows NT:

1. Log on to the Guest account and configure the desktop from that account, with desktop icons, color preferences, display settings, shortcuts, startup options, and any other desktop settings.

2. Open the **System** icon in the Control Panel to display the System Properties dialog box, then click the **User Profiles** tab, as shown in Figure 7-15.

3. Highlight the **Guest** profile and click the **Copy To** button.

4. In the Copy To dialog box, enter the path in which to store the profile and the name of the profile, such as **\Winnt\Profiles\Usersall**.

5. Click the **Change** button to enable all accounts to use the profile.

6. In the Choose User dialog box, highlight the **Everyone** group (which includes all users) and click **Add**.

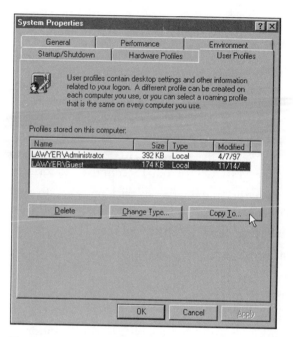

Figure 7-15   Creating a user profile

7. Click **OK** in the Choose User dialog box.

8. Click **OK** in the Copy To dialog box, and then click **OK** in the System Properties dialog box. The profile is now ready to use.

 PROJECT 7-6

In this activity you make the Guest profile a roaming profile.

To change a profile to a roaming profile:

1. Open the **System** icon from the Control Panel and click the **User Profiles** tab in the System Properties dialog box.

2. Highlight the **Guest** profile and click the **Change Type** button.

3. Click the **Roaming Profile** radio button in the Change Type dialog box. There is an optional check box to download the profile into the client workstation's cache if there is a slow network connection. You might use this option if the workstation is connecting to the network remotely or through a wireless hookup.

4. Click **OK** in the Change Type dialog box, and click **OK** in the System Properties dialog box.

PROJECT 7-7

In this activity you use Network Client Administrator to make a boot disk for Windows 95.

To make the boot disk:

1. Format a blank floppy disk, including the system files, and insert it into drive A of a computer running Windows NT Server. (Select the **Format** option in the My Computer File menu, or type the MS-DOS **format /S** command to format the disk.)

2. Open Network Client Administrator on the server by clicking **Start, Programs, Administrative Tools (Common),** and **Network Client Administrator**.

3. Click **Make Network Installation Startup Disk,** and then click **Continue**.

4. In the Share Network Client Installation Files dialog box, click **Use Existing Path,** and then click **OK**.

5. Click the floppy disk type, such as **Drive A: is 3.5"**.

6. In the Network Client: box, select **Windows 95**.

7. Use the Network Adapter Card: list box to select the NIC (Figure 7-16), and click **OK**.

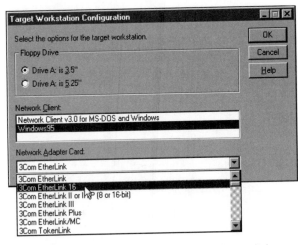

Figure 7-16   Creating a Windows 95 boot disk

8. A dialog box warns that you need to purchase a license to install Windows 95. Make sure that you have the license, and click **OK**.

9. Provide a computer name in the Network Startup Disk Configuration dialog box (Figure 7-17). Leave Administrator as the default username, and leave the default domain name.

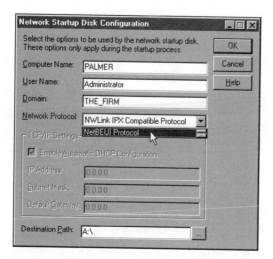

Figure 7-17   Configuring the Windows 95 boot disk

10. In the Network Protocol: list box, select **NetBEUI**. Enter **A:** (or another appropriate disk drive) as the destination path, and click **OK**.

11. Click **OK** again to accept the configuration settings.

12. After the disk is created, click **OK**. Click **Exit** in the Network Client Administrator dialog box, then click **OK**.

 PROJECT 7-8

In this activity you install a client operating system through the network. There must be a shared operating system folder, such as \Client, made available from an NT Server.

 Back up the workstation before starting, if it already contains an operating system and work files. Check the BIOS of the workstation and make sure that it is set up to boot from drive A: first (refer to Chapter 4).

To install a client operating system:

1. Log on to the network using Windows 95, Windows 3.11, or use the disk created in Project 7-7 to boot and log on to the network.

2. Access the shared folder that contains operating system files. Use **Network Neighborhood** to access the share, double-clicking on the server and then on the shared drive name.

3. Open the **\Win95\Netsetup** subfolder within the shared directory.

4. Open the shared folder and find the setup.exe program.

5. If you have backed up the workstation and want to actually load the operating system, double-click **setup.exe**. If you are just practicing, close the shared folder.

ASPEN CONSULTING: SETTING UP CLIENT WORKSTATIONS

This week you again work with Micro Electronics and Beckwith College. Your assignments are to help them select and install client workstations for their Microsoft networks.

1. Micro Electronics has over 100 client workstations that are to connect with the three Windows NT Servers and the client/server software they are preparing to use. They have twenty 80286 computers running MS-DOS 5.0, forty-five 80386 computers running Windows 3.11, twenty-four 80486 computers running Windows 95, and twelve Pentium computers running Windows 95. What are your recommendations in terms of reviewing these client resources and upgrading computers for networking with Windows NT Server and the client/server software?

2. The Micro Electronics server administrator has just installed NICs in their 80486 and Pentium computers. Explain to him how to set up the NICs and the NetBEUI protocol in these computers.

3. Two of the computers set up in Case Assignment 2 seem to have a hardware conflict with COM2. Explain how the server administrator can find and resolve these conflicts.

4. Beckwith College has just been funded for a new student lab in the science building. The computers in the lab will access a Windows NT Server for software such as a chemistry lab simulator, an engineering design system, Microsoft Office 97, a math problem solver system, a database of biological sciences information, and other lab software. They are funded to purchase 22 computers for the lab. Present your recommendations for selecting the type of computers to use, including NIC, memory, and disk storage specifications.

5. Beckwith College has an option to save money on the computers you have recommended by ordering them without operating systems. Explain how they might take advantage of this option by loading operating systems from Windows NT Server. Next, explain the steps involved to create boot disks and to set up the server so that an operating system can be loaded from it.

MANAGING THE SERVER THROUGH ACCOUNTS AND GROUPS

An essential part of configuring Windows NT Server is providing a managed way for clients to access it. Each user needs an account that serves as an individual doorway into servers and the domain resources managed by those servers. Accounts are known to servers by unique IDs and passwords. By dividing accounts into groups with similar access requirements, you simplify server maintenance. In this chapter you learn how to work with users to develop account setup guidelines. You also learn how domains and groups are established to make server management easier, and how to implement accounts and groups using the management tools provided in Windows NT Server.

AFTER READING THIS CHAPTER AND COMPLETING THE EXERCISES YOU WILL BE ABLE TO:

- WORK WITH USERS ON SETTING UP THEIR ACCOUNTS
- SET UP ACCOUNT-NAMING GUIDELINES
- DEVELOP GUIDELINES FOR USER ACCOUNT POLICIES AND SET UP ACCOUNT POLICIES
- EXPLAIN HOW TO MANAGE WINDOWS NT DOMAINS
- EXPLAIN HOW GROUPS ARE USED IN WINDOWS NT SERVER, AND CREATE AND CONFIGURE GROUP POLICIES
- CREATE, COPY, DISABLE, DELETE, AND RENAME USER ACCOUNTS
- SET UP ACCOUNT AUDITING

Obtaining Input from Users

Before establishing user accounts and groups, consult with those affected by the setup choices made for administering accounts and groups. Consulting with users about their needs gives you two advantages before you start creating accounts. The first is that by involving users, you help secure their interest in making the server installation work. No matter how hard you work on the installation, it will not be a complete success unless you have user support, which is more likely if users experience a degree of ownership in the project. Second, you need user input to make sure that you set up the server in a way that meets user needs, which is the reason that you are installing a server in the first place. There are several key issues that merit user input:

- Naming conventions for user accounts
- User account policies
- Use of the server for home directories
- Use and composition of groups
- Group policies
- Hours for the server to be available

There are several ways to obtain feedback from users. One way to gather input about setup possibilities in a small office is to have informal discussions with users over coffee or during an office meeting. In a large organization, you might consult with one or more management groups or compose a written description of the options for management to consider before providing their responses. Other organizations create an advisory group to provide input about policies governing computer resources.

Setting Up Account-Naming Conventions

Organizations set up account names based on the account user's actual name or function within the organization. For example, if the organization uses the user's actual name, it may adopt a particular naming convention, because it can be clumsy to use the full name. Also, server storage for the full name is limited by the operating system. Some IBM mainframe operating systems limit the length of the username to eight characters. Windows NT Server limits usernames to 20 characters. Some sample conventions for account names based on the user's actual name are as follows:

- Last name followed by the first name initial (for example, PalmerM)
- First name initial followed by the last name (for example, MPalmer)
- First name initial, middle initial, and last name (for example, MJPalmer)

When an organization creates usernames by position or function, it is often done using descriptive names. For example, the payroll office may use the names Paysuper (payroll supervisor), Payclerk (payroll clerk), and Payassist (payroll assistant). Another example is the way schools name accounts in student labs, such as Lab1, Lab2, Lab3, and so on. The advantage of naming accounts by function is that an account does not have to be purged when the account holder leaves or changes positions. The network administrator simply changes the account password and gives it to the new person in that position. The advantage of having accounts based on the user's name is that it is easier to know who is logged on to a server (if the naming convention is well designed). In Hands-on Project 8-1 you will investigate naming conventions.

 If you work in a large organization where computer systems and software are audited by independent financial auditors once a year, you will find that the auditors often prefer to have accounts named for individual users. This provides the best audit tracking of who has made what changes to data during the year.

8

USER ACCOUNT POLICIES

NT Server enables the network administrator to establish general password and logon security stipulations for some or all user accounts. The account policy options are the following:

- Password expiration
- Password length
- Password history
- Account lockout
- User home directories

There is no requirement to implement these security options, but most server administrators choose to use them. Many organizations like to have some guidelines to help computer users take advantage of computer security features, in order to protect company information from misuse by people inside or outside the organization. Security features also protect the domain server and printer resources from malicious activities.

PASSWORD SECURITY

The first line of defense for NT Server is password security, but it is only effective if users are taught to use it properly. Many users are careless about security, viewing it as an impediment to their work. They may tape passwords inside a desk drawer or use easily guessed passwords, such as the first name of a family member. Some users keep the same password for months or years, even though it may become known to several other people. Systems like Windows NT Server have built-in capabilities to help users become more conscious of maintaining passwords. One option is to set a password expiration period, requiring users to change passwords at regular intervals. Many organizations use this feature, by requiring, for example, that users change their passwords every 45 to 90 days. Server administrators should consider changing passwords every month for the Administrator account and for other accounts that can access sensitive information.

Some organizations require that all passwords have a minimum length, such as six or seven characters. This requirement makes passwords more difficult to guess. Another option is to have the operating system "remember" passwords that have been used previously. For example, the system might be set to recall the last five passwords, preventing a user from repeating one of these.

Windows NT Server is capable of monitoring unsuccessful logon attempts, in case an intruder attempts to break into an account by trying various passwords. The operating system can lock out an account after a number of unsuccessful tries. **Account lockout** means that no one is allowed to access the account, including the true account owner. The lockout can be set to release after a specified period of time, or by intervention from the server administrator. For example, at one university, a part-time custodian who had keys to computer center staff offices attempted to access a server administrator's personal accounts on Windows NT servers at night. Account lockout prevented him from accessing those sensitive accounts, and his surreptitious activities were discovered and stopped.

A common policy is to have lockout go into effect after five to ten unsuccessful logon attempts. Also, an administrator can set lockout to release after a designated time, such as 30 minutes. The 30 minutes creates enough delay to discourage intruders, while giving some leeway to a user who might have forgotten a recently changed password.

USER HOME DIRECTORIES

Another decision the server administrator must make is whether to make directory space available on the server for each user. This enables users to easily share files with other network users on a 24-hour basis, if they grant access to their home directory or one of its subfolders. Each account holder can have his or her own directory, called a **home directory**, in which to store files. An example of a home directory structure on a server in an office of 12 users is shown in Figure 8-1.

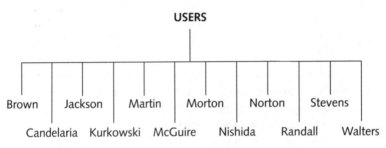

Figure 8-1   User home directories in a small office

As Figure 8-1 shows, each user's home directory is a subfolder of the main folder, USERS, which has no levels above it. Large organizations often create more elaborate directory structures to reflect the composition of units, divisions, or departments. For example, a company with accounting, sales, research, and production divisions might have a USERS folder with these four divisions as subfolders, with the user home directories under each division subfolder (Figure 8-2).

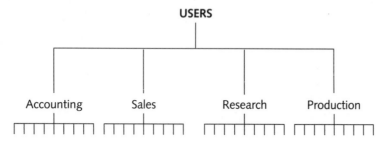

Figure 8-2 User home directories in a large organization

Every account holder can place information, such as a spreadsheet or a text document, in his or her home directory. The advantage of having home directories on the server is that the organization can spend less on hard disk storage at each client workstation. Users with overcrowded hard disks can be encouraged to take advantage of home directory storage, eliminating the need to purchase additional storage. Also, backing up and restoring user data is easier. The disadvantage is that home directories can fill up quickly, and it is necessary for the server administrator to closely monitor disk capacity. When home directories are on the server, the administrator must police disk space to encourage users to regularly delete unused files.

NT Server 4.0 does not have a built-in utility to limit the amount of disk space allocated to a particular user. If home directories are used on the server, the server administrator must closely watch to ensure that they do not grow too large. Another approach is to purchase software to limit disk space allocated to home directories.

DOMAIN SERVICES MANAGEMENT

One way to manage user accounts and network resources is through domains. The largest context in which domains are used is for country designations on the Internet. For example, the domain name for the U.S. is *.us*, and for Sweden it is *.se*. Another Internet domain representation is for organizational types, such as *.edu* for education and *.com* for commercial. Yet another type of domain is a network at a business or university, such as *microsoft.com* for Microsoft and *sewanee.edu* for the University of the South.

As you learned in Chapter 1, "Networking with Microsoft Windows NT Server," a Microsoft NT Server domain is a collection of resources and of users who have access to the resources, which can be servers, printers, CD-ROM arrays, and other equipment. A single domain can have one or more servers as members. Some servers may have generalized functions, such as PDCs and BDCs that provide logon services and logon authentication. Others may be specialized, such as print servers, database servers, or CD-ROM servers. Figure 8-3 shows an example of two domains, A and B.

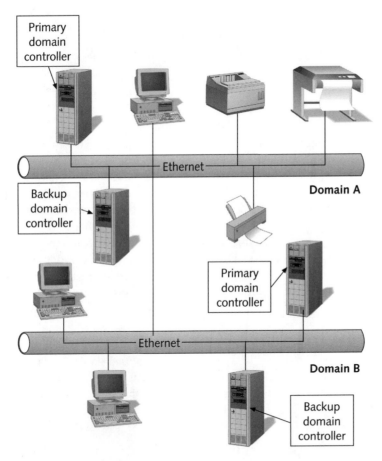

Figure 8-3 Two domains

Microsoft domains consist of clients and resources used by the clients. User accounts and user groups compose the client side. File servers, print servers, and other network services are the resources.

One or more groups can be defined as part of the domain, with a user having membership in any or all groups. The concept of the domain preserves the idea of work groupings, without the headaches of managing them individually from multiple workstations and file servers. The domain on an NT server allows the network administrator to manage resources and users as one unit. The user needs only to log on to the domain one time with one password. The domain has a record of the resources the user is allowed to access and makes those available at logon.

For example, if a business is interested in creating an executive management group with access to the accounting, sales, and inventory software, a group can be created to include each manager on that team. If a supervisor is promoted to a manager's position on the team, she or he is easily added by using the NT Server User Manager for Domains tool.

The domain concept saves time as the network administrator sets up users, privileges, and groups. One or more domains can be created to suit the management needs and styles of an organization. A domain is a powerful management tool because one domain can be home to as many as 26,000 users and 250 groups. Multiple domains can bring many more thousands of users and resources under one roof for centralized management. Multiple domains work well for businesses or colleges with branch sites in different cities or states. They also work well for organizations with foreign and domestic locations. With network administration centralized at the domain, only one SAM database is needed to store information about all users and their security privileges.

8

DOMAIN TRUST RELATIONSHIPS

In situations where there are two or more domains, users can access domains other than their own through trust relationships set up by the network administrator. Each trust relationship has two parties, the trusted domain and the trusting domain. The **trusted domain** is the one that is granted access to resources, whereas the **trusting domain** is the one granting the access. For example, suppose that a manufacturing business has a main office and branch offices in five states, each with its own Windows NT file server and domain. The main-office domain needs access to all five branch-office domains, which is granted. In this scenario, the main office is the trusted domain, and the branch offices are the trusting domains. There are several combinations of trust relationships, but three are most common: one-way trust, two-way trust, and universal trust relationships.

ONE-WAY TRUST

In a **one-way trust**, the trust relationship is not reciprocated. One domain is the trusted party, and the other is trusting. This might be the case in a manufacturing business where one domain, the business domain, is for business accounting, human resources, and sales data, and the manufacturing domain is intended for inventory control in the plant. In this case, members of the business domain may need to use resources on the manufacturing side, such as inventory and materials costs information. Access to the business domain from the manufacturing domain must be restricted because of the sensitive nature of the accounting and human resources information. Members of the business domain can access resources and belong to groups in the manufacturing domain. However, users in the manufacturing domain have no access to files, groups, or resources in the business domain. Figure 8-4 illustrates a one-way trust as signified by the arrow going from the trusting to the trusted domain.

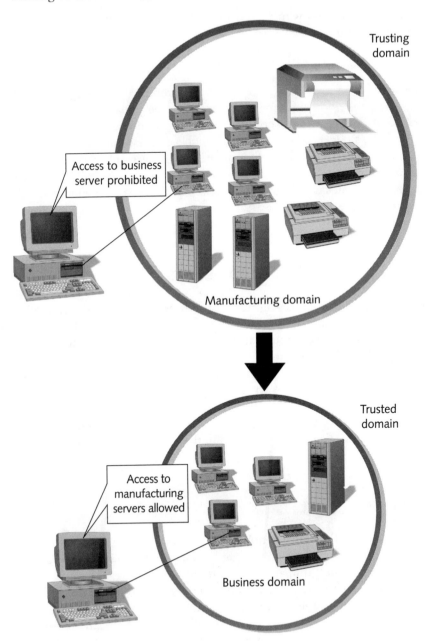

Figure 8-4   One-way trust

TWO-WAY TRUST

The trusting relationship is reciprocated in a **two-way trust**. For example, a chemical company might have its business office downtown and a production plant in an industrial park across town. Two separate domains might be established for the sake of routing e-mail and other electronic communications. However, members of each domain need to access resources in the other domain. A two-way trust enables full sharing of resources between domains (Figure 8-5). Also, members of one domain can belong to groups in the other domain. When two-way trusts are set up among more than two domains, this is called a **universal trust**.

DOMAIN MANAGEMENT

Trust relationships between domains can be set up in many combinations to make managing resources easier. For example, in a **single-master domain** model, several domains are controlled from one master domain, with all accounts in the master domain and the other domains containing only resources, such as servers. The domains may be separate divisions on one large campus or they may be across cities or states.

The advantage of the single-master domain is that all users access resources in all the domains. This model works particularly well for small organizations where several hundred users are spread across several branches or business units. The advantages are the following:

- Accounts and groups are centrally managed.

- Resources are available to all users (as determined by the network administrator).

- One consistent security policy applies across the organization.

- Groups can be tailored across organizational unit boundaries.

- The SAM data is easy to maintain and keep synchronized within the master domain.

For very large organizations that may span several states or countries, the **multiple-master domain** model may be used. This model consists of multiple single-master domains connected through two-way trust relationships. For example, an international foods company might have single-master domains established at company sites in the United States, Brazil, and Norway. The master domains at each site are linked in two-way trust relationships, as shown in Figure 8-6. In this instance, the Brazil master domain has a one-way trust with its two local domains. It has a two-way trust with the United States and Norway master domains. Because users are defined in the master domains in each country, all users can be granted access to the resources of each domain. Administration of this system can be centralized in one domain or decentralized to each master domain. The advantages of this model for a large organization are the following:

- Administration can be centralized or decentralized.

- Thousands of users can share resources across the country or around the world.

- Groups can be formed to span domains.
- Security policies can be standardized for thousands of users and resources.

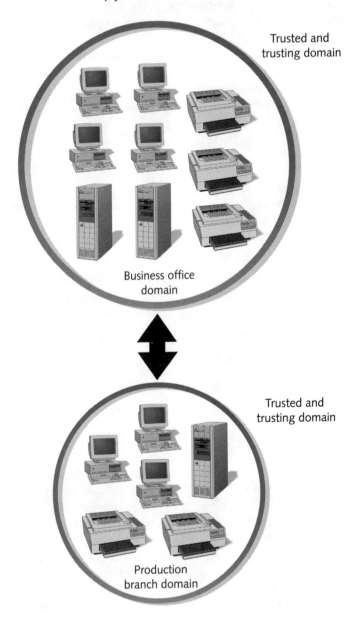

Figure 8-5   Two-way trust

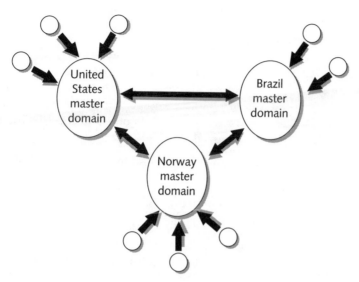

Figure 8-6   Multiple-master domain model

USING GROUPS

There are three ways administrators can manage domain resources: by individual user, by resource, or by group. Managing by individual user is the most labor-intensive method. This requires setting up security access customized for each user account. In an organization of 20 users, creating and managing individual accounts is not unmanageable, but can be time-consuming. On a network of 200 users, managing resources by individual account quickly becomes a nightmare.

Another way to manage network access is by the resource. Assume that the resources on a network are two file servers and one print server. One file server is for business applications and one is for scientific research applications. The business unit in the organization would have access to the business applications server and the print server. Scientists would have access to the server with science-related applications. Some managerial people would have access to all three resources. The problem with this security model is that access management is still labor-intensive because it is customized by user and by resource.

The group management concept saves time by eliminating repetitive steps in managing user and resource access. This arrangement is based on the idea that users can belong to one or more groups having the same access needs. Windows NT Server has two types of groups: local and global. Local groups are particularly useful for managing access to resources within a domain or on a single server. Global groups have user accounts as members and enable resource sharing across domains.

LOCAL GROUPS

Local groups are a resource management tool for a single server or a set of servers in a single domain. In an organization in which there is only one domain containing a single server (or more), local groups are applied to the resources and users of the domain. The resources include file servers (PDCs and BDCs), database servers, print services, fax services, and other network services. The users consist of accounts on PDC and BDC servers. The characteristics of local groups are the following:

- They are used to help manage rights and permissions on a server within a domain.

- User accounts can be members of local groups.

- Domain resources can be assigned to local groups.

- Global groups can belong to local groups.

- Local groups can be used to make domain resources accessible to trusted domains, for example in the master domain models.

Rights enable an account or group to perform predefined tasks in the domain. The most basic right is to have the privilege to access a server. More advanced rights give privileges to create accounts, manage server functions, and even modify the operating system. **Permissions** are associated with directories and files, controlling the way an account or group accesses information. For example, access can range from no permission to view files in a folder to full permission for adding or changing any files in the folder. Rights are a higher level of access than permissions. For instance, if the server administrator gives an account permission to access all software application files on the server but does not grant that user rights to access the server, the user cannot access the applications.

 Consider how groups can be paired with resources to give the greatest range of administrative control. This will make administrative tasks, as well as audits, more efficient. Company and organization auditors are receiving advanced training in the setup of security privileges on network systems, and they expect to find good security practices through group and account management.

Windows NT Server comes with several predefined local groups. These are groups common to most network applications, such as an administrator group to manage server functions, a user group for server users, and various operator groups to perform specific functions such as server backups. Table 8-1 shows the predefined Windows NT local groups with descriptions of their purpose.

GLOBAL GROUPS

Global groups are intended as a means to provide links between domains in a multiple-domain environment. Their purpose is to easily manage access rights among domains. Because global groups have access to trusting domains, they are a way to provide users access across domains. The access is made possible by adding a global group with trusting domain rights to a local group whose users need access to the trusting domain. The characteristics of global groups are the following:

- They provide rights access across domains by linking rights from trusting domains to groups in trusted domains.

- Global groups can have domain user accounts as members but not local groups, to avoid circular group relationships.

- Global groups can be members of local groups.

- Global groups cannot have resources as members. They gain rights to resources through belonging to a local group.

Table 8-1   Windows NT Predefined Local Groups

Local Group	Description
Account Operators	This group of users has rights to create, delete, and manage accounts on a server or domain.
Administrators	This group has access to all server and administrative functions.
Backup Operators	These operators have rights to back up all files on a server or within a domain.
Guests	This group has limited access to a server or domain, for example: temporary employees, part-time help, or Internet visitors.
Print Operators	This group can manage designated print services such as holding or deleting print jobs.
Replicator	This is a unique group for automating the replication of files, such as databases. For example, some application systems use two identical databases, one for updating data and one for reporting on data. The updating database is regularly copied to the reporting database so that they remain in synchronization.
Server Operators	This group has privileges to manage specific server functions, such as dismounting disk volumes or shutting down servers.
Users	These are the regular users on a server or domain who access server files and applications.

 Local groups can contain global groups, but global groups cannot contain local groups. Furthermore, although global groups are used to link resources across domains, they can also be used within a domain to manage access to resources even when no other domains are present. Microsoft recommends adding users to global groups instead of local groups for better management options.

Three global groups come predefined with NT Server: one administrator group and two user groups. These are described in Table 8-2.

8

Table 8-2   Windows NT Predefined Global Groups

Global Group	Description
Domain Administrators	This group enables network administrators to have administrative rights across domains. Domain Administrators is pre-established as a member of the Administrators group in the home domain.
Domain Users	This group is used to manage user access rights across multiple domains. The group is pre-established as a member of the Users group in the home domain. All new users are automatically added to the group to ensure domain access.
Domain Guests	This group enables network administrators to manage guest account access across multiple domains. The group is pre-established as a member of the Guest group in the home domain.

When there are multiple domains, the process for managing rights is to first assign resources to a local group. Next, you assign users who need cross-domain access to the appropriate global group in their domain. Access rights between domains are enabled by adding the global group of a trusted domain to the local group in the trusting domain. For example, consider a hypothetical situation in which an administrator manages three domains, CANADACORP, EASTCORP, and WESTCORP. Also, assume that there are two server administrators, Sabrina and her backup Curtis. Sabrina or Curtis can access all three domains as administrators by following these steps, in order:

1. Add Sabrina and Curtis to the Domain Administrators group (which is a default member of the local Administrators group) for CANADACORP.

2. Ensure that the EASTCORP Domain Administrators group is already a member of the EASTCORP Administrators group, which should be set up by default.

3. Check that the WESTCORP Domain Administrators group is already a member of the WESTCORP Administrators group.

4. Add the CANADACORP Domain Administrators to the Administrators group for EASTCORP.

5. Add the CANADACORP Domain Administrators to the Administrators group for WESTCORP.

Step 1 gives administrator rights and permissions to Sabrina and Curtis. Steps 2 and 3 ensure that administrator rights and permissions are already given to domain administrators on EASTCORP and WESTCORP. Finally, Steps 4 and 5 convey administrator rights and permissions from EASTCORP and WESTCORP to Sabrina and Curtis (Figure 8-7).

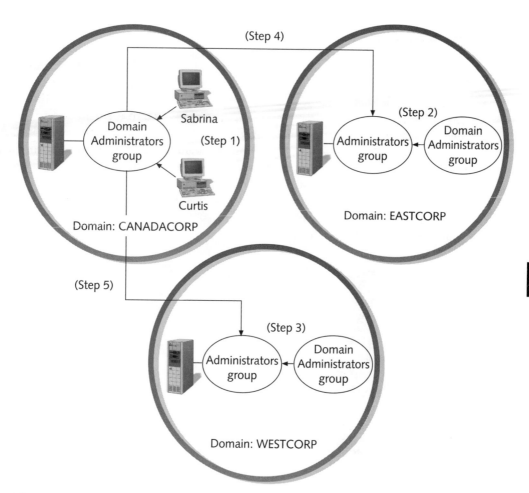

Figure 8-7 Managing administrator groups in multiple domains

Building groups represents some work initially, but it saves work once all the groups are set up. Many individual account management tasks are reduced by consolidating them into fewer group management tasks. For example, if Curtis leaves and Terry is promoted into Curtis's job, only two steps are required to make the change of administrator. Curtis is removed from the Domain Administrators group on CANADACORP, and Terry is added. Otherwise, without the local and global group setup, these two steps would be repeated for the Domain Administrators groups on EASTCORP and WESTCORP, adding four extra steps. Although the savings in this example are small, the savings are greatly multiplied when you are working with many users and large networks.

ADDING GROUPS

The server administrator can add new local and global groups at any time. For example, consider a 40-person office of accountants that is run by a management team of five people. The network administrator might create a local group called Managers, consisting of the five managers in the office. Special permissions can be granted to the managers to access confidential management reports and communications within the accounting firm. Another larger group, called Business, might consist of the managers plus the office coordinator and the human resources supervisor. The Business group would have access to office supplies expenses, equipment inventories, and human resources files. An easy way to set up these groups is to first create the Managers group and add its members. Then create the Business group, add to it the Managers group and the office coordinator and the human resources supervisor (Figure 8-8).

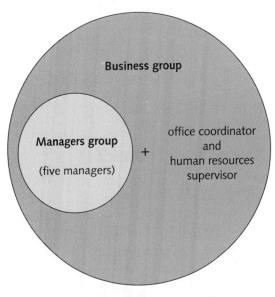

Figure 8-8   Business group composition

Plan in advance the groups you will implement, so that you are not performing extra administrative tasks for groups you do not need.

Do not create a global group with the same name as a local group, to avoid confusion. A global group will not be the same as a local group with the same name—members of one will not have the privileges of the other.

SETTING ACCOUNT POLICIES

After decisions are made about account-naming guidelines, account password and lockout procedures, and what groups are needed, the next phase is to set up the account policies. To set up account policies, open the Administrative Tools (Common) menu and click User Manager for Domains. From User Manager for Domains, click the Policies menu and select Account, as shown in Figure 8-9.

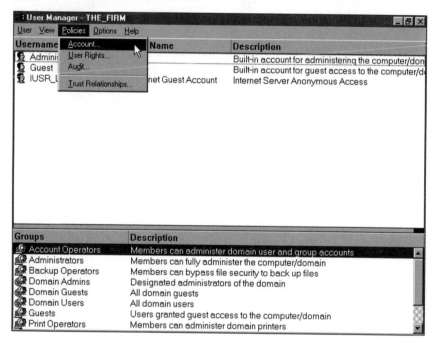

Figure 8-9   Setting up account policies

The Account Policy dialog box is where the administrator can implement the account policies established by an organization. For example, in the area called Maximum Password Age, enter the time allowed until a password expires, such as Expires in 60 Days. For Minimum Password Age, click one of the two options. Allow Changes Immediately enables passwords to be changed at any time and used immediately. Allow Changes In __ Days forces a new password to be used for a specified period until it can be changed.

A password length requirement is set in the Minimum Password Length area via the radio button At Least __ Characters. The Password Uniqueness area parameter, Remember __ Passwords, is used to have the system remember the specified number of previous passwords associated with a particular account. In the middle of the Account Policy dialog box, click the radio button for Account lockout, if you want to activate the area below it, in which you input the lockout parameters. Lockout after __ bad attempts limits the number of unsuccessful tries at logging on to an account. Reset count after __ minutes is for setting the time the system waits before resetting the number back to zero. Under Lockout Duration, click the radio button for Duration __ minutes, which enables the system to keep an account locked for the specified amount of time.

The second to last parameter applies to users who remotely access the server—for example, from a modem. When checked, it forces them to log off at times when the server is unavailable for general use. Use this parameter cautiously because users might lose work that has not been saved. The last parameter, Users must log on in order to change password, forces users to change their passwords before the last password has expired and they are unable to log on. When this is checked and a user's password is expired, the server administrator must change the password through User Manager for Domains. (You can practice setting account policies in Hands-on Project 8-2 at the end of the chapter.)

MANAGING ACCOUNTS

In addition to setting account policies, User Manager for Domains is used to create, copy, delete, disable, and rename user accounts. These functions are covered in the following sections.

CREATING ACCOUNTS

With the account policies established, the next step is to create accounts. New accounts are set up in User Manager for Domains. Two accounts already exist, Administrator and Guest, both created when Windows NT Server was installed. Also, if the Internet Information Server is installed at the same time as Windows NT Server, there is an anonymous Internet Guest account automatically created, using the name IUSR_*servername*. This account may be used as a way for Internet users to access a server in order to download data files.

The **Administrator account** is set up to provide complete access and control over the server. Some server administrators prefer to use this account for all work on the server. Others prefer to create their own account with the same rights and permissions as the Administrator account.

The **Guest account** can be set up with controlled access for guest users. Server administrators sometimes use Guest accounts to provide access for people who are temporary employees, or for financial auditors who visit a business once a year to audit the books.

 Many operating systems have a Guest account that should be checked to ensure that it has a password for the sake of security.

Each new account is created through the following basic procedure:

1. Enter the account information and password.

2. Establish password controls.

3. Assign the account to appropriate groups for security management.

4. Link user profiles, logon scripts, and home directories to the account.

5. Establish dial-in access security.

New accounts are created in User Manager for Domains by selecting the User menu (Figure 8-10) and clicking New User. The New User dialog box provides text boxes and check boxes to complete the information for creating an account. In the Username: text box, enter the name for the account, such as MPalmer. For Full Name, enter the user's full name, which is a vital reference in a server with several hundred accounts. Also enter a description for the account, such as the account holder's work title (for example, Server Administrator). Then enter the account password and the password confirmation. The next four parameters enable you to control the account further. For example, the User Must Change Password at Next Logon option forces users to enter a new password the first time they log on. This option is unnecessary for accounts used by the server administrator, but it is valuable for accounts created for others. Server administrators check this box when creating new accounts so that they will not know the passwords of account holders. Although the initial password is known, once it is given to the account holder, the administrator will not know the new password that the user is forced to enter at first logon.

Another way to create a new account in Windows NT 4.0 Server is to use the Add User Account Wizard. The administrative wizards are found in the Administrative Tools (Common) menu by clicking the Administrative Wizards option. The Add User Account Wizard takes you through the same process as in User Manager for Domains; however, dialog boxes are presented one after another until all information is entered.

Another option is to check User Cannot Create Password, which means that only the network administrator can assign the password to an account. Under most circumstances, it is best for users to create their own confidential passwords, so that they are the only ones using their accounts. Confidential passwords provide good security and ensure that if an account is audited, the audited activities are only those of the account holder. However, this option is used for special accounts, such as one that is used by the Windows NT Replicator for automatically copying files from one server to another server (the Replicator is discussed in Chapter 9, "Managing Server Folders, Permissions, and Software Installation"). Two other accounts for which the administrator may want to control the passwords are the Guest and IIS anonymous Guest accounts.

Account auditing may be performed by the server administrator or by financial auditors to determine which users are accessing or modifying specific files. Auditors view this as a means to track changes in financial information to a particular account holder.

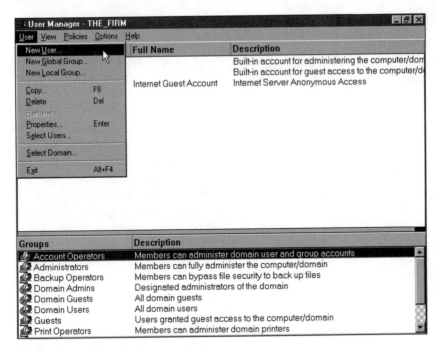

Figure 8-10   Creating a new account

The option to set a password that never expires is used in some situations in which an account must always be accessed, even if no one remembers to change the password. That would be true for a utility account needed to run a program process. The password would be hard-coded into the program for the purpose of accessing the account to start the process. For example, the administrator might create an account that automatically copies database files twice a day, which is done in client/server environments where one database is used for updating information throughout the day. A copy of the database is made—for example, each morning and each afternoon—and is used for creating reports on the data. That way, heavy demand from large reports never slows down database updating, because reports are generated from the separate, copied database. Another advantage of making periodic copies of a database is that a poorly written database query never halts critical updates to the main database. The disadvantage is that reports may not reflect the most up-to-the-minute information, because the database copy is updated only twice each day.

The Account Disabled option is used to stop activity on an account after the account holder leaves the organization. For example, if the payroll supervisor decides to go on a leave of absence for two months, the administrator might disable his or her account for that time period. That would secure the account until the supervisor's return. Figure 8-11 shows the New User dialog box with the information entered for an account. (You can practice creating an account in Hands-on Project 8-3 at the end of the chapter.)

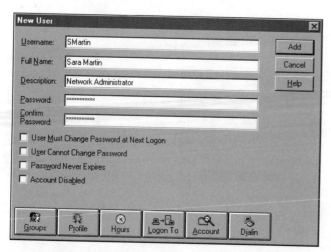

Figure 8-11 Completing the new account information

The six buttons at the bottom of the dialog box are used to customize information that pertains to an account: Groups, Profile, Hours, Logon To, Account, and Dialin. Each of these is described in the sections that follow.

Assigning Users to a Group

Accounts that have the same security and access requirements can be assigned as members of a group. Security access then is set up for the group instead of for each account. User groupings can save a significant amount of time when there are tens or hundreds of accounts to manage. For example, if 42 accounts all need full access to a folder, it is easier to create a group, add each account to the group, and give the group full access. The more time-consuming method would be to set up access permissions on individual accounts, repeating the same steps 42 times.

Management by using groups is particularly handy on a server where many accounts are managed. It saves time and provides an immediate point of reference when the security needs of a particular account must be recalled. For example, if there is a small programming group responsible for developing a software application in which there are specialized access requirements to test data, the administrator can set up a small group, such as Developers. Later, when there is a need for certain users to test the application before it is released for general use, it is easy to add new members without having to redetermine all the privileges needed to help with the development and testing.

To place an account in a group, click the Groups button from the New User dialog box. In the Group Memberships dialog box, highlight the group to which the user will belong in the Not member of: text box. Click the Add button to move that group into the Member of: text box (Figure 8-12). The Set button at the bottom of the dialog box is used to set the account's **primary group**, for accounts that are accessed from a Macintosh or POSIX workstation. NT Server requires that these systems be members of a global group in the

Member of: text box. After the group memberships are set up, click OK. (To practice adding an account to a group, try Hands-on Project 8-4.)

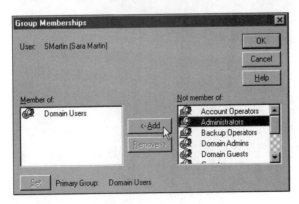

Figure 8-12   Setting group membership

Customizing User Access

The user account environment can be customized through user profiles, logon scripts, and home directories. Clicking the Profile button in the New User dialog box produces the User Environment Profile dialog box, in which each user account can be linked with a user profile, a logon script, a home directory, and a home drive. Many administrators begin with the home drive information.

When home directories are set up on the server, administrators often standardize the home directories of all users to a particular drive letter, such as H. To enter the home directory drive letter, click the Connect radio button and use the list box to select the drive letter. Enter the path to the home directory, such as \USERS\MARTIN, in the To box (Figure 8-13). Each time the user logs on, there will be an H drive shown in My Computer and in the Explorer, with a path to the user's home directory on the server. If the home directory is on the user's computer, enter the computer name and the path on the computer to be used as a home directory, such as \\Mycomputer\Mywork\ (using the Universal Naming Convention).

User profiles are needed in situations in which users have early versions of Windows, or when there are very inexperienced users, and in high-security situations. Profiles can be set up through the System icon for each user or for groups of users, to create a consistent desktop environment each time they log on. The path to the user profile located on the server is entered in the User Profile Path: text box.

A default user profile, Userdef, is provided by Windows NT Server as an example and is located in the server directory \Winnt\System32\Config.

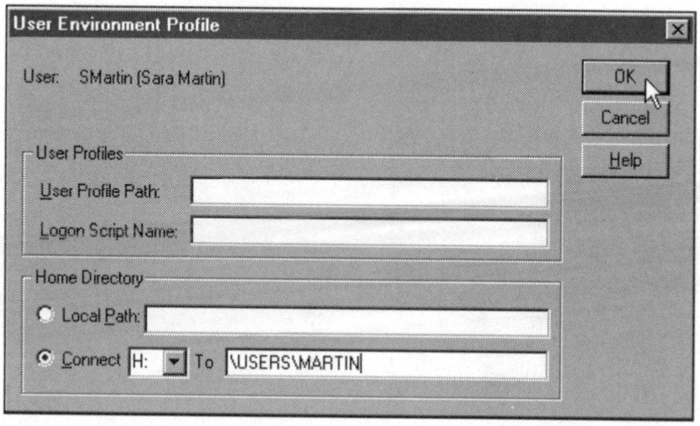

User Environment Profile

User: SMartin (Sara Martin)

OK Cancel Help

User Profiles

User Profile Path:

Logon Script Name:

Home Directory

○ Local Path:

● Connect H: ▼ To \USERS\MARTIN

Figure 8-13 Setting up the user environment

A **logon script** is a set of commands that automatically runs each time the user logs on to the domain. It is usually implemented as a DOS batch file, but it can also be an executable file. A summary of the commands is provided in Table 8–3.

Note Logon scripts and user profiles can require lots of maintenance work, such as large-scale changes when servers are added or when a group of users gets new computers. However, workstation operating systems are more advanced than in the past, creating less need for user scripts and profiles. If your network uses only Windows clients and users run few MS-DOS programs, you probably won't need to create logon scripts or user profiles.

Table 8-3 Windows NT Logon Script Commands

Script Command	Function
%Homepath%	Establishes the path to the user's home directory
%Homedrive%	Sets a drive letter for the system hard disk drive
%Username%	Specifies the user's logon name
%Userdomain%	Specifies the domain to which the user belongs
%OS%	Specifies the operating system being used
%Processor%	Specifies the type of processor
%Homeshare%	Specifies home directory on a shared drive

If a logon script exists for a user, it is downloaded from the server at each logon. Scripts are kept in the server directory \Winnt\System32\Repl\Import\Scripts. The following script commands would set a user's home directory to drive H, specify the home directory path, and specify her logon name so that she would not have to type it:

```
USERNAME=SMARTIN

HOMEDRIVE=H:

HOMEPATH=\USERS\MARTIN
```

A logon script is not likely to be needed for Microsoft networks because drive mappings and logon information are retained through other methods, such as the Welcome to Windows dialog box that appears when a user logs on (displaying the default username), and by making drive mappings permanent through My Computer and Windows Explorer by checking the Reconnect at logon option (Figure 8-14).

Figure 8-14   Making a drive mapping permanent

 Windows NT Server can process NetWare login scripts without changing them to Windows NT logon scripts.

Configuring the Server Hours

The server administrator can set up the user accounts so that they cannot access the server at designated times, such as during backups and at times designated for system work. For example, if the system service time is every Thursday evening from 8:00 to 10:00 P.M., you can reserve the server so that no one else can access it. Also, if no one uses the server over the weekend, logon access can be closed from Friday night to Monday morning, to make sure that information is not accessed by an intruder when no one is around. You do this by clicking the Hours button on the New Users dialog box. The Logon Hours dialog box with dates and times appears, where you can block out the system time, as in Figure 8-15. (Try Hands-on Project 8-5 to set server accessibility.)

 From the start, plan to have domain servers unavailable at designated hours for system activities such as installing software, performing backups, adding drivers, and changing or adding hardware.

 As system administrator, you should enable access during all hours to the domain from your personal account as well as from the Administrator account. This gives you alternate access in case there is a problem with the Administrator account.

Securing Account Access from Designated Workstations

The Logon To button on the New User dialog box enables the server administrator to limit where a user can log on to the domain. The Logon To option is a good security measure when you want to make sure that certain accounts can only be accessed from designated workstations. For example, you might want to guard the Administrator account and your own account with administrator privileges so that they are only accessed from the server, from a workstation in your office, and from your computer at home. At the same time, the employee who prepares the payroll in your organization may be required by the auditors to finalize the payroll from one computer only. These security stipulations are met by using the Logon Workstations dialog box (Figure 8-16).

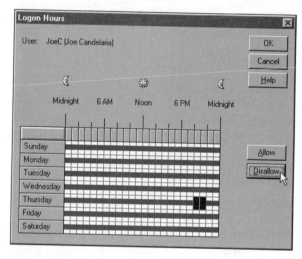

Figure 8-15 Logon Hours dialog box with 8 PM–10 PM disallowed

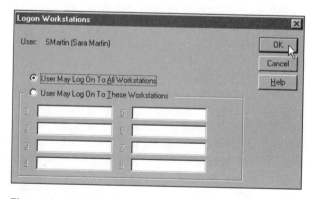

Figure 8-16 Logon Workstations dialog box

For example, consider that the payroll is finalized from the payroll clerk's workstation, which is assigned the computer name PAY. In the Logon Workstations dialog box, click User May Log On To These Workstations. Then in the top left box, enter the name PAY. Click OK to leave the Logon Workstations dialog box.

Account Expiration and Type

The Account button in the New User screen is used to set an expiration date for an account. This is a useful option when temporary employees, business auditors, or visitors need an account created for a specific period of time. The account can be set to expire on a given date by clicking the radio button labeled End of and entering the expiration date. The account expires at the end of the specified working day. Or to make sure that an account is set to never expire, click the Never radio button (Figure 8-17).

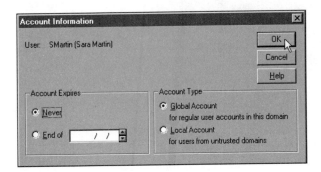

Figure 8-17   Account information

An account also can be designated as global or local. A **global account** is one that has normal domain membership and is recognized by other domains when it is in a trusted domain. A **local account** is one that is defined only to the home domain and is not recognized by other domains. The local account option is used for situations in which the user would never access another domain, such as when creating student accounts in an academic lab domain, where access to administrative domains must be restricted.

Remote Dial-In Security

The Dialin button in the New User dialog box is for controlling remote access to the domain, such as from dial-in modems. Remote access can be granted or disallowed, as shown in Figure 8-18. To enable an account holder to access the server domain from a home computer or while on the road, click Grant dialin permission to user, which causes the bottom portion of the screen to activate. The bottom portion has **call-back security** options for dial-in access, so that a server's modems can call back the accessing workstation after the initial request to log on is received. This enables the server to verify that the call is from a known location. The call-back can be set from the workstation's modem or from a prearranged number used by the server. (Dial-in security is covered in more detail in Chapter 11, "Remote Access.")

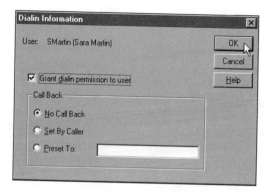

Figure 8-18 Dial-in security for an account

COPYING AN ACCOUNT

8

In many situations, you will create accounts that are virtually identical in terms of setup, except for the username, password, and home directory. Accounts can be modeled after a master account or a certain user's account by copying the account. Copying accounts can save time when there are many accounts to create.

To copy an account, open User Manager for Domains and highlight the account to be duplicated. Click the User menu and Copy. Enter the new account name, full name, title, password, and password confirmation in the New User dialog box. Click the box User Must Change Password at Next Logon, to force the user to enter his or her own new password at first logon. Click the Profile button in the New User dialog box and enter the user's home directory information plus the profile path and logon script name, if used. Save the new account information and repeat the same process to create additional accounts. (Hands-on Project 8-6 gives you practice in copying an account.)

If the home directory is on a FAT volume, it must be created manually before the directory is specified via the Profile button.

DELETING AN ACCOUNT

Sometimes an administrator wants to delete an account, for instance when an account holder permanently leaves an organization. An account can easily be deleted using User Manager for Domains. It is as simple as deleting a file. To delete an account, open User Manager for Domains and highlight that account. Click the User menu, then click Delete. Another way to delete the account after highlighting it is to press Del.

However, many security advisors and Microsoft recommend disabling an account rather than deleting it right away. Deleting an account completely erases it from the security database (SAM); it also deletes the account's unique **Security ID (SID)**, which can never be reused. This means that even if you immediately create a new user account with the same settings, you will have to reestablish all the access privileges and preferences of the deleted account.

 Before deleting an account, disable it for a period of time, in case there is a need to reactivate it for access at a later date. Also, back up that user's home directory before deleting the account. Reactivating an account is particularly common in a large networking environment in which a user has access to many computers with a variety of operating systems, such as Microsoft, Novell, and UNIX servers, as well as mainframes or minicomputers.

Consider for example, a case at a university where a department secretary left her job. The day after she left, her Microsoft NT and Novell accounts were deleted as well as her home directory on a Novell NetWare server. The secretary was in charge of keeping accounting records for the department, but when there was a question about an expenditure, there was no way to replicate her server access, and no accounting files were left with the information.

DISABLING AN ACCOUNT

As just mentioned, disabling an account is a good security practice. A disabled account cannot be used to log on to the system, but all other settings and configuration options remain intact. To disable an account, check the Account Disabled check box in the user's Properties dialog box (select the username, and click the Properties menu selection in User Manager for Domains). To reactivate the account, simply remove the check from the Account Disabled box.

RENAMING AN ACCOUNT

Every user account can be renamed, including the Administrator and Guest accounts. In fact you may want to change the names of these accounts to prevent intruders familiar with the default account names from gaining access to the system by guessing a password. Other situations in which you might want to rename an account might be:

- To change an account name if an account associated with a specific job is assigned to another individual
- To comply with changes in your organization's naming convention
- To reflect a user's name change

To rename an account, highlight the user account in User Manager for Domains, select User, and Rename from the menu.

ACCOUNT AUDITING

Once an account is set up, you can specify account **auditing** to track activity associated with that account. For example, some organizations need to track security changes to an account, while others want to track failed logon attempts. In a college setting, security changes might be tracked for part-time students who work in sensitive administrative areas such as the registrar's office. Many server administrators track failed logon attempts for the Administrator account, to be sure that an intruder is not attempting to access the server. Accounts that access an organization's financial information often are routinely audited to protect their users as well as the information they access. The events that can be audited are as follows:

- Logon and logoff activity

- Accesses to files and objects (for files and folders set up to be audited)

- How often user rights are exercised

- User and group management functions (such as when an account or group is created or modified)

- Security policy changes

- Restarting, shutting down, and other system activities

- Starting processes or software applications

Each listed activity is audited in terms of the success or failure of the event. For example, if failed logon attempts are audited, a record is made each time someone tries unsuccessfully to access an account. If successful process starts are tracked, a record is made each time a software application on the server is started from that account.

Use auditing sparingly. Each audited event causes a record to be made in an event log. For example, if you audit all started processes on 100 server accounts, the server will quickly become loaded down just in auditing events, and it will have fewer resources to perform other work.

Account auditing is configured from the Audit option in the Policies menu in User Manager for Domains. For example, consider a situation in which an account seems to have problems starting applications located on the server. You can audit the number of times applications fail to start for that account by clicking the Audit option in the Policies menu. Click Audit These Events and check the Failure box for Process Tracking. Auditing is covered in more detail in Chapter 9.

CREATING GROUPS

Global and local groups are created from Windows NT User Manager for Domains. Before you create a group, consider its purpose in the domain. Some types of groups that might be transformed into NT groups are:

- Organizational units, workgroups, or departments

- Authorized users of network resources or applications

- Events, projects, or special assignments

- Geographical or locational groups

- Individual job descriptions or functions

For example, in a situation in which there are company plants spread over four states, each with its own management, you might need to create a global Managers group at each site and make all four global groups members of a local Managers group that has access to resources at the headquarters site. Even in a small network with only one server and 20 users, all of the groups you create will likely be global groups with local groups used for resources. Placing users in global groups makes it easier to expand and add domains as the network grows.

To create a global group in User Manager for Domains, click the User menu and then the New Global Group option. Enter the group name and a description of the group in the text boxes at the top of the dialog box. Highlight each member in the Not Members: box and click Add to move them one by one into the Members: box. After all of the members are added, click OK (Figure 8-19). (You can create a global group in Hands-on Project 8-7.) The steps for creating a new local group are the same, except that you click New Local Group in the Users menu when starting.

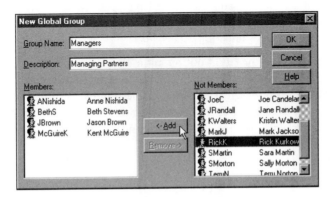

Figure 8-19   Creating a global group

Another way to create new groups is to use the Group Management Setup Wizard from the Start menu, Administrative Tools (Common), and Administrative Wizards. Double-click the Group Management Wizard in the Administrative Wizards dialog box. The wizard takes you step-by-step through the process of creating either a global or local group.

SETTING GROUP POLICIES

After groups are created, check the rights assigned to each group. Rights are assigned by using the Policies menu in User Manager for Domains. Click Policies, and then click User Rights. Windows NT Server has a wide range of rights that can be assigned. Click the down arrow to view the rights selections in the Right: list box, as shown in Figure 8-20.

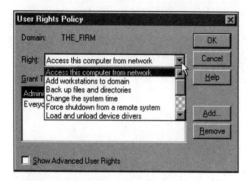

Figure 8-20   Setting user rights policies

Rights grant privileges to perform functions such as accessing the server, adding workstations to the domain, changing the system time, and backing up files. Only members of the Administrators group have authority to grant rights. The rights can be granted to users, groups, or a combination of both, but the easiest way to administer rights is through groups.

Two levels of rights can be granted. The standard rights are described in Table 8-4. These rights apply to everyday users and groups, and appear in the Rights: list box. More complex rights can be assigned by clicking the box labeled Show Advanced User Rights. The advanced rights are for programmers and system developers who have technical access needs, such as debugging programs, gaining access to operating system internals, and controlling memory swapping.

Table 8-4   Default NT Server User Rights

Right	Granted to by Default	Description
Access this computer from network	Administrators, Everyone	Allows connection to a server from a connection on the network
Add workstations to domain	No default group, but should be granted to Administrators	Ability to add a server or NT workstation to an existing domain with capability to interact with domain users, resources, and global groups
Back up files and directories	Administrators, Backup Operators, Server Operators	Includes permission to read all files and directories to be able to back them up
Change the system time	Administrators, Server Operators	Privilege to reset the server's time clock
Force shutdown from a remote system	Administrators, Server Operators	Reserved but not yet available on NT Server
Load and unload device drivers	Administrators	Privilege to copy device drivers to the server and remove device drivers from the server
Log on locally	Administrators, Backup Operators, Print Operators, Server Operators, Account Operators	Ability to log on to the server from the server console
Manage auditing and security log	Administrators	Privilege to specify what to audit and to maintain the audit logs kept on system and user activities
Restore files and directories	Administrators, Server Operators, Backup Operators	Permission to write to any file or directory on the server
Shut down the system	Administrators, Server Operators, Account Operators, Backup Operators, Print Operators	Privilege to shut down the server
Take ownership of files or other objects	Administrators	Ability to take ownership of files and folders created by another user

GRANTING RIGHTS TO A GROUP

To grant a right, select it in the Rights: list box (see Figure 8-20). Observe the Grant To: box to determine which groups and users are already granted those rights. To grant that right to another group or user, click the Add button to show a list of groups from which to select. If you want to add users as well, click the Show Users button. Highlight a group or user and click

Add. That group or user now appears in the Add Names box. Repeat that process, selecting additional groups or users to include. Click OK in the Add Users and Groups dialog box, then click OK in the User Rights Policy dialog box.

 If a user is granted conflicting rights through two separate groups, the most restrictive rights prevail. For example, suppose you belong to the Managers group that has the right to log on locally, and to the Exec group, which is denied this right. In this case, you cannot log on locally to that server.

CHAPTER SUMMARY

- Begin the process of setting up accounts and groups with some research about the organization in which a Windows NT server is used. The feedback you get from users and advisory bodies will help you make sure that accounts are set up to match the users' needs. As part of your preparations, develop guidelines for account names. Also develop account policies for setting up passwords and account lockout features in Windows NT Server.

- Windows NT domains are a tool to help manage a server. Understanding domains and domain relationships provides a good background for understanding how to set up user accounts and groups. Local and global groups play an important role in helping to manage domain resources and accounts. Groups offer a way to reduce time spent managing individual accounts by using common group characteristics to manage many accounts at one time.

- Creating an account is a multiple-step process. Basic information about the account is provided, such as user and password information. Account setup also involves assigning users to groups, assigning home directories, setting up hours to access the account, and configuring account security options. Accounts can also be copied, deleted, disabled, and renamed. Account activity can be audited in different ways to help locate problems or track account intruders.

- Before setting up groups, plan what groups are needed and their purpose. Access to server functions can be customized for groups and for individual accounts by setting up group policies. Always check the group policies before releasing a server for general use, to make sure that server access is properly set up for all groups and users.

KEY TERMS

- **account lockout** — Security measure that prohibits logging on to an NT server account after a specified number of unsuccessful attempts.

- **Administrator account** — A default account on a Windows NT system with complete and unrestricted access and privileges.

- **auditing** — Tracking the success or failure of events by recording selected types of events in an event log of a server or a workstation.

- **call-back security** — Used for remote communications verification; the remote server calls back the accessing workstation to verify that the access is from an authorized telephone number.

- **global account** — An account type that has regular domain membership and can be recognized by other domains.

- **global group** — A type of Microsoft NT Server grouping that is used to make one Microsoft domain accessible to another, so that resources can be shared and managed across two or more domains.

- **Guest account** — A default user account on Windows NT that has only limited access to network resources.

- **home directory** — A dedicated location on a file server or a workstation for a specific account holder to store files.

- **local account** — An account type that is recognized and used only in the home domain.

- **local group** — In Windows NT Server, a grouping of any combination of accounts, network resources, and global groups. It is used to manage accounts and resources within a single domain or on a single server or NT workstation.

- **logon script** — A file that contains a series of commands to run each time a user logs on to his or her account, such as a command to map a home drive.

- **multiple-master domain** — A domain model that consists of many domains, in which domain management is located in two or more domains.

- **one-way trust** — A domain trust relationship in which one domain is trusted and one is trusting.

- **permissions** — In Windows NT, privileges to access files and folders, such as to read a file or to create a new file.

- **primary group** — A group designation used in setting up a Windows NT Server account for workstations running Macintosh or POSIX. NT Server requires that these systems be members of a global group.

- **rights** — In Windows NT Server and Workstation, access privileges for high-level activities such as logging on to a server from the network, shutting down a server, and creating user accounts.

- **security ID (SID)** — The computer-generated identification code used by Windows NT to uniquely identify users, computers, groups, and other objects.

- **single-master domain** — A relationship model in a domain or domains in which trusts are set up so that management control is centralized in only one domain.

- **trusted domain** — A domain that has been granted security access to resources in another domain.

- **trusting domain** — A domain that allows another domain security access to its resources, such as file servers.

- **two-way trust** — A domain relationship in which both domains are trusted and trusting.

- **universal trust** — A domain relationship among three or more domains in which all domains are mutually trusting and trusted.

REVIEW QUESTIONS

1. A local account is used in the context of _____.
   a. one domain
   b. two or more domains
   c. a remote domain server
   d. all of the above
   e. only b and c

2. The privilege to access a server over the network is a _____.
   a. permission
   b. privilege
   c. right
   d. authority

3. Which of the following can be audited via account auditing?
   a. successfully starting a program
   b. failure to open a file
   c. successfully updating a database value
   d. all of the above
   e. only a and b

4. You want to set up accounts so that they cannot access the server on weekends. From where can you do this?
   a. Profile button in the New User dialog box
   b. Log To button in the Control Panel System icon
   c. Hours button in the New User dialog box
   d. Clock button in the Control Panel System icon

5. Call-back security is used by which of the following?
   a. the audit log to m ake a security check
   b. remote access services
   c. NetBEUI to test a workstation on the network
   d. all of the above
   e. only a and b

8

6. Account policies are set from _____.

    a. User Manager for Domains Policies menu

    b. User Manager for Domains Accounts menu

    c. User Manager for Domains Group menu

    d. Server Manager User menu

7. Account lockout is which of the following?

    a. when an account cannot be accessed because a user has not paid his or her access fee

    b. when a given number of bad logon attempts have been made

    c. when a user accidentally deletes the account access code

    d. when the server is set to deny remote access

8. Global groups can _____.

    a. be domains

    b. use trust inclusion

    c. be members of local groups

    d. all of the above

    e. only a and c

9. A one-way trust has which of the following?

    a. trusted domain

    b. trusting domain

    c. reverse trust domain

    d. all of the above

    e. only a and b

10. A single-master domain model has how many trusted domains?

    a. one

    b. two

    c. three

    d. two or more

11. A trusted domain is one that _____.

    a. has given access to its resources to another domain

    b. has access to the resources in another domain

    c. has only PDC servers

    d. has two or more workgroups

12. One domain can have up to _____ users.

    a. 1,000

    b. 5,000

    c. 10,000

    d. 26,000

13. Advanced user rights are needed for _____.
    a. client/server users
    b. backup operators
    c. expert programmers
    d. server operators

14. Which of the following groups can load and unload device drivers?
    a. Administrators
    b. Server Operators
    c. Backup Operators
    d. Managers
    e. all of the above
    f. only a and b

15. "Guests" is a _____.
    a. local group
    b. global group
    c. account group
    d. account type

16. You want to set a requirement that all passwords must be at least eight characters long. From where would you set this requirement?
    a. Account Creation dialog box
    b. Group Policies
    c. Account Policies
    d. Server Policies

17. "Userdef" is a(n) _____.
    a. default logon script
    b. account lock key
    c. account ID
    d. default profile

18. Which of the following might be used in a logon script?
    a. homepath
    b. username
    c. temppath
    d. all of the above
    e. only a and b

8

19. Which of the following is not a global group?

   a. Domain Users

   b. Domain Operators

   c. Server Operators

   d. all of the above

   e. only b and c

20. You are setting up groups in four domains to manage an accounting system on servers in each domain. Which types of groups would you likely need to set up?

   a. global

   b. local

   c. restricted

   d. all of the above

   e. only a and b

21. You are setting up users in a master domain that is trusted by another domain containing resources. To what type of group do you add users in the master domain for ease of management?

   a. Administrators group

   b. global group

   c. local group

   d. rights group

22. The right to force shutdown from a remote system is granted by default to which of the following groups?

   a. Administrators

   b. Server Operators

   c. Backup Operators

   d. all of the above

   e. only a and b

23. Which group(s) is(are) granted the right to manage auditing and security?

   a. Administrators

   b. Server Operators

   c. Backup Operators

   d. all of the above

   e. only a and c

HANDS-ON PROJECTS

 PROJECT 8-1

In this activity you have an opportunity to find out about an organization's account naming and password guidelines.

To learn about an organization's account naming and password conventions:

1. Contact the server or network administrator at a college or business and make an appointment for a visit or prepare a list of questions for a telephone interview.

2. Ask the administrator about her or his organization's guidelines for setting up user accounts on file servers.

3. Ask about guidelines for passwords, such as password length, history requirements, and account lockout.

4. Ask about any other guidelines relating to accounts or groups on servers.

5. Record the administrator's responses in a document.

 PROJECT 8-2

In this activity you practice setting the account policies on a Windows NT Server. You need access to the Administrator account or to a practice account with Administrator privileges.

To set account policies in Windows NT:

1. Log on to the server, click **Start**, **Programs**, and **Administrative Tools (Common)**.

2. Click **User Manager for Domains**.

3. Click the **Policies** menu and the **Account** option. The Account Policy dialog box opens, which contains options to set the password security and account lockout policies (Figure 8-21).

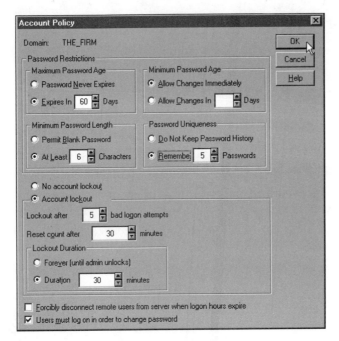

Figure 8-21 Account Policy dialog box

4. Under Maximum Password Age, click **Expires In ____ Days** and type **60** so that each user must change his or her password every 60 days.

5. Under Minimum Password Age, click **Allow Changes Immediately**, so that the account holder can use his or her new password the next time he or she logs on.

6. Under Minimum Password Length, click **At Least ____ Characters** and enter **6** to specify that users must have a password six characters or more in length.

7. Under Password Uniqueness, click **Remember ____ Passwords** and enter **5** to prevent the last five passwords from being reused.

8. Click the **Account lockout** radio button.

9. Enter **5** in the **Lockout after ____ bad logon attempts** scroll box, which means that the account cannot be accessed after someone enters the wrong password five times.

10. Enter **30** in the **Reset count after ____ minutes** scroll box. Thus, if there are five bad logon attempts within 30 minutes, the account is locked.

11. Under Lockout Duration, click **Duration ____ minutes** and enter **30** again, as the number of minutes the account will remain locked until it can be accessed again.

12. At the bottom of the screen, check **Users must log on in order to change password**, which means that a user must be able to log on to change a password. If the user waits to change his or her password until after the expiration date, then he or she will have to ask the network administrator to change it.

13. Click **OK** to confirm the settings and exit the Account Policy dialog box.

14. Close User Manager for Domains.

 PROJECT 8-3

In this activity you create an account on an NT Server.

To create an account:

1. Click **Start**, **Programs**, and **Administrative Tools (Common)**.
2. Click **User Manager for Domains**.
3. Click the **User** menu and **New User** (see Figure 8-10).
4. Enter an account name in the Username: box, such as your first initial and last name combined with no space (see Figure 8-11).
5. Enter your full name in the Full Name: box.
6. Enter a description, such as **Server Administrator**.
7. Enter a six-character or longer password in the Password: box.
8. Enter the password again in the Confirm Password: box.
9. Check the box **User Must Change Password at Next Login**.
10. Click the **Add** button.
11. Close User Manager for Domains.

 PROJECT 8-4

In this activity you add the account created in Hands-on Project 8-3 to the Administrators group.

To add an account to Administrators:

1. Click **Start**, **Programs**, and **Administrative Tools (Common)**.
2. Click **User Manager for Domains**.
3. Under the Username column, double-click the account you created in the last activity.
4. In the User Properties box (also called the New User box when an account is being created), click the **Groups** button.

8

5. Click **Administrators** in the Not member of: box (refer to Figure 8-12).

6. Click the **Add** button.

7. Click **OK** in the Group Memberships dialog box.

8. Leave the User Properties dialog box open for the next Hands-on Project.

 PROJECT 8-5

In this activity you reserve time five nights a week for backups, so that users cannot access the server.

To make the server inaccessible on certain nights:

1. In the User Properties dialog box left open in the last activity, click the **Hours** button.

2. In the Monday row, click the **6 PM** box and drag the cursor to **Midnight**, so that this block of time is highlighted (refer to Figure 8-15).

3. Repeat Step 2 for the Tuesday, Wednesday, Thursday, and Friday rows.

4. Click the **Disallow** button.

5. Click **OK**.

6. Click **OK** in the User Properties dialog box.

 PROJECT 8-6

In this activity you copy an existing account as a way to quickly create a new account.

To create a new account by copying an account:

1. In User Manager for Domains, highlight the **GUEST** account.

2. Click the **User** menu and click **Copy**.

3. In the Copy of Guest dialog box, enter the new user name (for example, MSanchez), a full name, description, password, and password confirmation.

4. Click to select the box for **User Must Change Password at Next Logon**, so that the new account user will have to create a new password as soon as she or he logs on.

5. Click the **Profile** button and note the information you would need to enter for the profile, logon script, and home drive. Click **Cancel**.

6. Click **Add** in the Copy of Guest dialog box to complete the account creation.

PROJECT 8-7

In this activity you create a global group called Payroll.

To create a global group:

1. Click **Start**, **Programs**, and **Administrative Tools (Common)**.
2. Click **User Manager for Domains**.
3. Click the **User** menu and **New Global Group**.
4. Enter **Payroll** in the Group Name: box and enter **Payroll staff at plant one** in the Description: box.
5. Click **Administrator** under Not Members: and click **Add**.
6. Click **Guest** under Not Members: and click **Add** (you use Administrator and Guest for practice because these are users on every server).
7. Click **OK** in the New Global Group dialog box.
8. Close User Manager for Domains.

8

 ASPEN CONSULTING: SETTING UP ACCOUNTS AND GROUPS

Today you are working with a large hardware store, Tools Unlimited, to help it set up accounts and groups for its staff, which uses a Windows NT server for sales, business, inventory, and purchasing activities.

1. Tools Unlimited has at least 30 sales representatives helping customers at a given time. All sales, inventory, and purchasing functions will soon be performed by means of programs and databases on an NT Server. There are 20 networked workstations on the sales floor that double as electronic cash registers. Also, the business office contains eight networked workstations for its eight-member staff. Tools Unlimited is contacting you for advice about setting up accounts on their server. Describe an account policy and naming scheme that would work for this company. What information would you get from the company in order to develop your recommendations?

2. The accounting and payroll information on the Tools Unlimited server will only be seen and used by the eight business office employees. Further, the store inventory and inventory purchasing are handled by only two people in the business office. Sales and cash register activity are handled only by the sales representatives. Explain how you might set up domains and groups for Tools Unlimited.

3. Tools Unlimited has selected a server administrator from among the business office staff members. Their administrator has lots of questions about setting up accounts. Make a table to summarize for their server administrator where to set up certain administrative functions. Set up the table with three columns: Function, Windows NT Server Tool, and General Instructions to Access the Tool. Place the following under the Function column:

   - Set up a new account
   - Set account policies
   - Set up a group
   - Add a right to a group
   - Restrict hours that an account can access the server
   - Set a pointer to an account's home directory
   - Restrict access to the Administrator account to only the server administrator's computer

   Complete the rest of the table to show which NT Server tool is used for each function, and provide general instructions to set up the function using that tool.

4. Explain how to copy an account and how this might make account setup go faster for Tools Unlimited.

5. Explain how to set up the groups you recommended in Case Assignment 2 for Tools Unlimited.

6. One of the sales representatives has already forgotten his password. Explain how to set a new password for that sales representative.

MANAGING SERVER FOLDERS, PERMISSIONS, AND SOFTWARE INSTALLATION

The primary purpose of a network is to provide access to shared resources. Windows NT servers seamlessly offer information and system resources to users in the form of shared folders and files. The server administrator's job is to set up folders and files so that they are easy to manage as well as accessible to clients. A well-planned folder structure is critical for managing a server. Another critical area is establishing folder security to make sure that only intended users can access folder contents.

Network software applications are some of the most accessed files on a server. Applications like Microsoft Office are designed for networking, while other applications require more work to install and use. Windows NT Server contains tools to help set up applications and customize them for network implementation. Two examples of these tools are the Registry and Microsoft License Manager. In this chapter you learn about these and other tools, such as Directory Replicator, which automatically copies folders from one computer to another. You also learn to design a folder structure and to manage folders on a server.

AFTER READING THIS CHAPTER AND COMPLETING THE EXERCISES YOU WILL BE ABLE TO:

- MANAGE FOLDERS ON A SERVER, INCLUDING THE FOLLOWING TASKS: PLANNING A FOLDER STRUCTURE, VIEWING AND CREATING FOLDERS, SETTING FOLDER PROPERTIES SUCH AS ATTRIBUTES, PERMISSIONS, AUDITING, AND OWNERSHIP, SETTING UP SHARED FOLDERS, AND MOVING AND COPYING FILES AND FOLDERS

- INSTALL AND MANAGE APPLICATION SOFTWARE

- USE THE REGISTRY TO CONFIGURE WINDOWS NT SERVER AND APPLICATION SOFTWARE, AND USE WINDOWS NT DIAGNOSTICS TO VIEW REGISTRY CONTENTS

- SET SYSTEM POLICIES USING THE SYSTEM POLICY EDITOR

- CONFIGURE AND USE THE LICENSE MANAGER

- CONFIGURE AND USE THE DIRECTORY REPLICATOR

MANAGING FOLDERS

Managing folders is one of the major and most important tasks of a network administrator. It includes designing the hierarchy and structure of folders, viewing existing folders and creating new folders, setting properties for folders (this is when security is implemented), setting up shared folders, and moving and copying files and folders.

DESIGNING A FOLDER STRUCTURE

It is easy for a hard disk to become cluttered and disorganized with different versions of files and software. Many PC users keep all their files in the computer's **root folder**, or they load all application software into the same folder. Application software programs often use an automated setup that suggests a folder for new programs, but some users still have difficulty organizing files. A chaotic file structure makes it difficult to run or remove programs, as well as to determine the most current versions.

To avoid confusion, carefully design file and folder structure from the start, especially on the server because it has an impact on all users. Chapter 8, "Managing the Server Through Accounts and Groups," provided a start by presenting ways to organize home directories under a Users folder in the root folder. Beyond home directories, there needs to be a place for the following:

- Software applications
- Confidential files shared by particular groups
- Public files shared by everyone
- Software utilities for all users
- Server management utilities

In deciding how to allocate folders for specific types of files, consider following some general practices. For instance, the root folder should not be cluttered with files or too many folders. Each software application should have its own folder or subfolder, so that updates and software removal are easy to administer. For easy access control, similar information should be grouped, such as accounting systems or office productivity software. Windows NT Server system files should be kept separate and protected so that important files are not accidentally deleted by a user. Folders should have names that clearly reflect their purpose. For example, consider a law office that uses legal time accounting software, legal forms software, Microsoft Office, shared spreadsheets and Word documents, and general utility applications for all users. Also, this law firm has a confidential folder containing human resources and other sensitive information available to the managing partners. Their folder structure from the root might be as follows:

- *Users* for home directories
- *App* for general software and utilities
- *Msoffice* for Microsoft Office applications

- *Data* for shared spreadsheets
- *Word* for shared Microsoft Word files
- *Forms* for legal forms software
- *Manage* for the managing partners
- *Ntserver* for server and network management utilities

 On DOS and Windows systems, the root folder or directory of the hard drive often is represented by C:\ and the first network drive as F:\.

Each major folder has subfolders to keep grouped files or application software separate. For example, the Msoffice folder might have the subfolders: Access, Clipart, Excel, Office, Queries, Templates, and Winword. The Forms folder might have subfolders containing legal forms software for different legal areas such as Contracts, Wills, Court, Bankruptcy, Tax, and RealEstate.

Figure 9-1 is a diagram of a sample folder structure for a law firm, showing the subfolders for the Forms and Msoffice folders on a server.

9

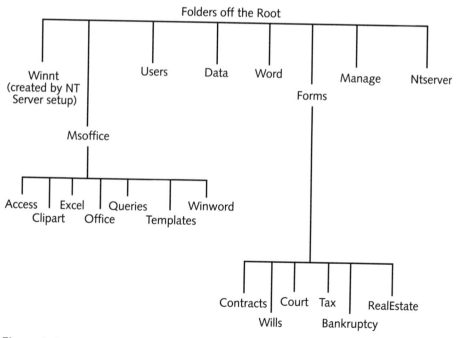

Figure 9-1   A sample folder structure

VIEWING AND CREATING FOLDERS

Use My Computer on the desktop or Windows NT Explorer from the Start button, Programs menu to view folders. For example, to view the folders in the root directory, double-click My Computer and then double-click drive C. To view the contents of one of these folders, such as Users, double-click it (Figure 9-2).

Figure 9-2   Viewing server folders

The files and folders displayed in My Computer or Windows NT Explorer can be customized by clicking the View menu and then Toolbar. The toolbar contains buttons that enable you to display the files and folders in different ways: as large icons, small icons, as a vertical list of small icons with no details, or as text with folders and files listed vertically with information about size, item type, modification date, and attributes.

A new folder can be created from My Computer or Windows NT Explorer. To create a folder, click the File menu, New, and then Folder (Figure 9-3). The folder display returns, highlighting a box in which to enter a title for the folder. Enter the title and press Enter. If the title is entered incorrectly, you can reenter it by right-clicking the new folder and selecting Rename. (You can practice creating and renaming a folder in Hands-on Project 9-1 at the end of the chapter.)

When creating a folder, be certain that the name is entered correctly from the start. It is confusing and time-consuming to change folder names after users have built mapped drives to the original ones.

SETTING FOLDER PROPERTIES

When a folder is created, there are several folder properties that can be set. To view the folder properties, right-click the folder in My Computer or in NT Explorer, and click Properties. There are three Properties tabs for any folder: General, Sharing, and Security. The General tab contains descriptive information about the folder and folder attributes, the Sharing tab enables the folder to be shared with network users, and the Security tab is for setting folder permissions.

Figure 9-3   Creating a new folder

General Properties

The General tab shows descriptive information about the folder, such as type of object, location, size, and number of files or folders contained within the folder (Figure 9-4). The folder name and creation date also appear on the screen. The bottom of the screen has folder attributes that can be assigned.

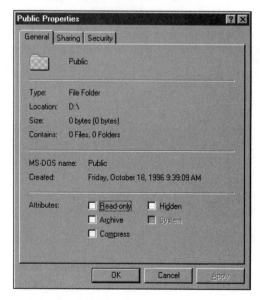

Figure 9-4   Folder properties

Attributes are folder and file characteristics and should not be confused with NT File System (NTFS) permissions.

Use of **attributes** is retained in NTFS as a carryover from earlier DOS-based systems and to provide a partial migration path to convert files and directories from a Novell NetWare file server. DOS and NetWare systems use file attributes as a form of security and file management. These attributes, except for backup purposes, are largely ignored by NT administrators in favor of rights and permissions. Attributes are stored as header information with each folder and file, along with other characteristics, including volume label, designation as a subfolder, date of creation, and time of creation. Table 9-1 provides a comparison of attributes for MS-DOS, NetWare, and Windows NT.

As Table 9-1 shows, folder and file attributes available in NTFS are Read-only, Archive, Compress, Hidden, and System. If you check Read-only, the folder is read-only, but not the files in the folder. This means that the folder cannot be deleted or renamed from the MS-DOS command line. Also, it cannot be deleted or renamed by a user other than one belonging to the Administrators group. If an administrator attempts to delete or rename the folder, a warning message states that the folder is read-only and asks whether to proceed. Most Windows NT server administrators leave the read-only box blank and set the equivalent protection in permissions instead, because the read-only permissions apply to the folder and its files.

Archive is checked to indicate that the folder or file needs to be backed up, because the folder or file is new or changed. Most network administrators ignore the folder Archive attribute, but instead rely on the Archive attribute for files. Files, but not folders, are automatically flagged to archive when they are changed. File server backup systems can be set to detect files with the Archive attribute, to ensure that those files are backed up. The backup system ensures that each file is saved, following the same folder or subfolder scheme as on the file server.

Table 9-1   MS-DOS, Novell NetWare, and Windows NT Attributes

MS-DOS Attribute	NetWare Attribute	Windows NT Equivalent Attribute	Purpose of Attribute
Read-only (R)	Read-only (RO)	Read-only (R)	Prevents directory or file from being changed or deleted
Archive (A)	Archive (A)	Archive (A)	Directory or file is new or changed and needs to be backed up
No equivalent	No equivalent	Compress (C)	Compresses files to save disk space
System (S)	System (SY)	System (S)	File is used by the operating system and should not be viewed with ordinary list commands — used by NetWare directories but not NT directories

Table 9-1   MS-DOS, Novell NetWare, and Windows NT Attributes (continued)

MS-DOS Attribute	NetWare Attribute	Windows NT Equivalent Attribute	Purpose of Attribute
Hidden (H)	Hidden (H)	Hidden (H)	Directory or file cannot be viewed with ordinary list commands
No equivalent —file is not flagged with an R	Read-Write (RW)	No equivalent—file is not flagged with an R	Directory or file can be viewed, changed, or deleted
No equivalent	Copy Inhibit (C)	Handled through NTFS permissions	Cannot copy a file
No equivalent	Delete Inhibit (D)	Handled through NTFS permissions	Cannot delete a directory or file
No equivalent	Execute only (X)	Handled through NTFS permissions	Can only execute a file (run the program)
No equivalent	Indexed (I)	Handled by the NT operating system	Flags large files for fast access
No equivalent	Purge (P)	Handled by the Recycle Bin	Purge deleted directories and files so that they cannot be salvaged
No equivalent	Rename Inhibit (RI)	Handled through NTFS permissions	Cannot rename a directory or file
No equivalent	Read Audit (RA)	No equivalent	Can be assigned, but has no function in NetWare 3.1 and later systems
No equivalent	Sharable (SH)	Handled by creating a network share	Files can be accessed by more than one user at a time
No equivalent	Transactional (T)	Handled by NTFS through directory and file recovery options	For recovery of data files after a system interruption, such as a power failure
No equivalent	Write Audit (WA)	No equivalent	Can be assigned, but has no function in NetWare 3.1 and later systems

9

A folder and its contents can be stored on the disk in compressed format, which is a property of NTFS. This attribute is used when disk space is limited, or for directories that are accessed infrequently, such as those used to store old fiscal year accounting data. Compression saves space, but it takes longer to access information because each file must be decompressed before it is read.

There also is the option to compress files in subfolders. Subfolders are not automatically compressed along with the folder's files, unless this option is checked. If you want to compress the folder files and the files in its subdirectories, check Compress and click the Apply button. A message appears warning that all files in the main folder will be compressed, accompanied by a box to check for compressing files in subfolders (Figure 9-5).

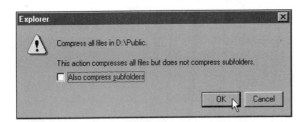

Figure 9-5   Compressing files and subfolders

Folders can be marked as Hidden to prevent users from viewing their contents. For example, one college server administrator placed zip code verification software on a network, but kept the folder hidden while several users tested it. After testing was completed, the Hidden attribute was removed.

    The Hidden attribute can be overridden by any Windows 95 or Windows NT Workstation or Server user by selecting to view hidden files from the View menu in Explorer or My Computer.

The System attribute is deactivated for folders and cannot be set. This attribute is used on system files to make them hidden and read-only for protection against accidental deletion.

Folder and Permission Security

Always set up or check folder security before releasing a folder for public access. Click the Security tab on the folder's Properties dialog box to set up permissions. There are three security options: Permissions, Auditing, and Ownership (Figure 9-6). Permissions control access to the folder and its contents. Auditing enables the administrator to audit activities on a folder or file, such as the number of times the folder or file has been read or changed. Ownership designates the folder owner who has full control of that folder.

Permissions are set on objects such as folders, subfolders, files, and shares. Shares are resources (objects), such as folders or printers, that are made available to network users. Because permissions can be set at several levels, there needs to be a way to determine what permission applies. For example, permissions on a folder may be different from permissions set on the network share of that folder. Or permissions on a file may be different from those of its parent folder. When there are multiple permissions, in general a principle of least allowed access applies as a way to err in favor of greatest security (see the following Note). For example, you might set up a shared folder called Public with full share permissions. At the same time, you might set basic permissions (through the Permissions button) to allow no access. It is unlikely that you would make this mistake, but if you did, users would have no access to the folder.

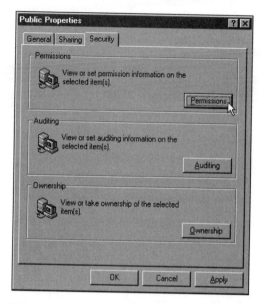

Figure 9-6   Folder Properties Security tab

 There are exceptions to the principle of least allowed access. For example, the owner of a folder has full access even though the owner belongs to a group that has no access. Ownership is usually associated with the account that created the folder and overrides the conflicting access. Also, members of the Administrators group always have authority to take ownership of any folder or other server object.

 Permissions can be set on individual files within a folder. However, managing these exceptions can become time-consuming and confusing. Instead, create a subfolder for exceptions, for easier management.

Ownership of a folder or subfolder gives the owner entire control, including the ability to set permissions. Many server administrators limit ownership to the Administrators group, except for a few situations. The folders typically owned by users include subfolders within their home directories and subfolders within publicly shared directories. Users can create and own subfolders within a folder for which they have appropriate permissions. When there are user areas on a server, it is wise to monitor available disk space, so that the disk does not fill up too quickly.

Permissions

Click the Permissions button to set folder permissions. The Directory Permissions dialog box has two check boxes at the top. The first check box sets permissions on all subfolders, and the second sets permissions on all files in the folder. You have the option to check one or both boxes. For example, if you check only Replace Permissions on Existing Files, from that point on, the permissions you set apply to the folder and its files. Table 9-2 lists the folder and file permissions supported by NTFS.

Table 9-2   NTFS Folder and File Permissions

Permission	Access and Abbreviation*	Description	Applies to
No access	None	No access to the folder for any users other than the owner	Folders and files
List	Read and execute files (RX)	Can list files in the folder or switch to a subfolder, but cannot access the file contents	Folders only
Read	Read and execute files (RX)	For existing and new files, can read their contents and can execute program files	Folders and files
Add	Write and execute files (WX)	Can write new files in the folder and execute program files, but cannot view the folder files	Folders only
Add & Read	Read, write, and execute files (RWX)	Can read files, add new files, and execute program files, but cannot modify the file contents	Folders only
Change	Read, write, execute, and delete files (RWXD)	Can read, add, delete, execute, and modify files	Folders and files
Full Control	All directory and file permissions	Can read, add, delete, execute, and modify files plus change permissions and take ownership of folders	Folders and files

*D = delete files; R = read files; W = write files; X = execute files

The permission with the broadest range of capabilities is Full Control. This permission is the default assigned to a folder at the time it is created. Most server administrators change Full Control to another permission, so that the ability to take ownership and assign permissions is kept with the Administrators group. Click the list arrow to display the permission options, as in Figure 9-7. For example, to set the permissions from Full Control to Change, highlight Change and click OK. In this example, members in the Everyone group will have permissions to read, add, delete, execute, and modify files. Click OK to accept the changes.

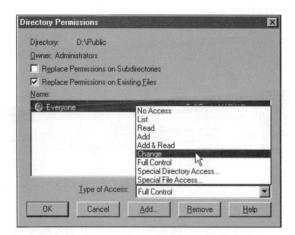

Figure 9-7   Directory Permissions dialog box

In the same dialog box, there is the option to specify which groups can access the folder with a specified set of permissions. The group Everyone, which includes all users, is set as the default; however, you may want to remove Everyone, so that this group does not have access, and replace it with Server Operators, for example. To do that, click Everyone in the Name: box and then click Remove. Next, click Add to access the Add Users and Groups dialog box. Make sure that the domain is listed in the List Names From: box. To view user accounts as well as groups in the Names: box, click the Show Users button. Click the group Server Operators and the Add button. Click Full Control in the Type of Access: list box, and then click OK. Click OK again in the Directory Permissions dialog box and OK in the Properties dialog box. (Practice setting folder permissions in Hands-on Project 9-2.)

You can add multiple groups or accounts in the Add Users and Groups dialog box by clicking each one and then clicking Add. When all of your selections are in the Add Names: box, select the type of access to apply to all of them, and then click OK.

Microsoft provides guidelines for setting permissions as follows:

- Protect the Winnt folder that contains operating system files on NT servers and workstations, and its subfolders, from general users through No Access or Read, but give the Administrators group Full Control access.

- Protect server utility folders, such as those used for backup software and network management, with access permissions only for Administrators, Server Operators, and Backup Operators.

- Protect software application folders with Add & Read to enable users to run applications and write temporary files, but not to alter files.

- Create publicly used folders with Change access, so that users have broad access except to take ownership and set permissions.

- Provide users Full Control of their own home directories.

- Remove the group Everyone from confidential folders, such as those used for personal mail, for sensitive files, or for software development projects.

 Always err on the side of too much security. It is easier, in terms of human relations, to give users more permissions later than it is to take away permissions.

The Special Folder Access and Special File Access options listed in the Directory Permissions dialog box for type of access enable you to customize folder or file access beyond the standard permissions. For example, by clicking Special File Access, you could click Read and Write access only, or Delete and Execute only (Figure 9-8).

In most cases you should stay with the standard permissions, unless a unique situation arises, such as meeting special software installation requirements. For example, there might be a situation in which a program only stores setup parameters in the program files folder, and you want to remove users' ability to change the setup file or to create their own customized setup. This may be necessary to ensure that everyone uses the program identically. In this case, you can set up the folder as Execute only through Special Folder Access. The option Access Not Specified means that files cannot be accessed. (NTFS security does not permit access to a folder or any other object when the type of access is not specified.)

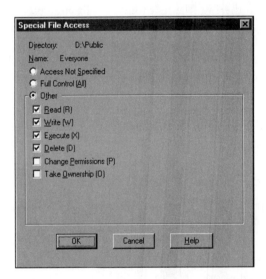

Figure 9-8   Special File Access parameters

Auditing

Accessing folders and files can be tracked by setting up auditing through the Audit button on the Security tab in the Properties dialog box. The Directory Auditing dialog box (Figure 9-9) enables you to audit the following successful and failed attempts:

- *Read* events, such as listing files and details about files
- *Write* events, including creating files and subfolders and changing folder attributes
- *Execute* events, such as changing from one subfolder to another and displaying folder permissions and ownership
- *Delete* events, such as deleting folders and subfolders
- *Change Permissions* events, including any time that permissions are modified
- *Take Ownership* events, which change the ownership of a folder

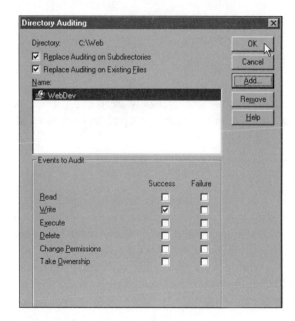

Figure 9-9   Folder and file auditing

To implement folder and file auditing, click the Auditing button and then check one or both of the check boxes at the top of the Directory Auditing dialog box. The option Replace Auditing on Subdirectories enables you to audit the listed events in all subfolders under the folder in which you are setting up auditing. The option Replace Auditing on Existing Files is used to audit events involving files in a folder, as well as to audit folder accesses. After selecting one or both of those options, click the Add button and select one or more groups to audit. Click Add and then check the type of auditing you wish to perform, such as auditing successful changes to folder permissions. If you have previously set up account auditing, then the system connects an audited event with an account.

For example, if account RJenson is set up for file and folder event auditing, and folder Utilities is set up to audit successful reads, then an event record is kept each time account RJenson lists files in folder Utilities or modifies any file in that folder. (Try Hands-on Project 9-3 to audit accesses to a folder.)

Besides tracking folder access, you also track file access through auditing. An audit record can be kept for each time a file is opened or each time a file is modified. The following are file audit activities:

- Reading events, such as displaying the contents of a file or viewing the file permissions and attributes
- Writing events, such as modifying the file contents or changing file attributes (also viewing the file permissions and attributes)
- Executing events, such as running a program file (also viewing the file permissions and attributes)
- Deleting a file
- Changing file permissions
- Changing file ownership

 Use folder and file auditing carefully because it can slow access to the server, for example, if an audit record must be written each time a popular file is accessed.

Ownership

With permissions and auditing set up, you may want to check the ownership of a folder. Folders are first owned by the account that creates them, such as the Administrator account. Folder owners have Full Control permissions for the folders they create. Also, ownership can be transferred only by having Full Control Permission. This permission enables a user to take control of a folder and become its owner. Taking ownership is the only way to shift control from one account to another. The Administrators group always has the ability to take control of any folder, regardless of the permissions.

To take ownership, click the Ownership button in the Securities tab in the Properties dialog box. The next dialog box (Figure 9-10) shows the folder name and the account that is the owner. If you need to take ownership, click the Take Ownership button. There are instances in which the server administrator needs to take ownership of a folder, such as when someone leaves an organization.

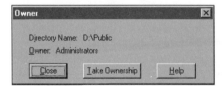

Figure 9-10   Taking ownership of a folder

SETTING UP A SHARED FOLDER

Along with setting permissions, auditing, and ownership, you can set up a folder as a shared folder for network users to access. To share a server folder, access the Sharing tab in the folder's Public Properties dialog box (from the desktop, highlight the folder in My Computer or NT Explorer, right-click it, and select Sharing). As Figure 9-11 shows, the Sharing tab has two main options: to share or not to share the folder. To share a folder so that network users can access or map it, click the Shared As: radio button. Figure 9-11 shows the folder Public, with the share name Public, for general sharing. The radio button Maximum Allowed enables as many accesses as there are Windows NT client access licenses. The other option, Allow _____ Users, enables you to specify a limit to the number of simultaneous users. This is one way to ensure that the licensing restrictions for software are followed.

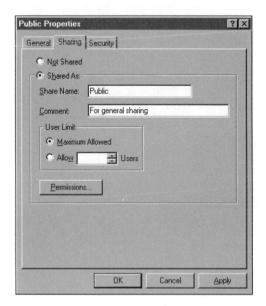

Figure 9-11   Sharing a folder

There is an option to hide a shared folder so it does not appear on a browser list, as in Network Neighborhood. To hide a share, place the $ sign just after its name. For instance if the Share Name: box contains the share name Budget, you can hide the share by entering Budget$. (This is an actual example of what one university does to discourage general scanning of a folder containing budget worksheets. However, department assistants who know of the folder's existence can access it to help with budget planning.)

For example, suppose that you have an accounting software package in a folder and have only two licenses. In this case you would set the Allow _____ Users parameter to 2, so that the license requirement is honored.

You can set permissions for the share from this tab by clicking the Permissions button. As explained earlier, share permissions can differ from basic folder permissions set through the Security tab, but the most restrictive permission takes precedence. There are four share permissions that are associated with a folder:

- *No Access* prevents access to the shared folder by the specified groups or users.

- *Read* permits groups or users to read and execute files.

- *Change* enables users to read, add, modify, execute, and delete files.

- *Full Control* provides full access to the folder, including the ability to take control or change permissions.

Before setting the share permissions, first make sure that you have selected the appropriate groups and users, for example by specifying the Everyone group for a publicly accessed folder. You can remove a group by highlighting it in the list box in the Access Through Share Permissions dialog box and clicking Remove. To set the share permissions, highlight a group, click the list arrow for Type of Access:, and select the permission, such as Change (Figure 9-12). (Practice setting share permissions in Hands-on Project 9-4.)

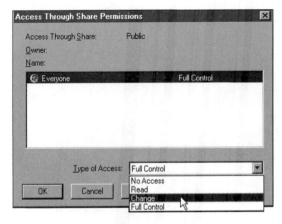

Figure 9-12   Setting share permissions

TROUBLESHOOTING A SECURITY CONFLICT

Sometimes you will set up access for a user, but find that the user does not actually have the type of access you set up. Consider the example of Cleo Jackson, a professor who maintains a shared folder, CompData, for his students from the account CJackson. CJackson needs to update files, copy in new files, and delete files. As Administrator, you have granted CJackson Change access permissions to CompData. However, you omitted the step of reviewing the groups to which CJackson belongs, such as the Profs group, which only has Read permissions to the CompData folder. When Cleo Jackson attempts to copy a file to the folder, he receives an "Access is denied" message.

To troubleshoot the problem, you should review the folder permissions and share permissions for the CJackson account and for the groups to which CJackson belongs. In this case, because Profs is limited to Read share permissions, group member CJackson is also limited to Read permissions. The easiest solution is to remove CJackson from Profs and put the account in a more appropriate group, or create a new group in which to put similar accounts, such as NetProfs for professors who maintain a shared folder for their classes.

This example also illustrates how you save both time and user aggravation when you carefully plan in advance the folder structure and user groups in light of the server security needs.

9

MOVING AND COPYING FILES AND FOLDERS

A common task is to move or copy files from one folder to another in the same volume or to a different volume. When a file is copied, the original file remains intact and a copy is made in another folder. Moving a file causes it to be deleted from the original location and placed in a different folder on the same or on a different volume. Copying and moving are done in the same way for a folder, but the entire folder contents (files and subfolders) are copied or moved.

When a file is created, moved, or copied, the file and folder permissions can be affected in the following ways:

- A *newly created* file takes on the permissions already set up in a folder.

- A file that is *copied* from one folder to another on the *same volume* inherits the permissions of the folder to which it is copied.

- A file or folder that is *moved* from one folder to another on the *same volume* takes with it the permissions it had in the original folder. For example, if the original folder had Read permissions and the folder to which it is transplanted has Change permissions, that file will still only have Read permissions.

- A file or folder that is *moved or copied* to a folder on *different volume* inherits the permissions of the folder to which it is moved or copied.

- A file or folder that is *moved or copied from an NTFS volume to a folder in a FAT volume* is not protected by NTFS permissions, but it does inherit share permissions if they are assigned to the FAT folder.

- A file or folder that is *moved or copied from a FAT volume to a folder in an NTFS volume* has no access permissions (other than to the owner who moved or copied it) and should be assigned permissions so it can be accessed.

Windows NT offers many ways to move and copy files and folders. You can use the right-click or left-click drag method. Right-click the file or folder you want to copy or move, and while holding down the right mouse button, drag it into the folder to which you want it copied or moved. When you release the right mouse button, click Copy Here or Move Here on the shortcut menu. If you use the left mouse button to click and drag a file or folder, it moves or copies it without presenting the shortcut menu. When you use the left mouse button, the file or folder is moved if the destination is on the same volume or disk; it is copied if the destination is on a different volume or disk. Another way to move and copy files or folders is to use the Cut, Copy, and Paste toolbar icons in My Computer and NT Explorer. (Practice moving and copying files and folders in Hands-on Project 9-5.)

If you discover that you have moved or copied the wrong file or folder, immediately click the Edit menu in My Computer or NT Explorer, and then click Undo Move.

All of these techniques can be used to move and copy files and folders between FAT and NTFS volumes. However, files and folders copied to FAT will not be protected by NTFS permissions, but FAT folders are protected by share permissions.

INSTALLING AND MANAGING APPLICATION SOFTWARE

There are several important issues to consider before installing application software for users to access or set up from a server. These include the following:

- Software licensing
- Network compatibility
- Network performance
- Location of temporary files
- Software testing
- Loading software from the network
- Restrictions for MS-DOS-based software

Application software is licensed to the user as explained in the software licensing agreement. The server administrator should carefully read and follow the licensing agreement before loading software. Some companies offer site licensing for unlimited access to the software through the network. Others restrict software licensing to groupings, such as "5-packs" or "10-packs." Some come with license monitoring built into the software, whereas others rely on the server administrator to monitor use, such as by using Microsoft's License Manager or by placing a user access limit on a shared folder. **License monitoring** involves creating a mechanism to ensure that network users do not access software in numbers larger than the software license allows.

Besides monitoring license use, the server administrator also is responsible for copy protecting the software as much as possible. This is accomplished in two ways. One is to set permissions on software directories so that it is difficult to copy the software from the network, for example protecting program files with permission to Execute only. Many software applications cannot be fully protected because of their runtime requirements, such as creating individual setup files. Therefore, the second way to protect software is often the best. This is to fully educate network users on their responsibility to honor software licensing.

Some applications, such as desktop publishing programs, are not designed to run from a network. In these cases, the best solution is to consult with the vendor about how to adapt the software for a network, if possible. The best advice is to check all applications to be certain that they are network-compatible. **Network-compatible** programs are designed for multi-user access, often with network capabilities such as options to send files through e-mail.

The network load generated by an application is another issue. Some database applications create high levels of traffic, particularly if the entire database is sent each time a user wishes to examine a small amount of information. Database reporting tools also may generate high traffic. Graphics and computer-aided design programs are other examples. Traffic is not likely to be a problem on a small network, but it is important to closely monitor network activity associated with applications.

Some applications create temporary or backup files while the application is running. For example, Microsoft Word creates backup files so that work can be restored after a power failure or computer problem. It is important to determine what extra files are needed to run an application and where to store them. For example, Word backup files can be directed to the user's home directory through Word setup or to the user's workstation hard drive. Plan to teach software users how to deploy temporary and backup files created by software. Also, show users how to delete old temporary and backup files no longer needed.

Microsoft Office programs create .TMP files that may not be automatically deleted when the user exits a program such as Microsoft Word. A fast way to delete these files is to use the Find utility from the Windows Explorer Tools menu, searching for all .TMP files from the root level and then deleting them.

Plan to test each software installation before releasing it to the users. You might test it from two or more special server accounts created for that purpose. Another way to test software is to first install and test it on a Windows NT Workstation and then port it to Windows NT Server, which is a common technique used by server and network administrators. Testing is important as a way to determine that the software is working, is network compatible, and that the permissions are correctly set.

Some applications, such as Microsoft Office, provide the option to install software application files from the network onto each client workstation. Another way is to install client software so that application files are loaded from the server each time the application is run. The second way might take a few seconds longer to run the application, because the files are shipped over the network instead of loaded from the user's hard drive. The advantage is a significant savings in disk space on the workstation. A disadvantage is the extra network traffic created on a large network.

Some organizations have MS-DOS software applications to load onto the server. Difficulties that may arise from this software include memory management problems, swap space requirements, lock files that lock the application to one user at a time, and drivers that are not compatible with Windows 95 or Windows NT. Often the best solution is to avoid networking these applications, instead running them independently on individual workstations. If it is necessary to run the application from the network, it is wise to fully test it to be sure that the application does not interfere with other NT Server operations.

Some applications use **swap space** on a hard disk to store data for manipulation or because the data won't fit in memory. Check to be sure that you know where the application writes the swap space and that it deletes old swap space.

There are instances in which software does not work properly in Windows 95 or Windows NT because of updates in **application program interfaces (APIs)** from Microsoft. APIs are portions of the operating system that perform specific functions or provide links to the operating system, such as for mail services or network communication services. Microsoft is standardizing the APIs for both Windows 95 and Windows NT through a common set of programming interfaces called WIN32, to address this issue. However, some applications might still introduce problems. Most vendors develop "fixes" for these problems, which are available at the vendors' Internet sites.

More and more software companies offer software through the Internet. Eventually most software may be purchased and loaded directly through the Internet, instead of from disks or CD-ROMs.

INSTALLING SOFTWARE USING ADD/REMOVE PROGRAMS

The best way to install software is to use the Add/Remove Programs icon in the Windows NT Server Control Panel. There are two important advantages in using the Add/Remove Programs utility:

- With this method, software configuration is stored in the Windows NT Registry. This makes software configuration easier, and configuration information can be updated to the Emergency Repair Disk in case problems develop later.

- The Registry tracks the location of all files associated with software, such as program, initialization, and **dynamic link library (DLL)** files. The Registry information makes it easier to remove all program pieces, if necessary.

Consider the installation of Microsoft Office. Before starting the setup, check the licensing information to be sure that you have purchased enough licenses for the installation on the server and for users to install it from the server. Before installing Microsoft Office, insert the Microsoft Office CD-ROM in the server's CD-ROM drive. Next, double-click the Add/Remove Programs icon in the Control Panel, and click the Install button (Figure 9-13).

9

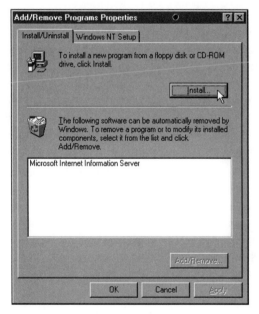

Figure 9-13   Installing software

The Installation Setup Wizard takes over with a request to install the setup disk in the floppy or CD-ROM drive. Click Next and then click the Browse button to provide the path to the Microsoft Office setup program on the CD-ROM drive. With the correct path and installation program name entered, click Finish. The Microsoft Office setup program takes over, providing different options to install the Office software. After the software is installed, create a shared folder, such as Msoffice, for network users to access.

Many server administrators advise users to map a permanent drive from their workstations, using a drive letter that represents the software, such as mapping drive M for Microsoft products.

RUNNING SOFTWARE APPLICATIONS IN USER MODE

When a software application is run on Windows NT Server it runs in **user mode**. This means that it does not have direct access to the system kernel, operating system services, CPU, or hardware. Each application runs in its own memory address space, which is the extent to which it affects Windows NT. The Windows NT kernel, consisting of operating system code and services, runs in the privileged **kernel mode**, which also is called the supervisor or protected mode. The operating system programs running in the kernel mode have access to hardware, CPU registers, and I/O functions. They also run in a protected area of memory that cannot be accessed by applications in user mode. If a software application needs to access hardware or an operating system service, it must go through an API that serves as a go-between.

The advantage of user mode and kernel mode architecture is that the Windows NT operating system is not affected when an application experiences a runtime error or coding bug. Also, the operating system is not affected when a program hangs or has a problem handling memory. The disadvantage is that extensive use of APIs by a program can create system overhead because of the drain on memory and CPU resources. Also, a software application designed to use an older API, such as an e-mail or network API, may not work properly when that API is upgraded to a new version. This is particularly a problem for software designed for Windows 95 and Windows NT, for example when an API is upgraded in a new version of Windows NT, but not in Windows 95 (or Windows 98).

When you run applications that use graphics, such as the OpenGL graphics screen savers mentioned in Chapter 5, "Server Configuration," they can put an extra load on a Windows NT server because graphics services run in kernel mode instead of user mode. The load is created when an application makes heavy use of the API that communicates between the kernel mode graphics services and the user mode graphics DLLs. Microsoft has developed a way to optimize memory for graphics communications between the kernel and user modes, but you still should watch the impact that graphics programs have on the server.

USING THE REGISTRY TO CONFIGURE THE OPERATING SYSTEM SETUP AND SOFTWARE

The Windows NT **Registry** is a very complex database containing all information the operating system needs about the entire server. For example, the initialization files used by other versions of Windows, including the critical SYSTEM.INI and WIN.INI files, are contained in the NT Registry. They also may exist as separate files, but this is only necessary for programs that are not designed for compatibility with the Registry, such as early MS-DOS and pre-Windows 95 programs. Some examples of data contained in the Registry are as follows:

- Information about all hardware components including the CPU, disk drives, network interface cards, CD-ROM drives, and more

- Information about NT services that are installed, which services they depend on, and the order in which they are started

- Data about all user accounts

- Data on the last current and last known setup used to boot the computer

- Configuration information about all software in use

- Software licensing information

- All Control Panel parameter configurations

There is the option to use either of two editors to view the contents of the Registry: Regedit or Regedt32. **Regedit** is an earlier non–32-bit version of the Registry editor and is preferred by some administrators because it has the most complete utility to search for keys, subkeys, values, data, and strings. A **key** is a category or division of information within the Registry. A single key may contain one or more lower-level keys called **subkeys**, just as a folder may contain several subfolders. A Registry **value** is a data parameter associated with a software or hardware characteristic under a key (or subkey). A Registry value consists of three parts: a name, the data type, and the configuration parameter, such as ErrorControl:REG_DWORD:0 (ErrorControl is the name, REG_DWORD is the data type, and 0 is the parameter setting). In this value, the option to track errors is turned off if the parameter is 0, and error tracking is turned on if the value is 1. There are three data formats: DWORD is hexadecimal, string is text data, and binary is two hexadecimal values.

The Regedit editor window is very straightforward, with common menu utilities such as Registry, Edit, View, and Help. **Regedt32** is a much fancier 32-bit editor, with cascading windows and twice the number of menu bar options as Regedit. It has added options to manage Registry security, see information in expanded views, set up auditing to track who has accessed the Registry, add keys or values, and set up to access the Registry in read-only mode to ensure against mistakes. (Explore using a Registry editor in Hands-on Project 9-6.)

Neither Registry editor is automatically available from a menu or icon in Windows NT Server. Regedit is located in the \Winnt folder, and Regedt32 is in the \Winnt\System32 folder. If you use one or both editors frequently, you will likely want to create a shortcut to access them. Otherwise, many administrators start them using the Run option from the Start button.

THE FIVE ROOT KEYS

The Registry data is stored in a top-down hierarchy with five root keys at the highest level:

- HKEY_LOCAL_MACHINE
- HKEY_CURRENT_USER
- HKEY_USERS
- HKEY_CLASSES_ROOT
- HKEY_CURRENT_CONFIG

A **root key**, also called a **subtree**, is a primary or highest-level category of data contained in the Registry. It might be compared to a main folder, such as the Winnt folder, which is at the root level of folders. All root keys start with HKEY to show they are the highest-level keys.

HKEY_LOCAL_MACHINE

Under the HKEY_LOCAL_MACHINE root key is information on every hardware component in the server. This includes information about what drivers are loaded and their version levels, what IRQs (interrupt requests) are used, setup configurations, the BIOS version, and more. Figure 9-14 shows the Registry contents using Regedt32 to view the HKEY_LOCAL_MACHINE root key information about serial ports.

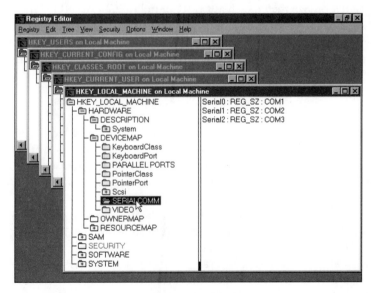

Figure 9-14 Registry information for the HKEY_LOCAL_MACHINE root key

Under each root key are **subkeys**, which are HARDWARE, SAM, SECURITY, SOFT-WARE, and SYSTEM for the root key in Figure 9-14. Each subkey may have subkeys under it, such as DESCRIPTION, DEVICEMAP, OWNERMAP, and RESOURCEMAP under the HARDWARE subkey in Figure 9-14.

A few subkeys are stored as sets, called **hives**, because they hold related information. This is true for the SAM and SOFTWARE subkeys, which hold information about user accounts and about installed software, respectively. For example, the user account data is stored in the SAM hive in the \Winnt\System32\Config folder as the SAM file. Stored with every hive file is a log file that contains information about changes to the hive, such as the SAM.LOG file. These files should only be edited using one of the Registry editors.

You can make hardware configuration changes directly from the Registry, although this is not recommended (see the following Caution). For example, if Windows NT Server has incorrectly detected three serial ports, but only two are actually installed, you can delete one by using the Registry editor. For instance, to delete serial port 3 you need to do it in two places. First, highlight the line in Figure 9-14, Serial2:REG_SZ:COM3, and then press Del, or open the Edit menu and click Delete. Next, delete the reference to this serial port under the System key. You do this by clicking SYSTEM under the HKEY_LOCAL_MACHINE root key. Then click the CurrentControlSet key, and click Service under it. Next, click Serial and Parameter. Finally, highlight the Serial2 parameter and delete it.

 Although it is possible to make hardware configuration changes directly from the Registry, this is a dangerous undertaking, because a wrong deletion may mean that you cannot reboot your server into Windows NT. It is better to use other options first, such as the Control Panel. Make changes in the Registry only under the guidance of a Microsoft technical note or a Microsoft support person.

Another useful application of the HKEY_LOCAL_MACHINE root key is to trace a problem in Windows NT Server, such as with the Server service. This service must be loaded at the time of installation in order for Windows NT Server to enable users to log on. If you boot the server after installation and see a message that the Server service, or another critical service, failed to start, you can use the Registry to determine if the service is installed, as shown in Hands-on Project 9-7. If the service is not installed, you can reinstall it through the Network icon on the Control Panel. If the service is installed, but not set to start, you can go into the Control Panel Services icon and use the Startup button to start the service automatically.

HKEY_CURRENT_USER

The HKEY_CURRENT_USER key contains information about the desktop setup for the account presently logged on to the server console. It contains data on color combinations, font sizes and type, the keyboard layout, the taskbar, clock configuration, and nearly any setup action you have made on the desktop. For example, if you want to change the environment parameter governing where temporary files are stored for applications, you would do it from here. The new path is set by clicking the Environment subkey under the HKEY_CURRENT_USER root key and changing the path shown as the value on the right side of the window. The sounds associated with a given event can be set by clicking the path \HKEY_CURRENT_USER\AppEvents\EventLabels and then changing the sound value for a particular event, such as the event to close a window, which is a single value in the Close subkey (\HKEY_CURRENT_USER\AppEvents\EventLabels\Close).

Another example is changing a program that runs in association with a particular file extension. For example, click the following path: \HKEY_CURRENT_USER\ Software\Microsoft\Windows NT\CurrentVersion\Extensions (Figure 9-15; notice that there are so many subkeys that not all of the path fits into a single screen display). If the Notepad program is associated with files ending in .TXT, you can make a change to have Wordpad start instead. To do this you would change the value "txt:REG_SZ:notepad.exe ^.txt" to "txt:REG_SZ:write.exe ^.txt," because WRITE.EXE is the file that starts the Wordpad application.

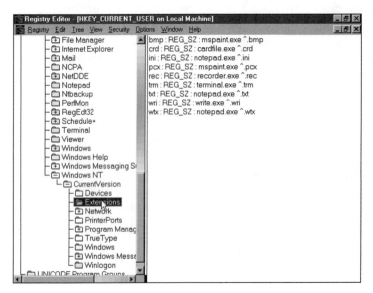

Figure 9-15   Changing Registry data for file associations

HKEY_USERS

The HKEY_USERS root key contains all of the user profiles kept on the server for all users. Each profile is listed under this root key. Within each user profile there is information identical to that viewed within the HKEY_CURRENT_USER root key. The profile used when you are logged on is one of the profiles stored under HKEY_USERS. You can make the same changes just examined, by finding the subkey for your profile and making the changes here instead of under the HKEY_CURRENT_USER root key.

HKEY_CLASSES_ROOT

The HKEY_CLASSES_ROOT key holds data to associate file extensions with programs. This is a more extensive list than the one viewed under HKEY_CURRENT_USER. Associations exist for executable files, text files, graphics files, clipboard files, audio files, and many more. These associations are used as defaults for all users who log on to Windows NT Server, whereas the associations in HKEY_CURRENT_USER and HKEY_USER are those that have been customized for a given user profile.

HKEY_CURRENT_CONFIG

The last root key, HKEY_CURRENT_CONFIG, has information about the current hardware profile. It holds information about the monitor type, keyboard, mouse, and other hardware characteristics for the current profile. On most servers, there is only a default hardware profile set up. Two or more profiles could be used, but this is more common for a portable computer running Windows NT Workstation that is used both with and without a docking station. One profile would have the keyboard and monitor used when it is on the road, and another would have a larger keyboard and monitor used when it is docked.

9

Backing Up the Registry

Because the Registry is vitally important to Windows NT Server, plan to back it up regularly when you back up other files. Some backup systems have a separate option that you must set up to make sure the Registry is backed up. Also, each time there is a change to the Registry, update the Emergency Repair Disk by running RDISK /s. If you do not specify the /s option, then RDISK does not fully copy the Registry contents to the Emergency Repair Disk.

You can obtain a Registry backup utility from Microsoft called REGBACK.EXE that enables you to back up the Registry without using a tape device. REGBACK.EXE can back up the Registry contents, even when portions of the Registry are open and in use. The program comes with a companion utility, REGREST.EXE, which is used to restore the Registry.

VIEWING REGISTRY INFORMATION USING THE WINDOWS NT DIAGNOSTICS UTILITY

The most common Registry parameters are easily viewed by opening the Windows NT Diagnostics utility. This utility reports information on what services are installed, the server's network setup, and other server environment data. The information cannot be changed from the NT Diagnostics utility, but problems can be quickly and safely identified by viewing the data in this tool. Table 9-3 shows what is contained in the Windows NT Diagnostics utility.

Table 9-3 Windows NT Diagnostics Utility

Windows NT Diagnostic Category	Information
Display	Contains information about the display adapter card and driver
Drives	Lists all known drives including floppy, hard, CD-ROM, and network drives
Environment	Lists all environment variables and environment information, such as the operating system, number of processors, and default path for system files
Memory	Presents information about available RAM, paging file use, and the location of the paging files (similar to the information provided in Task Manager)
Network	Lists information about the domain and server names, number of logged-on users, administrator access level, protocols in use, network settings, and network statistics
Resources	Shows IRQ assignments, the bus in use, the bus type, device I/O port addresses, and devices attached to the computer
Services	Lists services and devices and shows whether they are running or stopped; also provides information on which services are dependent on others (requiring others to be running along with them)
System	Displays information about the processor, BIOS version, and HAL
Version	Shows the Windows NT Server operating system version level and the software registration

You can take a quick look at the Windows NT Diagnostics tool by clicking the Start button, the Programs option, and Administrative Tools (Common). Click Windows NT Diagnostics and then the Resources tab, as shown in Figure 9-16. This is a good way to determine if there is an IRQ or I/O port addressing conflict. The figure shows that there are no IRQ conflicts, because each device has a different IRQ assigned.

If you detect a conflict, you can change the assignment through the Registry, or more safely, by using the Control Panel. For example, if one of the serial ports is assigned an IRQ also used by another device, you would open the Ports icon on the Control Panel, and highlight the serial port in conflict. Next, click the Settings button, and then the Advanced button to change the IRQ assignment for that port.

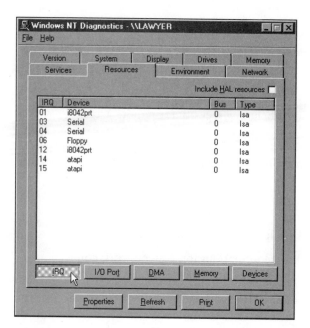

Figure 9-16   Windows NT Diagnostics

SETTING SYSTEM POLICIES

The system policies are tools provided to override Registry settings in Windows NT Server. They are used to set up special conditions for individual users, such as displaying a banner for certain users or groups when they log on. They also can be used to set up restrictions for all users, such as limiting the applications they can run from the server. Using the System Policy Editor, you can modify certain Registry settings, the default user profile, and information regarding how individual accounts are set up. Specifically, the System Policy Editor can change values contained in the Registry root keys HKEY_LOCAL_MACHINE and HKEY_CURRENT_USER. The changes made through the System Policy Editor are kept in the NTCONFIG.POL file.

Using the System Policy Editor, you can implement changes that affect all computers in a domain or only individual computers. The following policies can be set up to govern all users:

- Control Panel display options

- Desktop wallpaper and color schemes

- Operating system shell restrictions, such as removing the Start menu Run option, hiding drives in My Computer, hiding Network Neighborhood, and hiding all items on the desktop

- System restrictions such as permission to run only certain Windows applications and disabling Registry editing tools

- Windows NT Shell options such as customizing folders and desktop icons
- Windows NT System options that affect the use of AUTOEXEC.BAT and logon scripts

Policies that can be set up to govern individual users include:

- Remote access settings, including security for remote access
- Creation of hidden drive shares
- Network printer scheduling and error control options
- Customized shared folder setup
- Logon security and logon banner controls
- File-naming options, such as the use of extended characters
- User profile network timeout options for slow network connections

For example, to hide Network Neighborhood on the desktop for the Domain Guests group, click System Policy Editor in the Administrative Tools (Common) menu. Click the File menu and New Policy. Click the Add Group button in the tool bar and click Browse. Select Domain Guests and click Add and then OK. Double-click the newly added Domain Guests icon, double-click Shell, and double-click Restrictions. The grayed boxes with no checks show that those policies are not implemented. Check the box to hide Network Neighborhood and click OK (Figure 9-17). Close System Policy Editor for the change to take effect.

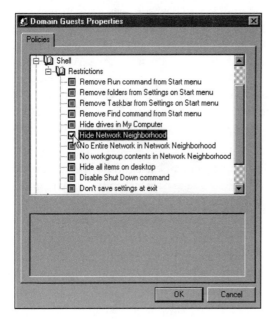

Figure 9-17 Using System Policy Editor

Use the System Policy Editor carefully because it is possible to lock out even the Administrator account.

SETTING UP AND USING LICENSE MANAGER

Microsoft includes a licensing monitor tool called License Manager in Windows NT Server. License Manager works for Microsoft products, such as Windows NT Server and Microsoft BackOffice products such as Microsoft Mail and Exchange Server for e-mail, Internet Information Server for Internet connectivity, Systems Management Server to help manage network workstations and software, and SQL Server for large databases.

License Manager is equipped to monitor licensing on a per seat or per server basis. Most software licensing is handled in one of two ways. **Per seat licensing** means that there needs to be a license to run a software application for the computer on which that software is loaded, no matter whether the executable files are loaded over the network from the server or from a folder on that workstation's hard disk. If there are 72 computers on a network that need to run a program, such as Microsoft Word, then there must be 72 licenses. The **per server licensing** approach places the licensing burden on the server instead of on the workstation. In the per server method, there only need to be enough licenses for the maximum number of workstations that use a software application at a given time. For example, in per server licensing, the highest number of people who use Microsoft Word simultaneously might be 22, even though there are 72 total workstations connected to the network. In this case, only 22 Microsoft Word licenses are needed for that server. When you purchase software licenses, make sure that you understand what type of licensing you are getting, and set up the license monitoring to match the type of license you have. Costs for per seat licenses are often different from costs for per server licenses. Also, some software vendors license only to a specific computer and have no per seat or per server arrangement, making that software difficult to employ in a network environment. Always read the license information or check with the software vendor to make sure that you understand the licensing stipulations.

Besides tracking the per seat and per server license privilege, License Manager is used to add new licenses or to delete licenses. Also, it can replicate licensing to other Windows NT servers in a domain. Thus if you have 1,000 licenses for Microsoft Word and 15 Windows NT servers, License Manager can spread the licenses across all servers or workstations (depending on the licensing mode). License Manager does not stop use of software when the number of users exceeds the number of licenses, it only keeps statistics on use and provides information when there is a need to purchase more licenses. However, it does have the capability to revoke a software license for a user or to limit licensing for a particular server.

The first step in setting up License Manager is to make sure that the License Logging Service is enabled and set to automatically start when the server is booted. To set up the License Logging Service:

1. Double-click the Control Panel Services icon.

2. In the Services dialog box, scroll to the License Logging Service and click it. Make sure that the status is set to Started and the startup is set to Automatic. If it is not set up in this way, click the Startup button and click the Automatic radio button as the Startup Type, and then click OK.

3. If the service is not already started, start it now by clicking the Start button in the Services tab.

The next step is to open Microsoft License Manager from the Administrative Tools (Common) menu. Click the License menu and New License. The New Client Access License dialog box opens, as shown in Figure 9-18. (Try Hands-on Project 9-8 to complete the process of adding new licenses.)

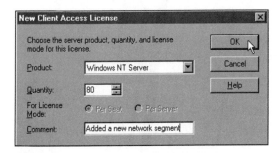

Figure 9-18   Adding new licenses

To view the software that is installed, click the View menu in License Manager and click Products View. The installed products are listed with information about the per seat and per server allocation of the licenses, plus the maximum license use that has been reached. Other information is available as well, such as the purchase history. To view the license usage statistics, click the View menu in License Manager and Clients, which shows the licensed and unlicensed usage.

SETTING UP AND USING DIRECTORY REPLICATOR

Directory replication services enable designated directories on one server to be copied to one or more servers or workstations on the network. The server with the original directories is the **export server**. An export server must have the Windows NT Server operating system. The computers that receive the directories and files are the **import servers** or **import computers**. Updates to files in the original directories also are automatically copied to the target directories on the import computers.

Directory replication has many uses in a domain, particularly if that domain has several BDC and member servers. One use is to copy an update database on a member server in a client/server system to a reporting database on a different member server. As discussed in previous chapters, this is done to ensure that access to the update database is not slowed by frequent queries or reporting on data. Another reason for replication is to create a backup copy of account-related information, such as profiles, system policies, and logon scripts. If the PDC server fails, the BDC is promoted quickly to a PDC so that there is little interruption to users. Some organizations use directory replication to distribute data files from a main server to several other servers in the network, as a way to evenly spread the user load among servers for best performance. This might be done on a large college campus of several hundred departments, in which each department needs to access budget information. The budget database can be replicated from the main accounting department's server to several other servers, such as a server for the natural science departments, a server for the humanities departments, a server for the engineering departments, and so on.

 When you set up directory replication, keep in mind that open files (files in use) cannot be replicated until they are closed.

The beginning steps to set up directory replication involve creating an account from which to export files, giving that account the necessary rights and permissions by adding it to the Replicator and Backup Operators groups, and then configuring the replication service. The steps are as follows:

1. Create an account on the export computer (running Windows NT Server) for directory replication services by using User Manager for Domains. You might name the account Replicate or Exporter.

2. Set the account password to never expire. Also make sure that the following boxes are not checked: User Must Change Password at Next Logon, User Cannot Change Password, and Account Disabled.

3. Add the account to the Replicator local group by using the Groups button in the New User dialog box in User Manager for Domains.

4. Add the account to the Backup Operators group.

5. Ensure that there are no time restrictions on the account, by using the Hours button in the New User dialog box.

6. Use the Control Panel Services icon to set the Directory Replicator service to start automatically when the server boots (click the Services icon Startup button). Another way to access services is to open Server Manager from the Administrative Tools (Common) menu, click the Computer menu, and click Services.

7. While in the Service dialog box in Step 6, associate the export computer's replication account with the startup. This is accomplished by entering the account name in the This Account: box under Log On As: and providing the account's password (Figure 9-19). Click OK to finish and click OK again to verify the logon access as a service right.

Figure 9-19   Configuring the Directory Replicator service

Also on the export server, it is necessary to configure the replication services. This involves designating the export computer (or computers), the import computers, and the export and import folder paths on the computers. The steps for configuring these services are as follows:

1. Double-click the Server icon in the Control Panel (or open Server Manager from the Administrative Tools (Common) menu, click the Computer menu, and click Services).

2. Click the Replication button.

3. Click the Export Directories radio button (Figure 9-20).

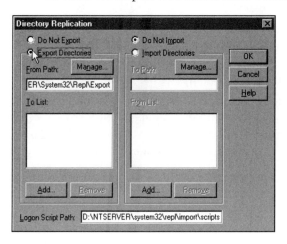

Figure 9-20   Setting up export and import parameters

4. Enter the export path into the From Path: text box. This is the path to the folder that will be copied to other computers.

5. Click the Add button to designate the domain of the export server. In the Select Domain dialog box, enter the domain in the Domain: box or double-click the domain name in the Select Domain: box and click the name of the export server, and then click OK. Back in the Directory Replication dialog box, you can use the Remove button to remove a computer as the export computer.

6. Use the Manage button to manage lock information. The number of locks must be 0 to export files in a folder or subfolder. For example, you might want to export a folder, but not the subfolders within the folder. In this case the main folder should not be locked, but you can place a lock on each subfolder that you do not want to export. Locks are set by using the Add Lock button. Subfolders are designated by using the Add button in the Manage Exported Directories dialog box. Locks are removed by using the Remove Lock button. Once locks are set, click OK to return to the Directory Replication dialog box.

7. After designating the export server, use the right side of the Directory Replication dialog box to set up the import server.

8. Click the Import Directories radio button.

9. Enter the path to which you want to write the files on the import computer (computer to receive the files).

10. Click the Add button to designate the name of each import computer within the domain (files can be sent to computers in more than one domain, but make sure that there is an appropriate high-speed connection, so that imports do not take excessive time). Click OK in the Select Domain dialog box when you are finished designating import computers. Back in the Directory Replication dialog box, the Remove button can be used to remove an import computer.

11. Use the Manage button to manage file lock information. Locks should be 0 to enable files to be imported to a folder, but you may want to lock certain subfolders in that folder, so that the files are not copied into them. Click OK in the Manage Imported Directories dialog box after you have set up locks.

12. Click OK in the Directory Replication dialog box.

13. Click the Alerts button in the Server dialog box. Add your account and the Administrator account to the Send Administrative Alerts To: box. This enables you to automatically receive a warning in case there is a problem with directory replication. Click OK in the Alerts dialog box.

14. Click OK in the Server dialog box.

After you have completed these steps, the Windows NT export server creates a shared folder called Repl$ from which to export the files.

9

CHAPTER SUMMARY

- Managing a Windows NT server is much easier when the folder structure is planned in advance. A sound folder structure involves creating distinct folders for user directories, software applications, server utilities, and other files that are stored on the server. As each folder is created, set up the folder properties to help manage their contents. Permissions are one of the most important properties and should be set up according to the purpose of the folder. For example, the folder containing system files needs to be protected from general access, so that an important file is not changed or deleted by a user. A public folder that will be shared among all users needs wide-ranging permissions so that its contents can be accessed and modified. Some server folders are set up to be shared over the network and have designated share permissions to enable access to files.

- Before installing application software in a folder, make sure that the software is network-compatible, because some application software is difficult to run in a network context. Always use the Add/Remove Programs tool to install software, so that the installation is coordinated with the Windows NT Registry. The Registry tracks the location of software and keeps configuration information. It also contains information about the server hardware and setup. The Registry can be used to correct a Windows NT Server installation problem or to reconfigure application software, but you should make sure that you know how to work on a problem before making a change.

- The system policies offer another way to change some Registry settings and to customize how users access Windows NT Server. Making changes through the system policies can be safer than directly changing the Registry, but the changes primarily affect desktop capabilities, logon access, security measures, and the programs that can be run by users.

- When Microsoft application software is installed, you can use License Manager to record and monitor the number of licenses. License Manager yields statistics to show when more licenses are needed as network use grows. Another useful tool is Directory Replicator, which copies folders from a server to other network computers. You might use this to copy database files or to spread the load among several network servers.

KEY TERMS

- **application program interface (API)** — Functions or programming features in a system that programmers can use for network links, links to messaging services, or interfaces to other systems.

- **attribute** — A characteristic associated with a folder or file, used to help manage access and backups.

- **dynamic link library (DLL)** — Executable program code that is stored as a .DLL file and called only when needed by a program.

- **export server** — A Windows NT Server from which files are copied by the directory replication services.

- **hive** — A set of related Registry keys and subkeys stored as a file.

- **import server** or **import computer** — A server or workstation to which files are written from an export server via Windows NT directory replication.

- **kernel mode** — Protected environment in which the Windows NT operating system kernel runs, consisting of a protected memory area and privileges to directly execute system services, access the CPU, run I/O operations, and conduct other basic operating system functions.

- **key** — A category of information contained in the Windows NT Registry, such as hardware or software.

- **license monitoring** — A process used on network servers to be certain that the number of software licenses in use does not exceed the number for which the network is authorized.

- **network-compatible** — Able to operate in a multiuser environment using network or e-mail communication APIs.

- **object** — Entity in NT Server that has properties and exists as a single unit. Files, folders, subfolders, printers, user accounts, and groups are examples of objects.

- **per seat licensing** — A server software licensing method that requires that there be enough licenses for all network client workstations.

- **per server licensing** — A server software licensing method based on the maximum number of clients that use an application at one time.

- **Regedit** — One of two Registry editors. It has limited display and menu options, but the best search options.

- **Regedt32** — One of two Registry editors. It has a large range of menu options to help view and manipulate data, and a read-only mode that can be used to guard against accidental changes.

- **Registry** — A database used to store information about the configuration, program setup, devices, drivers, and other data important to the setup of a computer running Windows NT or 95.

9

- **root folder** — The highest-level folder, with no folders above it in the tree structure of folders and files on a disk.

- **root key** — Also called subtree, the highest category of data contained in the Registry. There are five root keys.

- **subkey** — A key within a Registry key, similar to a subfolder under a folder.

- **subtree** — Same as root key.

- **swap space** — Temporary disk storage used by an application to supplement memory requirements and manipulate data.

- **user mode** — A special operating mode in Windows NT used for running programs in a memory area kept separate from that used by the kernel and in which the program cannot directly access the kernel or operating system services except through an API.

- **value** — A data parameter in the Registry stored as a value in decimal, binary, or text format.

REVIEW QUESTIONS

1. An export computer must be running which of the following?
   a. Windows NT Server
   b. Windows 95
   c. Windows 3.11
   d. any of the above
   e. only a and b

2. Which of the following can be audited on a folder?
   a. successful reads
   b. failed writes
   c. amount of time spent executing a file
   d. all of the above
   e. only a and b

3. Which of the following is not a capability of License Manager?
   a. logging off users when the number of software licenses is exceeded
   b. tracking per seat or per server licensing
   c. tracking software versions and providing a warning when an update is needed
   d. all of the above
   e. only a and c

4. There are ——————————— root keys in the Windows NT Registry.

   a. 2

   b. 3

   c. 5

   d. 10

5. ErrorControl:REG_DWORD:0 is an example of ———————————.

   a. a Registry value

   b. a Registry key

   c. a policy script command

   d. a replicator path

6. Which tool enables you to view information in the Registry?

   a. Microsoft Word

   b. Notepad

   c. Windows NT Diagnostics

   d. Wordpad

7. Which of the following is not a permission for a shared folder?

   a. Read

   b. Full Control

   c. Change

   d. Hidden

8. Graphics services in Windows NT Server run in which of the following?

   a. user mode

   b. kernel mode

   c. OpenGL mode

   d. API mode

9. Auditing can be set up on ———————————.

   a. accounts

   b. folders

   c. domains

   d. all of the above

   e. only a and b

10. Which attribute is deactivated on an NTFS folder?

   a. Compress

   b. Hidden

   c. System

   d. Read-only

11. When Directory Replicator is set up, —————————.

    a. it is necessary to create an account for Directory Replicator on the export computer

    b. the folder from which files are copied must have one lock for security

    c. the computer to receive the files must be in a different domain

    d. all of the above

    e. only a and b

12. Which of the following permissions includes the ability to change permissions?

    a. Change

    b. Replicate

    c. Add & Read

    d. Full Control

13. Which of the following permissions provide(s) the ability to execute a program file?

    a. Read

    b. Add

    c. Add & Read

    d. all of the above

    e. only a and b

14. Ownership of a folder is changed by —————————.

    a. granting ownership

    b. taking ownership

    c. setting special permissions to Add/Own

    d. the granting permission held by Administrators

15. Which of the following is (are) examples of NT Server objects?

    a. printer

    b. file

    c. folder

    d. all of the above

    e. only b and c

16. Your company's president wants each account that accesses Windows NT Server to view a banner warning against software misuse. What might you use to set this up?

    a. System Policy Editor

    b. Windows NT Diagnostics

    c. Control Panel System icon

    d. New User dialog box for an account

17. A shared folder is set up through —————————.

    a. the folder properties

    b. User Manager for Domains

    c. Control Panel Share icon

    d. the folder attributes

18. The SAM hive is part of the —————————.

    a. System Policies

    b. Registry

    c. kernel API

    d. key word cluster

19. The accounting manager at your university wants to track how often permissions are changed in the General Ledger data folder. What tool would you use to accomplish this?

    a. ownership tracking

    b. setting folder permissions

    c. setting folder auditing

    d. access tracking

20. From where do you set the Directory Replicator service to start automatically?

    a. Control Panel Services icon

    b. Control Panel Server icon

    c. User Manager for Domains

    d. Windows NT Diagnostics

21. Which Registry editor has the best search functions?

    a. Regedit

    b. Regedt32

    c. Registry Policy editor

    d. Notepad

22. You have moved a file from the Temp folder to the Words folder on the same volume in which users have Change permissions and that is shared with Change permissions, but now users cannot access it. Which of the following would explain the problem?

    a. you need to reset share permissions on the Words folder because folder permissions change when you copy in a new file

    b. you need to flag the file you copied as newly created

    c. the Temp folder has No Access permission and so the file still is assigned this permission

    d. the file still has the archive attribute assigned to it

9

HANDS-ON PROJECTS

PROJECT 9-1

In this activity you practice creating a folder. You need a computer running Microsoft Windows NT Server or Windows NT Workstation.

To create a folder:

1. Double-click **My Computer** on the desktop.
2. Double-click drive **(C:)** or another available drive.
3. Click the **File** menu, **New**, and then **Folder** (refer to Figure 9-3).
4. In the highlighted box, enter the name **Practce** for the folder and press **[Enter]**. (The name is intentionally misspelled.)
5. Next, rename the folder: right-click it, click **Rename**, then enter the new name, **Practice**, and press **[Enter]**.

PROJECT 9-2

This activity enables you to give the Server Operators group Read permissions for the system files in the Winnt folder on a Windows NT server.

To set folder permissions:

1. Log on to the server and double-click **My Computer** on the desktop.
2. Double-click drive **(C:)** (or the drive where the Winnt folder is located) in the My Computer window.
3. Right-click the **Winnt** folder and click **Properties** (Figure 9-21).
4. Click the **Security** tab on the Winnt Properties dialog box.

Figure 9-21   Accessing folder properties

5. Click the **Permissions** button.

6. Click the **Add** button and click the **Server Operators** group in the Add Users and Groups dialog box. Set the Type of Access: to **Read** (Figure 9-22).

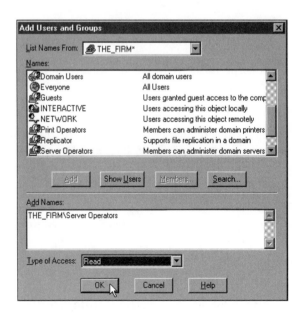

Figure 9-22   Assigning Server Operators Read access

7. Click **OK** in the Add Users and Groups dialog box.

8. Click **OK** in the Directory Permissions dialog box.

9. Click **OK** in the Winnt Properties dialog box.

 PROJECT 9-3

In this activity you configure the Winnt folder to audit each change to folder permissions.

To set up auditing:

1. Open NT Explorer and right-click the **Winnt** folder.

2. Click **Properties**.

3. Click the **Security** tab and then the **Auditing** button.

4. Check the boxes **Replace Auditing on Subdirectories** and **Replace Auditing on Files**.

5. Click the **Add** button.

6. Click **Administrators**, the **Add** button, and **OK**.

7. Check the **Success** box for Change Permissions.

8. Click **OK** in the Directory Auditing dialog box and **OK** in the Winnt Properties dialog box.

 PROJECT 9-4

In this activity you share a folder and set permissions for it. You remove the Everyone group and add Full Control access for the Domain Users group.

To set permissions for a shared folder:

1. In My Computer or NT Explorer, select the folder to be shared. (If you want to create a folder for this exercise, select **File**, **New**, **Folder**, and enter **Proj9-4** to name the new folder.) Right-click the folder and select **Sharing** from the menu.

2. Click the **Shared As** radio button. Enter a name for your shared folder if you don't want to use the default name (the folder's name).

3. Click the **Permissions** button to open the Access Through Share Permissions dialog box (refer to Figure 9-12).

4. Select the **Everyone** group from the Name: list, and click the **Remove** button.

5. Click the **Add** button.

6. Select **Domain Users** in the Names list box, and then click **Add**.

7. Select **Full Control** in the Type of Access: list box.

8. Click **OK**, and then click **OK** again. The folder is now shared to all members of the Domain Users group.

 PROJECT 9-5

In this activity you create two folders and move a file from one folder to the other.

To create the folders and then move the file:

1. Double-click **My Computer** on the desktop and double-click the **(C:)** drive, or whichever drive is available to you for creating folders. If the window occupies the whole screen (is maximized), click the **Maximize/Restore** button in the title bar (between the Minimize and Close buttons), so that other windows can be viewed.

2. Click the **File** menu, **New**, and **Folder**.

3. Enter the name **Folder1** and press **[Enter]**.

4. Repeat Step 2, enter the name **Folder2** and press **Enter**.

5. Click **Start**, **Programs**, **Accessories**, and **Notepad**.

6. Type a short string of words such as **My new file**. Click the **File** menu and **Save as**. In the Save in: box, find **Folder1** and double-click it, enter **Test** in the File name: box, and click **Save**. Close Notepad.

7. Double-click **Folder1** in My Computer, and right-click **Test**.

8. Drag the Test file to Folder2 while holding down the right mouse button.

9. Release the mouse button and click **Move Here** in the shortcut menu.

10. Move Folder1 inside Folder2 by right-clicking **Folder2** and dragging it on top of Folder1. Release the mouse button and click **Move Here**.

11. Click **Folder1** and press **[Del]** to remove the practice folders and Test file.

12. Close My Computer.

 PROJECT 9-6

In this activity you use a Registry editor to view subkeys under the HKEY_LOCAL _MACHINE root key.

To use the Registry editor to view a root key:

1. Click **Start** and **Run**.

2. Enter **Regedt32** in the Open: box and click **OK**.

3. Click the **Window** menu and **Cascade**.

4. Click the **Options** menu and check **Read Only Mode** (you would need to remove this check to make a change to the Registry).

5. Click the title bar **HKEY_LOCAL_MACHINE on Local Machine**.

6. Notice the subkeys in the dialog box. Double-click the **HARDWARE** subkey.

7. Double-click the **DEVICEMAP** key and then click the **SERIALCOMM** key to see information stored about the serial ports (refer to Figure 9-14). Each line on the right portion of the window is a value entry. There is one value entry for each serial port on the computer. For instance, port Serial0 might be mapped to COM1. REG_SZ indicates that it is a string value.

8. Double-click the **SOFTWARE** subkey.

9. Notice the subkeys for the software installed on the server.

10. Close the Registry editor.

PROJECT 9-7

In this activity you use the Registry editor to see if a service is installed.

To check the Registry to see if a service is installed:

1. Open Regedt32 as shown in Steps 1-2 of Project 9-6.

2. Double-click **HKEY_LOCAL_MACHINE**, if necessary, then double-click each of the following: **SYSTEM**, **CurrentControlSet**, and **Services**.

3. Click the **View** menu and make sure that **Tree and Data** is checked, then click **Find Key** on the View menu. Enter **server** in the Find what: text box. Make sure that Match whole word only and Match case are not selected, and click **Find next** until you find LanmanServer.

4. Close the Registry editor.

If the search does not find a subkey called LanmanServer, consider reinstalling the Server service via the Control Panel Network icon. If it finds the subkey and the Start:REG_DWORD value is not 0x2, the service may be set not to start. In this case, open the Control Panel Services icon and check to determine if the service is disabled, and if so, use the Startup button to set it to start automatically.

PROJECT 9-8

In this activity you view which products are installed via License Manager, and then you add 10 new Windows NT Server licenses.

To use License Manager:

1. Click **Start, Programs, Administrative Tools (Common)**, and **License Manager**.

2. Click the **View** menu and **Products View**.

3. Notice the products that are installed under the Product column. Also notice the number of licenses. The last column, Per Server Reached (which may be too long to show completely in your display; click the Options menu and change to a smaller font) shows the maximum number of users who have used the licenses at a given time (Figure 9-23).

4. Click a blank area in the Products View tab so that no selection is highlighted, or click **Windows NT Server**.

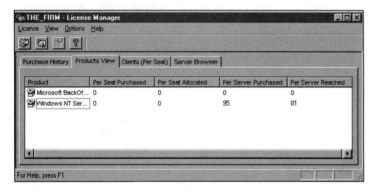

Figure 9-23   Viewing licensed software

5. Click the **License** menu and **New License**.

6. Click **Windows NT Server** in the Product: scroll box.

7. Enter **10** in the Quantity: box.

8. Click the radio button for the License mode, Per Seat or Per Server (unless this is already selected by default).

9. Add the comment **New licenses for student lab**.

10. Click **OK** and then close License Manager.

ASPEN CONSULTING: SETTING UP SERVER FOLDERS AND SOFTWARE

This week you are contacted by a server administrator at a business college who is setting up Windows NT Server for the first time. You help her to set up folders and install software.

1. Fatima Roy is the server administrator for the Collins Business Institute. She is setting up a server for the college administration, which is divided into the following units: president's office, accounting and business office, admissions office, and registrar's office. These offices use software that includes Microsoft Word, Great Coast Accounting for Colleges, an admissions system, and a student services system. Fatima also has network management software to put on the server and several utilities that she makes available to users. Collins Business Institute has decided to put home directories on their server for all 28 business office employees. Fatima has contacted you about recommending a directory structure for this server. What do you recommend?

2. Fatima also is interested in your recommendations for setting folder properties such as permissions, share permissions, auditing, and ownership. What properties do you recommend for the folder structure?

3. Practice creating and setting up a shared folder. Explain to Fatima how this is done, including setting permissions, auditing, share permissions, and ownership. Also explain an easy way to move folders and files.

4. Recommend to Fatima how to install software on the college's server. What should she find out about a software package before installing it?

5. Fatima has installed Microsoft Office and has found a technical note about deleting a value in the Registry to improve the performance of Microsoft Word. The value she needs to delete is under the key HKEY_ LOCAL_MACHINE and in the subkey SOFTWARE. Practice using a Registry editor and then explain to her how to access the SOFTWARE subkey.

6. Collins Business Institute has purchased 10 new Windows NT Server per server licenses. Explain how Fatima can use License Manager to implement these new licenses.

PRINTER MANAGEMENT

Network printing is often viewed with apprehension by server administrators. Multiuser computer systems are known for having a maze of printing utilities to install printer drivers, set up print services, and accommodate special forms. On these systems, maintaining printers is tedious, problem-ridden work, and this work sometimes is deferred by administrators in favor of easier and more interesting tasks. But to network users, printing is one of the most critical network services.

Fortunately, network printing has evolved as network operating systems have improved, especially with Windows NT Server. For instance, Microsoft has made printer setup intuitive by sharing printers as objects, in the same way that folders are shared. First of all, printer shares are created, named, and made available to the network with permissions similar to those used for folders. Second, printer setup is performed in one place within the operating system, instead of in three or four places, as with other operating systems. And last, all new printers are installed step by step through the Add Printer Wizard, making it difficult for the server administrator to make an error. In this chapter, you explore the Add Printer Wizard, learn how network printing works, learn to fine-tune network printing, and learn how to manage **print jobs**, which are print files that contain text and codes formatted to be sent to a printer for printing.

AFTER READING THIS CHAPTER AND COMPLETING THE EXERCISES YOU WILL BE ABLE TO:

- DESCRIBE THE PRINTING PROCESS USED BY WINDOWS NT
- INSTALL A LOCAL PRINTER IN WINDOWS NT SERVER
- EXPLAIN AND INSTALL PRINTER POOLING
- MANAGE PRINTER SERVICES AND CONFIGURE PRINT DEVICES
- CONTROL PRINT JOBS AND PRINTING STATUS
- INSTALL AND MANAGE A NONLOCAL PRINTER
- SOLVE A COMMON WINDOWS NT SPOOLER SERVICE PRINTING PROBLEM

WINDOWS NT PRINTING

The network printing process on NT Server LANs begins when a workstation user decides to print a file. For example, in a law firm, a Microsoft Word user prints a file, which goes to the printer designated in the user's Printer Setup configuration within Word. The Printer Setup may direct the printout to the user's local printer or to any network printer available through a printer share for which the user has permission. A shared printer can be a printer attached to a workstation, a printer attached to a file server, or a printer attached to a dedicated print server device. The workstation that initially generates the print job is the network **print client**, and the computer offering the printer share is the network **print server**.

A shared printer is an object, like a folder, that is made available to network users for print services. Microsoft also includes faxes as **print device** objects that can be treated in the same way as printers. The print device is offered from a server, workstation, or dedicated print server device. Several manufacturers make print server devices that connect directly to the network without the need of an attached PC. These devices eliminate dependence on a PC that may be shut off or inconveniently located. Some print server devices are small boxes that connect to the network at one end of the box and to one or more printers at the other. Another kind of print server is a card that is installed inside the printer, with a network port similar to a NIC on the card. One of the most commonly used print server cards is Hewlett-Packard's JetDirect card, used in many laser printers for network printing. Microsoft calls these printer and server combinations **network–interface printers** because the printer is connected directly to the network through its print server card instead of through a computer. Figure 10-1 shows examples of print server devices.

Figure 10-1   Print server devices

Some print server devices generate a large amount of network traffic because they frequently poll to determine whether print jobs are waiting. These devices may contribute to bottlenecks on busy networks. Find out about the network traffic generated before you buy a print server device. Also, check to make sure that the device is compatible with Windows NT.

When the printout goes to a printer share, it is temporarily spooled in specially designated disk storage and held until it is sent to be printed. **Spooling** frees the server CPU to handle other processing requests in addition to print requests. NT networks spool on the computer providing the print services. For example, if your organization's Windows NT server is also working as a print server and sharing its laser printer, spool space is made available on the server for users' print jobs. Print jobs are usually printed in the same order as received, unless an Administrator or Printer Operator (with appropriate permissions) changes the order because of a high-priority situation. The server administrator can disable spooling, but this is rare because it defeats the value of background print services, which free server resources for other tasks.

When its turn comes, the print file is sent to the printer along with formatting instructions. The formatting instructions are provided by a **printer driver** that holds configuration information for the given printer. The formatting and configuration information includes instructions to reset the printer before starting, information about printing fonts, and special printer control codes. Most printer drivers are composed of three elements:

- The *printer graphics driver*, which formats Graphical Device Interface (GDI) commands into graphics printing instructions that can be handled at the printer

- The *characterization data file*, which contains information about the particular features of a printer, such as paper drawers, color printing abilities, and sheet feeders

- The *printer interface driver*, which sets up the interface you view in the Properties dialog box for that printer, including such elements as special tabs for configuring the printer's capabilities

10

The printer driver resides on the computer offering the printer services (for local and network print jobs) and also can reside on the workstation client sending the print job. For example, when you send a print job to be printed on a Windows NT server print share, your printout is formatted by means of the printer driver at your workstation and then further interpreted by print services software on the print server. The printer driver is either contained on the Windows NT Server CD-ROM or obtained from the printer manufacturer.

When the user selects to use a printer share, the document to be printed is formatted for the driver on that share. The printer can start printing the file as soon as the first page is received, or it can be instructed to print the file only when all pages have been received. The advantage of printing immediately is that printing starts sooner than it does if the entire print file must be spooled first. The disadvantage is that, in offices where there are constant print requests, a pause at a workstation sending a print job may result in another job printing pages in the middle of the first job. If this is a problem, it is better to have the printer share wait until the entire file is spooled. This instruction is implemented at the shared printer. Figure 10-2 shows a summary of network printing stages.

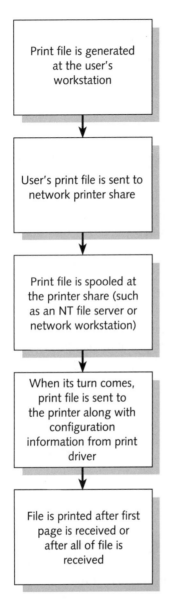

Figure 10-2   Printing stages

THE TECHNICAL PRINTING PROCESS

In technical terms both the network print client and the network print server run specific processes to finally deliver a print job to a printer. When the print server is Windows NT Server, the printing procedures start at the network print client. The network print client handles the following processes:

- Software application

- Graphics device interface

- Printer driver

- Spooler

- Remote print provider

In the first stage in the process, the software application at the client generates a print file. As it creates the print file, the application communicates with the Windows **Graphics Device Interface (GDI)**. The GDI integrates information about the print file—such as word-processing codes for fonts, colors, and embedded graphics objects—with information obtained from the printer driver installed at the client for the target printer, in a process that Microsoft calls **rendering**. When the GDI is finished, the print file is formatted with control codes to implement the special graphics, font, and color characteristics of the file. At the same time, the software application places the print file in the client's spooler, by writing the file, called the **spool file**, to a subfolder used for spooling. In the Windows 95 and Windows NT environment, a **spooler** is a group of DLLs, information files, and programs that processes print jobs for printing. Spool files are kept in the \Windows\Spool\Printers folder in Windows 95 and in the \Winnt\System32\Spool\Printers folder in Windows NT. MS–DOS and other clients use a similar process to prepare a print job to be sent to a print server, but the spool files and their location are not the same as for Windows 95 and Windows NT.

10

Large print files cannot be processed if there is inadequate disk space on which to store spooled files. Make sure that clients and the server have sufficient disk space to handle the largest print requests, particularly for huge graphics and color files that are targeted for a color printer or plotter.

The remote printer provider at the client makes a procedure call to the network print server to which the print file is targeted, communicating with the print server program SPOOLSS.EXE. If the print server is responding and ready to accept the print file, the remote printer transmits that file from the client's spooler folder to the Server service on Windows NT Server. The print file is sent by means of whichever protocol has been designated for communications between the print client and print server, such as NetBEUI, TCP/IP, NWLink, or DLC.

The network print server uses the following processes to receive and process a print file:

- Router

- Print provider

- Print processor

- Print monitor

The router, print provider, and print processor all are pieces of the network print server's spooler. Once it is contacted by the remote print provider on the print client, the Windows NT Server service calls its router (the print server service). The router directs the received print file to the print provider on the server, which writes the print file to disk (spools it) until it can be sent to the printer. The print provider also communicates with the server's print processors for different data types or formats used with print files. For example, some print files are sent as an enhanced data type used by Windows computers, and others are sent as an untouched or raw data type (data types are discussed in the next section). Once the appropriate print provider identifies the file by the data type it uses, it may make several changes to the file to prepare it for the printer. The print processor also may work with the separator page processor, if the print server is set up to insert a separator page between each printed spool file.

When the spool file is fully formatted for transmission to the printer, the print monitor pulls it from the spooler's disk storage and sends it off to the printer. The print monitor is in frequent contact with the printer to determine: (1) if the printer is online and (2) if the printer is ready to accept all or a portion of the print file (depending on how printer services are set up).

PRINT JOB DATA TYPES

Each print processor is designed to work with a specific data type. A **data type** is the way in which information is formatted and presented in the print file. Some data types involve minimal data formatting for printing, and others involve more extensive formatting. Different data types are used to accommodate printing from different kinds of clients, and are the following:

- RAW
- RAW with FF appended
- RAW with FF auto
- TEXT
- Enhanced metafile (EMF)
- PSCRIPT1

A print file formatted as the RAW data type is often used for files sent from MS-DOS, Windows 3.x, and UNIX clients. The print file is intended to be printed by the print server with no additional formatting. In the data type RAW with FF appended, the FF is a form-feed code placed at the end of the print file. Some non-Windows and old 16-bit Windows software does not place a form feed at the end of a print file. A form feed is used to make sure that the last page of the file is printed. When RAW with FF appended is designated, the print code for a form feed is written by the Windows NT Server print processor as the last thing in the print file. RAW with FF auto means that the print processor checks the print file for a form feed as the last character set, before appending a form feed at the end. If there already is a form feed, it does not add anything to the file.

Prior to having the ability to insert a form feed in the print file, many users found it necessary to press the form feed button on a printer or to send another print job, in order to print the last page.

The TEXT data type is used for printing text files formatted according to the ANSI standard, which uses values between 0 and 255 to represent characters, numbers, and symbols. You would use the TEXT data type for printing many types of MS-DOS print files, such as text files printed from older word processors or MS-DOS text editors such as EDLIN.

Windows NT and Windows 95 clients use the enhanced metafile (EMF) data type. This is the data type that is created when a print file is prepared by the GDI at the client. EMF files are prepared via a 32-bit system process that is well suited to handle files containing special fonts and graphics objects, such as a picture or a spreadsheet. EMF files are prepared by the network client and then further prepared by the network print server. EMF print files offer a distinct advantage in Windows NT and Windows 95 environments because they are very portable from computer to computer.

The PSCRIPT1 data type is intended for Macintosh clients that print on a Windows NT print server. The print processor uses this data type to translate a PostScript coded print file into one that can be printed on a non–PostScript printer. Using the PSCRIPT1 data type, the Windows NT print processor builds a bitmap file, which is again reformatted to be printed on the target printer. If you use this data type, keep in mind that bitmap files can be very large, requiring extra disk space for the spooler.

10

WINDOWS NT PRINT MONITORS

Microsoft provides a range of print monitors with Windows NT Server. The print monitors, located in the folder \Winnt\System32, are used for local printing and to print using specialized print servers such as those from Hewlett-Packard, Macintosh, Digital Equipment Corporation (DEC), and Lexmark. **Local printing** refers to printing on the same computer to which print devices are attached.

The local print monitor is the file LOCALMON.DLL, which handles print jobs sent to a physical port on the server, such as an LPT or COM port. It also sends print jobs to a file, if you specify FILE as the port. When a print job is sent to FILE, there is a prompt to supply a filename.

The line printer (LPR) print monitor consists of two files, LPRMON.DLL and LPR.EXE. It is used for transmitting files by means of the Microsoft TCP/IP Printing service. To use LPR, you first need to install the TCP/IP protocol through the Control Panel Network icon (use the Protocol tab) and the Microsoft TCP/IP Printing service (use the Services tab). Also, to use LPR, there must be a line printer daemon (LPD) server. The LPD server can be a UNIX computer, an MVS computer with TCP/IP, a computer running Windows NT, a Windows 3.11 computer running specialized software, or a print service device such as a Hewlett-Packard JetDirect card in a Hewlett-Packard printer. If you create an LPR port on the server, you will need to provide the IP address of the LPD server.

LPR combined with an LPD server provides a way to integrate printing on a mainframe, such as an IBM mainframe running open MVS, with network printers. It allows you to use Windows 95 or Windows NT, for example, to print a mainframe file to a network printer. Also, when using LPR, you may need to experiment with using either RAW or TEXT as the data type, depending on the software used at the clients.

There are several ways to send print jobs to a Hewlett-Packard printer, such as the 5Si, that has a JetDirect print server card. Hewlett-Packard provides print-handling software that employs options such as using DLC, NWLink (IPX), and TCP/IP. Another way to send print jobs to a JetDirect card is by using the Hewlett-Packard print monitor, HPMON.DLL, which is provided on the Windows NT Server CD-ROM. If you choose to use this monitor, make sure that you also install the Microsoft DLC protocol, because HPMON.DLL only works through DLC.

If you are working on a Microsoft network in which computers cannot send printouts to an HP printer connected to the network through a print server card, determine if the print share is set up to use HPMON.DLL. If it is, each workstation that needs to use the printer must have DLC installed.

The printer job language (PJL) print monitor, PJLMON.DLL, is primarily used for printers that have bidirectional printing (bidirectional printing is explained later in this chapter). It makes the two-way communications between the printer and the print server possible and enables the print server to automatically obtain information about the printer.

Many networks use DEC network-ready laser printers because many of these printers are designed for heavy duty-cycles, such as in a machine room or in a large, busy office. Microsoft provides the Digital Network Port print monitor, DECPSMON.DLL, for use with DEC's laser printers and print server devices. To implement DECPSMON.DLL, you also need to install the TCP/IP protocol or the DECnet protocol, which is obtained from DEC.

Lexmark International is another manufacturer of laser printers and print servers. The Lexmark Mark Vision print monitor, LEXMON.DLL, is designed for communications with these devices. If you install this print monitor, check the Lexmark documentation to find out which protocol to install, which is likely to be TCP/IP, IPX, or DLC.

Apple LaserWriter printers and print servers can be used on a Microsoft network by implementing the Macintosh print monitor, SFMMON.DLL. This monitor uses AppleTalk, which means that Services for Macintosh must be installed on Windows NT or Windows 95 clients that use this type of printer. Also, LaserWriters are PostScript printers, requiring that the client and print server software use a LaserWriter driver.

Table 10-1 summarizes the print monitors and their associated files.

Table 10-1   Windows NT Print Monitors

Print Monitor	File(s)
Local	LOCALMON.DLL
Line printer (LPR)	LPRMON.DLL and LPR.EXE
Hewlett-Packard	HPMON.DLL
Printer job language (PJL)	PJLMON.DLL
Digital Network Port	DECPSMON.DLL
Lexmark Mark Vision	LEXMON.DLL
Apple Macintosh	SFMMON.DLL

INSTALLING A LOCAL PRINTER IN WINDOWS NT SERVER

On a Microsoft network, any server or workstation with Windows NT Server, Windows NT Workstation, or Windows 95 can host a shared printer for others to use through network connectivity. Figure 10-3 is a simplified representation of how shared printers are connected to a network, including printers connected to servers, workstations, and print server devices.

10

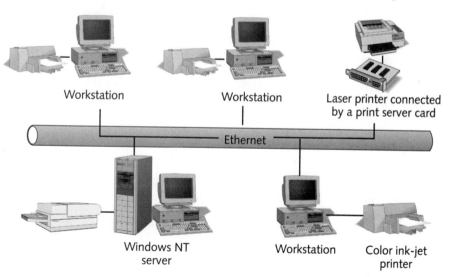

Figure 10-3   Printers used on a network

There are several ways to start a local printer installation in Windows NT Server. One is to open the Control Panel and click the Printers folder. The Printers folder also is available by clicking the Start button and Settings menu. Two other places in which it can be found are My Computer and NT Explorer. Open the Printers folder and click the Add Printer icon to start the Add Printer Wizard. Yet another way to start the wizard is from the Administrative Tools (Common) menu by clicking the Administrative Wizards and then the Add Printer Wizard. The Add Printer Wizard starts, as shown in Figure 10-4. There are two radio buttons on the dialog box, one for setting up a printer connected to the workstation and one for setting up a printer already shared on the network. The My Computer option configures a printer directly connected to the Windows NT server. The Network Printer Server option is used to set up a printer that is shared from another computer on the network. Click the My Computer radio button and click Next.

The next screen is used to select the printer port to which the printer is attached. There are options to use parallel ports LPT1, LPT2, or LPT3, and to use serial ports COM1 through COM4. Also, there is an option to direct print jobs to a file, rather than to print them. This option might be useful for capturing print output to send later to a fax or to store in a file for use by a graphics program. There also is an option to send a print job directly to a fax port. The Add Port button is used to add a print monitor, such as LPRMON.DLL or HPMON.DLL. To load a monitor that is not in the selection list, click the New Monitor button, insert the Microsoft Windows NT Server CD-ROM, and specify the path to the CD-ROM drive.

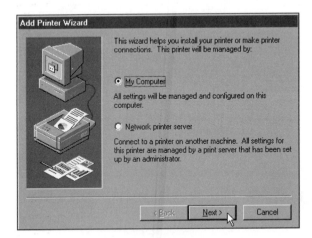

Figure 10-4   Selecting My Computer in the Add Printer Wizard

 Several companies, including Microsoft, are working on a new port standard known as **Universal Serial Bus (USB)**. This is a 32-bit data path to peripherals attached to the computer. This standard includes the capability to support nearly any type of peripheral through one port design, and to daisy-chain over 200 peripherals.

Click the Configure Port button to check the **port timeout** setting. This setting is the amount of time the workstation will continue to try sending a print file to a printer, while the printer is not responding. The default setting is normally 90 seconds (Figure 10-5). Consider increasing the setting to 120 seconds or more if you are installing a printer to handle large print files, such as for combined graphics and color printing. Set the transmission retry value and click OK. Click Next to proceed with the installation.

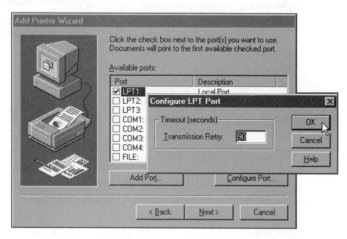

Figure 10-5   Setting the printer port and port timeout

The Add Printer Wizard requests information about the printer manufacturer and the printer model, as shown in Figure 10-6. In the Manufacturers: and Printers: selection boxes, scroll to the manufacturer and printer model. With both highlighted, insert the printer driver disk supplied by the manufacturer into drive A: (or use the Windows NT Server CD-ROM), and click Next.

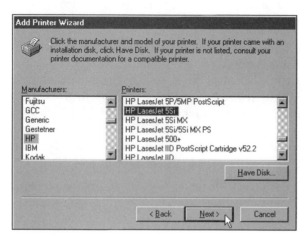

Figure 10-6   Entering the type of printer

Enter the path, such as A:\, to the driver disk in the Copy manufacturer's files from: box in the Install From Disk dialog box. Click OK and wait briefly for the wizard to load the driver to the server.

After the driver is loaded, you need to enter a name for the printer and to set it up as a shared printer. You also need to provide a name for the printer share. The printer name will appear as an icon in the Printers folder, while the share name is what users will see when they access the printer from the network. Many server administrators use the same name for both, simplifying management of the printer by reducing the confusion caused by having two names for one printer. As a rule, a printer and a printer share name are easiest to manage and use if some basic guidelines are followed, such as:

- Compose names that are easily understood and spelled by those who will use the printer.

- Include a room number, floor, or workstation name to help identify where the printer is located.

- Include descriptive information about the printer, such as the type, manufacturer, or model.

For example, if the server name is Lawyer and the printer is a Hewlett-Packard DeskJet color printer, the name and share name might be Lawyer_Deskjet. Or if the printer is located in the Administration Building and is a laser printer you might call it Admin_Laser.

Develop a printer-naming scheme for your organization from the beginning of the server installation. It is hard on users if you change names after a printer has been in use, because your users will have to reinstall those network printers at their workstations.

On networks in which there are MS-DOS workstations, it may be necessary to limit printer share names to eight characters or less, since this is the maximum MS-DOS can decipher.

Enter the printer name in the Printer Name: box and click Next. On the screen that follows, click the Shared radio button to share the printer on the network. Enter the printer share name in the Share Name: box. Also, click all of the operating systems on workstations that will be using the printer. For example, if the printer is accessed by Intel computers running Windows 95 and by DEC Alpha computers running Windows NT 4.0, click both of those selections. You do not need to click Windows NT 4.0, because the server is already set up for this. If additional operating systems are specified, then the Add Printer Wizard may request insertion of the Windows NT Server CD-ROM to load more printer drivers. Click Next to continue with the installation (Figure 10-7).

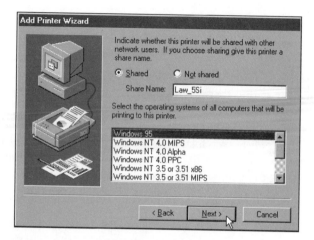

Figure 10-7   Creating a printer share

The reason for clicking all of the operating systems that will access the shared printer is to be able to load the server's printer driver to each type of client. For instance, when a workstation running Windows 95 or a DEC Alpha workstation running Windows NT installs the printer share, the installation first checks the server for the printer driver and then downloads the driver, if it is available from the server. If the driver is not available from the server, then the installation process checks the workstation client for a driver. Finally, if the driver is not loaded on the client, then users must find their operating system installation disks to load the driver.

There are two philosophies about loading the printer driver from the server to the workstation. On the positive side, loading the driver in this way saves users work because they do not have to find their operating system installation disks to load a printer driver. On the negative side, if the server administrator does not regularly update printer drivers at the server, then after several months these drivers may be out of date. In the latter case, it is better to leave additional operating systems unchecked to force new users to load more recent drivers from their own operating system disks.

The last wizard screen gives you an opportunity to print a test page, a practice you should follow to be sure that a newly installed printer is working. Click Yes (recommend) and then the Finish button. Verify the test page and click Yes. If there is a problem, click No and try the remedies suggested by the Windows NT help documentation. You can confirm that the share is available by checking for it in Network Neighborhood.

Allocating Virtual Memory for PostScript Printers

PostScript printers sometimes slow down when printing files containing several fonts and font sizes. A **PostScript printer** is one that has special firmware or cartridges that print using a **page-description language (PDL)**. PDL printing instructions are performed through PostScript programming code that produces extremely high-quality printing with extensive font options. Windows NT Server includes an option to make virtual memory available to a PostScript printer, to circumvent the purchase of extra RAM for that printer. The virtual memory is not part of the paging file that you tune to enhance the server performance. Instead it is a separate allocation of disk space for PostScript printing.

 Virtual memory is a useful way to extend memory capabilities, but keep in mind that disk access speeds (15 milliseconds or less) are slower than RAM access speeds (70 nanoseconds). Virtual memory can help server and printer performance, but it is still no match for the performance boost achieved when additional RAM is added to a server for server activities and/or to a printer for printing fonts, graphics, and colors.

To set up virtual memory for a PostScript printer, first use the Add Printer Wizard to install the printer. Next, open the Printers folder and right-click the new icon for the PostScript printer. Click Properties and the Device Settings tab. Click Available Postscript Memory and enter the virtual memory size in the __ KB box. Consider setting the virtual memory at 1MB or more. (You can practice setting up virtual memory for a PostScript printer in Hands-on Project 10-1.)

 A file called TESTPS.TXT is available from Microsoft, containing recommendations on which memory settings should be used with specific PostScript printers. The virtual memory option is available only for PostScript printers because they have such high memory requirements, and it is used for storing and managing fonts.

Setting Printer Share Permissions

With the printer installed and set up as a shared printer, the next step is to set the permissions on the printer share. In the Printers folder, right-click the icon for the new printer, and click Properties. Next, click the Security tab. There are three buttons on the tab: Permissions, Auditing, and Ownership (Figure 10-8). These buttons perform functions similar to those used in the Properties dialog box for a folder, with one important difference: with folders, you can set both permissions and share permissions, but with printers, you can set only share permissions. The Permissions button on the printer Properties dialog box sets printer share permissions only, whereas share permissions on a folder are set from the Sharing tab on the folder Properties dialog box.

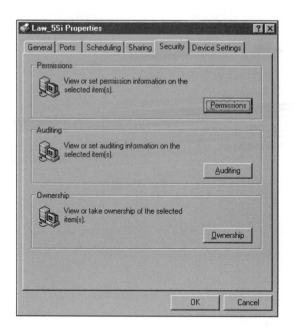

Figure 10-8   Printer Properties Security tab

10

The Auditing button is used to record printer events, such as printing a file or deleting a printout. Events may be audited by group or by user. The Ownership button is used to take ownership of the printer share. When you install a printer from the Administrator account, the printer is already owned by Administrators, so there is no need to take ownership. To set the share permissions, click the Permissions button.

Usually, the default permissions are set up so that the Everyone group is granted Full Control of the printer share. It is recommended that you change this to Print permissions only, which restricts printer share users from managing the print documents of others. To make the change, highlight the Everyone group, and then use the list arrow in the Type of Access: box to find Print, and click that selection. You also can use the Printer Permissions dialog box to add and remove groups or users, to further refine the access permissions. (You can practice setting up printer permissions in Hands-on Project 10-3.) Table 10-2 lists the printer share permissions that can be set.

Table 10-2   Printer Share Permissions

Permission	Access Capability
No Access	Users cannot access or print from the printer share.
Print	Users can connect to the printer share, send print jobs, and manage their own print requests (such as to pause, restart, or cancel a print job).
Manage Documents	Users can connect to the printer share, send print jobs, and manage any print job sent (including jobs sent by other users).
Full Control	Users have complete access to a printer share, including the ability to change permissions, turn off sharing, or delete the share.

PRINTER POOLING

Printer pooling involves configuring two or more identical printers with one printer object. For example, you might connect three identical laser printers (except for port access) to one parallel port and two serial ports on a Windows NT server. When you run the Add Printer Wizard, check the Enable printer pooling box in the second wizard dialog box, which is for selecting the ports. Once you check the box, the Add Printer Wizard enables you to click more than one port, such as LPT1, COM2, and COM3. If you want to create a printer pool by adding another printer to an existing printer setup, you can do this from the Ports tab in that printer's Properties dialog box.

All of the printers in a pool must be identical so that they use the same printer driver and handle print files in the same way. The advantage of having a printer pool is that the Windows NT print monitor can send print files to any of the three printers (or however many you set up). If two of the printers are busy, it can send an incoming file to the third printer. Printer pooling can significantly increase the print volume in a busy office, without the need to configure network printing for different kinds of printers. Hands-on Project 10-2 gives you practice installing pooled printers.

It is wise to locate pooled printers in close physical proximity, because users are not able to tell to which pooled printer a print job goes.

MANAGING PRINTER SERVICES

The setup information that you specify while stepping through the Add Printer Wizard can be modified and further tuned by accessing the Properties dialog box for a printer. The printer properties are available by opening the Printers folder, right-clicking the printer you want to modify, and clicking Properties. You can manage the following functions associated with a printer (or printer pool) from the Properties window:

- General printer information
- Printer port setup
- Printer scheduling
- Printer sharing
- Security
- Device settings

GENERAL PRINTER SPECIFICATIONS

The top portion of the General tab (Figure 10-9) shows the name of the printer. The Comment box is used to record special notes about the printer that might describe a particular feature, a common operational problem, or information about special use. Below the Comment box is a place to specify the location of the printer. This is convenient information for a large organization in which there may be several dozen network printers. Where there are many printers, comments in these boxes help current or new network administrators to have handy documentation about printers. The Driver list box enables you to select a driver that is already installed for any printer connected to the server; the New Driver button is used to install a new driver, in the event that the printer manufacturer issues a new driver, or the printer is upgraded or replaced with a different model.

The Separator Page button is used to place a blank page at the beginning of each printed document. This helps designate the end of one printout and the beginning of another, so that printouts do not get mixed together. Windows NT Server has three separator page files from which to choose, located in the \Winnt\System32 folder:

- SYSPRINT.SEP, which is used with PostScript-only printers and prints a separator page at the beginning of each document
- PCL.SEP, which is used to print a Printer Control Language (PCL) separator page on a printer that handles PCL and PostScript
- PSCRIPT.SEP, which is used to print a PostScript separator page on a printer that handles PCL and PostScript

10

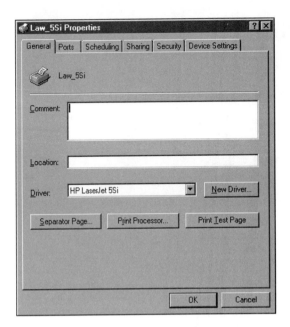

Figure 10-9 Printer Properties General tab

 Most non-PostScript laser printers use a version of the **Printer Control Language (PCL)** developed by Hewlett-Packard.

You can create a customized separator page file by using one of the three default files, adding your own control codes, and saving the file with a different name. Table 10-3 lists the control codes you can use.

 Consider the cost of paper before you set up separator pages. If you set up a separator page for each document and each user also specifies a banner page from the client, the resulting paper costs quickly mount in an office. For example, depending on the setup, there will be one or more extra pages printed per document, turning a one-page original document into two, three, or more printed pages. Many offices sharing a printer simply decide to forgo separator and banner pages, because each person usually knows what he or she has printed.

The Print Processor button is used to specify data types, such as EMF or RAW [FF appended]. (Try Hands-on Project 10-4 to practice changing the data type.) Also, there is a button to print a test page to help diagnose printing problems.

Table 10-3   Separator Page Customization Codes

Control Code	Result
\	Indicates that the file is a separator page file and must be the first character in the first line of the file
\B\M	Double-width block printing until turned off by \U
\B\S	Single-width block printing until turned off by \U
\D	Includes the date and time of the print job
\E	End of file marker or can be used to begin a new separator page when there are more than one
\F*path*	Prints a text file located in the *path* designation
\H*nn*	Sends the printer control code *nn* to the printer, but you need to read the printer documentation to find out what control codes can be used
\I	Includes the ID or job number of the print job
\L*mno*	Continuously prints one or more characters as specified, such as *mno*, until the next control code is found in the separator file
\N	Includes the name of the person who sent the print file
n	Skips *n* lines to enable formatting the separator page
\U	Stops single- or double-wide block printing

10

PORT SPECIFICATIONS

The Ports tab has options to specify which server port is used for the printer, such as LPT1, and to set up bidirectional printing and printer pooling (Figure 10-10). Bidirectional printing is used with printers that have bidirectional capability. A bidirectional printer can engage in two-way communications with the print server and with software applications, allowing the printer driver to determine how much memory is installed in the printer or if it is equipped with PostScript print capability, for instance. The printer also may be equipped with the ability to communicate that it is out of paper in a particular drawer, or that it has a paper jam. The Enable printer pooling box allows you to set up pooled printers, if you did not already do so when installing the printer with the Add Printer Wizard. Another option is to discontinue pooled printing by unchecking the Enable printer pooling box, and specifying just one printer port.

Before you connect a printer, consult the manual to determine whether or not the printer is bidirectional. If so, the printer requires a special bidirectional cable labeled as an IEEE 1284 cable, and the printer port may need to be designated as bidirectional in the computer's BIOS setup program.

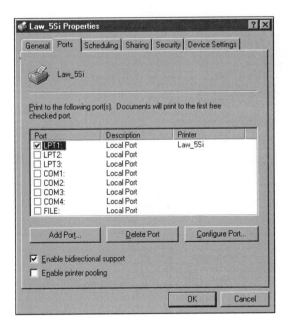

Figure 10-10   Printer Properties Ports tab

The Add Port button enables you to add a new port, such as a new print monitor or a fax port. The Delete Port button is used to remove a port option from the list of ports. The Configure Port button enables you to configure the port timeout value.

PRINTER SCHEDULING

The Scheduling tab allows you to have the printer available at all times or to limit the time to a range of hours (Figure 10-11). To have the printer available at all times, click Always or click From and set a time range. You can set the priority higher to give a particular printer or print pool priority over other printers attached to the server, which applies only if there are two or more printer icons set up in the Printers folder. The priority can be set from 1 to 99. For example, if the server is managing several printer shares, one may be set for higher priority because it prints payroll checks or is used by the company president.

Printer scheduling can be useful when there is one printer and two printer objects (shares) for that printer. One object can be set up for immediate printing and the other can be used for long print jobs that are not immediately needed. The object for the longer jobs that can wait might be set up so those print jobs are scheduled to print overnight between 6 PM and midnight. Another way to handle the longer jobs is to pause that printer object and resume printing when the printer has a light load, such as at noon or during slow times of the day (for information on pausing a printer, see the section "Controlling the Status of Printing").

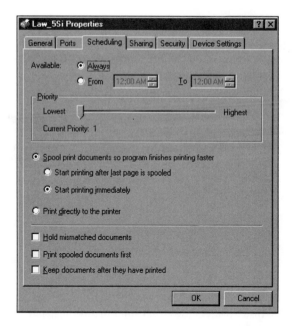

Figure 10-11   Printer Properties Scheduling tab

The Scheduling tab provides the option to use spooled printing or to bypass the spooler and send print files directly to the printer. It works best to spool print jobs so that they are printed on a first-come, first-served basis and to enable background printing so that the CPU can work on other tasks. Printing directly to the printer is not recommended, unless there is an emergency need to focus all resources on a specific printout. Print spooling also helps ensure that jobs are printed together, so that a long Word document is not interrupted by a one-page print job. Without spooling, such an interruption can happen if the one-page job is ready to print at the time when the Word job is pausing to read the disk. The spool option is selected by default, with the instruction to start printing before all the pages are spooled. This is an appropriate option in a small office in which most print files are not resource-intensive and there is infrequent contention for printers, reducing the odds of intermixing printouts.

If there is a problem with pages intermixing from printouts, click the option to "Start printing after last page is spooled."

The Hold mismatched documents option causes the system to compare the setup of the printer to the setup in the document. For example, if the printer is set in the share as a Hewlett-Packard 5Si and the document is formatted for a plotter, the print job is placed on hold. The job doesn't print until the document is released by the user, a member of the Print Operators or Server Operators group, or an administrator.

The Hold mismatched documents option is a good way to save paper in a heterogeneous situation, such as a student lab, where users have very differently formatted print jobs. One mismatch situation can use up hundreds of pages by printing one character per page.

The option to Print spooled documents first enables jobs that have completed spooling to be printed, no matter their priority. Where there is high-volume printing, this speeds the process by reducing the wait for long print jobs to spool. The Keep documents after they have printed option enables the network administrator to re-create a printout damaged by a printer jam or other problem. For example, if a large number of paychecks are printing and a printer problem strikes in the middle of the printout, this critical option makes it possible to reprint the damaged checks. However, this option should be accompanied by a maintenance schedule to delete documents no longer needed.

SHARING PRINTERS

The Sharing tab can be used to enable or disable a printer for sharing, as well as to specify the name of the share. You can use this if you decide to set up a printer for sharing after you have configured it in the Add Printer Wizard. Also, you can use the Alternate Drivers: box to add new types of clients. For example, if a new user wants to access the shared printer from a computer running Windows NT 3.51, you can click that option in the Alternate Drivers: box (Figure 10-12).

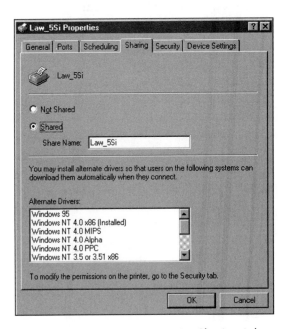

Figure 10-12 Printer Properties Sharing tab

SECURITY

The Security tab was discussed earlier, in the section "Setting Printer Share Permissions," where you learned about setting permissions via the Permissions button.

Printer auditing is set by using the Auditing button and tracks successful or failed attempts at:

- Printing jobs
- Using Full Control permissions
- Deleting jobs
- Changing permissions on the printer share
- Taking ownership of the printer

Ownership of a printer created on a Windows NT server is usually held by administrators, because ownership is first given to the account that set up the printer. The Ownership button enables anyone with Full Control permissions to take ownership.

DEVICE SETTINGS

The Device Settings tab enables you to specify printer settings such as printer trays, memory, paper size, and fonts (Figure 10-13). For example, in many cases if you have a multiple-tray printer you will leave the paper tray assignment on Auto Select and let the software application at the client specify the printer tray. However, if your organization uses special forms such as paychecks you can specify use of a designated paper tray when checks are printing.

The printer RAM is usually automatically detected in bidirectional printers, but if it is not, you can specify the amount of RAM on this tab. In Windows 95 and Windows NT printer clients, the workstation printer setup also can have information about how much memory is installed in the printer.

Make sure that the memory reported in the device settings matches the RAM installed in the printer, because this enables the print server to offload more work to the printer, improving the speed at which print jobs are completed. Most other settings are better left to the software at the client end to handle. For example, a client printing in Microsoft Word can specify font and paper tray instructions inside the document and in printer setup in Word.

Figure 10-13   Printer Properties Device Settings tab

MANAGING PRINT JOBS

In the time after a print job is sent and before it is fully transmitted to the printer, there are several options for managing that job. Users with Print permission can print and manage their own jobs. Also, Print Operators, Server Operators, and Administrators can manage the jobs of others through Manage Documents and Full Control permissions. The printer and print jobs management tool is accessed by opening the Printers folder and double-clicking the icon for the printer you want to manage. The following options are available to users with Print permission:

- Send print jobs to the printer

- Pause, resume, and restart their own print jobs

- Delete their own print jobs

Print Operators and Server Operators having Manage Documents permissions can:

- Send print jobs to the printer

- Pause, resume, and restart any user's print jobs

- Delete any user's print jobs

Administrators and any other groups having Full Control permissions can do all of the same things as Print Operators and Server Operators, but they also can change the status of the printer, such as starting and stopping sharing, setting printer properties, taking ownership, changing permissions, and setting the default printer for the Windows NT server.

CONTROLLING THE STATUS OF PRINTING

Printer control and setup information for a particular printer are associated with that printer's icon in the Printers folder. For example, if you have two printers installed, Law_5Si and Law_InkJet, there is a set of properties and printer control information for each printer. If you want to pause a print job on the Law_5Si printer, you need to first double-click its icon in the Printers folder, and if you want to delete a print job on the Law_InkJet printer, you need to double-click its icon.

If you work frequently at the console of a server, consider setting its default printer to the selection that suits your needs. For example, if you print mostly to a laser printer called Law_5Si, then make it the default printer for local printing on the server. You can do that by double-clicking the printer's icon, clicking the Printer menu, and checking Set As Default Printer (Figure 10-14).

10

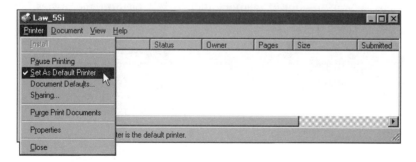

Figure 10-14   Designating a default printer

Sometimes you need to pause a printer to fix a problem, such as to reattach a loose cable or to power the printer off and on to reset it. You can pause printing to that printer by double-clicking its icon in the Printers folder, clicking the Printer menu, and checking Pause Printing. Remember that you need to uncheck Pause Printing for print jobs to be able to continue printing. The Pause Printing capability is particularly important if a user sends an improperly formatted document to the printer, such as a PostScript-formatted document to a non-PostScript printer. If you do not have Hold mismatched documents enabled, the printer may print tens or hundreds of pages with a single control code on each page. By pausing printing, you have time to identify and delete the document before too much paper is wasted. (Try Hands-on Project 10-5 to practice pausing a printer.)

Also, you can set up defaults for documents that are received with no setup information. Click the Printer menu and click Document Defaults. Through this option, you can set a default paper size, paper source, and paper orientation (portrait or landscape). The Printer menu also has a Properties option to access that printer's properties, and a Sharing option, which allows you to turn printer sharing on or off.

CONTROLLING SPECIFIC PRINT JOBS

You can pause, resume, restart, or view the properties of one or more documents in the print queue of a printer. A **print queue** is like a stack of print jobs, with the first job submitted at the top of the stack, the last job submitted at the bottom, and all of the jobs waiting to be sent from the spooler to the printer.

To pause a print job, open the Printers folder and double-click the icon for the target printer. The resulting window shows a list of jobs to be printed, the status of each job, the owner, the number of pages to be printed, the size of the print file, and when the print job was submitted. Click the document you want to pause, click the Document menu, and then click Pause. That print job will stop printing until you highlight the document and click Resume or Restart on the Document menu (Figure 10-15). Resume starts printing at the point in the document where the printing was paused. Restart prints from the beginning of the document. Keep in mind that portions or all of a document may already have been sent to the printer's memory. You only pause from the portion that is left in the print server's spooler. If the printer has a large amount of memory, such as 1, 2, or more megabytes, you may not be able to pause a document before it is loaded into the printer's memory.

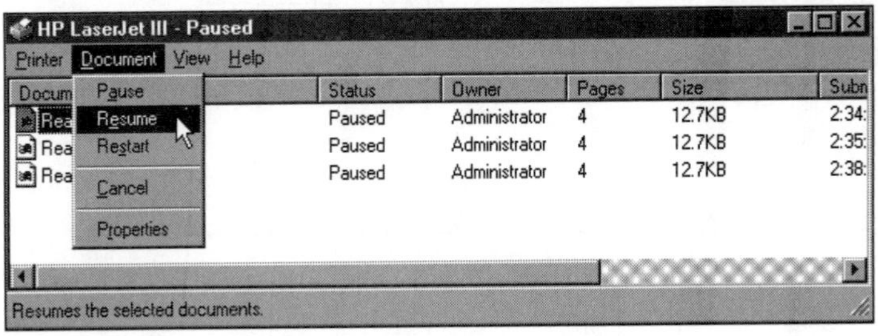

Figure 10-15   Resuming a paused document

You also can use the Document menu to cancel a print job. First click the job in the status window, click the Document menu, and click Cancel. Canceling a job deletes it from the print queue.

Jobs print in the order they are received, unless the administrator changes their priority. Jobs come in with a priority of 1, but can be assigned a priority as high as 99. For example, if you work for a university, the president may need to quickly print a last-minute report before going to a meeting with the trustees. You can give the president a 99 priority by clicking her print job in the window listing the print jobs. Next click the Documents menu, Properties, and the General tab. The Priority box is in the middle of the General tab. Move the priority bar from Lowest (1) to Highest (99) and click OK. (Practice setting print priority in Hands-on Project 10-6.)

You also can use the General tab to set a time for selected jobs to print on a printer. For example, if the server is very busy during the day, you can ease the load by setting jobs to print at a certain time of day, such as from noon to 1 PM. If you do schedule printing, plan to notify the users of that printer in advance.

Moving Print Jobs

Sometimes a printer can malfunction at the worst time, such as when your organization is working to meet a deadline for a project and is printing hundreds of pages for multiple copies of a report. In this or similar situations, you can move the unfinished print jobs to another shared printer that is working. You do this by adding a new port on the broken printer's setup that points to the working printer, then specifying the path to that printer. For example, consider a situation in which printer Pub_5Si is broken but Bus_5Si on server Business is working (also assume that both printers use the printer name for the share name, too). To move the print jobs, open the Printers folder, right-click the Pub_5Si icon, and click Properties. Click the Ports tab and the Add Port button. Click Local Port in the Available Printer Ports: box and click the New Port button. Enter the UNC path to the working printer, \\Business\Bus_5Si, and click OK. Click Close in the Printer Ports dialog box and OK in the Pub_5Si dialog box.

10

Connecting to a Nonlocal Printer

There are times when you want to enable Windows NT Server to connect to a printer that is not directly connected to one of its ports, such as a printer shared from a workstation, another server, or a print server device. You can connect to a network printer by using the Add Printer Wizard. Start the Add Printer Wizard, click the radio button Network printer server, and click Next. The Connect to Printer dialog box is displayed with Microsoft Windows Network in the Shared Printers: box (if you are configured as a NetWare client, there also is a heading for NetWare or Compatible Network). Double-click the type of network containing the printer you want to use, and double-click each icon displayed next, such as the domain and the server icons, until you view the desired printer. Double-click the printer; in the next dialog box, click Yes if you want to use it as the default printer, or click No. Click Finish to complete the installation.

You can change the properties of the shared printer you just installed, even though you are not logged on to its host computer. This means that you can manage any remote shared network printer, even though it is not connected to a port on the server. For example, open the Printers folder and right-click the remote printer you installed. Click the Properties option and make any changes you desire. This capability is very useful when you manage a large network with network printers located in distant buildings. If you need to change the print processor used by a shared printer that is a block away, you can do so without leaving your office.

SOLVING A COMMON PRINTING PROBLEM

One common printing problem occurs when the Windows NT Spooler service experiences a temporary problem, gets out of synchronization, or hangs. The result is that print jobs are not processed until the problem is solved. The Windows NT Spooler service consists of several pieces, as follows:

- WINSPOOL.DRV
- SPOOLSS.EXE
- SPOOLS.DLL
- LOCAL.DLL
- WIN32SP.DLL
- NWPROVAU.DLL (for NetWare printing)
- WINPRINT.DLL
- SFMPSPRT.DLL

Because the spooler contains these complex pieces, it is a common source of printer problems. If a print job is not going through, and you determine that the printer is not paused and the cable connection is good, then stop and restart the Spooler service. You do this by opening the Control Panel and clicking the Services icon. Scroll to the Spooler service and click it. Click Stop and click Yes in the warning dialog box. With the Spooler service still highlighted, click Start. Make sure that the status column shows that the service is started. Click Close to leave the Services dialog box.

 Warn users before you stop and restart the Spooler service, because queued print jobs will be deleted.

CHAPTER SUMMARY

- Network printing is as important as file access and file management for many users. Network printing gives them a hard-copy document to study, send to a colleague, or present before a committee. However, network printing is a complex area because it involves many elements such as clients, print servers, and printers. Behind the scenes are printing services that operate on each client and that must communicate with printing services on the print server. Also, there must be a means for the print server to communicate with one or more printers.

- Printing involves particular data types used to enable a document formatted by a software application to print successfully. There are data types designed for Windows environments, and others are used by UNIX and IBM systems. Also, Windows NT uses different print monitors to communicate with specialized printing devices and network-interfaced printers, such as Hewlett-Packard and Lexmark printers.

- Installing a local or nonlocal printer is handled by the Add Printer Wizard. The wizard takes you through the installation process step by step, including setting up a printer as shared. When you finish an installation, the printer properties can be customized to match the purpose of the printer. For example, the printer can be set up to print only during certain hours, or to print legal-size pages by default.

- Printers and print jobs can be managed according to your needs. If there is a printing problem, a printer can be paused so that nothing prints until the problem is solved. Also, specific print jobs can be paused and resumed or deleted; important jobs can be given a high priority so that they print before others in the queue.

KEY TERMS

- **data type** — Means by which information is formatted in a print file.

- **Graphics Device Interface (GDI)** — An interface on a Windows network print client that works with a local software application, such as Microsoft Word, and a local printer driver to format a file to be sent to a local printer or a network print server.

- **local printing** — Printing on the same computer to which print devices are attached.

- **network-interface printer** — A printer with its own print server card, which enables it to be connected directly to a network.

- **page-description language (PDL)** — Printing instructions involving a programming code that produces extremely high-quality printing with extensive font options.

- **port timeout** — A setting for a printer port, indicating the amount of time a print server will continue to try sending a print file to a printer when the printer is not responding.

- **PostScript** — A programming language that is used to code instructions for printers that can interpret page-description language (PDL).

- **PostScript printer** — A printer that has special firmware or cartridges to print using a page-description language (PDL).

- **print client** — Client computer that generates a print job.

- **print device** — A device, such as a printer or fax, that uses the Spooler services in Windows NT.

- **print job** — A print file that contains text and codes formatted to be sent to a printer for printing.

- **print queue** — A stack or line-up of print jobs, with the first job submitted at the top of the stack and the last job submitted at the bottom, and all of the jobs waiting to be sent from the spooler to the printer.

- **print server** — Network computer or server device that connects printers to the network for sharing and that receives and processes print requests from print clients.

- **Printer Control Language (PCL)** — A printer language used by non–PostScript Hewlett-Packard and compatible laser printers.

- **printer driver** — A file containing information needed to control a specific printer, implementing customized printer control codes, font, and style information.

- **printer pooling** — Linking two or more identical printers with one printer setup or printer share.

- **rendering** — Graphically creating a print job.

- **spool file** — A print file written to disk until it can be transmitted to a printer.

- **spooler** — In the Windows 95 and Windows NT environment, a group of DLLs, information files, and programs that process print jobs for printing.

- **spooling** — A process working in the background to enable several print files to go to a single printer. Each file is placed in temporary storage until its turn comes to be printed.

- **Universal Serial Bus (USB)** — An emerging standard for connecting peripherals, such as printers, to a computer, based on the idea that one port fits all. It replaces the use of multiple parallel and serial ports.

REVIEW QUESTIONS

1. Which of the following protocols might be used with a Hewlett-Packard JetDirect print server card?

   a. DLC

   b. TCP/IP

   c. DECnet

   d. any of the above

   e. only a and b

2. You work in an office area in which there is one shared laser printer attached to the centrally located Windows NT server, and another laser printer that is the same make and model attached to a supervisor's workstation, which runs Windows 3.11. What would you recommend to ease some of the burden on the printer attached to the server?

   a. install Printer Assist and make the supervisor's workstation double as a print server

   b. purchase a print server device to attach to the supervisor's workstation and to which you attach the printer

   c. set up a printer pool on the server

   d. set the properties for the server printer to print immediately instead of spooling

3. What is the default priority of a print job?

   a. 1

   b. 5

   c. 25

   d. 99

4. You have set up HPMON.DLL in order to enable communications with a Hewlett-Packard printer, but still cannot send a print job to it from your Windows NT server. What might you check?

   a. make sure the HP spooler service is installed

   b. check the jumpers on the HP JetDirect card

   c. make sure that the DLC protocol is installed at the server

   d. set up an IP address for HPMON.DLL

5. Which separator page file would you use for a printer that can print only PostScript?

   a. SYSPRINT.SEP

   b. PCL.SEP

   c. PSCRIPT.SEP

   d. COMBI.SEP

10

6. The network printer connected to your server is turned on and has a good cable connection, but print jobs are not printing. What might you do to solve the problem?

   a. check if the printer is paused

   b. stop and restart the Spooler service

   c. open the icon for that printer to make it active

   d. all of the above

   e. only a and b

7. From where can you disable a printer share?

   a. Properties dialog box Sharing tab

   b. Properties dialog box Security tab

   c. Control Panel Services icon

   d. Control Panel Server icon

8. A spooler is _____.

   a. a folder of spool files

   b. a program that polls printers to determine if they are ready to accept a print job

   c. a memory-handling DLL for printing

   d. a group of programs, DLLs, and processes used to handle printing

9. Which control code would you use in a separator page file to print the user's name on the separator page?

   a. /n

   b. /N

   c. /ID

   d. /I

10. A printer is an example of a(n) _____.

    a. folder

    b. object

    c. data set

    d. resource pool

11. You are the network administrator for a network with 20 remote printers. What would you do to administer these printers?

    a. designate a printer administrator at each location

    b. install the remote printer administrator

    c. set up each printer to use SNMP

    d. install each printer in Windows NT Server and manage its properties from the server

12. Which of the following can a Print Operator handle using the default permissions for this group?

    a. delete any user's print job

    b. reformat any user's print file

    c. specify a print monitor

    d. all of the above

    e. only a and b

13. You are setting up a plotter that will handle many extremely large print jobs. To what value would you set the port timeout?

    a. 20 seconds

    b. 50 seconds

    c. 90 seconds

    d. 120 seconds

14. You need to set up LPR printing. What other component must be set up?

    a. an LPD server

    b. an MS-DOS print server processor

    c. an IIS server

    d. more RAM for Windows NT Server

15. Which of the following can use virtual memory for a printer in Windows NT?

   a. a PCL printer

   b. a PostScript printer

   c. a plotter

   d. all of the above

   e. only a and b

16. There are three Windows NT Server groups defined on your server, Executives, Warehouse, and Sales. Sometimes members of the Executives and Sales groups inadvertently send print jobs to the Warehouse group's shared printer. How might you solve this problem?

   a. create a new local printer

   b. create a new remote printer

   c. set the shared printer permissions on the Warehouse group's printer to No Access for the Executives and Sales groups

   d. there is no way to control this situation other than through training

17. Which Document menu option commences a print job from the beginning after it has been paused?

   a. Reset

   b. Resume

   c. Restart

   d. Renew

18. Several UNIX workstations use a shared printer connected to your Windows NT server. One problem you have noticed is that often the last page of a print job is not printed. What would you do?

   a. set the data type to EMF

   b. set the data type to RAW [FF auto]

   c. use the /P option in the separator page file

   d. edit the Registry and change that printer share to UNIX Enabled

19. Who owns a printer share?

   a. all printer shares are owned by the Administrators group

   b. all printer shares are owned by the Printer Operators group

   c. the printer share is originally owned by the account that sets it up

   d. the domain owns the printer share

10

20. Which of the following can be set from the printer properties Device Settings tab?

    a. paper size

    b. printer port

    c. print auditing

    d. all of the above

    e. only a and b

21. What happens when a mismatched document is detected by a printer share set up to look for mismatches?

    a. the document is automatically deleted

    b. the document is automatically held

    c. the document is immediately sent to the printer

    d. the document is automatically reformatted

22. Where would you look to find out the size of a document waiting to be printed?

    a. in the system log

    b. in the window showing all queued print jobs for that printer

    c. in the Registry

    d. in User Manager for Domains under the user who sent the document

23. The separator page is set up from which of the following printer Properties tabs?

    a. Security

    b. Sharing

    c. General

    d. Scheduling

24. From which type of printer is the print server most likely to be able to automatically determine the amount of RAM in the printer?

    a. laser

    b. dot matrix

    c. bidirectional

    d. ink jet

25. The _____ integrates information in a print file with a printer driver to prepare a print job for printing.

    a. Graphics Device Interface (GDI)

    b. remote monitor

    c. Driver Application Interface (DAI)

    d. spooler monitor

26. Jake Field is accessing a shared printer at the server for the first time. When Jake connects to the shared printer in Network Neighborhood via Windows 95 to install the printer, where does the printer setup look first to find a printer driver?

    a. in Windows 95 on Jake's computer

    b. in the printer share set up on the server

    c. in the printer drivers folder on Jake's Windows 95 installation disk

    d. in the printers folder of the network workstation closest to Jake's

27. Right now, your office can only afford one printer. The problem is that some people occupy the printer by sending 100-page print jobs that do not need to print immediately. What solution can you use to solve this problem?

    a. develop a voluntary system so that users with print jobs over 50 pages will send the jobs after 5 PM.

    b. limit print jobs to 25 pages or less

    c. constantly monitor printing and pause long print jobs when you see them in the print queue

    d. set up two printer objects for one printer, but implement one object for long print jobs and schedule it to print overnight

10

HANDS-ON PROJECTS

 PROJECT 10-1

In this activity you set up virtual memory for a PostScript printer.

To set up virtual memory for a printer:

1. Open the **Printers** folder from the Control Panel, My Computer, NT Explorer, or the Settings option on the Start menu.

2. Right-click the icon for a PostScript printer (or install one for practice using the Add Printer Wizard, as illustrated in Hands-on Project 10-2).

3. Click **Properties** from the shortcut menu.

4. Click the **Device Settings** tab in the **Properties** dialog box for that printer.

5. Near the top of the Device Settings tab, click **Available Postscript Memory** (Figure 10-16).

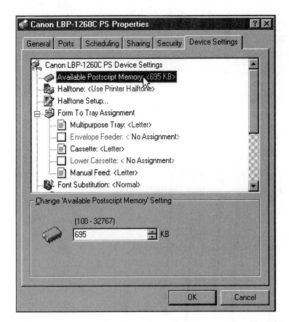

Figure 10-16   Setting virtual memory for PostScript printing

6. In the box on the lower portion of the tab, use the **up arrow** to increase the memory allocation.

7. Click **OK** to finish.

PROJECT 10-2

In this activity you set up two pooled network printers connected to a Windows NT server (or you can practice on Windows NT Workstation as an alternative). You also practice using alternate settings available in the Add Printer Wizard.

To set up two pooled network printers:

1. Click **Start**, **Settings**, and the **Printers** folder.

2. Double-click the **Add Printer** icon.

3. Click **My Computer** and click **Next**.

4. Check the **Enable printer pooling** box.

5. Use the scroll bar to view the available ports, and check two ports, such as **LPT2** and **LPT3** (Figure 10–17).

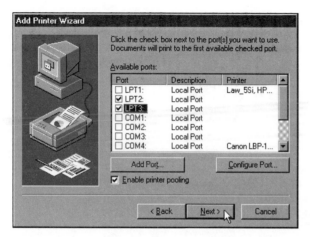

Figure 10-17   Selecting ports for printer pooling

6. Click the **Add Port** button to view the types of ports that can be set up, such as a local port on the computer, a port for a remote fax connection, or a port for a Lexmark print server (using the DLC or TCP/IP protocols). Click **Cancel**.

7. Click the **Configure Port** button and set the transmission retry to **120** seconds. Click **OK**.

8. Click **Next**.

9. Click the printer manufacturer and the model, such as **HP** and **HP LaserJet 5Si**. Click **Have Disk**, insert the driver disk (or Windows NT Server CD-ROM), enter the path to the disk, and press **OK**.

10. Enter a name for the printer in the Printer Name: box. Click **Yes** to make this the default printer used by those who print at the server, such as the server administrator when working at the console. Click **Next**.

11. Click the **Shared** radio button and enter a share name. Also, click **Windows 95** and click **Next**.

12. Click **Yes** to print a test page, and click **Finish**.

 PROJECT 10-3

In this activity you give print management permissions to the Server Operators group.

To set up permissions for the Server Operators group:

1. Click **Start**, **Settings**, and the **Printers** folder.

2. Right-click an existing printer icon, such as the one you created in Hands-on Project 10-2 to install pooled printers. Click **Sharing** or **Properties**.

3. Click the **Security** tab and click **Permissions**.

4. If Server Operators already has permissions, highlight that group and click **Remove**.

5. Click the **Add** button in the Printer Permissions dialog box.

6. In the Names: box, scroll to **Server Operators** and double-click this group so that it is moved into the Add Names: box.

7. Select **Manage Documents** in the Type of Access: box, and click **OK** in the Add Users and Groups dialog box (Figure 10-18).

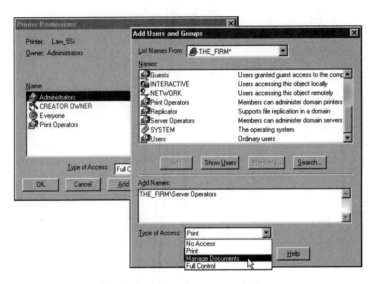

Figure 10-18   Setting printer share permissions

8. Make sure that the Server Operators group has Manage Documents permissions in the Names: box in the Printer Permissions dialog box, and click **OK**.

9. Click **OK** in the printer Properties dialog box.

PROJECT 10-4

In this activity you select the data type TEXT for a shared printer.

To specify the data type:

1. Click **Start**, **Settings**, and the **Printers** folder.

2. Right-click an existing printer icon, such as the one you created in Hands-on Project 10-2. Click **Properties**.

3. Click the **General** tab.

4. Click the **Print Processor** button.

5. Click **TEXT** in the Default Datatype: box, and click **OK**.

6. Click **OK** in the printer Properties dialog box.

 PROJECT 10-5

In this activity you practice pausing a printer.

To pause and resume printing:

1. Click **Start**, **Settings**, and the **Printers** folder.

2. Double-click an existing printer icon, such as the one you created in Hands-on Project 10-2.

3. Click the **Printer** menu.

4. Click **Pause Printing** (you will see a check next to the option after you click it) (Figure 10-19).

Figure 10-19   Pausing a print job

5. Click **Pause Printing** again to remove the check, so that the printer can continue printing jobs.

6. Click **OK** in the printer Properties dialog box.

 PROJECT 10-6

In this activity you reset the priority of a print job from 1 to 50.

To set the priority of a print job:

1. Click **Start**, **Settings**, and the **Printers** folder.

2. Double-click an existing printer icon.

3. Pause the printer as shown in Hands-on Project 10-5 (pausing the printer is just a way to prevent the job from printing long enough for you to change its priority; normally you do not need to pause the printer to change the priority of a job).

4. Use Microsoft Word or Notepad to create a small document, and send that document to the paused printer.

5. Return to the printer window showing the jobs in the print queue.

6. When you see the job you just created appear in the queue, click that job.

7. Click the **Document** menu and **Properties**.

8. Click the **General** tab and move the Priority bar until the Current Priority: value is 50 (Figure 10-20).

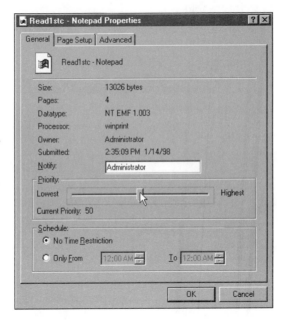

Figure 10-20   Setting the priority of a document

9. Click **OK** in the Properties dialog box for the document.

10. Click the **Printer** menu and remove the check from the **Pause Printing** option.

11. Close the window listing the print jobs.

ASPEN CONSULTING: NETWORK PRINTING SOLUTIONS

In these assignments you make a presentation to your Aspen Consulting colleagues about network printing. You also work with two companies to help them implement printing solutions.

1. Your boss, Mark Arnez, has asked you to make a presentation to the other consultants about Windows NT printing. He wants you to explain in general how Windows NT works as a print server. Explain the process of sending a print job, and focus on what happens at the client and what happens at the print server. Create a flow diagram or table to illustrate your points.

2. Supplement your presentation from Case Assignment 1 by listing the print monitors that come with Microsoft NT 4.0 Server. Provide a brief explanation of how they are used.

3. After the presentation, two of the consultants have some questions. Their questions are as follows:

   - Is there a way to set up large print jobs to print at night as a means to ease the load on a shared server printer? If so, how?

   - Is there a way to bypass creating a spool file and to send a print job directly to the printer? If so, how?

   - Can you temporarily stop a printer from printing? If so, how?

   - Does Windows NT Server have the ability to print using protocols other than NetBEUI? If so, which ones?

   Prepare a document that answers their questions.

4. The server administrator for Vancouver Tires is calling for help with installing a shared plotter on their Windows NT 4.0 server. The plotter is a large model designed to print in multiple colors. Vancouver Tires manufactures specialized snow tires for trucks and heavy equipment. The administrator has gone through the Add Printer Wizard and has already set up the printer. He can use the printer from the Administrator account and his own account with Administrator privileges. Also, he has set up an account for another employee with Print Operator privileges, and that account can use the printer. However, the Business, Sales, and Research groups cannot print on that printer. Explain what you would check and change to enable all three groups to use the print server.

10

5. Your advice to Vancouver Tires solved their initial problem; however, now there are some new ones. The Windows 95 and Windows NT 3.51 Workstation clients are experiencing frequent difficulties in (1) sending documents that are related to communicating with the shared printer and (2) finding printouts with a control code on the first page or two of their documents. The documents from Windows NT 4.0 Workstation clients are printing correctly, but those clients are experiencing occasional timeout messages from the printer. Advise them on what you would do to solve these problems.

6. Biological Research Services is a small water quality research and analysis company that consults with cities about water purification systems. They have a small network consisting of 20 Windows 95 workstations, 10 UNIX workstations, and one Windows NT server. They want to set up two shared printers on the server, one for the Windows 95 clients and one for the UNIX clients. Explain how they would set up both printers.

7. Vancouver Tires is pleased with the success of their network and network printing. They are expanding their network into several buildings on their business and manufacturing campus. Part of the expansion includes setting up networked printers in every building. The server administrator is asking you for a plan to manage those printers. Create a recommendation for managing the printers, and include an example of how to set up one printer.

REMOTE ACCESS

At one time if you worked in an organization that used computers, you had to travel every day to an office or building to do your work. Remote access techniques have changed the way we work, enabling many people to travel to an office only a few times per week or month. Millions of people access networks and host computers from workstations at home or from portable workstations while traveling. Remote access communications can also be used to diagnose computer system problems. For example, when an IBM mainframe or a large server has a hardware difficulty, it can be set up to remotely access a service center server that records the nature of the problem and contacts an engineer's pager, sometimes even sending information about what part is needed. When the repair is complete, the engineer can remotely connect to the service center server to record how the problem was solved and to enter billing data.

Microsoft has brought many improvements to remote access by incorporating remote access capabilities in its workstation operating systems (MS-DOS, Windows for Workgroups, and Windows 95, for example) and by enabling Windows NT servers to perform remote access tasks. In this chapter you learn about remote access methods, the use of modems, and to set up remote access in a Microsoft environment.

AFTER READING THIS CHAPTER AND COMPLETING THE EXERCISES YOU WILL BE ABLE TO:

- EXPLAIN THE CAPABILITIES OF RAS AND HOW IT WORKS
- EXPLAIN HOW MODEMS ARE USED FOR REMOTE COMMUNICATIONS, WHAT TYPES OF MODEMS ARE USED, AND HOW TO INSTALL AND CONFIGURE A MODEM IN WINDOWS NT SERVER
- EXPLAIN DIAL-UP VS. LEASED TELEPHONE LINES
- INSTALL AN ISDN OR X.25 ADAPTER
- CONNECT MODEMS USING COMMUNICATIONS AND ACCESS SERVERS
- DISCUSS REMOTE ACCESS COMMUNICATIONS PROTOCOLS
- SET UP A RAS SERVER AND RAS CLIENTS, MONITOR A RAS SERVER, AND SET UP RAS SECURITY
- TROUBLESHOOT RAS CONNECTION PROBLEMS
- INSTALL AND USE THE REMOTE ADMINISTRATION TOOLS FOR A SERVER

HOW REMOTE ACCESS WORKS

There are several ways to remotely access a server on a network. If you use the Internet, you already have experienced one method, which is using public telephone lines to dial in to your local Internet service provider (ISP). That method requires that you have a computer with a modem, a computer operating system, and an Internet browser such as Microsoft Internet Explorer. The servers you access may be UNIX, Windows NT, or other servers that offer a special remote access interface. The files and information that you access are strictly controlled by the capabilities of the interface on the server and by the Internet site manager or "Webmaster."

Before widespread use of the Internet, the only way that many people could access their organization's network was by dialing in to a network workstation running remote access software, such as pcANYWHERE or Carbon Copy. In this situation, that workstation is left running most of the time so that a single user can dial in to it from a remote computer, for example from home (Figure 11-1). The remote computer takes control of the network computer that is left turned on, accessing hosts, servers, or software available through the network. When this method was first used, access was frustrating because modems were slow, and someone might inadvertently turn off the computer connected to the network. Failing to leave the network workstation turned on is still a problem, and there are limitations because the mouse on the network workstation cannot be accessed by the user over the telephone connection.

Another way to set up remote communications is to configure TCP/IP, Telnet (a terminal emulator), and FTP (for file transfer) at the network workstation and leave the workstation turned on. The remote workstation that accesses the network workstation has the same elements configured, and obtains or sends files through FTP. This method also has disadvantages because it is complex to set up, has limited GUI support, and enables access to the remote workstation only. Also, many people fail to set a password because the software is hard to use and, there still is the problem that the network workstation may not be left turned on, or that a power failure will shut it down. Another disadvantage of this method is that the security is not robust and it is subject to intrusion.

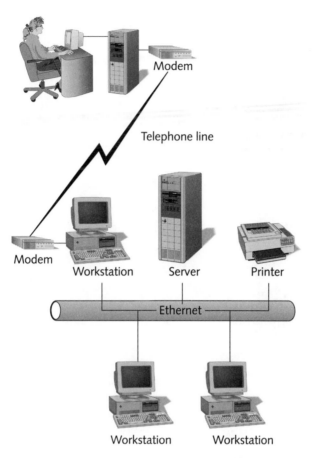

Figure 11-1   Remotely accessing a workstation on a network

In the early 1990s Novell improved on remote access technology by introducing the NetWare Access Server (NAS). The original concept of NAS was to make one node connected to the network act as many workstations in the same unit. For example, a network computer running NAS might contain five modem cards, enabling that number of users to dial in. On that system each user would have a specific portion of the computer to use, including CPU and hard disk space, with NAS acting like five small computers in one (Figure 11-2).

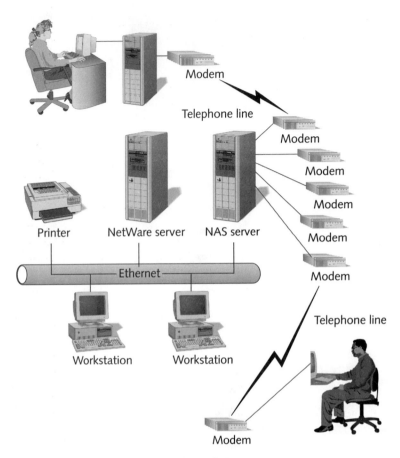

Figure 11-2   Remote access through NAS

Microsoft improved network access by making an NT network server double as a remote access server. A Windows NT server (or workstation) can be installed with **Remote Access Services (RAS)** to turn it into a RAS server capable of handling hundreds of simultaneous connections. The NT server performs its normal functions as a server, but serves remote access needs at the same time. A user dials in to the RAS server, providing her or his NT Server account name and password. If NWLink is set up at the user's workstation and NetWare Client Service is set up in the RAS server, that user also can provide a password to log on to a NetWare server at the same time.

MICROSOFT REMOTE ACCESS SERVICES

A Windows NT server that is also a RAS server offers flexible remote access into the server. Any computer with one or more modems and the Windows NT Server or NT Workstation operating system can be set up for RAS, because RAS is included on the

Windows NT CD-ROM for versions 3.51 and higher. Windows NT Workstation is a limited RAS server because it can handle only one caller at a time. Windows NT Server 4.0 enables up to 256 remote callers to connect at the same time. A RAS server offers remote connectivity to the following client operating systems:

- MS-DOS
- Windows 3.11 (Windows for Workgroups)
- Windows NT 3.1
- Windows NT Advanced Server 3.1
- Windows NT Workstation 3.5 or higher
- Windows NT Server 3.5 or higher
- Windows 95
- OS/2

Not only is it designed to work with many kinds of clients, a RAS server supports the following types of connections:

- Asynchronous modems (such as the modem you may already use in your PC)
- Synchronous modems through an access server
- Null-modem communications
- Regular dial-up telephone lines
- Leased telecommunications lines
- ISDN lines (and digital modems)
- X.25 lines

Integrated Services Digital Network (ISDN) is a standard for delivering data services over specialized digital telephone lines using 64 Kbps channels. The channels are combined to offer different types of services; for example, an ISDN basic rate interface consists of three channels. Two are 64 Kbps channels for data, voice, and graphics transmissions. The third channel is a 16 Kbps channel used for communications signaling. Many United States telecommunications companies offer ISDN, which is often used for industrial-strength Internet connectivity. **X.25** is an older WAN communications method used to transmit data over telecommunications lines at speeds up to 64 Kbps, and is more commonly used in Europe and in other countries than it is in the United States.

One of the most common ways to connect is by using asynchronous modems and dial-up telephone lines. When you employ RAS with this equipment, it supports different types of modem command languages, such as the widely used Hayes AT modem commands. It also supports the modem communications standards employed by most modems, such as the MNP and V communications and error control standards described later in this chapter.

11

Microsoft RAS is compatible with data compression standards, enabling faster communications over telecommunications lines. Microsoft also has developed a special RAS data compression capability that can be twice as fast as the modern V.42bis standard.

 Purchase modems listed in the Hardware Compatibility List (HCL). However, if you do have a modem that is not on the supported list or that does not fully use standard modem commands, there is an option to modify the Windows NT MODEM.INI file to enable the modem to work with RAS.

Microsoft RAS provides support for the standardized modem driver, **Universal Modem Driver**, used by recently developed modems. It also contains support for the **Telephony Application Programming Interface (TAPI)**. TAPI is an interface for line device functions, such as call holding, call receiving, call hang-up, and call forwarding. **Line devices** are communications equipment, such as modems, ISDN adapters, X.25 adapters, and fax cards, that directly connect to a telecommunications line.

Besides supporting different types of modems and communications equipment, RAS is compatible with the following network transport and remote communications protocols:

- NetBEUI
- TCP/IP
- NWLink
- SLIP
- CSLIP
- PPP
- PPTP

Modems, access methods, and communications protocols are discussed in the next sections.

USING MODEMS FOR REMOTE COMMUNICATIONS

Improvements in remote access have involved dramatic advances in remote communications devices such as modems. Modems are a key piece in making remote access possible and worthwhile. The term **modem** is a shortened version of the full name, modulator/demodulator. This device converts a computer's outgoing digital signal to an analog signal that can be transmitted over a telephone line. It also converts the incoming analog signal to a digital signal that the computer can understand. A modem is attached to a computer in one of two ways: internally or externally. An internal modem is installed inside the computer using an empty expansion slot on the main board. An external modem is a separate device that connects to a serial port on the computer (serial communications are explained later in this chapter). An external modem is attached by a cable designed for modem communications that matches the serial port connector on the computer. There are three types of connectors:

- DB-25, an older-style connector that has 25 pins and resembles a parallel port for a printer (but does not use parallel communications)

- DB-9, a connector with nine pins

- PS/2, a round connector for serial communications on an IBM PC

Both internal and external modems connect to a telephone outlet through a regular telephone cable with RJ-11 connectors at each end.

The modem data transfer rate is measured in two similar, but not identical, ways: baud rate and bits per second (bps). **Baud rate** is the number of changes per second in the wavelength of the signal transmitting the data. Baud rate was an appropriate way to measure the modem transmission rates when modems were first developed and could transmit only one data bit per signal change. Early modems were painfully slow at 300 and 1200 baud. 9600 baud modems were available, but at great expense. Modem technology has advanced rapidly, requiring a different measurement of modem transfer rates. Vendors have developed technologies to send multiple bits of data per each change in the signal. Because of new technologies, modem rates are now measured in **bits per second (bps)**. Modems are currently capable of up to 56 Kbps rates, and are soon expected to reach over 100 Kbps.

A main influence on modem technology has been Microcom, the company that pioneered the **Microcom Network Protocol (MNP)** for modems. MNP consists of communications service classes such as MNP classes 2 through 6 and a newer class 10 for cell phone transmission. MNP classes were developed to provide efficient communications, error-correction techniques, and data compression. However, MNP classes 2 through 5 are aging communications and compression techniques and do not provide the same advantages as the fastest modern communications standards.

 Windows 95 is the only client operating system that supports cellular communications that may use MNP class 10. Keep in mind that data communications through cellular means can become extremely slow, causing timeout problems with a RAS server.

The International Telecommunications Union (ITU) has also developed standards for modem communications with some of the MNP service classes (such as MNP class 10) included in its V.42 standard. Table 11-1 shows the ITU-Telecommunications (ITU-T) modem standards.

Table 11-1 ITU-T Modem Standards

ITU-T Modem Standard	Description
V.21	300 bps data transmission for dial-up lines
V.22	1200 bps data transmission for dial-up and leased lines
V.22bis	2400 bps data transmission for dial-up lines
V.23	600/1200 bps data transmission for dial-up and leased lines
V.26	2400 bps data transmission for leased lines
V.26bis	1200/2400 bps data transmission for dial-up lines
V.26ter	2400 bps data transmission for dial-up and leased lines
V.27	4800 bps data transmission on leased lines
V.27bis	2400/4800 bps data transmission on leased lines
V.27ter	2400/4800 bps data transmission on dial-up lines
V.29	9600 bps data transmission on leased lines
V.32	9600 bps data transmission on dial-up lines
V.32bis	14400 bps data transmission on dial-up lines using synchronous communications
V.33	14400 bps data transmission on leased lines
V.34	28800 bps data transmission on dial-up lines with the ability to drop to slower speeds when there are line problems
V.35	48000 bps data transmission on leased lines
V.42	Error detection and correction on noisy telephone lines
V.42bis	4:1 data compression for high-capacity transfer

At this writing, a standard for 56 Kbps modem transmissions is being formalized. Two incompatible approaches exist for 56 Kbps modems, one developed by U.S. Robotics and one by Rockwell Semiconductor Systems and Lucent Technologies. Also, you will find some references to V.FC (V. FastClass) as a modem "standard" for 28800 bps. V.FC is really a proprietary specification that was replaced by the more universal V.34 standard.

When a computer is connected to a modem, the data transfer speed is the **data terminal equipment (DTE)** communications rate. A workstation client and the RAS server are both examples of DTE because they prepare data to be transmitted. The modem is called the **data communications equipment (DCE)**, and its speed is the DCE communications rate. The computer's port setup for the modem (DTE rate) should be the same as or higher than the DCE rate of the modem. For example, if you have a 56 Kbps modem, select a maximum speed, of 57600 (the closest setting) in Windows 95 or NT when you configure the computer's modem port. (You can practice setting up a modem in Hands-on Project 11-1.)

To configure a port in Windows 95, open the Control Panel System icon, click the Device Manager tab, and click the port (for example COM2). Click Properties and the Port Settings tab. In Windows NT, open the Control Panel Ports icon. Click the port and the Settings button.

When two modems are communicating over a telephone line, for example the modem on a remote workstation communicating with a modem on a network, they may not actually communicate at the maximum speed for both modems. For example, two V.34 or V.42 modems may negotiate to transmit at 14400 bps instead of 28800 bps because of noise detected on the line.

Sometimes modems will not communicate because of how they are set. For example, a 2400/4800 bps V.27ter modem will not be able to establish communications with a 36600 bps V.42 modem if the 36600 bps modem is not set to negotiate down to a slower speed. Also, when telephone lines are very noisy, some V.42bis modems attempt to step down to MNP-5 for data compression. If one of the communicating modems does not have MNP-5 compression capability (which is used concurrently with MNP-4 error detection), they may not be able to establish a link-up, because V.42 error control will not work with MNP-5 data compression. Also, a modem using MNP-4 error control will not work with another modem using V.42 compression. Keep these cautions in mind when you set up network modems, and work with users to solve modem communications problems.

INSTALLING A MODEM IN WINDOWS NT SERVER

The first step in installing a modem is to identify an unused IRQ, I/O memory address, and communications port. You can find this information from the Windows NT Diagnostics tool (Start, Programs, Administrative Tools (Common), Windows NT Diagnostics) by checking its Resources tab. Once you have found resources that are available, shut down and turn off the computer. Set up the modem, for example by using DIP switches or jumpers, so that it is configured to use the available resources. The modem instructions will show you how to set it up. Install the modem in an open expansion slot that is compatible with that modem, again following the instructions provided with the modem. Power up the computer.

Windows NT 4.0 Server uses an installation wizard to install modems. You can start the wizard from the Control Panel or from the Administrative Wizards screen. To start it from the Control Panel, click Start, Settings, and Control Panel. On the Control Panel, click the Modems icon. If you want to use the Administrative Wizards screen, click Start, Programs, Administrative Tools (Common), and Administrative Wizards. On the Administrative Wizards screen, click Install New Modem. If a modem has not previously been installed, you are taken directly into the modem installation wizard. If another modem has already been installed, click the Add button in the Modem dialog box, which starts the Install New Modem Wizard.

After the Install New Modem Wizard is started, click Next to have the wizard automatically detect the modem installed in the computer (Figure 11-3). Click Next to use the modem setup determined by the wizard (if you use a modem from the HCL, the wizard is likely to correctly detect it). Click Finish to exit the wizard.

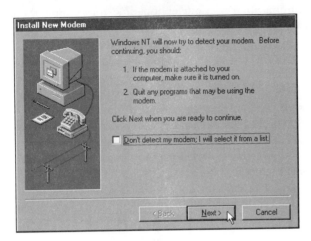

Figure 11-3 Installing a modem

If the wizard does not correctly detect the modem, click Back to return to the first dialog box. Check the box "Don't detect my modem; I will select it from a list." Click Next, and select the modem manufacturer and model. You may need a driver disk to install the modem. Click Finish when the installation is complete.

DIAL-UP AND LEASED TELEPHONE LINES

Most communications by modem still use **public dial-up lines**, which are the voice-grade lines you use to make a telephone call to a friend or relative. These lines compose part of what is known as the **Public Switched Telephone Network (PSTN)**, which is a global network of telecommunications companies that offer telephone services through an array of communications lines and switches. Those lines offer a temporary connection that lasts as long as your session on the modem. In some areas, they are subject to noise from other callers using portions of the line bandwidth for their calls and from electrical or magnetic interference.

Another term used for PSTN is Plain Old Telephone Service (POTS).

A **leased line** is a telephone line that is used exclusively for data transmissions and is a permanent connection between two sites. It bypasses the need to dial and select a circuit for a connection each time you send data, providing a high-quality signal. Another advantage of a leased line is that it is conditioned to reduce noise and provide reliable transmissions. There are different levels of conditioning, depending on the cost and type of line. Low-cost leased lines provide 56 Kbps transmission rates. More expensive fractional T1 and T1-based lines offer higher transmission speeds and more bandwidth for data communications. T-carriers use switching techniques to offer high-speed data transmission options. The smallest carrier service, T1, offers 1.544 Mbps data communications that can be switched to create multiple data channels for high-speed communication (Table 11-2). For example, switching T1 to the next level of service, T2, creates four channels. T3 has 28 channels, and T4 has 168 channels. Because T-carrier service is expensive, telephone companies offer fractional services that use a portion of the T1 service, utilizing subchannels with 64 Kbps speeds. This is possible because each T1 service consists of 24 64-Kbps subchannels, called data signal at level 0 (DS-0) channels.

Table 11-2   T-Carrier Services and Data Rates

T-Carrier	Data Transmission Rate	T1 Switched Channels	Data Signal Level
Fractional T1	64 Kbps	1 of 24 T1 subchannels	DS-0
T1	1.544 Mbps	1	DS-1
T2	6.312 Mbps	4	DS-2
T3	44.736 Mbps	28	DS-3
T4	274.176 Mbps	168	DS-4

11

Public telephone dial-up and leased lines are analog-based (except for ISDN and T-carrier lines) and require the use of asynchronous or synchronous modems to connect to computers. A popular alternative, where service is available, is to use ISDN links available from the local telephone company. ISDN provides a digital line for fast, high-quality data transmissions. ISDN requires using a **terminal adapter (TA)** to connect a computer to an ISDN line. A TA also is called a digital modem, even though it is not truly a modulator/demodulator, because it uses digital instead of analog technology. ISDN digital modems are available for about the same cost as a high-quality asynchronous or synchronous modem, but with higher data transfer capabilities (for example, 128 Kbps to 512 Kbps). Another alternative is to connect some or all of these devices using an access server (discussed later in this chapter).

Three interfaces are supported in ISDN: basic rate interface, primary rate interface, and broadband ISDN. The **basic rate interface (BRI)** has an aggregate data rate of 144 Kbps. Since many conventional LANs have data rates of 1–16 Mbps, ISDN BRI is not suitable for some network applications, such as file transfer, and graphics applications. The ISDN basic rate interface consists of three channels. Two are 64 Kbps channels for data, voice, voice, and graphics transmissions. The third is a 16 Kbps channel used for communications signaling.

The **primary rate interface (PRI)** supports faster data rates, particularly on a channel called H11, which offers switched bandwidth in increments of 1,536 Kbps. Also, as high-speed networks are developing, so are advances in **broadband ISDN (B-ISDN)** that provides data communications at 155 Mbps. The theoretical limit of B-ISDN is 622 Mbps.

TYPES OF MODEMS

When you purchase modems for remote communications, you likely will use asynchronous modems. An asynchronous modem sends information a bit at a time, in byte-sized packages. One byte represents a character, such as the capital letter *B* or the small letter *t*. There is a start bit in front of each byte package and a stop bit at the end, showing where each package of bits begins and ends. Asynchronous modems transmit at from 300 bps to 56 Kbps, depending on the modem you purchase.

Synchronous modems package data in streams. One data stream may contain several bytes of data, each contained in a single-byte unit within the stream. Each data stream is sent according to a timing or synchronized interval established by the communicating modems, called the clocking interval. Data streams are continuously clocked onto the line so that the streams are sent by one modem and received by the other at the pre-established synchronized intervals. A synchronous modem can potentially send and receive more data in a given time than an asynchronous modem, because a start and stop bit does not have to be placed at the beginning and end of each byte (although with some methods there is a start and stop indicator for each stream).

Synchronous modems are more expensive than asynchronous and are not of real advantage to the single user working remotely from home. Instead, they are used more commonly for remote communications between a site with multiple users and a host computer, such as a mainframe. For example, before networks were widely used, 10 researchers studying water quality in the Adirondack Mountains remotely connected to a mainframe computer at their city university through synchronous modems at each end. They connected five terminals to a multiplexer, which is a switching device that creates several channels on one line. The multiplexer was connected to a synchronous modem. The synchronous modem connected over a telephone line to another synchronous modem at the city university, also connected to a multiplexer. The multiplexer was connected to the mainframe, providing a channel for each terminal connected at the other end.

 Synchronous modems and asynchronous modems cannot directly communicate with one another except through intervening devices such as access servers, which are discussed later in this chapter.

INSTALLING ISDN AND X.25 ADAPTERS

An ISDN TA may connect internally or externally to the computer. An external TA connects to the computer's serial port. An internal TA is installed in an open expansion slot. The same applies to X.25 adapters. Both types of adapters are treated by Windows NT as NICs, and you must install drivers as part of their setup.

You can install the TA or X.25 adapter drivers by opening the Control Panel and then the Network icon. Click the Add button in the Adapters tab, select the adapter from the list, insert the drivers disk (or the Windows NT Server CD-ROM), and click Have Disk. Enter the bus type (ISA or PCI) and the number, such as 0, or accept the defaults. If you are installing a TA you will see an Adapter Configuration dialog box in which to enter:

- I/O base address

- IRQ

- Telco switch information (provided by the telephone company)

- Number of terminals (provided by the telephone company)

- Telephone number for the provider access (provided by the telephone company)

- Service Provider ID (SPID; provided by the telephone company)

If you are installing an X.25 adapter, enter the following in the Adapter Setup dialog box (Figure 11-4):

- I/O base address

- Memory base address

- IRQ level

- Other information for the attached lines as specified by the X.25 provider

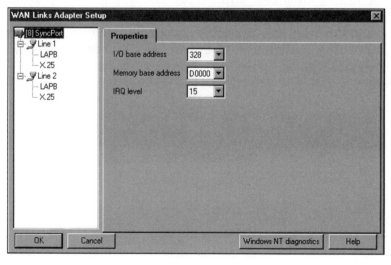

Figure 11-4 Installing an X.25 adapter

CONNECTING DIAL-IN MODEMS TO THE NETWORK

When you plan for remote network connections, find out how many people want to use this service on a regular basis. If there are only a few users, such as 10 or 20, and intermittent demand, one modem card in the server may be enough. More users require more modems and a telephone line for each modem. An organization of 100 users may need 10 modems for remote access to the network, while another organization of 500 users may need 40. One problem is that there are a limited number of expansion slots within a server for multiple modem cards. A common solution is to purchase a communications server to attach to the network.

A **communications server** is used to connect devices to the network that use asynchronous serial communications, such as modems and terminals. **Serial communications** are data transmissions using one channel to send data bits one at a time. Terminals and modems use serial communications. The serial communications port on a PC conforms to the EIA/TIA-232 (formerly RS-232) standard for communications up to 64 Kbps. The server contains a NIC with which to attach to the network and serial ports to connect the serial devices to the network. Communications servers are able to provide asynchronous routing for protocols such as IP and IPX.

Access servers are newer devices for serial connectivity. An access server connects synchronous and asynchronous devices, providing routing for both types of communications. This enables communications via X.25, T1, and ISDN. Some access servers are designed for small to midsized applications. Those servers have one Ethernet or token ring NIC to connect to the network. They also have a combination of synchronous and asynchronous ports, for terminal, modem, public telephone, ISDN, and X.25 connectivity. Smaller access servers typically have 8 or 16 asynchronous ports and one or two synchronous ports. Larger access servers are modular with slots (such as 10 to 20) for communications cards (Figure 11-5). For example, one card may have eight asynchronous ports and one synchronous port. Another card may be for T1 communications. There also may be modular cards with built-in modems, such as four modems per card. Some modular access servers can have nearly 70 modems. These servers also may have redundant power supplies for fault tolerance.

Microsoft RAS does not directly support synchronous communications, but those communications can be used through an access server connected to the network, or they can be used if the DCE providing the synchronous communications will accept a connection to the RAS server using an asynchronous null-modem cable. A **null-modem cable** is configured to disable specific communications signals that are normally sent by modems, and often is used to connect computers directly from serial port to serial port.

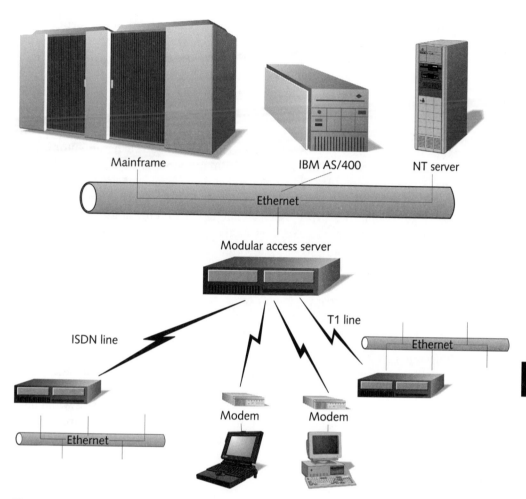

Figure 11-5   Access server connecting modems to a network

11

REMOTE ACCESS PROTOCOLS

Two protocols are used most frequently in remote communications: SLIP and PPP. **Serial Line Internet Protocol (SLIP)** was originally designed for UNIX environments for point-to-point communications between computers, servers, and hosts using TCP/IP. SLIP is an older remote communications protocol with more overhead than PPP. **Compressed Serial Line Internet Protocol (CSLIP)** is a newly developed extension of SLIP that compresses header information in each packet sent across a remote link. CSLIP reduces the overhead of a SLIP connection by decreasing the header size and thus increasing the speed of communications. However, the header still must be decompressed at the receiving end. Both SLIP and CSLIP are limited in that they do not support network connection authentication to prevent someone from intercepting a communication. They also do not support automatic negotiation of the network connection through multiple network connection layers at the same time. Another disadvantage is that SLIP and CSLIP are intended for asynchronous communications only, for example through a modem-to-modem type of connection.

Point-to-Point Protocol (PPP) is used more commonly than SLIP or CSLIP for remote communications because it has lower overhead and more capability. PPP supports more network protocols, such as IPX/SPX, NetBEUI, and TCP/IP. It can automatically negotiate communications with several network communications layers at once and supports connection authentication. PPP is supplemented by the newer **Point-to-Point Tunneling Protocol (PPTP)**, which enables remote communications to intranets or to a RAS server by way of the Internet. PPTP uses a technique called tunneling that enables one protocol to be transported through a network by another protocol. For example, through PPTP, you can use IPX communications to access a remote NetWare server through the Internet. The IPX protocol is encapsulated within PPTP and then transported over the Internet. By the same means, you can communicate with a Windows NT server using NetBEUI over the Internet. Through PPTP, a company manager can access a report housed on that company's in-house intranet by dialing into the Internet from a remote location. A server administrator can use PPTP to access a RAS server for files or to run an NT Server management tool.

PPP and PPTP support both synchronous and asynchronous communications, enabling connectivity through modems, dial-up telephone lines, leased lines, ISDN, and X.25 telecommunications. PPP is available in Windows 95 and Windows NT (3.5, 3.51, and 4.0). PPTP is available in Windows NT 4.0. When a Windows NT 4.0 server is also configured as a RAS server, it can be configured to accept remote connections through SLIP or PPP. PPP configuration is recommended on networks in which users perform remote access through computers running Windows 95 or NT. Table 11-3 compares SLIP to PPP. (You can practice setting up these remote access protocols in Hands-on Projects 11-2 and 11-3.)

Table 11-3   SLIP and PPP Compared

Feature	SLIP	PPP
Network protocol support	TCP/IP	TCP/IP, IPX/SPX, and NetBEUI
Asynchronous communications support	Yes	Yes
Synchronous communications support	No	Yes
Simultaneous network configuration negotiation and automatic connection with multiple levels of the OSI model between the communicating nodes	No	Yes
Support for connection authentication to guard against eavesdroppers	No	Yes

IMPLEMENTING REMOTE ACCESS SERVICES

Microsoft offers an effective way to connect multiple users to one network through Microsoft's RAS (Remote Access Services). Using RAS on a Microsoft-based network requires three important pieces:

- Making a Microsoft NT server a network's RAS server

- Installing RAS on workstations

- Installing Dial-Up Networking on workstations

CREATING A RAS SERVER

There are two parts to making an NT server double as a RAS server. You already have learned the first, which is to implement a way to connect multiple modems to a network. On a very small network you may only need to install one or two modems directly into an existing networked computer running Microsoft NT Server. For a larger network, you can install an access server with enough modems, T1, and ISDN connections for the type of communications required by users.

 Choose an access server that is designed to be compatible with Microsoft NT Server. A compatible access server will include software and drivers that can be used to coordinate communications between the NT server and the access server.

The second part of turning the NT server into a RAS server is to install the necessary software. You install RAS by opening the Control Panel and clicking the Network icon. Click the Add button, select Remote Access Service, insert the Windows NT Server CD-ROM, and click OK. If you have not yet installed and configured the modem, the RAS installation provides an opportunity to start the Install New Modem Wizard. There are options to activate each protocol already set up on the network or only certain ones. For example, if you have NetBEUI, TCP/IP, and NWLink installed, the setup will ask, one at a time, if you want to use the protocol and if you want to provide access via that protocol to the current server or to all servers on the network. If you employ TCP/IP, you need to provide the IP address and subnet mask or indicate that there is a DHCP server. If you use NWLink, you need to specify the network number or have it automatically assigned.

Once the installation is complete, you need to configure RAS, such as to dial out and receive calls. It is prudent to enable both, so that you can configure dial-up security later. Go to the Network dialog box and the Services tab, highlight Remote Access Service, and click Properties. On the Remote Access Setup dialog box, highlight the modem device and click Configure. In the Configure Port Usage dialog box, click the radio button for Dial out and Receive calls. Click Continue and then Close. (Try Hands-on Project 11-4 to practice setting up a RAS server.)

11

Monitoring RAS

Once RAS is installed on a Windows NT Server, the Dial-Up Monitor icon is added to the Control Panel. The Dial-Up Monitor contains three tabs: Status, Summary, and Preferences. The Status tab contains statistics, such as the number of bytes received, the number of bytes transmitted, and transmission errors. This tab can be particularly useful for troubleshooting RAS connection problems. The Summary tab reports information about specific accounts that are logged on, for example showing who is currently using RAS. The Preferences tab enables you to establish preferences for monitoring RAS connections, such as playing a sound when a connection is made or having it display as an icon next to the taskbar clock (Figure 11-6). (Try Steps 19–23 of Hands-on Project 11-4 to experiment with the Dial-Up Monitor.)

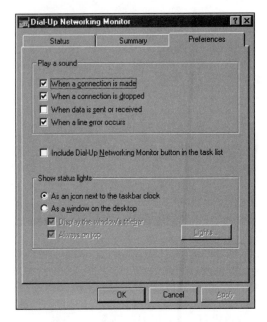

Figure 11-6 Dial-Up Networking Monitor

Installing Remote Access Services in Windows NT Workstation

Windows 95 and Windows NT workstations are connected to the RAS server by first installing RAS and Dial-Up Networking at the workstation. The RAS services support both SLIP and PPP, but PPP should be used as the remote access protocol in most cases because it supports more network transport protocols, such as TCP/IP, NetBEUI, and NWLink.

The general steps to install RAS on a Windows NT Workstation client are as follows:

1. Open the Control Panel, double-click the Network icon, and click the Services tab. Click Add, select the Remote Access Service, and click OK.

2. Insert the Windows NT Server CD-ROM, provide the path to the CD-ROM drive, and click Continue. The RAS setup will automatically detect the modem or offer to let you start the Install New Modem Wizard.

3. Check to make certain that the modem is correctly set up, and click OK.

4. In the next dialog box, highlight the modem and click Configure. Set up the modem to dial out and receive calls, so call-back security can be implemented. (Security is covered later in the chapter.) Click OK after you configure the modem.

5. Click Continue to finish the installation. Windows NT automatically configures bindings for the remote access; however, if it does not, click the Bindings tab in the Network dialog box, and then click OK. Binding is necessary because RAS connectivity at the workstation is treated similarly to the connectivity of a NIC.

(To practice setting up Remote Access Services on a Windows NT workstation, try Hands-on Project 11-5.)

INSTALLING DIAL-UP NETWORKING ON THE WINDOWS NT WORKSTATION CLIENT

After installing remote services on the remote workstation, it is necessary to create a dial-up configuration to automate the dialing procedures needed to connect to the NT server running RAS. Individual dial-up settings can be created for each type of remote access, such as one for RAS, one for America Online, and one for an Internet service provider.

To set up dial-up networking in Windows NT Workstation or NT Server, open My Computer and double-click the Dial-Up Networking folder. Click New and enter a name for the RAS connection. Click Next, and select "Send my plain text password if that's the only way to connect." Enter the telephone number for the dial-up connection, click Next, and click Finish. Back in My Computer, open the Dial-Up Networking icon, select the connection you just created, and click More. Click Edit entry and modem properties, and check the Server tab to make sure that PPP is selected. (Practice setting up dial-up networking in Hands-on Project 11-6.)

 Windows NT 4.0 RAS has an Autodial feature that maps network addresses to the RAS phonebook information. Autodial enables a RAS connection (such as a RAS server) to be dialed automatically from a software application or from the Windows NT command line window. RAS Autodial can use an IP address, NetBIOS name, or Internet URL to automatically dial a connection. Autodial works over NetBEUI and TCP/IP only.

SETTING UP DIAL-UP NETWORKING AND RAS ON A WINDOWS 95 CLIENT

Setting up dial-up networking on a Windows 95 RAS client is somewhat more involved than setting it up in Windows NT Workstation. The Windows 95 installation is a three-stage process:

1. Install the dial-up networking software.

   a. Open the Control Panel.

   b. Double-click the Add/Remove Programs icon.

   c. Click the Windows Setup tab.

   d. Click the Communications box and then the Details button.

   e. Click the Dial-Up Networking box and click OK.

   f. Click the Have Disk button on the Windows Setup tab.

   g. Insert the Windows 95 installation disk or the Windows 95 CD-ROM, if requested.

2. Create and configure the dial-up networking connection:

   a. Double-click My Computer.

   b. Double-click the Dial-Up Networking folder.

   c. Double-click the Make New Connection icon.

   d. The wizard will detect the modem installed at the workstation.

   e. Check the modem information and click Next after verifying that it is correct.

   f. Enter the area code, telephone number, and country code of the RAS server, and click Next.

   g. Enter a name for the dial-up connection, which will appear on its icon, such as RAS, and click Finish.

   h. An icon for the dial-up connection is created in the Dial-Up Networking folder in My Computer; open the Dial-Up Networking folder.

   i. Right-click the newly created icon and click Properties.

   j. Click the Server Type button.

   k. Specify PPP as the protocol for the dial-up server.

   l. Click the appropriate Advanced options, such as "Log on to network."

   m. Select the appropriate protocol, such as NetBEUI for an NT server.

   n. If TCP/IP is required, click the TCP/IP Settings button and enter the appropriate IP addresses for the workstation and the RAS server.

3. Establish networking settings.

   a. Open the Control Panel and double-click the Network icon.

   b. Click the Configuration tab, highlight Dial-Up Adapter, and click the Properties button.

   c. On the Driver Type tab select Enhanced mode (32-bit or 16-bit) NDIS driver.

   d. Click the Bindings tab and check the desired protocol, such as NetBEUI.

   e. In the Advanced tab, select the appropriate properties, and click OK to return to the Configuration tab.

   f. Select each protocol associated with the dial-up adapter (one at a time), such as NetBEUI —> Dial-Up Adapter, and click Properties.

   g. Check to make sure that the properties match the need for the dial-up service; for example, the Bindings tab for NetBEUI should have Client for Microsoft Networks checked.

   h. If TCP/IP —> Dial-Up Adapter is used, make sure that the necessary IP address information is provided for its properties.

   i. Click OK when you are finished entering the properties.

   j. Click OK in the Network dialog box.

11

SECURITY

With today's concerns about security, it is wise to set up protection on the remote access server. Microsoft NT Server has this capability through management of user accounts on the server. A user account can be set up to enforce dial-in permission each time a remote user attempts to log on to an NT server. This is accomplished by granting dial-in access to the server and through **call-back security**, which entails having the RAS server call back the workstation that is requesting access. For example, the remote workstation calls into the RAS server to access a particular NT server account. With call-back security set up, the server calls back the remote computer to verify its telephone number, in order to discourage a hacker from trying to access the server. The call-back options available in Windows NT 4.0 Server are the following:

- *No Call Back*, which means that the server allows access on the first call attempt

- *Set By Caller*, so that the number used for the call back is provided by the remote computer

- *Preset To*, so that the number to call back is entered into the text box

Set up call-back security for each account holder who will remotely access the RAS server. To set up call-back security, start User Manager for Domains (Start, Programs, Administrative Tools (Common), User Manager for Domains). Double-click the account that will be using

RAS. Click the Dialin button in the User Properties box to open the Dialin Information dialog box (Figure 11-7). Check Grant dialin permission to user, and select the type of call-back you want to use. Click OK in the Dialin Information dialog box and OK in the User Properties dialog box. (Practice setting call-back security in Hands-on Project 11-7).

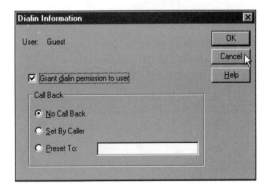

Figure 11-7 Setting up dial-in security

There is a way to set call-back security on more than one user at a time by using the Remote Access Admin option in the Administrative Tools (Common) menu. Open the Remote Access Admin tool, click the Users menu option, and then Permissions. Select the accounts to have dial-in permissions in the Users box, check Grant dialin permission to user, and select the type of call-back.

When you use PPP as the communications protocol, the RAS server can perform authentication of the connection with a client. Through PPP there are three means of authentication (not available in SLIP or CSLIP): the **Password Authentication Protocol (PAP)**, the **Challenge Handshake Authentication Protocol (CHAP)**, and **CHAP with Microsoft extensions (MS-CHAP)**.

- PAP can perform authentication, but does not require it. When you set up RAS to "Allow any authentication including clear text," you enable PAP, which means that operating systems without password encryption capabilities, such as MS-DOS, can connect.

- CHAP is enabled when you select "Require encrypted authentication." CHAP uses a generic form of password encryption, which enables UNIX computers to work with the RAS server.

- MS-CHAP is set as the default when you install a RAS server. If you select "Require Microsoft encryption authentication," this activates MS-CHAP, which means that clients must use MS-CHAP with PPP. Only Windows 95 and Windows NT clients support MS-CHAP. Along with using "Require Microsoft encryption authentication," you can select "Require data encryption," which encrypts data sent between the client and RAS server, an option you can use with Windows 95 and Windows NT clients.

RAS encryption security is set in Windows NT Server and Workstation by double-clicking the Network icon in the Control Panel. Click the Services tab, highlight Remote Access Service, and click Properties. In the Remote Access Setup dialog box, highlight the modem and click the Network button. You can set up security options, such as Require Microsoft encrypted authentication, in the Network Configuration dialog box. You also can further configure RAS from here, for example to add a protocol and configure the protocol for RAS (Figure 11-8).

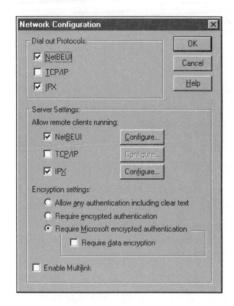

Figure 11-8 PPP-enabled security options

The Network Configuration dialog box also has an option to Enable Multilink. RAS supports Multilink for Windows NT Server and NT Workstation ISDN connections. **Multilink**, sometimes called **Multilink PPP**, is used to combine two or more ISDN channels or modems into one communications link. For example, if you are using two 64 Kbps channels, Multilink can combine them into one 128 Kbps channel. (See the next section for more detail on Multilink.)

On a computer running Windows 95, to use encrypted passwords, open the Dial-Up Networking icon in My Computer, right-click the icon for the RAS connection, click the General tab and the Server Type button, and then check Require encrypted password.

Password and data encryption for a RAS link are most important when you connect to RAS using PPTP over an Internet link. This is a feature introduced in Windows NT 4.0 Server and NT 4.0 Workstation. To use it you need Internet access through an ISP, and you need to install PPTP from the Control Panel Network icon. Click the Protocols tab and use the Add button to install PPTP from the list of protocols.

MULTILINK

Multilink provides a way to join two separate telecommunications or serial links into a "bundle" that looks like one link to RAS. For example, if you are using two 64 Kbps ISDN channels, Multilink can combine them into one logical 128 Kbps channel. Multilink can be used on ISDN, dial-up, leased, and X.25 lines and requires multiple ISDN, X.25, or modem adapters installed in the server. For example, two ISDN, X.25, or modem lines can be joined. Also, an ISDN link and a modem can be joined through Multilink. The remote communications for Multilink must be configured for PPP.

To use Multilink, the clients must be set up for this type of communications as well as the server. For the clients, there must be a phonebook entry containing the two numbers for the lines; or the ideal situation is to have two multilinked ISDN channels that use the same telecommunications number. When two numbers are used at the client, it is necessary to disable call-back security because the RAS server is only able to call back one number.

To set up a client for Multilink, modify the dial-up networking setup for the RAS connection. For example, to modify a Windows NT Workstation dial-up connection for Multilink, do the following:

1. Open My Computer and double-click the Dial-Up Networking icon.
2. Select the phonebook entry to edit and click More.
3. Click Edit entry and modem properties.
4. In the Dial using: box, select Multiple lines and click the Configure button.
5. Check each modem or adapter to bundle into one logical link.
6. When you check a modem or adapter, click Phone numbers to enter the number for the line to which it is connected.
7. Click OK and click OK again.
8. Close the Dial-Up Networking dialog box.

TROUBLESHOOTING RAS

Troubleshooting RAS problems can be divided into hardware and software troubleshooting tips.

HARDWARE SOLUTIONS

If no one can connect to the RAS server, try these hardware solutions:

- Use the Windows NT Diagnostics Resource tab to make sure that the modem is installed with no resource conflicts. If there is a conflict, fix it immediately.

- If you are using a communications or access server, make sure that it is properly connected to the network and to the telephone lines. Also, make sure that it has power.

- If you are using one or more internal or external modems connected to the server, make sure that the telephone line(s) is (are) connected to the modem(s) and to the wall outlet(s).

- For external modems, make sure that the modem cable is properly attached and that the modem has power.

- For internal modems, make sure that they have a good connection inside the computer. Reseat internal modem cards, if necessary.

- Check the Remote Access Service properties to be sure that RAS is set up for the modem(s) installed in the computer.

- Test the telephone wall connection and cable by temporarily attaching a telephone to the cable instead of the modem and making a call.

SOFTWARE SOLUTIONS

Try the following software solutions if no one can access the RAS server:

- Use the Control Panel Services icon or Windows NT Diagnostics to make sure that the Remote Access Server services are started.

- Use the Remote Access Admin tool in the Administrative Tools (Common) menu to check the port status. Open the tool, click the Server menu, and click Communication Ports. Next, click the Port Status button.

- If TCP/IP connectivity is used, make sure that the correct IP address and subnet mask are used, or if DHCP is used, make sure that the DHCP client is started as a service.

If only certain clients, but not all, are having connection problems, try these solutions:

- Check the Dial-Up Networking setup on the clients.

- Make sure that the clients are using the same communications protocol (PPP or SLIP) as the server and that they are using the same encryption method as the server.

- Make sure that the clients all have a server account and that each knows the correct account name and password. Also, make sure that accounts have the necessary rights and permissions to access files and folders on the server.

- Make sure that the client accounts have been granted dial-up access permission and have the correct call-back set up.

- Determine if the clients' modems are compatible with the modems on the RAS server (check the V and MNP capabilities).

11

USING REMOTE ADMINSTRATION TOOLS TO ADMINISTER A SERVER

Many server administrators find that it is practical to manage a server from a workstation in their office or via a RAS connection from home or while traveling. This is especially important if a problem requires immediate attention. The remote administration tools can be set up to administer a server over the network or from a RAS connection. The client workstation that runs the remote administration tools can have Windows 95 or Windows NT installed. The remote administration tools include (but are not limited to):

- User Manager for Domains
- Server Manager
- System Policy Editor
- Remote Access Administrator
- DHCP Administrator
- Directory Replication Manager
- IIS Manager
- WINS Administrator

To remotely administer a server from a workstation, you must first set up the remote administration tools on the server. To set up the remote administration tools, log on to the Administrator account from the server's console, and use the following steps:

1. Configure a RAS server on the network so that you can access the remote administration tools from a RAS connection as well as from a regular network connection.

2. Open Network Client Administrator from the Administrative Tools (Common) menu.

3. In the Network Client Administrator dialog box, click Copy Client-based Network Administration Tools, and click Continue.

4. In the next dialog box, click Share Files, and enter a share name, such as SetupAdm or RemoteAdm.

5. Click OK to create the share.

6. Set permissions on the share to ensure that only network administrators can access it.

With remote administration set up, you now have a shared folder on the server that contains the essential server administration tools. To access a tool, first permanently map a drive on your workstation for remote administration. For example, if you are using Windows NT Workstation, you might assign the drive letter R (for Remote Administration) and map it to Servername\\RemoteAdm\Winnt\I386 using Network Neighborhood.

In the shared folder, there are subfolders for Windows 95, called \Win95, or for Windows NT Workstation, called \Winnt. The \I386 folder within \Winnt has programs designed to run on Intel computers. For example, open that folder to view the administrative tools that can be run on the server, and double-click *usrmgr*, which is the remote version of User Manager for Domains (Figure 11-9). The program works as it does when you are logged on to the server console. Now, you have the option to manage Windows NT servers from your office or remotely using RAS.

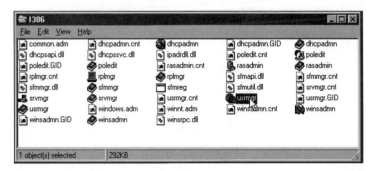

Figure 11-9 Remote Administration tools

CHAPTER SUMMARY

- Remote access to a network through Windows NT Server RAS is accomplished by installing RAS on the server and configuring it to be accessed by remote clients running workstation operating systems such as Windows 95 and Windows NT 3.1. Windows NT RAS supports many kinds of modems and communications devices. When you select modems for the server, check their specifications to make sure that they will communicate with all types of client modems. ISDN and X.25 communications require special adapters and configuration techniques, as well as information from the telecommunications provider about how to set them up.

- If you need to enable many users to access a RAS server, consider purchasing an access server with modem cards and other capabilities such as ISDN and T1 communications. Also, consider using the PPP communications protocol because it enables connection authentication, which is particularly important if users plan to use PPTP over the Internet to access the RAS server.

- Windows NT Server comes with tools to monitor and administer RAS, including Dial-Up Monitor and the Remote Access Admin tool. Dial-Up Monitor is particularly useful for tracking RAS communication problems, and the Remote Access Admin tool gives you the ability to check on the port status. Although not part of RAS, the remote administration tools provide the ability to manage a server from your office workstation or through a RAS dial-up connection. As more people work from home or have the need to access a headquarters server while they are on the road, there is more need to implement and manage RAS for all types of organizations.

KEY TERMS

- **access server** — A device that connects synchronous and asynchronous communications devices and telecommunications lines to a network, providing routing for these types of communications.

- **basic rate interface (BRI)** — An ISDN interface consisting of three channels. Two are 64 Kbps channels for data, voice, video, and graphics transmissions. The third is a 16 Kbps channel used for communications signaling.

- **baud rate** — An older modem speed measurement reflecting the fact that one data bit is sent per each signal change (signal oscillation).

- **bits per second (bps)** — Number of binary bits (0s or 1s) sent in one second, a measure used to gauge network, modem, and telecommunications speeds.

- **broadband ISDN (B-ISDN)** — An ISDN interface that is being developed to initially provide a data transfer rate of 155 Mbps. The theoretical limit is 622 Mbps.

- **call-back security** — A security measure used for remote communications verification, whereby the remote server calls back the accessing workstation to verify that the access is from an authorized telephone number.

- **Challenge Handshake Authentication Protocol (CHAP)** — An encrypted handshake protocol designed for standard IP- or PPP-based exchange of passwords. It provides a reasonably secure, standard, cross-platform method for sender and receiver to negotiate a connection.

- **CHAP with Microsoft extensions (MS-CHAP)** — A Microsoft-enhanced version of CHAP that can negotiate encryption levels and that uses the highly secure RSA RC4 encryption algorithm to encrypt communications between client and host. This is the highest level of security and authentication that RAS offers, but it works only with Windows 95 and Windows NT machines.

- **communications server** — A device that connects asynchronous serial devices to a network, providing only asynchronous routing.

- **Compressed Serial Line Internet Protocol (CSLIP)** — An extension of the SLIP remote communications protocol that provides faster throughput than SLIP.

- **data communications equipment (DCE)** — A device that converts data from a DTE, such as a computer, to a format that can be transmitted over a telecommunications line.

- **data terminal equipment (DTE)** — A computer or computing device that prepares data to be transmitted over a telecommunications line to which it attaches by using a DCE, such as a modem.

- **Integrated Services Digital Network (ISDN)** — A telecommunications standard for delivering data services over telephone lines with a current practical limit of 64 Kbps and a theoretical limit of 622 Mbps.

- **leased line** — A line that is conditioned for high-quality transmissions and forms a permanent connection without going through a telephone switch.

- **line device** — A DCE such as a modem or ISDN adapter that connects to a telecommunications line.

- **Microcom Network Protocol (MNP)** — A set of modem service classes that provides efficient communications, error correction, data compression, and high-throughput capabilities.

- **modem** — A modulator/demodulator that converts a transmitted digital signal to an analog signal for a telephone line. It also converts a received analog signal to a digital signal for use by a computer.

- **Multilink** or **Multilink PPP** — A capability of RAS to aggregate multiple data streams into one network connection for the purpose of using more than one modem or ISDN channel in a single connection.

- **null-modem cable** — A serial communications cable configured to disable specific communications and handshaking signals that are normally sent by modems, often used to establish a direct serial-port-to-serial-port connection between computers.

- **Password Authentication Protocol (PAP)** — A nonencrypted plain-text password authentication protocol. This represents the lowest level of security for exchanging passwords via PPP or TCP/IP.

- **Point-to-Point Protocol (PPP)** — A widely used remote communications protocol that supports IPX/SPX, NetBEUI, and TCP/IP for point-to-point communications (for example, between a remote PC and an NT server on a network).

- **Point-to-Point Tunneling Protocol (PPTP)** — A remote communications protocol that enables connectivity to intranets (private virtual networks).

- **primary rate interface (PRI)** — An ISDN interface that consists of switched communications in multiples of 1,536 Kbps.

- **public dial-up line** — Voice-grade, standard telephone connection used only for the duration of the communication session.

- **Public Switched Telephone Network (PSTN)** — A global network of telecommunications companies that offer telephone services through an array of communications lines and switches.

- **Remote Access Services (RAS)** — Microsoft software services that enable off-site workstations to access an NT server through modems and analog telephone or ISDN telecommunications lines.

- **serial communications** — Data transmissions that use one channel to send data bits one at a time. Terminals and modems use serial communications. The serial communications port on a PC conforms to the EIA/TIA-232 (formerly RS-232) standard for communications up to 64 Kbps.

11

- **Serial Line Internet Protocol (SLIP)** — An older remote communications protocol that is used by UNIX computers.

- **Telephony Application Programming Interface (TAPI)** — An interface for line device functions, such as call holding, call receiving, call hang-up, and call forwarding.

- **terminal adapter (TA)** — Popularly called a digital modem, links a computer or a fax to an ISDN line.

- **Universal Modem Driver** — A modem driver standard used on recently developed modems.

- **X.25** — A packet-switching communications technique for connecting remote networks at speeds up to 64 Kbps.

REVIEW QUESTIONS

1. You want to set up RAS to use password and data encryption. What authentication should you select?

    a. Require Microsoft encrypted authentication

    b. Require data encryption

    c. Require encrypted authentication

    d. all of the above

    e. only a and b

2. When you set up RAS to use the NWLink network transport protocol, you need to provide _____.

    a. the IP address of the server

    b. the subnet mask

    c. the network number

    d. all of the above

    e. only a and b

3. Which protocol would you need to set up a secure connection to a RAS server through the Internet?

    a. SLIP

    b. PPTP

    c. DECnet

    d. DLC

4. Which of the following operating systems can be used to access a Microsoft RAS server?

   a. MS-DOS

   b. Windows NT 3.1

   c. Windows 95

   d. all of the above

   e. only b and c

5. You are working with a client who has a modem that switches to MNP-4 and MNP-5 communications when it detects interference on a telephone line. There are times, especially in bad weather, when that client cannot connect to the RAS server, or is disconnected. What might be the problem?

   a. the client's modem needs to have MNP-12 installed

   b. the modem on the RAS server cannot step down to MNP-4 and MNP-5

   c. the client's modem cannot switch from baud rate communications to bps communications

   d. the client's modem needs to be able to switch to digital mode

6. Which of the following is (are) used to enable and coordinate call receiving and hang-up on a telephone line connected to a modem in a computer?

   a. Telephony Application Programming Interface (TAPI)

   b. Universal Modem Coordination (UMC) services

   c. Telephone Device Interface

   d. line adapter driver

   e. only a and b

7. Which of the following network transport protocols is (are) supported by SLIP?

   a. NetBEUI

   b. NWLink

   c. TCP/IP

   d. all of the above

   e. only a and b

8. Which modem communications mode transmits a byte at a time, with each new byte prefaced by a start bit?

   a. synchronous

   b. asynchronous

   c. bidirectional

   d. digital

11

9. Which of the following is (are) an advantage of a leased line compared to a dial-up line?

   a. it is conditioned for data communications

   b. it does not go through a central switch

   c. it is a permanent connection

   d. all of the above

   e. only b and c

10. One way to make sure that a remote connection request is from a user authorized to access a RAS server is through _____.

   a. call forwarding

   b. caller ID

   c. call analysis

   d. call-back

11. The NT Server remote administration tools are set up by using which of the following?

   a. Network Client Administrator

   b. Windows NT Diagnostics

   c. Control Panel Services icon

   d. purchasing the remote administration tools separately from Microsoft

12. The speed of a port in a computer running Windows NT Server should be _____.

   a. lower than the maximum speed of the modem

   b. as high as or higher than the maximum speed of the modem

   c. exactly the same as the maximum speed of the modem

   d. 1200 bps lower than the maximum speed of the modem

13. RAS call-back is set from which of the following?

   a. user account properties

   b. Remote Access Admin tool

   c. Dial-Up Security tab

   d. all of the above

   e. only a and b

14. One Microsoft NT Server 4.0 RAS server can support how many remote clients at the same time?

   a. 1

   b. 64

   c. 144

   d. 256

15. There are 17 users currently accessing RAS at your server. The 18th user is attempting to access RAS with no success. What might you do to find the problem?

    a. determine if RAS services are started

    b. make sure your access server has power

    c. have the user check what communications protocols are set up

    d. send a RAS ping to that user's telephone connection

16. When you connect the RAS server to an ISDN line, it is necessary to use a(n)
_____.

    a. terminal adapter

    b. X.25 adapter

    c. synchronous modem

    d. communications server

17. Your boss wants you to make the organization's NT Server a RAS server as well, and to provide some way to authenticate communications. Which communications protocol offers that ability?

    a. SLIP

    b. CSLIP

    c. PPP

    d. RPC

18. One limitation of a Microsoft RAS server is that it cannot work directly with
_____.

    a. asynchronous modems

    b. digital modems

    c. X.25

    d. synchronous modems

19. What type of device enables you to connect 24 modems and an ISDN line to the network for remote access communications?

    a. digital modem

    b. access server

    c. X.25 combination card

    d. digital line conditioner

20. Which of the following is an example of DCE?

    a. terminal

    b. modem

    c. RAS server

    d. RAS client

11

21. With which protocol is a Microsoft RAS server not compatible?

    a. DECnet

    b. TCP/IP

    c. NetBEUI

    d. NWLink

22. RAS permissions are set _____.

    a. by a RAS connection device

    b. at the client

    c. from the user account

    d. by ownership

23. ISDN is often used for _____.

    a. Internet connectivity

    b. establishing a direct connection between two PCs without using a special interface, such as a modem

    c. connecting multiple modems to a network

    d. none of the above

24. PSTN is a(n) _____.

    a. communications protocol

    b. authentication protocol

    c. public telephone network

    d. private switched network

25. Windows NT treats dial-up RAS similarly to _____.

    a. a network interface card

    b. a router

    c. a print queue

    d. a host computer

HANDS-ON PROJECTS

 PROJECT 11-1

In this activity you view the modem setup for a workstation running Windows 95 or Windows NT 4.0 Workstation. You need a workstation with a modem.

To view the modem setup:

1. Click **Start**, **Settings**, and **Control Panel**.

2. Double-click the **Modems** icon.

3. View the type of modem installed and set as the default—it is highlighted in the box entitled "The following modems are set up on this computer:" (Figure 11-10).

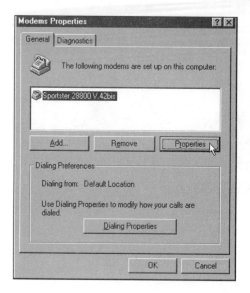

Figure 11-10   Viewing installed modems

4. Click the **Properties** button to see what modem speed is set up.

5. If the speed is less than the maximum speed of the modem (the maximum speed is often part of the modem description in the title bar of the dialog box), click the **Maximum speed** list arrow and select a speed as high as or higher than that of the modem (Figure 11-11).

6. Click **OK** in the Modems Properties dialog box.

7. Click **Close** in the Modems Properties dialog box.

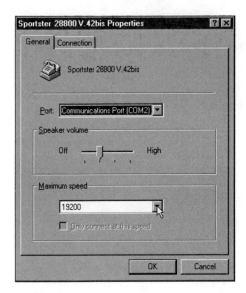

Figure 11-11   Determining the modem speed setup

 PROJECT 11-2

In this activity you learn where to set up a client computer running Windows NT 4.0 and using PPP to communicate remotely with an NT server also configured as a RAS server using PPP. The client computer must already be set up for Dial-Up Networking (go through Hands-on Project 11-5 to set up Dial-Up Networking, if necessary).

To check the remote protocol setup in Windows NT 4.0, and set it to PPP:

1. Double-click **My Computer** on the desktop.
2. Double-click the **Dial-Up Networking** icon.
3. On the Dial-Up Networking dialog box, click the **More** button.
4. Click the menu option **Edit entry and modem properties**.
5. Click the **Server** tab on the Edit Phonebook Entry dialog box (Figure 11-12).

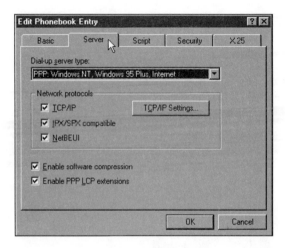

Figure 11-12   Remote networking protocol setup

6. Observe the entry in the Dial-up server type: list box, which should be PPP: Windows NT, Windows 95 Plus, Internet. If it is not, click the Dial-up server type **list arrow** and select this option.

7. Also observe which network protocols are checked for Dial-Up Networking under Network protocols (such as TCP/IP, IPX/SPX, and NetBEUI).

8. Click **OK** when you are finished with the Edit Phonebook Entry dialog box.

9. Click **Close** on the Dial-Up Networking dialog box.

 PROJECT 11-3

In this activity you check the remote access protocol in use by a RAS client running Windows 95. You will need a workstation already configured for Dial-Up Networking, such as one configured for a RAS server, America Online, or The Microsoft Network.

To check the remote access protocol setup in Windows 95, and set it to PPP:

1. Double-click **My Computer** on the desktop.

2. Double-click the **Dial-Up Networking** icon.

3. Right-click an existing Dial-Up Networking icon, such as The Microsoft Network.

4. Click **Properties**.

5. Click the **Server Type** button.

6. Click the **list arrow** on the Type of Dial-Up Server: list box to view the remote network protocol options (Figure 11-13).

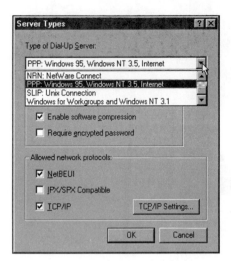

Figure 11-13   Windows 95 remote protocol setup

7. Make sure that the option **PPP: Windows 95, Windows NT 3.5, Internet** is selected.

8. Also notice the network protocols that are checked to be used over the PPP-based connection.

9. Click **OK** on the Server Types dialog box.

10. Click **OK**.

 PROJECT 11-4

In this activity you install the RAS Server software on a computer already running Windows NT 4.0 Server and with a modem that is already installed. You need access to the Administrator account or its equivalent to install the software. Also, you need the Windows NT 4.0 Server CD-ROM.

To install the RAS Server software:

1. Double-click the **Network** icon from the Control Panel.

2. Click the **Services** tab and click the **Add** button.

3. Scroll to the **Remote Access Service** on the Select Network Service dialog box and highlight it (Figure 11-14).

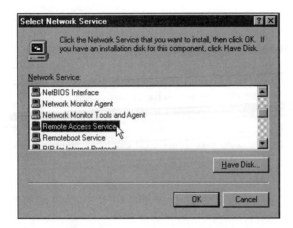

Figure 11-14   Installing the Remote Access Service

4. Insert the Windows NT Server 4.0 CD-ROM.

5. Click **OK** on the Select Network Service dialog box.

6. Make sure that the confirmation box contains the drive letter for the CD-ROM drive and the path **\i386**. Click **Continue**. The setup process now loads files onto the server.

 If your modem had not been previously installed, the system at this point would have asked if you wanted to start the Modem Wizard to install the modem.

7. The Add RAS Device dialog box shows the remote connection options, such as all installed modems. Select the modem or modems to link with RAS and click **OK** (Figure 11-15).

Figure 11-15   Adding the modem device for RAS

8. Click **Continue**.

11

9. Dialog boxes appear, indicating whether the RAS and the previously installed protocol access options are for all servers on the network (if there is more than one NT server) or only for the server with RAS. A dialog box is used for each active protocol, such as TCP/IP, NetBEUI, and IPX (NWLink). On each dialog box, click **Entire network**. If the server is configured for TCP/IP, a dialog box requests addressing information. Ask your instructor or technical support person what information to use for the IP addressing. If the computer is already configured for IPX (NWLink), the setup will ask for a network number for the remote connection. Select **Allocate network numbers automatically** in this dialog box. NetBEUI does not require additional connection information. After the information is entered, click **OK** on each dialog box.

10. Click **OK** on the Setup Message dialog box announcing that you have made a successful installation.

11. After the setup is complete, configure the modem for remote access. Back on the Services tab, highlight **Remote Access Service** in the Network Services: scroll box, and click the **Properties** button.

12. On the Remote Access Setup dialog box, highlight the modem device and click **Configure**.

13. On the Configure Port Usage dialog box, click the radio button for **Dial out and Receive calls**, as in Figure 11-16 (this enables the RAS server to receive incoming calls and to call out to a number as a means to authenticate the connection).

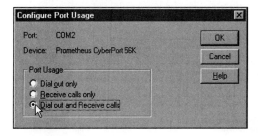

Figure 11-16 Configuring the modem port

14. After the modem is configured, click the **Continue** button on the Remote Access Setup dialog box.

15. Click **Close** on the Services tab (the system will automatically configure bindings for a minute or two).

16. Click **Yes** on the Network Setting Change dialog box to restart the server to enable the new settings to go into action.

17. Once the server is restarted, log on again using an account with Administrator privileges.

18. Click **Start**, **Settings**, and **Control Panel**.

19. Notice that there is a new Dial-Up Monitor icon. Double-click that icon.

20. Click the **Status** tab and notice that you can view connection statistics for the RAS server.

21. Click the **Summary** tab, as in Figure 11-17, for information about specific users who have logged on, including currently logged-on users (you won't have any yet).

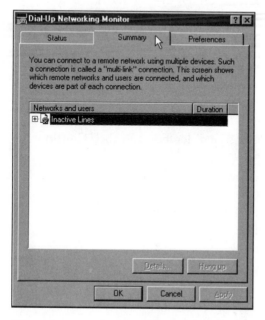

Figure 11-17   Dial-Up Networking Monitor, Summary tab

22. Click the **Preferences** tab to see where to set up preferences for monitoring RAS connections on the server.

23. Click **OK** on the Dial-Up Networking Monitor dialog box when you are finished.

PROJECT 11-5

In this activity you practice installing RAS on a computer running Windows NT 4.0 Workstation. Notice how similar this process is to the one used to install the RAS Server software.

To install RAS in Windows NT 4.0 Workstation:

1. Double-click the **Network** icon in the Control Panel and click the **Services** tab.

2. Click **Add** on the Services tab.

3. Highlight **Remote Access Service** in the Network Service: selection box, and click **OK**.

4. Enter the path to the CD-ROM and the **\i386** directory name. Insert the Windows NT Workstation CD-ROM, and click **Continue**. The RAS files are loaded from the CD-ROM.

5. The RAS setup program detects the modem card in the computer or the modem attached to the computer. Check to be certain that the modem is correctly detected in the Add RAS Device dialog box. If no modem is detected, click the **Install Modem** button to run the Modem Installation Wizard. Click **OK**.

6. On the Remote Access Setup dialog box, highlight the modem and click the **Configure** button. Set the port to "Dial out only" or to "Dial out and Receive calls." For example, the modem needs to be able to receive calls if the RAS server at work is set up to call back the user as a security measure, to ensure that a known user is requesting access.

7. Click **OK** on the Configure Port Usage dialog box, and click **Continue** on the Remote Access Setup dialog box.

8. Windows NT Workstation should automatically configure bindings for the remote access. If there is no message confirming that it is configuring bindings, click the Bindings tab on the Network dialog box to initiate the Bindings configuration.

9. Click **Close** on the Network dialog box.

PROJECT 11-6

In this activity you create a dial-up configuration for a RAS connection on a workstation running Windows NT 4.0 Workstation.

To set the dial-up configuration:

1. Double-click **My Computer** and then double-click the **Dial-Up Networking** folder.

2. Click **New** on the Dial-Up Networking dialog box.

3. Enter **RAS** as the name for the automated dial-up connection, and click **Next**.

4. Check **Send my plain text password if that's the only way to connect.** Your plain text password is the password for your account on the NT server. Leave the other boxes blank because you are not connecting through the Internet, and there are no non-Windows servers that you are planning to connect to at this time. Click **Next**.

5. Enter the telephone number of the line attached to the RAS server's modem in the Phone number: text box on the Phone Number dialog box. Do not click the box for telephony dialing properties because the line is a basic telephone line and does not require specialized information. Click **Next**.

6. Click **Finish** on the last dialog box, to complete the installation wizard.

7. Back in the Dial-Up Networking dialog box, select the connection you just made as the Phonebook entry to dial, click the **More** button, and click **Edit entry and modem properties**.

8. Click the **Server** tab, and make sure that **PPP: Windows NT**, **Windows 95 Plus**, **and Internet** is selected in the Dial-up server type: box. Click **OK.**

9. Click **Close** in the Dial-Up Networking dialog box.

PROJECT 11-7

In this activity you use the Guest account to view where to set up call-back security on an NT server account. You need access to a Windows NT server through an account with Administrator privileges.

To view where to set up call-back security for an account:

1. Click **Start**, **Programs**, and **Administrative Tools (Common)**.

2. Click the **User Manager for Domains** menu option.

3. Double-click one of the accounts, such as **Guest.**

4. Click the **Dialin** button on the User Properties dialog box.

5. Notice the three dial-in security options in the Call Back section of the Dialin Information dialog box. Also, notice that dial-in access can be denied to an account holder by removing the check from Grant dialin permission to user.

6. Click **Cancel** on the Dialin Information dialog box and **Cancel** on the User Properties dialog box.

7. Close User Manager for Domains.

11

ASPEN CONSULTING: REMOTE ACCESS

This week you are working again with your colleagues at Aspen Consulting to explain RAS and to help Mark Arnez set up RAS. You also work with Vancouver Tires to help them set up to remotely administer Windows NT Server.

1. The presentation to your colleagues explaining Windows NT printing was well received, and Mark Arnez is now asking you to make a presentation on the capabilities of RAS. Specifically, he has asked you to address the following:

   ■ Briefly provide an overview of how RAS works.

   ■ Explain which remote clients can use RAS.

   ■ Describe the connectivity equipment that works with RAS.

   ■ Explain what protocols work with RAS.

2. Aspen Consulting has decided to install RAS on one of its Windows NT servers. Currently, Mark Arnez anticipates that there will be up to 15 consultants who will remotely access the server at the same time, while on the road. The consultants all use either Windows 95 or Windows NT Workstation, and the headquarters network uses TCP/IP. Mark is asking you to prepare specifications for modems and any other equipment needed to set up RAS. Prepare specifications for the following:

   - DCE equipment

   - Network equipment

   - Telephone lines

3. Mark Arnez is planning to install RAS himself. However, he needs some advice from you about several issues, as follows:

   - What communications protocol do you recommend he use, and why?

   - What security do you recommend?

   - What network transport protocols should he configure?

   - Where can he configure a new transport protocol after installing RAS?

4. Mark Arnez has installed RAS, but no one can connect to it. What would you recommend that he check to troubleshoot the problem?

5. The server administrator for Vancouver Tires is wondering if there is a way to administer a Windows NT server from home. Explain step by step how this can be done. List at least four Windows NT Server tools that can be used remotely.

INTEROPERATING WITH NOVELL NETWARE

Many networks host a combination of network operating systems that need to interoperate for file sharing, printer services, and running software applications. One of the most common combinations of network operating systems is Microsoft Windows NT Server and Novell NetWare. NetWare emerged in the 1980s as a prominent network operating system. The two most common versions of NetWare are 3.x, often used in smaller networks having only a few servers, and version 4.x, which is used in multiple-server networks.

There are several roles that NetWare servers may fulfill on a network. If an organization started with NetWare servers, it may have a significant investment in those servers and simply want to interconnect NetWare with a few Windows NT servers. In other situations, there might be a business or university campus in which part of the organization has NetWare servers and another part is using Windows NT servers, with a need to have the servers communicate. Another scenario is that an organization is converting its NetWare servers to Windows NT Server and wants to migrate files, accounts, and application software.

In this chapter, you learn about the alternatives for interconnecting with NetWare, including facilitating direct communication between Windows NT and NetWare using Client Service for NetWare and setting up a Windows NT server to operate as a gateway to NetWare. You also learn how to migrate NetWare information to Windows NT Server.

AFTER READING THIS CHAPTER AND COMPLETING THE EXERCISES YOU WILL BE ABLE TO:

- EXPLAIN GENERAL CHARACTERISTICS OF NOVELL NETWARE
- EXPLAIN THE OPTIONS FOR INTEROPERATING BETWEEN NETWARE AND NT SERVER
- SET UP WINDOWS NT AS A NETWARE CLIENT AND A GATEWAY TO NETWARE
- SET UP PRINTING USING NETWARE PRINTERS
- MIGRATE A NETWARE SERVER TO A WINDOWS NT SERVER

AN OVERVIEW OF NOVELL NETWARE

The services provided by NetWare are similar to those available through Windows NT Server, but each operating system uses different tools and management techniques. Like Windows NT Server, NetWare employs accounts and groups to manage access to the server, with each group containing one or more accounts, which makes server management easier. In NetWare version 3.x, a set of files called the **bindery** contains information about user accounts, groups, printers, security, and other server data. Each NetWare 3.x server has its own bindery that authenticates accounts when they log on. Periodically the bindery files get slightly out of synchronization because accounts have been deleted and security parameters are changed. The server administrator runs a tool to restructure the bindery and reboots for the restructuring to take effect. NetWare 4.x consolidates information formerly stored in individual server binderies by using a single database called **Novell Directory Services (NDS)** for all NetWare servers on the same network.

When a user logs on to a NetWare server, the user's account is authenticated through an account name and password. Files and applications are stored in a directory tree structure similar to the folder structure used by Windows NT Server. Access to directories, files, and applications is controlled through a combination of security privileges called property rights, attributes, access rights, and trustee assignments.

A NetWare server can be configured to offer network printing through print queues. When printers are configured, they are assigned to a print queue, which manages the print jobs. NetWare uses capture commands to direct print jobs to specific queues. Printers and print queues are managed by using the PCONSOLE utility or the NetWare Administrator (NWADMIN).

NetWare file servers contain boot and operating system files on a volume called the Sys: volume. This volume contains the bindery or NDS files. It also contains system files, user utilities, mail files, and space allocated to spool print files. NetWare servers use IPX/SPX as the main protocol to communicate between servers and client workstations. Also, software applications and clients use the **NetWare Core Protocol (NCP)** for communications with NetWare server services.

NetWare versions 3.x and 4.x can have enhanced services loaded, to link into the operating system through **NetWare Loadable Modules (NLMs)**, for e-mail services, for example. In some versions of NetWare, loading too many NLMs can make a server unstable because the server system files and the NLMs vie for the same memory. NetWare 4.x offers greater stability and adds the **Virtual Loadable Module (VLM)**, which is used for the server's network communications with clients. Novell uses ODI drivers for communications that combine multiple protocols, such as IPX/SPX and TCP/IP. It also offers **Client32**, used for communications between NetWare and 32-bit operating systems such as Windows 95 and OS/2.

CONNECTIVITY OPTIONS

There are several ways to set up a link between a Microsoft server environment and NetWare servers. If you only need to connect a Windows NT server as a NetWare client, the solution is to install the **Client Service for NetWare (CSNW)**, a service included with Windows NT that enables a Windows NT server or workstation to connect to a NetWare server as a client. In Windows NT Server it is loaded as part of the **Gateway Service for NetWare (GSNW)**, and in Windows NT Workstation it is loaded separately as Client Service for NetWare.

Another alternative is to set up an NT server as a NetWare gateway using GSNW. A **gateway** is software or hardware that converts data from one format to another, such as from a NetWare format to a Microsoft-based format. Clients access the NetWare files and folders by going through Windows NT Server, without the need to load IPX/SPX or NWLink. This method reduces the amount of IPX/SPX traffic to a NetWare server, as compared to using CSNW. The gateway includes the ability for Microsoft NT Server clients to use NetWare printer resources.

 The term "gateway" is used in several contexts. The most common is as software or hardware that converts data from one format to another, for example converting data from a NetWare environment to be used in a Microsoft-based environment.

A third option is to migrate NetWare accounts and files to a Windows NT server, because you want to retire the NetWare server. All of these options are explained in the sections that follow.

12

SETTING UP MICROSOFT WINDOWS NT SERVER AS A NOVELL NETWARE CLIENT

When you log on to Windows NT Server from its console, you may find that it is convenient to be able to access NetWare servers on the same network. Or if you plan to copy or migrate files from a NetWare server, you will need a way to access it from NT Server. The most direct method is to make the Windows NT server a NetWare client by setting up Client Service for NetWare (CSNW), which is part of Gateway Service for NetWare (GSNW). The requirements on the client consist of the following:

- Client Service for NetWare

- NWLink IPX/SPX Compatible Transport

- NWLink NetBIOS

All three services and protocols are needed for Windows NT Server to directly access a NetWare file server as a client. The CSNW includes a Novell NCP requester to run applications on a NetWare server. NWLink IPX/SPX Compatible Transport is the Microsoft-developed IPX/SPX protocol emulation for seamless communications with a NetWare server. NWLink NetBIOS provides a NetBIOS link for NetWare applications requiring NetBIOS, including DOS-based applications. All three pieces are installed when you install Gateway (and Client) Services for NetWare on NT Server, or Client Service for NetWare on NT Workstation. (In Hands-on Project 12-1, you install CSNW on NT Workstation.)

A workstation running Windows 95 can also access a NetWare file server if you install Client for NetWare Networks. It is installed by opening the Control Panel, clicking the Network icon, and clicking the Add button in the Configuration tab. Select Client, click Add, and select Microsoft in the Manufacturers: box and Client for NetWare Networks in the Network Clients: box.

In the following sections, the term *directories* is used when discussing NetWare file structures, and *folders* is used when referring to similar structures in Windows NT, in keeping with the terminology of each operating system.

CREATING A GATEWAY TO NOVELL NETWARE

Another way to enable access to files stored on a Novell NetWare server in an enterprise network is to make a Microsoft Windows NT server a gateway to NetWare. Used in this context, "gateway" means that the server acts as a go-between for Windows-based workstations and a NetWare file server. The workstations do not need to be NetWare clients using NWLink, because they access the directories and files through the gateway. The advantage of installing a gateway is that it reduces the network traffic of multiple protocols. This is especially helpful because IPX/SPX is a "chatty" protocol that can yield extra network overhead. Also, the SPX portion of the protocol suite is very sensitive to timing, causing applications to fail on busy networks.

However, there are some limitations to keep in mind. All users of the gateway are assigned the same access rights and account privileges on the NetWare side of the connection, because all users are aggregated into a single virtual NetWare account. In addition, GSNW allows only a single gateway per NT Server machine; to set up gateways with differing account privileges and access rights, each gateway must be on a separate NT server. And finally, a gateway can become a bottleneck, since multiple logical connections pass through a single physical connection. A Windows NT Server gateway to NetWare is not intended for heavy access to information on a NetWare server, and may bog down if more than 10 users try to access NetWare resources at once. The gateway is better suited for light or occasional NetWare access.

When it acts as a gateway, the Windows NT server has an account on the NetWare server and a corresponding account on the NT server. The accounts stay in constant communication while the NT server runs Gateway Service for NetWare. Acting as a window to a

NetWare hard drive or to specific directories, the Windows NT server makes available to its users a shared folder containing the NetWare directories. To NetWare, the Windows NT server is just another client accessing files and directories. With the right permissions, any Windows NT Server client accesses the shared folder in the same way that it would access any other shared folder, without needing to use NWLink.

Before installing Gateway Service for NetWare, you must make sure that there is no NetWare redirector already set up, such as **File and Print Service for NetWare (FPNW)**. A **redirector** is a Windows NT kernel mode driver that enables an NT computer to access another network computer. You can check for File and Print Service for NetWare by opening the Control Panel Network icon and clicking the Services tab. Highlight any existing NetWare services (unless Gateway Service for NetWare is already installed), and click the Remove button. Click Yes to confirm the action, and reboot the server, if necessary.

File and Print Service for NetWare can be installed to make the Windows NT folders and printers available to NetWare clients without adding special software to the client. File and Print Service for NetWare is part of a product called Services for NetWare, that can be purchased separately from Microsoft. It is installed via the Control Panel Network icon in the same way as other network services.

You need to contact the NetWare server administrator or have NetWare Supervisor rights to create the account on the NetWare server. Also, it is necessary to log on to the Windows NT server using an account that belongs to the Administrators group. The steps for making a Windows NT Server computer a gateway to Novell NetWare are summarized as follows. (Try Hands-on Project 12-2 to practice installing Gateway Service for NetWare.)

1. Create an account on the NetWare server for the Windows NT server to access (using SYSCON or NWADMIN). The appropriate directory and file attributes and access rights or group membership should be granted to the account as determined by the directories and files that will be made available for the users. For example, the NetWare account might be granted Read and File Scan access rights, which enable users to read files, run programs, and view file and subdirectory names.

2. Create a group on the NetWare server called NTGATEWAY, which has access rights to the files and directories that need to be used.

3. Make the NetWare user account a member of the NTGATEWAY group.

There are two places from which to control access to NetWare resources offered by a gateway. You can set up security through the access rights on the NetWare server or you can set up security using share permissions on the Windows NT server. If you set up security in both places, keep in mind that the Windows NT gateway's access is first restricted by the NetWare access rights and that user access is next restricted by the NT share permissions.

4. Create a corresponding account on the Windows NT server through User Manager for Domains.

5. Install Gateway Service for NetWare on the NT server by opening the Network icon from the Control Panel, clicking the Services tab, and double-clicking Gateway (and Client) Services for NetWare. Load the services from the Windows NT Server CD-ROM (Figure 12-1).

 When you load the GSNW service on Windows NT Server, it is listed as Gateway (and Client) Services for NetWare. Once it is loaded it displays on the Service tab as Gateway Service for NetWare.

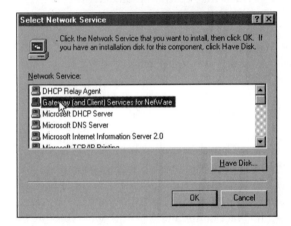

Figure 12-1   Installing Gateway (and Client) Services for NetWare

6. Ensure that the NWLink IPX/SPX Compatible Transport and NWLink NeBIOS protocols are installed on the NT server as part of the installation of Gateway Service for NetWare (check the Protocols tab in the Network icon).

7. Reboot the NT server and provide a preferred server name in the dialog box that is displayed.

Gateway Administration

After Gateway (and Client) Services for NetWare is loaded, a new GSNW icon is added to the Control Panel. The GSNW icon enables you to configure the gateway, for example establishing a path to the NetWare server directories that will be offered as shared directories to clients. The steps for configuring the gateway are as follows:

1. Open the GSNW icon on the Control Panel, and click the Gateway button.

2. Enter the NetWare account name and password, if requested.

3. Check **Enable Gateway** and click Add to create a shared folder (Figure 12-2).

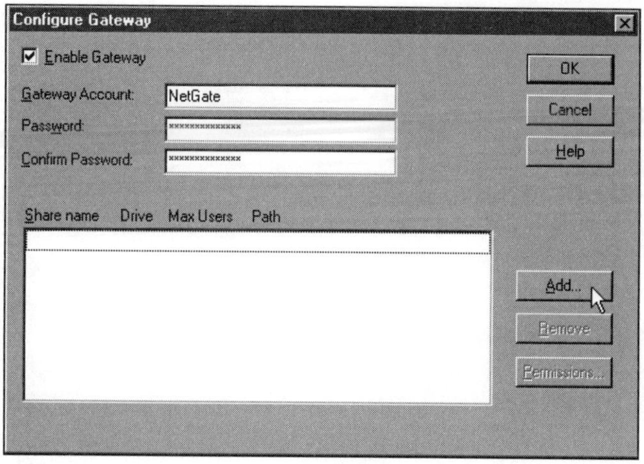

Figure 12-2   Configuring the gateway

4. Enter the share name, path to the NetWare server, drive, and user limit.

5. Set the share permissions.

6. Close the GSNW utility.

You can create multiple shared folders to different drives or directories by using the Add button and specifying a different share name, network path, and drive letter each time. (Try Hands-on Project 12-3 to practice configuring a gateway.)

When you configure the gateway, you have the option to specify a preferred server or a default tree and context. A **preferred server** is the NetWare server that the gateway accesses by default, and that authenticates the logon. **Tree and context** is used when the NetWare environment supports NDS, and refers to the user account object and directory tree that will be set by default.

When you install Gateway Service for NetWare, there also is an option to set default options for print queues that are accessed through the gateway. The print options are as follows:

- Add a form feed to each printout to make sure that the last page prints

- Send a notification to users when a job has printed

- Print a banner page with each print job

There also is an option to run a login script on the NetWare server each time the gateway account logs on. The login script is a text script similar to NT Server's logon script, containing commands that automatically run, such as specifying the operating system, account name, and other information. The preferred server, tree and context, print, and login script options are set from the Gateway Service for NetWare dialog box that appears when you first open the GSNW icon (Figure 12-3).

 NetWare uses the term *login*, which is equivalent to the term *logon* in Windows NT.

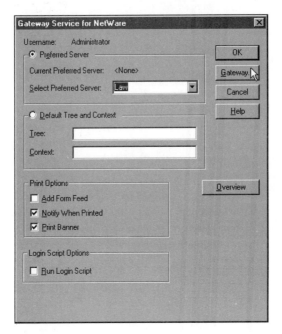

Figure 12-3   Gateway options

Printing on NetWare Printers

You can set up NetWare printers (print queues in NetWare terminology) to be shared, like files. However, NetWare shared print queues are set up using the Windows NT Printers folder instead of the GSNW icon in the Control Panel. Gateway Service for NetWare must be installed before you can give NT Server clients access to shared NetWare print queues. Open the Printers folder and double-click the Add Printer icon. Click the radio button for Network printer server, and click Next. In the Shared Printers: box, double-click NetWare or Compatible Network (Figure 12-4). Double-click the printer you want to share. Click Yes to install a print driver, if requested. Click No to make this the default printer, click Next, and then click Finish.

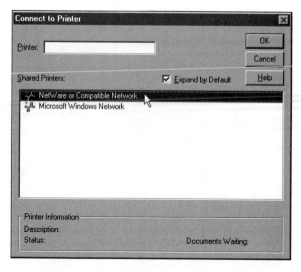

Figure 12-4 Connecting to a NetWare printer

After the printer is set up, right-click it in the Printers folder, and click Properties. Click the Sharing tab, click Shared, and enter a share name (Figure 12-5). Also specify alternate drivers, such as Windows 95. Next, click the Security tab and set the share permissions for the printer.

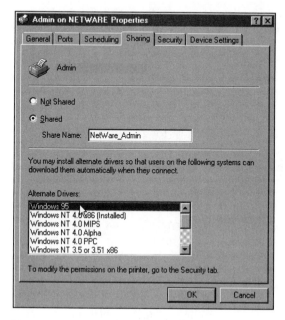

Figure 12-5 Configuring printer sharing

MIGRATING FROM NETWARE TO WINDOWS NT SERVER

A mixed network of Microsoft NT and NetWare servers can be expensive and confusing to maintain. Each operating system requires different knowledge about how to set up and maintain it. For example, setting up a printer in the NetWare environment is a several-stage process involving configuring printers, queues, and forms. In Windows NT the process is centralized from the Add Printer Wizard. Setting up security in NetWare involves attributes, access rights, and trustee rights. Windows NT uses rights and permissions, without relying on attributes. NetWare uses IPX/SPX (new versions can use other protocols), and Windows NT can use NetBEUI, IPX/SPX, TCP/IP, and other protocols, depending on the setup of the network.

Many organizations decide to convert NetWare servers to Windows NT as a way to simplify network and server management, as well as to reduce network congestion. Converting to one network operating system also creates fewer difficulties for the users. A Windows NT Server environment makes sense to many organizations because it takes full advantage of the GUI interface and object-oriented Microsoft operating system. The reduction in the number of systems to maintain makes the network and server administrators' jobs much easier. For example, maintaining printers in two or more operating systems can involve much work and expertise. Consolidating printing into one system saves the administrator's time and makes it easier to troubleshoot printing problems. Also, tuning operating systems is easier, and the load on the network is less because there are fewer protocols to handle.

 If you need to convert a number of servers from NetWare to Microsoft Windows NT Server, consider starting with one new server freshly loaded with Windows NT Server. Back up one of the NetWare servers and migrate it to the new NT server. Once that migration is complete, remove NetWare from that server, install Windows NT Server, and migrate the next NetWare server. Continue migrating NetWare servers one at a time until the job is complete. Make sure that you back up each NetWare server before you migrate its files!

Windows NT Server comes with Migration Tool for NetWare, which is installed when you install Gateway Service for NetWare. The migration tool can transfer accounts, groups, directories (folders), and files from a NetWare server to a Windows NT server. It can even transfer account setup information, such as a required length for passwords.

When you migrate accounts and groups to Windows NT Server, they are automatically added to the domain in which the NT server resides. Account information is recorded to the SAM, and it is replicated to all BDCs in the domain. If your organization is divided into different domains, using the single-master domain model, for example, then you should migrate accounts and groups to the master domain.

When you use the migration tool, transfer information from only one NetWare server at a time; otherwise, you may transfer duplicate information. Also, plan in advance the order of migration when there are two or more NetWare servers. For example, you might start with the server that contains the least critical information and applications. This gives you an opportunity to work out any transfer problems in a low-impact situation. Also, plan other elements of the migration as follows:

- Take an inventory of the security setup on the NetWare server to make sure that you establish a similar setup on the Windows NT Server. NetWare comes with a tool that enables you to print out security information.

- Take an inventory of the account and group setup on the NetWare server.

- Determine where files and folders will be moved to, on the Windows NT Server.

- Identify directories that should not be migrated from NetWare. For example, the NetWare-specific folders \Login, \Etc, \System, \Public, and \Mail on the Sys: volume should not be migrated (by default, those folders will not be migrated unless you modify the file migration options).

- Identify files that should not be migrated from NetWare, such as system files and hidden files (by default, those files will not be migrated unless you modify the file migration options).

- Identify NetWare print queues that will need to be reproduced in the Windows NT Printers folder.

- Identify any NetWare setups you would like to change on the new server, such as the folder structure or security.

- Determine a time for the migration that will have the least impact on users, such as over a weekend. Also, migrating over the network will result in heavy network traffic. This is another good reason to migrate at a time when users are absent.

- Back up the NetWare server and the Windows NT server before starting.

 Plan to migrate files into NTFS instead of FAT, because NTFS can replicate NetWare file and folder security more completely than FAT.

When you migrate files and folders to NTFS, the migration tool translates the NetWare access rights to Windows NT permissions. Table 12-1 shows how the translation is performed on files, and Table 12-2 shows how folders are translated.

Table 12-1 NetWare File Access Rights Converted to NTFS File Permissions

NetWare File Access Right*	Windows NTFS File Permission
Read (R)	Read (RX)
Write (W)	Change (RWXD)
Erase (E)	Change (RWXD)
Modify (M)	Change (RWXD)
Access Control (A)	Change (P to change file permissions)
Supervisory (S)	Full Control (All permissions)

*The migration tool disregards the NetWare File Scan (F) and Create (C) file access rights.

Table 12-2   NetWare Directory Access Rights Converted to NTFS Folder
              Permissions

NetWare Directory Access Right	Windows NTFS Folder Permission
Read (R)	Read (RX) (RX)
Write (W)	Change (RWXD) (RWXD)
Erase (E)	Change (RWXD) (RWXD)
Create (C)	Add (WX) (not set for subfolders)
Modify (M)	Change (RWXD) (RWXD)
File Scan (F)	List (RX) (not set for subfolders)
Access Control (A)	Change (P to change folder permissions)
Supervisory (S)	Full Control (All permissions)

The traditional file attributes are converted directly from NetWare to NTFS. These are Read
Only, Archive, Hidden, and System. Other NetWare file attributes are not converted because
they are not supported in NTFS, or because NTFS handles them through permissions or
rights. The specialized NetWare attributes that are not converted are as follows:

- Copy Inhibit (C)
- Delete Inhibit (D)
- Execute Only (X)
- Indexed (I)
- Purge (P)
- Rename Inhibit (R)
- Read Audit (Ra)
- Shareable (SH)
- Transactional (T)
- Write Audit (Wa)

NetWare user accounts are migrated in a way that keeps many of the characteristics associated with each account. If you do not want to retain the account characteristics, you can create a **mapping file** to specify new account names and passwords for each user. Unless your
organization has mandated that account names should be changed, consider avoiding this
option, because it may cause confusion for users who attempt to log on after the migration.
However, passwords are not converted in the migration, so you may need to use the mapping file if specific passwords must be set for accounts. A simpler way to handle passwords is
to have the migration tool set the password to each account's username, or to use the same
password for all accounts (both are options in the migration tool) and then to require users
to change their passwords when they log on. Emphasize to the account holders that they
need to log on right away after the migration and change their passwords. If you need to
create a mapping file, you can do so after you have started the migration tool. The mapping

file is a simple text file. If you do not use the mapping file, the following NetWare account characteristics can be retained:

- Username
- Password expiration period
- User permission to change a password
- Account expiration date
- Account disabled status
- Time restrictions

It also is possible to migrate NetWare login scripts to Windows NT logon scripts, but that option is not recommended because you will need to change drive mappings, printer setups, and other information used in the scripts. A simpler method is to use tools in the Windows client operating systems to configure these settings.

 Migrating login scripts can introduce extra problems because of the differences between NetWare and Windows NT Server, and may generate lots of work for the server administrator in identifying problems and modifying scripts.

Before starting the migration, make sure you have provided users with training about the changes they will encounter. Also, be sure that all users have instructions about how to reconfigure their workstations for new protocols, drive mappings, and printers. Develop a testing plan for the new Windows NT Server after files, folders, accounts, and groups are migrated. Some areas you might test are as follows:

- Test a sampling of accounts, groups, and applications that were on the NT server before the migration.
- Test a sampling of new accounts, groups, and applications migrated from the NetWare server.
- Test your own account and the Administrator account to make sure that both work properly.
- Test permissions and rights.
- Have a representative group of users test their accounts by accessing them before you release the server to all users.
- Have a representative group of users test software applications.
- Have a few users test printing.

12

IMPLEMENTING THE MIGRATION

When you are ready to start the migration, open Migration Tool for NetWare from the Administrative Tools (Common) menu. The general steps for implementing a migration are as follows:

1. In the Select Servers for Migration dialog box, which appears when you start the migration tool, specify the NetWare server to migrate from and the Windows NT server to migrate to (Figure 12-6). Enter the NetWare supervisor account and password, if you are prompted by the migration tool for this information.

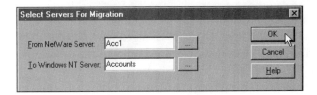

Figure 12-6   Selecting the source and destination servers for migration

2. You can add more NetWare servers to migrate (not recommended) by using the Add button in the Migration Tool for NetWare dialog box (Figure 12-7).

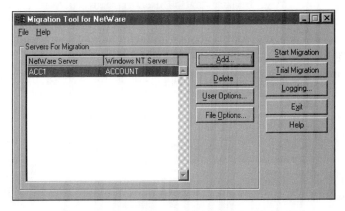

Figure 12-7   Migration Tool for NetWare dialog box

3. Click the User Options button, and check or uncheck Transfer Users and Groups. If you remove the check, then only volumes, directories, and files are migrated. The User and Group Options dialog box is also used to create a mapping file, specify where to locate the mapping file, set password conversion rules, set username and group conversion options, and choose how to convert NetWare Supervisors to NT Server Administrators. Use the Create button to set up a mapping file, or use the Edit button to edit an existing mapping file. The other options are available through tabs.

4. In the User and Group Options dialog box, click the Passwords tab and select the password option, such as Password is Username. The other password options are No Password, Password Is (specify a password to use for all accounts), or Use Mappings in File (specify the mapping file name). Also, select User Must Change Password, to make sure that each account holder changes his or her password when first logging on. If you use a mapping file, keep in mind that Windows NT Server passwords are limited to 14 characters and are case sensitive.

5. It is possible that there will be username conflicts, if there are accounts already on the NT server with the same usernames as are on the NetWare server. If you are concerned about conflicts, you can designate how conflicts are to be handled or reported, such as by logging conflicts in the ERROR.LOG file. The way to handle conflicts is set up in the User and Group Options Usernames tab. The ERROR.LOG file tracks information about migration problems. The options for handling conflicts are as follows:

   ■ *Log Error* to record the error in the error log

   ■ *Ignore*, which disregards the conflict

   ■ *Overwrite with new Info*, which overwrites the NT account with the NetWare account

   ■ *Add prefix* to attach a prefix onto the NetWare account so that it does not conflict

   A safe way to avoid conflicts is to use the option to add a prefix to each migrated username. For example, you might use the prefix n_, which would convert the NetWare username mpalmer to n_mpalmer. Keep in mind that usernames can be up to 20 characters. Another way to avoid conflicts is to create a mapping file for complete control of which usernames and passwords are used in the migration.

6. Problems with name conflicts also may exist for migrated groups. The conflict resolution options for groups are the same as for usernames (except that the Overwrite with new Info option is not offered), and are set from the Group Names tab in the User and Group Options dialog box.

7. On the Defaults tab in the User and Group Options dialog box, you can select to apply the account policies already set up in NT Server to the migrated accounts. If you want to use the NT Server account policies, remove the check in the box Use Supervisor Defaults (note that this option is confusingly named). If you want to use the account privileges as set up in NetWare instead of the NT Server account policies for the migrated accounts, place a check in the Use Supervisor Defaults box. There also is an option to add the NetWare accounts with Supervisor rights to the NT Server Administrator's group. Click OK to leave the User and Group Options dialog box and return to the Migration Tool for NetWare dialog box.

8. Click the File Options button to customize which volume, file, and folder resources will be migrated. For example, you can select to transfer only certain

12

directories or files (avoiding checking the Sys: volume folders \Mail, \System, \Login, \Public, and \Etc, and the system and hidden files). The directories and files with checks in the boxes are the ones that will be migrated. Return to the Migration Tool for NetWare dialog box.

9. Click the Trial Migration button to run a test of the migration without really migrating files. Click Logging and View Log Files. Examine the SUMMARY.LOG file to check general statistics about what will be migrated, such as the number of users, groups, files, and anticipated username and group conflicts.

10. After you leave the SUMMARY.LOG, return to the Migration Tool for NetWare dialog box, and click Start Migration.

When the migration is finished, examine the three logs that are created about the migration results. LOGFILE.LOG contains detailed data about the groups, accounts, folders, and files that are migrated. It shows successful and failed transfers. SUMMARY.LOG contains gross statistics about how long the migration took, total number of users, groups and files transferred, total number of conflicts, and errors. Finally, ERROR.LOG contains errors that were encountered, such as user and group name conflicts, transmission errors from network problems, and system errors related to hardware problems or lack of disk space. (Try migration in Hands-on Project 12-4.)

After the migration is complete, put your testing plan into action. When you make the Windows NT server accessible to users, plan to take time to help them with questions and to provide further training about how to use the new features available to them.

CHAPTER SUMMARY

- NetWare servers are used in many networks, particularly in enterprise contexts. There are some significant differences between NetWare and Windows NT Server in terms of operating system files, server management, handling printers, use of protocols, and setting up security. Microsoft recognizes the need to interoperate with NetWare servers by offering Client Service for NetWare (CSNW) and Gateway Service for NetWare (GSNW). These services provide the ability for a Windows NT server to access a NetWare server as a client for the purpose of copying files, running applications, or even remotely managing a NetWare server.

- Another option of Gateway Service for NetWare is the ability to make NetWare files and directories available to NT Server clients. The NetWare directories appear to the NT Server client as shared folders on the network. NetWare printers also can be shared so that NT Server clients can send print files to them. Gateway Service for NetWare comes with a management tool to control what is shared and the security on each share.

- Many organizations decide to consolidate the network enterprise by converting NetWare servers to Windows NT servers. Migration Tool for NetWare enables you to transfer accounts, groups, folders, and files from a NetWare server to a Windows NT server. Many of the security settings on a NetWare server are migrated in the process. Migration can represent a cost savings in terms of reducing the equipment costs, operating system costs, network traffic, and administrative costs of maintaining different network operating systems.

KEY TERMS

- **bindery** — A set of files in NetWare versions 3.x and lower that contains data about user accounts, groups, printers, and security, and other server information.

- **Client Service for NetWare (CSNW)** — A service included with Windows NT that allows Windows NT computers to connect as clients to NetWare servers.

- **Client32** — Software used for communications between NetWare and 32-bit operating systems, such as Windows 95 and OS/2.

- **File and Print Service for NetWare (FPNW)** — Service for Windows NT Server that allows NT clients to use NetWare print services; part of a product called Services for NetWare, which can be purchased separately from Microsoft.

- **gateway** — Software or hardware that converts data from one format to another for an entire network, for example converting data from a NetWare environment to be used in a Microsoft-based environment.

- **Gateway Service for NetWare (GSNW)** — A service included with Windows NT Server that provides connectivity to NetWare resources for NT servers and NT clients via a gateway.

- **mapping file** — A file containing instructions for migrating NetWare accounts, groups, and other information to Windows NT Server.

- **NetWare Core Protocol (NCP)** — A protocol used by applications to access NetWare server services.

- **NetWare Loadable Module (NLM)** — An application module, such as for e-mail, that can be loaded to link with the NetWare operating system.

- **Novell Directory Services (NDS)** — A consolidated database of user account, group, security, and other information shared by all NetWare servers on a network.

- **preferred server** — NetWare server that a Windows NT Server gateway accesses by default, and that authenticates the logon.

- **redirector** — A Windows NT kernel mode driver that enables an NT computer to access another network computer.

- **tree and context** — Used when the NetWare environment supports NDS, this term refers to the user account object and directory tree that will be set by default for an NT gateway.

- **Virtual Loadable Module (VLM)** — A module used by NetWare for the server's network communications with clients.

12

REVIEW QUESTIONS

1. Information about NetWare 3.x accounts is stored on a NetWare server in _____.

   a. the registration files

   b. the bindery

   c. the Sys: volume Login directory

   d. tape backups only

2. When you set up a gateway to NetWare, _____.

   a. an account must be created in NetWare for the NT server

   b. an account must be created on the NT server

   c. an NT Server group, called NetWare, must be created

   d. all of the above

   e. only a and b

3. Which of the following is used for communications between a Windows 95 computer and NetWare?

   a. Client32

   b. Net3.10

   c. ODI32

   d. DLC

4. You are working to set up a gateway to NetWare and see that Gateway Service for NetWare is already installed. However, when you try to connect to a NetWare server, there seems to be no communication. What might you check?

   a. that the NetWare server has enough communications buffers

   b. that page file size on the NT server is sufficient

   c. that NWLink is installed on the NT server

   d. all of the above

   e. only b and c

5. An e-mail system on a NetWare server might be loaded as _____.

   a. a protocol device

   b. NLM

   c. a group server

   d. VBM

6. Which of the following NetWare attributes is not available in Windows NT Server as an attribute?

a. Copy Inhibit

b. Execute Only

c. Purge

d. all are not available

e. only a and b are not available

7. From where do you manage a Windows NT gateway to NetWare?

a. through the services properties in the Windows NT Control Panel Network icon

b. on the NetWare server

c. from the client that accesses the gateway

d. through the GSNW icon in the Windows NT Control Panel

8. When migrating accounts from NetWare to Windows NT, what might you do to prevent a conflict from occurring, when there is already an NT Server account using the name of an account that you are migrating from NetWare?

a. log the conflict

b. add prefixes to accounts that will be migrated

c. select the No conflict option

d. delete all accounts on the NT server first, even though this will be an inconvenience to users

9. What must be installed on the client computer in order for a Windows NT client to run a NetWare server application that uses NetBIOS?

a. NWLink NetBIOS

b. NDS

c. file services for IPX/SPX

d. NetBEUI

10. When you migrate NetWare directories and files, _____.

a. the access rights are not converted to permissions

b. the directory access rights are converted to permissions, but not the file access rights

c. the file access rights are converted to permissions, but not the directory access rights

d. the file and directory access rights are converted

11. When migrating from NetWare to NT Server, _____.

a. migrate several servers at the same time

b. minimal network traffic is created because the migration tool uses a special protocol compression

c. migrate only one server at a time

d. purge the trustee rights on the NetWare server because they cause migration errors

12

12. You have completed the migration of a NetWare server to Windows NT Server, but discover in User Manager for Domains that several accounts did not come across. How might you track down the problem?

    a. check the access rights associated with all NetWare accounts

    b. shut down and reboot the NT server because it does not recognize the new accounts until after it is rebooted

    c. check the ERROR.LOG file

    d. check the migration speed set in the migration tool, which should be 5 Mbps

13. When you migrate from NetWare to Windows NT, _____.

    a. you must bring across all files and directories on the NetWare server

    b. the Sys: volume should not be migrated

    c. migrate the \Public and \Etc directories, but not the \System directory

    d. do not migrate hidden and system files

14. You are planning a migration, and your boss has provided instructions to set up new account names and a different password for each account. What tool would enable you to do this?

    a. mapping file

    b. Password and Username tabs in the User and Group Options dialog box

    c. setup script

    d. password redirector

15. You have set up an NT server as a gateway to NetWare, and now you want to make the NetWare printers available to the NT Server clients. What tool would you use to make the printers available?

    a. User Manager for Domains in Windows NT Server

    b. PCONSOLE in NetWare

    c. Printers folder in Windows NT Server

    d. NWPR icon in the Control Panel

16. When you migrate NetWare to Windows NT Server, what file system should be set up in Windows NT Server?

    a. FAT

    b. NTFS

    c. OS/2

    d. NetWare File System (NWFS)

17. How might you test a NetWare migration to Windows NT Server before actually transferring the data?

    a. do a test run on accounts only

    b. migrate directories only

    c. use the trial migration option in the migration tool

    d. there is no way to perform a test in advance

18. NetWare Supervisory access rights on a directory are most similar to
_____ in NT Server.

   a. Full Control permissions

   b. Change permissions

   c. Ownership rights

   d. Log on locally rights

19. When you migrate NetWare accounts, _____.

   a. they can inherit the account policies already set up in NT Server

   b. they can bring over the account settings used in NetWare

   c. it is necessary to set up migration account specifications

   d. none of the above is true

   e. only a and b are true, depending on specifications set up in the migration tool

20. You have configured a NetWare printer in NT Server, but no one can use it other than
Administrators who log on to the NT Server console. What should you check first?

   a. the printer access rights in NetWare

   b. the printer properties in Windows NT, to make sure that sharing is enabled

   c. the print queue form assigned in NetWare

   d. the NetWare Printers configuration tab in the Windows NT printer properties

HANDS-ON PROJECTS

12

 PROJECT 12-1

In this activity you practice installing Client Service for NetWare in Windows NT 4.0
Workstation.

To install Client Service for NetWare for Windows NT 4.0 Workstation:

1. Click **Start**, **Settings**, and **Control Panel**.

2. Double-click the **Network** icon.

3. Click the **Services** tab on the Network dialog box and click **Add**.

4. On the Select Network Service dialog box, double-click **Client Service for
NetWare** (Figure 12-8).

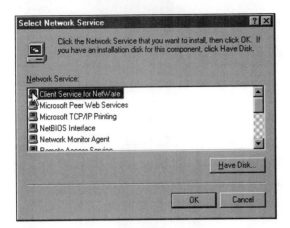

Figure 12-8   Installing Client Service for NetWare

5. Insert the Windows NT CD-ROM. On the Windows NT Setup dialog box, enter the CD-ROM drive letter (such as **D:**) and the **\I386** path (containing files for Intel-based computers). Click **Continue** to begin loading the NetWare client drivers.

6. Click the **Bindings** tab to automatically bind the protocol (this is an optional step, because the setup will automatically bind NWLink when you exit; however, clicking the Bindings tab causes it to make sure that the automatic binding takes place).

7. Click **Close** when you are finished.

8. A message appears to say that you will need to reboot the computer for the protocol to take effect. Click **Yes** to reboot.

PROJECT 12-2

In this activity you set up Gateway (and Client) Services for NetWare. You need access to a NetWare account that has Supervisor access rights and to a Windows NT Server account with Administrator privileges.

To set up Gateway (and Client) Services for NetWare:

1. Set up NetWare for access by the Windows NT Server gateway:

   a. Start the NetWare server's **SYSCON** or **NWADMIN** utility.

   b. Create a new user account in NetWare, such as **NetGate**.

   c. Require that a password be used for the account.

   d. Enter the new password and confirm it.

   e. Save the new account information.

   f. Use SYSCON or NWADMIN to create the **NTGATEWAY** group for the gateway services.

g. Add the new NetWare account (for example, NetGate) to the NTGATEWAY group.

h. Designate the volumes or directories that will be accessible to the NTGATEWAY group.

2. Create a user account in Windows NT Server that has the same name as the account you created in NetWare.

a. Open **User Manager for Domains** and create the account, such as **NetGate**.

b. Enter the same password that you used for the NetWare account, and confirm it.

c. Set the password to never expire.

3. Install the Gateway (and Client) Services for NetWare on the NT Server:

a. Click **Start**, **Settings**, and **Control Panel**.

b. Double-click the **Network** icon.

c. Click the **Services** tab and then the **Add** button.

d. Click **Gateway (and Client) Services for NetWare**, and click **OK**.

e. Insert the Microsoft Windows NT Server CD-ROM, and specify the path to the CD-ROM (for example, the drive letter and **I\386**). Click **Continue**.

If NWLink IPX/SPX Compatible Transport and NWLink NetBIOS have not been installed previously, they are installed now.

f. Click **OK** in the Network dialog box (if NWLink IPX/SPX Compatible Transport and NWLink NetBIOS were installed, they will be bound to the NIC when you leave the Network dialog box).

g. Shut down the server and reboot.

h. When you reboot and log on, the Select a Preferred Server For NetWare dialog box prompts for the NetWare preferred server name. Enter the name of the NetWare server on which you created the account for the gateway. You do this by clicking the Preferred Server radio button and selecting the name of the preferred server in the text box.

PROJECT 12-3

In this activity you configure a newly installed gateway for NetWare.

To configure the gateway in Windows NT Server:

1. Click **Start**, **Settings**, and **Control Panel**, and double-click the **GSNW** icon.

2. Click the **Gateway** button in the Gateway Service for NetWare dialog box.

3. In the Configure Gateway dialog box, check **Enable Gateway**.

4. If requested, enter the name of the account you created on the NetWare server, such as **NetGate**. Enter the password and confirm it.

5. Click the **Add** button to create a share for the resources on the NetWare server.

6. In the New Share dialog box, enter the name of the share (Figure 12-9).

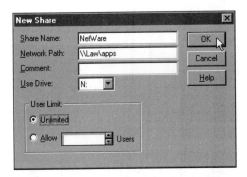

Figure 12-9 Establishing the share information

7. Enter the network path to the shared NetWare volume, such as **\\Law\apps**.

8. Enter a comment to describe the share.

9. Enter a drive letter, such as **N** for NetWare.

10. Set the user limit to **Unlimited** (unless there is a reason to limit access).

11. Click **OK**.

12. Back in the Configure Gateway dialog box, select the share, and click **Permissions**.

13. In the Access Through Share Permissions dialog box, give the desired permissions to the Everyone group, such as **Read** or **Change**. Click **OK**.

14. Click **OK** in the Configure Gateway dialog box.

15. Click **OK** in the Gateway Service for NetWare dialog box.

 PROJECT 12-4

In this activity you practice a simple NetWare migration to Windows NT Server. You will need a NetWare server and an NT server for practice. Make sure that you back up both servers before starting, and that no one is logged on to one of the servers. Also, be sure that Gateway Service for NetWare is already loaded and configured on the NT server. In this activity you have the option to discontinue the migration in the trial run stage without actually migrating data.

To migrate from NetWare to Windows NT Server:

1. Click **Start**, **Programs**, and **Administrative Tools (Common)**.

2. Click **Migration Tool for NetWare**.

3. In the Select Servers for Migration dialog box, enter the NetWare server name in the From NetWare Server: box or click the ... (ellipsis) button to search for the NetWare server you want to migrate. Enter the name of the Windows NT server in the To Windows NT Server: box, or use the ... button to search for it. Click **OK**.

4. Enter the supervisor account name (or equivalent) and its password if requested by the NetWare server.

5. In the Migration Tool for NetWare dialog box, click the **User Options** button, and check **Transfer Users and Groups**.

6. Click the **Passwords** tab and select the password option **Password is Username**. Also, check **User Must Change Password**.

7. Click the **Usernames** tab. Click the option **Log Error** (logs an error when there is a name conflict and does not migrate that account).

8. Click the **Group Names** tab. Click the option **Log Error** (logs an error when there is a name conflict and does not migrate that group).

9. Click the **Defaults** tab. Remove the check from Use Supervisor Defaults, but check **Add Supervisors to the Administrators Group**. Click **OK** to return to the Migration Tool for NetWare dialog box.

10. Click the **File Options** button. Choose the NetWare volume and click **Files**. Click the folders you want to migrate (do not select the SYS: volume folders \Mail, \System, \Login, \Public, and \Etc). Click **OK** and **OK** again to return to the Migration Tool for NetWare dialog box.

11. Click the **Logging** button, and check **Verbose User/Group Logging** and **Verbose File Logging** (the verbose options provide the most detailed reporting).

12. Click the **Trial Migration** button to run a test of the migration without really migrating files. Click **Logging** and **View Log Files**. Examine the **SUMMARY.LOG file**.

13. Close the log viewer and click **OK**.

14. If you just want to practice the migration without continuing, click **Exit** now to leave the migration tool.

15. If you want to continue with a real migration, click **Start Migration**.

16. Click **OK** when the migration is complete, and click **Logging** to view log file results.

17. Close the log viewer, click **OK**, and close Migration Tool for NetWare.

12

ASPEN CONSULTING: NETWARE CONNECTIVITY AND MIGRATION

Today Mark Arnez has some questions for you about NetWare. He also assigns you to work with Greenville Paper to handle NetWare interoperation issues.

1. Mark Arnez has never worked with NetWare and is curious about some of the differences from and similarities to Windows NT Server. Compare the operating systems in terms of the following:

   - Where information about accounts is kept

   - Protocols used

   - Printer setup

   - Logon authentication

   - File and directory security

2. Greenville Paper makes paper products, such as paper towels and napkins. They have a network consisting of eight NetWare servers and two Windows NT servers, and would like to set up Gateway Service for NetWare on one of the NT servers. Summarize the steps they need to follow to load Gateway Service for NetWare.

3. Greenville Paper has loaded Gateway Service for NetWare. However, there are no shared folders on the Windows NT server. What must they do to set up shared folders?

4. The server administrator for Greenville Paper is unsure about how security works for NetWare folders and files that are available through a gateway on an NT server. Explain how security is set up to protect the folders and files.

5. A follow-up question from Greenville Paper is about setting up NetWare printers to be used in Windows NT. Their server administrator is asking you to write step-by-step instructions for setting up NetWare printer access through a Windows NT gateway.

6. Greenville Paper has decided to migrate four of their NetWare servers to Windows NT Server. They are asking for your help in developing a strategy for the migration. Provide them with your recommendations for the following:

   - How many servers to migrate at a time

   - How to prepare for a migration

   - How to choose a time for the migration

   - How to anticipate and prevent possible migration problems

   - How to develop a testing plan

   - How to locate problems in case they occur

INTERNET AND INTRANET SERVICES

Few computer technologies have had the rapid impact of the Internet. Now an internationally popular way to communicate, the Internet has spawned an interest in personal computers, modems, and networks. TV news programs and advertisements encourage viewers to go to the Internet for more information. Thousands of organizations and individuals have their own Web sites or home pages. You can order clothes, cars, refrigerators, books, music, and just about anything else through the Internet. Individuals post family pictures, resumes, recipes, or even a short clip of their favorite music. Students earn degrees through the Internet, and physicians use it to learn about new medical techniques. The Internet has become a major international tool for communication, commerce, education, and research.

Microsoft products have played a role in the growth of the Internet by offering tools such as Internet Explorer and Internet Information Server (IIS). Complementing these tools, Microsoft has laid a foundation for Internet connectivity by providing operating systems that are Internet friendly, such as Windows 95 and Windows NT. The computers that host many Internet sites, large and small, are often doing so with Microsoft Windows NT Servers and IIS. In this chapter you learn about Microsoft Internet tools and connectivity, and about applying these tools to private networks (intranets) as well.

AFTER READING THIS CHAPTER AND COMPLETING THE EXERCISES YOU WILL BE ABLE TO:

- EXPLAIN HOW THE INTERNET WORKS AND HOW IT IS USED
- EXPLAIN INTRANETS
- DESCRIBE THE FEATURES OF MICROSOFT INTERNET EXPLORER
- DESCRIBE, INSTALL, AND CONFIGURE MICROSOFT INTERNET INFORMATION SERVER (IIS)
- INSTALL MICROSOFT DNS SERVER

THE INTERNET

The **Internet** is a vast collection of thousands of networks connected worldwide. Millions of computer users are attached to these networks in every part of the United States and in countries all over the world. The Internet brings together governmental, educational, business, and research organizations. Internet participants share in discussion groups, work on leading-edge technological developments, conduct business, publish news stories, and access weather information.

Although it seems like an overnight success, the Internet and its predecessors were carefully developed over several years. In the mid-1980s a few researchers, academics, government personnel, and military users took advantage of early long-distance networks such as BITNET for communications, using very basic e-mail systems and file-transfer capabilities. Many of these communications were handled through dial-up telephone lines and slow 300 and 1200 bps modems. Others used slow dedicated telecommunications lines or unreliable microwave links. By the mid-1990s, communications equipment had been vastly improved, diverse long-distance networks were uniting into the Internet, e-mail systems had matured, and GUI interfaces had made using the Internet possible for many more users.

Also, the corporate world began to realize the business potential of the Internet. As mentioned earlier, you can order or find information about any type of product you can imagine. Thousands of companies have scrambled to establish Web sites from which to advertise and sell products. Some publications are now electronic only, available through subscription on the Internet. The Internet has also become a personal banking and investment resource, where people can manage their bank accounts, apply for a loan, or trade in the stock market.

For all of these uses, Internet users access text, voice, and video files that are typically presented through a format called Hypertext Markup Language (HTML). **Hypertext Markup Language (HTML)** is a formatting process used to enable documents and graphics images to be read on the World Wide Web. **Hypertext** is a method of establishing routes through an electronic document to enable the reader to go quickly from one section to another. HTML provides for fast links inside a document, to other documents, to graphics, and to World Wide Web sites.

The **World Wide Web (Web** or **WWW)** is a series of file servers with software such as Microsoft's Internet Information Server (IIS), that make HTML and other Web documents available for workstations. HTML files are read by Internet users with the help of client software called a **Web browser**, such as Netscape Communicator and Microsoft Internet Explorer.

The Web browser employs a **Uniform Resource Locator (URL)**, which is a special addressing format, to find particular Web sites. A URL is like a house number, street, city, state, and zip code combined on one line to locate a specific destination. The first part of a URL is the communication search method. The next part is the actual address, which may specify a WWW format, the name of the site, and type of site. For example, the URL *http://www.microsoft.com* indicates the use of the Hypertext Transfer Protocol to find the WWW-formatted site Microsoft, which is a commercial site (com). The combined name *microsoft.com* is called a domain name.

A URL is one form of the **Universal Resource Identifier (URI)**, which is a convention for locating an Internet site. The other form is a **Relative URL (RELURL)**, which is typically a document name such as *mypage.html* that is treated as a resource in the same directory as the browser specifying the RELURL.

The **Hypertext Transport Protocol (HTTP)** is a communications protocol that obtains HTML-formatted documents on the Internet and objects embedded in those documents, such as .GIF picture files and .WAV sound files. HTTP works over TCP/IP, which is the network transport protocol of the Internet. It also works with FTP to send and receive files over the Internet. (See Chapter 2, "Basic Network Design and Protocols," for more information on TCP/IP and FTP.)

Access to the Internet is made possible through an Internet service provider (ISP). A large or small business is likely to have an Internet connection to an ISP through dial-up modem access or through ISDN and a TA (terminal adapter). Many colleges and universities have had Internet access for years, as it evolved from participation in a network structure using BITNET and later the Internet.

As the Internet has become more commercialized and busy, colleges and universities are moving toward establishing Internet II to focus on and facilitate noncommercial and research interests.

INTRANETS

An **intranet** is like the Internet in that it provides access to HTML-formatted documents from one or more servers and uses HTTP, TCP/IP, and FTP. The difference is that an intranet uses tight controls to limit who has access, forming a private network within an organization. Many organizations make sales, performance, human resources, and accounting reports available to their managers through an intranet. Other organizations use an intranet to enable employees to update personal information, such as a new address or a change in health benefits. Colleges use intranets to enable students to look up grade and degree progress information.

13

Some intranets are established in such a way that they can be accessed through the Internet. That access is made possible, in part, by remote access communications protocols such as PPP and PPTP. Other intranets are set up so that they are accessible only within a closed network and are **private virtual networks** available to selected workstations, subnets, and IP addresses. Intranets are popular because their information is protected and because they employ Web browsers and Web formats that make users instantly productive. For example, an intranet might offer a range of executive-level reports that a college president can access immediately from her or his office or remotely from a portable computer while in a meeting with the college trustees.

MICROSOFT INTERNET TOOLS

Microsoft offers several tools to enable users and server administrators to take advantage of the Internet and of intranets. One of the earliest Internet tools from Microsoft is the Internet Assistant, which is an add-on for early versions of Microsoft Word. The Internet Assistant works within Word to format a document with HTML tags and to save the document as a text file. Bookmarks, hypertext links, headings, and pictures are inserted into a document by means of point-and-click techniques. Later versions of Microsoft Word have Internet Assistant capabilities built into the software and include a wizard to guide users through creation of an HTML document. Also, existing Word documents can be converted to HTML. Other Microsoft Office products, such as Excel (for spreadsheets) and Access (for databases), also have Web capabilities that can be set up.

Microsoft FrontPage is a full-scale Web site development tool that is used to create Web documents or a complete Web site. It has tools for image editing, implementing a database on the Web, integration of Microsoft Office files, table creation, and managing a Web site. FrontPage supports both ActiveX and Java. Developed by Microsoft, **ActiveX** is a set of controls that enables Internet access to advanced sound, video, graphics, text, and 3-D capabilities. **Java** is a programming language developed by Sun Microsystems that is designed for writing programs to use on the Internet that will run on a variety of client platforms. Many Web pages now use small Java programs, called **applets**, which can perform just about any task that a regular program on a computer can perform. An applet might present an animation or enable you to calculate the interest on a loan.

Two other Microsoft tools used with the Internet are Microsoft Internet Explorer and the Microsoft Internet Information Server. Included with Windows NT Server, these tools are explained in the next sections.

MICROSOFT INTERNET EXPLORER

Internet Explorer is a Web browser that comes with Windows NT Server and is installed as an application at the same time as the operating system. Internet Explorer provides an interface that communicates with the Internet and can read Web-formatted files. Internet Explorer has several capabilities that include the following:

- An address line to enter a URL for a specific Internet site or page, such as the Microsoft Web site (Figure 13-1)
- Animated displays, sound, and video capabilities
- Internet e-mail access
- Internet channel access
- Moving forward and back between pages that have already been viewed
- Ability to recall previously visited sites and to set bookmarks to return to favorite sites

- Option to download Internet files and to browse at the same time

- Support for ActiveX documents in order to view Microsoft Office files in Internet Explorer

- Support for Java applets

- Access to Internet search services

- Access to newsgroups

- Ability to customize the browser interface

- Security capabilities

- Option to chat with other Internet participants

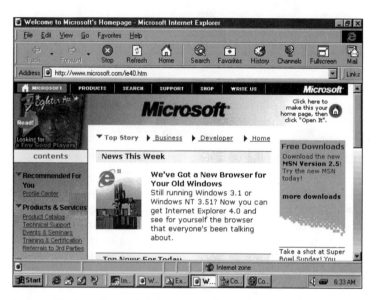

Figure 13-1   Microsoft Internet Explorer showing the Microsoft home page

Microsoft Internet Explorer version 4 has been adapted to work in Windows 3.1, 3.11, Windows 95, and Windows NT 3.51, as well as in Windows NT 4.0. Internet Explorer 4 has several new capabilities such as the option to set up a default search engine and a new history option that displays the Web sites you have visited by the day of the week. Internet mail can be imported into Microsoft Outlook as a way to manage your mail. Internet Explorer 4.0 introduces the use of security zones, which set different levels of security. An Internet site that is designated as restricted has high security that must be validated each time you access a file. For example, you would restrict a site in which you provide your credit card number to order a product. A local intranet site or a site from which you simply obtain information might be designated as a trusted site zone. Another new feature is the option to load the Windows Desktop Update, which gives elements of your desktop the same features that are used in Internet Explorer, such as an address bar and a Favorites menu. Figure 13-2 shows how My Computer includes the address line, Favorites menu, Internet Explorer-type icons, and an information box that appears on the left of the screen when you click an object such as Dial-Up Networking.

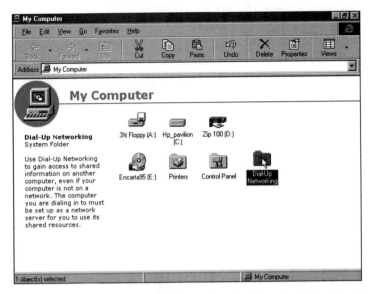

Figure 13-2 My Computer using the Windows Desktop Update

Internet Explorer 4.0 has another new option called channels, which are used for dynamic Web sites that you access frequently. Channels provide enhanced visual and audio presentations. NetMeeting is another addition that is intended for conducting a meeting over the Internet. NetMeeting employs several different media options such as electronic chat, video, voice, and exchanging data files. A small video conference is made possible by attaching a video camera to a specialized card in the computer.

MICROSOFT INTERNET INFORMATION SERVER

Microsoft Internet Information Server (IIS) is included on the Windows NT Server CD-ROM. IIS enables you to offer a complete Web site from an NT Server. Your Web site might fulfill any number of functions. On a college campus you might use it to enable applicants to apply for admission, or to allow currently enrolled students to view their progress toward completing degree requirements. Another use is to train company employees to use an inventory or order entry system. Many companies use their Web sites for multiple purposes such as to announce new products, provide product support, take product orders, and advertise job openings.

IIS is compatible with several application programming goals. It can be used as a key part of a client/server system by implementing the Internet Server API (ISAPI) set. The ISAPI set provides a performance enhancement for communications with the NT kernel by implementing new calls, such as TransmitFile( ), which make IIS an efficient software application. Through the IIS filter capability, programs can be built to automatically trigger other programs, and security can be set up to control who accesses a Web site.

IIS contains three critical services for a Web site:

- World Wide Web
- Gopher
- FTP

Gopher is a program available on the Internet that provides menus of information for users to access as files. Gopher slightly predates WWW, and Gopher servers have largely been replaced by WWW servers. Gopher files do not use the popular HTML format and do not provide much beyond a basic text presentation of information. FTP is an application protocol that works over TCP/IP to handle file transfers over a network (see Chapter 2).

There are several reasons that Windows NT Server makes a good candidate as a Web server. One reason is that Windows NT Server's privileged-mode architecture and fault-tolerance capabilities make it a reliable server platform. Another reason is that Windows NT Server is compatible with small databases, such as Microsoft Access, and large databases, such as SQL Server and Oracle. Also, users can log directly into a database through the IIS ODBC drivers. This makes it very compatible for integration with Web-based client/server applications. IIS also is compatible with the **Secure Sockets Layer (SSL)** encryption technique. SSL is a dual-key encryption standard for communications between a server and a client and is also used by Internet Explorer. IIS enables security control based on username and password, IP address, and folder and file access controls.

IIS is designed to handle a large number of users because it uses what Microsoft calls the "worker thread" model. In this model, all three services (WWW, Gopher, and FTP) run as part of one process, INETINOF.EXE, which enables them to work more efficiently by sharing the same cache and other program resources.

13

Microsoft has two other Microsoft Web site applications, similar to, but less capable in some areas than, IIS: Microsoft Peer Web Services and Microsoft Personal Web Server. Microsoft Peer Web Services is a limited version of IIS that runs on Windows NT Workstation. Microsoft Personal Web Server for Windows 95 also is a scaled-down version of IIS. Peer Web Services and Personal Web Server are intended to develop and manage low-volume Web sites for a limited number of users.

Installing IIS

There are several requirements for installing and using IIS, as follows:

- Windows NT 4.0 Server installed on the computer to host IIS
- TCP/IP installed on the IIS host
- Access to an ISP (ask the ISP for your IP address, subnet mask, and default gateway IP address)

- A CD-ROM drive from which to load IIS

- Sufficient disk space for IIS and for Web site files—50 MB is the minimum requirement, but you should have three or four times this much space

- Disk storage formatted for NTFS—IIS can run on FAT, but NTFS has better performance and security

- A method for resolving IP addresses to computer or domain names, such as DNS or WINS

One way to install IIS is to do so when you install Windows NT Server. In the initial setup, there is a dialog box with a check box to Install Microsoft Internet Information Server. (See Chapter 4, "Server Installation.") Another way to install IIS is from the Network icon on the Control Panel, as with any other network service. After you open the Network icon, click the Services tab and then the Add button. In the Network Service: scroll box, double-click Microsoft Internet Information Server (Figure 13-3; the version will vary depending on when you purchased Windows NT Server). A dialog box is displayed in which to enter the location of the files to install. Insert the Windows NT Server CD-ROM, provide the CD-ROM drive letter and the path, \I386. Click OK to load the files from the CD-ROM.

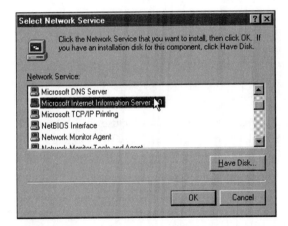

Figure 13-3   Installing Microsoft Internet Information Server

 A third way to start the IIS installation is to use the Control Panel Add/Remove Programs icon. Insert the Windows NT Server CD-ROM, click the Install button, and load IIS from the CD-ROM folder \I386\Inetsrv\Inetstp.exe (if you are installing on an Intel-based computer). The Microsoft Internet Information Server Setup dialog box may appear, advising that all applications running on the server should be closed before continuing with the setup.

The next Setup dialog box shows that there are many services to install as part of IIS (Figure 13-4). Check all of the services. These services are described in Table 13-1. Accept the default selection to install the files in \Winnt\System32\inetsrv, and click OK.

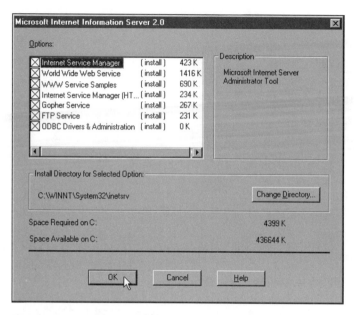

Figure 13-4   Selecting the services to install

Table 13-1   IIS Services

Service Option	Purpose
FTP Service	Used to set up FTP server services for file transfers between the server and a client
Gopher Service	Used to set up a menu system enabling network users to view regularly formatted text files through the network
Internet Service Manager	A tool used to manage all installed IIS services, including FTP, Gopher, and World Wide Web services
Internet Service Manager (HTML)	HTML help documentation for the Internet Service Manager
ODBC Drivers & Administration	Loads Open Database Connectivity (ODBC) drivers for connecting to databases through IIS services such as a Microsoft Access or SQL Server database
World Wide Web Service	Used to set up a World Wide Web server offering access to Web-formatted (HTML) documents
WWW Service Samples	Loads sample Web files

If the \Inetsrv folder does not exist, a dialog box will query if you want to create it. Click Yes. Next, specify in which folders to place files for World Wide Web access, for FTP access, and for Gopher access. It is recommended that you choose to use the default subfolder selections, \wwwroot, \ftproot, and \gophroot, and click OK (Figure 13-5). If these subfolders do not exist, click Yes to create them. The files are loaded, and the Setup program starts the Microsoft World Wide Web Publishing Service, the Gopher Publishing Service, and the FTP Service. (You can practice installing Microsoft IIS in Hands-on Project 13-1.)

13

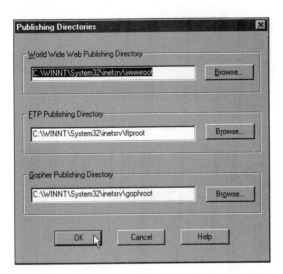

Figure 13-5   Selecting the installation folders

 When you install IIS, it automatically sets up the services you selected so that they start each time the server is booted. The services are: FTP Publishing Service, Gopher Publishing Service, and World Wide Web Publishing Service. Confirm that they are started by opening the Control Panel Services icon. Also, consider disabling the Gopher service so that it does not use server resources. (Hands-on Project 13-2 shows how to disable the Gopher Publishing Service.)

Configuring World Wide Web Services

With IIS installed, a new menu item is available from the Start button Programs option called Microsoft Internet Server (Common). There are four IIS management tools that you can use (Figure 13-6):

- Internet Information Server Setup

- Internet Service Manager

- Key Manager

- Product Documentation

Figure 13-6   IIS management options

The Internet Service Manager is used to manage WWW, Gopher, and FTP services. When you install all three services, they appear in the Internet Service Manager, as shown in Figure 13-7. In most instances you will not use the Gopher service, but it is useful to have it installed for older Internet applications, and to learn more about Gopher. From the Internet Service Manager, you can double-click a service to view its properties. Table 13-2 summarizes the four tabs on the WWW Service Properties dialog box.

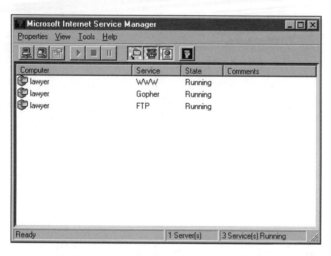

Figure 13-7 Microsoft Internet Service Manager

Table 13-2 WWW Service Properties Tabs

Tab	Purpose
Service	Sets information about the WWW network port, connection timeout, maximum number of connections, and a username and password for the anonymous FTP logon and password authentication data
Directories	Specifies where directories are located on the server for Web files, script files for automated services, and administration files; and determines the type of access users have to browse Web directories
Logging	Creates log files to track access of the server in logs that are created daily, weekly, monthly, or when a certain log size is reached
Advanced	Controls, by IP address and subnet mask, which computers can access the Web server; all computers can be allowed access, or access can be limited to only selected computers on the network

13

If you click the Service tab, it shows several parameters that you can set (Figure 13-8). The TCP Port is a unique port number for IIS, which is set to 80 by default. It is unlikely that there will be a port conflict, so the best approach is to leave the port number at 80. If you change it, you will need to reboot the computer. The Connection Timeout is a useful parameter to set, because it disconnects users who have been inactive. Disconnecting inactive users improves the IIS response for those who are actively using the Web site. The Maximum Connections parameter enables you to set a limit on how many users can access your site simultaneously.

For the sake of the server's performance, consider lowering the Maximum Connections value, for example to 100.

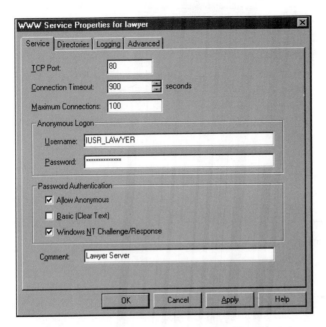

Figure 13-8   WWW Service Properties Service tab

Anonymous users are able to access IIS via the anonymous logon account. The default name is IUSR_servername, and a default password is randomly generated to ensure that the account has a password. All anonymous connections are able to come in through this account, which also must exist in User Manager for Domains. The name of the account and its password, as specified in the Service tab, must match the account and password in User Manager for Domains. Also, the account must have the right to log on locally in order for anonymous users to access IIS. Anonymous access is a common way for Internet users to access a Web site.

The Password Authentication box is used to determine how IIS users are granted access. Allow Anonymous enables users to come in through the anonymous guest account without using authentication from the browser on the client. Basic (Clear Text), used by many browsers, means that passwords are encrypted if the client's browser employs SSL, and otherwise passwords are likely to be sent unencrypted. Windows NT Challenge/Response ensures that usernames and passwords are encrypted, a function that is supported by Internet Explorer. Any text entered in the Comment: box will appear in the Internet Service Manager main dialog box, next to the WWW service.

The Directories tab shows the locations of directories published by the WWW. Double-click any of the directories to view the properties of that directory. The default directories include: \Inetpub\wwwroot (alias \Home) for files you want to publish, \Inetpub\scripts (alias \Script) for scripts that run in conjunction with programs, and \Winnt\System32\iinetsrv\iisadmin (alias \iisadmin) for IIS administration files. The directory access permissions are Read, Execute, or both. Use Read for directories containing informational files, and use Execute for directories containing scripts and programs.

An **IIS home directory** is a main or IIS root directory containing the WWW service, such as \Inetpub\wwwroot. Place files that will be accessed by the IIS users in subfolders under the home directory. You also can set up virtual directories to be accessible from IIS. A **virtual directory** is one that does not reside on the IIS server, but is made to appear as though it does. For example, at a college, the Web site files might be on the computer that is home to IIS, but the alumni association might have files that they maintain on their server and that are set up as an IIS virtual directory. All virtual directories must reside on computers in the same domain as IIS. Another option is to set up **virtual servers** to make one IIS server appear to be many Web sites. For example, one parent company may consist of three smaller companies and want to make IIS appear as though it is three different Web sites. To accomplish this, a virtual server is set up for each company, but the files are really on one IIS server in different folders. Each virtual server is assigned its own IP address, which must be bound to the NIC in the IIS server. Also, the path to the Web files folder is specified. Use the Add button in the Directories tab to open the Directory Properties dialog box in which to set up a virtual directory or server (Figure 13-9).

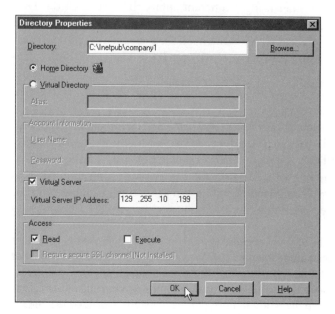

Figure 13-9   Setting up a virtual server

13

If you select to use virtual servers, you need to open the Control Panel Network icon and configure the NIC for multiple IP addresses. Click the Protocols tab, click TCP/IP Protocol, and click Properties. Click the Advanced button to set up additional IP addresses. Make sure that the IP addresses first have been registered by your ISP. Also, consider installing an additional NIC to improve server performance when virtual servers are configured.

Use the Logging tab (see Figure 13-8) to keep a record of how IIS is used. Keeping a log is a good practice for several reasons. It enables you to determine the activity on IIS to help plan for growth as you offer more information and services. Also, the log is a valuable way to troubleshoot problems. IIS starts logging data when you click the Enable Logging radio button. You can log the information to a file or to an ODBC-compliant database. If you log to a file, select the way you want to keep logs, such as starting a new one each day, week, or month, or when the log reaches a certain size. Logs are kept in the \Winnt\System32\Logfile folder. If you choose to log the information directly into a database, specify the source name, table, user access name, and password. (Try Hands-on Project 13-3 to practice configuring IIS password authentication and logging.)

The Advanced tab (see Figure 13-8) enables you to control access to IIS by IP address and subnet mask. If you are offering IIS to all Internet users, then in most cases you will simply click the Granted Access radio button on the tab. However, you can deny users access by adding them to the exception list. To do that, click Add, single computer, and enter the IP address of the first user, or click the ... (ellipsis) button and enter the DNS name of the user. Repeat the process for each user that you want to keep from accessing IIS. If you are creating a restricted intranet, consider using a different approach. First, click the Denied Access radio button and add the private intranet group as exceptions. You can use the Add button to specify a group of users, for example by subnet mask for users on a certain portion of the network. (You can practice setting advanced security for IIS in Hands-on Project 13-4.)

Key Manager

Key Manager is used to secure data transmission between IIS and clients accessing it through the network. Microsoft IIS uses an SSL public/private key method for communications. The **public key** is a password that is obtained from a public file or by another public means. Any client has access to the public key. The **private key** is a data decryption key used by the server. Key Manager is used to generate a public and private key pair, both needed for communications between a server and its client.

The public/private key data encryption method used by Microsoft is consistent with the **Data Encryption Standard (DES)** developed by the National Institute of Standards and Technology. The public key is published for any network station to view, while the private key is reserved only for the sending and receiving stations. Both keys are necessary to decrypt data. Look for expanded use of DES security in all network communications as security needs increase in proportion to the importance of the data that is routinely transmitted.

INSTALLING MICROSOFT DNS SERVER

One of the requirements for running IIS is some sort of domain name resolution service, such as DNS or WINS. If there is not a DNS Server on your network, you will need to install Microsoft DNS Server or WINS. This section shows you how to install Microsoft DNS Server. **DNS Server** is a Microsoft service that resolves IP addresses to computer names, for example resolving 129.77.1.10 to the computer name Brown; it also resolves computer names to IP addresses. Microsoft DNS Server is installed from the Control Panel Network icon. Once you have opened the icon, click the Services tab and the Add button. Click Microsoft DNS Server, insert the Windows NT Server CD-ROM, and click OK. In the Windows NT Setup dialog box, provide the path to the CD-ROM and the folder, such as \I386, and click Continue. After the DNS files are installed, click Yes to shut down and reboot the server.

After you install DNS Server, a new DNS Manager option is added to the Administrative Tools (Common) menu. When the computer reboots, you need to use DNS Manager to create two primary zones of DNS information. One zone holds host name records, called address records, to map a computer name to the IP address. Another zone, called the reverse zone, holds the PTR resource record, which contains the IP-address-to-host-name translation. Open DNS Manager, click the DNS menu, New Server, and enter the name of the server that is to be the DNS server. After the server is added, click that server in the Domain Name Service Manager dialog box (Figure 13-10).

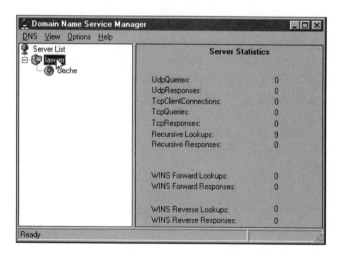

Figure 13-10   Selecting the DNS server

With the server highlighted, click the DNS menu again, and click New Zone. Click the Primary radio button and then click Next. Enter the name of the zone (which is your Internet domain name, such as *mycompany.com*), press Tab to set the zone file name (a default is entered for you), and click Next and then Finish.

The next step is to create the reverse zone, which is called the "in-addr.arpa" name. Click the server again, click the DNS menu, and click New Zone. Click Primary and then Next. Enter the in-addr.arpa domain name for the reverse zone, which consists of your zone network address in reverse with in-addr.arp at the end. For example, if your zone network address is 129.77.10, then the in-addr-arpa name is 10.77.129.IN-ADDR.ARPA (Figure 13-11). Click Next and then Finish. (You can practice creating a primary zone in Hands-on Project 13-5.)

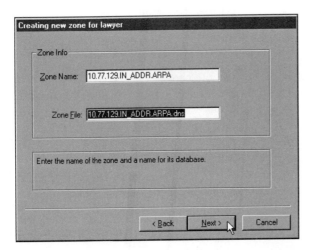

Figure 13-11 Creating the reverse primary zone

After the two primary zones are created, it is necessary to enter a record for each host-to-IP-address translation (address resolution). Click the DNS menu and New Host. In the New Host dialog box, enter the host name and its IP address. For example, if the DNS server name is Lawyer and its IP address is 129.77.10.100, enter that information. Place a check in the Create Associated PTR Record box and click Add Host. Continue entering a record for each computer in the domain. Click Done when you are finished.

CHAPTER SUMMARY

- The Internet has become a pervasive tool for obtaining information, communicating electronically, and purchasing products. Some users, such as colleges and universities, have been using the Internet and its forerunners for years. Other users are part of the growing wave of new Internet "surfers" and commerce sites. Microsoft has become part of this fast-developing environment by making available an array of new Internet and intranet-based software.

- Microsoft Internet Explorer is one example of an Internet product that has reached large numbers of computer users. Internet Explorer is a Web browser with built-in features such as e-mail capability and access to folders containing links to favorite Internet sites.

- Microsoft Internet Information Server (IIS) has taken hold as popular Web site development and management software. IIS is used to set up and manage large and small Web sites. It comes with several management tools to enable the server administrator to configure it, set up security, and offer access to Web documents that are on other computers. Microsoft DNS Server and WINS software are vital companions to IIS, providing IP and name resolution services.

KEY TERMS

- **applet** — A small Java program that runs on the Internet.

- **ActiveX** — A set of controls that enables Internet access to advanced sound, video, graphics, text, and 3-D capabilities.

- **Data Encryption Standard (DES)** — A network encryption standard developed by the National Institute of Standards and Technology (NIST) and IBM.

- **DNS Server** — A Microsoft service that resolves IP addresses to computer names (for example, resolving 129.77.1.10 to the computer name Brown) and computer names to IP addresses.

- **Gopher** — A set of programs available on an Internet server that makes information available to users through a menu format.

- **hypertext** — A method of establishing routes through an electronic document to enable the reader to go quickly from one section to another. The fast routes are created by placing bookmarks at specific locations, such as at section headings, and by placing transfer links to those bookmarks at another location, such as in a table of contents.

- **Hypertext Markup Language (HTML)** — A formatting process that is used to enable documents and graphics images to be read on the World Wide Web. HTML also provides for fast links to other documents, to graphics, and to Web sites.

- **Hypertext Transport Protocol (HTTP)** — A communications protocol that obtains HTML-formatted documents and that works with FTP to transport files over the Internet.

- **IIS home directory** — An IIS root directory containing the WWW service, such as Inetpub\wwwroot, and subfolders for the published IIS files.

- **Internet** — A global network of diverse Gopher, Web, and information servers offering voice, video, and text data to millions of users by means of the TCP/IP protocol.

- **intranet** — A private network within an organization. It uses the same Web-based software as the Internet, but can be restricted from public access.

- **Java** — A programming language developed by Sun Microsystems that enables you to write programs for use on the Internet from a variety of platforms.

- **private key** — A data decryption key known only to authorized network stations that are sending and receiving data to and from each other.

13

- **private virtual network** — An intranet that is closed to access through the Internet, restricting access to specific workstations, subnets, and IP addresses.

- **public key** — A data decryption key that is publicly available to any station on a network.

- **Relative URL (RELURL)** — Document name, such as *mypage.html*, that is treated as a resource in the same directory as the browser specifying the RELURL.

- **Secure Sockets Layer (SSL)** — A dual-key encryption standard for communications between an Internet server and a client.

- **Uniform Resource Locator (URL)** — An addressing format used to find an Internet Web site or page.

- **Universal Resource Identifier (URI)** — A convention for locating an Internet site.

- **virtual directory** — A folder of Web documents that does not reside on the IIS server, but is made to appear as though it does.

- **virtual server** — One IIS server that is made to appear as many Web sites.

- **Web browser** — Software that uses HTTP to locate and communicate with Web sites and that interprets HTML documents, video, and sound to give the user a sound and video GUI presentation of the HTML document contents.

- **World Wide Web (Web or WWW)** — A vast network of servers throughout the world that provide access to voice, text, video, and data files.

REVIEW QUESTIONS

1. Which communications protocol is used with the World Wide Web?

    a. HTTP   **b.** NetBEUI   **c.** PPP   **d.** DLC

2. Which of the following is an example of a private network that uses Web-like features?

    a. Internet   **b.** intranet   **c.** linknet   **d.** multinet

3. Microsoft Internet Explorer can be installed in which of the following?

    a. Windows 3.1   **d.** all of the above

    b. Windows 95   **e.** only b and c

    c. Windows NT

4. An applet is used with which of the following?

    a. Java   **c.** NCP

    b. virtual machine code   **d.** URL

5. Which of the following services is (are) included with IIS?

   a. World Wide Web   **d.** all of the above

   b. Gopher   **e.** only a and b

   c. DNS

6. Which of the following options is (are) used for logging WWW activity?

   a. starting a new log daily

   b. starting a new log weekly

   c. starting a new log when the older one reaches a designated size

   d. all of the above

   e. only a and b

7. SSL is a(n) _____.

   a. shell used for an Internet server

   b. Internet gateway for NetWare servers

   c. dual-key encryption method

   d. e-mail server

8. Your boss wants you to set up an intranet available only to users having IP addresses that start with 122.88.19. How might you most easily set up IIS to restrict access according to your boss's wishes?

   a. by using the WWW service Advanced tab to restrict individual IP addresses

   b. by using the WWW service Advanced tab to grant access by subnet

   c. by setting access authorization to Windows NT Challenge/Response

   d. by requiring a unique access code in Internet Explorer

9. Your organization is really two companies in one, and you want it to appear that there are two Web sites on your NT Server. How might you do this?

   a. by setting up virtual servers

   b. by installing the IIS in two separate directories so that two versions are running at all times

   c. by linking a workstation running Peer Web Services with a server running IIS

   d. by purchasing an SMP dual-processor server

10. From where do you install IIS?

   a. Control Panel Add/Remove Programs icon

   b. Control Panel Network icon

   c. as part of the Windows NT Server installation

   d. all of the above

   e. only a and b

13

11. How many primary zones are created to set up a DNS server to work in conjunction with IIS?

    a. one   **b.** two   **c.** four   **d.** eight

12. While operating Internet Explorer, you want to access Microsoft's Internet site. What do you use to access it?

    a. URL   **b.** subnet mask   **c.** UNC   **d.** RELURL

13. You have set up a Web site that accepts credit card numbers when users place orders for your products. What security can an Internet Explorer 4.0 user set up to help protect her or his card number?

    a. trusted   **b.** clear text   **c.** restricted   **d.** dial-back

14. An in-addr.arpa name is used in a _____.

    a. security zone   **c.** computer name

    b. reverse zone   **d.** DNS server to identify it as unique

15. Who accesses the NT Server username, IUSR_servername?

    a. IIS users

    b. administrators when working on IIS

    c. IIS operators to print the activity logs

    d. IIS print operators

16. Documents are formatted to be read via the WWW by means of _____.

    a. RPC   **c.** the Microsoft Help compiler

    b. rich text formatting   **d.** HTML

17. There is a document on your Web site that contains a small picture of your newest product. When users click the picture to learn more about the product, they go back to your home page instead. What would you check?

    a. IIS security set up

    b. size of the file containing the product information, because it may be too large

    c. hypertext links in the document containing the small picture

    d. IIS protocol set up

18. With which file system does IIS work best?

    a. NTFS   **b.** FAT   **c.** OS/2   **d.** open MVS

19. Your organization has decided to set up IIS with the most secure form of password authentication. Which of the following would match that requirement?

    a. Allow Anonymous   **c.** Password Logging

    b. Windows NT Challenge/Response   **d.** Basic (Clear Text)

20. What level of access would you set on an informational home page?

    a. Read & audit   **b.** Anonymous   **c.** Read   **d.** Execute

21. Which of the following Microsoft Office products contain(s) Web capabilities?

a. Word
b. Access
c. Excel
d. all of the above
e. only a and b

22. It is possible for a user to offer a limited personal Web site in Windows NT Workstation through _____.

a. Microsoft Peer Web Service
b. Microsoft FrontPage
c. Microsoft Personal Web Server
d. Microsoft Internet Explorer

HANDS-ON PROJECTS

 PROJECT 13-1

In this activity you install IIS on a Windows NT 4.0 Server.

To install IIS:

1. Log on using the Administrator account and close any applications that are running.
2. Click **Start**, **Settings**, and **Control Panel**.
3. Double-click the **Network** icon.
4. Click the **Services** tab in the Network dialog box and click **Add**.
5. In the Select Network Service dialog box, double-click **Microsoft Internet Information Server** (see Figure 13-3).
6. Insert the Windows NT CD-ROM. In the Windows NT Setup dialog box, enter the CD-ROM drive letter (such as **D:**) and the **\I386** path (containing files for Intel-based computers). Click **Continue** to begin loading IIS.
7. Check all of the services in the Options: box, and leave the default folder path as \Winnt\System32\inetsrv. Click **OK**.
8. Click **Yes** to create the \Inetsrv folder (if it already exists, you will skip this step).
9. Accept the default locations and names for the publishing directories \Winnt\System32\inetsrv\wwwroot, \Winnt\System32\inetsrv\ftproot, and \Winnt\System32\inetsrv\gophroot (refer to Figure 13-5). Click **OK**. If these folders do not exist, click **Yes** to create each one.
10. Click **OK** after the files are loaded and the publishing services are started.

13

PROJECT 13-2

In this activity you confirm that the IIS services are loaded and started. You also disable the Gopher Publishing Service.

To check the status of the IIS services and disable the Gopher Publishing Service:

1. Click **Start**, **Settings**, and **Control Panel**.

2. Double-click the **Services** icon.

3. Scroll to the **FTP Publishing Service** and make sure that its status is *Started* and that the startup is set to *Automatic* (Figure 13-12).

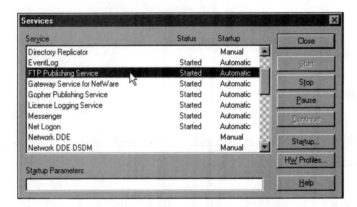

Figure 13-12   Checking the FTP Publishing Service

4. Repeat Step 3 for the **World Wide Web Publishing Service**.

5. If either of the two services is disabled or set to start manually, highlight the service and click the **Startup** button to change the Startup Type to Automatic, and click **OK**.

6. Scroll to **Gopher Publishing Service**, click it, then click **Startup**.

7. Click the **Disabled** radio button in the Service dialog box and click **OK**.

8. Make sure that the Startup column shows that the Gopher service is *Disabled*.

9. Click **Close** in the Services dialog box.

PROJECT 13-3

In this activity you configure the WWW service to specify the number of connections, set up password authentication, and set up logging.

To configure the WWW service:

1. Click **Start**, **Programs**, and **Microsoft Internet Server (Common)**.
2. Double-click the computer name associated with the WWW service.
3. Click the **Service** tab, and enter **100** in the Maximum Connections: box.
4. Check **Windows NT Challenge/Response**.
5. Click the **Logging** tab (Figure 13-13) and click the **Enable Logging** check box.

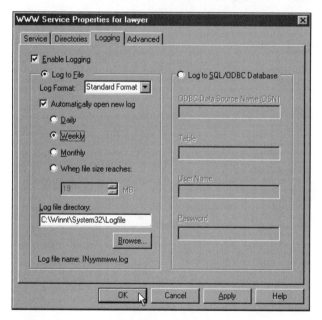

Figure 13-13 Configuring IIS logging

6. Click **Log to File**, and click **Automatically open new log**.
7. Click **Weekly** and the interval in which to start a new log.
8. Click **OK** in the WWW Service Properties dialog box.
9. Close Microsoft Internet Service Manager.

PROJECT 13-4

In this activity you practice setting advanced security for IIS.

To set advanced security:

1. Click **Start**, **Programs**, and **Microsoft Internet Server (Common)**.
2. Double-click the computer name associated with the WWW service.
3. Click the **Advanced** tab, then click the **Granted Access** radio button.
4. Click the **Add** button (Figure 13-14) to view where you would limit access to a single computer or a group of computers by IP address or subnet mask.

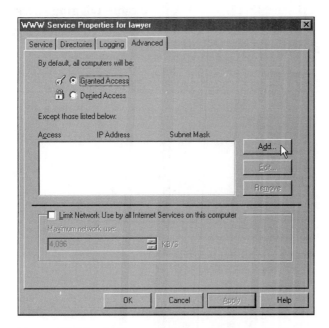

Figure 13-14   Setting up IIS advanced security

5. Click the **...** (ellipsis) button to see where you would enter the DNS name of a computer to look up the IP address.
6. Click **Cancel** in the DNS Lookup dialog box.
7. Click **Cancel** in the Deny Access On dialog box.
8. Click **Apply** in the WWW Service Properties dialog box, and click **OK**.
9. Close Microsoft Internet Service Manager.

PROJECT 13-5

In this activity you create a DNS server primary zone.

To create the primary zone:

1. Click **Start**, **Programs**, and **Administrative Tools (Common)**.
2. Double-click **DNS Manager**.
3. If no server is in the Server List, click **DNS menu**, **New Server** and enter the DNS server name.
4. Click the server under the Server List, then click **DNS menu** and **New Zone**.
5. Click the **Primary** radio button and click **Next** (Figure 13-15).

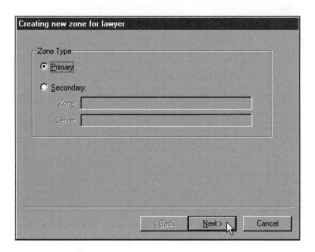

Figure 13-15   Configuring a primary zone

6. Enter the zone name **Test**, press **[Tab]**, then click **Next** and then **Finish**.
7. To delete the practice zone you created, click it under the server name (click **Test**). Make sure that you click the right zone name, or else you may delete someone's host records!
8. Click the **DNS** menu and click **Delete**. Click **Yes** to delete the zone and its records (again, make sure that you delete the right one), and close DNS Manager.

ASPEN CONSULTING: USING INTERNET TOOLS

In these assignments you help two of your established clients to use the Internet. First you work with Tools Unlimited to help them understand Internet capabilities, Web browsers, and how to set up IIS. Also, you assist Vancouver Tires in their setup of IIS.

1. Tools Unlimited, the giant hardware store for which you worked in Chapter 8, "Managing the Server Through Accounts and Groups," is interested in learning more about the Internet. They have asked you to make a presentation to their staff about how the Internet works. Develop a small presentation for them, including the following topics: 1) Explain what makes up the Internet; 2) Provide some examples of how the Internet is used; 3) Describe how the Internet is accessed; 4) Explain the purpose of a Web browser.

2. Tools Unlimited is investigating a browser for all of their networked computers. They need your advice about how to select a browser. Develop a list of capabilities that a browser should include. Use the Internet to research the latest versions of browsers such as Microsoft Internet Explorer and Netscape Communicator. Add to your list these browsers' features and how they might be useful to the employees of Tools Unlimited.

3. The president of Tools Unlimited is interested in selling electric and hand tools over the Internet by accepting credit card payments. He is concerned about security to protect the customers. Explain how IIS can be set up to help protect clients. Also, how might Tools Unlimited advise clients to set up Internet Explorer for security?

4. The server administrator at Tools Unlimited has set up IIS with your help. Now the administrator wants to link several Web pages on the marketing manager's computer, because she will be posting weekly special offers for customers. Explain how you can make those Web pages appear as though they are part of the Tools Unlimited Web site on the IIS computer. What is this capability called? What tool do you use to set it up and how is it set up?

5. Vancouver Tires, your client from Chapter 12, "Interoperating with Novell NetWare," also is setting up IIS on an NT server. Their server administrator is not sure what is required to set up IIS and is calling you. Explain what is needed.

6. Vancouver Tires has installed IIS according to your advice, and now they need to configure it. Explain how to configure the following:

- Authentication   ▪ Folder access   ▪ Logging   ▪ IP access

SERVER AND NETWORK MONITORING

Monitoring your server can make the difference between being caught off guard when a problem strikes and anticipating and correcting an impending problem before the users notice. For example, a server administrator at a university developed a Web site where students could obtain information about closed classes during registration. The administrator tracked the performance of the server and CPU on the first day of registration, and discovered that the CPU was taxed at peak periods during the day. After the second day of monitoring, the administrator upgraded the server memory, resulting in a performance boost for the remainder of the registration period and good reviews from users.

Monitoring the performance of multiuser systems is a complex process. Many factors interact to affect the total performance of a server. These range from the size of the CPU to the efficiency of applications. Problems in one area can disguise problems in another. For example, a problem that initially shows up as high CPU utilization may actually be caused by a poorly written software application. Perfecting your monitoring skills helps you to identify the true cause of a problem and apply the proper corrective action. In this chapter you learn how to monitor the server and the network, using tools included with Windows NT Server, such as Task Manager, Performance Monitor, and Network Monitor. Projects at the end of the chapter give you hands-on experience in monitoring and diagnosing server and network problems.

AFTER READING THIS CHAPTER AND COMPLETING THE EXERCISES YOU WILL BE ABLE TO:

- UNDERSTAND THE BENEFITS OF PERFORMANCE MONITORING

- ESTABLISH SERVER PERFORMANCE BENCHMARKS

- MONITOR SERVER PERFORMANCE USING WINDOWS NT SERVER SERVICES, TASK MANAGER, AND PERFORMANCE MONITOR

- MONITOR THE NETWORK USING NETWORK MONITOR AGENT, THE SNMP SERVICE, PERFORMANCE MONITOR, AND NETWORK MONITOR

MONITORING THE SERVER

Server monitoring accomplishes several purposes. One reason to monitor is to become familiar with your server's performance so that you know how to interpret a problem. It may be difficult to diagnose a problem or to determine if there is a resource shortage unless you first know what performance is typical for your server. A second reason to monitor the server is to prevent problems before they occur and to diagnose existing problems to resolve them. Monitoring enables you to pinpoint problems and identify solutions, for example tracking disk errors and replacing a hard disk before it fails. Table 14-1 shows some typical performance areas to monitor. Each area plays a significant role in a server's response and is monitored through the tools included with NT Server.

Table 14-1   Server Activities to Monitor

Monitoring Area	Factors Causing the Problem
Server services	Hung service or one using a high percentage of CPU resources
Logged-on users	Number of users logged on and types of resources they are accessing
Software	Server resources used by software applications
Paging	Page file sizing and performance
RAM	Memory shortage or damaged memory
CPU	CPU utilization and performance
Hard disk	Disk performance, capacity, and errors
Caching	Cache allocation and performance

ESTABLISHING SERVER BENCHMARKS

The most important way to get to know your server is to use monitoring tools to establish normal server performance characteristics. This is a process that involves establishing benchmarks. **Benchmarks**, or baselines, provide a basis for comparing data collected during problem situations with data showing normal performance conditions. This creates a way to diagnose problems and identify components that need to be upgraded. Benchmarks are acquired in the following ways:

- By generating statistics about CPU, disk, memory, and I/O with no users on the system, to establish a baseline for comparison to more active periods. Keep a spreadsheet or database, and performance charts of this information.

- By using performance monitoring to establish slow, average, and peak periods. Keep records on these periods.

- By gathering performance statistics each time a new software application is installed, on slow, average, and peak periods during its use.

- By establishing benchmarks to track growth in the use of servers, such as increases in users, increases in software, and increases in the average amount of time users are on the system.

The best way to get a feel for a server's performance is to gather benchmarks and then to frequently monitor server performance after you have the benchmark data. Performance indicators can be confusing at first, so the more time you spend observing them, the better you'll understand them. For example, viewing the CPU utilization on a server the first few times does not tell you much, but viewing it over a period of two or three months, noting slow and peak periods, helps develop knowledge about how CPU demand varies for that server.

USING WINDOWS NT SERVER SERVICES

Windows NT Server automatically starts a range of system services that run in the background as the server is running and that should be monitored periodically. Many are default services provided with NT. Other services can be installed or added by the server administrator from the Windows NT Server CD-ROM or from independent software sources. Some are automatically started when the server boots, and others are started manually as needed. There are several default services that provide for messaging, logging, scheduling, server, and printer activities. If the server is having performance problems, you have the option to check the services and determine if one is stopped or possibly hung. You also have the option to stop an unused service to ease the server load. The default services are summarized in Table 14-2 and described in the following paragraphs.

Table 14-2   Windows NT Server Default Services

Service	Description
Alerter	Sends notification of alerts or problems on the server to users designated by the network administrator
AT	Schedules NT Server to run designated programs or commands at a specified time
ClipBook Server	Acts as server for the remote clipbook viewer, enabling clipbook pages to be shared
Computer Browser	Keeps a listing of computers and domain resources to be accessed
Directory Replicator	Creates a duplicate of specified directories on different computers, such as designated databases
EventLog	Enables server events to be logged for later review or diagnosis in case problems occur
Messenger	Handles messages sent for administrative purposes
Net Logon	Maintains logon services such as verifying users who are logging on to the server and synchronizing the server SAMs

14

Table 14-2 Windows NT Server Default Services (Continued)

Service	Description
Network DDE	Enables dynamic data exchange on the network for objects such as graphics
Network DDE DSDM	Enables conversion of object formats across the network
NTLM Security Support Provider	Provides security on remote procedure calls from UNIX and other systems
Remote Procedure call locator service	Locates available programs to run; used in communications with clients using remote procedure calls
Remote Procedure Call service	Provides remote procedure call services
Server	Supports shared objects, logon services, and remote procedure calls; critical to the server
Spooler	Enables print spooling
UPS	Used with a UPS to supply power to the server during power failures
Workstation	Enables workstation activities at the server

The Alerter service is used to send a notification when a problem is detected at the server, such as a failed NIC, a disk problem, or a hung service. The notification is sent to anyone designated by the server administrator, but typically is sent to those who would fix the problem, such as the Administrators and Server Operators groups. Establishing who will be notified is performed through the Server icon (discussed later in this chapter) or through Server Manager. The Alerter service requires that the Messenger and Workstation services have also been started.

The AT or scheduling service enables Administrators to run jobs at specified times. For example, the service can be used to run a database update at a given time each day. Another use is to automatically reset the NT Server's system time once each week from an Internet time server.

The ClipBook Server enables users to share graphics images, files, and other information. Each entity, such as a picture or text, is stored as a page. The images are viewed by means of the ClipBook Viewer on the server. The ClipBook Viewer can store up to 127 pages for users to share. Any page within the Viewer can be designated as a share, with share permissions. The ClipBook service requires the Network DDE service to be running as well.

Computers on a network can be viewed within Windows NT by means of the Computer Browser service. The service is used by tools such as Network Neighborhood, User Manager, and Server Manager to view computers. Any Windows 3.1, 3.11, 95 or NT computer configured for network access is a part of the Browser system. A Windows NT server is selected through the Computer Browser service to be the **master browser**, keeping the main list of logged-on computers, while the other browsers play a support role, such as **backup browsers**, which maintain a copy of the list in case the master browser is offline. There are also potential browsers that can be promoted to backup browsers, if more are needed, and nonbrowsers, which are computers that do not maintain a list. Services upon which Computer Browser depends are the Server and Workstation services.

 If a LAN Manager client is attached to the network, it will not receive a browse list from Windows NT Server, unless NT Server is configured to send the list. To configure NT Server, open the Control Panel Network icon and click the Services tab. Next, click Server and the Properties button. Check the box, Make Browser Broadcasts to LAN Manger 2.x Clients.

Another service, Directory Replicator, copies files and directories from one server to another server or workstation (refer to Chapter 9, "Managing Server Folders, Permissions, and Software Installation"). It is set up to start automatically when the Directory Replicator service is installed and configured to be used. Directory Replicator relies on the Server and Workstation services.

EventLog is a monitoring service that is of critical importance to network administrators. Server events, such as logon activity and hardware problems, are tracked and recorded in logs, which run from the EventLog service. The server administrator uses these logs to trace and solve problems.

The Messenger service provides communications to deliver messages, such as those sent by Alerter. Also, this service is linked to e-mail and other applications that use messaging, including print and fax service messages. Messaging requires that the Workstation service be working as well. Another service, Net Logon, interacts with the SAM to verify each account and its password when a user logs on. Net Logon is used by each domain controller and also has responsibility for synchronizing the domain SAM databases. Like many other services, Net Logon requires that the Server and Workstation services have been started.

The Network DDE and DSDM services provide capabilities to handle data exchange over the network between two programs. For example, data used by one program may be in a spreadsheet format and linked for use by another that is using Microsoft Access. Or a graphics object in the ClipBook server can be brought into Microsoft Word on a client workstation. The Network DDE service does not work unless Network DDE DSDM is already started.

NTLM and the associated remote procedure call services enable an application on a remote computer to access functions on NT Server, such as file transfer or messaging capabilities. The Remote Procedure Call service makes this option possible. The Locator service enables client applications to find functions they can access. And the NTLM Security Support Provider enables access security for the functions.

The Server service is critical to enabling shared services on NT Server, such as shared printers, directories, and network services. Without the Server service, users cannot access and use the server as a server. Another critical service is the Spooler, which enables printer services at the server, as discussed in Chapter 10, "Printer Management."

14

The UPS service is used when an uninterruptible power supply (UPS) is connected to the server to protect it from power failures. Many UPS systems have the ability to communicate with the server, for instance to warn it that there is a power failure. To make communications possible, the UPS service also needs the Messenger service to be active (refer to Chapter 6, "Configuring Server Storage, Backup, and Performance Options").

Last, the Workstation service provides network connectivity for clients. It acts as the user-mode interface to the kernel mode when a request is issued over the network for a particular action at the server, such as obtaining a file from a shared folder.

MONITORING SERVER SERVICES

The Windows NT services are viewed and controlled from either Server Manager or the Services icon in the Control Panel. If you use Server Manager, start it from the Administrative Tools (Common) menu. After Server Manager opens, click the Computer menu and then Services. Alternately, you can double-click the Control Panel Services icon, which resembles two gears meshed together. The Services dialog box opens, as shown in Figure 14-1. Services are displayed in a list box containing three columns. The leftmost column shows services listed alphabetically. The Status column indicates the condition of the service as follows:

- *Started* shows that the service is running.

- *Paused* means that the service is started, but is on hold to the users.

- A blank means that the service is stopped or has not been started.

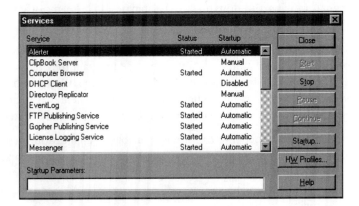

Figure 14-1   Monitoring services

The Startup column shows how a service is started. Most services are started automatically when the server is booted. Some services are started manually because they may not be needed until a given time. In Figure 14-1, the Directory Replicator service is not currently running and is set to start manually when needed by the administrator. The DHCP Client service is disabled.

The buttons on the right of the screen are used to manage the services. For example, the Start button is used to manually start a service, such as Directory Replicator. The button is not active in Figure 14-1 because the highlighted service, Alerter, is already started. The Stop button is used to stop a service. Use Stop carefully, because some services are linked to other ones. Stopping one service will stop the others that depend on it. For instance, stopping the Messenger service affects the Alerter. The system gives the administrator a warning when other services are affected by stopping a particular service. (Try stopping a service in Hands-on Project 14-1.)

 Many services are linked to the Server service, along with logged-on users. If it is necessary to stop the Server service, for instance to diagnose a problem, give the users advance warning or stop it after work hours.

The Pause button takes services offline to be used only by Administrators or Server Operators. For example, if the ClipBook Server is sending error messages to users, you can pause the service so that it is only available to the Administrator for testing until the problem is resolved. A paused service is restarted by highlighting the service and clicking Continue. As you have learned in earlier chapters, the Startup button is used to change how a service is started. For instance, if you want to make Alerter a manually started process, click Startup, select Manual, and click OK. The last button, HW Profiles, is used to enable or disable a service for a given hardware unit. The bottom of the screen has a box to enter special startup parameters. For example, if there is a service that only runs from a CD-ROM in drive E, then you would enter the drive letter and path in the box.

Occasionally, a service, such as the Spooler service, does not start properly when the server is booted, or hangs while the server is running. The Services icon provides a way to monitor this situation. For example, suppose that a message at the server console says that the Server service is suspended because of a problem, and you cannot log on to the server from the workstation in your office. When you log on to the console as Administrator, the logon process takes four minutes, and when you click the Printers folder for a shared printer, the folder hangs for a minute and aborts with a message that the Server service is suspended. One way to address the problem is to double-click the Services icon to view the currently started services and to check the Server service to see if it is stopped or paused. If it is stopped, you can start it by clicking the Server service and the Start button.

MONITORING LOGGED-ON USERS AND SERVER ACCESS INFORMATION

Network administrators frequently monitor the number of users logged on to the system, for several reasons. One is to develop an indication of how many users are typically logged on at given points in time, which provides the administrator with information about normal user load. Also, if a problem develops and the server needs to be shut down, the administrator can determine when the shutdown will have the least impact. Another reason is to be aware of security or misuse problems, such as an account that is in use when the owner is not at his or her workstation. On large networks, it is a good idea to frequently check the number of users on a server. An especially popular server may need to be upgraded as more users log on for extended periods.

To view logged-on users, start Server Manager from the Administrative Tools (Common) menu, click the Computer menu, and click Properties. Alternately, you can go to the Control Panel and double-click the Server icon to view information about connections to the server. The Server dialog box shows the number of active sessions, as in Figure 14-2. The dialog box also shows the number of open files, file locks, and named pipes. The open file information shows the number of files in use. A **file lock** means that no one else can access a specified file, and **named pipes** are open communication links.

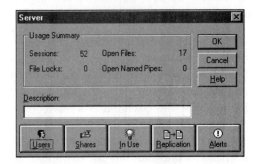

Figure 14-2   Viewing logged-on users

The Description box is for an optional description of the server computer, such as the name, brand, or location. The buttons at the bottom of the screen are used to view information about connections in use or to set service parameters. For example, when you click Users, a list appears of all users connected to the server, along with a list of resources in use by each user, such as shared folders and printers (try viewing users and resources in Hands-on Project 14-2). The Users button also enables you to disconnect one or more users. You might disconnect a user when his or her logon session fails to close even after the user has logged off, or to perform an emergency server shutdown. The Shares button enables you to view the same information, but by resource instead of by user. For example, you can view users who are accessing a shared folder or printer. You can also disconnect a user from this button. Each resource is shown with an icon; for example a shared folder is represented as a folder inside a hand. The contents of drive C are shown to be shared from the root by the dollar sign. A connector icon represents a named pipe, such as IPC, which is a network communications pipe. A shared printer is shown with a printer icon.

The In Use button provides information about all resources, such as printers, that are currently being used. The Replication button enables the network administrator to designate information about replication services, as explained in Chapter 9. The Alerts button is used to specify which users should receive warning messages about problems at the server, also as shown in Chapter 9. For example, as server administrator you will add your account name to receive alerts (Figure 14-3).

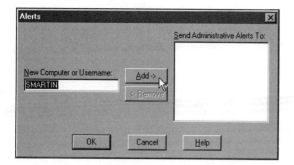

Figure 14-3   Adding your name to receive alerts

Monitoring Applications with Task Manager

Not all software applications are designed equally. Some have an extremely inefficient design that places unnecessary demands on the server. For example, an application may generate excessive network traffic by transporting more data than it needs between the server and the client. Another source of demand is reports that run against a database, requiring the system to read all of the records in the database instead of the limited few needed for the report. An inefficient program is often signaled by high CPU, memory, or disk utilization each time the program runs.

 Some applications advertised to be client/server-based are not truly designed according to these standards and can be inefficient when using server and network resources. For example, client/server design is intended to efficiently spread the workload between server and clients, but some place excessive work on the server or use poor database design at the server. Check on actual performance before you buy.

You can use Task Manager to view applications running on the server by pressing Ctrl-Alt-Del while logged on as Administrator. After you press this key combination, the following options appear:

- *Lock Workstation* to secure the file server console for access
- *Change Password* to change the Administrator account password
- *Logoff* to exit the Administrator account
- *Task Manager* to view information about tasks and services currently running
- *Shutdown* to shut down the server
- *Cancel* to return to the NT Server desktop

Click the Task Manager button, which displays a dialog box with three tabs: Applications, Processes, and Performance. The Applications tab, shown in Figure 14-4, displays all of the software applications running from the server console, including 16-bit applications. Any of the applications can be stopped by highlighting it and pressing the End Task button. If an application is hung (no longer responding to user input), you can press End Task to release more resources for the server. The Switch To button brings the highlighted application to the front so that you can work in it. New Task enables you to start another application at the console using the Run option, which is the same option that you would access from the Start button. The status bar at the bottom of the screen shows information about the total number of processes, the CPU usage, and minimum/maximum available memory. For example, in Figure 14-4, there are 24 total processes running, using 100% of the CPU and 39232K out of 97304K total memory. As used in the context of Task Manager, a **process** is one or more executable programs that run from a main program. For example, when you click Help from the Microsoft Word menu bar, the WINHLP32.EXE process runs along with WINWORD.EXE.

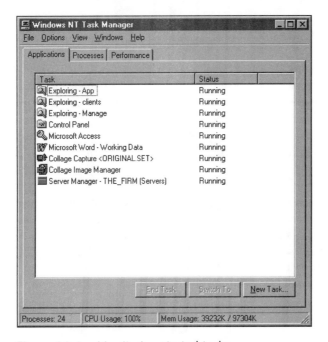

Figure 14-4   Monitoring started tasks

As you will learn as you monitor a server, CPU utilization at 100% is not cause for immediate concern, because it may simply mean that a process is using the CPU very efficiently. However, if utilization frequently stays at 100% for several minutes instead of several seconds, this is cause for concern and may indicate a software or hardware problem.

If you right-click a task, or highlight a task and right-click the heading in the Task or Status column, several options appear in a shortcut menu, as follows:

- *Switch To* takes you into the highlighted program.

- *Bring to Front* maximizes and brings to the front the highlighted program, but leaves you in Task Manager.

- *Minimize* causes the program to be minimized.

- *Maximize* causes the program to be maximized but leaves you in Task Manager.

- *End Task* stops the highlighted program.

- *Go To Process* takes you to the Processes tab and highlights the process associated with the program.

The Processes tab lists the processes being used by all running applications. If you need to stop a process, you can stop it from this screen by highlighting it and clicking End Process. Also, the Processes tab shows information about each started process, as summarized in Table 14-3.

Table 14-3   Task Manager Information on Processes

Process Information	Description
Image Name	The process name, such as WINWORD.EXE for Microsoft Word
PID	The process identifier (PID), which is an identification number assigned to the process so the operating system can track information on it
CPU	The percentage of the CPU resources used by the process
CPU Time	The amount of CPU time used by that process from the time the process started
Mem Usage	The amount of memory the process is using

For example, if you suspect that a program is causing a bottleneck at the CPU, go to the Applications tab, right-click the program, and click Go To Process, which identifies its process on the Processes tab. Next look in the CPU and CPU Time columns to see how much of the CPU that program's process is using. Also, check the figure in the Mem Usage column to see if it is causing a memory bottleneck. If the program is using too many resources, such as 90% of the CPU, consider stopping it and discontinuing its use until you know the source of the problem.

Also, you can increase the priority of one or more processes in the list so that the process has more CPU priority than the level that is set as its default. Suppose, for example, that you want to increase the priority for Microsoft Word, which is process WINWORD.EXE. To start, right-click WINWORD.EXE, displaying a shortcut menu in which you can end the process or reset the priority. Click Set Priority to reset the priority (Figure 14-5).

Normally, the priority at which a process runs is set in the program code of the application, which is called the **base priority class**. If the base priority class is not set by the program, a normal (average) priority is set by the Windows NT Server operating system. The server administrator always has the option to set a different base priority. As shown in Figure 14-5, the administrator can change the priority to any of four options: Low, Normal, High, and Realtime. A Low priority means that if a process is waiting in a queue, such as for processor time, disk access, or memory access, all processes with a higher priority will go first. This might be equated to waiting in line for a movie. Assume that you have no ticket, but that all ten other people in line have a ticket or a free pass. The movie house manager comes out and announces that the ticket holders can come in first, then the holders of a free pass, and finally those who don't have a ticket. Even if you are first in line, you will be the last in because you have the lowest priority. Like the free pass holder, if a process has a normal priority, it will get to use the resource before a low-priority process and after a high-priority process. Those processes with a High priority are like the ticket holders, because they go first. Also, a Realtime priority always goes first, no matter what. This might be like having the star of the movie show up and the manager decide to shut down entrance into the theater until the star is seated. (Try Hands-on Project 14-3 to practice resetting a priority and stopping a task.)

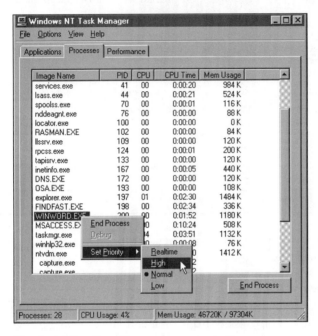

Figure 14-5 Resetting a process priority

 Use the Realtime priority with great caution. If it is assigned to a process, that process may completely take over the server, preventing work by any other processes. A situation in which you might want to assign a Realtime priority is one in which you detect a disk drive that is about to fail and you want to give all resources over to the backup process so that you can back up files before the disk fails.

The Performance tab shows vital CPU and memory performance information through bar charts, line graphs, and performance statistics (Figure 14-6).

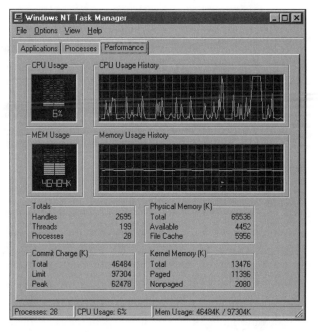

Figure 14-6   Task Manager performance information

The CPU Usage and MEM Usage bars show the current use of CPU and memory. To the right of each bar is a graph showing the immediate history statistics. (Practice using this tab in Hands-on Project 14-4.) The bottom of the Performance tab shows more detailed statistics, for example for **handles** and **threads**, which are described in Table 14-4.

Table 14-4   Task Manager Performance Statistics

Statistic	Description
Handles	The number of objects in use by all processes, such as open files
Threads	The number of code blocks in use; one program or process may be running one or more code blocks at a time
Processes	The number of processes that are active or sitting idle
Physical Memory Total	The amount of RAM installed in the computer
Physical Memory Available	The amount of RAM available to be used
Physical Memory File Cache	The amount of RAM used for file caching
Commit Charge Total	The size of virtual memory allocated on disk
Commit Charge Limit	The maximum virtual (disk) memory that can be allocated
Commit Charge Peak	The maximum virtual memory that has been used during the current Task Manager monitoring session
Kernel Memory Total	The amount of memory used by the operating system
Kernel Memory Paged	The amount of virtual memory used by the operating system
Kernel Memory Nonpaged	The amount of RAM used by the operating system

14

Notice that in Figure 14-6 the Physical Memory Total is 65536 KB, but the Commit Charge Total is only 46484 KB, which is the setting for the initial page size. Also, notice that the Commit Charge Peak for this monitoring session is 62478 KB, which shows that the initial page size has already been exceeded. As discussed in Chapter 6, the initial page file size should be equal to the amount of installed RAM plus 12 MB. Thus, the performance statistics show that the page file size is set too low at 46484 KB because it should be about 77000 KB, which means that the virtual memory needs to be tuned for this server. The page file is tuned by opening the Control Panel System icon, clicking the Performance tab, and then the Change button.

USING PERFORMANCE MONITOR

The most vital tool used to detect and fix problems on a Windows NT computer is **Performance Monitor (PM)**. Performance Monitor is like a window into the inner workings of just about every aspect of the server, such as hard disks, memory, the processor, disk caching, started processes, or the paging file. For example, you might monitor memory and paging to determine if you have fully tuned the paging file for satisfactory performance, and to determine if you have adequate RAM for the server load.

PM is opened from the Administrative Tools (Common) menu. Click Performance Monitor to view an inactive screen, as shown in Figure 14-7. The screen is in the chart mode, showing a grid that you use for graphing activities on the server. To begin tracking, you must select one or more objects to monitor. A Performance Monitor object may be memory, the processor, or another part of the computer. Table 14-5 lists the main objects that can be monitored. Other objects are added as you add server services. For example, when you install IIS, objects are added to monitor Internet Information Services, the HTTP Service, and FTP Server activity.

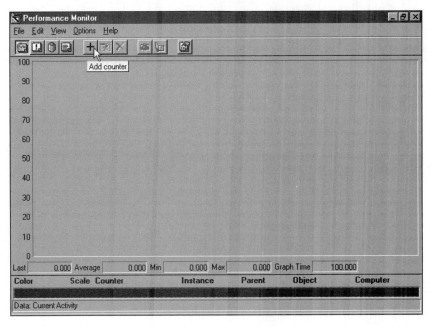

Figure 14-7   Performance Monitor

Table 14-5   Performance Monitor Objects

Object	Description
Browser	Tracks the activity of the browser service that enables Network Neighborhood to communicate and exchange information with other computers on the network
Cache	Supplies performance information on data caching for the hard disks
LogicalDisk	Tracks information about one or more physical disks that are linked as a single logical disk (one assigned drive letter for multiple disks), such as queue length for disk requests and data transfer speeds
Memory	Provides information about RAM use, such as percent of memory in use, input and output activity, and peak usage
Objects	Tracks the activities of special objects, such as started processes and started threads
Paging File	Supplies data on page file performance, such as current usage and peak usage
PhysicalDisk	Provides data on each hard disk drive, such as the length of queues to access a disk and the data access speeds
Process	Supplies performance data on a specific process that is running
Processor	Tracks demands on the processor, such as the percentage in use, the number of requests from hardware components, and the percentage in use by the operating system
Redirector	Monitors network connection information, such as folder access requests from other computers on the network and information about workstations presently connected
Server	Tracks information about the Server service, such as number of bytes sent out and received, logon errors, and logged-off sessions
System	Monitors file access, system calls, operating system activities, and the percentage of the processor used by the system
Thread	Tracks a specific thread running within a process, such as the processor time used by the thread

14

For each object, there are one or more counters that can be monitored. A **counter** is an indicator of a quantity associated with the object that can be measured in some unit, such as percentage, rate per second, or peak value, depending on what is appropriate to the object. For example, the % Processor time counter for the Processor object measures the portion of the processor that is in use by non-idle processes. Current Disk Queue Length is an example of a counter for the PhysicalDisk object that measures the number of disk read or write requests in the queue that are waiting to be processed. The processor is one of the common objects to monitor when a workstation or server is slow. Table 14-6 gives examples of counters for the Processor object.

Monitoring Page File and Memory Performance

To monitor the server's page file performance (recall that a page file is disk space reserved for use when memory requirements exceed the available RAM), click the Add counter (plus sign) button, as shown in Figure 14-7. This brings up the Add to Chart dialog box, in which you can select objects to monitor. At the top of the box, you can select the network computer you want to monitor by clicking the button with three dots and selecting the UNC for that computer, such as \\Lawyer (the \\ indicates a workstation or server) from the list. The server from which you start Performance Monitor is already inserted as the default computer. This is a powerful option for a server administrator, because it means that you can monitor other network servers or workstations from one place. Many network administrators monitor a server from PM on their Windows NT workstation.

Table 14-6   Sample Processor Counters in Performance Monitor

Counter	Description
% DPC time	Processor time used for deferred procedure calls, for example for hardware devices
% Interrupt time	Time spent on hardware interrupts by the CPU
% Privileged time	Time spent by the CPU for system activities in privileged mode, which is used for the operating system
% Processor time	Time the CPU is busy on all non-idle activities
% User time	Time spent by the CPU in user mode running software applications and system programs
Interrupts/sec	Number of device interrupts per second

After selecting the computer to monitor in the Computer: box, go to the Object: list box and click the list arrow to select an object to monitor, such as Memory as shown in Figure 14-8 to monitor paging. For the counter, select Pages Input/sec. This counter measures the number of virtual memory pages read back into memory per second. After selecting the counter, click the Add button to start monitoring. While still in the Add to Chart dialog box, select to monitor the Memory object and the Pages Output/sec counter, which shows the number of pages written to the paging file each second. Also, select to monitor the % Usage and % Usage Peak counters for the Paging File object, to show the amount in use and the peak usage. When you finish, click Done to view a graph of the four objects you are monitoring.

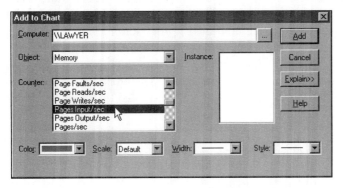

Figure 14-8   Selecting an object and its counter

Gather data for a short time before checking on the progress of Performance Monitor. Each object and counter combination is charted using a different color so that one can be separated from the other. For instance, % Usage is red, % Usage Peak is green, Pages Input/sec is blue, and Pages Output/sec is yellow. As shown in Figure 14-9 (not shown in color), the counters are displayed at the bottom of the screen with a key to indicate the graphing color for each one. The status bar just above the counters shows the following:

- *Last* is the current value of the monitored activity.

- *Average* is the average value of the monitored activity for the elapsed time.

- *Min* is the minimum value of the activity over the elapsed time.

- *Max* is the maximum value of the activity over the elapsed time.

- *Graph Time* is the amount of time to complete a full graph of the activity.

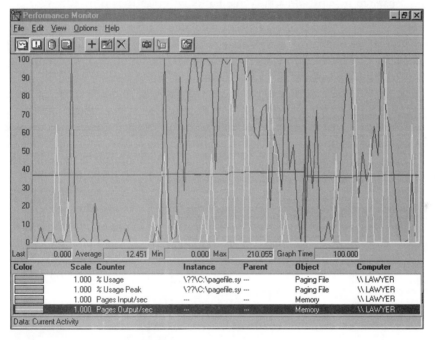

Figure 14-9   Monitoring page file performance

In Figure 14-9, the charting shows that paging looks good. The % Usage and the % Usage Peak are not much over 40% at any point in time. But, the extreme peaks for the Pages Input/sec and Pages Output/sec are a concern. To follow up in this situation you might close the two paging-related counters, Pages Input/sec and Pages Output/sec by highlighting each, one at a time, in the bottom of the screen, then clicking the Close button (the x) in the toolbar.

In this example, you would further monitor the two counters for the Paging File object: % Usage and % Usage Peak. You can save these settings and start and stop monitoring at different times. To save the settings, click the File menu, Save Chart Settings, and specify the file in which to save the settings. The next time you start Performance Monitor, you would click the File menu, Open, and open that file.

Also, you can keep a log of the information charted for an object by clicking the View menu and Log. For example, to log data for memory, click the plus button, click the Memory object, Add, and then Done. Highlight the Memory object on the screen, click the Options menu and Log. In the Log Options dialog box, enter a filename and click the Start Log button, and then Save. Log the data for the desired period of time, then click the Options menu again, click Log, and click the Stop Log button. You can add to the log again at other times, to collect cumulative data, by opening that log and starting to log information on the same object. Data from the log can be viewed through the report feature of Performance Monitor, or a log can be exported by first opening it and then clicking the File menu and Export Log. The file formats are designed to be used with a spreadsheet or database. A TSV file contains columns separated by tabs, and a CSV file has columns separated by commas.

Another option is to gather data in a report format on the screen. For example, to monitor the Paging File object counters % Usage and % Usage Peak, click the View menu and Report. Next, click the Options menu and click Data From, click Current Activity (or if you want to display a report from a log file instead, you can click Log File and specify the file). Click the Add counter button and select the objects and counters you want to view, clicking Add after each selection, such as Paging File as the object and % Usage and % Usage Peak as the counters. Click Done to begin gathering information collected at a specified interval (Figure 14-10). If you want to change the interval, click the Options menu, Report, and set the interval in seconds. A report also can be exported to a TSV or CSV file by clicking the File menu and Export Report.

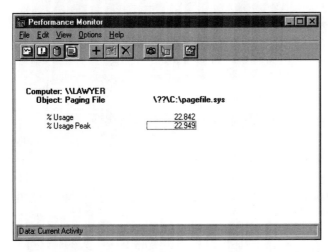

Figure 14-10 Using the Performance Monitor report mode

Assume that you have periodically monitored the Paging File counters % Usage and % Usage Peak over a period of a few days and found that the % Usage is almost always over 90% and that the % Usage Peak goes up to 100%. In addition you monitor the Memory counter Page Faults/sec and continue checking the results. A hard page fault occurs when a program does not have enough physical memory to execute a given function. If there are frequently over five hard page faults per second, this is another strong indication of a memory bottleneck. In this situation, the combination of statistics indicates the need to add memory to the server. Chapter 16, "Troubleshooting," contains additional examples of how to monitor for CPU, hard disk, and other problems.

Another situation resulting in a page fault occurs when two processes share the same 4 MB block of paged data. One process may read the block from disk into memory, just before the other process is about to do the same. The second process is unable to access the paged block, because it is in use. A page fault also results when there is not enough RAM to be shared by virtual memory and caching. All of these page fault problems are monitored by using Memory as the object and Page Faults/sec as the counter. One way to reduce page faults and improve performance is to increase RAM. This is especially important if database systems such as Microsoft SQL Server or Oracle are installed, because they are designed to share memory blocks when there is limited RAM.

A page fault in a kernel (operating system) process may occur if a reference to a page location is lost or corrupted. If this happens, the NT system may crash with the message: STOP 0x0000000A IRQL_NOT_LESS_OR_EQUAL. The error may be caused by a small power fluctuation, a damaged memory module, or a corrupted operating system file. Try rebooting to determine if the error recurs. If it does not, it was most likely caused by a transient situation, such as a power fluctuation. If it persists, test the computer's memory and replace damaged memory modules, or contact a Microsoft technician for information on how to read a crash dump to determine which process is linked to the crash.

Setting an Alert

Another feature of PM is the ability to set alerts to warn you of a problem when it occurs. For example, you may want Windows NT to send you an alert each time that the CPU is at 100% utilization. To set an alert, first open the Control Panel Server icon and click the Alerts button, making sure that your account is on the list of users to receive alerts. In Performance Monitor, click the View menu and Alert. Next click the Add counter button, select Processor as the object, and % Processor Time as the counter. Under Alert If, click Over, and enter 99. Click Add and then Done in the Add to Alert dialog box (Figure 14-11). (Try Hands-on Project 14-5 to practice setting an alert.)

Monitoring the Processor

Besides monitoring the processor in Task Manager, you also can use Performance Monitor, for diagnosing processor overload. There are three important components to studying the processor load:

- The percentage of time the processor is in use

- The length of the queue containing processes waiting to run

- The frequency of interrupt requests from hardware

Performance Monitor has processor counters to measure each type of processor load.

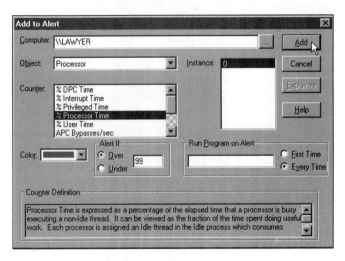

Figure 14-11 Setting an alert

Start monitoring the processor load by selecting Processor as the object and % Processor time as the counter. This counter measures how much the processor is being used at the present time. It is normal for processor use to fluctuate between 50% and 100%. If processor use constantly remains at a high percentage, such as between 90% and 100%, this is an indication that there is a problem.

When processor use is high, it is time to collect additional data by monitoring the number of processes waiting in line for their turn on the processor. Use the Processor Queue Length counter for the System object to determine if there is a queue of waiting processes. If the processor use is often at 100%, but there are no processes waiting in the queue, the processor is handling the load. If four or five processes are always in line, this suggests that it is time to consider a faster processor.

Before concluding that you need to purchase a new processor, make sure that the processor load is not due to a malfunctioning hardware component, such as a NIC or disk adapter. When you monitor the processor load, add two additional counters, %Interrupt Time and Interrupts/Sec, for the Processor object. A high frequency of interrupts per second, over 1000 for example, is an indication that there is a problem with a hardware component. Also, frequently high %Interrupt Time, over 80% for example, is another indication of a hardware problem. These counters do not locate the component, but they do show that the overload problem is unlikely to be solved by a new processor. If you encounter a high level of hardware interrupts, check the system log (refer to Chapter 16) for information about hardware problems. (Practice monitoring the processor in Hands-on Project 14-6.)

Collect benchmarks on the level of hardware interrupts so as to have comparative data for diagnosing problems later.

Monitoring Disk Performance

You can use PM to monitor disk activity by selecting LogicalDisk or PhysicalDisk as the object to monitor. Use LogicalDisk to observe activity on a set of disks, such as a striped set. Use PhysicalDisk if you want to monitor a specific disk, such as disk 0 in a set of five disks. Watch at least two counters, % Disk Time and Current Disk Queue Length. The first counter shows the amount of activity on a disk, and the second shows the number of waiting requests to access the disk. If one disk frequently is busy at the 100% level, information on the number of waiting requests helps to diagnose the problem. If there are zero or one requests normally in the queue, the disk load is acceptable. If the queue generally has two or more requests, it is time to move some files from the overloaded disk to one less busy.

The best way to determine which files to move is to understand which applications and data are on the server and how they are used. If all of the server disks are constantly busy, it may be necessary to purchase disks with more spindles or to add additional data paths. A **spindle** is a rod attached to the center of a hard disk platter and to a motor used to rotate the rod and disk.

Individual drives typically have one spindle; RAID drives have multiple spindles within the disk array. A RAID array is a good investment for growing servers because of the combined performance and redundancy features.

Another source of disk activity is the page file. Monitor the Memory counter Pages/sec and the PhysicalDisk counter % Disk Time simultaneously. This shows the paging activity in relationship to the activity on the disk. Sometimes the disk data transfer rate also is a problem, which is measured by the PhysicalDisk counter Disk Bytes/sec. Use all three counters to track page file activity and how fast the page file is written to disk. This gives you a good idea of the page file activity and the disk speed at the same time, particularly since the page file is a very large file. Also, experiment with the disk transfer rate by copying a large file from floppy drive A: to the hard disk you are monitoring. Another option is to monitor the transfer rate when a large number of records are written to a database on the disk. If page file activity is a problem, consider increasing RAM or implementing a page file on more than one disk. If paging activity is low, but the transfer rate is slow when handling large files, such as the page file or a database file, consider upgrading to faster disks.

14

Summary of Significant PM Objects and Counters

The following is a list of some important PM objects and associated counters for server monitoring that are likely to appear on the certification exam. They are listed by object, then counter.

- *LogicalDisk: Current Disk Queue Length.* Indicates how many system requests are waiting for disk access. If the queue length is greater than two for any logical drive, consider redistributing the load across multiple logical disks, or if this is not possible, upgrading the disk subsystem. Also check the corresponding PhysicalDisk counters.

- *LogicalDisk: % Disk Time.* Measures the percentage of time that a disk is busy with read or write requests. If this level is sustained at 80% or greater, redistribute files to spread the load across multiple logical drives. Also check the corresponding PhysicalDisk counter.

- *LogicalDisk: Disk Bytes/sec.* Measures the average number of bytes transferred between memory and disk during Read and Write operations. If the value is at or near 4 KB, this might mean excessive paging activity on that drive. A larger number indicates more efficient transfers than a smaller one, so watch for declines from the baseline as well.

- *Memory: Available Bytes.* Measures the bytes of memory available for use on the system. Microsoft recommends that this value be 4096 KB or higher. If values stay at or below this, your system will benefit from additional RAM. This figure is also available on the Task Manager Performance tab.

- *Memory: Cache Faults/sec.* Measures the number of times the page file is called from disk or relocated in memory. Higher values indicate potential performance problems. (Higher values will be about double or more than that of baseline values on a lightly loaded system.) Remedy by adding more memory; in this case, adding L2 cache is better than adding main RAM.

- *Memory: Page Faults/sec.* Returns a count of the average number of page faults per second for the current processor. Page faults occur whenever memory pages must be called from disk, which explains how memory overload can manifest as excessive disk activity. If the value is more than double that in a light-load baseline, consider adding more RAM.

- *Memory: Pages/sec.* Tracks the number of pages written to or read from disk by Virtual Memory Manager plus paging traffic for the system cache. If this value is more than double the light-load baseline, it indicates a need for additional RAM.

- *PhysicalDisk: Current Disk Queue Length.* Tracks activity per hard disk, but provides much of the same kind of information that the logical disk counters do. However, the problem threshold for physical disks is different than for logical ones. For physical disks, the threshold is between 1.5 and 2 times the number of spindles on the hard drive. For ordinary drives, this is the same as for logical disks. But for RAID arrays (which Windows NT treats as a single drive), the number is equal to 1.5 to 2 times the number of drives in the array.

- *PhysicalDisk: % Disk Time.* Measures the percentage of time that a hard drive is kept busy handling read or write requests. The sustained average should not exceed 80%, but even if sustained averages are high, this value is not worrisome unless the corresponding queue length numbers are in the danger zone as well.

- *PhysicalDisk: Disk Bytes/sec.* Measures the average number of bytes transferred by read or write requests between the drive and memory. Here, smaller values are more worrisome than larger ones, because they can indicate inefficient use of drives and drive space. If a small value is caused by inefficient applications, try increasing file sizes. If it's caused by paging activity, an increase in RAM or cache memory is a good idea.

- *Processor: % Processor Time.* Measures the percentage of time since PM started during which the CPU is busy handling non-idle threads. Sustained values of 80% or higher indicate a heavily loaded machine; consistent readings of 95% or higher indicate a machine that needs to have its load reduced, or its capabilities increased (with a new machine, a motherboard upgrade, or a new CPU).

- *Processor: Interrupts/sec.* Measures the average number of times per second that the CPU is interrupted by devices requesting immediate processing. Network traffic and system clock activity establish a kind of background count against which this number should be compared. Problem levels occur when a malfunctioning device begins to generate spurious interrupts, or when excessive network traffic overwhelms a network adapter. In both cases, this will usually create a count that's five times or more greater than a lightly-loaded baseline situation.

- *System: Processor Queue Length.* Measures the number of execution threads waiting for access to a CPU. If this value increases to more than double the number of CPUs present on a machine, it indicates a need to distribute this machine's load across other machines, or the need to increase its capabilities, usually by adding additional CPU speed (where possible) or by upgrading the machine or the motherboard.

Monitoring the Network with Microsoft Tools

14

In addition to monitoring the server itself, you can also monitor the network with several software-based monitoring tools available either in the NT operating system or from Microsoft, such as the following:

- Network Monitor Agent
- SNMP Service
- Performance Monitor
- Network Monitor

Network Monitor Agent

Network Monitor Agent is a service that can be installed on a network computer running Windows NT Workstation, Windows NT Server, or Windows 95. Once installed, it enables a computer to collect statistics about network performance, such as the number of packets sent and received at that workstation. The computer running Network Monitor Agent gathers the information through its NIC. With Network Monitor Agent loaded, the NIC gathers information about NetBEUI and NWLink (IPX/SPX) traffic that passes through it. A workstation or server running Microsoft analysis software, such as Performance Monitor or Network Monitor, can connect to the computer running Network Monitor Agent and use that computer's NIC to capture data for examination. Table 14-7 shows the type of information that can be captured by the Network Monitor Agent for use by Performance Monitor.

Table 14-7   Information Collected Through Network Monitor Agent

Network Object Being Monitored	Information Collected
NetBEUI	Data on NetBEUI communications, such as communications errors, bytes sent, and data packets sent
NetBEUI Resource	Data on resources used, such as data about the storage areas (buffers) used by a NIC transmitting NetBEUI data packets
Network Interface	Data that travels through the workstation or server NIC, such as the number of bytes transmitted and received, number of packets sent, and packet transmission and receipt errors
Network Segment	Data on the network segment to which the workstation or server is attached, such as broadcast and network utilization data
NWLink IPX	Data on IPX communications sent from a Novell NetWare server or workstation, or from an IPX-enabled print server
NWLink NetBIOS	Data on NetBIOS communications, such as bytes sent, packet transmissions, and communications errors
NWLink SPX	Data on SPX communications sent from a Novell NetWare server or workstation

THE SNMP SERVICE

A computer running Windows NT Server or Workstation can be turned into an SNMP network data gathering agent by loading the SNMP service at that computer. The **Simple Network Management Protocol (SNMP)** is a protocol that enables computers and network equipment to gather standardized data about network performance, and it is part of the TCP/IP suite of protocols. With the SNMP service loaded, a computer can communicate with an SNMP-based network management station that obtains and distills data about network performance. Microsoft's SNMP service provides support for Management Information Base (MIB) information gathering. **Management Information Base (MIB)** is a database of network performance information that is stored on a network agent that gathers information for a network management station.

Although SNMP includes network monitoring for TCP/IP and IPX/SPX traffic, the Microsoft SNMP service monitors TCP/IP only, because Microsoft's Network Monitor Agent is used to gather information on NWLink (IPX/SPX). Table 14-8 shows the SNMP monitoring information that is available to Performance Monitor.

Table 14-8 Information Collected Through the SNMP Service

Network Object Being Monitored	Information Collected
ICMP	Data on network communications using the Internet Control Message Protocol (ICMP), which is used by TCP/IP-based computers to share TCP/IP addressing and error information
IP	Data on Internet Protocol (IP) activity and addressing
NetBT (NBT)	Data for NetBIOS communications that are performed via TCP/IP data communications
Network Interface	TCP/IP performance data on a network interface such as a NIC, including the number of bytes or data packets sent
TCP	Data on TCP activity, including transmission or connectivity errors
UDP	Data on the User Datagram Protocol (UDP), which is the protocol used by network management stations and network agents for sending messages between one another

 Internet Control Message Protocol (ICMP) is a network maintenance protocol used within the Internet Protocol (IP) to assist in building information about routing network packets, including determining the shortest path to use for transmitting data. It also is used to help determine if a network station is live, to help locate network problems, and to reduce the flow of packets when the network is congested with traffic.

With the SNMP service loaded, the following can be remotely controlled by a management station:

- NT servers
- NT workstations
- WINS servers
- DHCP servers
- Internet Information Server computers

You can practice loading Network Monitor Agent and the SMNP service in Hands-on Project 14-7.

14

USING PERFORMANCE MONITOR TO MONITOR NETWORK PERFORMANCE

A second important function of Performance Monitor, besides monitoring the server performance, is to gather data about network performance with the help of servers and workstations that have Network Monitor Agent and SNMP services. The server administrator can use Performance Monitor to examine the load on the network at peak, average, and slow periods. For example, if the average range of utilization is 30% or less, then network performance is in an acceptable range. However, if the average range is 40 to 70% utilization, with frequent peaks over 90%, this may indicate a serious problem, such as a malfunctioning network component, poor network design, or the need to expand the network capability. Average utilization over 70% is a cause for immediate network troubleshooting, to locate a defective network device, for example.

To determine network load, monitor the following counters for the Network Segment object:

- *% Broadcast Frames*: Shows how much network traffic is due to broadcasts from servers, workstations, and print servers

- *% Network utilization*: Shows how much of the network bandwidth is in use

For example, a workstation or server NIC might be sending continuous broadcasts, causing high network traffic or a **broadcast storm**, which could be diagnosed by monitoring these counters. (Chapter 16 discusses more about how to diagnose a broadcast storm.) Try Hands-on Project 14-8 to practice monitoring network traffic.

If you want to view specifics about protocol traffic, you can use Performance Monitor for this purpose, too. For example, you might compare NetBEUI traffic with NWLink IPX traffic. To monitor the traffic, select NetBEUI as the object and Bytes Total/sec as the counter; then, select NWLink IPX as the object and Bytes Total/sec as the counter. You might add the object Network Segment and the counter % Network utilization to watch the full amount of network traffic at the same time. If you suspect that there is a problem with NetBEUI, NWLink, or TCP/IP traffic, you can monitor problem-reporting statistics for these protocols, such as rejected and re-sent frames, connection failures, and adapter failures.

NETWORK MONITOR

Network Monitor is included with the Windows NT Server CD-ROM and is installed from the Network icon Services tab. To run, it requires that Network Monitor Agent be installed. Network Monitor also gathers SNMP-related data when the SNMP service is installed on the server and on other workstations or network devices. Network Monitor tracks information such as the following:

- Percent network utilization

- Frames and bytes transported per second

- Network statistics

- Statistics captured during a given time period

- Transmissions per second information

- NIC statistics

- Error data

- Addresses of network nodes

Network Monitor can be customized to present many different pictures of network activity, because it displays four windows of data, and because **filters** can be set to collect specific types of information. Filters can be built on the basis of addresses, protocols, and properties. You can choose to capture data for a short or long period of time.

The steps for starting Network Monitor are as follows:

1. Click Start, Programs, Administrative Tools (Common), and Network Monitor.

2. Maximize one or both Network Monitor screens, if the display is not maximized.

3. Click the Capture menu and Start, in order to start capturing network performance data.

4. View the data capture on the screen, for % Network Utilization or Network Statistics, for example (Figure 14-12).

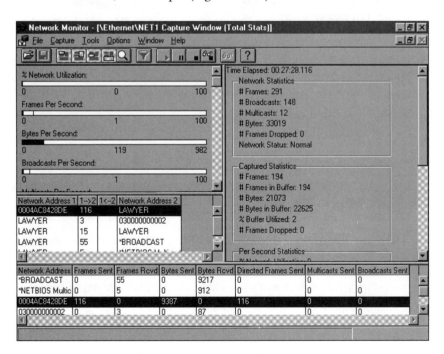

Figure 14-12 Network Monitor capturing data

5. Use the scroll bars in each of the four windows to view the information they offer.

6. When you are finished, click the Capture menu and Stop.

7. Close Network Monitor.

 Both Network Monitor and Performance Monitor create a load on the CPU of the computer on which they are running. As a server administrator, when you implement these, plan to run them only on a limited basis from a server so that time spent gathering the data does not interfere with the server's other activities. Many server and network administrators run Windows NT Workstation on their personal workstation and gather network data from there, by using the workstation's NIC or by briefly attaching to a server's NIC.

Network Monitor supports event management, which enables a server administrator to set up filters to capture a certain event or type of network activity. For example, the administrator may want to watch only activity between the server and a workstation. Another possibility is to track only TCP/IP activity related to Internet traffic into the server, or to track NWLink traffic between a NetWare server and a Windows NT Gateway for NetWare. The steps to set a filter are as follows:

1. Start Network Monitor from the Administrative Tools (Common) menu.

2. Click the Capture menu and Filter.

3. Double-click the SAP/ETYPE line to specify a protocol to monitor. Use the Disable All button to disable the protocols, then select only the protocols you want to monitor, and use the Enable button to be able to capture them.

4. Double-click Address Pairs to specify certain workstations or servers to monitor. You can use the Direction option to monitor only one-way traffic or traffic both ways between the stations you select to monitor.

5. Double-click the Pattern Matches option if you want to capture frames containing only certain types of data, reading data either from the beginning of a frame or offset a designated number of bytes from the frame's beginning. A specific hexadecimal or ASCII pattern of data can be captured for study.

6. Return to the main Network Monitor screen and click the Start Capture button to start capturing data based on the filter you constructed.

 The Network Monitor Agent enables a NIC to capture frames in the promiscuous mode for analysis by Performance Monitor and Network Monitor. The promiscuous mode makes it possible to view the contents of every frame transmitted on the network. For this reason, it is prudent to set up capture and display passwords for the Network Monitor Agent to control who can capture data and view saved capture information. Open the Control Panel Monitoring Agent icon and click the Change Password button to set up password protection.

CHAPTER SUMMARY

- Monitoring servers and related network performance is an integral part of the network administrator's work, because it is one of the best ways to identify problems as early as possible. The best way to monitor effectively is to establish benchmarks of server performance. Benchmarks give you a basis by which to compare normal circumstances to those that indicate a problem, enabling you to identify some problems before they become critical.

- One place to start monitoring is the server services. There are many services that must be running for the server to perform normally. Occasionally a service hangs or does not properly start, and so it must be stopped and restarted. Another area to monitor is the number of users on the server and how resources, such as shared printers and folders, are deployed. As you monitor users, there is an option to disconnect them in case a user session is hung and will not properly log off.

- Task Manager provides an instant look at server functions of great interest, such as programs and processes that are running, plus CPU and memory usage. It enables the server administrator to stop a hung program or to monitor how the CPU is being used while a specific software function is under way.

- Performance Monitor is one of the most versatile and widely used Windows NT Server monitoring tools. It enables the server administrator to monitor key component functions such as memory, CPU, and disk performance. Performance Monitor is able to gather statistics in several modes for immediate analysis or for analysis at a later time. With the right services loaded, Performance Monitor can be used as a network monitoring tool.

- Network monitoring also is performed through Microsoft Network Monitor. This tool can provide general network monitoring or be set up to monitor only specific activities, such as TCP/IP network traffic. With the right software, it can be equipped to view network traffic from other network servers or workstations.

14

KEY TERMS

- **backup browser** — A computer in a domain or workgroup that maintains a static list of domain/workgroup resources to provide to clients browsing the network. The backup browser periodically receives updates to the browse list from the master browser.

- **base priority class** — The initial priority assigned to a program process or thread in the program code by Windows NT when the program is started.

- **benchmark** — A measurement standard for hardware or software used to establish performance baselines under varying loads or circumstances. Also called a baseline.

- **broadcast storm** — Saturation of network bandwidth by excessive broadcasts from devices attached to that network.

- **counter** — Used by Performance Monitor, this is a measurement technique for an object, for instance measuring the processor performance by percentage in use.

- **file lock** — Flagging a file as temporarily inaccessible because it is in use. Files in use are locked to prevent two users from updating information at the same time.

- **filter** — A capacity in network monitoring software that enables a network or server administrator to view only designated protocols, network events, network nodes, or other specialized views of the network.

- **handle** — A resource such as a file, used by a program, that has its own identification so the program is able to access it.

- **Internet Control Message Protocol (ICMP)** — A protocol used to build information about the location of network workstations, servers, and other network equipment.

- **Management Information Base (MIB)** — A database of network performance information that is stored on a network agent that gathers information for a network management station.

- **master browser** — On a Microsoft network, the computer designated to keep the main list of logged-on computers.

- **named pipe** — A communication link between two processes, which may be local to the server or remote, such as between the server and a workstation.

- **Network Monitor Agent** — A utility that enables a Microsoft workstation or server NIC to gather network performance data.

- **Performance Monitor (PM)** — The Windows NT utility used to track system or application objects. For each object type there are one or more counters that can be logged for later analysis, or tracked in real time for immediate system monitoring.

- **process** — An executable program, such as Microsoft Word, that is currently running. A process may launch additional processes that are linked to it, such as a help process to view documentation or a search process to find a file.

- **Simple Network Management Protocol (SNMP)** — A protocol that enables computers and network equipment to gather standardized data about network performance and is part of the TCP/IP suite of protocols.

- **spindle** — A rod or shaft with a hard disk platter at one end and a motor at the other to rotate the platter.

- **thread** — A block of program code within a program.

REVIEW QUESTIONS

1. Your boss is considering the purchase of an additional printer for those who are using one called Admin_HP. However, first she wants to quickly determine if there is enough use of this printer to merit purchasing an additional one. Which tool would help you determine existing use of the Admin_HP printer?

   a. Control Panel Server icon   **c.** Network Monitor

   b. Task Manager   **d.** Control Panel Services icon

2. What software is necessary to enable a Windows NT server to gather data about TCP/IP traffic on a network?

   a. TPC/IP Net Watcher   **c.** IPX Agent

   b. SNMP service   **d.** SNMP Manager

3. You want to track network utilization. Which of the following tools would enable you to do this?

   a. Network Monitor   **d.** all of the above

   b. Performance Monitor   **e.** only a and b

   c. Task Manager

4. Once installed, Network Monitor Agent enables network data to be gathered
   _____ .

   a. through a NIC

   b. through a channel attachment device on the network cable

   c. by sending repeated tracer signals throughout the network

   d. through a customized net monitor device

5. Network Monitor Agent runs from which of the following?

   a. Windows NT Workstation   **d.** all of the above

   b. Windows NT Server   **e.** only a and b

   c. Windows 95

6. You have set up Windows NT Server to send a message to your account when CPU utilization is over 100%, but you are not receiving messages even though you have verified that utilization has gone this high several times. What would you try to fix this problem of alerts not being sent?

   a. open Performance Monitor because alerts are not sent unless it is running

   b. reboot the server because the kernel may be having problems

   c. stop and start the Alerter and Messenger services

   d. start Alerter Manager from the Administrative Tools (Common) menu

14

7. As server administrator, you need to disconnect a user account. What tool would you use?

   a. Control Panel System icon   **c.** User Manager for Domains

   b. Control Panel Services icon   **d.** Control Panel Server icon

8. Which of the following cannot be done to a server service?

   a. stop it   **c.** link it to another service

   b. start it   **d.** pause it

9. How many counters can be monitored at one time using Performance Monitor?

   a. up to four

   b. up to seven

   c. as many as are available to select from

   d. the number is limited by the size of the server CPU

10. You find that the server CPU utilization often is at 100%. This means you should:

    a. upgrade to a faster CPU

    b. check other measures, such as hardware interrupt requests

    c. add more RAM

    d. reboot the server to re-initialize the CPU

11. Which process priority adjustment should be used with the most caution?

    a. High   **b.** Realtime   **c.** Low   **d.** Normal

12. You want to study NetBEUI traffic on your network from Performance Monitor, but when you start it there is no NetBEUI object. What should you do?

    a. install Network Monitor Agent

    b. make sure that the server NIC has a good connection to the network cable

    c. start Network Monitor because you can view NetBEUI traffic only from there

    d. first open the Performance Monitor filter option to set up a NetBEUI filter

13. In Task Manager, Commit Charge Peak refers to _____.

    a. the amount of RAM in the computer

    b. the amount of virtual memory configured for the initial page file size

    c. the highest page file size reached during the current monitoring session

    d. the highest amount of RAM used by the kernel

14. You are using Performance Monitor to study CPU activity. Which object would you use to determine if processes are waiting in line to use the processor?

    a. Processor   **b.** LogicalDisk   **c.** Memory   **d.** System

15. You want to collect Performance Monitor data over a period of several days. Which would be the best method to use so that you can review all of the data?

a. run Performance Monitor continuously on the server

b. run Performance Monitor off and on for short periods, collecting data in a log

c. set Performance Monitor to chart activity only at night

d. run Performance Monitor in report mode, taking periodic screen shots using the clipboard to save them for later reference

16. Which NT Server service enables you to schedule the backups to start at 8 P.M.?

    a. Alerter   **b.** Directory Replicator   **c.** Server   **d.** AT

17. You are monitoring the object PhysicalDisk and find that %Disk Time is often at 100. What other measure(s) would you check for more information about disk performance?

  a. Disk Spindle Rotation   **d.** only b and c

  b. Disk Bytes/sec   **e.** all of the above

  c. Current Disk Queue Length

18. _____ enable you to compare the current server performance with performance statistics recorded in known situations, such as when traffic is normal or unusually slow.

  a. Benchmarks   **c.** User comments

  b. Test bytes   **d.** Server averaging statistics

19. Your company is interested in finding out how much traffic comes into your IIS from the Internet. How might you study this?

a. use Performance Monitor to gauge TCP/IP traffic

b. gather network utilization statistics through Network Monitor

c. set up a filter in Network Monitor

d. use Performance Monitor to compare TCP/IP traffic to NetBEUI traffic

20. When you came in this morning, the server and network were working fine. Now they are still working, but no one can log on to the server. Which of the following should you check?

a. make sure that the page file is not over its initial setting

b. check the Server service to see if it is paused or having a problem, then stop and start it, if it is

c. reboot the server immediately

d. use Performance Monitor to check the Logon Buffers object

14

21. Your organization has purchased a new program to run on the server. After it has been in use for a short period, the server seems to slow down a bit. You think that the software program is using too much of the CPU. How might you quickly monitor this?

    a. check the shared resources through the Control Panel System icon

    b. use Performance Monitor to view processor utilization

    c. look at the CPU and CPU Time data for that program's process or processes in Task Manager

    d. use Performance Monitor to check paging

22. Which of the following data is immediately available for the counter you are monitoring in Performance Monitor?

    a. average data

    b. minimum data

    c. maximum data

    d. all of the above

    e. only b and c

23. A Performance Monitor alert is set on _____.

    a. objects only

    b. objects and counters

    c. color codes

    d. none of the above

    e. only b and c

24. A named pipe is _____.

    a. a communication link between two processes

    b. an event management tool

    c. a network protocol

    d. a monitoring driver

25. Which of the following is not a default service on an NT server?

    a. Messenger   **b.** Eventlog   **c.** UPS   **d.** Task Logon

HANDS-ON PROJECTS

 PROJECT 14-1

In this activity you stop the Server service as one way to determine which other services depend on it. Try this activity on a server with no users logged on, or on one that is intended only for practice. (Note that you later learn a safer way to determine service dependencies.)

To stop the Server service and view dependencies:

1. Click **Start**, **Settings**, and **Control Panel**, and double-click the **Services** icon.

2. Scroll to the **Server** service (which supports shared objects and logon services) and click it.

3. Click **Stop**. Notice which services will also be stopped, such as Computer Browser and Net Logon (Figure 14-13).

4. Click **Cancel**, and close the Services dialog box.

Figure 14-13 Service dependencies

 PROJECT 14-2

In this activity you view the number of users logged on to a server and then the users connected to a particular share.

To check the user connections:

1. Click **Start**, **Settings**, and **Control Panel**, and double-click the **Server** icon.

2. Click the **Users** button. Notice the connected users. Click a user to see what resources that user is using. Notice the buttons to disconnect one user and all users. Click **Close**.

3. Click the **Shares** button. Click a shared resource under Sharename, and look under Connected Users for those accounts using the resource. Also, notice that you can disconnect one or more users from this screen. Click **Close**.

4. Click the **In Use** button. The Open Resources dialog box shows which resources are in use, the type of use (such as reading a folder), if any locks are set, and the path to the resource. You can disconnect a user from a resource via the Close Resource button, or you can disconnect users from all resources through the Close All Resources button (Figure 14-14). Click **Close**.

5. Click **OK** in the Server dialog box.

14

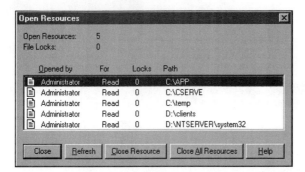

Figure 14-14 Monitoring open resources

PROJECT 14-3

In this activity you set a process's priority and stop a task. To perform this activity, open the Control Panel and then My Computer before starting.

To set the priority and stop a task:

1. Press **[Ctrl]–[Alt]–[Del]**.
2. Click the **Task Manager** button in the Windows NT Security dialog box.
3. Click the **Applications** tab, if necessary.
4. Right-click **My Computer** and click **Go To Process**. (This takes you to the Processes tab.)
5. Right-click the **explore.exe** process.
6. Click **Set Priority**, then **High**. Click **Yes** in the Task Manager Warning dialog box.
7. Click the **Applications** tab, then click **Control Panel** and then the **End Task** button.
8. Close Task Manager.

PROJECT 14-4

This activity enables you to practice monitoring CPU utilization from Task Manager.

To monitor CPU utilization:

1. Press **[Ctrl]–[Alt]–Del]**.
2. Click the **Task Manager** button in the Windows NT Security dialog box.
3. Click the **Performance** tab, and monitor CPU usage for a minute or two, checking memory usage.
4. Determine the highest peaks for both measures, then close Task Manager.

PROJECT 14-5

In this activity you set a Performance Monitor alert to warn when someone tries more than five times to access a file or folder that he or she does not have permissions to access.

To set the alert:

1. Click **Start**, **Settings**, and **Control Panel**, double-click the **Server** icon, and click **Alerts**.
2. Enter your username in the New Computer or Username: box, and click **Add**.
3. Click **OK** and **OK** again. Close the Control Panel.
4. Click **Start**, **Programs**, and **Administrative Tools (Common)**.
5. Click **Performance Monitor**, click the **View** menu, and click **Alert**.
6. Click the **Add counter** button, and select **Server** in the Object: box.
7. Select **Errors Access Permissions** in the Counter: box.
8. Click the **Over** radio button and enter **5** in the text box.
9. Click **Add**, then click **Done**, and close Performance Monitor.

PROJECT 14-6

In this activity you monitor CPU activity.

To monitor the CPU:

1. Click **Start**, **Programs**, and **Administrative Tools (Common)**.
2. Click **Performance Monitor**.
3. Near the top of the screen, click the **Add** counter button.
4. Leave the default selection in the Computer: box.
5. Click the **list arrow** in the Object: box, and select **Processor** (which is usually the default).
6. Click **% Processor Time** in the Counter: box, then click **Add**.
7. Leave Processor as the object, click **% Interrupt Time** as the counter, and click **Add**.
8. Again leave Processor as the object, click **Interrupts/sec** as the counter, and click **Add**.
9. Select **System** in the Object: box and **Processor Queue Length** as the counter.
10. Click **Add** and then **Done**.
11. View the active charting for a few minutes, and close Performance Monitor.

14

PROJECT 14-7

In this activity you practice installing Network Monitor Agent and the SNMP service on a computer running Windows NT 4.0 Server or NT 4.0 Workstation. You need access to the Windows NT CD-ROM for version 4.0. To start, log on using the Administrator or equivalent account.

To load Network Monitor Agent and the SNMP service:

1. Click **Start**, **Settings**, and **Control Panel**, and double-click the **Network** icon.
2. Click the **Services** tab and **Add**.
3. In the Network Service: scroll box, double-click **Network Monitor Agent**.
4. The Windows NT Setup dialog box requests the path of the disk from which to install the service. Enter the CD-ROM drive letter, the path **\I386**, and click Continue.
5. Back on the Network dialog box, click the **Add** button to view the list of services. This time, find the SNMP service in the Network Service: box and double-click **SNMP Service**.
6. In the Windows NT Setup dialog box, enter the CD-ROM drive letter, the path **\I386**, and click **Continue**.
7. If TCP/IP or Internet services are already loaded, the SNMP agent installation displays the Microsoft SNMP Properties dialog box. Click the **Security** tab. Click **Add** under Accepted Community Names, and enter a community name, such as topsecurity. A community name is used like a password for communications between a network agent and the network management station. Click **Add** on the Service Configuration dialog box, and then **Apply**. Click **OK**.
8. Click **Close** at the bottom of the Network dialog box.
9. A warning message notes that the changes will not be implemented until you restart the workstation. Click **Yes** to restart.

PROJECT 14-8

In this activity you see how Performance Monitor is used to monitor network utilization. You need access to a computer running Windows NT Workstation or Server that also has the Network Monitor Agent loaded (the SNMP Agent is optional). You also need access to the Administrator or an equivalent account.

To view network utilization with Performance Monitor:

1. Click **Start**, **Programs**, and **Administrative Tools (Common)**.
2. Click **Performance Monitor**.
3. Click the **Add counter** button on the empty Performance Monitor tracking screen.

4. Notice that the Add to Chart dialog box shows your computer in the Computer: text box, which means that Performance Monitor is set by default to monitor from your computer's NIC. This is where you can tell it to monitor from another agent, such as a network server or a workstation on another part of the network. Leave your computer as the default for this activity.

5. Click the **list arrow** in the Object: text box, and select **Network Segment**.

6. Click **% Broadcast Frames** in the Counter: text box. On a Microsoft-based network, this counter shows how much of the network traffic is due to servers (Windows NT) and workstations (Windows 95 and NT Workstation). Click **Add**.

7. Click **% Network utilization** in the Counter: text box. This counter enables you to view the network utilization statistic (Figure 14-15). Click **Add**.

8. Click **Done** in the Add to Chart dialog box.

9. View the network utilization compared to the broadcast frames for information on the utilization and the amount of traffic due to broadcasts from servers and workstations. Notice that each counter is graphed in a different color. Spend a few minutes viewing the information to see how it changes.

10. Close Performance Monitor when you are finished viewing the information.

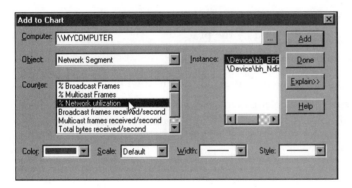

Figure 14-15 Monitoring the network with Performance Monitor

ASPEN CONSULTING: MONITORING SERVERS AND NETWORKS

This week you work with two regular clients, Greenville Paper and Tools Unlimited, helping them to set up monitoring and use monitoring to diagnose problems.

1. Greenville Paper, your client from Chapter 12, "Interoperating with Novell NetWare," has Windows NT and Novell file servers, and needs some help in monitoring the Windows NT servers. As a start, they would like to obtain some benchmarks on their

Windows NT servers. Recommend how they might establish benchmarks, and discuss why this is important.

2. Greenville Paper uses both NetBEUI and IPX/SPX on the network. They are particularly interested in monitoring how much network traffic is related to each protocol. Also, they want to gather data on how much NWLink traffic goes out via Gateway Service for NetWare. To help them, explain the following:

- The tools or services they will need to install

- The Windows NT tools that can be used for this type of monitoring

- How to set up the tools for monitoring

- How often to monitor, and under what conditions

3. Tools Unlimited has some basic questions about using Task Manager. To provide them with some quick training, you suggest that they start three applications on the server: Notepad, Performance Monitor, and My Computer. Explain how to do the following in Task Manager:

- Set the priority of Performance Monitor to Low

- Stop Notepad

- Determine which processes are used by My Computer, and the amount of CPU and memory used by the processes

- Determine the total RAM in the server

- Determine how much memory is used in total by the kernel

4. Greenville Paper has just implemented a new client/server system in which a large database is kept on one of the servers. The program files are started from the other server. Each day around 10 A.M. the database server slows down a little. They are attempting to determine if they need a faster CPU for the database server. Explain how they might do the following on the database server to help with the decision:

- Monitor the number of users

- Monitor the CPU activity

- Monitor memory and paging

- Monitor disk response

5. While you are working at Greenville Paper, their server administrator asks how to collect Performance Monitor data and store it in a file. Explain how this is done.

6. You suspect that a hard disk is failing on one of the Greenville Paper servers. What monitoring tool would you use to track the problem, and how would you set up the monitoring?

PERFORMANCE TUNING

Chapter 14, "Server and Network Monitoring," introduced basic methods for tuning a server. This chapter builds on Chapter 14 and provides even more techniques to help optimize a server for varying requirements. For example, a server can be tuned to emphasize application or file access, print services, or Internet services, depending on the demand. Windows NT Server includes many automatic tuning features, such as adjusting the number of communication buffers, shifting complex memory and disk buffers for more users, and marking large files for faster access. There are other areas, however, where the network administrator can intervene to improve performance and prevent problems, such as expanding virtual memory to help relieve contention for RAM, setting lower priorities on applications that are demanding, or modifying applications to work more efficiently. Files on a busy disk can be moved to another disk; full system logs can be cleared and saved to disk. All of these are options to try before purchasing more hardware, such as memory or disk drives.

AFTER READING THIS CHAPTER AND COMPLETING THE EXERCISES YOU WILL BE ABLE TO:

- Tune critical server elements such as software and memory
- Tune file system cache
- Identify processor bottlenecks
- Tune disk storage
- Tune network parameters
- Tune the Recycle Bin and event logs

TUNING A SERVER

Whether a server is newly installed or has been running for a period of time, it requires tuning to help it perform optimally. One of the most common reasons that a server needs to be tuned is the emergence of bottlenecks. A **bottleneck** is any impediment that slows the movement of data. Often a bottleneck is caused by only one component, such as a software application, but it can involve two or more components, making analysis of what to tune or fix more difficult. The most visible symptom of a bottleneck is an increase in a server's response time. Sometimes server administrators purchase new hardware, such as more memory, instead of determining the source of the bottleneck. Some undiagnosed bottlenecks persist even though more memory is added, or a faster CPU is purchased. In some instances, more hardware is needed, but the best approach is to first locate the source of the bottleneck and tune the server to handle the problem. If tuning does not solve the problem, then use a different solution, such as purchasing more hardware.

There are many places to look for bottlenecks and other performance problems. These include the following:

- Software
- Memory
- Paging
- Cache
- Processor
- Disk storage
- NIC

SOFTWARE TUNING

One of the first places to look for bottlenecks is the software running at the server. This is a good place to start because many bottlenecks caused by software are solved at no cost, other than the server administrator's time and effort to locate the problem. One common bottleneck is running software that has an unnecessarily high overhead. For example, check the screen saver used on the server. The 3D Maze and 3D Pipes screen savers are more resource-intensive than others. If one of these screen savers is running, it is easy to improve server performance by implementing a low-overhead screen saver such as Mystify or Beziers. Also, avoid using third-party screen savers unless you first test their impact. Some third-party screen savers not only are resource-intensive, but they also occupy significant disk space and slow down the server while decompressing complex pictures or graphics files each time the screen display changes.

Ironically, running performance monitoring tools such as Task Manager, Performance Monitor, and Network Monitor can cause server bottlenecks. In Windows NT 4.0 Server, Performance Monitor is redesigned to produce less load than in earlier versions, but it still has an effect on server performance. Task Manager and Network Monitor also produce a load when monitoring. Use these tools only when you are tracking a problem or temporarily gathering benchmarks. Also, use the tools thoughtfully to gather only the performance data you need. In Performance Monitor, monitor the minimum objects and counters necessary to diagnose a problem. Using two to four counters at the same time is reasonable. Monitoring seven to ten counters produces extra load on the server, along with confusing results.

Monitoring with too many tools at the same time is another source of load and confusion. For example, one university used Performance Monitor and Task Manager to test the performance of a new client/server system. Besides running these tools on the server, several system programmers monitored the server through Performance Monitor at their Windows NT workstations, attaching to the server's NIC. The server and program response was significantly slowed by all the monitoring, initially giving a false indication that there was a problem with the server or client/server software.

Some network monitoring tools used from remote network administration computers also can create an unnecessary server load. Many network monitoring packages continually poll servers, workstations, and network equipment to watch for problems. A disadvantage of this software is that it may be set to constantly poll a particular network node, such as a server. The constant polling creates a bottleneck at that server's NIC, giving a spurious indication that there is a server problem.

ADJUSTING PROGRAM PRIORITY

Consider adjusting task and process priorities when it is necessary to run a program on the server while users are accessing the server for their work. All servers have finite resources and can be adjusted to give some resources priority. For example, if one server is used primarily to handle print jobs, you might give the Spooler service, SPOOLSS.EXE, a High priority through Task Manager. Similarly, if you need to run Performance Monitor to analyze server performance, you can give it a Low priority on that server.

Windows NT handles task and process priorities by assigning ready threads for time on the processor. A ready thread can have a priority number from 1 to 31, with 31 yielding the most processor time. The ready thread with the highest priority runs before one with a lower priority. For example, suppose that the Spooler service is assigned a ready thread of 25, and NT Explorer has a ready thread of 9. NT Explorer is already accessing the processor when someone sends a print job to the server. Because the Spooler service has a ready thread with a higher priority, it interrupts NT Explorer's processor access until the print job is finished.

When the server administrator sets a process priority, Windows NT assigns a ready thread within a range of values which is the base class priority, as follows:

- *Realtime* has a priority range of 16–31.
- *High* has a priority range of 11–15.
- *Normal* has a priority range of 6–10.
- *Low* has a priority range of 1–5.

15

Once the base class priority is set for a process, the Windows NT operating system decides the specific priority number within the range that will be used for that process and for the individual threads within the process. Consider a process that runs three threads and for which the server administrator has set a High base class priority. The operating system may then assign 12 as the process's priority, and 11, 14, and 15 as the priorities of that process's three threads.

A program can be started from the Command Prompt window at a designated base class priority (Realtime, High, Normal, or Low) by using the following syntax: start [/priority] [program or command].

Another way to manage the priority of software running at the server is to adjust resources given to programs running in the foreground and in the background. A **foreground process** is one that is currently interactive with the user, whereas a **background process** is running but not currently interactive. For instance, while entering text in Microsoft Word, you may also decide to print two pages of that document and then continue typing in text. The process with which you are interacting while typing the document is WINWORD.EXE, which is in the foreground. The process that is spooling the pages to be printed, SPOOLSS.EXE, operates in the background.

Consider, for example, adjusting the resources given to the Regedt32 Registry editor while you are using it from the server console. If you use Regedt32 while you are doing system work and no users are logged on, you can give Regedt32 a priority boost as a foreground program, so that you can complete your work faster. You might do the same to speed up backups, particularly for situations in which the server is in high demand and there is a limited window of time for backups. Likewise, you can set the system to reduce the impact of a foreground process you are using at the console while there are many users accessing the server.

To change the foreground application's performance, open the System icon in the Control Panel and click the Performance tab (Figure 15-1). The performance boost for the foreground application is set on a slider bar as follows:

- *None* distributes processor time equally among all running programs.

- The middle setting gives the foreground application more processor time, but the background programs still have ample access to the processor.

- *Maximum* gives most processor time to foreground processes.

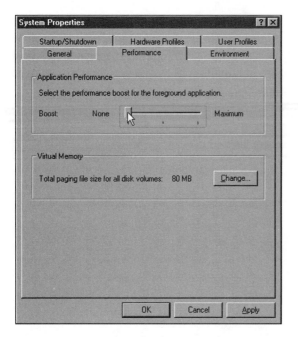

Figure 15-1   Tuning the foreground priority

If performance for users is slow on a server, try setting the foreground boost to None, and see if that improves user access to the server. (You can practice adjusting the foreground priority in Hands-on Project 15-1.)

INTERACTION BETWEEN SOFTWARE AND MEMORY USE

Software applications sometimes use the server's RAM very inefficiently, causing performance problems. Inefficient use of memory occurs in two primary ways: poor program design and failure to return memory to the server after a process is complete.

Consider an inefficient program that needs to obtain four different data values from a database table. For each value, the program loads the database table, extracts the value, and works on that value, loading the entire table and using a significant amount of memory four times. A more efficient program would create a view of the table that would include only the type of data that the program accesses, such as the four data values. When the program needed the data, it would load only the view, and extract the four data values at the same time, a technique that uses much less memory than loading the entire table four times.

Another way in which programs use memory inefficiently is by **leaking memory**, which means that the application fails to release memory when it is no longer needed. This is a very common problem that has a cumulative impact, because the program may go through several cycles in which it repeatedly accesses blocks of memory that are not released. The result is that the page file continually grows, resulting in slower and slower server performance.

15

Adding RAM or increasing the page file size to combat the inefficiency of a program is not likely to address the server's performance problem. A better solution is to identify the program and redesign it or purchase one that is more efficient. Performance Monitor is an effective tool for identifying an inefficient program. In Performance Monitor, track the Process object and the Page Faults/sec counter for each process that you suspect is causing a problem. All of the currently running processes are listed in the Instance: box in Performance Monitor's Add to Chart dialog box (Figure 15-2). As you select processes to monitor, also add Total in the Instance: box to monitor the combined page faults for all processes. A high rate of page faults for one process is a strong indicator there is a problem with that process. (Try Hands-on Project 15-2 to monitor for problems due to the inefficient use of memory.)

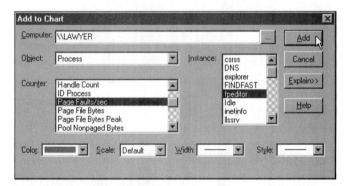

Figure 15-2   Using Performance Monitor to find an inefficient program process

TUNING DATABASES

A client/server system that accesses a database may yield slow server performance because the database needs to be restructured or tuned. Restructuring a database involves redesigning tables and other data structures so that data can be accessed more quickly. The structure of the database determines how many routes must be taken through a database to obtain the data that is sought. Obviously, server performance is better if data is obtained quickly through one or two routes than if seven complex routes through database structures must be taken to reach particular data.

 Optimizing a database is a distinct art that belongs to the realm of a database administrator. However, if you notice server performance problems on a database server, do not hesitate to involve the database administrator.

Another database function that must be performed on a regular schedule is tuning the database itself. A database administrator should be aware of tuning mechanisms such as tuning views, triggers, data structures, queries, and database statistics. Database statistics provide information about the fastest database retrieval routes.

These entities should be tuned once a month or more. For example, some automated queries that create SQL statements may not use the most efficient path to reach data, or data paths may change over time. The database administrator can periodically examine these queries to make sure that they use the best combination of SQL statements and paths to the data. A poorly generated query can take up nearly all of the server resources so that only a few users are able to do their work; a query that goes in a loop can render a server unable to process any other work.

OPTIMIZING 16-BIT WINDOWS PROGRAMS

Sometimes it is necessary to run 16-bit Windows programs on a Windows NT server. A common mistake is to run two or more 16-bit Windows programs in the same NT virtual DOS machine (NTVDM; virtual DOS machines were introduced in Chapter 1, "Networking with Microsoft NT Server"), which results in the following problems:

- The programs occupy the same memory space, and if one program aborts, it is likely to abort the NTVDM process, causing all programs running in that process to abort.

- When two or more 16-bit Windows programs are started in a single NTVDM session, only one of the programs can be active at a time.

- It is difficult to monitor a single 16-bit Windows program running inside an NTVDM process, because you must first determine its thread ID and monitor that thread.

For best performance, always run 16-bit Windows programs in their own NTVDM process and memory space. You can do this by using the Start button Run option. Specify the program name and click the Run in Separate Memory Space box. The Task Manager display in Figure 15-3 shows two NTVDM process sessions, each running a different Windows 16-bit program inside the process, along with WOWEXEC.EXE, the program that is used to simulate a 16-bit environment for a Windows 16-bit program.

When you use the Start button Run option, you can enter a "/" command switch whether or not you are running a 16-bit Windows program. For example, if you want to load Microsoft Word so that it instantly starts without a pre-set template or default information, enter WINWORD.EXE /A in the Open: box of the Start, Run option. Also, if a 16-bit program is run from the Command Prompt window, it can be started in its own NTVDM session by using this command syntax: start /separate [program].

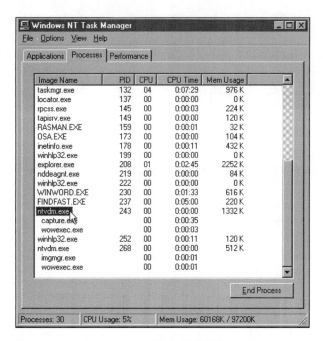

Figure 15-3 Running multiple NTVDM sessions

FILE SYSTEM CACHE

Windows NT Server uses a portion of RAM for file system cache as a way to enhance a server's performance. **Cache** is employed by computer systems to store frequently used data in quickly accessed storage, such as memory. In Windows NT Server, file system cache operates as an intermediary between disk operations and an application that requests data. When the application requests data, the operating system first checks cache, and then it checks disk storage to locate the data.

In Windows NT Server, the operating system attempts to store both program code and data that has a high probability of being accessed in the file system cache, including code and data that have been used most recently. In some cases, if the operating system determines that records in a particular file are likely to be accessed, it may cache the entire file. When working with file systems, Windows NT does not load the data itself into cache, but creates maps or pointers to the disk location of the data. The pointers enable the system to quickly access data without engaging in a search process to obtain its disk location, and then to load the data. The cache pointers are kept in RAM only, relieving the stress on page file resources.

The success of file system caching is measured through cache hits and misses. A **cache hit** is an instance in which an application goes to cache, and there is a pointer to the disk location of the data that the application needs. A **cache miss** occurs when there is no pointer, and a disk search process is used to find the data location. A low cache miss rate means that there is low disk I/O activity used to obtain data, because there is less searching to find the data. When the operating system determines that there is no longer a need to store certain information in file system cache, it performs a **cache flush** to make that cache area available for the next cached information.

File system cache performance is influenced by the way in which an application obtains data and by how data is stored in a file. The best performance results when an application accesses data sequentially and when data is stored sequentially in a file and on disk. The sequential storage of data makes it easier to access than when it is necessary to jump to different disk locations for data. A program's caching efficiency can be measured through Performance Monitor by watching the Cache object and the Copy Read Hits % counter. Microsoft recommends that this counter should be in the 80–90% range.

The Windows NT Server operating system controls the amount of RAM that is allocated to file system cache. The amount allocated is determined by the amount of RAM in the server. For example, if there is 16 MB of RAM, the amount allocated to cache is likely to be about 5 MB. For 24 MB of RAM, cache is likely to be around 6–8 MB, and for 128 MB RAM, cache will be around 30–40 MB. The Performance tab in Task Manager shows the amount of RAM allocated for file system cache in the Physical Memory area, as shown in Figure 15-4. (Try Hands-on Project 15-3 to monitor file system cache.)

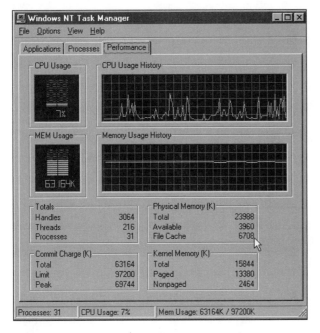

Figure 15-4   Monitoring file system cache

Too little file system cache equates to a system bottleneck, particularly on servers in which software applications make extensive use of the cache. There are only limited ways to tune the cache on a server. The best way is to install more memory. A second option is to increase the priority given to file system cache in memory. To increase the priority:

1. Open the Network icon in the Control Panel, click the Services tab, click the Server service, and then click the Properties button.

2. Click Maximize Throughput for File Sharing to give a higher priority to file system caching, so that more RAM is allocated by the operating system for this purpose.

If, instead, you click Maximize Throughput for Network Applications, priority (RAM space) is taken away from file system cache and is used for working sets. A **working set** is the amount of RAM allocated to a running process. Thus, when you tune the server you need to determine whether you need more RAM allocated to file system cache or more to running processes. One way to determine how RAM should be allocated is to use Performance Monitor to study cache needs for memory compared to cache needs for working sets. To make a comparison, monitor cache using the following object and counter combinations:

- Cache and Copy Read Hits %

- Memory and Available Bytes

- Process and Page Faults/sec (use Total as the Instance)

Next, monitor the working sets activity using these process and counter combinations:

- Process and Working Set (use Total as the Instance)

- Process and Page Faults/sec (use Total as the Instance)

- Memory and Available Bytes

 As a general rule, if the server is used mostly to run applications and to access data files, consider tuning it to give priority to cache. If the server is mostly used to run processes, tune it for working sets.

PROCESSOR BOTTLENECKS

Chapter 14 presented several Performance Monitor object/counter pairs to monitor to determine if there is a bottleneck at the processor:

- Processor and % Processor Time

- System and Processor Queue Length

- Processor and % Interrupt Time

- Processor and Interrupts/Sec

These measures provide general information to determine if there is a bottleneck at the processor. If % Processor Time is frequently over 90%, the Processor Queue Length is always over 5, and there are insignificant interrupt requests, then it is time to investigate further the nature of the processor bottleneck.

A bottleneck at the processor may be caused by overloading from one or more processes, or by process priorities that are set too high. To find out more about a bottleneck at the processor, try monitoring with additional objects and counters:

- To check for one or more processes that may be causing the load, monitor Processor / % Processor Time and the Process object / % Processor Time counter. You can select different processes to monitor in the Instance: box in the Add to Chart dialog box.

- To see if the processor load is due to priorities set for certain processes, monitor Process / Priority Base for each process (selected as the Instance) that may be set too high. This method enables you to determine the exact priority of any process.

If the bottleneck is due to a priority that is set too high, the solution to the bottleneck may be as simple as lowering the priority. However, if you determine that a bottleneck is focused on one process and that its priority is not set too high, monitor the threads used by that process by using the Thread object and % Processor Time counter. Each thread is displayed in the Instance: box. For example, if the process CSRSS looks like the culprit, monitor each thread from CSRSS ==> 0 to CSRSS ==> 6, as shown in Figure 15-5.

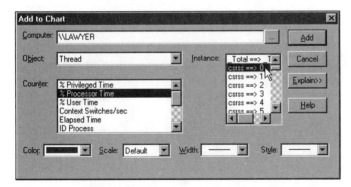

Figure 15-5   Selecting each thread within a process to monitor

15

Sometimes the processor bottleneck is due to multiple processes running on the server. In this situation, for each process, determine the number of threads that are placing a load on the processor. For example, if the processes use an average of two or three threads, then the processing load is likely to be alleviated by upgrading to a faster processor. However, if the combined processes are using a high number of threads on average, such as 6 to 8 threads, then implementing a faster processor may not provide enough performance enhancement to solve the bottleneck. In this situation, it is necessary to upgrade to a multiple-processor (SMP) computer on which the processing load is equalized across processors.

DISK TUNING

Before using Performance Monitor to study hard disk performance, it is necessary to install the Disk Performance Statistics Driver, which includes counters for disk monitoring. The driver is installed by running the program DISKPERF, which is located in the \Winnt\System32 folder. Figure 15-6 shows the installation screen for the driver, which can be installed from Start, Programs, Command Prompt, or from the Start button Run option. After the driver is installed, the server needs to be rebooted. (Hands-on Project 15-4 shows how to check that DISKPERF is installed, and what its parameters are.) The parameters for DISKPERF are as follows:

- DISKPERF displays whether or not the driver is installed and if the counters are started.

- DISKPERF –Y installs the driver and disk performance counters.

- DISKPERF –YE installs the driver and counters for a striped disk set.

- DISKPERF –N disables the counters.

Figure 15-6 Running DISKPERF

 Microsoft warns that when you use Performance Monitor disk counters, some values, particularly those used with the PhysicalDisk object, may total more than 100% (for example, when you are monitoring a counter for three separate disks). The discrepancy occurs because the counters are designed to monitor objects separately without regard to their combined totals. Once you have practiced monitoring your disks, you will be able to factor the small discrepancy into your analysis of the statistics.

Chapter 14 presented basic steps showing how to use the LogicalDisk and PhysicalDisk counters % Disk Time and Current Disk Queue Length to monitor disk activity. You can track information about paging by monitoring the following object/counter combinations simultaneously:

- Memory and Pages/sec
- LogicalDisk and % Disk Time or PhysicalDisk and % Disk Time

A visible indication that a disk may be a bottleneck is that its LED is lighting constantly and you can hear the disk busily reading and writing data. There are three general reasons why a disk is busy. One reason is simply that it is experiencing heavy sustained use. Heavy use is not an automatic indication that there is a problem, if the disk is handling the load. If the Current Disk Queue Length and Avg. Disk Queue Length values generally stay in the 1 to 2 range, the disk is handling the load, even though you may see its light on frequently. If the queue length is often in the 3 and over range, then you need to explore more about the problem, which leads to the other reasons for a disk to be busy.

The second reason is that there is a memory shortage causing disk activity because of heavy use by the page file. Use the techniques you learned in Chapter 14 and earlier in this chapter to monitor memory, paging, and file system cache to determine if there is a memory shortage. Also, monitor the following to check the link between paging and disk activity:

- Memory and Pages/sec
- LogicalDisk object and the counters % Disk Time, Avg. Disk Queue Length, Avg. Disk Read Queue Length, and Avg. Disk Write Queue Length

Figure 15-7 is a dramatic illustration of a disk bottleneck caused by a memory shortage. In this graph, the Performance Monitor histogram option is used to track the counters so that it is easier to distinguish their values. All counters are at their peak, and the server is nearly paralyzed with disk and paging activity.

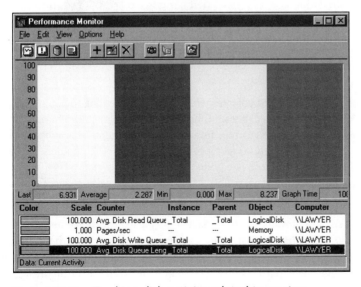

Figure 15-7 Tracking disk activity related to paging

To use the histogram tracking option in Performance Monitor, click the Options menu, Chart, and then click the Histogram radio button in the Chart Options dialog box.

The third reason for one or more disks to be busy is that they themselves may be a bottleneck. If hard disks are having difficulty handling the load and you have eliminated shortage of memory as the problem, the next step is to study the disk load, which is influenced by the following:

- Fragmentation
- Disk fault-tolerance method
- Location of files
- Disk speed

Perhaps the most common reason for a disk bottleneck is that one or more disks are heavily fragmented. Disks read and write data much faster when the data is sequentially or contiguously arranged on each disk. Read and write times escalate as a disk becomes fragmented, because the read/write head must jump all over the disk with every read and write operation. Defragmenting disks is an often-neglected task, but it is vital because it significantly improves disk performance and extends the life of disks. Set up a regular defragmentation schedule, such as once a week or month, and strictly follow it. Windows NT 4.0 Server does not come with a defragmenting tool, but you can purchase one from several third-party vendors. Besides defragmenting disks, these tools also generate statistics to show how badly a disk is fragmented.

After the defragmenting tool is installed, it can be accessed through My Computer or Windows NT Explorer. For example, to start the defragmenting tool from Windows NT Explorer, right-click the volume you want to defragment, click Properties, and click the Tools tab. Click the Defragment Now button in the Tools tab (Figure 15-8). The Tools tab also has a Check Now button that is used to scan a disk for file system errors and bad sectors. (Try Hands-on Project 15-5 to practice accessing a defragmenting tool and scanning a disk for errors.)

There is a way to defragment volumes without a defragmenting tool, but it is a lot of work. To defragment volumes: (1) back up each volume, (2) reformat the volumes, and (3) restore the volumes from the backup. This old-fashioned way of defragmenting is still used on all types of large and small computers in the absence of defragmenting software. One advantage of this method is that bad disk areas are found and circumvented through the formatting, before they become a problem.

If you have configured disk storage as stripe sets with parity, the bottleneck may be linked to more active disk writing than you initially estimated. Stripe sets with parity are able to read data faster than they can write it, because they must take time to calculate and write parity and fault-tolerance data with each write operation. You can compare read to write activity by using the following Performance Monitor measures:

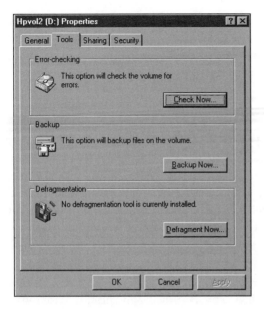

Figure 15-8 Defragmenting a volume from Windows NT Explorer

- For read activity, monitor the LogicalDisk and PhysicalDisk counters Avg. Disk Bytes/Read and Avg. Disk sec/Read.

- For write activity, monitor the LogicalDisk and PhysicalDisk counters Avg. Disk Bytes/Write and Avg. Disk sec/Write.

The Avg. Disk Bytes/Read or /Write counter measures the average number of bytes transferred to or from the disk per each read or write activity. The Avg. Disk sec/Read or /Write shows the average number of seconds it takes to perform the disk read or write activity. If the disk write activity is much more frequent than read activity, and the users report delays in their work, consider using disk mirroring or duplexing instead of stripe sets with parity.

On disks that employ no fault-tolerance measures or that are mirrored, the location of disk files can be important to diagnosing a bottleneck. Frequent visual inspection may show that one set of mirrored volumes is busier than another set. Suppose you have two mirrored volumes, disks 0 and 1, and your visual inspections indicate that disk 0 is often busy, but disk 1 is not. You can study the discrepancy further by monitoring on both disks the LogicalDisk counters % Disk Time, Avg. Disk Queue Length, Avg. Disk Read Queue Length, and Avg. Disk Write Queue Length. If you find, for example, that disk 0 is nearly always busier than disk 1, consider moving files. This tuning requires knowledge of the files and their purpose. For example, disk 0 may contain a set of Microsoft Access databases that are used constantly, while disk 1 has only sparse data. In this situation, you can spread the load of the databases between the two disks (consulting first with the users).

In some situations, a hard disk simply may have a slow transfer rate and may need to be upgraded, particularly if it is an older disk. As discussed in Chapter 14, measure the disk transfer rate by monitoring the PhysicalDisk counter Disk Bytes/sec along with % Disk Time. Set

15

up a test by transferring large files to that disk or by developing a large query of a database. Disk performance is related to the data transfer rate of the disk adapter and controller, and the disk access time is the speed of the disk in accessing data. It can be very worthwhile to replace old disk technology with newer disks that use high-speed SCSI adapters and that have fast disk access times.

NETWORK-RELATED TUNING

One of the best ways to tune a server is to tune the protocols used on the network. For example, if you started out with 75 users and NetBEUI, but have expanded to 250 users, consider switching to TCP/IP for the larger network needs. Or if you have implemented an intranet and use NetBEUI and TCP/IP, investigate the option to convert all users to TCP/IP and reduce network traffic to one protocol. Also, remove from the server any protocols that are no longer in use.

Another way to tune the server's performance as it relates to the network is to establish the network access order when there are multiple network provider and print services installed on the server. For example, if the server is configured as a NetWare gateway, and it provides access to NetWare print servers, tune the server by configuring the order in which it accesses those services over the network. If Microsoft-based servers are accessed the most by the server and its clients, give those services the top access order position, and give NetWare services the second position. Also, determine which print services are used most and set their order of access. The network access order is viewed from the Control Panel Network icon. Upon opening the icon, click the Services tab and then the Network Access Order button. The services listed first are those that the server accesses first over the network. To change the order, click the service and then click the Move Up or Move Down button, as shown in Figure 15-9. (You can practice changing the network access order in Hands-on Project 15-6.)

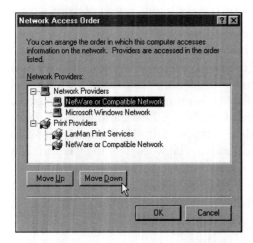

Figure 15-9   Changing the network access order

TUNING THE RECYCLE BIN SIZE

The Recycle Bin contains files, shortcuts, and other items that have been deleted but not purged from Windows NT Server. Its purpose is to provide the opportunity to restore one or more deleted items, in case certain items are inadvertently deleted. Items occupy disk space until they are purged from the Recycle Bin. Plan to regularly clear the Recycle Bin, for example once a week or more, by double-clicking Recycle Bin on the desktop, clicking the File menu, and then clicking Empty Recycle Bin.

By default, the Recycle Bin can grow to be as large as 10% of the hard disk storage. If there are two or more volumes, a Recycle Bin is kept for each one. You can tune the maximum size of the Recycle Bin by right-clicking the Recycle Bin icon and selecting Properties. Click the Global tab, and if there are multiple volumes, click the Use one setting for all drives: radio button. Move the slider bar to decrease or increase the maximum size of the Recycle Bin for each drive. If you want deleted files to be immediately purged (not recommended), click Do not move files to the Recycle Bin.

TUNING EVENT LOGS

Windows NT Server maintains event logs to track system, security, and software application events, such as reporting a hardware problem or a software error. The event logs quickly fill with information, and you should establish from the beginning how you want the logs maintained. There are several ways to maintain the logs, as follows:

- Size each log to prevent it from filling too quickly.

- Regularly clear each log before it is full.

- Automatically overwrite the oldest events when a log is full.

Some network administrators prefer to save the log contents on a regular basis, such as weekly or monthly. Others prefer to allow the logs to overwrite the oldest events. It is recommended that you develop a maintenance schedule to save the log contents for a designated time period, because the logs contain valuable information about historical server activity. For example, if a financial auditor needs to see information about who is accessing the payroll folder, you would set up auditing on that folder and then save the security log data that contains the audited events.

To tune the event logs, start the Event Viewer from the Administrative Tools (Common) menu. Click the Log menu and then Log Settings. In the Change Settings for ____ Log list box, there are three logs from which to choose: System, Security, and Application. Adjust the setting for each of those logs. Set the maximum log size to match the way you want to handle the logs. The default size is 512 KB. For example, if you want to accumulate two weeks of information, set the size to enable that much information to be recorded, for instance to 1024 KB (Figure 15-10). You will need to test this setting for a few weeks to make sure that the size you set is adequate. A common way to set event log wrapping is to use the

15

Overwrite Events Older than ___ Days option. For instance, entering 14 means that two weeks of events are stored.

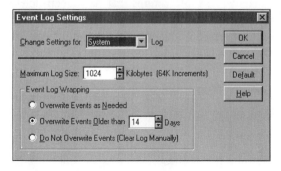

Figure 15-10   Tuning event logs

There also are options to save and clear the individual event logs. To save a log, click the Log menu, check the log to save, and click Save As. In the Save As box, specify the filename for the log and a folder in which to save it. Logs often are named to reflect the date or time period of their contents, such as 101598A.EVT for October 15, 1998 and application log. After a log is saved, clear its contents by clicking the Log menu, checking that event log, and clicking Clear All Events. (You can practice maintaining logs in Hands-on Project 15-7.)

CHAPTER SUMMARY

- After a Windows NT Server is set up and running, it is important to tune it regularly, for the best performance. Tuning can be somewhat complicated, but the results are very worthwhile. All servers can be tuned to match changing circumstances such as evolving software needs, the installation of new disks, and the growth in the number of users.

- One area that requires tuning is software. Server software can be tuned to run at higher or lower priorities, to match the needs of users and of the server administrator working at the console. In other situations, what appears as a memory shortage may really be the impact of software that uses memory inefficiently. Databases and 16-bit Windows programs are additional examples of software elements that require tuning for optimal performance.

- Other tuning areas include file system cache and the processor. The file system cache can benefit from monitoring and tuning because it affects the performance of the server and of applications that run on the server. A processor bottleneck can have many causes, such as a process or a thread that occupies a high percentage of processor resources. Applications can be tuned to reduce their impact on the processor, but there also are times when the best tuning solution is to purchase a faster processor or to implement multiple processors.

- Server disk storage can be tuned in several ways to reduce a bottleneck. One of the most effective tuning methods is to defragment disks. Sometimes the disk fault-tolerance method is a bottleneck that requires changing. The server's interaction with the network requires that parameters be tuned to help network performance at the server, for example evaluating the protocol needs as a network grows, and establishing network service access priorities.

- Two additional areas to consider for performance tuning are the Recycle Bin and event logs. If the Recycle Bin is not regularly cleared, it can grow to occupy a significant amount of disk space. Also, event logs grow over time and need to be managed so that only valuable historical data is retained to help troubleshoot problems and audit server activities.

- Table 15-1 summarizes information presented in this chapter on using Performance Monitor to detect many types of tuning problems.

Table 15-1   Using Performance Monitor to Detect Tuning Problems

Problem	Performance Monitor Object / Counter
Leaking memory	Process / Page Faults/sec (select the process(es) to monitor in the Instance: box)
Cache performance	Cache / Copy Read Hits %
Comparing cache memory needs to cache working set needs	*(1) First study cache for memory:* Cache / Copy Read Hits % Memory / Available Bytes Process / Page Faults/sec *(use Total as the Instance)* *(2) Next, study cache for working processes:* Process / Working Set *(use Total as the Instance)* Process / Page Faults/sec *(use Total as the Instance)* Memory / Available Bytes
Processor bottleneck (general performance monitoring)	Processor / % Processor Time System / Processor Queue Length Processor / % Interrupt Time Processor / Interrupts/Sec
One or more processes overloading the processor	Processor / % Processor Time Process / % Processor Time (select different processes to watch in the Instance: box)
Priority setting that is causing the processor load	Process / Priority Base (for each process as selected in the Instance: box)
Process that is causing load on the processor, but not because of the priority setting	Thread / % Processor Time (monitor individual threads as selected in the Instance: box)
Starting disk monitoring counters	Run DISKPERF and set the counters to start when the server boots (DISKPERF -Y or DISKPERF -YE for a striped set)

15

Table 15-1   Using Performance Monitor to Detect Tuning Problems (continued)

Problem	Performance Monitor Object / Counter
Disk performance	LogicalDisk / % Disk Time LogicalDisk / Current Disk Queue Length PhysicalDisk / % Disk Time PhysicalDisk / Current Disk Queue Length
Disk load due to paging	Memory / Pages/sec LogicalDisk / % Disk Time or PhysicalDisk / % Disk Time
Sustained disk load	LogicalDisk / Current Disk Queue Length LogicalDisk / Avg. Disk Queue Length or PhysicalDisk / Current Disk Queue Length PhysicalDisk / Avg. Disk Queue Length
Disk load because of excessive paging	Memory / Pages/sec LogicalDisk / % Disk Time LogicalDisk / Avg. Disk Queue Length LogicalDisk / Avg. Disk Read Queue Length LogicalDisk / Avg. Disk Write Queue Length
Active disk writing compared to reading on a stripe set with parity	*For read activity, monitor:* LogicalDisk or PhysicalDisk / Avg. Disk Bytes/Read LogicalDisk or PhysicalDisk / Avg. Disk sec/Read *For write activity, monitor:* LogicalDisk or PhysicalDisk / Avg. Disk Bytes/Write LogicalDisk or PhysicalDisk / Avg. Disk sec/Write
Uneven load on a disk without fault-tolerance	LogicalDisk / % Disk Time LogicalDisk / Avg. Disk Queue Length LogicalDisk / Avg. Disk Read Queue Length LogicalDisk / Avg. Disk Write Queue Length
Disk(s) with a slow transfer rate and access time	PhysicalDisk / Disk Bytes/sec PhysicalDisk / % Disk Time

KEY TERMS

- **background process** — A process that is not currently interactive with the computer user.

- **bottleneck** — Any impediment that slows the movement of data in a computer or on a network.

- **cache** — Storage used by a computer system to house frequently used data in quickly accessed storage, such as memory.

- **cache flush** — Clearing the cache of old information to make it available for new data.

- **cache hit** — A situation in which the data needed by an application is found in cache.

- **cache miss** — A situation in which the desired data is not found in cache.

- **foreground process** — A process with which the user is currently interactive, such as the program in the open window that the user is accessing.

- **leaking memory** — Failing to return memory for general use after a process is finished using a specific memory block.

- **working set** — Amount of RAM allocated to a running process.

REVIEW QUESTIONS

1. The default size of an event log is _____.
   - **a.** 64 KB
   - **b.** 512 KB
   - **c.** 1024 KB
   - **d.** 2048 KB

2. A 16-bit Windows application runs _____.
   - **a.** 10% faster than a 32-bit application
   - **b.** using the NTLDR.DLL
   - **c.** as a NTVDM process
   - **d.** in file system cache

3. Which of the following screen savers is (are) better to run in Windows NT Server in terms of resource consumption?
   - **a.** 3D Pipes
   - **b.** Mystify
   - **c.** third-party 4GL compressed images
   - **d.** all of the above use about the same resources
   - **e.** only a and b

4. When tuning applications in Windows NT Server, the maximum setting gives _____.
   - **a.** priority to foreground applications
   - **b.** priority to background applications
   - **c.** all applications equal priority
   - **d.** priority to the kernel

5. An event log is sized from _____.
   - **a.** Event Viewer
   - **b.** Performance Monitor
   - **c.** WordPad
   - **d.** Windows NT Diagnostics

6. You suspect that your disk drive has a fairly slow data transfer rate. What would you use to measure it?
   - **a.** Task Manager Performance tab
   - **b.** Performance Monitor Processor and Disk objects monitoring % Processor Time and % Disk Time
   - **c.** Disk Administrator Performance Evaluator
   - **d.** Performance Monitor Disk object using the counters Disk Bytes/sec and % Disk Time

15

7. When the Windows NT Server operating system no longer needs to keep certain information in file system cache, it _____.

    a. performs a controlled purge

    b. reinitializes the file system cache

    c. flushes the information

    d. performs a clear-start process

8. The Recycle Bin by default can _____.

    a. use up to 20% of disk space

    b. use up to 10% of disk space

    c. use up to 5% RAM and 5% disk space

    d. automatically purge files at an interval set by the server administrator

9. File system cache uses which of the following for its storage?

    a. RAM

    b. virtual memory

    c. hard disk space

    d. unpartitioned hard disk

10. From where do you set the network access order?

    a. Control Panel System icon

    b. User Manager for Domains

    c. Control Panel Network icon

    d. NETACCESS program

11. The alerter has sent a message that the application log is full. What should you do?

    a. delete and recreate the log

    b. save and clear the log

    c. set the log monitor to the maximum size

    d. regenerate all of the logs

12. You have just installed Gateway Services for NetWare, but the primary use of the server is for Microsoft networking services. What should you do to optimize performance for Microsoft services?

    a. make NWLink a secondary protocol

    b. make NetBEUI a primary protocol

    c. set the network access order so that Microsoft Windows Network is listed first

    d. set the Gateway Services for NetWare so that they are automatically disabled when they are not in use

13. You are using Performance Monitor to study disk traffic, but the information is all zeros. What should you do next?

    a. restart Performance Monitor

    b. monitor the processor activity first because disk activity is linked to it

    c. click the instance parameter called Total

    d. run the DISKPERF program

14. You want to scan a disk for file system errors. What tool would you use?

    a. Performance Monitor file system cache counter for the PhysicalDisk object

    b. disk defragmenter in the Control Panel System icon

    c. Check Now button in that volume's Properties dialog box and on the Tools tab

    d. disk scan option in Windows NT Diagnostics

15. What is the value range of the High priority used for a process?

    a. 1-31   **b.** 11-15   **c.** 6-18   **d.** 25-31

16. How many event logs are there to tune?

    a. 1   **b.** 2   **c.** 3   **d.** 4

17. You have noticed that disk performance seems to be getting a bit slower. What might you try first?

    a. defragment the disks

    b. implement a different fault-tolerance method

    c. increase the disk queue size

    d. all of the above

    e. both a and b

18. You are charting five counters in Performance Monitor, and the graphed lines are getting difficult to read. What can you do?

    a. set the charting to have a shorter interval

    b. use the Link chart option to join counters

    c. limit your charting to only three counters at any one time

    d. use the Histogram option

19. Your organization has purchased a new program, but you have found that it does not return memory it no longer needs while processing. This is called _____.

    a. memory management   **c.** leaking memory

    b. memory lag   **d.** blocking memory

20. Your network started as a NetBEUI-based network with 35 users. Today you have about 172 users and have implemented an intranet, resulting in a multiprotocol network. What might you do to improve network communications?

    a. convert all users to NetBEUI only

    b. convert all users to TCP/IP only

    c. optimize the protocol communications by using a 64-bit version of NDIS

    d. optimize the network communications with a NetBEUI gateway

21. You are assessing the performance of file system cache by using Performance Monitor. Which of the following indicates an acceptable percentage of cache hits?

    a. 50%   **b.** 60%   **c.** 72%   **d.** 85%

22. Your monitoring shows that one process is taking a very high amount of CPU resources. What would you try first?

    a. rewrite the code of that process

    b. determine if one thread in that process is using more resources than other threads

    c. monitor to determine the exact base priority assigned to that process

    d. move the program associated with that process to a different volume

15

23. You have noticed that there is heavy disk activity and want to determine if that activity is related to the page file. Which of the following LogicalDisk counters would be included in your monitoring?

    a. % Disk Time
    d. all of the above
    b. Avg. Disk Read Queue Length
    e. only b and c
    c. Avg. Disk Write Queue Length

24. In the absence of a defragmenting tool, you can defragment a disk by
    _____ .

    a. clearing its Recycle Bin each day

    b. backing it up, reformatting it, and restoring it

    c. regularly deleting old files

    d. fixing bad disk clusters

25. You have set up a stripe set with parity, but find that disk write activity is very significantly higher than read activity, and users report that this slows their work. Which of the following might you try?

    a. convert to mirrored volumes
    c. increase memory for working sets
    b. give parity writing a higher priority
    d. ask the users to be patient

HANDS-ON PROJECTS

 PROJECT 15-1

In this activity you minimize the performance boost for foreground applications in Windows NT Server.

To tune the foreground performance boost:

1. Click **Start**, **Settings**, and **Control Panel**, and double-click the **System** icon.
2. Click the **Performance** tab, and move the slider bar in the Boost: continuum to **None**.
3. Click **Apply**, then click **OK**, then close the **Control Panel**.

 PROJECT 15-2

In this activity you monitor three program processes to look for inefficient use of memory.

To monitor processes for inefficient memory use:

1. Click **Start**, **Programs,** and **Accessories**, then click **Calculator**.

2. Repeat Step 1 to start **Paint** and then **WordPad**.

3. Click **Start**, **Programs**, and **Administrative Tools (Common)**.

4. Click **Performance Monitor**, then click the **Add counter** button.

5. Select **Process** in the Object: box, and click **Page Faults/sec** in the Counter: box.

6. Click **calc** in the Instance: box, and then click **Add**.

7. Repeat Steps 7–9 for the processes **mspaint** and **wordpad**. Also, add **Total** via the Instance: box to view the page faults for all combined running processes (Figure 15-11).

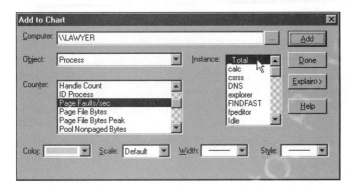

Figure 15-11   Monitoring page faults for all combined processes

8. Click **Done**, monitor the processes for a short time and then close Performance Monitor, Wordpad, Paint, and Calculator.

 PROJECT 15-3

In this activity you check the amount of RAM allocated to file system cache and then you monitor the file system cache.

To study the file system cache:

1. Press **[Ctrl]-[Alt]-[Del]**.

2. Click the **Task Manager** button in the Windows NT Security dialog box.

3. Click the **Performance** tab.

4. Write down or note the amount of allocated file system cache, which is listed as the value for File Cache, and close Task Manager.

5. Start Performance Monitor by clicking **Start**, **Programs**, **Administrative Tools (Common)**, and **Performance Monitor**, and click the **Add counter** button.

6. Select **Cache** as the object and **Copy Read Hits %** as the counter. Click **Add**, then click **Done**.

7. Monitor for a few minutes and determine if Copy Read Hits % is in the 80–90 % range, and close Performance Monitor.

PROJECT 15-4

In this activity you determine whether or not the DISKPERF driver is installed and the Performance Monitor disk counters are activated.

To check on DISKPERF's status:

1. Click **Start**, **Programs**, and **Command Prompt**.
2. In the Command Prompt window type **diskperf**.
3. Read the first line after the command you entered. If the counters are installed, it will say *Disk Performance counters on this system are currently set to start at boot.*
4. Notice the information about switches you can use with DISKPERF.
5. Type **exit** and press [**Enter**] to close the Command Prompt window.

PROJECT 15-5

In this activity you view where to start a disk defragmenting tool and how to check a disk for errors.

To view where to start the defragmenter and how to check for disk errors:

1. Double-click **My Computer** on the desktop.
2. Right-click volume **(C:)** (or another available volume on which to practice).
3. Click **Properties**, then click the **Tools** tab.
4. Notice the location of the Defragment Now button, which is where you would start the defragmenting tool, then click the **Check Now** button.
5. Notice that there are two disk-error-checking options: Automatically fix filesystem errors, and Scan for and attempt recovery of bad sectors.
6. Click **Cancel** to return to the volume's Properties dialog box (or if the server has no one logged on, check both boxes and try the disk check utility).
7. Close the volume's Properties dialog box.

PROJECT 15-6

In this activity you tune the server by placing Microsoft Windows Network services at the top of the network access order list.

To change the network access order:

1. Click **Start**, **Settings**, and **Control Panel**, and double-click the **Network** icon.
2. Click the **Services** tab, and click the **Network Access Order** button (Figure 15-12).

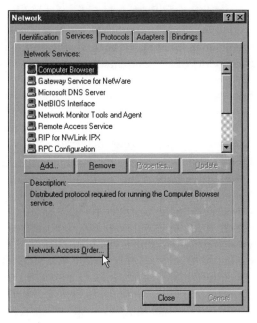

Figure 15-12   Tuning the network access order

3. Click **Microsoft Windows Network**, click the **Move Up** button, then click **OK**.
4. Close the Network dialog box, and click **Yes** to restart your computer.

 PROJECT 15-7

In this activity you practice saving and clearing the application event log.

To maintain the application event log:

1. Click **Start**, **Programs**, and **Administrative Tools (Common)**.
2. Click **Event Viewer**.

15

3. Click the **Log** menu and place a check in front of **Application**.

4. Click **Save as** in the Log menu.

5. Enter a filename, such as **Test**, and select a folder in which to save the log.

6. Click **Save**, and then click the **Log** menu and make sure that **Application** is selected.

7. Notice the option to **Clear All Events**. Do not click the option unless you are truly ready to clear the log, and close the Event Viewer.

ASPEN CONSULTING: PERFORMANCE TUNING

This week you assist three clients: Press Plastics, Greenville Paper, and Tools Unlimited. All three are working on finding and solving performance bottlenecks.

1. Press Plastics, your client from Chapter 4, "Server Installation," has one server that seems to have a bottleneck related to memory or disk, but they are not sure of the cause. What questions might you ask about the hardware setup of the computer having problems? What steps do you recommend they take to determine the source of the bottleneck?

2. Your advice helped Press Plastics solve their problem, but a new one has developed on another server. Each afternoon at 4 P.M. they close down the accounting system to take a backup of its database before they perform an end-of-the-day closing and reconciliation. The backup is a special program written in Visual Basic by a Press Plastics programmer. Each time the backup runs, other users of that server can hardly complete their work because the server is so slow. What course of action do you recommend to find the source of the problem? What would you recommend to solve the problem?

3. Greenville Paper, the client that has a combination of Windows NT and NetWare file servers, finds that access to their NetWare gateway on one of the servers is fast, but that most users who regularly access other non-NetWare shared server drives find that access is a little slow. What might you tune on that NT server?

4. Press Plastics is back on the telephone to discuss how to tune the server that has the accounting database, in an effort to enhance the server's performance for database access. What questions would you ask to help them decide how to tune it?

5. The server administrator from Tools Unlimited wants to collect event log data on a weekly basis. Explain how to set this up, along with other event log management techniques.

6. Press Plastics is considering an upgrade of memory for all of its 15 Windows NT Servers. Before they purchase the memory, they have called you for ideas on how to tune their servers and then upgrade only the servers that truly need more memory. Prepare a list of tuning ideas for them.

TROUBLESHOOTING

Troubleshooting is an integral part of working with computers and is closely linked to the skills you have learned for monitoring and tuning. Sometimes problems can be prevented through monitoring, but at other times problems strike without warning, such as when a hard disk fails. In nearly all cases, troubleshooting a server problem is accompanied by a sense of urgency because users depend on servers. At the same time, troubleshooting is an opportunity to learn more about a server and its network.

In this chapter, you learn about troubleshooting from many angles. You learn to use Windows NT Diagnostics and event logs to help locate problems. Also, you learn to resolve server and network connectivity problems, including NIC and cable difficulties. Some other areas that are the focus of troubleshooting involve printing, hard disk, memory, and boot problems. Finally, you learn where to turn for additional help in troubleshooting Windows NT Server problems.

AFTER READING THIS CHAPTER AND COMPLETING THE EXERCISES YOU WILL BE ABLE TO:

- DEVELOP A PROBLEM-SOLVING STRATEGY
- USE WINDOWS NT DIAGNOSTICS AND EVENT VIEWER TO TROUBLESHOOT PROBLEMS
- SOLVE DIFFERENT TYPES OF PROBLEMS WITH ACCESS AND PERMISSIONS, NETWORK CONNECTIVITY, NETWORK PRINTING, BOOTING OR FAILED SYSTEM DISK, AND MEMORY
- DEAL WITH PROBLEMS WITH MIRRORED DISKS AND STRIPE SETS WITH PARITY
- USE SERVER MANAGER FOR TROUBLESHOOTING
- LEARN WHERE TO OBTAIN ADDITIONAL TROUBLESHOOTING HELP

DEVELOPING A PROBLEM-SOLVING STRATEGY

The best approach in solving server and network problems is to develop troubleshooting strategies. Three general strategies are to:

- Know how a server and the network interact
- Train your users about how to help you solve problems
- Know the business processes of your organization

KNOW HOW SERVERS AND THE NETWORK INTERACT

There are many steps you can take to better understand the environment in which a server operates. Many server and network administrators create a diagram of the entire network and update the diagram each time an aspect of the network changes. The network diagram should include the following elements:

- Servers
- Host computers
- Workstations and network printers (unless the network has too many to include these)
- Network devices
- Telecommunications links
- Remote links
- Building locations
- Cable link types, such as copper or fiber, link speeds, and cable distances

A server does not exist in a vacuum, but instead is a member of a larger community of networked workstations and their users. Gathering benchmarks, as discussed in Chapter 14, "Server and Network Monitoring," helps you understand your server and how the network context affects the server. For example, slow server performance can look like a network problem, and slow network performance can look like a server problem. The more you know about the server's network context, the faster you will be able to resolve a problem such as slow server performance.

TRAIN USERS TO HELP

Another valuable strategy is to train network users to be your partners in reporting problems. If you encourage users to be troubleshooting allies, they are more likely to feel that they can take action on a problem than to wait impatiently for you to detect and solve the problem. When you train users to gather information and report it to you, they become troubleshooting partners who can advance you several steps ahead to the solution. The following are some actions you can train users to take to help you and themselves:

- Save their work at the first sign of a problem.

- Carefully record information about a problem, such as the exact wording of error messages, the impact on their workstation, and the impact on others working nearby.

- Report any protocol information, such as error messages about a protocol or an address.

- Quickly report a problem to you by telephone or by voice mail, if you cannot be reached immediately.

- Avoid sending e-mail about urgent problems.

KNOW THE BUSINESS PROCESSES OF YOUR ORGANIZATION

Your knowledge of how your organization works is another weapon in solving problems. For example, assume that you are the server administrator at a college library, and the catalog server is reported to be slow just before 1:00 P.M. and 6:00 P.M. Your knowledge of library activities might indicate that the network or a server is slow because large numbers of students are checking out books just before going to afternoon classes or to the dorms for dinner. In another case, you might work at a business where network problems occur each morning when the company president downloads a huge database or runs several giant reports. Your understanding of how people work in your organization can help you take the appropriate steps in finding solutions, such as tuning a server.

SOLVING PROBLEMS STEP BY STEP

Armed with knowledge of your network context, trained users, and an understanding of your organization, you can use the following step-by-step techniques to solve network problems.

16

1. *Get as much information as possible about the problem.* If the problem is reported by a network user, listen carefully to his or her description. Even if he or she does not use the right terminology, the information is still valuable. Part of your challenge is to ask the right questions to get as much information as possible.

2. *Record the error message at the time it appears or when a user reports it to you.* This is an obvious, but sometimes overlooked, step. If you try to recall the message from memory, you may lose some important information. For example, the error, "Network not responding" can lead you to a different set of troubleshooting steps than the message, "Network timeout error." The first message might signal a damaged NIC, whereas the second message could mean that a database server is overloaded and the application is waiting to obtain data.

3. *Start with simple solutions.* Often the solution to a problem is as simple as connecting a cable or power cord.

4. *Determine if anyone else is experiencing the problem.* For example, several people may report that they cannot load a word-processing software package. This may be due to a problem at the server they use to load the software. If only one person is experiencing this problem, it may point to trouble on his or her workstation.

5. *Check to see if any recent alerts have been sent to your account.* If you have set up Performance Monitor alerts, check to determine if any have been sent, warning you of a problem.

6. *Check the event logs.* Regularly check the Windows NT Server event logs for signs of a problem.

7. *Use Performance Monitor filtering.* Perfect your skills at using Performance Monitor filters to trap detailed information about a problem.

8. *Check for power interruptions.* Power problems are a common source of server and network difficulties. Even though the server is on a UPS, its network connection can still be a source of problems, because the network cable can carry current to the server's NIC during a lightning storm, or because of another major power-related problem.

TRACKING PROBLEMS AND SOLUTIONS

One effective troubleshooting tool is to keep a log of all network problems and their solutions. Some server administrators log problems in a database created for that purpose. Others build problem logging into help desk systems maintained by their organization. A **help desk** system is application software designed to maintain information about computer systems, user questions, problem solutions, and other information that members of the organization can reference.

The advantage of tracking problems is that you soon accumulate a wealth of information on solutions. For example, to jog your memory about a solution, you can look up how you handled a similar problem six months ago. The log of problems also can be used as a teaching tool and reference for other computer support staff. Problems that show up repeatedly in the log may indicate that special attention is needed, for example for a server that experiences frequent hardware problems.

WINDOWS NT DIAGNOSTICS

A central place to check to determine if there is a server problem is the Windows NT Diagnostics utility introduced in Chapter 9, "Managing Server Folders, Permissions, and Software Installation." This utility, accessed from the Administrative Tools (Common) menu, is helpful not only in diagnosing resource conflicts and viewing the Registry contents, but also provides troubleshooting information. Windows NT Diagnostics has information about server hardware and software. All information is arranged within the tabs: Display, Drives, Environment, Memory, Network, Resources, Services, System, and Version. The Services tab, for example, shows all services and whether they are running or stopped. If you click a service in the Services tab and then click the Properties button, you can view information in the resulting General tab about where that service resides, such as in the \Winnt\System32 folder. Also, there is information about how the service is started and if it has a dependency on other services. Click the Dependencies tab to view the dependencies (Figure 16-1).

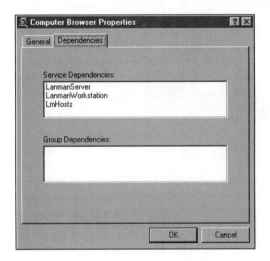

Figure 16-1 Service dependencies shown in Windows NT Diagnostics

This is useful information in case there is a problem with a service, or in case you need to stop a service but want to first determine if stopping it will affect other services. The Devices button on the NT Diagnostics Services tab shows if hardware, protocols, and hardware-linked activities are running. For example, if the server has trouble loading a file from the floppy drive, you can use the Devices button to quickly determine if the drive is recognized by the server. If the server printer refuses to communicate, you can use the same button to check on the parallel port to which the printer is attached. Another reason to check device information is to find out where drivers are located, for example the NetBEUI driver NBF.SYS, which is in the \Winnt\System32 folder.

The Network tab shows information about network communications settings stored in the Registry. To view these, click the Network tab and the Setting button. Click the Network tab Statistics button for information about network communications, such as the number of bytes received by the server and the number of bytes it has transmitted (Figure 16-2). The statistics also show when there are problems, including hung user sessions, server disconnects, network errors, and user sessions that have timed out or errored out. The Statistics button provides an instant snapshot of network and server communications statistics in a single location. (Try using NT Diagnostics to check network statistics in Hands-on Project 16-1.)

16

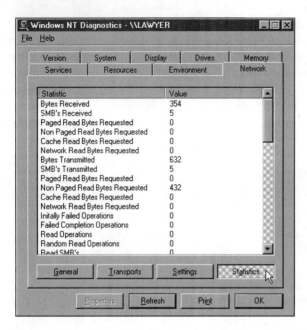

Figure 16-2   Server and network performance statistics in Windows NT Diagnostics

USING EVENT VIEWER TO SOLVE PROBLEMS

Another way to diagnose a server problem is through the event logs displayed in Event Viewer. There are three **event logs** available on Windows NT Server: the system, security, and application logs. The **system log** records information about system-related events such as hardware errors, driver problems, and hard drive errors. The **security log** records access and security information about logon accesses and file, folder, and system policy changes. If you choose to audit an account or folder, the audit data is recorded in the security log. The **application log** records information about how software applications are performing, if the programmer has designed the software to write information into the log. For example, if a software error occurs it may be recorded in the log.

Log events are displayed with an icon that indicates the seriousness of the event. An informational message, for example that a service has been started, is prefaced by an "i" icon. A warning, for instance that a CD-ROM is not loaded, is depicted by an "!" (exclamation point) icon; and an error, like a defective disk adapter, is indicated with a "stop sign" icon (Figure 16-3). Each log displays descriptive information about individual events, such as the following information provided in the system log:

- Date and time of the event

- Source of the event, which is the software application or hardware reporting it

- Category or type of event, if one applies, such as a system event or logon event

- Event number, so that the event can be tracked if entered into a database

- User account involved in the event, if applicable

- Name of the computer on which the event took place

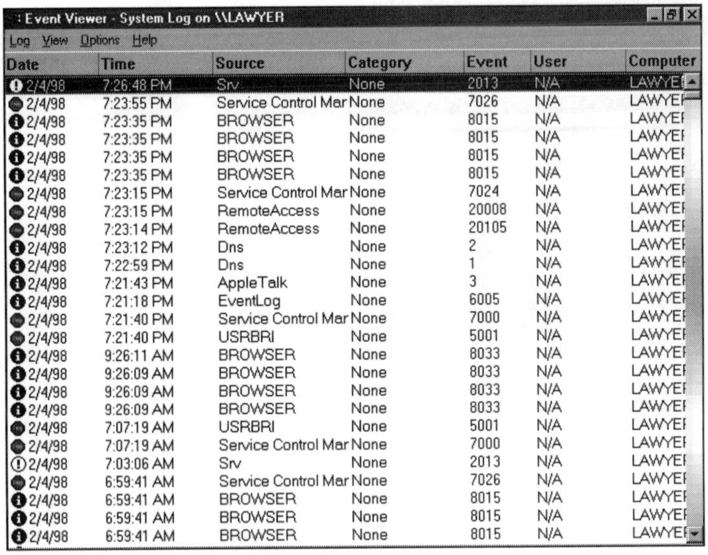

Figure 16-3   System log

Event Viewer is started from the Administrative Tools (Common) menu. It contains options to view all events or to set a filter so that only certain events are viewed, such as only error events.

The first time you start Event Viewer, it shows the system log by default, as in Figure 16-3. To view one of the other logs, click the Log option on the menu bar and select the desired log. To view detailed information about an event, double-click the event. Check the description of the event for more information. In Figure 16-4, the Event Detail dialog box shows that RAS cannot communicate through COM2. This is an error that should be corrected as soon as possible. One way to diagnose the error is to go to Windows NT Diagnostics, click the Services tab, Devices button, and double-click Serial to see if the driver is installed. If the Pathname is reported as unavailable, this means that the driver cannot be located, and it is necessary to reinstall it.

16

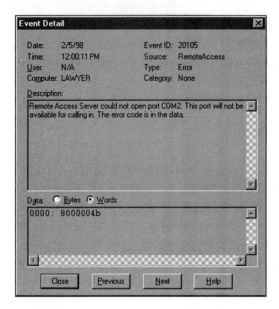

Figure 16-4   Event details

 Event logs are a good source of information to help troubleshoot a software or hardware problem. For example, if Windows NT Server crashes unexpectedly, reboot and look at the logs as a first step. A memory allocation or disk problem may be found quickly through the help of the system log. If a software application hangs, check the application log for information.

All three event logs in Event Viewer have a filter option to help quickly locate a problem. For example, you can design a filter to show only events associated with the disk drives, or only events that occurred on the previous afternoon. The events can be filtered according to the following criteria:

- Date range

- Time of day range

- Event type, such as information, warning, or error

- Source of the event, such as a particular service or hardware component

- Category of event, such as a security change

- User associated with the event, including the server

- Event ID, which is a number assigned by Event Viewer to identify the event

For instance, to build a filter to view only error events in a specified time period for the Server service, you would use the following steps:

1. Start Event Viewer and display the system log.
2. Click View on the menu bar and select Filter Events.
3. Enter the start and end dates and times for which to view events.
4. Click the Error box on the Filter screen under Types.
5. Click the Source list box and select Server.
6. Click OK to view the system log showing only those events specified by the filter.

SOLVING USER ACCESS AND PERMISSION PROBLEMS

One of the most common network problems is that users are not able to log on or to access desired resources. Users can forget their passwords, they can change their passwords but not remember the new ones they created, or they may be assigned inappropriate permissions. As a security precaution, Windows NT Server does not allow the administrator to look up a user password; the password is hidden by asterisks. As administrator, you do, however, have the ability to change a user's password through User Manager for Domains in the Administrative Tools (Common) menu. If a user cannot remember a password, you can set a new password with the provision that the user must change the password at next logon, allowing him or her to enter (and hopefully remember!) the password. To change a password, follow these general steps:

1. Open User Manager for Domains and double-click the account that has the password that needs to be changed.
2. Enter a new password in the Password: box, and enter it again in the Confirm Password: box.
3. Check the User Must Change Password at Next Logon box, so that the user will have to replace the password you created with a new one at the next logon.
4. Click OK to save the change.

Many organizations have policies about how to communicate a new or changed password to a user because of recommendations made by their financial auditors. In those organizations, the server administrator may hand-deliver the password to the user instead of communicating it over the telephone or through e-mail, as a way to ensure that the password directly reaches the account owner. Another method is to send the password in a sealed envelope through the company mail. Also, some auditing recommendations suggest that the server administrator keep a record of each newly created account and of all password changes made by the server administrator for that account.

Sometimes a user or a group of users is unable to access a resource, such as a shared folder, subfolder, or printer, because there is a problem with the permissions. One way to diagnose the problem is to temporarily audit the resource to show failed access and then have the user try to access the resource. Next, check the security log, because it creates an event that reports on the access problem.

16

Some administrators have one or more test accounts that enable them to replicate an access problem, particularly when the problem involves a group membership. This also is a good way to test the security available to a group of users before releasing the resources to those users, for instance when you implement a new application or database. Another way to test the problem is to log on to the Administrator account and determine whether or not that account can access the resource. While you are logged on as administrator, check the share permissions and the folder and file permissions assigned to each group that accesses the resource, and change the permissions, if necessary, to grant user or group access. Keep in mind, for example, that there may be a mismatch between the different types of permissions so that the user or group has access at the share level, but not at the folder or file level. Also, check for conflicts created because a user belongs to one group that has the right permissions and to one group that does not, such as a group that has No Access. (Permissions are covered in detail in Chapter 9.)

If the Administrator account cannot access the resource, the next step is to take ownership of the resource and then grant permissions to the appropriate groups and users. Ownership is taken by opening the Properties dialog box for that resource and clicking the Ownership button in the Security tab. (You can practice taking ownership of a folder in Hands-on Project 16-2.)

NETWORK CONNECTIVITY PROBLEMS

There are many kinds of network connectivity problems, but some of the most common are as follows:

- Client and server connectivity
- NIC broadcasts
- TCP/IP connectivity
- Cable connectivity

Each of these is discussed in the following sections, along with ways to troubleshoot and solve the problem.

CLIENT AND SERVER CONNECTIVITY

A server or workstation may have problems connecting to the network or to other computers on the network for several reasons. When you experience a connection problem, try the following:

- Check to see if that node is the only one having problems.

- Check that the NIC driver is properly installed and is a current version.

- Use the NIC test software to determine that the NIC is functioning and reseat or replace the NIC if it fails the test.

- Verify the protocol setup through the Network icon.

- Make sure that network bindings are set up for each NIC and dial-up connection.

- Check to ensure that the correct packet type is in use for the NIC setup.

- Check the cable connection into the NIC, or reconnect the cable.

- Examine the network cable to the NIC for damage.

For example, if you are using an out-of-date NIC driver, the server or workstation may have difficulty connecting to the network, it may experience intermittent slow performance, or it may periodically lose connection. Another problem on Ethernet networks is that computers may be using different versions of Ethernet packet types. On a Microsoft-based network, check the protocol setup to make sure that all computers are using either frame type I or frame type II (802.3 or Ethernet-II), because both types should not be used on the same segment. The same is true if the server and workstations are configured for NWLink IPX/SPX Compatible Transport. For example, to check NWLink, open the Network icon in the Control Panel and double-click NWLink IPX/SPX Compatible Transport (or click the Properties button). Check the frame type and network number to make sure that they are the same as those used by the NetWare servers (Figure 16-5; try Hands-on Project 16-3). Also, if the network uses IPX routing, an internal network number must be specified. An **internal network number** is used to create a logical network between a server or workstation and a NetWare server, providing a unique identification for the NetWare server. The internal network number is in hexadecimal format. Also, if the network uses **Routing Information Protocol (RIP)** for NWLink, check the Routing tab of the Properties dialog box to make sure that RIP routing is enabled. RIP is used to help determine the shortest path from a computer on one network to a computer on another, and two versions are supported by Windows NT 4.0. One version is used for IP routing when TCP/IP is employed, and the other is used for NWLink routing. A server can be equipped with one or both forms of RIP. For either protocol suite, RIP is installed on Windows NT Server from the Control Panel Network icon, by using the Services tab. Microsoft also recommends that you install RIP if there is more than one NIC in the server on a network that uses TCP/IP or NWLink.

16

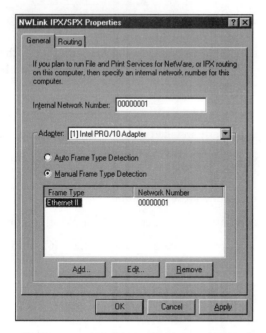

Figure 16-5   Checking the frame type and network number

 NetWare also uses an external network number that identifies the network on which the server resides and is in decimal format. For example, if there are 15 NetWare servers on one network, they all will use the same external network number, 1 for example. The external network number is specified with the Ethernet packet type.

 When RIP is installed for NWLink and it is enabled on a Windows NT server, the server becomes a router for IPX. Use this option with caution because it can create additional network traffic. It is often best to leave routing tasks to dedicated network routers on a medium-sized or large network.

RIP is no longer the routing protocol of choice for many network equipment vendors because of its high overhead and because there are other more efficient routing protocols. Network Monitor can help you determine the extra traffic that results.

Another problem to check is the cable medium setting in the software. A NIC set for coaxial cable will not communicate if it is connected to twisted-pair cable. In Windows NT and 95 you can check this through the Control Panel Network icon by looking at the properties of the NIC.

When multiple users have trouble accessing a server, check to make sure that the server is on, is completely booted, and has a good network connection in terms of the NIC, connector, and cable. Always make sure that servers have the latest NIC drivers. Sometimes users cannot connect to a server because one or more disk drives have failed or because a SCSI adapter is malfunctioning. Also, check the network equipment that the user must pass through to reach the server. Table 16-1 presents a variety of connectivity problems and their solutions.

Table 16-1   Troubleshooting Connectivity Problems

Connectivity Problem	Solutions
The NIC will not connect to the network (no computers are visible in Network Neighborhood).	(1) Check the system log for reported problems. (2) Check the cable and cable connection to the NIC for damage or for a loose connection. Do the same for the connection into the wall or hub. Also, check to make sure that intermediate network equipment (such as hubs and routers) is working. (3) Check that the media type (cable type) set for the NIC is the same as is used on the network. (4) Check to make sure that the NIC driver is installed and that bindings are set. (5) Check to make sure that the correct protocol is installed and that all NIC parameters are correct. (6) Check to make sure that the correct packet type is in use. (7) Run the NIC manufacturer's NIC diagnostics program to locate problems. (8) Replace the NIC with one you know is working.
Windows NT Server periodically disconnects from the network, or it experiences a connectivity problem when a particular computer is logged on.	(1) Check the cable segment to make sure that it is within IEEE specs for distance and cable type. Also, check for electrical interference on the cable segment, check the cable and connector for damage, check for a problem with that port on the network hub, and check for a problem with the workstation NIC. (2) Make sure that no other station on the network has the same computer name. (3) If using TCP/IP, make sure that no other station is using the same IP address.
Windows NT Server has difficulty maintaining a reliable connection as a client to a NetWare server via NWLink.	Try resetting the MaxPktSize for IPX communications. To do this, edit the Registry path: \HKEY_LOCAL_MACHINE\System\CurrentControlSet\Nwlnkipx\Netconfig, and change the MaxPktSize value from 0 to a decimal 1000 (highlight the value, click the Edit menu DWORD option, and set it to work in decimal format).
Computers on a Microsoft network experience Network Neighborhood display problems when Windows 3.11 clients are logged on.	Windows 3.11 clients may compete with an NT Server or Workstation to act as the Master Browser. On every Windows 3.11 client, edit the SYSTEM.INI file to have the line: MaintainServerList=no.

16

Table 16-1 Troubleshooting Connectivity Problems (continued)

Connectivity Problem	Solutions
Windows 3.11 clients frequently disconnect or experience general protection faults when connected to Windows NT Server.	The KeepAliveTimeout value for these connections may need to be increased. To do so, edit the Registry path: \HKEY_LOCAL_MACHINE\ System\CurrentControlSet\Services\Nwlnknb\ Parameters, and decrease the KeepAliveTimeout value by half, from a decimal 60 to 30, for example (record the current value first, as a precaution). This doubles the communication rate at which Windows NT sends connection keep-alive messages to the client. (On networks with large numbers of clients—several hundred—be careful when adjusting this value, because it creates more network traffic. Monitor the additional traffic and adjust the value higher—to 45, for example—if network traffic is a problem.)
Clients cannot run logon scripts when connecting to a Windows NT server.	Check to make sure that the location of logon scripts matches the location specified via User Manager for each account.
Clients cannot access a shared directory or printer.	Check the rights, group memberships, share permissions, and regular permissions associated with the shared resource.
Clients cannot log on to the Windows NT server.	Make sure that the Windows NT computer is powered on and properly connected to the network, and that the Server and Computer Browser services are started (use the Services icon on the Control Panel).
Windows NT is not responding as an SNMP agent.	(1) Make sure that SNMP services are installed and are set to automatically start when the computer is booted. (2) Make sure that the SNMP and SNMP Trap services are started (use the Services icon on the Control Panel). (3) Make sure that the community names are set correctly.
Windows NT generates excessive Routing Information Protocol (RIP) packets via NWLink, causing excessive network traffic.	When configured as a server, Windows NT can be set up as an IPX router on a network that also has Novell NetWare servers. Normally, it is better to allow the NetWare servers and network routers to handle IPX routing, and to leave this function turned off in Windows NT. To turn it off, open the Control Panel Network icon, click the Protocols tab, highlight NWLink IPX/SPX Compatible Transport, click Properties, click the Routing tab, and remove the check from the Enable RIP Routing box.

Table 16-1 Troubleshooting Connectivity Problems (continued)

Connectivity Problem	Solutions
TCP/IP packets sent from Windows NT are not routed.	Enable routing by opening the Control Panel Network Icon, click the Protocols tab, highlight the TCP/IP protocol, click Properties, click the Routing tab, and check the Enable IP Forwarding box. (IP forwarding enables a data packet to be routed from one subnet to another, and enables IP routing on single and multihomed RIP host servers.)

NIC BROADCAST PROBLEMS

Sometimes a NIC malfunctions and broadcasts continuously, creating a broadcast storm that causes the entire network to slow down. A broadcast storm is a condition in which so many broadcasts are sent at the same time that the network bandwidth is saturated, and the network slows significantly or times out. Use Network Monitor or Performance Monitor to trace a malfunctioning NIC. For example, using Network Monitor, check the network utilization and the number of broadcasts per second in the upper left and upper right windows. In the bottom window, watch for a workstation or server sending a large number of broadcasts. Once you identify the malfunctioning NIC, reseat it in the computer and check the network traffic again. If this does not work, the next step is to replace the NIC. (Try Hands-on Project 16-4 to practice an alternate way to identify excessive NetBEUI traffic on a network using Performance Monitor.)

TROUBLESHOOTING TCP/IP CONNECTIVITY

One area that network administrators often troubleshoot is TCP/IP connectivity. For example, a common problem is the use of duplicate IP addresses. This can happen in situations in which static IP addressing is used, with the network administrator or user typing in the IP address and subnet mask when the computer is set up. If two computers are using the same IP address, one or both will not be able to connect to the network if they are used at the same time; or, both are likely to experience unreliable communications such as sudden disconnections.

Some TCP/IP utilities, such as Telnet, have IP troubleshooting tools built in. The same is true for workstations and servers running TCP/IP-compatible operating systems, such as Windows NT and Windows 95. You can test the IP address of a Windows 95 computer by opening the MS-DOS window from the Start button, Programs option. Type *WINIPCFG*

16

to view a dialog box showing the adapter address, IP address, subnet mask, and other information for that workstation (Figure 16-6). You can run a similar test on a Windows NT server or workstation from the MS-DOS window (Click Start, Programs, Command Prompt) by typing IPCONFIG. If the server is using an IP address that is identical to the address used by another networked computer that is turned on, the subnet mask value is 0.0.0.0 when you run one of these utilities.

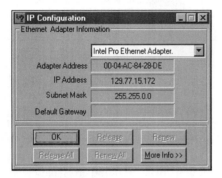

Figure 16-6   Checking the IP address on a Windows 95 workstation

Another tool for testing TCP/IP connections is the PING utility. You can poll the presence of another TCP/IP computer from the Windows 95 MS-DOS Prompt or Windows NT Command Prompt window by typing *ping* and the address or computer name of the other computer. Many server administrators use PING to quickly test the presence of a server or mainframe from their office, when there are reports of connection problems to that computer. Pinging a server on a network in another state or remote location also enables you to quickly test whether or not your Internet connectivity is accessible from your office workstation. Figure 16-7 illustrates the PING utility as used from Windows NT.

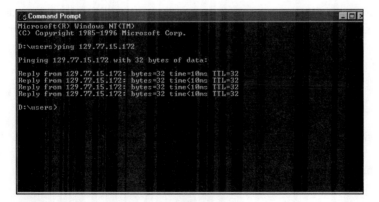

Figure 16-7   Using the PING utility

NETSTAT is a utility for Windows NT and Windows 95 that is a quick way to verify that a workstation or server has established a successful TCP/IP connection. This utility provides information about TCP and UDP connectivity. Sometimes a TCP/IP session to a server or mainframe computer hangs. You can determine that this is the case by entering *NETSTAT -e* from the Command Prompt window at that computer. Two columns of send and receive data are displayed. If these columns contain 0 bytes, it is likely that the session is hung. If it is, reboot the computer and try again. Rebooting will reset the NIC and the TCP/IP connectivity to make sure that you have a clean connection. The *NETSTAT -e* command also provides a quick indication of the number of transmission errors and discarded packets detected at that computer's NIC. For a more comprehensive listing of communications statistics, type *NETSTAT -s*. (You can practice using NETSTAT in Hands-on Project 16-5.) Table 16-2 lists some useful diagnostics available from the Command Prompt window in Windows 95 and NT.

Table 16-2   Windows 95 and NT Diagnostic Commands for TCP/IP Connectivity

Diagnostic Command	Function
WINIPCFG (Windows 95) IPCONFIG (Windows NT)	Displays information about the TCP/IP setup at that computer
PING	Polls another TCP/IP node to verify that you can communicate with it
NETSTAT (-a, -e, -s)	Displays information about the TCP/IP session from that computer
NBTSTAT (-n)	Shows the server and domain names registered to the network
TRACERT (server or host name)	Shows the number of hops and other routing information on the path to the specified server or host

The Windows 95 and NT TCP/IP diagnostics come with switches that enable you to display different kinds of information. To learn more about those switches, type the command and "all," such as: *NETSTAT all*.

TROUBLESHOOTING CABLE PROBLEMS

Network cabling is one of the most common sources of network problems. Cabling problems have many symptoms, such as disconnecting workstations, slow network services, a high level of packet errors, and unreliable data transmission. If you have reports of any of those problems, one way to start troubleshooting is by investigating the network cabling. There are several things to check related to cabling problems, such as cable length, cable type, cable impedance, terminators, connectors, and opens and shorts.

Network problems may show up on Network Monitor as dropped frames, CRC errors, or other error conditions. A **cyclic redundancy check (CRC)** is an error-checking technique used in network protocols to signal a communication problem. **Dropped frames** are those that are discarded because they are improperly formed, such as those that fail to meet the appropriate packet size.

16

On a small network, it is good practice for the server or network administrator to periodically inspect the visible cabling for damage. Cable may be pinned under a table leg, excessively bent or knotted, or damaged from exposure to a portable heater. Also, cable connectors may be broken or have an exposed wire. The best solution for damaged cable is to replace it immediately. On large networks, cable problems can be traced through the use of network test equipment or by means of enterprise-wide network monitoring software.

There is a wide array of network test equipment that ranges from inexpensive multimeters to very expensive network analyzers. The simplest place to start is with a multimeter to measure cable voltages and perform rudimentary tests on cable continuity. A multimeter can be purchased for under $100.

The next step is to obtain a cable scanner, for several hundred dollars. A cable scanner transmits an electrical signal, which it times to determine the cable length. Scanners also show if there is an open or short on a cable, along with the distance to the problem. An intermittent open or break on a cable segment prevents workstations on that segment from connecting to the network. A short, when one wire touches another, may cause intermittent problems, network errors, and disconnection problems. Cable scanners are especially suited to providing help in determining if the cable length meets network specifications.

Another network testing device is a time domain reflectometer (TDR). This device works like an oscilloscope to show a representative signal pattern (normal or faulty) on network communication cable. It shows cable distance, signal strength, electrical interference, impedance, and other information about cable communications. TDRs can record cable data to be played back later for analysis. These devices are more expensive than cable scanners because they have better analysis features.

Protocol analyzers are very expensive tools that provide an impressive range of data about network performance. They supply information about protocols, packet collisions, CRC errors, dropped packets, addresses of network nodes, network bottlenecks, broadcast problems, and many other kinds of information. Some vendors offer network protocol analysis software that can be installed on a server or workstation, or in network equipment. The software is a low-cost solution for protocol analysis, but creates performance overhead in its host.

The most economical solution for a small network is to use Network Monitor and Performance Monitor along with a multimeter or cable scanner. For a small to medium-sized network, if a network problem cannot be found immediately, it may be more cost-effective to hire a network professional than to purchase equipment and spend many personnel hours locating a problem. The network professional will likely have equipment to help quickly locate and solve a problem, including problems with fiber-optic cable.

Table 16-3 lists common cable problems that you should look for and ways to troubleshoot them.

Table 16-3   Troubleshooting Cable Problems

Cable Problem	Solutions
A cable segment is too long.	If a network segment is extended beyond the IEEE specifications, there will be communication problems affecting all nodes on that segment. Use a cable scanner, which is a device that tests network cable, to measure the distance of the cable.
Mismatched or improper cabling	Check the labeling on the cable jacket to make sure that it is right for your network. For example, coaxial cable should be labeled RG-58A/U.
Defective or missing terminator on coaxial cable	A segment with a defective or missing terminator responds like one that is too long, and usually does not work. Workstations on the segment may disconnect, experience slow network response, or receive network error messages. If your cable scanner or TDR shows that the segment distance is invalid or reports an open at the end of the segment, check the terminators.
Improper grounding	Proper grounding is critical to packet transmission on the cable. Without it, the network packet transmissions will have many CRC errors. Ethernet frames include this check to ensure the reliability of data transfer from the source node to the recipient node. Network Monitor reports CRC errors in the error statistics box.
Opens and shorts	Use a cable scanner or TDR to find opens and shorts. Also, check Network Monitor error statistics for CRC errors and dropped frames.
Electrical and magnetic interference	Electrical and magnetic interference result in excessive noise or jabber on the cable. This happens when the cable is run too close to an electrical field, above fluorescent lights in the ceiling, for example, or through a machine shop with heavy electrical equipment. Check the cable for these possibilities.
Defective connector	A faulty connector can cause a short or open on the cable. If several workstations on a segment are experiencing problems, or if a segment is automatically shut down by network equipment, this may be due to a cable connector on a workstation or server. Use a cable scanner or TDR to identify shorts and opens due to a faulty connector. Also, Network Monitor can help by identifying a high rate of CRC errors and dropped frames.

16

Table 16-3   Troubleshooting Cable Problems (continued)

Cable Problem	Solutions
Improper coax connectivity at the wall outlet	A T-connector should not be placed directly on a wall outlet because then the topology for the coax segment is not in a true bus configuration.
Improper distance between connections	Two adjacent stations may have network communication problems, if the distance between their connectors is too short. The same is true if the distance is too short between a node and a hub. For example, on a thinnet coaxial Ethernet segment, the minimum distance between nodes is 0.5 meters. For STP and UTP the minimum distance between two nodes, between a node and a hub, or between the wall outlet and a node is 3 meters. Check to be certain that all workstations are separated according to IEEE specifications.

For more complete information on IEEE network cabling specifications, refer to Ed Tittel, David Johnson, *A Guide to Networking Essentials* (ISBN 0-7600-5097-X) Course Technology, 1998; or Michael Palmer, *Hands-On Networking Essentials with Projects* (ISBN 0-7600-5089-9) Course Technology, 1998.

NETWORK PRINTING PROBLEMS

Network printing problems are common difficulties. The best advice is to check out the simplest solutions first. These include the following:

- Make sure that the printer has power.
- If the printer is physically connected to a workstation or server, check to make sure that the computer is turned on and working.
- Be certain that the printer is online (i.e., that the online light or button is active).
- Press the printer reset button, in case the printer has not fully reset after the last print job.
- Make certain that all printer trays have paper.
- Check that the printer data cable is properly connected between the computer and the printer.
- Check that the network cable is properly connected when a printer server card is used in the printer.
- Stop and restart the Spooler service.

These are obvious solutions, but they are not always checked first. Perhaps the most overlooked solution is to press the reset button on the printer. When several people share one printer, it may be printing documents with different fonts and formats. A slight misqueue at the printer or in a printer connection may cause it to miss the software reset instruction sent at the beginning of each document.

If the problem is related to the server or workstation, the most likely problems to check for are the following:

- The printer driv s improperly installed and selected for the print job.
- The printer share is not enabled.
- The printer share permissions are set incorrectly.
- The software used to produce the print job is incorrectly installed at the workstation.
- The wrong print job data type is set up.
- The wrong print monitor is installed.
- The wrong protocol is installed (for example, Microsoft DLC may need to be installed at the print server and at workstations for some types of Hewlett-Packard printers).

Table 16-4 provides a series of concrete steps you can take to resolve different types of network printer problems.

Table 16-4   Troubleshooting Network Printing Problems

Printing Problem	Solutions
Only one character prints per page.	If only one workstation experiences this problem, reinstall the printer driver on that workstation, using the Add Printer Wizard. If all workstations are experiencing the problem, reinstall the printer and printer driver at the computer or print server offering the printer share (using the Add Printer Wizard). Also, check the print monitor and data-type setup.
Some users get a no-access message when trying to access the printer share.	Check the share permissions. Make certain that the clients belong to a group for which at least Print permission has been granted.
Printer control codes are on the printout.	If only one workstation experiences the problem, reinstall the printer driver on that workstation, using the Add Printer Wizard. Also, make sure that the software generating the printout is installed correctly. If all workstations are experiencing the problem, reinstall the printer and printer driver at the computer or print server offering the printer share (using the Add Printer Wizard). Make sure that the share is set up for all operating systems that access it, that the right print monitor is installed, and that the right data type is used.
A print server card is used on the printer and shows an amber or red data error light.	Power off the printer. Disconnect the network cable to the printer. Reconnect the network cable and turn on the printer.

16

Table 16-4   Troubleshooting Network Printing Problems (continued)

Printing Problem	Solutions
A print job shows that it is printing, the printer looks fine, but nothing is printing.	Open the Control Panel and click the icon for the printer. Check for a problem with the print job at the top of the queue. If it shows that the job is printing but nothing is happening, delete the print job because it may be hung (and resubmit the print job). Also, try stopping and restarting the Spooler service.
The wrong print form is used.	Check the setup of the document in the software at the client.
A workstation cannot view the printer share in Network Neighborhood.	Check the network connection to that workstation, including connectors, cable, network hub, and the workstation's NIC. Also, check the protocol setup at the workstation.
Some clients find that the ending pages are not printed for large print jobs.	Check the disk space on the server or workstation in which the job is spooled. It may not have enough space to fully spool all jobs.
On some long print jobs, pages from other print jobs are found in the printout.	Set the printer properties for the printer so that it starts printing only after all pages are spooled. To do that, open the Control Panel, open the Printers folder, right-click the icon for the printer, click Properties on the shortcut menu, click the Scheduling tab, click the radio button for Spool Print documents so program finishes printing faster, click the radio button for Start printing after last page is spooled, click OK.
Extra separator pages are printed, or print jobs seem to get stuck in the printer for all users.	Check the print processor in use. To do that, open the Control Panel, open the Printers folder, right-click the icon for that printer, click Properties, click the General tab, click the Print Processor button, and check the print processor in use. Also check the data type. If the problem continues, try a different data type or print processor.
A document is sent that prints garbage on hundreds of pages before anyone notices and can stop the printing.	Have the spooler automatically hold printer jobs that contain the wrong printer setup information. To do that, open the Printers folder, right-click the icon for that printer, click Properties, click the Scheduling tab, click the check box to Hold mismatched documents, and click OK on the Properties dialog box.

RESOLVING BOOT PROBLEMS

Sometimes the server encounters a hardware problem and cannot be booted, displays a blue error screen during the boot process, or hangs. There are several possible causes of boot failures such as the following:

- Disk failure on the drive or drives containing the system and boot files

- A corrupted partition table

- A corrupted boot file

- A disk read error

- A memory error

In most cases the first step is to power off the computer and try rebooting. Often this will work in instances where there is a temporary disk read error during the first boot attempt, which is corrected on the second try. Also, one or more data storage registers may be out of synchronization in the CPU, causing a transient problem. Rebooting resets the CPU registers. If there are multiple drives in the computer, a disk controller may need to be reset, which is accomplished by rebooting.

The best way to reboot for clearing a temporary error is to turn the power off, wait several seconds for the hard disk drives to fully come to a stop, and then turn on the power. This causes all components to completely reset. If, instead, you reboot using a reset button, some components may not fully reset.

If rebooting does not work, then an alternative is to use the Emergency Repair Disk, which contains a copy of the boot files, such as the BOOT.INI file, and information about the configuration of the computer. When started, the disk will step you through the repair steps according to the type of problem it detects. To use the Emergency Repair Disk, perform the following steps:

1. Power off the computer.

2. Insert the Windows NT floppy disk labeled Setup Disk 1.

3. Power on the computer, enabling it to boot from the floppy disk.

4. Follow the instructions to insert Setup Disk 2.

5. On the Welcome to Setup screen, press R for repair (Figure 16-8).

6. Insert the Emergency Repair Disk.

7. Follow the instructions on the screen to repair the problem.

8. Reboot the computer.

16

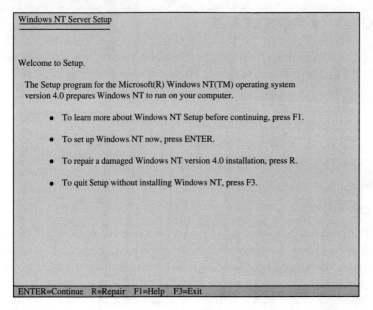

Figure 16-8 The repair option in the Welcome to Setup screen

 This is the time when keeping your Emergency Repair Disk updated with every change on the server really pays off.

Table 16-5 presents troubleshooting tips for different kinds of boot problems.

Table 16-5   Troubleshooting Boot Problems

Boot Problem	Solutions
A message appears when booting, such as one of the following: *Stop 0x0000007B Inaccessible Boot Device; Invalid Partition Table; Hard Disk Error; Hard Disk Absent or Failed*.	The boot sector on the System partition is corrupted, or the hard drive is damaged. This may be caused by a virus, a corrupted partition table, a BIOS setting change, a malfunctioning CD-ROM drive, or a corrupted disk. (1) Check the BIOS setup to make certain that it is correct and recognizes all hard disks and CD-ROM drives. Correct any improper settings (also make sure that the CMOS battery is working). (2) If there are no BIOS problems, boot the system from drive A using a copy of the Windows NT Setup Disk 1 or the startup disk you create in the section that follows. Insert a virus scanner in drive A and attempt to scan the hard disk for viruses. If a virus is found, remove it. (3) Whether or not a virus is found, reboot from the Setup Disk 1 and use the Emergency Repair Disk to replace corrupted files. If the disk cannot be accessed, determine if the problem is the hard disk, disk controller, or a SCSI adapter, and replace the defective part (make sure to check that a SCSI adapter is properly terminated). If the hard disk must be replaced, reinstall the operating system.
The system hangs when booting.	(1) Power the computer off and on to reboot. Try rebooting a couple of times. (2) If rebooting does not work, check the BIOS settings to be sure that they have not changed, and that the CMOS battery is working. If many of the BIOS settings are incorrect, replace the battery and restore the proper settings. (3) Boot from drive A using Setup Disk 1 and use the repair option for the Emergency Repair Disk, having it check the boot sector, startup, and system files. (4) For an SMP computer, the HAL.DLL file may be corrupted. Use the Boot Disk to reboot from drive A, reinstall HAL.DLL from the manufacturer's disk at the point when Setup checks the computer's configuration, select the Custom setup, and install files in the same directory that already exists.
You see the message: *Non-System disk or disk error — Replace and press any key when ready*.	(1) Remove any disks from drive A and reboot. (2) If Step 1 does not work, and the computer is set up to boot from MS-DOS, the BOOTSECT.DOS file may be corrupted on the boot drive. Reinstall the BOOTSECT.DOS file by booting from your MS-DOS disk in drive A, and then use the *Sys C:* command to copy the file to the boot drive. Next, reboot from the Windows NT Setup Disk 1 and use the Emergency Repair Disk to check the boot sector and startup environment.

16

Table 16-5 Troubleshooting Boot Problems (continued)

Boot Problem	Solutions
You see the message, *Couldn't open boot sector file*.	If the computer is set up to boot from MS-DOS, the BOOTSECT.DOS file may be corrupted on the boot drive. Reinstall the BOOTSECT.DOS file by booting from your MS-DOS disk (or the startup disk created in the next section) in drive A, and then use the *Sys C:* command to copy the file to the boot drive. Next, reboot from the Windows NT Setup Disk 1 and use the Emergency Repair Disk to check the boot sector and startup environment.
Changes were made to the system configuration when you last logged on, and now the computer will not boot.	Stop the boot process immediately and reboot using the Last Known Good option (press the space bar) on the boot screen. Once logged on, check the configuration and fix any problems, such as a bad or removed device driver.
The screen display goes blank or is jumbled as the computer begins booting Windows NT.	(1) Immediately stop the boot process. Restart the computer, accessing the BIOS Setup before starting Windows NT. Check the video BIOS setup to make sure that it is correct, and restore any settings that are changed. Reboot the computer. (2) If there are no BIOS problems, reboot selecting the Last Known Good option on the boot screen, or if booting an Intel-based computer from MS-DOS select the Windows NT Server Version 4.00 [VGA mode] (which sets the computer to standard VGA). Once you have booted, check for IRQ conflicts, video device driver problems, and changes to video settings.
Boot problems on RISC computers	(1) Try rebooting as the first alternative. (2) If Step 1 does not work, insert the Setup Disk 1 in drive A, reboot, and use the repair option to access the Emergency Repair Disk to check for corrupted or missing boot and startup files, replacing any files with problems. (3) Or, check with the manufacturer to make sure that you have the latest firmware and drivers, installed according to the manufacturer's instructions.
A driver is missing, but you are not sure which one.	Modify the BOOT.INI file on the system partition to display the drivers that are loaded as the system boots. The */sos* switch is used to display this information. Here is a sample line from the BOOT.INI file, showing how to use the switch (also note that the /basevideo switch forces use of default video settings in case of video problems): multi(0)disk(0)rdisk(1)partition(1)\WINNT="Windows NT Server Version 4.00 [VGA mode]" /basevideo /sos

Table 16-5   Troubleshooting Boot Problems (continued)

Boot Problem	Solutions
The operating system is having trouble recognizing all hardware components on the computer when NTDETECT runs at the start of the boot process.	Rename the NTDETECT.COM file in the root directory to something like NTDETECT.ORG. Copy NTDETECT.CHK from the Windows NT CD-ROM folder Support\Debug\ I386 to the root directory. Rename the file NTDETECT.COM (this is a special debug version of NTDETECT.COM that should not be copied over the regular version already in the computer's root directory). Boot Windows NT to run the new version of NTDETECT.COM to locate a hardware problem. Make sure that you put back the original version of NTDETECT after you have examined the debug information and located the problem.
A dual-boot system will not start from the MS-DOS partition.	Boot the computer from drive A with an MS-DOS system disk or the startup disk you make in the next section. Run FDISK to make sure that the MS-DOS partition is intact and is selected as the boot partition. Also, if there are corrupted boot sectors, use *FDISK /mbr* to write a new master boot record (the /mbr switch will not harm the disk if the problem is not corrupted boot sectors).
One or more hard drives show continuous access or disk thrashing, slowing down the server.	(1) Check for auditing at the root level of the hard disk. If it is writing an audit record for each successful access, it may not have time for any other work. Turn off the auditing and set it at a lower level, for instance on a specific folder. (2) Check to make sure that there is enough memory for overall server and application uses of the server.

CREATING A STARTUP DISK FOR BOOT PROBLEMS

16

It is a good idea to create a floppy boot disk in case a workstation or server cannot boot from its hard disk. This is especially useful if you have a dual-boot system, sharing Windows NT Server with MS-DOS or Windows 95. If the computer will not boot from the hard disk, you can set the BIOS to boot first from the floppy drive, and then boot using the disk you created.

To make a Windows 95 boot disk, use the following steps:

1. Boot the workstation to start Windows 95.

2. Click the Start button, Settings, and open the Control Panel.

3. Click Add/Remove Programs and the Startup Disk tab.

4. Insert a formatted disk in drive A.

5. Click the Create Disk button. The create disk process copies system files to make the disk bootable. It also copies utilities, including: ATTRIB, CHKDSK, COMMAND, DEBUG, EDIT, FDISK, FORMAT, REGEDIT, SCANDISK, SYS, and UNINSTALL (see Table 16-6 for a description of these utilities). (Once the disk is created add two other utilities found in the \Windows\Command folder: MEM and XCOPY; see Table 16-6.)

6. Click OK on the Add/Remove Programs Properties dialog box, after the files are written to the disk.

To create an MS-DOS boot disk, follow these steps:

1. Start the workstation from MS-DOS.

2. Insert a disk in drive A.

3. At the MS-DOS command prompt, enter FORMAT A: /S and press Enter. The /S switch is used to copy system files to the disk to make it bootable.

4. Use the COPY command to copy the utilities from the \DOS directory (or equivalent). Make sure that you copy the following utilities: ATTRIB, CHKDSK, COPY or XCOPY, DEBUG, EDLIN (or an equivalent line editor), FDISK, FORMAT, MEM, and SYS.

Table 16-6   Utilities for an MS-DOS or Windows 95 Floppy Startup Disk

Utility/Operating System	Description
ATTRIB	Sets attributes on or off such as read only and archive
CHKDSK	Displays information about the disk (for FAT and NTFS partitions); identifies and corrects disk errors
COMMAND	Needed to boot from the disk; contains utilities such as DIR (list directory contents) and CD (change directories)
COPY	Copies one or more files from one directory or disk to another
DEBUG	Similar to an editor; it enables you to access and change the contents of the disk
EDIT	An MS-DOS-based screen editor
EDLIN	An MS-DOS-based line editor
FDISK	Creates disk partitions and sets the boot and active partitions
FORMAT	Formats a hard disk with sectors and tracks
MEM	Displays information about how memory is used
REGEDIT	A Windows-based utility used to access and modify the Registry
SCANDISK	A utility used to identify disk errors and fix them
SYS	Copies the system files to a disk to make it bootable
UNINSTALL	Used to remove Windows 95 from a system that has been upgraded from MS-DOS
XCOPY	Copies groups of files or subdirectories from one location to another

RESTORING A FAILED SYSTEM VOLUME

If the system volume fails, use the following steps:

1. Replace the failed hardware.
2. Perform an emergency repair using the Emergency Repair Disk created as described in the section "Resolving Boot Problems."
3. Restore that volume using the most recent backup tapes.

If you are using only normal backups, then the restore simply involves using the most current normal backup tape or tapes. If you have designed the backups to combine normal and incremental backups, then there will be additional steps after restoring from the last normal backup. You will need to restore from each incremental backup taken that week, progressing from the oldest to the most recent.

TROUBLESHOOTING A FAILED MIRRORED VOLUME OR STRIPED SET WITH PARITY

Sometimes the main disk in a mirrored set fails, or the mirrored disk fails. In a duplexed set, an adapter or disk controller may fail. In this situation, the first step is to power off the computer and replace the failed disk, adapter, or controller, if a spare one is available. If the problem is an adapter or controller, the system will then be back in service.

However, if there is no spare adapter or controller, and the main drive is unavailable, use the startup disk (described in the section "Creating a Startup Disk for Boot Problems") to boot the server; you can do the same thing if the main drive has gone out. Once the server is running, use Disk Administrator and the Fault Tolerance menu to break the mirrored set (Figure 16-9). Next, click the Partition menu to mark the shadowed volume as active, so that it is bootable. Reboot the computer and run it until you obtain a replacement disk, adapter, or controller for the one that failed. When the new part arrives, install it, and re-mirror the drives as described in Steps 4, 5, and 6 in the technique discussed next.

Figure 16-9   Breaking a mirrored set

16

 When the main disk fails in a mirrored set, you can set up the BOOT.INI file on the remaining (mirror) volume to reference the system files on that volume. Change the ARC path (see Chapter 4), to find the remaining volume. For example, if that volume is the second disk drive on a single SCSI adapter, change the path from scsi(1)disk(0)rdisk(0)partition(1)\WINNT to scsi(1)disk(1)rdisk(0)partition(1)\WINNT—notice that disk (0) is changed to disk(1).

If a disk, controller or adapter fails and you have a spare available immediately, use the following steps:

1. Power off the computer and replace the failed drive, controller, or adapter (if you are replacing a SCSI disk, make sure that you use the right ID to identify it to the adapter and that you terminate the cable).

2. Reboot using the floppy startup disk you made, if the main drive has failed.

3. Use the Disk Administrator Fault Tolerance menu to break the mirrored set.

4. If you are installing a new drive, use Disk Administrator to delete the partitions on that drive, if any are present (click the drive, click the Partition menu, and click Delete).

5. While still in Disk Administrator, hold Ctrl and click the free space on the newly installed disk.

6. Click the Fault Tolerance menu and click Establish Mirror.

The steps are similar for replacing a disk in a stripe set with parity, and are as follows:

1. Power off the computer after you see the error message that a disk in the set has failed.

2. Replace the defective drive.

3. Restart the server and access Disk Administrator.

4. Use Disk Administrator to delete the partitions on the newly installed drive, if any are present.

5. Press Ctrl and click the stripe set and then click the free space on the newly installed disk.

6. Click the Fault Tolerance menu and click Regenerate.

SOLVING MEMORY PROBLEMS

Failing memory is often an intermittent problem in a server. One way to trace a memory problem is by checking the system log. However, memory problems are difficult to track without software designed to search for failing memory. One step in being prepared for memory problems is to purchase third-party software to analyze memory, or to obtain software from the manufacturer of the memory in a server. Also, try the solutions listed in Table 16-7 for dealing with memory difficulties.

Table 16-7   Troubleshooting Memory Problems

Memory Problem	Solutions
You suspect that there are memory problems, but still want to boot using the minimum memory in order to investigate the problems with tools available in Windows NT and using a third-party memory analysis program.	Windows NT will boot with a minimum of 8 MB of memory, although performance will be sluggish. Try setting the operating system to boot using only 8 MB of RAM so that you can run tests and access Windows NT Diagnostics. To boot with this minimum, modify the BOOT.INI file to use the MAXMEM switch, as follows: multi(0)disk(0)rdisk(1)partition(1)\WINNT="Windows NT Server Version 4.00" /MAXMEM=8. After the server is booted, run the third-party memory analysis tool.
One or more hard disks are continuously active or are thrashing when you access certain applications.	It is likely that you need to check RAM and paging. Use Performance Monitor to study memory and paging data. Also check the performance of processes and threads. Upgrade RAM or increase the page file size if your investigation warrants this step.
Memory errors are reported by an application or by the system log.	(1) Check the power-on memory diagnostics to be certain that all memory is recognized. Also, use Task Manager or Windows NT Diagnostics to check on what memory is recognized. (2) Reseat the SIMMs installed in the computer. (3) Check the numbers printed on the SIMMs with your computer vendor to make sure that all memory is running at the same speed. Also, make sure that the SIMMs are installed in the increments recommended by the computer manufacturer. (4) Run the manufacturer's diagnostics to identify malfunctioning memory. Replace all mismatched or malfunctioning SIMMs.
You have tried various tools, but still cannot determine which SIMM is defective.	If each SIMM is 8 MB or more, you can isolate the problem by setting the MAXMEM switch to 8 MB (see the solution to the first problem). Next, remove all SIMMs except the minimum required to boot the computer (make sure the SIMMs are in the first slots). Boot the computer. When you find a combination from which the computer will not boot, replace one of the SIMMs with a new one. If the computer boots, discard the SIMM you replaced. If the computer does not boot, leave the new SIMM in the combination and replace a different SIMM until the computer boots. Discard any SIMMs that you determine are bad. Return the computer to the original amount of memory and remove the MAXMEM switch.

16

USING SERVER MANAGER TO TROUBLESHOOT PROBLEMS

When you suspect that there is a problem with a server, open Server Manager from the Administrative Tools (Common) menu, if it is available. Server Manager contains a list of all servers in the domain. If one of the domain servers does not appear in the list, then suspect a problem with that server and go to the server to determine what it is.

Sometimes you need to send a message to all users of a server to inform them that there is an immediate problem and that you will be taking down the server to fix it. To send a message to all users, click the server and then click the Computer menu. Click Send Message and enter a message in the Message: box. Click OK to send the message to all users (Figure 16-10). (Practice sending a message in Hands-on Project 16-6.)

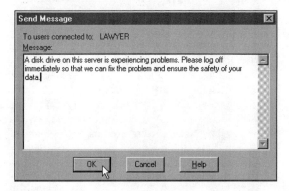

Figure 16-10 Sending a message through Server Manager

Another function of Server Manager is to manually update the BDCs in a domain to ensure that all BDCs have the most recent copy of the PDC. You update the BDCs from the Computer menu by clicking Synchronize Entire Domain. Or, if you want to add a new BDC to the domain, click the Computer menu and click Add to Domain. Click the Windows NT Backup Domain Controller radio button, enter the computer's name, and click OK.

When the PDC server is having problems or needs to be replaced, first use Server Manager to synchronize the BDCs. Then remove the PDC and promote one of the BDCs into the function of the PDC. To promote a BDC by using Server Manager, click the BDC you want to promote, click the Computer menu, and then click Promote to Primary Domain Controller. (Practice this procedure in Hands-on Project 16-7.) Make sure the BDC that is promoted is a large enough system to handle its new PDC tasks for the domain.

GETTING ADDITIONAL HELP

Sometimes you will need to turn to other resources to help you troubleshoot. One of the first places to turn is the Windows NT Help files. Other Microsoft resources include:

- *Microsoft Web site*, found at *http://www.microsoft.com/ntserver.*

- *TechNet CDs* are periodical CDs distributed by subscription to technical support professionals, an invaluable resource for white papers, FAQs (frequently asked questions), troubleshooting documents, articles and other written materials, plus software utilities, patches, upgrades, fixes, and drivers. The cost of a subscription at this writing is $300/yr; subscribe by calling 1-800-344-2121.

- *Microsoft Knowledge Base*, the predecessor to and resource for the TechNet CD; Knowledge Base is the official repository for Microsoft support information. It is an online resource that can be accessed through the Microsoft Web site at *http://www.microsoft.com/kb.*

- *NT Resource Kits* are available as a whole through the TechNet CDs and in portions through the Microsoft Web site. Resource Kits include information not found in the manuals, and often include software utilities to enhance product use.

In addition to these Microsoft resources, try the following Internet indexes and search engines. You can search either through general categories (for example, Computers and Internet, Operating Systems) or with specific search phrases, such as "Windows NT" + troubleshooting.

- Yahoo! *www.yahoo.com*

- Altavista: *www.altavista.digital.com*

- Lycos: *www.lycos.com*

CHAPTER SUMMARY

- Troubleshooting begins by developing a strategy for solving server and network problems. Elements of the strategy include developing an understanding of normal server functioning and of all devices on the network. Users can be important troubleshooting allies as you work to solve problems. Your knowledge of the business processes in your organization can also help significantly.

- Once your troubleshooting strategy is developed, you can develop your skills in using troubleshooting tools such as Windows NT Diagnostics and Event Viewer. Windows NT Diagnostics is valuable for checking on services, devices, and networking statistics. Event Viewer is your access to the Windows NT event logs that enable you to identify problems. Both of these tools provide information to supplement data you can obtain from Performance Monitor and Network Monitor.

16

- There are a number of network connectivity problems that you will encounter and solve as you work with a server. These include client and server connectivity difficulties, NICs that flood the network with unwanted traffic, TCP/IP connectivity issues, and cable problems. Of these, cable problems are likely to be the most commonly encountered. Many problems can be fixed by visually inspecting the cable and replacing damaged sections.

- Another common problem area is network printing. As with cable problems, some of these are solved by direct solutions, such as reattaching a printer cable or pressing the online button. Others are more difficult and require tuning printer properties. Boot and hard disk problems can represent some of the most dramatic troubleshooting because they have an impact on the entire server and all of its users. Keeping the Emergency Repair Disk updated and creating a floppy startup disk are two good ways to be prepared for boot and hard disk problems.

- Memory problems are another source of difficulty and fortunately do not occur often. The suggestions in this chapter show how to reduce bootup memory so that you can access the server and run memory diagnostic software. Server Manager is a useful tool to help identify a malfunctioning server and to promote a BDC when the PDC malfunctions.

- In addition to Windows NT resources for troubleshooting, there are other sources of information. Microsoft offers free support via its Web site and Knowledge Base documents, or advanced support on a subscription basis through the TechNet CDs. Internet search engines can help you locate other sources of troubleshooting information.

- Your journey as a server administrator will include many opportunities to troubleshoot problems and provide services to your users. Problems require patience and clear thinking, but they also offer a wide spectrum of opportunities to expand your knowledge of servers and computing.

KEY TERMS

- **application log** — An event log that records information about how software applications are performing.

- **cyclic redundancy check (CRC)** — An error-checking technique used in network protocols to signal a communication problem.

- **dropped frames** — Frames that are discarded because they are improperly formed, for example failing to meet the appropriate packet size.

- **event log** — One of three logs in which Windows NT Server records information about server events, such as errors, warnings, or informational events.

- **help desk** — Software that is used to keep data about hardware and software problems, how problems are solved, hardware and software setup information, and general computer documentation.

- **internal network number** — A number used to create a logical network between a Microsoft-based server or workstation and a NetWare server, providing a unique identification for the NetWare server.

- **Routing Information Protocol (RIP)** — A protocol that is used to help determine the shortest path from a computer on one network to a computer on another.

- **security log** — An event log that records access and security information about logon accesses and file, folder, and system policy changes.

- **system log** — An event log that records information about system-related events such as hardware errors, driver problems, and hard drive errors.

REVIEW QUESTIONS

1. Which of the following are common printer problems encountered by a server administrator?
   a. printer is out of paper
   b. printer needs to be reset
   c. print cable needs to be reversed
   d. all of the above
   e. only a and b

2. The server has just crashed unexpectedly. You are able to reboot without problems and are unsure about the cause of the crash. What should you do first?
   a. use Performance Monitor to check disk drive performance and paging
   b. call a Microsoft technician
   c. check the system log for errors
   d. use Disk Administrator to run an error check on the system volume

3. A CRC is _____.
   a. a measurement of CPU queuing
   b. a test available in Windows NT Diagnostics
   c. an error related to network communications
   d. a memory test

4. A Windows NT server is having problems staying connected when it is a NetWare client. What can you try to fix the problem?
   a. increase the number of communications buffers in NetWare
   b. increase the number of NWLink communications buffers in Windows NT Server
   c. reset the MaxPktSize for IPX communications in the Windows NT Registry
   d. move the Windows NT server closer to the NetWare server in terms of its network location

16

5. You have just run IPCONFIG on a Windows NT server, and the subnet mask is reported as 0.0.0.0. What does this most likely mean?

   a. the IP address configuration contains only two dotted values instead of four

   b. another networked computer is using the same IP address as the server

   c. the subnet mask is set up correctly in TCP/IP on the server, but not the default gateway address

   d. there is a high rate of collisions occurring on the network

6. You have changed the configuration of Windows NT Server and now it will not boot. What should you do?

   a. use the Emergency Repair Disk to fix configuration problems

   b. boot using the Last Known Good option and fix the configuration

   c. reinstall Windows NT Server

   d. replace the Windows NT Server key and reboot the system

7. A user has forgotten his password. How can you help as the server administrator?

   a. create a new password for that user's account

   b. create a new account for that user

   c. look up the password and give it to the user

   d. have the alerter send a copy of the password to the user through its messaging function

8. RIP can be installed in Windows NT Server for which of the following?

   a. TCP/IP

   b. NWLink IPX/SPX compatible transport

   c. DLC

   d. all of the above

   e. only a and b

9. Sometimes many pages of paper are wasted printing garbage characters, when some careless users send print jobs to a network printer. What can you do to prevent this problem?

   a. have the spooler automatically hold mismatched documents

   b. only give Print permission to those users

   c. limit print jobs to a maximum of 20 pages

   d. all of the above

   e. only a and c

10. Your server will not boot, and when you check the BIOS setup, it seems to have all the wrong settings for the hard drives and memory. What should you do next?

    a. boot from a mirrored drive because the main drive has failed

    b. use any BIOS settings for the hard disks and try booting again

    c. replace the CMOS battery

    d. replace the SCSI adapter in the server

11. There is a problem in a Microsoft network in which clients use Windows 3.11, Windows 95, and Windows NT Workstation. Sometimes clients cannot properly display other computers in Network Neighborhood. What might be the source of the problem?

a. computers running Windows NT Workstation may be using too many Windows sockets

b. computers running Windows 3.11 may be competing as master browsers

c. there are too many backup browsers on the network

d. the version of Windows NT Explorer needs to be upgraded on the Windows 95 and Windows NT computers

12. What tool is used to break a mirrored set when one of the disks fails?

a. Windows NT Diagnostics   **c.** Disk Administrator

b. Server Manager   **d.** Emergency Repair Disk

13. You want to determine the number of hung sessions at a server that seems to be experiencing a problem. Where would you locate this information?

a. Windows NT Diagnostics Resources tab

b. Windows NT Diagnostics Network tab

c. Server Manager Computer menu

d. Server Manager Statistics menu

14. The file containing the driver for your tape drive has gotten corrupted because of a power problem, and so it will not load properly. Which of the following logs would give you information about this problem?

a. application   **b.** security   **c.** system   **d.** services

15. Four users report to you that they cannot access a newly shared applications folder that others are successfully accessing. What step should you take first to determine the problem?

a. check the permissions assigned to the group or groups to which those four users belong

b. take ownership of the folder and reassign permissions

c. check the shared folder to make sure that it is not hidden

d. give the Everyone group Change permissions to that shared folder

16. Which of the following might you check for communications problems associated with network cable?

a. length of the cable   **d.** all of the above

b. type of cable   **e.** only a and b

c. cable distance between workstations

17. Which tool would you use to determine if a NIC is broadcasting excessively?

a. Network Monitor, by watching network utilization and broadcast traffic

b. Windows NT Diagnostics, by checking the network statistics

c. Server Manager Computer menu and Broadcasts option

d. System log

16

18. You need to correct a boot problem by using the Emergency Repair Disk. What do you do first?

    a. boot the server from the Emergency Repair Disk in floppy drive A

    b. boot the server from Setup Disk 1 in floppy drive A

    c. use the startup disk to change the BOOT.INI file, and then boot from the Emergency Repair Disk

    d. set the BIOS to boot from the CD-ROM drive, and then start the Emergency Repair Disk

19. The server is having trouble loading software from its CD-ROM drive. Which of the following tools would enable you determine if the CD-ROM drive is recognized by the server, and if the CD-ROM drive's driver is loaded on Windows NT Server?

    a. Disk Administrator   **c.** Windows NT Diagnostics

    b. Server Manager   **d.** Control Panel System icon

20. What tool can you use to determine if you can connect to a computer at another location?

    a. NETROUTE   **c.** IPCONFIG

    b. PING   **d.** WINIPCFG

21. In which of the following ways can users help resolve a server or network problem?

    a. save their work when problems occur

    b. report error messages they see at their workstations

    c. reset a hub when the amber light is on

    d. all of the above

    e. only a and b

22. Which of the following might be part of your problem-solving strategy?

    a. check the event log   **d.** all of the aboves

    b. reboot the server at the first sign   **e.** only a and c
    of trouble

    c. look for the simple solutions first

23. Which of the following would you include in a diagram of your network?

    a. servers   **d.** all of the above

    b. workstations   **e.** only a and b

    c. telecommunications links

24. The Windows NT Server operating system is having difficulty recognizing the hardware components on a server when you boot. Which of the following utilities can be used to help diagnose which components are and are not detected?

    a. NTDETECT.CHK   **c.** NTFIND.COM

    b. CHKDSK.EXE   **d.** REPAIR.COM

25. You believe that there is a security problem related to the access of the accounting folder. Which of the following would help you track the problem?

    a. set up auditing on the accounting folder   **d.** all of the above

    b. check the security log   **e.** only a and b

    c. check the account policies log

HANDS-ON PROJECTS

PROJECT 16-1

In this activity you use Windows NT Diagnostics to check the network statistics.

To view the network statistics:

1. Click **Start**, **Programs**, and **Administrative Tools (Common)**.

2. Click **Windows NT Diagnostics**, click the **Network** tab, then click the **Statistics** button.

3. Determine how many bytes the server has transmitted (Server Bytes Sent).

4. Next determine how many users are logged on to the server (Sessions).

5. Check if there are any Hung Sessions, then close Windows NT Diagnostics.

PROJECT 16-2

In this activity you practice taking ownership of a folder (even though it may already be owned by the Administrator account).

To take ownership of a folder:

1. Double-click **My Computer**, then double-click drive **(C:)** or whichever drive contains the Winnt folder.

2. Right-click the **Winnt** folder, click **Properties**, then click the **Security** tab.

3. Click the **Ownership** button, then click **Take Ownership** in the Owner dialog box.

4. Click **Yes**, then close the Winnt Properties dialog box, the drive (C:) window, and My Computer.

16

Project 16-3

In this activity you check the network number and frame type in NWLink IPX/SPX Compatible Transport.

To check the network number and frame type:

1. Click **Start**, **Settings**, and **Control Panel**, then double-click the **Network** icon.

2. Click the **Protocols** tab, then double-click **NWLink IPX/SPX Compatible Transport** and click the **General** tab, if necessary.

3. Check the frame type and network number information. In some cases automatic frame detection is used, and in others there is manual detection. If manual detection is used, make sure that the information is set up correctly for your network.

4. Click **OK** to leave the NWLink IPX/SPX Properties dialog box.

5. Close the Network dialog box and Control Panel.

Project 16-4

In this activity you use Performance Monitor to assess network traffic related to NetBEUI. You need access to a computer running Windows NT Server or NT Workstation that also has Network Monitor Agent installed.

To view the network utilization:

1. Click **Start**, **Programs**, and **Administrative Tools (Common)**.

2. Click **Performance Monitor**, then click the **Add counter** button.

3. Click the scroll arrow in the Object: box and select **NetBEUI**.

4. Click **Frame Bytes Received/sec** in the Counter: box to chart the total bytes received from the network per second in NetBEUI frames that contain data.

5. Click **Add**, then click **Network Segment** in the Object: box.

6. Click **% Network utilization** in the Counter: box to track network utilization as you track packet traffic from NetBEUI.

7. Click **Add**. Leaving Network Segment as the object, click **Total bytes received/ second** so that you can compare this with bytes received from NetBEUI frames.

8. Click **Add**, then click **Done** in the Add to Chart dialog box.

9. View the network utilization and NetBEUI traffic for a few minutes, then close Performance Monitor.

PROJECT 16-5

In this activity you have an opportunity to try the NETSTAT utility for a computer running Windows NT Server or Workstation that is already set up for TCP/IP communications.

To test TCP/IP connectivity with NETSTAT:

1. Click **Start**, **Programs**, and **Command Prompt**.

2. At the MS-DOS prompt, enter **netstat -a** (to view all connections including your own).

3. If your computer is successfully connected to the network, the TCP state will be reported as established (Figure 16-11).

4. Enter **Exit** at the prompt to close the Command Prompt window.

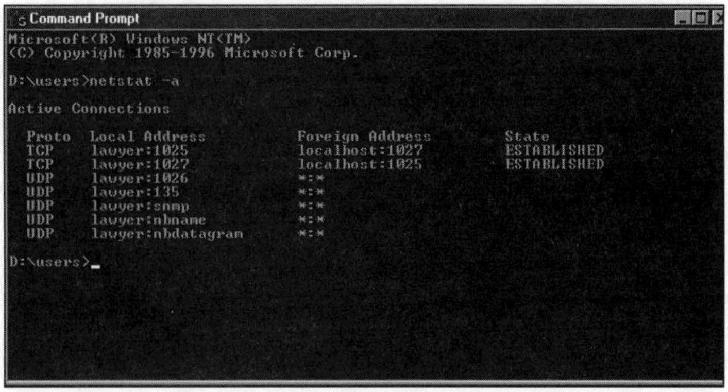

Figure 16-11   Using NETSTAT to test connectivity

 PROJECT 16-6

16

In this activity you send a message to all users on a server.

To send the message:

1. Click **Start**, **Programs**, and **Administrative Tools (Common)**, then click **Server Manager**.

2. Click a server in the list of servers, click the **Computer** menu, then click **Send Message**.

3. Type the message **Please disregard - this is just a test of the server communications** in the Message: box.

4. Click **OK**, then close Server Manager.

PROJECT 16-7

In this activity you view where to promote a BDC to a PDC.

To view the promote option:

1. Click **Start**, **Programs**, and **Administrative Tools (Common)**.

2. Click **Server Manager**. Notice the computers listed in the Domain.

3. Click a computer (a BDC if one is available), then click the **Computer** menu.

4. Notice the option Promote to Primary Domain Controller. This is the option you would click to promote a BDC, then close Server Manager.

ASPEN CONSULTING: TROUBLESHOOTING

You are still assisting Press Plastics, Greenville Paper, and Tools Unlimited. However, this week you help them troubleshoot and solve different server problems.

1. The server administrator for Tools Unlimited is calling with an urgent problem. Their server will not boot. Give the administrator a list of solutions to try, starting with the simplest and going to more complex alternatives.

2. Greenville Paper seems to have a very high rate of network utilization. Suggest what to look for to solve this problem. How can they use Network Monitor to help in diagnosing and solving the problem? What other tools should they use? Suggest one cause of the problem.

3. The server administrator for Tools Unlimited has fortunately solved the boot problem by using the advice you provided. However, the administrator is a bit unsure about how to use Event Viewer to check information about this problem and about problems that may come up in the future. Prepare a document for the administrator explaining the following:

   - The logs in Event Viewer and what they contain

   - The different types of events reported

   - How to view the details of an event

   - How to set up a filter

4. Greenville Paper has a server that will not boot, and the server is reporting a memory problem. Explain the steps they should take to solve this problem.

5. The primary drive in a mirrored set has failed at Press Plastics. They do not have a spare drive at the moment, but they want to boot the server and bring it back online until they can get a new drive. Explain how they can bring the server back online to process off of the mirrored volume. Also, explain how to re-mirror the drives once the new one comes in.

SERVER AND NETWORK
ADMINISTRATION UTILITIES

There are many utilities available for Microsoft Windows NT Server to assist with server and network administration. The utilities include Web server and administration tools as well as utilities to maintain hard disks, set disk quotas, and to check for disk fragmentation. For instance, Windows NT Server does not come with disk defragmenting software, but the software is available from third-party vendors. The defragmenter rearranges files to eliminate empty pockets that develop over time, yielding more disk space and reducing wear on the disks' moving parts because data can be accessed with less work. For a server that has home directories, it is important to set a disk quota for each user, to make sure that the server does not run out of disk space.

There are also tools for monitoring networks and network resources. For example, some tools can track the event logs on all Windows NT servers and workstations on a network, checking for critical errors. These monitors also watch network performance. Some tools provide connectivity to mainframes, and others can schedule jobs on an NT server as if it were a mainframe. Scheduled batch jobs start at a particular time without an interactive response from the server administrator, such as issuing the commands to start backups or to write data to a database. The tables that follow list many popular tools, along with a short description of each tool's purpose. In addition to the tools listed in this appendix, Microsoft offers several utilities that are free or are included with the Microsoft Windows NT 4.0 Option Pack, Microsoft Developer's Network, Microsoft Resource Kits, and with Microsoft's System Management Server (a good investment for medium and large networks). Consult Microsoft's Web site (*http://www.microsoft.com*) for more information about these utilities.

WEB SERVER TOOLS

Table A-1 lists tools for running a Web site and for Web development.

Table A-1 Web Server Tools

Company	Software	Description
Microsoft	Internet Information Server (IIS)	Full Internet services including WWW, FTP, and Gopher Services
Microsoft	Peer Web Services	Offers Internet services similar to Microsoft Internet Information Server, but scaled down for use on Microsoft Windows NT Workstation
Microsoft	FrontPage	Web development tool for maintaining a Web site
Microsoft	Internet Explorer	Web browser
O'Reilly & Associates	WebSite	Web development tool for maintaining a Web site
Edinburgh University	EMWAC Web Site Utilities	Utilities for Gopher and World Wide Web servers
Netscape	Netscape Communicator	Web browser

DISK MANAGEMENT UTILITIES

The utilities listed in Table A-2 provide disk management capabilities for setting disk quotas, defragmenting disks, data recovery, and enhanced disk access.

Table A-2 Disk Management Utilities

Company	Software	Description
Argent Software	Disk Quota Management	Sets user disk quotas and monitors disk use
NTP Software	Quota Manager	Sets and manages disk quotas for user accounts
Executive Software International	Fragmentation Analysis	Analyzes hard drives to determine the amount of fragmentation
Executive Software International	Diskeeper and Diskeeper Lite	Utilities for defragmenting hard disks
Symantec	Norton Utilities 2.0 for Windows NT	Disk defragmentation, file recovery, and monitoring of system resources
Octopus	Octopus for Windows NT	Hard disk data mirroring and data disaster recovery
EEC	SuperDisk-NT	Creates a RAM disk for fast data access, for example for Web services
EEC	SuperCache for Windows NT	Enhances caching for faster disk access

SCHEDULING UTILITIES

The utilities in Table A-3 are used to schedule jobs and other activities to run automatically at a designated time.

Table A-3   Scheduling Utilities

Company	Software	Description
Argent	Queue Manager with Job Scheduling option	Provides utilities to manage noninteractive scheduling of batch jobs; the Job Scheduling option is an add-on that enables scheduling an NT server job from a client, such as an IBM mainframe
BEI Corporation	Ultrabac	Includes software for scheduling tape backups
Camellia Software Corporation	Batch Job Server and Client	Provides utilities to manage the scheduling of batch jobs
Intergraph Corporation	Batch Services	Schedules jobs to run noninteractively
Seagate	AshWin Automated Scheduling for PC Networks	Schedules jobs to run noninteractively

UTILITIES TO COMMUNICATE WITH MAINFRAMES OR MINICOMPUTERS

The Windows NT utilities in Table A-4 are used for communications and data sharing with mainframes and minicomputers.

Table A-4   Utilities to Communicate with Mainframes or Minicomputers

Company	Software	Description
Intergraph Corporation	DiskShare	Enables a UNIX system to mount files from a Windows NT disk
Intergraph Corporation	DiskAccess	Enables a Windows NT system to mount files from a UNIX system
Newhart Systems	Blues for Windows NT	Provides connectivity to mainframe computers through existing gateways
Digital Equipment Corporation	SuperLAT for Windows NT	Connects Windows NT users to Digital Equipment Corporation computers, for both applications and peripherals

A

UTILITIES FOR VIRUS DETECTION

Popular virus–checking software is presented in Table A-5.

Table A-5   Virus-Detection Utilities

Company	Software	Description
Carmel	Anti-Virus for Windows NT	Performs virus scanning
McAfee Associates, Inc.	BootShield, NetShield, VirusScan, WebScan	Performs virus scanning
Norman Data Defense Systems	Norman Virus Control for Windows NT	Performs virus scanning
Symantec	Norton AntiVirus for Windows NT	Performs virus scanning
Symantec	Norton AntiVirus for E-Mail Gateways	Performs virus scanning for electronic mail services
Alternative Computer Technology, Inc.	InterCheck Client-Server Technology	Provides virus protection for a network

UTILITIES FOR EVENT LOG MANAGEMENT

The utilities in Table A-6 help server administrators manage logs and assess server and workstation security.

Table A-6   Utilities for Event Log Management

Company	Software	Description
Somarsoft	DumpEvt	Used to manage event logs
Somarsoft	DumpAcl-NT	Provides information about permissions settings to enable the server administrator to find security problems
Kane	Security Analyst for Windows NT	Does an analysis of NT security to find security holes
Mission Critical Software	SeNTry EEM	Centralizes management event alerts from multiple Windows NT Server and Workstation computers

NETWORK MAIL TOOLS

The tools listed in Table A-7 are for network mail, group discussions, and fax services.

Table A-7   Network Mail Tools

Company	Software	Description
Microsoft	Mail, Exchange, and Outlook	Mail systems for Microsoft networks
Software Com	Post Office	A post office and e-mail system for networks
Trax Softworks, Inc.	TeamTalk	Compatible with Microsoft Exchange, provides a group-discussion capability through e-mail
TSP Companies	Zetafax	Provides network fax services
Gold	Fax for Windows NT	Provides network fax services

NETWORK ANALYSIS TOOLS

The tools listed in Table A-8 are used to track server, workstation, and network performance.

Table A-8   Network Analysis Tools

Company	Software	Description
Network Instruments	Analyst Probe and Observer	Tools for monitoring network activity
Castle Rock Computing	SNMPc	Tools for TCP/IP and SNMP network monitoring
WhatsUP	TCP/IP Network Monitoring for Windows	Tools for TCP/IP and SNMP network monitoring
The Information Systems Manager, Inc.	PerfMan	Provides network and server performance data on networked NT servers, and workstations
Argent	Global Alert	Monitors workstations, servers, network services, and other resources on a network

A

MISCELLANEOUS UTILITIES

The Windows NT tools listed in Table A-9 are used to manage software licensing, scripts and RAS server use, and to set up the time on servers and workstations.

Table A-9   Miscellaneous Utilities

Company	Software	Description
ABC Systems and Development Ltd.	LanLicenser for Windows NT	Manages software licensing on a large network
Advanced Systems Concepts	XLNT	Offers an extended language for Windows NT for writing scripts and commands
Argent	RASTracker	Provides data about RAS Server use
Cheyenne Software	ARCserve Backup Agent for Open Files	Software for backing up Windows NT systems, including files that are open during backups
SomarSoft	ACTSNT	Synchronizes a server or workstation's internal clock with the National Institute of Standards and Technology time

An Overview of
Windows NT Commands

The two sections in this appendix present an overview of general commands and network-related commands that you can execute from the Windows NT command prompt, which is opened by clicking the Start button, Programs, and Command Prompt. Some of these utilities are helpful for administering a Windows NT server, such as the AT command that enables you to schedule server activities, and the CHKDSK command for checking file systems. Other utilities, such as the NET commands, are used to configure accounts, services, and resources offered from a server. In each section the commands are presented along with a description of their purposes.

GENERAL COMMANDS

The commands presented in Table B-1 are general commands for viewing or controlling different aspects of Windows NT Server. To find out more about a command, open the Command Prompt window and enter HELP [command], such as *HELP ASSOC*.

Table B-1   General Windows NT Server Commands

Command	Description
ASSOC	Used to view and change file associations in Windows NT
AT	Enables you to schedule one or more programs to run at a designated date and time
ATTRIB	Used to view the attributes set for a file and to change one or more attributes
BREAK	Used for MS-DOS programs to set break points for debugging a problem
CACLS	Enables you to view the attributes set for a file and to change one or more attributes
CALL	Used to call a batch file from within another batch file
CD or CHDIR	Enables you to change to a different folder or to view the name of the current folder
CHCP	Used to view the currently active code page number or to set a different code page number
CHKDSK	Used to report the disk file system statistics and to correct file system errors such as lost clusters
CLS	Clears the information currently displayed on the screen
CMD	Used to start a new NTVDM session
COLOR	Sets up the foreground and background screen colors
COMP or FC	Enables you to compare the information in two files or in two sets of files, to determine the differences in content
COMPACT	Compresses files and subfolders within a folder or removes the compression attribute
CONVERT	Converts a FAT formatted volume to NTFS at the time a server is booted
COPY	Copies files from one disk location to another
DATE	Enables you to view the date and to reset it
DEL or ERASE	Deletes specified files on a volume
DIR	Lists files and subfolders within a folder
DISKCOMP	Checks the contents of one floppy disk against the contents of another
DISKCOPY	Copies information on a floppy disk to another floppy disk
DISKPERF	Installs, starts, or stops the Performance Monitor disk counters

Table B-1   General Windows NT Server Commands (continued)

Command	Description
DOSKEY	Starts the recall of previously used MS-DOS commands and is used to create command macros
ECHO	Shows an associated message or turns screen messages off or on
ENDLOCAL	Used in batch files to terminate the storage of command process extensions, such as error level information
EXIT	Used to close the Command Prompt window session
FIND	Used to find a designated set of characters contained in one or more files
FINDSTR	Used to find one or more sets of characters within a set of files
FOR	Used within a batch file to continually run a designated command for a list of character strings or for a group of files
FORMAT	Formats a floppy disk for FAT or NTFS
FTYPE	Provides detailed information about file associations, and is used to change associations so as to link them with a designated program
GOTO	Used in a batch file to modify the order for running designated lines of commands
GRAFTABL	Displays characters and code-page switching for a color display monitor
HELP	Provides a list of the Windows NT command line commands, and is used to display help about a particular command
IF	Used to perform a conditional test in a batch file
KEYB	Enables you to set the keyboard language or layout
LABEL	Modifies the label on a disk volume
MD or MKDIR	Sets up a new folder
MODE	Sets up parameters for a device or a communications port
MORE	Limits the display to one screen at a time so that information does not rush by faster than it can be read
MOVE	Enables you to move files from one disk location to another on the same volume
PATH	Establishes the path or list of folders to search in order to run a program or command
PAUSE	Pauses a running batch file and displays a message until a keyboard key is pressed
POPD	Deletes a specified drive letter that was temporarily created by PUSHD
PRINTS	Prints a designated file
PROMPT	Modifies the format of the command prompt shown in the Command Prompt window
PUSHD	Creates a temporary drive letter to a network resource
RD or RMDIR	Deletes a folder or subfolder

B

Table B-1   General Windows NT Server Commands (continued)

Command	Description
RECOVER	Enables you to try recovering files and data from a damaged or unreadable disk
REM	Precedes comment lines to document the contents of a batch file
REN or RENAME	Renames a file or a group of files
REPLACE	Compares files in two disks or folders and synchronizes the files in one with those in another (similar to My Briefcase)
RESTORE	Restores files from another computer that were backed up via the BACKUP command on that computer
SET	Shows a list of currently set environment variables and is used to modify those variables
SETLOCAL	Used to start command process extensions via a batch file, for example for detecting error-level information
SHARE	Enables two programs to share use of the same file on one computer, while ensuring that both programs do not write to that file at the same time
SHIFT	Used within a batch file to shift command extensions from one position to another
SORT	Sorts lines input into a file, written to the screen, or sent to a printer from a file
START	Starts a new Command Prompt window in which to run a program or a command
SUBST	Used to link a path or volume with a designated drive letter
TIME	Used to view the time of day and to reset it
TITLE	Modifies the title in the title bar of the Command Prompt window
TREE	Used to show a graphic of the folder and subfolder tree structure
TYPE	Shows a file's contents on the screen or sends the contents to a file
VER	Shows the current version of the operating system
VERIFY	Instructs the operating system to verify that each file is accurately written to disk when it is created, copied, moved, or updated
VOL	Used to view the volume label, if there is one, and the volume serial number
XCOPY	Designed as a fast copy program for files, folders, and subfolders

NETWORK-RELATED COMMANDS

The commands in Table B-2 are used to test network connectivity and to manage network functions such as configuring services, checking shared files and file locks, and managing print jobs. Information about these commands is obtained by opening the Command Prompt window and typing the command followed by "/?," such as *IPCONFIG /?*.

Table B-2   Windows NT Server Network Testing and Management Commands

Command	Description
IPCONFIG (WINIPCFG in Windows 95)	Displays information about the TCP/IP setup at the server
NET ACCOUNTS	Used to change account policy settings and to synchronize BDCs
NET COMPUTER	Adds or removes a computer in a domain
NET CONFIG	Shows the started services that can be configured from this command, such as the Server and Workstation services
NET CONTINUE	Resumes a service that has been paused
NET FILE	Shows the currently open shared files and file locks, and is used to close designated files or to remove file locks
NET GROUP	Shows the existing global groups and is used to modify those groups
NET HELPMSG	Used to determine the meaning of a numeric network error message
NET LOCALGROUP	Shows the existing local groups and is used to modify those groups
NET NAME	Used to display, add, or remove computer names that can participate in the Messenger service
NET PAUSE	Pauses a service
NET PRINT	Used to view and manage queued print jobs by computer, share name, and job number
NET SEND	Sends a message to designated users or to all users currently connected to the server
NET SESSION	Shows the users currently connected to the server, and is used to disconnect designated user sessions or all user sessions
NET SHARE	Used to create, delete, or show information about a shared resource
NET START	Shows the started services or is used to start a designated service
NET STATISTICS	Shows the accumulated statistics about the Server or Workstation service
NET STOP	Stops a network service on the server
NET TIME	Used to synchronize the server's clock with that of a another computer in the same or in a different domain, or to view the time as set on another computer in the same or in a different domain

B

Table B-2 Windows NT Server Network Testing and Management Commands (continued)

Command	Description
NET USE	Shows information about shared resources or is used to configure, connect, and disconnect shared resources
NET USER	Used to view, add, or modify a user account set up on the server or in a domain
NET VIEW	Presents a list of domains, the computers and servers in a domain, and all resources shared by a computer in a domain
NBSTAT	Shows the server and domain names registered to the network
NETSTAT	Used to display information about the TCP/IP session at the server
PING	Used to poll another TCP/IP node to verify that you can communicate with it
TRACERT	Used to view the number of hops, and other routing information, on the path to the specified server or host

GLOSSARY

A

access server A device that connects synchronous and asynchronous communications devices and telecommunications lines to a network, providing routing for these types of communications.

account lockout A security measure that prohibits logging on to an NT server account after a specified number of unsuccessful attempts.

active partition The partition from which a computer boots, or starts.

ActiveX A set of controls that enables Internet access to advanced sound, video, graphics, text, and 3-D capabilities.

Administrator account A default account on a Windows NT system with complete and unrestricted access and privileges.

answer file A text file that contains a complete set of instructions for installing Windows NT.

applet A small Java program that runs on the Internet.

AppleTalk A peer-to-peer protocol used on networks for communications between Macintosh computers.

application log An event log that records information about how software applications are performing.

application program interface (API) Functions or programming features in a system that programmers can use for network links, links to messaging services, or interfaces to other systems.

attribute A characteristic associated with a folder or file, used to help manage access and backups.

auditing Tracking the success or failure of events by recording selected types of events in an event log of a server or a workstation.

B

backbone A high-capacity communications medium that joins networks on the same floor in a building, on different floors of a building, and across long distances.

background process A process that is not currently interactive with the computer user.

backup browser A computer in a domain or workgroup that maintains a static list of domain/workgroup resources to provide to clients browsing the network. The backup browser periodically receives updates to the browse list from the master browser.

backup domain controller (BDC) An NT server that acts as a backup to the primary domain controller and has a copy of the security accounts manager database containing user account and access privilege information.

base priority class The initial priority assigned to a program process or thread in the program code by Windows NT when the program is started.

basic input/output system (BIOS) A program on a read-only memory chip that establishes basic communications with components such as the monitor and disk drives.

baud rate An older modem speed measurement, reflecting that one data bit is sent per each signal change (signal oscillation).

bayonet navy connector (BNC) A connector, used for coax cable, that has a bayonet-like shell. The male BNC connector has two small knobs that attach to circular slots in the female connector. Both connectors are twisted on for a connection.

benchmark A measurement standard for hardware or software, used to establish performance baselines under varying loads or circumstances. Also called a baseline.

bindery A set of files in NetWare versions 3.x and lower that contains data about user accounts, groups, printers, security, and other server information.

bits per second (bps) Number of binary bits (0s or 1s) sent in one second, a measure used to gauge network, modem, and telecommunications speeds.

boot partition The partition that holds the Windows NT \Winnt folder containing the system files.

bottleneck Any impediment that slows the movement of data in a computer or on a network.

broadcast storm Saturation of network bandwidth by excessive broadcasts from devices attached to that network.

bus A pathway in a computer, used to transmit information. This pathway is used to send CPU instructions and to perform other data transfer within the computer.

bus mastering A process that reduces the reliance on the CPU for input/output activities on a computer's bus. Interface cards that have bus mastering can take control of the bus for faster data flow.

bus topology A network configured so that nodes are connected to a segment of cable in the logical shape of a line, with a terminator at each end.

C

cable plant The total cabling that composes a network.

cache Storage used by a computer system to house frequently used data in quickly accessed storage, such as memory.

cache flush Clearing the cache of old information to make it available for new data.

cache hit A situation in which the data needed by an application is found in cache.

cache miss A situation in which the desired data is not found in cache.

call-back security A security feature used for remote communications verification; the remote server calls back the accessing workstation to verify the access is from an authorized telephone number.

carrier sense The process of checking a communications medium, such as cable, for a specific voltage level indicating the presence of a data-carrying signal.

Carrier Sense Multiple Access with Collision Detection (CSMA/CD) A network transport control mechanism used in Ethernet networks, regulating transmission by sensing the presence of packet collisions.

Challenge Handshake Authentication Protocol (CHAP) An encrypted handshake protocol designed for standard IP- or PPP-based exchange of passwords. It provides a reasonably secure, standard, cross-platform method for sender and receiver to negotiate a connection.

CHAP with Microsoft extensions (MS-CHAP) A Microsoft-enhanced version of CHAP that can negotiate encryption levels and that uses the highly secure RSA RC4 encryption algorithm to encrypt communications between client and host. This is the highest level of security and authentication that RAS offers, but it works only with Windows 95 and Windows NT machines.

Client Service for NetWare (CSNW) A service included with Windows NT that allows Windows NT computers to connect as clients to NetWare servers.

Client32 Software used for communications between 32-bit operating systems (such as Windows 95 and OS/2) and NetWare.

clock speed Rate at which the CPU sends bursts of data through a computer's buses.

cluster remapping A fault-tolerance technique used by Windows NT that flags a damaged cluster and finds an undamaged cluster on which to write data.

coaxial cable Also called coax, a cable with a copper core surrounded by insulation. The insulation is surrounded by another conducting material, such as braided wire, which is covered by an outer insulating material.

collision A situation in which two or more packets are detected at the same time on an Ethernet network.

communications server A device that connects asynchronous serial devices to a network, providing only asynchronous routing.

Component Object Model (COM) Standards that enable a software object, such as a graphic, to be linked from one software component to another one. COM is the foundation that makes Object Linking and Embedding (OLE) possible.

Compressed Serial Line Internet Protocol (CSLIP) An extension of the SLIP remote communications protocol that provides faster throughput than SLIP.

conventional memory The lower 640 KB of memory on a PC, designated for software applications. Early small computers and operating systems reserved memory above 640 KB and below 1 MB for system use.

counter An indicator used by Performance Monitor, this is a measurement technique for an object, for example, for measuring the processor performance by percentage in use.

cyclic redundancy check (CRC) An error-checking technique used in network protocols to signal a communications problem.

D

data communications equipment (DCE) A device that converts data from a DTE, such as a computer, to a form that can be transmitted over a telecommunications line.

Data Encryption Standard (DES) A network encryption standard developed by the National Institute of Standards and Technology (NIST) and IBM.

Data Link Control (DLC) protocol Available through Microsoft NT 4.0 and Windows 95, this protocol enables communications with an IBM mainframe or minicomputer.

data terminal equipment (DTE) A computer or computing device that prepares data to be transmitted over a telecommunications line to which it attaches by using a DCE, such as a modem.

data transfer rate Speed at which data moves through the disk controller along the data channel to a disk drive.

data type The way in which information is formatted in a print file.

date stamp Documents, files, and other important information are permanently imprinted by a date stamp to record their creation date and time and to record modification dates and times.

default gateway A computer or router that forwards a network communication from one network to another, acting as a gateway between networks.

defragmentation A software process that rearranges data to fill in the empty spaces that develop on disks, and to make data easier to obtain.

disk access time Amount of time it takes for a disk drive to read or write data by moving a read/write head to the location of the data.

disk duplexing A fault-tolerance method similar to disk mirroring in that it prevents data loss by duplicating data from a main disk to a backup disk; however, disk duplexing places the backup disk on a different controller or adapter than is used by the main disk.

disk fragmentation A normal and gradual process in which files become spread throughout a disk, and empty pockets of space develop between files.

disk mirroring A fault-tolerance method that prevents data loss by duplicating data from a main disk to a backup disk. Some operating systems also refer to this as disk shadowing.

distributability Dividing complex application program tasks among two or more computers.

Distributed Component Object Model (DCOM) A standard built upon COM to enable object linking to take place over a network.

DNS Server A Microsoft service that resolves IP addresses to computer names (for example, resolving 129.77.1.10 to the computer name Brown) and computer names to IP addresses.

domain A grouping of network users and file servers to simplify the performance of common administrative and security management tasks.

Domain Name Service (DNS) A TCP/IP application protocol that resolves domain computer names to IP addresses, or IP addresses to domain names.

driver Software that enables a computer to communicate with devices such as network interface cards, printers, monitors, and hard disk drives. Each driver has a specific purpose, such as handling network communications.

dropped frames Frames that are discarded because they are improperly formed, for example failing to meet the appropriate packet size.

dual-boot system A computer set up to boot from two or more different operating systems, such as Windows NT Server and MS-DOS.

dynamic addressing An addressing method whereby an IP (Internet Protocol) address is assigned to a workstation without the need for the network administrator to "hard code" it in the workstation's network setup.

Dynamic Host Configuration Protocol (DHCP) A network protocol that provides a way for a server to automatically assign an IP address to a workstation on its network.

dynamic link library (DLL) Executable program code that is stored as a .DLL file and called only when needed by a program.

E

electronic mail (e-mail) Using mail software on a client to compose a message and send it to mail or post office software on one or more servers that forward the message to the intended destination. E-mail is made possible by networks and can span the globe thanks to the Internet.

Emergency Repair Disk (ERD) A disk created when you install Windows NT and updated after the installation, containing repair, diagnostic, and backup information for use in case there is a problem with Windows NT.

Enhanced Small Device Interface (ESDI) An early device interface for computer peripherals and hard disk drives.

enterprise network A network that reaches throughout a large area, such as a college campus or a city, or across several states, connecting many kinds of local area networks and network resources.

error checking and correcting memory (ECC) Memory that can correct some types of memory problems without causing computer operations to halt.

Ethernet A transport system that uses the CSMA/CD access method for data transmission on a network. Ethernet is typically implemented in a bus or star topology.

event log One of three logs in which Windows NT Server records information about server events, such as errors, warnings, or informational events.

export server A Windows NT server from which files are copied by the directory replication services.

Extended Industry Standard Architecture (EISA) A computer bus design that incorporates 32-bit communications within a computer. It is an industry standard used by several computer manufacturers.

extended partition A partition that is created from unpartitioned disk space and is linked to a primary partition in order to increase the available disk space.

F

fiber optics Communications cable consisting of one or more glass or plastic fiber cores inside a protective material and covered by a plastic outer jacket. Signal transmission along the inner fibers is accomplished using infrared light or in some cases, visible light.

File Allocation Table (FAT) file system A file system based on the use of a file allocation table, a flat table that records the clusters used to store the data contained in each file stored on disk. FAT is used by several operating systems, including MS-DOS, Windows 95, and Windows NT. Security and auditing are not supported on FAT partitions.

File and Print Service for NetWare (FPNW) Service for Windows NT Server that allows NetWare clients to use NT file and print services; part of a product called Services for NetWare that can be purchased separately from Microsoft.

file lock Flagging a file as temporarily inaccessible because it is in use. Files in use are locked to prevent two users from updating information at the same time.

File Transfer Protocol (FTP) Available through the TCP/IP protocol, FTP enables files to be transferred across a network or the Internet between computers or servers.

filter A capacity in network monitoring software that enables a network or server administrator to view only designated protocols, network events, network nodes, or other specialized views of the network.

foreground process A process with which the user is currently interactive, such as the program in the open window that the user is accessing.

format A process that prepares a hard disk partition for a specific file system by marking small sections called tracks and sectors to identify their location for storage of that file system's files.

free space Disk space not yet partitioned for use by a file or operating system.

full backup A backup of an entire system, including all system files, programs, and data files.

full duplex The ability to send and receive a signal at the same time.

G

gateway Software or hardware that converts data from one format to another for an entire network, for example converting data from a NetWare environment to a format that can be used in a Microsoft-based environment.

Gateway Service for NetWare (GSNW) A service included with Windows NT Server that provides connectivity to NetWare resources for NT servers and NT clients via a gateway.

global account An account type that has regular domain membership and can be recognized by other domains.

global group A type of Microsoft NT Server grouping that is used to make one Microsoft domain accessible to another, so that resources can be shared and managed across two or more domains.

Gopher A set of programs available on an Internet server that makes information available to users through a menu format.

Graphics Device Interface (GDI) An interface on a Windows network print client that works with a local software application, such as Microsoft Word, and a local printer driver to format a file to be sent to a local printer or to a network print server.

Guest account A default user account on Windows NT that has only limited access to network resources.

H

half duplex The ability to both send and receive a signal, but not simultaneously.

handle A resource, such as a file, used by a program, that has its own identification so the program is able to access it.

Hardware Abstraction Layer (HAL) A set of program routines that enables an operating system to control a hardware component, such as the processor, from within the operating system kernel.

Hardware Compatibility List (HCL) The list of computer hardware tested by Microsoft and determined to be compatible with Windows NT 4.0.

hardware profile A consistent setup of hardware components associated with one or more user accounts.

help desk Software that is used to keep data about hardware and software problems, solutions to problems, hardware and software setup, and general computer documentation.

High Performance File System (HPFS) A file system used by the OS/2 operating system. Although previous versions of Windows NT supported HPFS, Windows NT 4.0 does not.

hive A set of related Registry keys and subkeys stored as a file.

home directory A dedicated location on a file server or a workstation for a specific account holder to store files.

hot fix A data recovery method that automatically stores data when a damaged area of disk prevents that data from being written. The computer operating system finds another, undamaged area on which to write the stored data.

hub A network device that acts as a central unit to link workstations, servers, networks, and network equipment.

hypertext A method of establishing routes through an electronic document to enable the reader to go quickly from one section to another. The fast routes are created by placing bookmarks at specific locations, such as at section headings, and by placing transfer links to those bookmarks at another location, such as in a table of contents.

Hypertext Markup Language (HTML) A formatting process that is used to enable documents and graphics images to be read on the World Wide Web. HTML also provides fast links to other documents, to graphics, and to Web sites.

Hypertext Transport Protocol (HTTP) A communications protocol that obtains HTML-formatted documents and that works with FTP to transport files over the Internet.

I

IIS home directory An IIS root directory containing the WWW service, such as Inetpub\wwwroot, and subfolders for the published IIS files.

import server or **import computer** A server or workstation to which files are written from an export server via Windows NT directory replication.

incremental backup A backup of new or changed files.

Industry Standard Architecture (ISA) An older expansion bus design dating back to the 1980s, supporting 8-bit and 16-bit cards and having a data transfer rate of 8 MB per second.

Institute of Electrical and Electronics Engineers (IEEE) An organization of scientists, engineers, technicians, and educators that issues standards for electrical and electronic devices, including network interfaces, cabling, and connectors.

Integrated Device Electronics (IDE) An inexpensive hard disk interface that is used on Intel-based computers from the 80286 to Pentium computers.

Integrated Service Digital Network (ISDN) A telecommunications standard for delivering data services over telephone lines, with a current practical limit of 64 Kbps and a theoretical limit of 622 Mbps.

internal network number A number used to create a logical network between a Microsoft-based server or workstation and a NetWare server, providing a unique identification for the NetWare server.

Internet A global network of diverse Gopher, Web, and information servers offering voice, video, and text data to millions of users by means of the TCP/IP protocol.

Internet Control Message Protocol (ICMP) A protocol used to build information about the location of network workstations, servers, and other network equipment.

Internet Packet Exchange (IPX) A protocol developed by Novell for use with its NetWare file server operating system.

interrupt request (IRQ) line A hardware line that a computer component, such as a disk drive or serial port, uses to communicate to the processor that it is ready to send or receive information. Intel-based computers have 16 IRQ lines, with 15 of those available for computer components to use.

intranet A private network within an organization. It uses the same Web-based software and protocols as the Internet but is highly restricted from public access. Intranets are currently used to enable managers to run high-level reports, to enable staff members to update human resources information, and to provide access to other forms of private data.

I/O address The address in memory through which data is transferred between a computer component and the processor.

J

Java A programming language developed by Sun Microsystems that enables you to write programs for use on the Internet.

K

kernel An essential set of programs and computer code that allows a computer operating system to control processor, disk, memory, and other functions central to the basic operation of a computer.

kernel mode A protected environment in which the Windows NT operating system kernel runs, consisting of a protected memory area and privileges to directly execute system services, access the CPU, run I/O operations, and conduct other basic operating system functions.

key A category of information contained in the Windows NT Registry, such as hardware or software.

L

leaking memory Failing to return memory for general use after a process is finished using a specific memory block.

leased line A line that is conditioned for high-quality transmissions and provides a permanent connection without going through a telephone switch.

license monitoring A process used on network servers to ensure that the number of software licenses in use does not exceed the number for which the network is authorized.

line device A DCE, such as a modem or ISDN adapter, that connects to a telecommunications line.

local account An account type that is recognized and used only in the home domain.

local area network (LAN) A series of interconnected computers, printers, and other computer equipment that shares hardware and software resources. The service area is usually limited to a given floor, office area, or building.

local group In Windows NT Server, a grouping of any combination of accounts, network resources, and global groups. It is used to manage accounts and resources within a single domain or on a single server or NT workstation.

local printing Printing on the same computer to which print devices are attached.

logon script A file that contains a series of commands to run each time a user logs on to his or her account, such as a command to map a home drive.

low-level format A software process that marks tracks and sectors on a disk. A low-level format is necessary before a disk can be partitioned and formatted.

M

Management Information Base (MIB) A database of network performance information that is stored on a network agent that gathers information for a network management station.

mapped drive A disk volume or folder that is shared on the network by a file server or workstation. It gives designated network workstations access to the files and data in its shared volume or folder. The workstation, via software, determines a drive letter for the shared volume, which is the workstation's map to the data.

mapping file A file containing instructions for migrating NetWare accounts, groups, and other information to Windows NT Server.

master boot record (MBR) Data created in the first sector of a disk, containing startup information and information about disk partitions.

master browser On a Microsoft network, the computer designed to keep the main list of logged-on computers.

member server An NT server that does no account logon verification and that is used as a special-purpose server, such as a server used to store databases.

metropolitan area network (MAN) A network that links multiple LANs within a large city or metropolitan region.

microchannel architecture (MCA) A bus architecture that is used in older IBM Intel-based computers. It provides 32-bit communications within the computer.

Microcom Network Protocol (MNP) A set of modem service classes that provides efficient communications, error correction, data compression, and high-throughput capabilities.

mission-critical A term for a computer software application or a hardware service that has the highest priority in an organization.

modem A modulator/demodulator that converts a transmitted digital signal to an analog signal for a telephone line. It also converts a received analog signal to a digital signal for use by a computer.

Multilink or **Multilink PPP** A capability of RAS to aggregate multiple data streams into one network connection for the purpose of using more than one modem or ISDN channel in a single connection.

multiple-master domain A domain model that consists of many domains, in which domain management is located in two or more domains.

multistation access unit (MAU) A central hub that links token ring nodes into a topology that physically resembles a star, but where packets are transferred in a logical ring pattern.

multitasking The capability of a computer to run two or more programs at the same time.

multithreading Running several program processes or parts (threads) at the same time.

N

named pipes A communications link between two processes, which may be local to the server or remote, for example between the server and a workstation.

NetBIOS Extended User Interface (NetBEUI) A communications protocol native to Microsoft network communications. It is an enhancement of NetBIOS, which was developed for network peer-to-peer communications among workstations with Microsoft operating systems installed on a local area network.

NetWare Core Protocol (NCP) A protocol used by applications to access NetWare server services.

NetWare Loadable Module (NLM) An application module, such as one used for e-mail, that can be loaded to link with the NetWare operating system.

Network Basic Input/Output System (NetBIOS) A combination software interface and network naming convention. It is available in Microsoft operating systems through the file NETBIOS.DLL.

network binding Part of the NT Server system used to coordinate software communications among the NIC, the network protocols, and network services. Bindings ensure that communications are established to optimize performance of the hardware and software.

network-compatible A term for software that can operate in a multiuser environment using network or e-mail communication APIs.

Network Device Interface Specification (NDIS) A set of standards developed by Microsoft for network drivers that enables communication between a NIC and a protocol, and that enables the use of multiple protocols on the same network.

Network File System (NFS) A UNIX-based network file transfer protocol that ships files as streams of records.

network interface card (NIC) A PC adapter board designed to connect a workstation, file server, or other network equipment to some sort of network medium.

network-interface printer A printer with its own print server card, enabling it to be connected directly to a network.

Network Monitor Agent A tool that enables a Microsoft workstation or server NIC to gather network performance data.

network operating system Software that enables computers on a network to communicate and to share resources and files.

network traffic The number, size, and frequency of packets transmitted on the network in a given amount of time.

Novell Directory Services (NDS) A consolidated database of user account, group, security, and other types of information shared by all NetWare servers on a network.

NT File System (NTFS) The native Windows NT file system, which has more stability than FAT and also supports security measures. It also supports large disks, long filenames, and file compression.

NT Virtual DOS machine (NTVDM) In Windows NT, a process that emulates an MS-DOS window in which to run MS-DOS or 16-bit Windows programs in a designated area of memory.

null modem cable A serial communications cable configured to disable specific communication and handshaking signals that are normally sent by modems; often used to directly connect computers, serial port to serial port.

NWLink A network protocol that simulates the IPX/SPX protocol for Microsoft Windows 95 and NT communications with Novell NetWare file servers and compatible devices.

O

objects Entities in NT Server that have properties and exist as single units. Files, folders, subfolders, printers, user accounts, and groups are examples of objects.

offline UPS A battery backup system that waits until there is a power decrease or sag before switching to battery power.

one-way trust A domain trust relationship in which one domain is trusted, and one is trusting.

online UPS A battery backup system that provides power to equipment directly from its batteries at all times.

Open Database Connectivity (ODBC) A set of rules developed by Microsoft for accessing databases and providing a standard doorway to database data.

Open Datalink Interface (ODI) A driver that is used by Novell NetWare networks to transport multiple protocols on the same network.

OpenGL A standard for multidimensional graphics used in Microsoft's 3-D screen savers.

P

packet A unit of data formatted for transmission over a network. A packet normally consists of a header containing information about its source and destination, the data to be transmitted, and a footer containing error-checking information.

page description language (PDL) Printing instructions involving a programming code that produces extremely high-quality printing with extensive font options.

page file Disk space reserved for use when memory requirements exceed the available RAM.

paging Moving blocks of information from RAM to virtual memory on disk.

partition A block of tracks and sectors to be used by a particular file system, such as FAT or NTFS.

partition table A table containing information about each partition on a disk, such as the type of partition, size, and location. Also, the partition table provides information to the computer about how to access the disk.

partitioning A process in which a hard disk section or a complete hard disk is set up for use by an operating system. A disk can be formatted after it is partitioned.

Password Authentication Protocol (PAP) A nonencrypted plain-text password authentication protocol. This represents the lowest level of security for exchanging passwords via PPP or TCP/IP.

peer-to-peer network A network in which any computer can communicate with other networked computers on an equal or peer-like basis without going through an intermediary, such as a server or host.

per seat licensing A server software license that requires that there be enough licenses for all network client workstations.

per server licensing A server software license based on the maximum number of clients that use software at one time.

Performance Monitor (PM) The Windows NT utility used to track system or application objects. For each object type, there are one or more counters that can be logged for later analysis, or tracked in real time for immediate system monitoring.

Peripheral Computer Interface (PCI) A computer bus design that supports 32-bit and 64-bit bus communications for high-speed operations.

permissions In Windows NT, privileges to access files and folders, for example to read a file or to create a new file.

Personal Computer Memory Card International Association (PCMCIA) card A credit-card-sized adapter used in portable computers and in desktops to connect disk drives, CD–ROM drives, network interfaces, and other computer peripherals.

Plug and Play (PnP) The ability of added computer hardware, such as an adapter or modem, to identify itself to the computer operating system for installation.

Point-to-Point Protocol (PPP) A widely used remote communications protocol that supports IPX/SPX, NetBEUI, and TCP/IP for point-to-point communications (for example, between a remote PC and an NT server on a network).

Point-to-Point Tunneling Protocol (PPTP) A remote communications protocol that enables connectivity to intranets (private virtual networks).

port timeout Set for a printer port, the amount of time a print server will continue to try sending a print file to a printer when the printer is not responding.

portable operating system interface (POSIX) A set of standards established by the Institute of Electrical and Electronics Engineers (IEEE) for portability of applications.

PostScript A programming language that is used to code instructions for printers, allowing them to interpret page description language.

PostScript printer A printer that has special firmware or cartridges that allow it to print using a page description language (PDL).

preferred server NetWare server that a Windows NT Server gateway accesses by default, and that authenticates the logon.

primary domain controller (PDC) An NT server that acts as the master server when there are two or more NT servers on a network. It holds the master database (called the SAM) of user accounts and access privileges.

primary group A group designation used when a Windows NT Server account is set up for workstations running Macintosh or POSIX. NT Server requires that these systems be members of a global group.

primary partition The partition, or portion, of a hard disk that is bootable.

print client A client computer that generates a print job.

print device A device, such as a printer or fax, that uses the Spooler services in Windows NT.

print job A print file that contains text and codes formatted to be sent to a printer for printing.

print queue A stack or line-up of print jobs, with the first job submitted at the top of the stack and the last job submitted at the bottom, and all of the jobs waiting to be sent from the spooler to the printer.

print server A network computer or server device that connects printers to the network for sharing and that receives and processes print requests from print clients.

Printer Control Language (PCL) A printer language used by non-PostScript Hewlett-Packard and compatible laser printers.

printer driver A file containing information needed to control a specific printer, implementing customized printer control codes, font, and style information.

printer pooling Linking two or more identical printers with one printer setup or printer share.

private key A data decryption key known only to authorized network stations that are mutually sending and receiving data.

private virtual network An intranet that is closed to access through the Internet, restricting access to specific workstations, subnets, and IP addresses.

process An executable program that is currently running, such as Microsoft Word. A process may launch additional processes that are linked to it, such as a help process to view documentation or a search process to find a file.

protocol A strictly defined set of rules for communication across a network.

proxy server A server used to help convert a workstation or logon ID to an IP address.

public dial-up line A voice-grade, standard telephone connection used only for the duration of a communication session.

public key A data decryption key that is publicly available to any station on a network.

Public Switched Telephone Network (PSTN) A global network of telecommunications companies that offer telephone services through an array of communications lines and switches.

R

redirector A Windows NT kernel mode driver that enables an NT computer to access another network computer.

reduced instruction set computer (RISC) A computer that has a CPU that requires fewer instructions for common operations. The processor works faster because the commands to the CPU are reduced.

redundant array of inexpensive disks (RAID) A data storage method designed to extend the life of hard disk drives and to prevent data loss caused by a hard disk failure.

Regedit One of two Registry editors. It has limited display and menu options, but the best search options.

Regedt32 One of two Registry editors. It has a large range of menu options to help the user view and manipulate data, and has a read-only mode that can be used to guard against accidental changes.

Registry A database used to store information about the configuration, program setup, devices, drivers, and other data important to the setup of a computer running Windows NT or 95.

Relative URL (RELURL) Document name, such as *mypage.html*, that is treated as a resource in the same directory as the browser specifying the RELURL.

Remote Access Services (RAS) Microsoft software services that enable off-site workstations to access an NT server through modems and analog telephone or ISDN telecommunications lines.

rendering Graphically creating a print job.

request for information (RFI) A general planning document that is sent to vendors to obtain information about what services and products they can offer, and that may be used to develop an RFP (request for proposal).

request for proposal (RFP) A detailed planning document, often developed from responses to an RFI (request for information), that is sent to vendors and contains exact specifications for services and products that an organization intends to purchase.

resolution A process used to translate a computer's domain name to an IP address, and vice versa.

resource On a workstation or server, an IRQ, an I/O address, or memory that is allocated to a computer component, such as a disk drive or communications port. On an NT server network, a resource is a file server, shared printer, or shared directory that can be accessed by users.

rights In Windows NT Server and Workstation, access privileges for high-level activities such as logging on to a server from the network, shutting down a server, and creating user accounts.

ring topology A network in the form of a continuous ring or circle, with nodes connected around the ring.

roaming profile Desktop settings that are associated with an account in such a way that the same settings are employed no matter what computer is used to access the account (the profile is downloaded to the client).

root folder The highest-level folder, with no folders above it in the tree structure of folders and files on a disk.

root key Also called subtree, the highest category of data contained in the Registry. There are five root keys.

Routing Information Protocol (RIP) A protocol that is used to help determine the shortest path from a computer on one network to a computer on another.

S

scalable A term for a computer operating system that can be used on a range of computers, from small computers (such as those with a single Intel-based processor) to larger computers (such as those with multiple Intel or RISC processors).

sector A portion of a disk track. Disk tracks are divided into equal segments, or sectors.

sector sparing Available in Windows NT Server and Workstation for SCSI drives, a fault-tolerance method that reserves certain hard disk sectors so that they can be used when a bad sector is discovered.

Secure Sockets Layer (SSL) A dual-key encryption standard for communications between an Internet server and a client.

security accounts manager (SAM) database Also called the directory services database, it stores information about user accounts, groups, and access privileges on a Microsoft Windows NT server. The master database is kept on the PDC (primary domain controller) and regularly backed up to the BDCs (backup domain controllers).

security ID (SID) The computer-generated identification code used by Windows NT to uniquely identify users, computers, groups, and other objects.

security log An event log that records access and security information about logon accesses and file, folder, and system policy changes.

Sequence Packet Exchange (SPX) A Novell connection-oriented protocol used for network transport when there is a particular need for data reliability.

serial communications Data transmissions that use one channel to send data bits one at a time. Terminals and modems use serial communications. The serial communications port on a PC conforms to the EIA/TIA-232 (formerly RS-232) standard for communications up to 64 Kbps.

Serial Line Internet Protocol (SLIP) An older remote communications protocol that is used by UNIX computers.

shielded twisted-pair (STP) A type of cable that contains pairs of insulated wires that are twisted together and surrounded by a shielding material for added EMI and RFI protection, all inside a protective jacket.

Simple Mail Transfer Protocol (SMTP) An e-mail protocol used by systems having TCP/IP network communications.

Simple Network Management Protocol (SNMP) A protocol that enables computers and network equipment to gather standardized data about network performance, and that is part of the TCP/IP suite of protocols.

single-master domain A relationship model in a domain or domains in which trusts are set up so that management control is centralized in only one domain.

Small Computer System Interface (SCSI) A 32- or 64-bit computer adapter that transports data between one or more attached devices (such as hard disks) and the computer. There are several types of SCSI adapters, including SCSI, SCSI-2, SCSI-3, SCSI wide, SCSI narrow, and Ultra SCSI. All are used to provide high-speed data transfer to reduce bottlenecks within the computer.

spindle A rod or shaft with a hard disk platter at one end and a motor to rotate the platter at the other end.

spool file A print file written to disk until it can be transmitted to a printer.

spooler In the Windows 95 and Windows NT environments, a group of DLLs, information files, and programs that process print jobs for printing.

spooling A process that works in the background to enable several print files to go to a single printer. Each file is placed in temporary storage until its turn comes to be printed.

standalone server A server that is not part of an existing domain.

star topology A network configured with a central hub and individual cable segments connected to the hub in the shape of a star.

static addressing An IP (Internet Protocol) addressing method that requires the network administrator to manually assign and set up a unique network address on each workstation connected to a network.

stripe set Two or more disks set up so that files are spread in blocks across the disks.

stripe set with parity Three or more disks in which files are spread across the disks in blocks, and a parity block is written on each disk to enable data recovery should one disk in the set fail.

striping A data storage method that breaks up data files across all volumes of a disk set to minimize wear on a single volume.

subkey A key within a Registry key, similar to a subfolder under a folder.

subnet mask A method to show which part of the IP address is a unique identifier for the network, and which part uniquely identifies the workstation.

subtree Same as root key.

swap space Temporary disk storage used by an application to supplement memory requirements and to manipulate data.

symmetric multiprocessor (SMP) A type of computer with two or more CPUs that share the processing load.

system log An event log that records information about system-related events such as hardware errors, driver problems, and hard drive errors.

system partition Partition that contains boot files, such as BOOT.INI and NTLDR in Windows NT Server.

T

Telephony Application Programming Interface (TAPI) An interface for line device functions, such as call holding, call receiving, call hang-up, and call forwarding.

Telnet A TCP/IP application protocol that provides terminal emulation services.

terminal A device that consists of a monitor and keyboard with which to communicate with a host computer that runs the programs. The terminal does not have a processor to use for running programs locally.

terminal adapter (TA) Popularly called a digital modem, this device links a computer or a fax to an ISDN line.

thread A block of program code within a program.

token ring A network transport method that passes a token from node to node, using a ring topology. The token is used to coordinate transmission of data, because only the node possessing the token can send data.

topology The physical layout of the cable and the logical path followed by network packets sent on the cable.

tracks Concentric rings that cover an entire disk like grooves on a phonograph record. Each ring is divided into sectors in which to store data.

Transmission Control Protocol/Internet Protocol (TCP/IP) A protocol that is particularly well suited for medium and large networks. The TCP portion was originally developed to ensure reliable connections on government, military, and educational networks. It performs extensive error checking to ensure that data is delivered successfully. The IP portion consists of rules for packaging data and ensuring that it reaches the correct destination address.

tree and context A term used when the NetWare environment supports NDS, referring to the user account object and directory tree that is set by default for an NT gateway.

trusted domain A domain that has been granted security access to resources in another domain.

trusting domain A domain that allows another domain security access to its resources, such as file servers.

twisted-pair A type of flexible communications cable that contains pairs of insulated copper wires that are twisted together for reduction of EMI and RFI and covered with an outer insulating jacket.

two-way trust A domain relationship in which both domains are trusted and trusting.

U

Uniform Resource Locator (URL) An addressing format used to find an Internet Web site or page.

uninterruptible power supply (UPS) A device built into electrical equipment or a separate device that provides immediate battery power to equipment during a power failure or brownout.

uniqueness database file (UDF) A text file that contains an answer set of unique instructions for installing Windows NT.

Universal Modem Driver A modem driver standard used on recently developed modems.

Universal Resource Identifier (URI) A convention for locating an Internet site.

Universal Serial Bus (USB) An emerging standard for connecting peripherals, such as printers, to a computer, with the idea that one port fits all. It replaces the use of multiple parallel and serial ports.

universal trust A domain relationship among three or more domains in which every domain is trusting and is trusted by every other domain.

unshielded twisted-pair (UTP) A type of communications cable that has no shielding material between the pairs of insulated wires twisted together and the cable's outside jacket.

user mode A special operating mode in Windows NT used for running programs in a memory area kept separate from that used by the kernel and in which the program cannot directly access the kernel or operating system services except through an API.

user profile A desktop setup that is associated with one or more accounts to determine which startup programs and additional desktop icons are used, and other customizations. A user profile is local to the computer on which it is stored.

V

value A data parameter in the Registry, stored in decimal, binary, or text format.

virtual directory A folder of Web documents that does not reside on the IIS server, but is made to appear as though it does.

Virtual Loadable Module (VLM) A feature of NetWare used for the server's network communications with clients.

virtual memory Disk space allocated to link with memory to temporarily hold data when there is not enough free RAM.

virtual server One IIS server that appears to users to be many Web servers.

volume A partition that has been formatted for a particular file system, a primary partition, a volume set, an extended volume, a stripe set, a stripe set with parity, or a mirrored set.

volume set Two or more formatted partitions (volumes) that are combined to look like one volume with a single drive letter.

W

Web browser Software that uses the HTTP to locate and communicate with Web sites and that interprets HTML documents, video, and sound to give the user a sound and video GUI presentation of the HTML document contents.

wide area network (WAN) A far-reaching system of networks that can extend across state lines and across continents.

Windows Internet Naming Service (WINS) A Windows NT Server service that enables the server to convert workstation names to IP addresses for Internet communications.

workgroup In Microsoft networks, a number of users who share drive and printer resources in an independent peer-to-peer relationship.

working set Amount of RAM allocated to a running process.

workstation A computer that has its own CPU and may be used as a standalone computer for word processing, spreadsheet creation, or other software applications. It also may be used to access another computer, such as a mainframe computer or file server, as long as the necessary network hardware and software are installed.

World Wide Web (WWW) A vast network of servers throughout the world that provide access to voice, text, video, and data files.

X

X.25 A packet-switching communications technique for connecting remote networks at speeds up to 64 Kbps.

Xerox Network System (XNS) A protocol developed by Xerox in the early networking days for Ethernet communications.

INDEX